T0214200

Lecture Notes in Computer Science 11230

Commenced Publication in 1973
Founding and Former Series Editors:
Gerhard Goos, Juris Hartmanis, and Jan van Leeuwen

Editorial Board

More information about this series at http://www.springer.com/series/7408

Hervé Panetto · Christophe Debruyne
Henderik A. Proper · Claudio Agostino Ardagna
Dumitru Roman · Robert Meersman (Eds.)

On the Move to Meaningful Internet Systems

OTM 2018 Conferences

Confederated International Conferences:
CoopIS, C&TC, and ODBASE 2018
Valletta, Malta, October 22–26, 2018
Proceedings, Part II

 Springer

Editors
Hervé Panetto
CNRS
University of Lorraine
Vandoeuvre-les-Nancy, France

Christophe Debruyne
Trinity College Dublin
Dublin, Ireland

Henderik A. Proper
Luxembourg Institute of Science
    and Technology
Esch-sur-Alzette, Luxembourg

Claudio Agostino Ardagna
Università degli Studi di Milano
Crema, Italy

Dumitru Roman
SINTEF and University of Oslo
Oslo, Norway

Robert Meersman
TU Graz
Graz, Austria

ISSN 0302-9743   ISSN 1611-3349 (electronic)
Lecture Notes in Computer Science
ISBN 978-3-030-02670-7   ISBN 978-3-030-02671-4 (eBook)
https://doi.org/10.1007/978-3-030-02671-4

Library of Congress Control Number: 2018957822

LNCS Sublibrary: SL2 – Programming and Software Engineering

This Springer imprint is published by the registered company Springer Nature Switzerland AG
The registered company address is: Gewerbestrasse 11, 6330 Cham, Switzerland

General Co-chairs and Editors' Message for OnTheMove 2018

The OnTheMove 2018 event held October 22–26 in Valletta, Malta, further consolidated the importance of the series of annual conferences that was started in 2002 in Irvine, California. It then moved to Catania, Sicily in 2003, to Cyprus in 2004 and 2005, Montpellier in 2006, Vilamoura in 2007 and 2009, in 2008 to Monterrey, Mexico, to Heraklion, Crete in 2010 and 2011, Rome in 2012, Graz in 2013, Amantea, Italy, in 2014, and lastly to Rhodes in 2015, 2016, and 2017.

This prime event continues to attract a diverse and relevant selection of today's research worldwide on the scientific concepts underlying new computing paradigms, which of necessity must be distributed, heterogeneous, and supporting an environment of resources that are autonomous yet must meaningfully cooperate. Indeed, as such large, complex, and networked intelligent information systems become the focus and norm for computing, there continues to be an acute and increasing need to address the software, system, and enterprise issues involved and discuss them face to face in an integrated forum that covers methodological, semantic, theoretical, and application issues. As we all realize, e-mail, the Internet, and even video conferences are not by themselves optimal or even sufficient for effective and efficient scientific exchange.

The OnTheMove (OTM) International Federated Conference series has been created precisely to cover the scientific exchange needs of the communities that work in the broad yet closely connected fundamental technological spectrum of Web-based distributed computing. The OTM program every year covers data and Web semantics, distributed objects, Web services, databases, information systems, enterprise workflow and collaboration, ubiquity, interoperability, mobility, as well as grid and high-performance computing.

OnTheMove is proud to give meaning to the "federated" aspect in its full title1: it aspires to be a primary scientific meeting place where all aspects of research and development of internet- and intranet-based systems in organizations and for e-business are discussed in a scientifically motivated way, in a forum of interconnected workshops and conferences. This year's 15th edition of the OTM Federated Conferences event therefore once more provided an opportunity for researchers and practitioners to understand, discuss, and publish these developments within the broader context of distributed, ubiquitous computing. To further promote synergy and coherence, the main conferences of OTM 2018 were conceived against a background of their three interlocking global themes:

- Trusted Cloud Computing Infrastructures Emphasizing Security and Privacy
- Technology and Methodology for Data and Knowledge Resources on the (Semantic) Web
- Deployment of Collaborative and Social Computing for and in an Enterprise Context.

Originally the federative structure of OTM was formed by the co-location of three related, complementary, and successful main conference series: DOA (Distributed Objects and Applications, held since 1999), covering the relevant infrastructure-enabling technologies, ODBASE (Ontologies, DataBases and Applications of Semantics, since 2002) covering Web semantics, XML databases and ontologies, and of course CoopIS (Cooperative Information Systems, held since 1993), which studies the application of these technologies in an enterprise context through, e.g., workflow systems and knowledge management. In the 2011 edition, security aspects, originally started as topics of the IS workshop in OTM 2006, became the focus of DOA as secure virtual infrastructures, further broadened to cover aspects of trust and privacy in so-called Cloud-based systems. As this latter aspect came to dominate agendas in this and overlapping research communities, we decided in 2014 to rename the event to the "Cloud and Trusted Computing (C&TC) Conference," and it was originally launched in a workshop format.

These three main conferences specifically seek high-quality contributions of a more mature nature and encourage researchers to treat their respective topics within a framework that simultaneously incorporates (a) theory, (b) conceptual design and development, (c) methodology and pragmatics, and (d) applications in particular case studies and industrial solutions.

As in previous years, we again solicited and selected additional quality workshop proposals to complement the more mature and "archival" nature of the main conferences. Our workshops are intended to serve as "incubators" for emergent research results in selected areas related, or becoming related, to the general domain of Web-based distributed computing. We were very glad to see that our earlier successful workshops (EI2N, META4eS, FBM) re-appeared in 2018. The Fact-Based Modeling (FBM) workshop in 2015 succeeded and expanded the scope of the successful earlier ORM workshop. The Industry Case Studies Program, started in 2011, under the leadership of Hervé Panetto, Wided Guédria, and Gash Bhullar, further gained momentum and visibility in its seventh edition this year.

The OTM registration format ("one workshop and/or conference buys all workshops and/or conferences") actively intends to promote synergy between related areas in the field of distributed computing and to stimulate workshop audiences to productively mingle with each other and, optionally, with those of the main conferences. In particular EI2N continues to so create and exploit a visible cross-pollination with CoopIS.

We were very happy to see that in 2018 the number of quality submissions for the OnTheMove Academy (OTMA) noticeably increased. OTMA implements our unique, actively coached and therefore very time- and effort-intensive formula to bring PhD students together, and aims to carry our "vision for the future" in research in the areas covered by OTM. Its 2018 edition was organized and managed by a dedicated team of collaborators and faculty, Peter Spyns, Maria-Esther Vidal, inspired as always by the OTMA Dean, Erich Neuhold.

In the OTM Academy, PhD research proposals are submitted by students for peer review; selected submissions and their approaches are presented by the students in front of a wider audience at the conference, and are independently and extensively analyzed and discussed in front of this audience by a panel of senior professors. One may readily appreciate the time, effort, and funds invested in this by OnTheMove and especially by the OTMA Faculty.

As the three main conferences and the associated workshops all share the distributed aspects of modern computing systems, they experience the application pull created by the Internet and by the so-called Semantic Web, in particular developments of big data, increased importance of security issues, and the globalization of mobile-based technologies.

The three conferences seek exclusively original submissions that cover scientific aspects of fundamental theories, methodologies, architectures, and emergent technologies, as well as their adoption and application in enterprises and their impact on societally relevant IT issues.

- CoopIS 2018, Cooperative Information Systems, our flagship event in its 26th edition since its inception in 1993, invited fundamental contributions on principles and applications of distributed and collaborative computing in the broadest scientific sense in workflows of networked organizations, enterprises, governments, or just communities
- C&TC 2018 (Cloud and Trusted Computing 2018) the successor of DOA (Distributed Object Applications), focused on critical aspects of virtual infrastructure for cloud computing, specifically spanning issues of trust, reputation, and security
- ODBASE 2018, Ontologies, Databases, and Applications of Semantics covered the fundamental study of structured and semi-structured data, including linked (open) data and big data, and the meaning of such data as is needed for today's databases; as well as the role of data and semantics in design methodologies and new applications of databases

As with the earlier OnTheMove editions, the organizers wanted to stimulate this cross-pollination by a program of engaging keynote speakers from academia and industry and shared by all OTM component events. We are quite proud to list for this year:

- Martin Hepp, Universität der Bundeswehr Munich/Hepp Research GmbH
- Pieter De Leenheer, Collibra
- Richard Mark Soley, Object Management Group, Inc. (OMG)
- Tom Raftery, SAP/Instituto Internacional San Telmo

The general downturn in submissions observed in recent years for almost all conferences in computer science and IT has also affected OnTheMove, but this year the harvest again stabilized at a total of 173 submissions for the three main conferences and over 50 submissions in total for the workshops. Not only may we indeed again claim success in attracting a representative volume of scientific papers, many from the USA and Asia, but these numbers of course allow the respective Program Committees (PCs) to again compose a high-quality cross-section of current research in the areas covered by OTM. Acceptance rates vary but the aim was to stay consistently at about 1 accepted full paper for 3 submitted, yet as always these rates are subordinated to professional peer assessment of proper scientific quality.

As usual we separated the proceedings into two volumes with their own titles, one for the main conferences and one for the workshops and posters. But in a different approach to previous years, we decided the latter should appear post-event and so allow workshop authors to eventually improve their peer-reviewed papers based on critiques by the PCs and on live interaction at OTM. The resulting additional complexity and effort of editing the proceedings were professionally shouldered by our leading editor, Christophe Debruyne, with the general chairs for the conference volume, and with Hervé Panetto for the workshop volume. We are again most grateful to the Springer LNCS team in Heidelberg for their professional support, suggestions, and meticulous collaboration in producing the files and indexes ready for downloading on the USB sticks. It is a pleasure to work with staff that so deeply understands the scientific context at large, and the specific logistics of conference proceedings publication.

The reviewing process by the respective OTM PCs was performed to professional quality standards: Each paper review in the main conferences was assigned to at least three referees, with arbitrated e-mail discussions in the case of strongly diverging evaluations. It may be worthwhile to emphasize once more that it is an explicit OnTheMove policy that all conference PCs and chairs make their selections in a completely sovereign manner, autonomous and independent from any OTM organizational considerations. As in recent years, proceedings in paper form are now only available to be ordered separately.

The general chairs are once more especially grateful to the many people directly or indirectly involved in the setup of these federated conferences. Not everyone realizes the large number of qualified persons that need to be involved, and the huge amount of work, commitment, and the financial risk in the uncertain economic and funding climate of 2018, that is entailed in the organization of an event like OTM. Apart from the persons in their roles mentioned above, we therefore wish to thank in particular explicitly our main conference PC chairs:

- CoopIS 2018: Henderik A. Proper, Markus Stumptner and Samir Tata
- ODBASE 2018: Dumitru Roman, Elena Simperl, Ahmet Soylu, and Marko Grobelnik
- C&TC 2018: Claudio A. Ardagna, Adrian Belmonte, and Mauro Conti

And similarly we thank the PC (co-)chairs of the 2018 ICSP, OTMA, and Workshops (in their order of appearance on the website): Wided Guédria, Hervé Panetto, Markus Stumptner, Georg Weichhart, Peter Bollen, Stijn Hoppenbrouwers, Robert Meersman, Maurice Nijssen, Gash Bhullar, Ioana Ciuciu, Anna Fensel, Peter Spyns, and Maria-Esther Vidal.

Together with their many PC members, they performed a superb and professional job in managing the difficult yet vital process of peer review and selection of the best papers from the harvest of submissions. We all also owe a serious debt of gratitude to our supremely competent and experienced conference secretariat and technical admin staff in Guadalajara and Dublin, respectively, Daniel Meersman and Christophe Debruyne.

The general conference and workshop co-chairs also thankfully acknowledge the academic freedom, logistic support, and facilities they enjoy from their respective institutions: Technical University of Graz, Austria; Université de Lorraine, Nancy, France; Latrobe University, Melbourne, Australia—without which such a project quite simply would not be feasible. Reader, we do hope that the results of this federated scientific enterprise contribute to your research and your place in the scientific network, and we hope to welcome you at next year's event!

September 2018

Robert Meersman
Tharam Dillon
Hervé Panetto
Ernesto Damiani

Organization

OTM (On The Move) is a federated event involving a series of major international conferences and workshops. These proceedings contain the papers presented at the OTM 2018 Federated conferences, consisting of CoopIS 2018 (Cooperative Information Systems), C&TC 2018 (Cloud and Trusted Computing), and ODBASE 2018 (Ontologies, Databases, and Applications of Semantics).

Executive Committee

OTM Conferences and Workshops General Chairs

Robert Meersman   TU Graz, Austria
Tharam Dillon   La Trobe University, Melbourne, Australia
Hervé Panetto   University of Lorraine, France
Ernesto Damiani   Politecnico di Milano, Italy

OnTheMove Academy Dean

Erich Neuhold   University of Vienna, Austria

Industry Case Studies Program Chairs

Hervé Panetto   University of Lorraine, France
Wided Guédria   LIST, Luxembourg
Gash Bhullar   Control 2K Limited, UK

CoopIS 2018 PC Co-chairs

Henderik A. Proper   LIST, Luxembourg
     University of Luxembourg, Luxembourg
     Radboud University, The Netherlands
Markus Stumptner   University of South Australia, Australia
Samir Tata   IBM Reasearch, USA

C&TC 2018 PC Co-chairs

Claudio A. Ardagna   Università degli Studi di Milano, Italy
Adrian Belmonte   ENISA, Greece
Mauro Conti   University of Padua, Italy

ODBASE 2018 PC Chair and Vice-chairs

Dumitru Roman   SINTEF and University of Oslo, Norway
Elena Simperl   University of Southampton, UK
Ahmet Soylu   NTNU and DNV GL, Norway
Marko Grobelnik   Jozef Stefan Institute, Slovenia

Publication Chair

Christophe Debruyne   Trinity College Dublin, Ireland

Logistics Team

Daniel Meersman

CoopIS 2018 Program Committee

Agnes Nakakawa
Alex Norta
Amal Elgammal
Amel Bouzeghoub
Amel Mammar
Andreas Opdahl
Athman Bouguettaya
Baazaoui Hajer Baazaoui
Barbara Pernici
Barbara Weber
Bas van Gils
Beatrice Finance
Bruno Defude
Carlo Combi
Chengzheng Sun
Chirine Ghedira
Daniel Florian
Daniela Grigori David Aveiro
Djamal Benslimane
Doing Hai Eduard Babkin
Elisa Yumi Nakagawa
Epaminondas Kapetanios
Ernesto Damiani
Ernesto Exposito
Eva Kühn
Faouzi Ben Charrada
Francisca Peréz
Francisco Moo Mena
Francois Charoy
George Feuerlicht
Gerald Oster
Gil Regev
Hamid Motahari Nezhad
Huemer Christian
Jan Mendling

Janusz Szpytko
Jean-Sebastien Sottet
Jian Yang
Joao Paulo Almeida
Jolita Ralyte
Joonsoo Bae
Josephine Nabukenya
Joyce El Haddad
Juan Manuel
Julius Köpke
Kais Klai
Khalid Belhajjame
Khalil Drira
Laura Margarita Rodríguez Peralta
Liang Zhang
Lijie Wen
Lucinia Heloisa Thom
Luis Garrido Jose
Manfred Reichert
Marcelo Fantinato
Marco Aiello
Marco Comuzzi
Markus Stumptner
Marlon Dumas
Massimo Mecella
Matulcvicius Raimundas
Mehdi Ahmed-Nacer
Messai Nizar
Michael Mrissa
Michael Rosemann
Michael Sheng
Michele Missikoff
Mohamed Graiet
Mohamed Mohamed
Mohamed Sellami

Mohand-Said Hacid
Narjes Bellamine-Ben Saoud
Nour Assy
Noura Faci
Oana Balan
Olga Nabuco
Olivier Perrin
Oscar Pastor
Pnina Soffer
Raibulet Claudia
Richard Chbeir
Rik Eshuis
Romero David
Rüdiger Pryss
Salima Benbernou
Sami Bhiri
Sami Yangui
Sanjay K. Madria

Saul Pomares
Schahram Dustdar
Sebastian Steinau
Selmin Nurcan
Shazia Sadiq
Sietse Overbeek
Stefan Jablonski
Stefan Schönig
Stephan Aier
Stijn Hoppenbrouwers
Sybren de Kinderen
Valérie Issarny
Walid Gaaloul
Xavier Blanc
Yemna Sayeb
Zhangbing Zhou
Zohra Bellahsene

CoopIS 2018 Additional Reviewers

Amartya Sen
Azadeh Ghari Neiat
Bryden Da Yang Cho
Carlos Azevedo
Carlos Habekost dos Santos
Chahrazed Labba
Chaima Ghribi
Chamseddine Hamdeni
Diego Toralles Avila
Duarte Gouveia
Elio Mansour
Emna Hachicha Belghith
Fadoua Ouamani
Georg Grossmann
Geri Joskowicz
Guillaume Rosinosky
Haithem Mezni
Joaquin Garcia Alfaro
Josephine Nabukenya
Julio Cesar Nardi
Karamjit Kaur
Kevin Andrews
Lara Kallab

Laura Rodríguez
Lil Rodríguez Henríquez
Maha Riad
Marc Schickler
Marco Franceschetti
Martina Sengstschmid
Matt Selway
Michael Zimoch
Mohamed Ramzi Haddad
Olga Nabuco
Pavel Malyzhenkov
Quentin Laporte-Chabasse
Robin Kraft
Sarra Slimani
Sebastian Steinau
Slim Kallel
Stefan Crass
Victorio Carvalho
Wei Steve Wang
Weiliang Zhao
Weiwei Cai
Yemna Sayeb

C&TC 2018 Program Committee

Alberto Compagno
Belmonte Adrian
Chia-Mu Yu
Christos Xenakis
Claudio A. Ardagna
Claus Pahl
Conti Mauro
Daniele Sgandurra
David Chadwick
Ernesto Damiani
Eugenia Nikolouzou
Francesco Di Cerbo
George Karabatis
Gwanggil Jeon
Joerg Schwenk

Julian Schutte
Luca Vigano
Luis Vega
Marco Anisetti
Marit Hansen
Meiko Jensen
Michele Bezzi
Miguel Vargas Martin
Nabil El Ioini
Patrick Hung
Pierluigi Gallo
Rasool Asal
Scharam Dustdar
Stefan Schulte
Stefanos Gritzalis

CTC 2018 Additional Reviewers

Cedric Hebert
Christos Kalloniatis
Vaios Bolgouras

ODBASE 2018 Program Committee

Ademar Crotti Junior
Ahmet Soylu
Alessandra Mileo
Alfredo Maldonado
Andreas Harth
Anna Fensel
Annika Hinze
Antonis Bikakis
Axel Ngonga
Carlos A. Iglesias
Christoph Bussler
Christoph Benzmuller
Christophe Debruyne
Costin Badica
Cristina Feier
Csaba Veres
Dieter Fensel
Dietrich Rebholz
Dimitris Plexousakis

Divna Djordjevic
Dumitru Roman
Elena Simperl
Evgenij Thorstensen
Fabrizio Orlandi
Flavio De Paoli
Georg Rehm
George Vouros
George Konstantinidis
Giorgos Stoilos
Giorgos Stamou
Grigoris Antoniou
Guido Governatori
Harald Sack
Harry Halpin
Ioan Toma
Irene Celino
Irini Fundulaki
Jacek Kopecky

James Hodson
Jan Jurjens
Juan Miguel Gomez Berbis
Judie Attard
Kai-Uwe Sattler
Luis Ibanez Gonzalez
Manolis Koubarakis
Marko Tadic
Marko Grobelnik
Markus Stumptner
Markus Luczak-Roesch
Martin Hepp
Matteo Palmonari
Mihhail Matskin
Nick Bassiliades
Nikolay Nikolov

Oscar Corcho
Paul Fodor
Ruben Verborgh
Simon Scerri
Simon Krek
Soeren Auer
Stefano Pacifico
Stefano Modafieri
Steffen Lamparter
Sung-Kook Han
Till C. Lech
Tomi Kauppinen
Uli Sattler
Vadim Ermolayev
Vladimir Alexiev
Witold Abramowicz

ODBASE 2018 Additional Reviewers

Blerina Spahiu
Federico Bianchi
Mohammed Nadjib Mami
Volker Hoffmann
Yuchen Zhao

OnTheMove 2018 Keynotes

Web Ontologies: Lessons Learned from Conceptual Modeling at Scale

Martin Hepp

Universität der Bundeswehr Munich/Hepp Research GmbH, Germany

Short Bio

Martin Hepp is a professor of E-business and General Management at the Universität der Bundeswehr Munich and the CEO and Chief Scientist of Hepp Research GmbH. He holds a master's degree in business management and business information systems and a PhD in business information systems from the University of Würzburg (Germany). His key research interests are shared data structures at Web scale, for example Web ontology engineering, both at the technical, social, and economical levels, conceptual modeling in general, and data quality management. As part of his research, he developed the GoodRelations vocabulary, an OWL DL ontology for data interoperability for e-commerce at Web Scale. Since 11/2012, GoodRelations is the e-commerce core of schema.org, the official data markup standard of major search engines, namely Google, Yahoo, Bing, and Yandex. Martin authored more than 80 academic publications and was the organizer of more than fifteen workshops and conference tracks on conceptual modeling, Semantic Web topics, and information systems, and a member of more than sixty conference and workshop program committees, including ECIS, EKAW, ESWC, IEEE CEC/EEE, ISWC, and WWW.

Talk

Ever since the introduction of the term "ontology" to Computer Science, the challenges for information exchange, processing, and intelligent behavior on the World Wide Web, with its vast body of content, huge user base, linguistic and representational heterogeneity, and so forth, have been taken as a justification for ontology-related research. However, despite two decades of work on ontologies in this context, very few ontologies have emerged that are used at Web scale in a way compliant with the original proposals by a diverse, open audience.

In this talk, I will analyze the differences between the original idea of ontologies in computer science, and Web ontologies, and analyze the specific economic, social, and technical challenges of building, maintaining, and using socially agreed, global data structures that are suited for the Web at large, also with respect to the skills, expectations, and particular needs of owners of Web sites and potential consumers of Web data.

Data Governance: The New Imperative to Democratize Data Science

Pieter De Leenheer

Collibra, USA

Short Bio

Pieter De Leenheer is a cofounder of Collibra and leads the company's Research & Education group, including the Collibra University, which offers a range of self-paced learning and certification courses to help data governance professionals and data citizens gain new skills and expertise. Prior to co-founding the company, Pieter was a professor at VU University of Amsterdam. Today he still serves as adjunct professor at Columbia University in the City of New York and as visiting scholar at several universities across the globe including UC San Diego and Stanford.

Talk

We live in the age of abundant data. Through technology, more data is available, and the processing of that data easier and cheaper than ever before. Data science emerged from an unparalleled fascination to empirically understand and predict societies businesses and markets. Yet there is an understated risk inherent to democratizing data science such as data spills, cost of data exploration, and blind trust in unregulated, incontestable and oblique models. In their journey to unlock competitive advantage and maximize value from the application of big data, it is vital that data leaders find the right balance between value creation and risk exposure. To realize the true value of this wealth of data, data leaders must not act impulsively, but rethink assumptions, processes, and approaches to managing, governing, and stewarding that data. And to succeed, they must deliver credible, coherent, and trustworthy data and data access clearing mechanisms for everyone who can use it. As data becomes the most valuable resource, data governance delivers a imperative certification for any business to trust one another, but also increasingly sets a precondition for any citizen to engage in a trustworthy and endurable relationship with a company or government.

Learning to Implement the Industrial Internet

Richard Mark Soley

Object Management Group, Inc. (OMG), USA

Short Bio

Dr. Richard Mark Soley is Chairman and CEO of the Object Management Group (r), also leading the Cloud Standards Customer Council (tm) the Industrial Internet Consortium (r). Previously cofounder and former Chairman/CEO of A. I. Architects, he worked for technology companies and venture firms like TI, Gold Hill, Honeywell & IBM. Dr. Soley has SB, SM and PhD degrees in Computer Science and Engineering from MIT.

A longer bio is available here: http://www.omg.org/soley/

Talk

- The Industrial Internet Consortium and its members develop testbeds to learn more about Industrial Internet implementation: hiring, ecosystem development, standards requirements
- The Object Management Group takes real-world standards requirements and develops standards to maximize interoperability and portability
- The first insights into implementation and the first requirements for standards are underway
- Dr. Soley will give an overview of both processes and talk about the first insights from the projects

The Future of Digital: What the Next 10 Years Have in Store

Tom Raftery

SAP/Instituto Internacional San Telmo, Spain

Short Bio

Tom Raftery is a Global Vice President for multinational software corporation SAP, an adjunct professor at the Instituto Internacional San Telmo, and a board advisor for a number of start-ups.

Before joining SAP Tom worked as an independent industry analyst focusing on the Internet of Things, Energy and CleanTech and as a Futurist for Gerd Leonhardt's Futures Agency.

Tom has a very strong background in technology and social media having worked in the industry since 1991. He is the co-founder of an Irish software development company, a social media consultancy, and is co-founder and director of hyper energy-efficient data center Cork Internet eXchange – the data centre with the lowest latency connection between Europe and North America.

Tom also worked as an Analyst for industry analyst firm RedMonk, leading their GreenMonk practice for over 7 years. Tom serves on the Advisory Boards of Smart-Cities World and RetailEverywhere.com.

Talk

Digital Transformation, the Internet of Things and associated technologies (block-chain, machine learning, edge computing, etc.) are the latest buzz words in technology. Organisations are scrambling to get up to speed on them before their competitors, or some young start-up gets there first and completely disrupts them.

Right now, these digital innovation systems are, roughly speaking at the same level of maturity as the web was in 1995. So where are these new digital technologies taking us? What is coming down the line, and how will these changes affect my organisation, my wallet, and the planet?

Join Tom Raftery for our OnTheMove keynote as he unpacks what the Future of Digitisation is going to bring us.

Contents – Part II

Cloud and Trusted Computing (C&TC) 2018

International Conference on Ontologies, DataBases, and Applications of Semantics (ODBASE) 2018

ODBASE Regular Research Papers

ODBASE Short Papers

Contents – Part I

International Conference on Cooperative Information Systems (CoopIS) 2018

CoopIS 2018 PC Co-chairs' Message

CoopIS 2018 (the 26th CoopIS) takes place in Valetta on the beautiful island of Malta. The CoopIS series of conferences can look back upon a quarter of a century of scientific excellence and industrial success. The longevity of CoopIS demonstrates its continuing success in addressing the key challenges in the engineering of Cooperative Information Systems, a topic which is as relevant as it ever was.

Over the past quarter of a century, the CoopIS conference series has witnessed a plethora of IT trends come and go. Above, and beyond these trends, the CoopIS conference remains committed to the deeper challenge of achieving seamless cooperation of the socio-cyber-physical mix of actors that make up the ecosystem involved in the execution, development, and maintenance of modern day information systems.

As in previous years, this year we also were able to produce a high quality conference programme, thanks to the many high-quality submissions. A total of 123 papers were submitted, of which 37 were accepted as regular papers, and 12 as research in progress papers. The authors of the accepted papers originate from many countries and cultures around the world, in keeping with the tradition of the international nature of CoopIS.

We would like to thank everyone who contributed to the success of CoopIS 2018. In particular We thank both the authors who contributed their papers on their research to CoopIS 2018, and the PC members and additional reviewers who have reviewed the submissions in a timely manner while providing valuable and constructive feedback to the authors.

September 2018

Henderik A. Proper
Samir Tata
Markus Stumptner

Optimized Container-Based Process Execution in the Cloud

Philipp Waibel[1,2](✉) (iD), Anton Yeshchenko[1] (iD), Stefan Schulte[2] (iD),
and Jan Mendling[1] (iD)

[1] Institute for Information Business, WU Wien, Vienna, Austria
{philipp.waibel,anton.yeshchenko,jan.mendling}@wu.ac.at
[2] Distributed Systems Group, TU Wien, Vienna, Austria
{p.waibel,s.schulte}@infosys.tuwien.ac.at

Abstract. A key challenge for elastic business processes is the resource-efficient scheduling of cloud resources in such a way that Quality-of-Service levels are met. So far, this has been difficult, since existing approaches use a coarse-granular resource allocation based on virtual machines.

In this paper, we present a technique that provides fine-granular resource scheduling for elastic processes based on containers. In order to address the increased complexity of the respective scheduling problem, we develop a novel technique called GeCo based on genetic algorithms. Our evaluation demonstrates that in comparison to a baseline that follows an ad hoc approach a cost saving between 32.90% and 47.45% is achieved by GeCo while considering a high service level.

Keywords: Elastic processes · Optimization · Scheduling
Business process management · Software containers

1 Introduction

Business process management (BPM) is concerned with the efficient and effective organization of business processes [9]. Business Process Management Systems (BPMS) and other types of process-aware information systems help to flexibly redesign business processes, but have paid less attention to flexibility during process execution [28]. The advent of cloud computing provides new opportunities to make process execution at runtime more flexible by providing the means to scale the underlying computational resources in an ad hoc manner [26]. It is the ambition of elastic BPMS (eBPMS) to dynamically lease and schedule cloud resources on-demand in order to meet Quality-of-Service (QoS) levels while avoiding over- or under-provisioning [10,28]. While an over-provisioning scenario, i.e., more resources are allocated than required, leads to a waste of resources and, therefore, unnecessary cost, an under-provisioning scenario, i.e., less resources are available than required, can lead to decreased QoS [10].

© Springer Nature Switzerland AG 2018
H. Panetto et al. (Eds.): OTM 2018 Conferences, LNCS 11230, pp. 3–21, 2018.
https://doi.org/10.1007/978-3-030-02671-4_1

Recent approaches to eBPMS utilize virtual machines (VMs) in order to achieve scalability, e.g., [13,14]. One of the downsides of VMs is their coarse-granular packaging of functionality at the level of a full-fledged operating system. Beside the additional computational resources that are allocated by the operating system, also the deployment and start time of a VM are affected by the requirement of an own operating system, which reduces the ad hoc elasticity of VM-based systems [21]. To eliminate this problem inherent with VMs, the concept of *containers* is a promising solution. In comparison to a VM, a container eliminates the requirement of an own operating system, thus offering a lightweight virtualization solution [8,24].

While the usage of containers as an execution environment for business processes already offers a solution that helps to reduce resource consumption (in comparison to VM-based process execution) further reductions can be achieved by performing resource and task scheduling, aiming at resource efficiency [14]. However, state-of-the-art resource optimization and task scheduling approaches rely on VMs. The according optimization approaches aim for more coarse-grained solutions and are not tailored for the usage of containers, thus not fully mobilizing the potential of elastic business processes with regard to efficient resource utilization.

In this paper, we present a fine-granular task scheduling and resource allocation optimization approach, called *GeCo* (Genetic Container). This approach provides a cost-efficient process execution on containers that are deployed in a cloud environment while considering user-defined Service Level Agreements (SLAs). We address the increased complexity of the scheduling problem by using a genetic algorithm to meet our requirements. The evaluation demonstrates the efficiency of our approach and its capability to consider SLAs. In comparison to a baseline that follows an ad hoc approach, GeCo achieves a cost saving of 32.90% and 47.45% while considering the user-defined SLAs.

The remainder of the paper is organized as follows: Sect. 2 provides background information on containers and elastic business processes and discusses the preliminaries of our approach. Section 3 discusses our genetic algorithm optimization approach. The evaluated of our approach is presented in Sect. 4. The related work is discussed in Sect. 5 and Sect. 6 concludes this paper and presents our future work.

2   Background

Next, we discuss some necessary background information about containers, elastic process execution, as well as further preliminaries needed to comprehend the approach presented in this paper.

2.1   Containers

A container is, similar to a VM, a virtualization solution that bundles custom software and required dependencies (e.g., a database or specific libraries) together to form an executable package [24]. However, in comparison to a VM, a container uses the operating system of the host environment and, thus, needs less computational resources than a VM. This is achieved by partitioning the host operating system and computational resources to create isolated user space instances for each container [1,8,24]. This leads to configurable virtualization solutions similar to VMs but with smaller resource requirements and shorter deployment and startup times [29].

A *container image* configures and holds the custom software and possible required additional software (e.g., a database, or libraries) [24]. The distribution of those container images is done by so-called *container registries* such as Docker Hub, by uploading (*push*), sharing, and downloading (*pull*) the container images. By deploying a container image, a *container instance* is created.

2.2 Elastic Business Process Execution

A business process is composed of activities, called *process steps* (in the following called *steps*), and transitions, described in a *process model* [33]. The structure of a process model can contain sequential steps, parallel branches, called *AND-blocks* (started by an AND-split and closed by a join), exclusive branches, called *XOR-blocks* (started by an XOR-split and closed by a join), and *loops*. By executing a business process, a *process instance* is generated corresponding to the specific process model. Unless explicitly stated otherwise, the term process denotes a process instance in the remainder of this paper. A process is called an *elastic process* when cloud resources are used for the elastic execution of the process [10]. In the work at hand we concentrate on structured process models.

For a step to be executed, a software *service* is used. By deploying the service on a container, a *service instance* is created. To fulfill a specific step, the corresponding service instance is *invoked*. Each invocation runs for a specific *execution time* to complete its task.

2.3 Preliminaries

For our optimization approach, we assume that an eBPMS exists that serves as a middleware between the process owner, which requests the execution of a process, and the cloud, which is used for the execution of the processes. An example for such a middleware is presented in [27]. Furthermore, we assume that the process contains only software-based process steps, respectively that all human-based process steps are represented by a software-based service.

Similar to the concept of a microservice, each container image holds exactly one service of a specific type, with this service representing a particular step. Each container image can be deployed at any time (also several times in parallel) in the cloud. The service instance which is deployed with the container, can then be invoked several times simultaneously (i.e., as part of different process instances) as long as the container has sufficient computational resources. Once the service instance is not needed anymore, the container instance is removed.

The process owner defines for each process execution the required SLAs. If these SLAs are not fulfilled, penalty cost are charged by the process owner. In the current state the deadline until when the execution has to be finished is defined as a SLA. The deadline is also most commonly regarded in the related work [28]. The aim of our optimization approach is to optimize the process execution in a cost-efficient way by considering the computational resource *and* penalty cost.

3   The GeCo Algorithm

Our algorithm, called GeCo, aims to reduce the resource consumption of the process execution by performing scheduling of the steps in a way that a timely overlapping is achieved. Thus, the steps can share a container instance that can be invoked several times simultaneously (see Sect. 2.3). This results in a reduced resource consumption and, as a consequence, in reduced computational resource leasing cost. To also minimize the penalty cost, which are part of the overall process execution cost, the algorithm also considers the user-defined SLA, i.e., process execution deadline, during scheduling. Therefore, the result of GeCo is a schedule when each step should be executed in which particular software container, to minimize execution cost while considering the user-defined SLA.

Since the problem of task scheduling is NP-hard [14], we use the concept of genetic algorithms in order to find a cost-efficient task scheduling. Genetic algorithms have shown their capability for task scheduling in different areas [16, 36].

3.1   Genetic Algorithms

A genetic algorithm mimics an iterative, evolutionary process that applies the genetic operations *selection*, *mutation*, and *crossover* on each generation of possible solutions to a problem [34]. A generation contains several individual possible solutions called chromosomes, and each chromosome is a composition of several genes. For each iteration, the selection operator selects some chromosomes from the previous generation according to the fitness score of a chromosome. The fitness score is calculated by the *fitness function* for each chromosome and determines how well the chromosome solves a given problem (here: task scheduling). The selected chromosomes are then altered by the crossover and mutation functions to form a new generation. The crossover function swaps the genes of two chromosomes to form an offspring. The mutation function changes random genes to maintain the diversity of the generations. In addition to those newly created chromosomes a small number of elite chromosomes, i.e., chromosomes with the best fitness score, are added unaltered to the new generation. This process is repeated until a stop criterion, e.g., a defined optimization duration, is reached. At this point, the chromosome with the best fitness score is returned as a result. By this iterative approach, a genetic algorithm can browse a large search space to find a near-optimal solution in polynomial time [35].

3.2   Concepts of GeCo

As input, GeCo gets the current running and requested processes, their single steps (including the information if the execution of the step is currently ongoing, or has to be scheduled), the defined deadlines of the processes, and the status of the already running container instances. Furthermore, GeCo gets the information how long the service execution duration is and how much computational resources, with respect to CPU and RAM, are required for a particular amount of invocations. The execution duration and required computational resources have to be known upfront, e.g., via historical data [4].

The optimization is performed by GeCo each time a new process execution request is received. Furthermore, a re-optimization takes place if the execution times calculated by GeCo cannot be met, e.g., due to a longer execution duration of a preceding step. Otherwise, the calculated execution time is waited for before the execution of a step starts.

To further minimize the execution duration of the processes, GeCo deploys the container instance, required by a step, already during the execution of the preceding step to ensure that the container instance is up and running at the time it is needed. However, for the first step after the optimization, this is not possible since only after the optimization it is known which container instances have to be deployed. To consider this, GeCo schedules the execution time of the first steps in a way that there is enough time to deploy a container if needed.

Stopping Criteria. As stopping criteria, we employ time-based criteria. These criteria can be of two kinds, i.e., according to the number of iterations or according to the calculation time of the genetic algorithm [3]. In GeCo, we employ a stopping criterion based on the execution time of the algorithm, since the execution time of the algorithm plays an important role in the problem at hand, as it affects the actual schedule of the service start times.

Chromosome Representation. Our chromosome is a composition of all running and not yet running steps, which are the genes of the chromosome, and presents the schedule of the steps. Each gene holds the information when the execution of the step should start. This time is calculated by GeCo. Figure 1a shows a simplified example of a chromosome with a detailed representation of the process shown in Fig. 1b.

Initial Population. In GeCo, the initial population, i.e., first generation of chromosomes that is used as an input for the genetic algorithm [7], consists of randomly assigned task scheduling plans and, thus, already encodes possible solutions to the problem. As *a priori* knowledge, GeCo uses the deadlines of the processes and limits the random movement of the steps in a way that the deadlines are not violated in the initial population [3].

Algorithm 1 shows the process of creating a chromosome. This algorithm is executed several times, depending on the defined population size, to form the

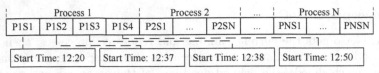

(a) Example Chromosome with a Detailed Representation of Process 1

(b) Process 1 in BPMN

Fig. 1. Example chromosome representation

Algorithm 1. Initial Population

Require: *processes, optEndTime*
 1: **function** GENERATEINITIALCHROMOSOME
 2:      *chromosome* ← NULL
 3:      **for all** *process* ∈ *processes* **do**
 4:          *lastStep* ← *getLastProcessStep(process)*
 5:          *maxBufferTime* ← (*process.deadline* − *lastStep.endTime*)/*process.steps.size*
 6:          **for all** *step* ∈ *process.steps* **do**
 7:              *randomTime* ← *getRandomNumber(0, maxBufferTime)*
 8:              *newStartTime* ← *getPrecedingStepEndTime(step)* + *randomTime*
 9:              **if** *timeForDeployment(newStartTime, optEndTime)* is false **then**
10:                  *newStartTime* ← *newStartTime* + *getReqTime(step, optEndTime)*
11:              **end if**
12:              *moveStep(step, newStartTime)*
13:          **end for**
14:          *chromosome* ← *chromosome.add(process)*
15:      **end for**
16:      **return** *chromosome*
17: **end function**

---

initial population. As an input, the algorithm gets all running and requested processes (*processes*), including the corresponding steps and the deadlines, and the end time of the optimization (*optEndTime*). The end time of the optimization is known since we use time-based stopping criteria. As a preliminary step (not shown in Algorithm 1), all start times of the steps are preset by setting the start time of a step to the end time of the preceding step. If a step is after a join gateway of an AND- or XOR-block, the end time of the latest step is used.

Beginning with line 3, Algorithm 1 iterates over all running and requested processes. The method *getLastProcessStep* returns the process step with the latest end time. To ensure that the deadline of a process is not violated, a maximal time that the execution start time of a step can be moved (*maxBufferTime*) is defined in line 5. This time is calculated by dividing the time between the process deadline (*process.deadline*) and the execution end time of the last step of the process (*lastStep.endTime*, as defined in line 4) by the number of process steps (*process.steps.size*). In case the process contains a loop structure, the algorithm uses a default amount of loop iterations, since the correct amount of loop iterations is not known at that point in time. This default amount of loop iterations has to be known upfront, e.g., via historical data.

In lines 6–13, the random movement of the steps takes place. In line 7, a random number between 0 and *maxBufferTime* is selected and assigned to *randomTime*. This random number is then added to the end time of the latest preceding step of a step leading to the new start time *newStartTime* (line 8). The latest preceding step of a step is found by the method *getPrecedingStepEndTime*. If a step does not have a preceding step, i.e., it is the first step of a process, *optEndTime* is returned since this marks the time when the execution of the process can start.

As discussed before, the algorithm has to ensure that there is enough time to deploy the required container instances after the optimization is done. For this, the method *timeForDeployment* checks if *newStartTime* allows enough time for the deployment. If this is not the case, line 10 adds the time required to deploy the container instance, calculated by *getReqTime*, to *newStartTime*.

The start time of the *step* is then moved to the new start time in line 12. Eventually, the new process is added to the chromosome (line 14), and the chromosome is returned (line 16).

Fitness Function. The fitness function assigns to each chromosome a fitness score. Finding a chromosome with the lowest container leasing cost and lowest penalty cost essentially yields a minimum fitness score.

The container leasing cost are the combination of all cost that arise due to the leasing of the required containers for the execution of the steps:

$$\sum_{c \in C} (c_{cpu} * p_{cpu} + c_{ram} * p_{ram}) * c_{duration} * f_{leasing} \qquad (1)$$

In Eq. (1), C determines the list of required container deployments for the execution of the steps represented by the chromosome. One container is defined as $c \in C = \{c_1, c_2, \ldots\}$ and $c = (cpu, ram, duration)$ defines the required CPU and RAM of this container, and the duration how long the container has to be deployed. The price of a container is defined by p_{cpu}, i.e., the price for one CPU core, and p_{ram}, i.e., the prize for one GB of RAM. Finally, the configurable weighting parameter $f_{leasing}$ determines how much the leasing cost should be considered in the final fitness score.

The penalty cost is the combination of all cost that arise due to missed deadlines, i.e., the time between the termination of the last step and the deadline:

$$\sum_{w \in W} x(w) * (w_{end} - w_{deadline}) * f_{penalty} \qquad (2)$$

In Eq. (2), W is the set of all processes of the chromosome and one process is defined as $w \in W = \{w_1, w_2, \ldots\}$. Each process contains the tuple $w =$

(*end*, *deadline*), where *end* is the execution end time of the process, i.e., the end time of the latest executed step, and *deadline* defines the deadline of the process. The weighting factor $f_{penalty}$ defines how much the penalty should be considered in the final fitness score. The term $x(w) \in \{0, 1\}$ considers if process w violates the deadline ($x(w) = 1$) or not ($x(w) = 0$).

The final fitness score is the sum of Eqs. (1) and (2).

Mutation. The mutation operation varies the start time of a step represented by a randomly selected gene of the chromosome. The resulting service execution time may not overlap the execution time of a preceding or upcoming step, which would violate the control flow defined by the process model.

How much the start time of a selected step (*step*) is changed is random. However, to ensure that no overlapping happens, the selection of how much the start time should be changed is bound by a lower (b_{lower}) and upper (b_{upper}) bound. There are three situations for b_{lower} and b_{upper}:

1. *step* is the first one in the process: In this situation, b_{lower} and b_{upper} are defined as shown in Eq. (3). If the container is not running, b_{lower} is defined by $opt_{endTime} + c_{deployDur}$, where $opt_{endTime}$ is the optimization end time and $c_{deployDur}$ the container deployment duration. Otherwise, i.e., the container was started by an already running step from another process, $b_{lower} = opt_{endTime}$. The bound b_{upper} is defined by the earliest start time of the next steps ($step_{ens}$) minus the duration of *step* ($step_{duration}$).

$$b_{lower} = \begin{cases} opt_{endTime} + c_{deployDur}, & \text{if deployment needed} \\ opt_{endTime}, & \text{otherwise} \end{cases} \qquad (3)$$

$$b_{upper} = step_{ens} - step_{duration}$$

2. *step* is between two other steps: This situation is defined by Eq. (4) whereas $step_{lps}$ defines the latest end time of the preceding steps. Again for b_{lower} it has to be considered that maybe an additional deployment time is needed for the container, e.g., *step* is the second step in the process and the preceding step duration is shorter than the deployment time. This is considered by $additionalDeployDur = c_{deployDur} - (step_{lps} - opt_{endTime})$, where $c_{deployDur}$ and $opt_{endTime}$ are defined as for Eq. (3).

$$b_{lower} = \begin{cases} step_{lps} + additionalDeployDur, & \text{if deployment needed} \\ step_{lps}, & \text{otherwise} \end{cases} \qquad (4)$$

$$b_{upper} = step_{ens} - step_{duration}$$

3. *step* is the last one in the process: This situation is defined by Eq. (5) whereas *deadline* is the deadline of the process and *additionalTime* a configurable time (e.g., 1 h). The remaining terms are defined as for Eqs. (3) and (4).

$$b_{lower} = \begin{cases} step_{lps} + additionalDeployDur, & \text{if deployment needed} \\ step_{lps}, & \text{otherwise} \end{cases} \qquad (5)$$

$$b_{upper} = deadline + additionalTime$$

The final random time, which lies in the interval (b_{lower}, b_{upper}), is then used to adapt the start time of *step*, which resolves in a new chromosome.

Crossover. The crossover operation is a genetic algorithm operation that creates a new chromosome by splitting two chromosomes, called parent chromosomes, and combining them to create a new chromosome, called offspring chromosome. Our crossover operation is a two-point crossover [34] where the first point is a random gene in the chromosome, i.e., a random step of a random process, and the second position is the end of the process to which the step belongs.

Figure 2 shows an example two-point crossover operation. The parent chromosomes are depicted in Fig. 2a. The highlighted genes show the genes that are selected for the crossover, i.e., P1S3 is the randomly selected gene and P1S4 is the end of the process (P1S3' and P1S4' are the representative steps in Parent 2). Eventually, the crossover operation results in the chromosome represented by Fig. 2b. It can be seen that the selected genes are taken from Parent 2 (i.e., P1S3' and P1S4') and the remaining genes are taken from Parent 1.

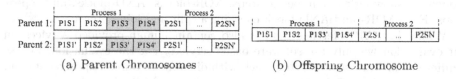

	Process 1				Process 2		
Parent 1:	P1S1	P1S2	P1S3	P1S4	P2S1	...	P2SN
Parent 2:	P1S1'	P1S2'	P1S3'	P1S4'	P2S1'	...	P2SN'

	Process 1				Process 2		
	P1S1	P1S2	P1S3'	P1S4'	P2S1	...	P2SN

(a) Parent Chromosomes   (b) Offspring Chromosome

Fig. 2. Two-point crossover operation

After the crossover is performed, a check if the offspring chromosome does violate the process structure, defined by the process model, or does not consider the deployment duration of the first container, is performed. If one of those constraints is violated, another crossover point, i.e., another gene, is selected. If both constraints are fulfilled, the offspring chromosome is returned.

4   Evaluation

As a proof of concept, GeCo has been thoroughly evaluated with respect to its allocation efficiency and SLA compliance. As underlying eBPMS, we apply the platform ViePEP [14,27]. A process owner can request the execution of processes by ViePEP, which then uses VMs on cloud resources for the execution of the services corresponding to the steps. Each service type has thereby an own VM image, similar to a container image as discussed in Sect. 2. Each VM can be deployed at any time, and the corresponding services can be invoked several times concurrently.

For our evaluation, we extend ViePEP in a way that it uses containers for the execution of the services. ViePEP and the services are written in Java.

As application server for the services, we use Jetty. Each service uses the load generator library *fakeload*[1], which simulates a configurable RAM and CPU load for a given time span. For the evaluation, ViePEP is running on a VM on the Microsoft Azure Cloud[2] and the containers are deployed on the Azure Cloud by using the functionality Container Instances. As container registry, the Azure Cloud Container Registry is used. The source code of ViePEP, the services, and the evaluation client are available at https://github.com/piwa/ViePEP-C, https://github.com/piwa/ViePEP-C-Backendservice, and https://github.com/piwa/ViePEP-C-Testclient.

4.1   Evaluation Setting

The evaluation is based on an adapted version of the settings used in [14].

Test Collection. For the evaluation, we choose 10 representative process models from the SAP reference process models [6,18]. The SAP reference models are a common testset in the BPM field [22]. The 10 selected process models possess different levels of complexity. Table 1a presents the characteristics of the selected models by showing the number of steps, XOR-blocks, AND-blocks, and repeat loops. Each XOR- and AND-block contains a split and join gateway.

While the SAP reference models also contain human-provided services, in our evaluation we only use software-based services. For the evaluation, we use 8 different software service types, each with different resource requirements and execution durations. Table 1b summarizes the required CPU load (in percentage) and total makespan (in seconds) of the services for one invocation. We further consider that the actual CPU load and execution duration of a service can vary to some extend. To consider this variation, we assume a normal distribution $\sigma_1 = \mu_{cpu}/10$ of the CPU load and $\sigma_2 = \mu_{makespan}/10$ of the total makespan, both with a lower bound of 95% and an upper bound of 105%.

To consider that a service needs more computational resources when it is invoked several times in parallel, we add for each invocation 2/3 of μ_{cpu} defined in Table 1b. For instance, if a service of type 1 is invoked two times in parallel the resource requirements are $\mu_{cpu} = 15 + 15 * 2/3 = 25$, while the service makespan stays the same. This way we consider that for a second invocation no additional resources are required for secondary software, e.g., the application server. Since most cloud providers have a upper resource limit for container instances (e.g., the CPU limit is 4 cores at Azure) a second container is deployed if the amount of invocations requires more resources than this limit.

In addition, we assume that each service is stateless and fully parallelizable among the available CPUs. For instance, if a service has a load of 100% on a single-core CPU, then the same service has a 50% load on a dual core (i.e., 50% on each core) with the same execution time.

---

[1] https://github.com/msigwart/fakeload.
[2] https://azure.microsoft.com.

Table 1. Evaluation process models and service types

(a) Evaluation Process Models

Name	|Steps|	|XOR|	|AND|	|loops|
1	3	0	0	0
2	2	1	0	0
3	3	0	1	0
4	8	0	2	0
5	3	1	0	0
6	9	1	1	0
7	9	1	0	0
8	3	0	1	1
9	4	1	1	1
10	20	0	4	0

(b) Evaluation Services

Service No.	CPU Load in % (μ_{cpu})	Service Makespan in sec. ($\mu_{makespan}$)
1	15	40
2	20	320
3	25	480
4	40	80
5	55	400
6	65	120
7	80	160
8	135	80

Applied SLAs. To tolerate some execution delay, due to the container deployment time and service start-up time, we apply a *lenient* and a *strict* SLA level as process execution deadline. In the lenient scenario, the deadline is 2.5 times of the average makespan of the whole process. The average makespan is the time that the execution of the whole process needs by considering the historical execution duration of each step and the order of them defined by the process model. In the strict scenario, the deadline is 1.5 times of the average makespan.

Process Request Arrival Patterns. For the evaluation, we apply two different process request arrival patterns. The first one, called *constant* arrival pattern, requests in a 240 s interval the execution of 5 different processes. The processes are selected from Table 1a in a round-robin fashion. This is repeated 20 times, which results in the execution of 100 processes.

The second request arrival pattern, called *pyramid* arrival pattern, follows the pattern shown in Eq. (6), where n represents a point in time and a the amount of process execution requests at this time. The processes are again selected from Table 1a in a round-robin fashion in a 120 s interval.

$$f(n) = a \begin{cases} 1 & \text{if } 0 \leq n \leq 3 \text{ and } 20 \leq n \leq 35 \\ \lceil (n+1)/4 \rceil & \text{if } 4 \leq n \leq 17 \\ 0 & \text{if } 18 \leq n \leq 19 \\ \lceil (n-9)/20 \rceil & \text{if } 36 \leq n \leq 51 \end{cases} \tag{6}$$

Baseline. We compare our optimization approach against a baseline that uses an ad hoc process execution approach. The baseline executes each process without task scheduling, but by executing one step after another according to the process model. However, for each new container that has to be deployed, it is checked if a compatible container is already deployed. If this is the case, this container is used, otherwise, a new container is deployed. When applying the baseline, containers are also deployed while a possible preceding step is running. This baseline is an adapted version of the *OneVMPerTask* provisioning strategy presented in [11].

Genetic Algorithm Parameter Setting. For the evaluation, we use a population size of 2,000 with 100 elite chromosomes per population. The optimization duration is set to 40 s. Furthermore, we set $f_{leasing} = 10$ (see Eq. (1)), $f_{penalty} = 0.001$ (see Eq. (2)), and *additionalTime* = 1 h (see Eq. (5)). These settings resolved in promising results in several pre-evaluation executions.

Metrics. As evaluation metrics we use the average *process makespan*, the *SLA adherence*, and the *total cost* of the execution. The process makespan is the duration between receiving a process execution request and the termination of the final step in minutes. The SLA adherence determines how many processes terminated without violating the deadline in percentage.

The total cost is composed of the *leasing cost*, i.e., the charged cost due to the leasing of the cloud resources, and the *penalty cost*, i.e., the charged cost due to a deadline violation. The penalty cost is calculated by a linear model based on [19]. This model assigns 1 unit of penalty cost for a delay of 10% of time units, i.e., seconds, of delay. For the leasing cost we use €0.0043 per GB-second and €0.0127 per CPU-second which are adapted real-world values from Azure prizing model[3]. For all evaluation results, we provide the mean value and the standard deviation.

4.2   Results and Discussion

In the evaluation, we evaluate the efficiency of our optimization approach, in comparison to the baseline, with both process request patterns and both SLA levels. Each evaluation step is performed three times over a timespan of 7 days to minimize external influences. The results of the evaluation are presented in Table 2. In addition, the constant arrival pattern results are presented in Fig. 3a and b and the pyramid arrival pattern results in Fig. 3c and d.

First, we discuss the constant arrival pattern results for both SLA levels, i.e., strict and lenient. In Table 2, it can be seen that our GeCo approach results in a lower SLA adherence than the baseline. This is due to the fact that the baseline executes each step directly after the preceding one without any delay between them. GeCo, in contrast, postpones the execution of a step if a more resource-efficient execution can be achieved. The postponing of the step execution in case of GeCo also results in a longer process makespan as observable in Table 2. While the process makespan stays nearly the same for both SLA levels in case of the baseline (i.e., 16.96 and 16.90 min), it varies in case of GeCo. Since GeCo has less room to postpone a step (before the deadline is violated) in case of the strict

---

[3] https://azure.microsoft.com/en-us/pricing/details/container-instances/.

Table 2. Evaluation results (Standard deviation in parenthesis)

| | Constant arrival pattern | | | | Pyramid arrival pattern | | | |
| | GeCo | | Baseline | | GeCo | | Baseline | |
SLA level	Strict	Lenient	Strict	Lenient	Strict	Lenient	Strict	Lenient
SLA adherence	82.67	96.67	90.00	100.00	83.67	97.67	90.00	100.00
(%)	(3.06)	(2.08)	(0.00)	(0.00)	(2.31)	(1.15)	(0.00)	(0.00)
Process	21.02	30.16	16.96	16.90	21.42	31.75	17.01	17.03
makespan (min)	(15.20)	(22.97)	(12.74)	(12.69)	(15.92)	(25.46)	(12.73)	(12.75)
Leasing cost	360.25	330.00	547.69	554.50	316.74	300.67	612.58	624.54
	(19.71)	(15.22)	(16.26)	(9.32)	(2.67)	(13.90)	(17.67)	(31.94)
Penalty cost	52.67	5.33	13.33	0.00	35.0	3.0	10.00	0.00
	(5.77)	(5.13)	(0.58)	(0.00)	(4.58)	(1.0)	(0.00)	(0.00)
Total cost	412.91	335.34	560.70	554.50	351.74	303.67	622.58	624.54
	(14.56)	(17.82)	(16.26)	(9.32)	(7.13)	(14.60)	(17.67)	(31.94)

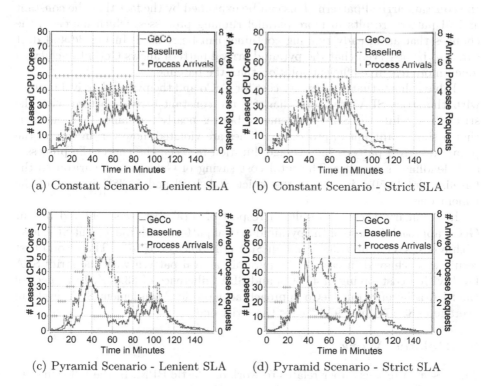

(a) Constant Scenario - Lenient SLA   (b) Constant Scenario - Strict SLA

(c) Pyramid Scenario - Lenient SLA   (d) Pyramid Scenario - Strict SLA

Fig. 3. Evaluation results

SLA level the process makespan is shorter for this SLA level, i.e., 21.02 min, than for the lenient one, i.e., 30.16 min.

While the baseline SLA adherence is better than in case of GeCo, GeCo achieves in average 37.37% lower leasing cost than the baseline. This cost-saving results from a better resource utilization achieved by GeCo. This can also be seen in Fig. 3a and b, where GeCo leases fewer CPU cores than the baseline.

The lower SLA adherence, achieved by GeCo, results in higher penalty cost. However, the baseline results for both SLA levels in higher total cost, due to higher leasing cost. The total cost saving of GeCo, in comparison to the baseline, is 26.35% in case of the strict SLA level and 39.52% in case of the lenient one. This cost saving was achieved despite higher penalty cost than in case of the baseline. This shows us that in some situations accepting some penalty cost can help to reduce the leasing cost, and thus the total cost, to quite some extent.

Second, we discuss the pyramid arrival pattern results. As can be observed in Table 2, the SLA adherence and process makespan stayed nearly the same, in comparison to the results of the constant arrival pattern. However, the leasing cost of GeCo and the baseline changed significantly. In case of GeCo, it can be seen that the pyramid arrival pattern allows GeCo to reduce the resource requirements even more. For the baseline the leasing cost increased, in comparison to the constant arrival pattern. This can be explained by the fact that the constant arrival pattern results in more parallel running processes, which increases the chances that an already running container can be re-used. In Fig. 3c and d, it can also be observed that the pyramid arrival pattern allows GeCo to achieve a much more resource-efficient solution than the baseline.

Table 2 shows that the penalty cost for GeCo and the pyramid arrival pattern with the strict SLA are lower than for the constant arrival pattern with the strict SLA, while the SLA adherence of both is nearly the same. This shows us that a similar amount of process deadlines are violated, however, in case of the pyramid arrival pattern the average duration between the end of the processes and deadlines is smaller. The total cost saving of GeCo in comparison to the baseline are 43.50% in case of the strict SLA level and 51.38% in case of the lenient one.

In summary, the best result, in respect of total cost, was achieved by our GeCo approach in case of the pyramid arrival pattern with the lenient SLA level with a cost saving of 51.38% and an SLA adherence of 97.67%. The second best result was achieved in case of the pyramid arrival pattern with the strict SLA level with a cost saving of 43.50% and SLA adherence of 83.67%. In respect of the SLA adherence our GeCo approach achieved for both lenient SLA levels an average of 83.17% and 97.17% for the strict one.

5   Related Work

The research in this paper relates to work on elastic BPM. In the following, we discuss selected contributions to this research field.

In our former work, we have presented the eBPMS platform ViePEP [27]. ViePEP offers several resource optimization and task scheduling approaches.

Those approaches perform a resource allocation optimization and task scheduling for cost-efficient process execution while considering predefined SLAs. Especially, the work presented in [14] has to be mentioned, where the task scheduling and resource optimization problem is formulated as a Mixed Integer Linear Program (MILP). However, until now ViePEP relies on VMs as an execution environment for the services, which results in a much more coarse-grained deployment and may increase cost in comparison to the work at hand.

In [17], the authors present a BPEL engine containing a scheduling algorithm for the cost-efficient execution of process steps on cloud resources in the form of VMs. The scheduling algorithm is based on a genetic algorithm and allows the execution and optimization of several processes in parallel. The presented scheduling algorithm considers the leasing cost of the VMs and the data transfer duration. However, since the approach uses VMs instead of containers, it results in a much more coarse-grained solution and may increase resource cost. Furthermore, in comparison to our work, it does not consider user-defined SLAs, e.g., the deadline until when the process has to be done. The same applies to the approach presented in [2]. In this work, the authors present a process scheduling approach that allows parallel execution of processes. The presented approach aims for a cost or execution time optimization or a pareto-optimal solution covering both, cost and execution time. Again, this approach uses VMs as the execution environment of the process steps and does not consider the process execution deadline. Hence, it is not possible to perform an optimization by postponing the execution of particular steps to the future as GeCo allows.

Wei and Blake present in [32] a resource utilization optimization approach that considers service levels. However, in contrast to our work, the approach does not consider a deadline for the process execution. Furthermore, while our approach follows the "classic" service composition model that allows the invocation of a service instance from different processes, this is not allowed in [32].

An approach for supporting a customer in finding the optimal cloud pricing strategy is presented in [13]. The approach selects a cost-efficient resource configuration (i.e., RAM and CPU size), the cloud provider, and the cloud pricing model (e.g., on-demand VM or reserved VM). Similar to our approach, the aim of the approach is to reduce the execution cost, including possible penalty cost, while considering QoS constraints and without violating temporal constraints. However, in comparison to our approach, the temporal constraints are on process step level and not on the process level.

In [25], the author's present migration-aware optimization strategies for multi-tenant process execution in the cloud. The presented strategies migrate a tenant, including the corresponding processes, from one BPMS to a different BPMS if the process execution needs more cloud resources or a new cost-efficient solution can be achieved. The BPMSs are thereby executed on VMs. The paper presents a linear optimization model and a heuristic optimization approach. The optimization aims to minimize the resource consumption while maintaining an acceptable migration amount for each tenant. While our approach considers the structure of the process and optimizes the execution of the steps on containers, the approach presented in [25] is more coarse-grained since it migrates the process as a whole and does not consider the single steps.

In [30] an approach for optimal resource provisioning for enterprise applications on cloud resources is presented. The authors present a linear program that finds the optimal setup of VM instances that minimizes the resources consumption while still able to fulfill all incoming requests. In comparison to our approach, which performs task scheduling to reduce the execution cost, their approach reduces the cost by finding the optimal VM instance configuration.

All of the aforementioned approaches are using VMs as an underlying execution environment and do not consider containers. As has been mentioned before, this leads to a more coarse-grained resource allocation, which may result in increased resource cost. For the usage of containers for scheduling and resource allocation of arbitrary services, several solutions have been proposed, e.g., [15,23,24,31]. Those publications discuss the usage of containers for scalable and isolated application execution in the cloud. However, none of them consider the execution of processes that are composed of several, interdependent steps.

In [5], the authors present a linear program that finds a global optimal cost-efficient solution for the deployment of a business process on containers. These containers are then deployed on VMs running on cloud resources. While this approach is the most comparable to the work at hand, the algorithm does not consider SLAs and considers only one process at a time. Thus, the usage of the same container for several service invocations is not facilitated. Moreover, in comparison to our work, the containers are deployed on VMs. For the evaluation, the authors extended ContainerCloudSim, while we make use of a cloud-based testbed for the evaluation.

In [12], the scientific workflows (SWF) platform Skyport is presented. The platform uses Docker containers for the deployment of the workflow services to achieve a reproducible software deployment solution with isolated software applications. In [37], the authors present a two-level resource scheduling model for an efficient resource sharing among different SWFs. They show that a container-based scheduling platform increases the system efficiency while decreasing the risk of performance issues. However, the differences between SWFs and business processes prevent a direct adaptation of the approaches for our purposes [20].

To sum things up, most of the presented publications are considering VMs as execution environment. This leads to rather coarse-grained deployment solutions in comparison to a container-based deployment as provided by GeCo. In addition, most of the above-discussed publications do not consider the usage of an already deployed container, respectively the deployed service instance, several times. This further reduces the resource consumption and, thus, the overall cost.

6   Conclusion

Within this paper, we present a novel scheduling approach for the fine-granular execution of process steps on containers, which are deployed on cloud resources.

This scheduling approach aims for a resource-efficient execution while considering user-defined SLAs, by scheduling the execution times of the steps of a complete process landscape. The resulting schedule minimizes the overall execution cost, which is a composition of the cloud resource leasing cost and penalty cost. The presented optimization approach, called GeCo, is based on a genetic algorithm. Our evaluation has shown that using such an optimization approach results in reduced leasing cost in comparison to an ad hoc baseline solution: In average our optimization approach issues 47.45% less cost for the pyramid arrival pattern and 32.90% less cost for the constant arrival pattern.

In our future research, we want to further analyze different genetic algorithm parameter settings. Furthermore, we want to examine different approaches for an automatic selection of the genetic algorithm parameter settings by using, for instance, machine learning. Another crucial point is the prediction of the service execution duration and the required computational resources. We will analyze in this respect how a combination of monitoring and prediction can be made.

Acknowledgments. This work is partially funded by FFG – Austrian Research Promotion Agency (FFG – project number: 866270).

References

1. Bernstein, D.: Containers and cloud: from LXC to docker to Kubernetes. IEEE Cloud Comput. **1**(3), 81–84 (2014)
2. Bessai, K., Youcef, S., Oulamara, A., Godart, C.: Bi-criteria strategies for business processes scheduling in cloud environments with fairness metrics. In: 7th International Conference on Research Challenges in Information Science (RCIS), pp. 1 10 (2013)
3. Bhandari, D., Murthy, C., Pal, S.K.: Variance as a stopping criterion for genetic algorithms with elitist model. Fundamenta Informaticae **120**(2), 145–164 (2012)
4. Borkowski, M., Schulte, S., Hochreiner, C.: Predicting cloud resource utilization. In: 2016 IEEE/ACM 9th International Conference on Utility and Cloud Computing (UCC), pp. 37–42 (2016)
5. Boukadi, K., Grati, R., Rekik, M., Abdallah, H.B.: From VM to container: a linear program for outsourcing a business process to cloud containers. In: Panetto, H. (ed.) OTM 2017. LNCS, vol. 10573, pp. 488–504. Springer, Cham (2017). https://doi.org/10.1007/978-3-319-69462-7_31
6. Curran, T.A., Keller, G.: SAP R/3 Business Blueprint: Understanding the Business Process Reference Model. Prentice Hall PTR, Upper Saddle River (1997)
7. Diaz-Gomez, P.A., Hougen, D.F.: Initial population for genetic algorithms: a metric approach. In: Proceedings of the 2007 International Conference on Genetic and Evolutionary Methods (GEM 2007), pp. 43–49 (2007)
8. Dua, R., Raja, A.R., Kakadia, D.: Virtualization vs Containerization to Support PaaS. In: 2014 IEEE International Conference on Cloud Engineering, pp. 610–614 (2014)
9. Dumas, M., Rosa, M.L., Mendling, J., Reijers, H.A.: Fundamentals of Business Process Management, 2nd edn. Springer, Heidelberg (2018). https://doi.org/10.1007/978-3-662-56509-4

10. Dustdar, S., Guo, Y., Satzger, B., Truong, H.L.: Principles of elastic processes. IEEE Internet Comput. **15**(5), 66–71 (2011)
11. Frincu, M.E., Genaud, S., Gossa, J.: On the efficiency of several VM provisioning strategies for workflows with multi-threaded tasks on clouds. Computing **96**(11), 1059–1086 (2014)
12. Gerlach, W., et al.: Skyport: container-based execution environment management for multi-cloud scientific workflows. In: 5th International Conference on Data-Intensive Computing in the Clouds, pp. 25–32 (2014)
13. Halima, R.B., Kallel, S., Gaaloul, W., Jmaiel, M.: Optimal cost for time-aware cloud resource allocation in business processes. In: 14th International Conference on Services Computing, pp. 314–321 (2017)
14. Hoenisch, P., Schuller, D., Schulte, S., Hochreiner, C., Dustdar, S.: Optimization of complex elastic processes. IEEE Trans. Serv. Comput. **9**(5), 700–713 (2016)
15. Hoenisch, P., Weber, I., Schulte, S., Zhu, L., Fekete, A.: Four-fold auto-scaling on a contemporary deployment platform using Docker containers. In: Barros, A., Grigori, D., Narendra, N.C., Dam, H.K. (eds.) ICSOC 2015. LNCS, vol. 9435, pp. 316–323. Springer, Heidelberg (2015). https://doi.org/10.1007/978-3-662-48616-0_20
16. Hou, E.S., Ansari, N., Ren, H.: A genetic algorithm for multiprocessor scheduling. IEEE Trans. Parallel Distrib. Syst. **5**(2), 113–120 (1994)
17. Juhnke, E., Dörnemann, T., Bock, D., Freisleben, B.: Multi-objective scheduling of BPEL workflows in geographically distributed clouds. In: 4th International Conference on Cloud Computing, pp. 412–419 (2011)
18. Keller, G., Teufel, T.: SAP R/3 Process Oriented Implementation: Iterative Process Prototyping. Addison-Wesley Longman Publishing Co., Boston (1998)
19. Leitner, P., Hummer, W., Satzger, B., Inzinger, C., Dustdar, S.: Cost-efficient and application SLA-aware client side request scheduling in an infrastructure-as-a-service cloud. In: 5th International Conference on Cloud Computing, pp. 213–220 (2012)
20. Ludäscher, B., Weske, M., McPhillips, T., Bowers, S.: Scientific workflows: business as usual? In: Dayal, U., Eder, J., Koehler, J., Reijers, H.A. (eds.) BPM 2009. LNCS, vol. 5701, pp. 31–47. Springer, Heidelberg (2009). https://doi.org/10.1007/978-3-642-03848-8_4
21. Mao, M., Humphrey, M.: A performance study on the VM startup time in the cloud. In: 5th International Conference on Cloud Computing, pp. 423–430 (2012)
22. Mendling, J., Verbeek, H., van Dongen, B.F., van der Aalst, W.M.P., Neumann, G.: Detection and prediction of errors in EPCs of the SAP reference model. Data Knowl. Eng. **64**(1), 312–329 (2008)
23. Nardelli, M., Hochreiner, C., Schulte, S.: Elastic provisioning of virtual machines for container deployment. In: 8th ACM/SPEC on International Conference on Performance Engineering Companion, pp. 5–10 (2017)
24. Pahl, C.: Containerization and the PaaS cloud. IEEE Cloud Comput. **2**(3), 24–31 (2015)
25. Rosinosky, G., Youcef, S., Charoy, F.: Efficient migration-aware algorithms for elastic BPMaaS. In: Carmona, J., Engels, G., Kumar, A. (eds.) BPM 2017. LNCS, vol. 10445, pp. 147–163. Springer, Cham (2017). https://doi.org/10.1007/978-3-319-65000-5_9
26. Schulte, S., Hoenisch, P., Hochreiner, C., Dustdar, S., Klusch, M., Schuller, D.: Towards process support for cloud manufacturing. In: International Enterprise Distributed Object Computing Conference, pp. 142–149. IEEE (2014)

27. Schulte, S., Hoenisch, P., Venugopal, S., Dustdar, S.: Introducing the Vienna platform for elastic processes. In: Ghose, A., et al. (eds.) ICSOC 2012. LNCS, vol. 7759, pp. 179–190. Springer, Heidelberg (2013). https://doi.org/10.1007/978-3-642-37804-1_19

28. Schulte, S., Janiesch, C., Venugopal, S., Weber, I., Hoenisch, P.: Elastic business process management: state of the art and open challenges for BPM in the cloud. Future Gener. Comput. Syst. **46**, 36–50 (2015)

29. Seo, K.T., Hwang, H.S., Moon, I.Y., Kwon, O.Y., Kim, B.J.: Performance comparison analysis of Linux container and virtual machine for building cloud. Adv. Sci. Technol. Lett. **66**(105–111), 2 (2014)

30. Srirama, S.N., Ostovar, A.: Optimal resource provisioning for scaling enterprise applications on the cloud. In: 2014 IEEE 6th International Conference on Cloud Computing Technology and Science (CloudCom), pp. 262–271. IEEE (2014)

31. Vaquero, L.M., Rodero-Merino, L., Buyya, R.: Dynamically scaling applications in the cloud. ACM SIGCOMM Comput. Comm. Rev. **41**(1), 45–52 (2011)

32. Wei, Y., Blake, M.B.: Proactive virtualized resource management for service workflows in the cloud. Computing **96**(7), 1–16 (2014)

33. Weske, M.: Business Process Management: Concepts, Languages, Architectures, 2nd edn. Springer, Heidelberg (2012). https://doi.org/10.1007/978-3-642-28616-2

34. Whitley, D.: A genetic algorithm tutorial. Stat. Comput. **4**, 65–85 (1994)

35. Ye, Z., Zhou, X., Bouguettaya, A.: Genetic algorithm based QoS-aware service compositions in cloud computing. In: Yu, J.X., Kim, M.H., Unland, R. (eds.) DASFAA 2011. LNCS, vol. 6588, pp. 321–334. Springer, Heidelberg (2011). https://doi.org/10.1007/978-3-642-20152-3_24

36. Yoo, M.: Real-time task scheduling by multiobjective genetic algorithm. J. Syst. Softw. **82**(4), 619–628 (2009)

37. Zheng, C., Tovar, B., Thain, D.: Deploying high throughput scientific workflows on container schedulers with makeflow and mesos. In: 17th IEEE/ACM International Symposium on Cluster, Cloud and Grid Computing, pp. 130–139 (2017)

ChIP: A Choreographic Integration Process

Saverio Giallorenzo[1(✉)], Ivan Lanese[2,3], and Daniel Russo[3]

[1] University of Southern Denmark, Odense, Denmark
saverio@imada.sdu.dk
[2] Focus Team, Inria, Sophia Antipolis, France
ivan.lanese@gmail.com
[3] University of Bologna, Bologna, Italy
daniel.russo@unibo.it

Abstract. Over the years, organizations acquired disparate software systems, each answering one specific need. Currently, the desirable outcomes of integrating these systems (higher degrees of automation and better system consistency) are often outbalanced by the complexity of mitigating their discrepancies. These problems are magnified in the decentralized setting (e.g., cross-organizational cases) where the integration is usually dealt with ad-hoc "glue" *connectors*, each integrating two or more systems. Since the overall logic of the integration is spread among many glue connectors, these solutions are difficult to program correctly (making them prone to misbehaviors and system blocks), maintain, and evolve. In response to these problems, we propose ChIP, an integration process advocating choreographic programs as intermediate artifacts to refine high-level global specifications (e.g., UML Sequence Diagrams), defined by the domain experts of each partner, into concrete, distributed implementations. In ChIP, once the stakeholders agree upon a choreographic integration design, they can automatically generate the respective local connectors, which are guaranteed to faithfully implement the described distributed logic. In the paper, we illustrate ChIP with a pilot from the EU EIT Digital project SMAll, aimed at integrating pre-existing systems from government, university, and transport industry.

1 Introduction

Over the years organizations acquired several software systems, each satisfying one specific need. Traditionally these systems hardly integrate with each other due to incompatible technology stacks [20,22]. It has been empirically observed that this leads to system stratification and increasing technical debt [40].

Contrarily, the high level of automation and consistency achievable by the integration of such systems could satisfy new requirements, maximize business/service performance, and avoid duplication of resources. This is confirmed by the thriving economics of Enterprise Resource Planners (ERPs) [24]. ERPs offer a closed, rigid yet highly structured environment for system integration.

H. Panetto et al. (Eds.): OTM 2018 Conferences, LNCS 11230, pp. 22–40, 2018.
https://doi.org/10.1007/978-3-030-02671-4_2

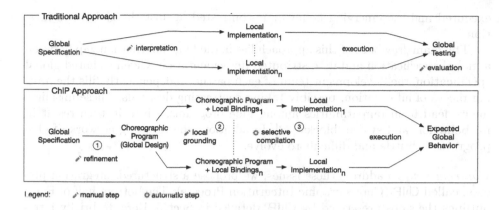

Fig. 1. Schemes of the traditional and the ChIP approaches.

However, ERPs are rarely a solution for cross-organizational integration, where the enforcement of a unique platform is nearly impossible.

In cross-organizational settings, the only possible approach is given by mediating applications, usually called "glue" programs [18] or connectors, that mitigate discrepancies among disparate technology stacks. The interest in this scenario has recently increased thanks to a new revenue model, called API Economy [19]. Adopting API Economy, many companies, among which Google, Facebook, eBay, and Sabre, started to sell to other organizations the access (under subscription, license, etc.) to their internal services. Although API Economy founds its model on integration, its practice is left to unstructured glue programming.

Both centralized and distributed glue programs are used [30]. In the centralized approach a unique glue program interacts with all the integrated systems. This entails all classical drawbacks of centralized systems in terms of scalability and reliability. Furthermore, this centralized connector has full access to the integrated functionalities, yet it resides on the premises of one of the involved organizations (or on third-party premises), hence issues of trust among organizations arise.

In the distributed approach, each stakeholder provides one or more connectors. Each connector interacts with both (*i*) other connectors, to realize the intended logic of integration and (*ii*) a set of local functionalities, which may not be accessible by the other connectors. In essence, each connector acts as an adapter for other glue programs. Each connector runs on the premises of one of the collaborating partners, providing a controlled access towards one or more of its resources. The traditional approach in developing distributed glue programs [22] is represented in Fig. 1, top half. First, a global specification of the integration is agreed upon by the stakeholders, using (frequently informal or semi-formal) notations such as Message Sequence Charts [28] (MSC), UML Sequence Diagrams [12] or BPMN choreographies [3]. The development team of each partner uses such a global specification as a reference to build the local implementation of the glue programs. Finally, the network of glue programs is executed and the emerging behavior is contrasted against the global specification.

The main drawback of this approach lies in the huge information gap between a global specification and its distributed implementation. Given a shared global specification, the development team of each partner independently fills the missing pieces of information, possibly taking contrasting decisions. These misalignments lead to incompatibilities among glue programs, which in turn result in misbehaviors and system blocks [32]. In addition, the resulting network of glue programs is brittle and difficult to evolve.

Contribution. To address these issues, we propose a structured integration process, called ChIP (Choreographic Integration Process). The bottom half of Fig. 1 outlines the steps prescribed by ChIP, detailed in Sect. 3. Here, to briefly introduce the ideas behind ChIP, we comment the two main artifacts built during the process. The first one to be produced is a *global specification* of the integrated system. It is intended for domain experts and gives a very abstract view of the system, omitting many details of the actual implementation. ChIP does not impose the use of a particular modeling notation to define the global specification. Examples of notation for global specification that we consider suitable within ChIP are MSCs, BPMN choreographies, and UML Sequence Diagrams. The second artifact is a *global design*, refinement of the global specification. The global design is the focal point of ChIP: it must be defined in a choreographic programming language [14,16,34] that (*i*) supports the compilation of a choreography into a set of connectors that faithfully implement the designed global interactions—so that *local connectors can be automatically generated from a global design*—and (*ii*) it is able to express at the global level when and how a given local connector invokes a local functionality, so that *the global design describes the whole integration within a unique artifact.*

Structure of the Paper. Section 2 discusses the positioning of the ChIP approach in the literature. Section 3 outlines ChIP, while Sect. 4 applies it to a real-world pilot from the EU EIT Digital project SMAll, aimed at integrating functionalities from the Emilia Romagna (Italy) regional government, University of Bologna, and a transport company. In this presentation we decided to use UML Sequence Diagrams to define the *global specification* and the AIOCJ choreographic programming language [2,15] for the *global design*. Section 5 clarifies how to exploit tools like AIOCJ within ChIP. Section 6 discusses the impact of ChIP on the evolution of integration solutions. Section 7 presents final remarks and future developments.

2   Related Work

Information systems that evolve over pre-existing legacy applications have always been a concern of system integration [21]. However, no definitive solution exists.

Choreographic programming, that is the use of choreographies to generate executable code, as advocated in ChIP, is quite recent and the literature on the topic is extremely limited [9, 14, 16, 17, 33, 34, 38]. Notably, among the approaches above, only [16], on which ChIP is built, provides a way of describing interactions with systems external to the choreographic program. The present paper complements the technical results and the tool presented in [16] by proposing a software development process where such results and tool are exploited. The other approaches listed above, since they cannot represent interactions with external systems, can be used to generate distributed systems but not distributed integrations.

More in general, choreographic programming can be framed in the setting of choreographic descriptions of communicating systems. Choreographies have been introduced in the area of business process management to support the description of business-to-business collaborations [1]. While the idea of the approach is not far from ours, they consider models such as Petri Nets that are more abstract and have less emphasis on communication than choreographic programming. Also they do not specifically target integrations of pre-existing systems.

More recently, approaches sharing our communication-centric view have appeared. Broadly, ChIP can be classified as a top-down approach: the integration is specified and designed at the global level, declaring which functionalities it will integrate and the logic of the integration. Locally, deployment information is added to link the desired functionalities to actual services providing them. Finally, local code for the connectors is automatically generated.

Other approaches we are aware of are not top-down, but mixed: they assume both a choreographic specification and an existing running integration. We divide them into two categories:

- *Type-based approaches* rely on multiparty session types [27], cannot be directly used to implement connectors but are a non-invasive solution to statically check [25] or dynamically monitor [11] the correctness of the integrations. Among the various approaches, Compositional Choreographies [36], which however have never been implemented neither applied to system integration, would be the closest to ours: thanks to compositionality, Compositional Choreographies describe both the glue connectors and the systems to be integrated, as we do.
- *Model driven approaches*, such as [5, 6] concentrate on realizability enforcement. Namely, they are used to build coordination delegates that limit the possible interactions between integrated services, avoiding undesired communication patterns. However, they cannot provide added behavior, hence limiting the forms of integration that can be specified.

In principle, instead of choreographic programs, one could use other formal coordination languages able to describe a global system and that support code generation, such as BIP [7], Reo [4], Dynamic Condition Response Graphs [23] or Let's Dance [43]. We choose choreographic programs since they are closer to UML Sequence Diagrams and BPMN choreographies, which are frequently used as starting point of the development process. Among those approaches, to the best of our knowledge, BIP is the only one that has a description of its intended use in the software development process from a software engineering perspective [7], as done here for choreographic programs. The two approaches are quite different in practice since BIP is a declarative model, while choreographic programs are operational descriptions.

3   A Choreographic Integration Process: Outline

In this section we give a general definition of the three-step process that characterizes ChIP, as outlined in the bottom half of Fig. 1. In the next section we will apply ChIP to a real-world integration project.

The main innovation of ChIP consists in filling the information gap between global specification and local implementations present in the traditional approach, using a three-step structured process:

1. a collective refinement process that, from an abstract global specification, leads to a global design expressed as a *choreographic program*. The obtained choreographic program formally defines the expected global behavior and clarifies which tasks are delegated to which stakeholder. The first step of ChIP is highly non trivial, nevertheless it provides a well-defined, limited task to users: defining an agreed global design of the logic of the integrated system. This contrasts with the unstructured, "open" task of the classical case, where from a global specification users should come up with their local implementations. In the ChIP approach, this step considers descriptions of the system from a global perspective, hence issues related to synchronization and distribution can still be abstracted away. The design is agreed upon by the participants and includes the whole logic of integration.
2. a local grounding separately performed by each stakeholder, which links the functionalities that each participant promised to deliver to actual resources in its IT system. Hence, this phase is straightforward. The information on which internal resources are used needs not to be shared with the other stakeholders: the access to these functionalities is provided via the local glue programs, which are under the control of the stakeholder and which run in its own system.
3. the fully automatic generation of the local connectors from the grounded global design (i.e., the grounded choreographic program). Making this step automatic is far from trivial, but it is tackled relying on well-known techniques called choreographic programming [14,16,34], endpoint projection [25] or choreography realizability [9]. Here, in particular, we exploit for this step the notion of endpoint projection described in [16], which is implemented in the AIOCJ tool [2,15]. Notably, the global behavior emerging from the execution of the glue programs is compliant with the global design by construction: synchronization and distribution issues are automatically managed. This avoids misalignments among the local implementations; a renowned problem of the traditional approach.

Remarkably, the process proposed in ChIP eases also the evolution of integration solutions. For example, it is relatively simple to take a choreographic program

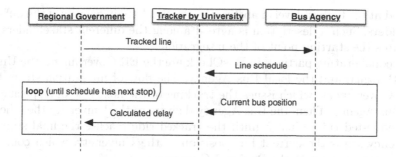

Fig. 2. Sequence diagram of the pilot.

belonging to a previous ChIP iteration and to modify it by including new stake-holders and/or changing the logic of interaction. In step ②, users can possibly reuse local groundings defined in the previous iteration. In step ③ users either obtain a connector that replaces an existing one or a completely new one, useful for integrating new functionalities. We further discuss the impact of ChIP on system evolution in Sect. 6.

4   A Choreographic Integration Process at Work

Running Example. We illustrate ChIP via a real-world pilot developed within the recent European EIT Digital project SMAll[1] The focus of SMAll is the creation of the namesake platform[2] [13] aimed at marketing functionalities for transportation owned, managed, and offered by diverse transport operators. The revenue model underlying the SMAll platform is based on the API Economy, where players whose core business is not that of information systems (e.g., in the context of SMAll, bus/train agencies, taxi associations) can publish and sell their functionalities within a global market. Some pilots have been developed as part of the SMAll project. Each pilot integrates pre-existing services, owned by diverse organizations, to provide new applications.

Below we refer to one of these pilots as a real-world example of application of the ChIP approach. The considered pilot is called BusCheck, it was commissioned by the Department of Transportation of the government of the Emilia-Romagna (ER) region (Italy) to the University of Bologna, and it is aimed at recording and displaying the punctuality of buses in Bologna county.

Global Specification. Both the traditional approach and ChIP start with an informal or semi-formal description of the intended global behavior, such as the UML Sequence Diagram in Fig. 2. In this phase the intended behavior is

---

[1] Project   description: https://forumvirium.fi/en/small-develops-mobility-as-a-service/.

[2] Deployable platform: https://hub.docker.com/u/smallproject/
Documentation: https://github.com/small-dev/SMAll.Wiki/wiki.

described at the highest level of abstraction by the domain experts of the different stakeholders. Such a description is agreed among the different stakeholders and constitutes the starting point of the integration.

The collaborating partners in BusCheck are the ER Government, the University of Bologna, and the local Bus Agency. The flow of integration starts from the ER Government, which issues the tracking of the next ride of a specific line to the Bus Agency. Then, the Bus Agency delivers to the University the schedule of the requested ride. Finally, until the tracked ride reaches the final stop, the Bus Agency sends the current bus position to the University, which computes the delay and sends it to the Regional Government.

① **Global Specification Refinement.** In this first step the abstract global specification is refined to obtain a global design. This phase ends when the global design is complete and agreed upon by the different stakeholders. Given the technical background necessary at this stage, we assume the collaboration of personnel from each stakeholder IT department. Following ChIP, IT personnel uses a full-fledged, high-level programming language, implementing the choreographic programming paradigm [16,34], to formalize the integration design. Choreographic programs are the key feature of the ChIP approach, since they provide two benefits:

1. they preserve a global view over the integrated systems, hence they are conceptually close to the original global specification, and
2. they already contain all the logic of the integration in a formal notation, hence they can later on be used to automatically generate the local code of each glue program, without the need for any additional behavioral information. This is particularly relevant since the addition of further behavioral information at the local level may create inconsistencies.

At this stage, choreographic programs are artifacts that support the transition from an informal global specification to a formal global design. The precise methodology used for this refinement step is not key in ChIP, provided that at the end of the phase the global design is formalized as a choreographic program. However, we advocate for this step an iterative approach, where details are added to the specification and technical decisions are recorded. Notably, at some point during the refinement, one should move from the specification notation (UML Sequence Diagram in this example) to the choreographic program notation. While a complete description of the step goes beyond the scope of the present paper, we remark that choreographic programs easily capture the information contained in UML Sequence Diagrams, yet require more information to be added. We will show this in detail in the case of our pilot. Further refinement steps can be performed both before, at the level of UML Sequence Diagram, and after, at the level of choreographic program. In our running example, we first translate the UML Sequence Diagram into the choreographic specification in Listing 1.1, where we use question marks as placeholders for missing information.

```
1  setLine: Government(line) -> BusAgency(line);
2  passSchedule: BusAgency(shd) -> Tracker(shd);
3  while(hasNext)@? {
4    passPosition: BusAgency(pos) -> Tracker(pos);
5    storeDelay: Tracker(delay) -> Government(delay)
6  }
```

Listing 1.1. Choreographic specification of the BusCheck pilot, first version.

Notably, the communications represented in the UML Sequence Diagram are directly mapped into *interactions* in the choreographic specification. An interaction represents a full message exchange, where one participant sends a message and another participant receives it, storing it in one of its local variables. For instance passPosition: **BusAgency**(pos) -> **Tracker**(pos) represents the interaction between the **BusAgency** and the **Tracker** provided by the University of Bologna to send the information on the position of the bus. We remark here that variables are local, hence the two occurrences of pos in the interaction refer to distinct variables: the left one is local to the **BusAgency** connector and the right one belongs to the **Tracker**.

Commenting the choreographic specification in Listing 1.1, the question mark at line 3 is a placeholder for the name of the participant that coordinates the distributed while loop, i.e., the one that at each iteration evaluates the condition hasNext and coordinates whether the participants involved in the loop shall enter another iteration or exit. Beyond missing the information replaced by the question mark, the choreographic specification also misses all the computational information regarding which local functionalities are needed and how values are computed. This is why we still call it a choreographic specification and not a choreographic design.

However, before adding the missing details, the ER Government decides to refine the system representation by splitting its behavior between two connectors: an **Admin**istrator, representing the official requesting the tracking of a certain line, and a **DatabaseConnector** which stores the data on delays of the tracked line for later analysis (the latter not in the scope of the pilot). The resulting choreographic specification is represented in Listing 1.2. Note the new interaction at line 1, which represents a communication internal to the ER Government, exposed by the refinement step (the interaction is composed with the one at line 3 using the parallel operator |, which models the fork-and-join pattern). All the stakeholders need to approve this refined specification, since all the choreographic specifications are shared documents.

Finally, the stakeholders prepare and agree on a concrete version of the choreographic description, containing all the behavioral information: only at this stage we can call it a global design. The main novelty in the global design is that it describes which functionalities need to be invoked, and when. For instance, with the invocation shd@**BusAgency** = *getSchedule*(line) the **BusAgency** promises to deliver a functionality named *getSchedule*, that, given

```
1  { setLine: Admin(line) -> DatabaseConnector(line)
2    |
3    setLine: Admin(line) -> BusAgency(line)
4  };
5  passSchedule: BusAgency(shd) -> Tracker(shd);
6  while(hasNext)@? {
7    passPosition: BusAgency(pos) -> Tracker(pos);
8    storeDelay: Tracker(delay) -> DatabaseConnector(delay);
9  }
```

Listing 1.2. Choreographic specification of the BusCheck pilot, refined.

a line, returns its schedule. At this stage, the semantics of the functionality is undefined. However, the invocation already specifies which variables the functionality will use (`line`) and where the result will be stored (`shd`).

Summarizing, the main ingredients of a choreographic program are interactions, describing the expected communications among the glue programs, and placeholders for invocations of local functionalities. Interactions and local functionalities can be composed using an arbitrarily complex logic, including conditionals, loops, etc. The resulting global design of our running example is represented in Listing 1.3, and described in detail below.

A condition for the refinement phase to be finished is that the resulting global design is *realizable* [9] (or connected, according to the terminology in [16]), i.e., it contains enough information on how the interaction is coordinated. This can be checked automatically using the approaches in [9,16]. If this is not the case, refinement should continue by adding the missing information. This aspect of refinement has been described in [8,31].

Global Design. The global design is a choreographic program [16,34] defining the expected behavior of the integration. Here, in particular, we use a variant of the AIOCJ [2,15] choreographic programming language.

At lines 1–5 the partners declare the location where their local connectors will be reachable. This is the only deployment information that the partners have to share and, as a consequence, it is inserted in the global design.

Lines 8–11 compose with operator | two interactions in parallel: the **Admin**istrator sends to both the **DatabaseConnector** and the **BusAgency** the bus `line` that the official wants to track (inserted at line 7) in a specific execution of the program. Since the composition is within braces, the system proceeds to line 12 only after both messages are stored in their respective local variables `line`. At line 12, the **BusAgency** retrieves the schedule of the tracked bus `line`, using the functionality *getSchedule*, and passes it to the **Tracker** (line 13).

Finally, lines 15–23 describe a loop among the **Tracker**, the **BusAgency**, and the **DatabaseConnector**. We recall the description of Listing 1.1, where a question mark indicates the need to define which participant should evaluate the condition of the loop and coordinate the other participants in its body. In the refined global design the coordinator of the loop is the **Tracker** and the

```
1   locations {
2     Admin: "reg-gov.org:80/BusCheckAdmin"
3     DatabaseConnector: "reg-gov.org:80/BusCheckDB"
4     Tracker: "university.edu:80/Tracker"
5     BusAgency: "bus-agency.com:80/BusCheck" }
6
7   line@Admin = getInput("Insert line to track");
8   { setLine: Admin(line) -> DatabaseConnector(line)
9     |
10     setLine: Admin(line) -> BusAgency(line)
11  };
12  shd@BusAgency = getSchedule(line);
13  passSchedule: BusAgency(shd) -> Tracker(shd);
14  hasNext@Tracker = hasNextStop(shd);
15  while(hasNext)@Tracker {
16    pos@BusAgency = getPosition(line);
17    passPosition: BusAgency(pos) -> Tracker(pos);
18    delay@Tracker = calculateDelay(shd, pos);
19    storeDelay: Tracker(delay) -> DatabaseConnector(delay);
20    { res@DatabaseConnector = insertDelay(line, delay)
21      |
22      hasNext@Tracker = hasNextStop(shd)
23  } }
```

Listing 1.3. Global design of the BusCheck pilot.

condition it evaluates depends on the result of the invocation of the *hasNextStop* functionality. The *hasNextStop* functionality is also used to pace the loop: when invoked to check the presence of another stop, it also waits until it is time to poll again the position of the tracked line (e.g., when the bus is expected to be approaching a stop).

Inside the loop, at each iteration, the **BusAgency** retrieves the position of the current bus on the observed bus line (line 16) and passes it to the **Tracker** (line 17). Then, at line 18, the **Tracker** invokes function *calculateDelay*. At line 19, the calculated delay is sent to the **DatabaseConnector**. Finally, two external functionalities are invoked in parallel: the **DatabaseConnector** inserts the delay for the observed bus line in the database (line 23) and the **Tracker** invokes functionality *hasNextStop* to check if and when a new iteration has to start.

Note that our choreographic program does not detail how to perform distributed synchronizations. For instance, the loop at lines 15–23 involves different distributed connectors, but it is unspecified how to ensure that all the connectors follow the prescribed behavior, i.e., looping or exiting when the **Tracker** decides so. This level of abstraction can be kept thanks to the selective compilation (described later), which automatically generates correct message-based synchronization algorithms, as detailed in [16].

② **Local Grounding.** The global design is the last document agreed upon by all the stakeholders. The local grounding is performed by each participant in isola-

```
1  deployment {
2    getSchedule from "socket://intranet.schdls:8000" with SOAP
3    getPosition from "socket://intranet.GPS:8001" with HTTP }
```

Listing 1.4. Deployment for the Bus Agency.

tion. For instance, the Bus Agency IT personnel grounds the global design by providing the binding for its internal functionalities *getSchedule* and *getPosition*. These functionalities are only invoked by the local connector, which acts as an intermediary by providing to the other participants access to the local functionalities as prescribed by the global design. Concretely, the deployment information for the Bus Agency is represented in Listing 1.4. The `deployment` declares the internal address where each functionality is available, possibly specifying the communication medium and the data protocol to be used. For instance, at line 2, the prefix `"socket://"` specifies the usage of TCP/IP as medium while SOAP specifies the used data protocol. This flexibility on communication media and data protocol is fundamental to enable the integration of disparate preexisting functionalities.

③ **Selective Compilation.** Finally, at this stage, the Bus Agency has specified all the information needed to automatically generate its local connector. The generation of the connector for the **BusAgency** takes the global design and the deployment information for the **BusAgency** and produces an executable program implementing the local logic of the connector.

Selective compilation hides most of the complexity of developing distributed glue connectors that interact with each other, without a central coordinator. This step is far from trivial, however it is well understood: it corresponds to the notion of endpoint projection in choreographic programming [14,16]. In particular, AIOCJ programs can be projected [16] by automatically creating web services in the Jolie [29, 35] language.

As an illustrative example, we report in Fig. 3 an excerpt of the pseudo-code of the compiled connectors of the **BusAgency**, the **DatabaseConnector**, and the **Tracker**[3]. The pseudo-code shows the result of the selective compilation of lines 14–23 in Listing 1.3. In the reported code, programs communicate through `send` and `recv` (short for "receive") instructions. External functionalities are invoked through the `call` instruction. In addition to the communications created by interactions in the global design, we also show the auxiliary communications used to ensure a coordinated execution of the while loop. Auxiliary communications are prefixed with an underscore "_", e.g., _wG1 (standing for while guard) and _wE1 (standing for while end) indicate the auxiliary communications used by the **Tracker** and the **BusAgency** to coordinate within the distributed loop.

---

[3] The compiled connectors are available at http://www.cs.unibo.it/projects/jolie/ aiocj_examples/ChIP_example/ChIP_example.zip.

```
1   recv _wG1(hasNext) from Tracker;        1   recv _wG2(hasNext) from Tracker;
2   while(hasNext){                         2   while(hasNext){
3     pos = call getPosition(line);         3     recv storeDelay(delay) from Tracker;
4     send passPosition(pos) to Tracker;    4     res = call insertDelay(line,delay);
5     send _wE1() to Tracker;               5     send _wE2() to Tracker;
6     recv _wG1(hasNext) from Tracker        6     recv _wG2(hasNext) from Tracker
7   }                                       7   }
```

BusAgency   DatabaseConnector

```
1    hasNext = call hasNextStop(shd);
2    send _wG1(hasNext) to BusAgency;
3    send _wG2(hasNext) to DatabaseConnector;
4    while (hasNext){
5      recv passPosition(pos) from BusAgency;
6      delay = call calculateDelay(shd,pos);
7      send storeDelay(delay) to DatabaseConnector;
8      recv _wE1() from BusAgency;
9      recv _wE2() from DatabaseConnector;
10     hasNext = call hasNextStop(shd);
11     send _wG1(hasNext) to BusAgency;
12     send _wG2(hasNext) to DatabaseConnector
13   }
```

Tracker

Fig. 3. From top-left to bottom, an excerpt (lines 14–23 of Listing 1.3) of the compiled connectors of the **BusAgency**, the **DatabaseConnector**, and the **Tracker**.

Expected Global Behavior. A main feature of ChIP is that no behavior is defined by the single stakeholder: all the behavior is described globally and agreed by all the stakeholders. This avoids the possibility that different stakeholders take contrasting decisions.

Furthermore, the generation of local connectors from the choreographic program has been proved correct in [16], hence no error can be introduced in this step. Of course, the stakeholders may agree on a wrong integration behavior. However, in choreographic programs, interactions are represented as atomic entities, hence it is syntactically impossible to express deadlocks and races on communications, avoiding by design the presence of such infamous bugs in the agreed integration behavior and, as a consequence, in the generated distributed network of connectors.

5   A Choreographic Integration Process: Tool Support

The ideas described in the previous sections are quite general, relying on key features of global specification languages and choreographic programs. The running example instantiated these ideas using UML Sequence Diagrams and the AIOCJ choreographic programming language. We do not describe support for UML Sequence Diagrams since there are many tools that support them. On the contrary, we dedicate this section to describe AIOCJ, which is less known yet it is fundamental for the approach. Furthermore, it has been adapted to support ChIP. While referring to [15,16] for a detailed description of AIOCJ, we clarify here why it is suitable for ChIP, and how it has been updated to support it. AIOCJ has been created to program adaptive applications [15], but the main reason why we build on it is that it supports not only choreographic programming and realizability checking (as done, for instance, by Chor [14] or Scribble [41]), but also interaction with external services. This last feature is fundamental to speak about integration, and, as far as we know, AIOCJ is currently the only choreographic language providing it. AIOCJ generates code for the local connectors in the Jolie [29,35] programming language. A relevant feature that AIOCJ inherits from Jolie is the possibility of supporting multiple communication media (TCP/IP sockets, Bluetooth L2CAP, Java RMI, Unix local sockets) and data protocols (HTTP, SOAP, ...) in a uniform way. This is convenient to integrate heterogeneous functionalities, as done, e.g., in Listing 1.4.

AIOCJ takes a choreographic program and generates code for all connectors at once, hence it needs full deployment information. This is not suitable for ChIP, where each stakeholder (i) generates its own connectors and (ii) can provide only deployment information on the other connectors and its local functionalities— i.e., it ignores the deployment of functionalities owned by the other stakeholders. Thus, we have extended AIOCJ with support for separate compilation: one can select which connectors to generate, and only the needed deployment information is required. Like AIOCJ, its extension with support for separate compilation is released as an open-source project[4].

We currently do not provide tool support for step ① of ChIP. Step ② does not require any tool support: deployment information and choreographic program can simply be concatenated. Finally, step ③ can be performed using AIOCJ with separate compilation. To this end, both the choreographic program and the deployment information need to fit AIOCJ syntax, reported in [2].

Note that the original version of AIOCJ can be used for testing: if full information for a local deployment is provided (and stubs for required functionalities are in place), AIOCJ will provide a fully working local network of connectors, that can be immediately tested to check whether the behavior is as expected. Changing the deployment information does not change the behavior (provided that required functionalities are available), hence this local test is relevant.

6   Evolution of Integrated Systems

Another important aspect of system integration, besides the design of new solutions, is the evolution of existing ones [21]. On the one hand, the rigidity of the integration imposes constraints on the network topology and the functionalities of the internal system of each stakeholder; on the other hand, each stakeholder strives to evolve its internal system independently, adapting it to environmental changes and newly-adopted business policies. Finally, integration solutions may also need to adapt to mirror changes in business relationships between the stakeholders, e.g., when some stakeholders leave or join the partnership.

---

[4] https://github.com/thesave/aiocj/tree/SeparateCompilation.

Managing these elements of software evolution is an essential aspect of software management, strongly supported by modern engineering approaches such as continuous delivery [26] and continuous deployment [39]. ChIP can be easily integrated into such modern approaches, offering a structured process for system design and evolution. Concretely, in ChIP, the generation of connectors is already automatic, hence automation can go directly from the global design to the deployment. Furthermore, the artifacts developed during the ChIP process, namely the global specification, the global design, and the local bindings, can be reused and updated during evolution. More in detail, in ChIP, updates to the integration are either done from the design step and/or locally, at the step of local grounding (e.g., starting from a pre-existing global design and reiterating from step ②)).

As expected, reiterating ChIP from step ② concerns only the local resources of single stakeholders and it is transparent to the other stakeholders. Contrarily, changes at the design level may influence many participants in the integration. In this case, partners can decide to update the integration either from the level of global specification or from that of global design. Such a decision is based on the visibility of the modifications. If the update regards only some technical details that are abstracted away in the global specification, partners can just have their IT personnel agree on a new version of the pre-existing global design, automatically generating the new connectors that implement the updated design (to replace the previous ones). On the contrary, if the update is visible at the level of the global specification, the domain experts of each stakeholder should reiterate over the whole ChIP process, first agreeing upon an updated version of the pre-existing global specification and then revising steps ①, ②, and ③ to obtain the updated integration solution.

We contrast this situation with what would be needed in the traditional integration process: the global specification is updated — provided that the change is relevant enough to be visible at the specification level — and then developers of each stakeholder need to update their local connectors accordingly. There, understanding which local changes are needed to enable a new desired global behavior is far from trivial, it requires good coordination among the involved teams, and it is prone to misbehaviors.

Example of System Evolution in ChIP. To illustrate how the ChIP process simplifies the evolution of existing integration solutions, we consider our running example and assume that, due to administrative data-provenance regulations, the Bus Agency must digitally sign each bus position sent to the University, while the University is asked to discard any unsigned data it receives.

According to the evolution process described in the previous paragraphs, first the stakeholders should agree upon a revised version of the global specification. To exemplify this, we report in Fig. 4 a possible revision of the UML Sequence Diagram in Fig. 2. In Fig. 4 in the loop fragment the Bus Agency sends a message labeled "signed current bus position" to the University. The data, if validated, is used to calculate the delay sent to the Regional Government. In the other

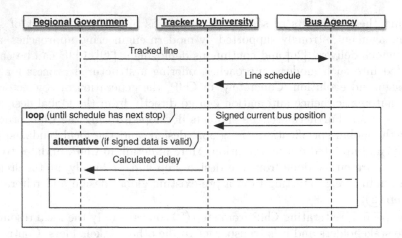

Fig. 4. Evolved sequence diagram of the pilot.

```
15   while(hasNext)@Tracker {
16     pos@BusAgency = getPosition(line);
17     signed_pos@BusAgency = sign(pos);
18     passPosition: BusAgency(signed_pos) -> Tracker(pos);
19     valid@Tracker = validate(pos);
20     if( valid )@Tracker{
21       delay@Tracker = calculateDelay(shd, pos);
22       storeDelay: Tracker(delay) -> DatabaseConnector(delay);
23       _@DatabaseConnector = insertDelay(line, delay)
24     };
25     hasNext@Tracker = hasNextStop(shd)
26   }
```

Listing 1.5. Global design of the updated BusCheck pilot.

case—the empty lane in the alternative fragment in Fig. 4—the received data is not used and therefore discarded.

Once the updated global specification is agreed upon by all the stakeholders, they can proceed with step ① by just modifying the second half of the global design in Listing 1.3. We report in Listing 1.5 the updated code of Listing 1.3. The most relevant changes are: (*i*) at line 17 the **BusAgency** invokes a new functionality to *sign* the retrieved position of the current bus, (*ii*) at line 19 the **Tracker** invokes a new functionality to *validate* the data sent by the **BusAgency**, and (*iii*) at lines 20–24 the **Tracker** decides, based on the result of the validation, whether to use the data for delay calculation or to discard it and proceed with the next iteration.

After agreeing upon the global design in Listing 1.5, the stakeholders proceed to the individual local grounding (as of step ②). In the example, only the **BusAgency** and the **Tracker** have to modify their pre-existing groundings, respectively defining the location of functionalities *sign* and *validate*. Following step ③, each partner automatically generates its own updated connectors. Finally, to start the updated version of the integration, all the partners have to terminate the previously deployed connectors and deploy their respective replacements.

Dynamic Evolution. As exemplified above (as well as in the traditional approach), when updating a pre-existing system, the stakeholders have to shutdown the deployed connectors, replace them, and restart the whole integrated architecture. In many application contexts these downtimes are acceptable, however when the integrated systems need to be always online, it is imperative to avoid or at least minimize these downtimes.

Shutdown can be avoided by resorting to live update techniques, such as the ones described in [42]. However, as shown in [42], only a few of these techniques support the live update of distributed systems. Indeed, while the centralized case entails the update of just one program, in the distributed case a protocol must be in place to coordinate the update of the distributed components, avoiding unexpected behaviors that may arise when updated components interact with components which have not been updated yet.

Notably, AIOCJ provides one of the few techniques for live updates of distributed systems, that is of the distributed connectors it generates. We refer to [16] for a full description of the technique, since it is out of the scope of the present paper. Essentially, selected parts of the choreographic program can be replaced by new choreographic program fragments at runtime thanks to AIOCJ runtime support. As proved in [16], AIOCJ guarantees correctness of the behavior after the update, and avoids unexpected behaviors while the update is applied.

7   Conclusion

We presented ChIP, a novel integration process suited for distributed, cross-organizational scenarios. The main highlight of ChIP is that it provides a structured way to refine abstract global specifications (e.g., UML Sequence Diagrams) into corresponding concrete implementations. The refinement process relies on choreographic programs to represent a global design agreed upon by all partners of the integration. The global design is used by each stakeholder to selectively compile its own set of executable connectors.

In ChIP, choreographies provide the main benefits of (*i*) enabling a simpler and less error-prone refinement process, since they are closer to the high-level global specifications with respect to low-level implementations; (*ii*) structuring how the integrated functionalities of each partner are accessed, without disclosing relevant information, like the internal topology of partners (which can even change dynamically, provided it preserves the interface expected by connectors); (*iii*) supporting a correctness-by-construction approach that guarantees the faithful implementation of the agreed global design, also avoiding hard-to-debug misbehaviors such as deadlocks; (*iv*) simplifying the evolution of the system, thus matching nicely continuous delivery and continuous deployment approaches.

While ChIP provides an innovative framework for integration, many aspects need further study. The global refinement phase should be fully specified (taking into account the different possible notations for the global specification) and equipped with suitable tool support. Integration should also be type safe, by declaring types both for variables in the global design and for external functionalities, relying, e.g., on XML Schema [37] type system. Other relevant issues include how to deal with exceptional behavior, transactions, large and complex data structures, security and non-functional properties. While a detailed study of each of these topics would be long and challenging, we deem ChIP able to help dealing with them. The broad idea is that desired behaviors, e.g., transactional or security properties, can be specified at the global level and then advanced projections ensure that specifications are matched by the running system. An approach along these lines for security properties is described in [10].

References

1. van der Aalst, W.M.P., Weske, M.: The P2P approach to interorganizational workflows. In: Dittrich, K.R., Geppert, A., Norrie, M.C. (eds.) CAiSE 2001. LNCS, vol. 2068, pp. 140–156. Springer, Heidelberg (2001). https://doi.org/10.1007/3-540-45341-5_10
2. AIOCJ website. http://www.cs.unibo.it/projects/jolie/aiocj.html
3. Allweyer, T.: BPMN 2.0: introduction to the standard for business process modeling. BoD-Books on Demand (2016)
4. Arbab, F.: Reo: a channel-based coordination model for component composition. MSCS **14**(3), 329–366 (2004)
5. Autili, M., Inverardi, P., Tivoli, M.: CHOREOS: large scale choreographies for the future Internet. In: CSMR-WCRE, pp. 391–394. IEEE (2014)
6. Autili, M., Di Ruscio, D., Di Salle, A., Inverardi, P., Tivoli, M.: A model-based synthesis process for choreography realizability enforcement. In: Cortellessa, V., Varró, D. (eds.) FASE 2013. LNCS, vol. 7793, pp. 37–52. Springer, Heidelberg (2013). https://doi.org/10.1007/978-3-642-37057-1_4
7. Basu, A., et al.: Rigorous component-based system design using the BIP framework. IEEE Softw. **28**(3), 41–48 (2011)
8. Basu, S., Bultan, T.: Automated choreography repair. In: Stevens, P., Wąsowski, A. (eds.) FASE 2016. LNCS, vol. 9633, pp. 13–30. Springer, Heidelberg (2016). https://doi.org/10.1007/978-3-662-49665-7_2
9. Basu, S., Bultan, T., Ouederni, M.: Deciding choreography realizability. In: POPL, pp. 191–202. ACM (2012)
10. Bhargavan, K., et al.: Cryptographic protocol synthesis and verification for multiparty sessions. In: CSF, pp. 124–140. IEEE Computer Society (2009)
11. Bocchi, L., et al.: Monitoring networks through multiparty session types. Theor. Comput. Sci. **669**, 33–58 (2017)
12. Booch, G.: The Unified Modeling Language User Guide. Pearson Education, New Delhi (2005)
13. Callegati, F., et al.: Smart mobility for all: a global federated market for mobility-as-a-service operators. In: ITSC, pp. 1–8. IEEE (2017)
14. Carbone, M., Montesi, F.: Deadlock-freedom-by-design: multiparty asynchronous global programming. In: POPL, pp. 263–274. ACM (2013)

15. Dalla Preda, M., Giallorenzo, S., Lanese, I., Mauro, J., Gabbrielli, M.: AIOCJ: a choreographic framework for safe adaptive distributed applications. In: Combemale, B., Pearce, D.J., Barais, O., Vinju, J.J. (eds.) SLE 2014. LNCS, vol. 8706, pp. 161–170. Springer, Cham (2014). https://doi.org/10.1007/978-3-319-11245-9_9

16. Dalla Preda, M., et al.: Dynamic choreographies: theory and implementation. Log. Methods Comput. Sci. **13**(2) (2017)

17. Decker, G., Zaha, J.M., Dumas, M.: Execution semantics for service choreographies. In: Bravetti, M., Núñez, M., Zavattaro, G. (eds.) WS-FM 2006. LNCS, vol. 4184, pp. 163–177. Springer, Heidelberg (2006). https://doi.org/10.1007/11841197_11

18. Endres, A., Rombach, H.D.: A Handbook of Software and Systems Engineering: Empirical Observations, Laws, and Theories. Pearson Education, London (2003)

19. Evans, P.C., Basole, R.C.: Revealing the API ecosystem and enterprise strategy via visual analytics. Commun. ACM **59**(2), 26–28 (2016)

20. Garlan, D., Allen, R., Ockerbloom, J.: Architectural mismatch or why it's hard to build systems out of existing parts. In: ICSE, pp. 179–185. ACM/IEEE (1995)

21. Hasselbring, W.: Information system integration: introduction. Commun. ACM **43**(6), 32–38 (2000)

22. He, W., Da Xu, L.: Integration of distributed enterprise applications: a survey. IEEE Trans. Ind. Informat. **10**(1), 35–42 (2014)

23. Hildebrandt, T., Mukkamala, R.R., Slaats, T.: Nested dynamic condition response graphs. In: Arbab, F., Sirjani, M. (eds.) FSEN 2011. LNCS, vol. 7141, pp. 343–350. Springer, Heidelberg (2012). https://doi.org/10.1007/978-3-642-29320-7_23

24. Hitt, L.M., Wu, D., Zhou, X.: Investment in enterprise resource planning: business impact and productivity measures. JMIS **19**(1), 71–98 (2002)

25. Honda, K., Yoshida, N., Carbone, M.: Multiparty asynchronous session types. J. ACM **63**(1), 9:1–9:67 (2016)

26. Humble, J., Farley, D.: Continuous Delivery: Reliable Software Releases Through Build, Test, and Deployment Automation. Pearson Education, London (2010)

27. Hüttel, H., et al.: Foundations of session types and behavioural contracts. ACM Comput. Surv. **49**(1), 3 (2016)

28. International Telecommunication Union: Message Sequence Chart (MSC). Series Z: Languages and General Software Aspects for Telecommunication Systems (2011)

29. Jolie website. http://www.jolie-lang.org/

30. Jongmans, S., Arbab, F.: Global consensus through local synchronization: a formal basis for partially-distributed coordination. SCP **115**, 199–224 (2016)

31. Lanese, I., Montesi, F., Zavattaro, G.: Amending choreographies. In: WWV. EPTCS, vol. 123, pp. 34–48 (2013)

32. Leesatapornwongsa, T., et al.: TaxDC: a taxonomy of non-deterministic concurrency bugs in datacenter distributed systems. ACM SIGPLAN Not. **51**(4), 517–530 (2016)

33. McIlvenna, S., Dumas, M., Wynn, M.T.: Synthesis of orchestrators from service choreographies. In: APCCM. CRPIT, vol. 96, pp. 129–138. Australian Computer Society (2009)

34. Montesi, F.: Kickstarting choreographic programming. In: Hildebrandt, T., Ravara, A., van der Werf, J.M., Weidlich, M. (eds.) WS-FM 2014-2015. LNCS, vol. 9421, pp. 3–10. Springer, Cham (2016). https://doi.org/10.1007/978-3-319-33612-1_1

35. Montesi, F., Guidi, C., Zavattaro, G.: Service-oriented programming with Jolie. In: Bouguettaya, A., Sheng, Q., Daniel, F. (eds.) Web Services Foundations, pp. 81–107. Springer, New York (2014). https://doi.org/10.1007/978-1-4614-7518-7_4

36. Montesi, F., Yoshida, N.: Compositional choreographies. In: D'Argenio, P.R., Melgratti, H. (eds.) CONCUR 2013. LNCS, vol. 8052, pp. 425–439. Springer, Heidelberg (2013). https://doi.org/10.1007/978-3-642-40184-8_30
37. Peterson, D., et al.: W3C XML Schema Definition Language (XSD) 1.1 Part 2: Datatypes. W3C (2012)
38. Qiu, Z., Zhao, X., Cai, C., Yang, H.: Towards the theoretical foundation of choreography. In: WWW, pp. 973–982. ACM (2007)
39. Rodríguez, P., et al.: Continuous deployment of software intensive products and services: a systematic mapping study. JSS **123**, 263–291 (2017)
40. Russo, D., et al.: Software quality concerns in the Italian bank sector: the emergence of a meta-quality dimension. In: ICSE, pp. 63–72. ACM/IEEE (2017)
41. Scribble website. http://www.jboss.org/scribble
42. Seiifzadeh, H., et al.: A survey of dynamic software updating. J. Softw.: Evol. Process **25**(5), 535–568 (2013)
43. Zaha, J.M., Barros, A., Dumas, M., ter Hofstede, A.: Let's dance: a language for service behavior modeling. In: Meersman, R., Tari, Z. (eds.) OTM 2006. LNCS, vol. 4275, pp. 145–162. Springer, Heidelberg (2006). https://doi.org/10.1007/11914853_10

PerceptRank: A Real-Time Learning to Rank Recommender System for Online Interactive Platforms

Hemza Ficel[✉], Mohamed Ramzi Haddad[✉], and Hajer Baazaoui Zghal[✉]

Riadi Laboratory, École Nationale des Sciences de l'Informatique,
University of Manouba, Manouba, Tunisia
hemza.ficel@ensi-uma.tn, haddad.medramzi@gmail.com,
hajer.baazaouizghal@riadi.rnu.tn

Abstract. In highly interactive platforms with continuous and frequent content creation and obsolescence, other factors besides relevance may alter users' perceptions and choices. Besides, making personalized recommendations in these application domains imposes new challenges when compared to classic recommendation use cases. In fact, the required recommendation approaches should be able to ingest and process continuous streams of data online, at scale and with low latency while making context dependent dynamic suggestions. In this work, we propose a generic approach to deal jointly with scalability, real-time and cold start problems in highly interactive online platforms. The approach is based on several consumer decision-making theories to infer users' preferences. In addition, it tackles the recommendation problem as a learning-to-rank problem that exploits a heterogeneous information graph to estimate users' perceived value towards items. Although the approach is addressed to streaming environments, it has been validated in both offline batch and online streaming scenarios. The first evaluation has been carried out using the MovieLens dataset and the latter targeted the news recommendation domain using a high-velocity stream of usage data collected by a marketing company from several large scale online news portals. Experiments show that our proposition meets real world production environments constraints while delivering accurate suggestions and outperforming several state-of-the-art approaches.

Keywords: Recommender systems · Stream processing
Online learning · Real-time recommendation · Learning to rank
Knowledge graphs

1 Introduction

Thanks to the Internet and to online services, most people in the world are able to access content, goods and services via tablets, smartphones or computers. Moreover, real-world commerces and medias have been migrating to the virtual

H. Panetto et al. (Eds.): OTM 2018 Conferences, LNCS 11230, pp. 41–59, 2018.
https://doi.org/10.1007/978-3-030-02671-4_3

world resulting in online interactive platforms that bring and engage people. The ubiquitous access and overload of choices have led providers to focus on personalizing the customer's experience by assisting them individually through their journey. This requirement has given more interest to personalization and recommendation systems that try to infer users' interests and needs to better fulfill them.

Recommender systems are continuously embracing personalization in order to better model the consumers' "perception of value" [6] which is driven by several factors that influence their judgments and consumption decisions [16,34,36]. However, due to the different hypothesis, complexities and objectives of existing recommendation approaches, systems designers are required to have a deep understanding of state-of-the-art recommenders in order to choose the ones that meet their application domain requirements and constraints. In this work, we propose a domain agnostic recommendation approach based on the concept of "perceived value". The approach enables the cooperation between service providers and the centralized recommendation platform. In addition, it address not only the usual problems of personalization, accuracy and cold start but also scalability, real-time and continuous recommendation in online highly interactive platforms. In fact, these platforms add several harder constraints on recommender systems due to their higher volume and velocity of content and behavioral data streams. Moreover, suggestions need to be generated dynamically, with low latency and under tight time constraints in order to better assist users in this context of rapid content creation and consumption.

In order to tackle the recommendation problem while coping with additional constraints of highly interactive application domains, we design our proposal around the concepts of accuracy, real-time, scalability and continuous streams which leads to the following challenges:

1. **Real-time processing and scalability:** Interactive online platforms require robust and low complexity approaches in order to efficiently deal with the massive amount of items and users streams with respect to the real-time delay constraint.
2. **Preferences modeling with incomplete data:** Efficiently model users' preferences facilitates the inference of their interests. However, highly interactive platforms have generally a free publicly available content which leads to mainly anonymous users. Therefore, there are no guarantee of deterministic users tracking and profiling which leads to a continuous cold start problem for users.
3. **Rapid content creation and obsolescence:** In highly interactive platforms, there is a higher rate of content creation, adoption and obsolescent than in other recommender systems application domains such as e-commerce. With continuous and frequent content creation and obsolescence, other challenges arise such items cold start where newly created items lack feedback and usage data which makes them more difficult to evaluate and recommend with confidence. Besides, recommendation approaches should take into account this time-dependent content lifecycle where items' novelty, adoption or rejec-

tion over time due to rapidly or slowly changing trends have different impacts on their perceived utility.

4. **Users' perceived utility scoring:** User's preferences are measured with their perceived value towards items. It may have little or nothing to do with the item's cost, however, it largely depends on the item's ability to satisfy the user's requirements or needs within a given context. Therefore, continuously inferring, quantifying and updating users' preferences and perceived items value while taking into account the temporal context may help predict and anticipate their intention and choices.

To take up these research challenges, we try to efficiently model users' preferences by estimating their perceived utility value towards items. Drawing our inspiration from decision-making theories and by relying upon the success of heterogeneous information network, we adopt a graph data model to represent connections between diverse artifacts, entities or factors. The aim is to quantify users' attitudes towards available items while taking into account the influence of external factors on their perception. Two evaluations scenarios have been carried out to evaluate our proposal's genericity, quality and usefulness in different use cases requiring offline, online, one time, continuous or large-scale recommenders. The first evaluation was conducted in a batch, offline, one time setup using the MovieLens dataset while the second tackled a large-scale, stream-based, continuous online recommendation using real streams of data describing interactions with news content collected in several large-scale news publishers.

The remainder of this paper is organized as follows. Section 2 gives an overview of related work. Section 3 outlines the proposed learning to rank recommendation system and its underlying approach. Section 4 presents a brief overview of the evaluation configurations and discusses both the batch and the stream experimentations results. The last section concludes the paper and gives an outlook on future work.

2   Related Work

Endowing online platforms with efficient recommendation systems has being the target of intensive research in the last years. Since we propose a ranking based recommendation approach for online streaming environments, we review in this section several previous works on stream-based and learning to rank recommendation methods. In the following, the abbreviations of algorithms were generated based on their names.

Learning to rank approaches attempt to solve a ranking problem on a list of items. The goal is to come up with an optimal ordering of those items. In contrast to predictive approaches, this class of approaches does not care much about the exact score of items, but cares more about their relative ordering. Most previous work in that area focus mainly on collaborative filtering methods [14]. They generally enhance matrix factorization models with other methods. For example, BPR-MF [26] exploits a matrix factorization as the learning model with Bayesian personalized ranking optimization criterion. In the same way,

MCMC-FM [27] adopts Markov chain Monte Carlo inference and MF [15] minimizes RMSE using stochastic gradient descent. In addition, RankingMF [33] uses a matrix factorization model for item ranking with ordinal regression score as loss function. Acting on the same principle, BPRLin [8] learns a linear mapping on the user-item features based purely on positive implicit feedback. Once again, SLIM [21] and its extension BPR-SSLIM [22] adopt a sparse linear method for learning a sparse aggregation coefficient matrix that is used for scoring items. However, BPR-SSLIM incorporates item side information within the sparse linear method. Furthermore, due to the success of heterogeneous information networks, others work such as HeteRec [35] and SPrank [23] uses meta-path features to represent users-items relationships in order to compute Top-K recommendations. The difference is that SPrank exploits Linked Open Data to extract the metapath-based features. Finally, PathRank [17], the random-walk based ranking algorithm, extends the Personalized PageRank algorithm to generate Top-K recommendations.

Stream-based approaches try to cope with the specific characteristics of real-world recommender systems under streaming settings. Indeed, real-time aspect, scalability issue and cold start problem are the main challenges facing steam-based recommendation approaches. To deal with these research challenges, Chang et al. [2] provided a framework that adopts a variational Bayesian approach to manage stream inputs via a continuous-time random process. Huang et al. [13] proposed a generic real-time stream recommender system built on the stream processing computation framework "Storm". They developed a data access and a data storage component to manage the large amount of data streams. In addition, they presented an incremental version of the item-based collaborative filtering algorithm to cope with implicit feedback problem and real-time aspect. Furthermore, Lommatzsch and Albayrak [19] presented a framework optimized for providing recommendations for online news portals. They combined various algorithms in an ensemble-based approach that selects the most appropriate recommendation strategy based on the requested data and their context. In the same field, Das et al. [5] addressed the large data (i.e. million users and items) and dynamic settings (i.e. item set is continually changing) in online news portals. They proposed an online collaborative model to recommend news articles that were read by users with similar click history. After a few years, this model has been combined with another content-based approach that adopts a Bayesian framework for predicting users' current news interests [18]. Recently, Haddad et al. presented an adaptation of a generic probabilistic model to the news recommendation context [10]. This model rely on the text semantic analysis and incremental segmentation techniques in order to process news stories and provide relevant recommendations to users.

Learning to rank approaches focus on large user-item matrices and resort to complex methods in order to extract knowledge about users while minimizing noise. Although they are robust for making recommendations, currently, they mismatch the requirements of online interactive platforms due to tight time constraints and the cold start problem in these environments. Otherwise, stream-based approaches are well suited for that scenario. Despite all their improvements, real-time delay constraint and cold start problem continue to be challenging in online interactive platforms. In addition, it is important to note that these approaches do not focus on the ranking nature of the online streaming recommendation problem, while there is a real-world need for Online learning to rank recommender systems [24]. By contrast, our proposal is stemmed from this real-world need.

3   PerceptRank: A Real-Time Recommender System for Online Interactive Platforms

The objective of the proposed approach is to provide relevant recommendations by efficiently modeling users' preferences in an incremental an continuous manner. The main idea here is to model the interrelationships between features' values describing items, users and the context in order to predict consumers' preferences and choices. Several researches on consumer decision-making domain suggest that users' preferences and decisions may be explained by the value they perceive towards a given item within a specific context [6]. The concept of perceived value is also defined as the user's opinion towards the added value or the usefulness of an item which may have little or nothing to do with its cost. In fact, it depends on the item's ability to satisfy the user's requirements or needs within a given context which makes it highly predictive of his future attitude, intention and choices. Theories such as Means End Chain (MEC) [9] and value-repurchase intention [3] support the idea of the consumer's perceived value and claim that it motivates purchase or repurchase decisions [32]. However, no universal formulation is adopted since various factors can influence the consumer's perceived value and hence its decision-making process [16, 34, 36].

In view of these theories, we believe that inferring users' preferences using a quantitative formulation of the perceived utility value concept may help predict their choices and anticipate them in a recommendation scenario. Therefore, the recommendation approach we proposed in this work is based on the following hypothesis:

Proposition 1. *The perceived utility value of an item is:*

- *personal: it varies between consumers.*
- *dynamic: it varies over the time with regard to the consumer's acquired experiences.*
- *contextual: depends on the current context.*
- *influenced by a local power derived from the compatibility between the user and the item internal descriptors which determines the perceived satisfaction if the acquisition or purchase is realized.*
- *influenced by a global power derived from several external factors independent from the item and the user.*

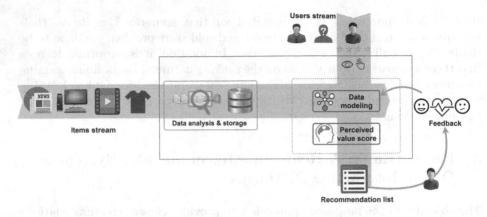

Fig. 1. A schematic representation of the proposed approach.

In this work, our proposal is built upon five types of utility values, namely, product utility, time weight, place utility, social influence and finally a post-suggestion factor.

The local power of an item depends on its utility value which quantifies the influence of its features in the user's decision. These features can be derived from the items' unstructured textual content (e.g. topic, subject, keywords, named entities, etc...) or structured descriptors (e.g. size, color, volume, price, quality, etc...). Moreover, these features would determine the item's ability to satisfy the user's needs and desires. Indeed, in real world scenarios, it is common to see consumers search for products using features or brands as keywords. Similarly, content consumers may search and filter news articles using named entities (i.e. persons' names, places, organizations, dates, etc...) as confirmed by a recent report from Google Trends[1].

The Global power is related to all external factors that may influence users' decisions or actions such as social trends and behaviors. For example, consumers can explore content, build opinions and make purchase decisions based on other users' opinions, experiences, reviews or trends [16,29]. The global power of an item depends also on its adequacy with the consumer's context with regard to the time, location, current task and motivations. In fact, relevant recommendations should align with the consumer's objectives and current task which may be inferred from his behaviors, interaction with the system, feedbacks and attitudes towards the available and the recommended resources.

The proposed recommendation approach integrates all the discussed factors and follows two stages, namely, (1) data modeling and (2) users' perceived utility scoring. Figure 1 illustrates the proposed approach and its processes.

---

[1] https://trends.google.com/trends/yis/2017/GLOBAL.

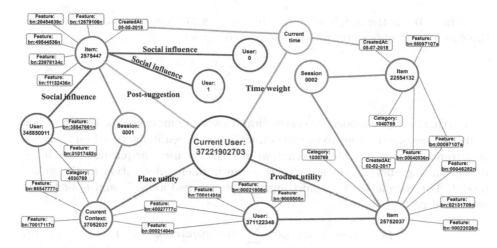

Fig. 2. Example of our heterogeneous information network.

3.1 Data Modeling

It has been shown that heterogeneous information graph have solid abilities to model connections between entities of recommender systems [23, 30]. Since our proposal relies on the relationships between multiple utility factors, we adopt a graph data model to represent connections between items and users' preferences.

We model items and users' preferences as a self organizing information network represented by means of a labeled, directed graph $G - (V, E)$ where $V - (v_1, v_2, \ldots, v_n)$ is the vertex set representing items, their features and users. $E \subseteq V \times V$ is the edge set where a directed pair $\langle v_1, v_2 \rangle$ indicates there is a connection from v_1 to v_2 in the graph. Each edge $e \in E$, is assigned to a weighting function $w : E \to R^+$ to indicate the quantitative strength of connection between two vertex. Correspondingly, we denote the weighting adjacency matrix W of size $|V| \times |V|$ for our graph G with each element $W_{ij} = w(\langle v_i, v_j \rangle)$ if the directed path $\langle v_i, v_j \rangle \in E$ and 0 otherwise. In this paper, we always use $\langle v_i, v_j \rangle$ to denote a directed vertex-to-vertex path from the vertex v_i to vertex v_j. Figure 2 shows an example of this defined information graph data model.

We model the streaming nature of online recommenders by considering a continuously time-varying set of $\langle user, feature \rangle$, $\langle item, item \rangle$ and $\langle user, item \rangle$ edges. Each edge measures the strength of connection between two vertex at a given time t. We assume that time is continuous; $t \in R^+$. In addition, the number of vertex are dynamically changing over time. In light of all this, we define the conditional in-degree of a vertex $v \in V$ given a specific path $\langle v, u \rangle$ at a given time t as:

$$d^{t^-}(v_i \mid U) = \sum_{j=1}^{|U \subset V|} w_{ij}^t \tag{1}$$

Where W^t is the weighting adjacency matrix at time t. Similarly, we define the conditional out-degree for the same vertex v as:

$$d^{t+}\left(v_i \mid U\right) = \sum_{j=1}^{|U \cup V|} w_{ji}^t \tag{2}$$

Furthermore, we model the correlation between items over time keeping track of users' sessions in order to create connection between items based on their co-occurrence. Hence, the choices that were made by users acquiring consecutive items whiting short times are stored as an implicit information in the graph model. The correlation (i.e. pairCounts) between two items i_1 and i_2 at time t is defined as:

$$pC^t\left(i_1, i_2\right) = w_{i_1,i_2}^t = \sum co - acquiring\left(i_1, i_2\right) \tag{3}$$

3.2   Perceived Utility Scoring

Based on the previous definitions, we formulate the recommendation problem as a learning to rank problem where user-item pairs, denoted $\langle user, item\rangle$, are associated with a perceived value score. The formulation may be stated as follows:

Considering connections $\langle user, feature\rangle$, $\langle item, item\rangle$ and $\langle user, item\rangle$ from our heterogeneous information graph, representing behaviors history (clicks, ratings, browsing history, etc...) for N users ($U = \{u_1, u_2, \ldots, u_n\}$) over M items ($I = \{i_1, i_2, \ldots, i_m\}$), and given an active user u at time t with profile P_u consisting of connections u-items and u-features $\{\langle u, f_1\rangle, \langle u, f_2\rangle, \ldots, \langle u, f_{|P_u|}\rangle\}$, recommend the most relevant K items that he/she may be interested in acquiring in the near future.

During the user's journey on the online platform, the approach ingests the stream of all users interaction events, updates its underlying model and tries to resolve the stated problem in order to continuously recommend the list of the k most relevant items for each individual. The list is generated based on the available items' personalized perceived utility scores which depends on the user. The Perceived utility scoring function $ps(i, u) : U \times I \to R$ is continuously learned from the evolving heterogeneous information graph in a way that enables it to estimate the perceived utility value of each user. The recommendation list is then built from the items having the highest estimated utility scores.

In batch offline recommendation, the previously inferred models or knowledge are discarded and regenerated before every recommendation campaign or periodically when new batches of data are collected. In contrast, our methodology ensures the dynamic nature of the proposed approach which makes it able to take into account all the freshly available data or updates concerning users, the content or the context. In fact, relationships and therefore the knowledge model are updated incrementally as time goes and as events, observations or updates arrive. Moreover, these updates are processed online as they occur and with low latency in order to rapidly react and adapt suggestions to the current users' needs, objectives and attitudes towards the content. This makes a significant advantage over batch, offline and non incremental approaches where users' recent feedbacks are not taken into account until the following update of the recommendation model. Besides such updates are generally consuming in time and processing power since they generally start from scratch and analyze the old collected data each time.

To learn the Perceived utility scoring function for each pair $\langle user, item \rangle$ we rely on our aforementioned hypothesis (cf. Proposition 1). First, to estimate the local power for a given user, we model their preferences to items' characteristics in various levels of abstraction and at different times. The low level preferences is represented by the edge itself (i.e. $\langle user, feature \rangle$) and a higher level based on how the user makes decisions (e.g. user attribute the importance to features n, or feature m) is represented by the weighting function w^t. Weights are dynamically adjusted based on users' behaviors to capture their real-time interests. Hereby, the local power is calculated by the following formula:

$$LP\,(item, u) = \frac{1}{|P_u|} \sum_{f \in \{\langle item, Features \rangle\}} w^t_{uf} \tag{4}$$

To estimate the global power we turn to a timely weighted schema of the items' in-degree to represent the society's tendency (cf. Time weight & Social influence). Additionally, we model a post-suggestion factor by a dynamic feedback variable $Aw\,(u, item)$ in order to take into account the implicit negative feedback where a user, totally aware of a recommended item, decides to ignore it and not to interact with it. This attitude towards that item indicates its low perceived utility for the active user and the need for the recommendation approach to avoid recommending it again later to that same user. This factor increases recommendations' diversity by lowering the scores of non interesting suggestions that do not seem to attract the user's attention. Furthermore, we take also into consideration the correlation between the current task for the current user (i.e. the current acquired item cAI) and the targeted items (cf. Place utility). Hereby, the final score of the global power can be calculated as follow:

$$GP\,(item, u) = d^{t-}\,(item \mid U) \cdot pC^t\,(cAI, item) \cdot e^{-\lambda Age(item) - \delta Aw(u, item)} \tag{5}$$

The exponential form is used to describe the gradual decay of items' trending and utility over time. λ and δ are parameters to control, respectively, the period after which the popularity of items plummets over time and the decay rate of the utility of items that was recommended several times without inducing a positive attitude. It is important to highlight that the choice of this formulation has been motivated by our previous work [7].

Finally, analogically to the statistical measure "term frequency–inverse document frequency" (TFIDF) form Information Retrieval [28] where TF measures how important a word in a document while IDF measures how important a word in the overall collection of documents, we estimate the final score of the perceived value of an active user u towards a candidate item as:

$$ps\,(item, u) = LP\,(item, u) \cdot GP\,(item, u) \tag{6}$$

4   Experimentations

In this section, we detail our experiments' settings and results while evaluating the effectiveness of our approach. The evaluation has been carried out in two distinct scenarios related to two different use cases. The first is a batch offline setup using the MovieLens dataset for movies recommendation and the second is a large-scale low latency recommendation setup simulating online news articles recommendation using a real stream of interaction events collected from several online news publishers.

4.1   Batch Recommendation of Movies

In order to compare our results with state-of-the-art learning to rank approaches, we reproduce the same configuration proposed by Noia et al. [23] using a processed version of the movielens 1M dataset originally introduced by Harper et al. [11]. In this configuration, they used 80% of ratings to build a training set and they took the remaining 20% as a test set to measure recommendations' accuracy. To this end, the "all unrated items" methodology [31] is adopted. It consists in creating a top-K recommendation list for each user by estimating a score for every item not rated by that particular user, whether the item appears in his test set or not. Next, the generated recommendations are compared with the test dataset to measure recommendations' accuracy. Steck [31] claim that this is a better methodology than the "rated test-items" one where only rated test items are considered for generating recommendations. Furthermore, they also removed the top 1% of the most popular items in order to avoid popularity biases from the evaluation [4]. In addition, they retained only users with at least fifty ratings to minimize sparsity degree. The final dataset contains 3 196 items and 822 597 ratings from 4 186 users.

In this experiment, we adopted standard performance metrics namely Precision, Recall and nDCG at N to measure recommendations' accuracy. In addition, we considered only items rated with four and five stars as relevant ones in the evaluation processes as well as in our recommendation approach. Besides, items features (i.e. movies' genres, actors, tags and directors) have been recovered from the "hetrec" extension of MovieLens dataset [1]. Hereby, the weighting function w adopted in this evaluation configuration is based on how much a user likes movies connected to each of the recovered features.

Figure 3 presents the obtained results from the benchmarking of our proposal against state-of-the-art learning to rank recommendation algorithms [8,15,17, 21–23,25–27,33,35] detailed in Sect. 2, a popularity-based baseline algorithm (PopRank) [4] and a hybrid factorization machine algorithm (Ranking-FM) [23].

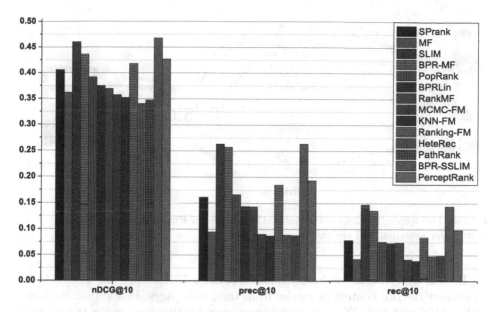

Fig. 3. Comparative results between the PerceptRank approach and state-of-the-art learning to rank recommendation algorithms.

4.2   Stream Recommendation of News Articles

This second experiment is based on the NewsREEL challenge of the CLEF News REcommendation Evaluation Lab [12]. NewsREEL is a campaign-style evaluation lab whose objective is to evaluate recommender systems with real-world data and conditions issued from a large scale news recommender system managed by the Plista GmbH company[2]. NewsREEL offers a near-to-online task named *NewsREEL Replay* in which participant systems are asked to predict in real-time which article each user will read in the near future. This task is based on a stream of real data and events issued from the historical logs collected from several news publishers in Germany. Figure 4 illustrates communications between this Platform, partner news publishers, participants' recommender systems and real users. In this network, registered participants' systems are asked to maintain a strict response delay constraint that shall not exceed 100 ms. The NewsREEL Replay task tries to simulate this live setting using the recommender system reference framework Idomaar[3]. Hereby, the recommendations quality is measured by the "near-to-online" click-through rate (CTR) measure referring to the ratio of successful recommendations that were read by a targeted user in the following 10 min.

---

[2] https://www.plista.com.
[3] http://www.clef-newsreel.org/tasks/.

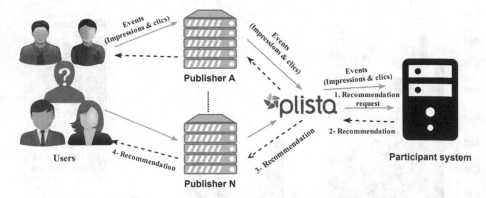

Fig. 4. The figure illustrates communications between Plista server, participants' recommender systems, and real users.

In this experiment, we have exploited articles URLs using the aylien API[4] to extract the full content of stories from their web pages. In addition, we have utilized Babelfy API [20] to derive relevant named entities and concepts from this extracted content. These artifacts are considered as item features in the proposed approach. Moreover, as we deal with more noisy data in this evaluation setup, the weighting function w adopted in this configuration considers only click events to measure how much a user likes stories connected to the previously extracted features. Besides, it attributes more weight to titles' features since titles that raise more in-depth named entities and concepts attract the most interest as recent study from Plista GmbH points[5].

In this setup, we measure the CTR per hour across one week ranging from February 1st to February 7th 2016. This subset contains 40 805 334 events, 14 931 news articles updates and 19 748 764 users belonging to the news publishers tagesspiegel[6], ksta[7] and sport1[8]. In this subset, 88% of users are anonymous since they disallowed tracking their sessions and we only known their current context.

In this experiment, "Most Recent", "Most Popular" and "Most Recently Requested" recommendation strategies [19] are used as baseline algorithms. Besides, items' statistics in Most popular strategy are reset on a daily basis in order to avoid recommending outdated items. Concerning our proposed approach, referred to as PerceptRank (**Perception Ranking**), the parameters λ and δ were empirically estimated (i.e. $\lambda = 1/50, \delta = 1/3$). The mean Click-Through Rates for each of the benchmarked recommenders is reported in Tables 1, 2 and 3 while their corresponding hourly measures are presented in Figs. 5, 6 and 7.

---

[4] https://aylien.com.
[5] https://blog.plista.com/articletitlesrelevanceforperformance/.
[6] https://www.tagesspiegel.de.
[7] https://www.ksta.de.
[8] https://www.sport1.de.

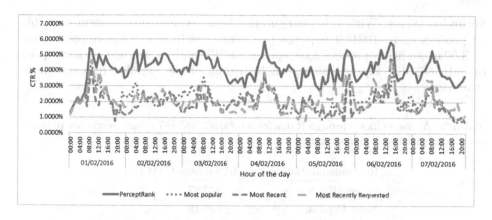

Fig. 5. Hourly Click Through Rates for the publisher tagesspiegel.

Table 1. Average Click Through Rates for a total of 5 159 641 recommendation requests over 7 days for the publisher tagesspiegel.

Recommendation approach	Average CTR (%)
PerceptRank	4.4333
Most Popular	2.2529
Most Recent	2.1452
Most Recently Requested	2.4406

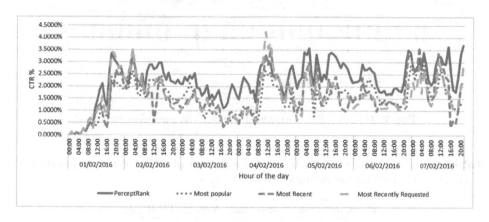

Fig. 6. Hourly Click Through Rates for the publisher ksta.

In this evaluation scenario, we simulate both the Plista server as well as our recommender system server by two Amazon EC2 m5.large instances[9]. Each instance have 8 GB of RAM and runs two Intel Xeon Platinum processors with 2.5 GHz each. The network average latency between this two Linux servers is

---

[9] https://aws.amazon.com/ec2/instance-types/m5.

around 0.185 ms. With this configuration, our recommender system was able to process up to 102 000 requests per minute with an average response time of 3.50 ms, a mean processor occupancy of 31% and an average memory space of only 887 MB. Figure 8 shows an histogram of the detailed response times statistics.

Table 2. Average Click Through Rates for a total of 3 255 887 recommendation requests over 7 days for the publisher ksta.

Recommendation approach	Average CTR (%)
PerceptRank	2.2787
Most Popular	1.4918
Most Recent	1.6040
Most Recently Requested	1.6375

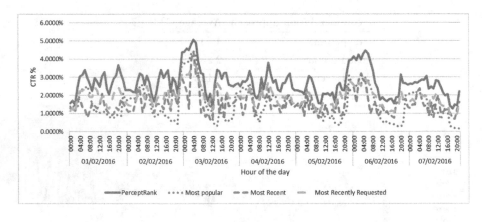

Fig. 7. Hourly Click Through Rates for the publisher sport1.

Table 3. Average Click Through Rates for a total of 31 254 089 recommendation requests over 7 days for the publisher sport1.

Recommendation approach	Average CTR (%)
PerceptRank	2.6808
Most Popular	1.2832
Most Recent	1.4899
Most Recently Requested	1.9003

4.3   Discussion of Results

In this section, we analyze the evaluation results and discuss the strengths and weaknesses of the compared approaches based on their recommendation quality and performances.

Regarding the obtained results on the MovieLens dataset (cf. Fig. 3), the proposed PerceptRank approach outperforms the popularity baseline and nearly all collaborative ranking based approaches with regard to the accuracy metrics (i.e. precision, recall and nDCG). In addition, PerceptRank outperforms the other graph-based approaches, namely, HeteRec, SPrank and PathRank. Nevertheless, this downgraded version of PerceptRank did not outperform BPR-MF, SLIM and its extension BPR-SSLIM. However, in this experiment using a static dataset, we were not able to utilize all the modeled factors such as time weight, place utility and post-suggestion when estimating the Perceived utility score. We believe that the recommendation problem is an incremental process by nature where items, users and interactions evolve continuously and that real-world, live and interactive benchmarks are more informative than static datasets [19].

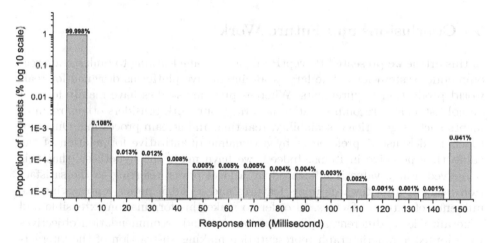

Fig. 8. Histogram of the detailed response time statistic of the PerceptRank approach.

With NewsREEL evaluation scenario, we were able to validate our proposal under real data and conditions. Indeed, in this setup, the time constraints in addition to the data streams volume, velocity and variety have raised more awareness of the issues and the challenges facing production scale recommenders. In this context, results show that our system was able to process high throughputs while maintaining low latency and a response time around few milliseconds (cf. Fig. 8). This is largely sufficient to meet the 100 ms response delay constraint imposed by the challenge. Furthermore, the obtained results show that PerceptRank outperforms the baseline algorithms which are largely adopted in the industry whether in the general portals with varied subjects like tagesspiegel and ksta or in more the specialized sport domain with homogeneous news. The advantage over is more noticeable in the tagesspiegel and sport1 publishers since they contain more recommendation requests and data streams (more than 93% of total users and items streams).

The experiments show that our approach may improve the experience of anonymous users who have disallowed tracking their sessions while partially resolving several facets of the cold start problem. In fact, even anonymous users represent 88% of total users, the approach was able to deliver better results by relying on their global power scores. This has also contributed to alleviate the cold start problem for new users who are initially considered as anonymous users. However, they have progressively received personalized suggestions that react to their current needs and attitudes towards the content as more of their behavioral data was collected. Furthermore, experiments show also that PerceptRank results are aligned with the CTR burst of the most recent strategy reflecting the occurrence of recent items of general interest. Thereupon, we can conclude that our approach have successfully integrated new items on which users have not yet expressed preferences thanks to the connection between users' preferences models and content information nodes linking various items.

5   Conclusions and Future Work

In this article we presented PerceptRank, a real-time learning to rank stream recommender system for online large-scale interactive platforms designed for real-world production requirements. Whereas previous studies have mainly focused on cold start and recommendation accuracy, our work considers others requirements such as genericity, scalability, real-time and stream processing. Our approach models users' preferences by a dynamic quantitative formulation of the value they perceive in items. Indeed, we have made the hypothesis that this perceived utility value is influenced by a local power referring to the satisfaction users express towards items features and a global power representing the influence of external factors. In order to make this formulation extensible and generalizable to different application domains and recommendation objectives we adopted a generic graph representation making abstraction of the interacting/interfering entities and factors.

The obtained results validate the interest of our proposal under different recommendation contexts, objectives, domains and constraints. Indeed, the scaled down version of the approach was able to provide high quality results in the batch offline evaluation with the MovieLens dataset when compared to state-of-the-art learning to rank approaches. Besides, in the online more realistic evaluation scenario, our approach was able to deliver quality recommendations and outperform some largely adopted algorithms known for their performances in online news portals.

Although the obtained results are promising, further improvements are still possible. Indeed, it has been shown that consumer demographic characteristics such as gender and age, also influence consumption behaviors, intentions and attitudes [6,36]. Integrating this knowledge, if available and shared by users, when estimating their perceived utility scores may lead to more accurate modeling and recommendations for users and increasing ROI for enterprises. Besides, our proposal needs to be applied in other application domains where user, items, interactions or contexts may exhibit other correlations, causalities or patterns in order to better validate its genericity and compare its results with other specialized state-of-the-art approaches.

References

1. Cantador, I., Brusilovsky, P., Kuflik, T.: 2nd workshop on information heterogeneity and fusion in recommender systems (HetRec 2011). In: Proceedings of the 5th ACM conference on Recommender systems, RecSys 2011. ACM (2011)
2. Chang, S., et al.: Streaming recommender systems. In: Proceedings of the 26th International Conference on World Wide Web, pp. 381–389 (2017)
3. Chiu, C.M., Wang, E.T., Fang, Y.H., Huang, H.Y.: Understanding customers' repeat purchase intentions in B2C e-commerce: the roles of utilitarian value, hedonic value and perceived risk. Inf. Syst. J. **24**(1), 85–114 (2014)
4. Cremonesi, P., Koren, Y., Turrin, R.: Performance of recommender algorithms on top-n recommendation tasks. In: Proceedings of the Fourth ACM Conference on Recommender Systems, pp. 39–46. ACM (2010)
5. Das, A.S., Datar, M., Garg, A., Rajaram, S.: Google news personalization: scalable online collaborative filtering. In: Proceedings of the 16th International Conference on World Wide Web, pp. 271–280. ACM (2007)
6. Fang, J., Wen, C., George, B., Prybutok, V.R.: Consumer heterogeneity, perceived value, and repurchase decision-making in online shopping: the role of gender, age, and shopping motives. J. Electron. Commer. Res. **17**(2), 116 (2016)
7. Ficel, H., Haddad, M.R., Baazaoui Zghal, H.: Large-scale real-time news recommendation based on semantic data analysis and users' implicit and explicit behaviors. In: Benczúr, A., Thalheim, B., Horváth, T. (eds.) ADBIS 2018. LNCS, vol. 11019, pp. 247–260. Springer, Cham (2018). https://doi.org/10.1007/978-3-319-98398-1_17
8. Gantner, Z., Drumond, L., Freudenthaler, C., Rendle, S., Schmidt-Thieme, L.: Learning attribute-to-feature mappings for cold-start recommendations. In: Proceedings of the 2010 IEEE International Conference on Data Mining, ICDM 2010, pp. 176–185. IEEE (2010)
9. Gutman, J.: Means-end chains as goal hierarchies. Psychol. Market. **14**(6), 545–560 (1997)
10. Haddad, M.R., Baazaoui, H., Ficel, H.: A scalable and interactive recommendation model for users' interests prediction. Int. J. Inf. Technol. Decis. Making **17**(05), 1335–1361 (2018). https://doi.org/10.1142/S0219622018500256
11. Harper, F.M., Konstan, J.A.: The MovieLens datasets: history and context. ACM Trans. Interact. Intell. Syst. (TiiS) **5**(4), 19 (2016)
12. Hopfgartner, F., et al.: Benchmarking news recommendations: The CLEF NewsREEL use case. SIGIR Forum **49**(2), 129–136 (2016)
13. Huang, Y., Cui, B., Zhang, W., Jiang, J., Xu, Y.: TencentRec: real-time stream recommendation in practice. In: Proceedings of the 2015 ACM SIGMOD International Conference on Management of Data, pp. 227–238. ACM (2015)
14. Koren, Y., Bell, R.: Advances in collaborative filtering. In: Ricci, F., Rokach, L., Shapira, B., Kantor, P. (eds.) Recommender Systems Handbook, pp. 145–186. Springer, Boston (2011). https://doi.org/10.1007/978-0-387-85820-3_5

15. Koren, Y., Bell, R., Volinsky, C.: Matrix factorization techniques for recommender systems. Computer **42**(8), 30–37 (2009)
16. Krishnan, S., Patel, J., Franklin, M., Goldberg, K.: Social influence bias in recommender systems: a methodology for learning, analyzing, and mitigating bias in ratings. In: Proceedings of the 8th ACM Conference on Recommender Systems, pp. 137–144 (2014)
17. Lee, S., Park, S., Kahng, M., Lee, S.G.: PathRank: a novel node ranking measure on a heterogeneous graph for recommender systems. In: Proceedings of the 21st ACM International Conference on Information and Knowledge Management, pp. 1637–1641. ACM (2012)
18. Liu, J., Dolan, P., Pedersen, E.R.: Personalized news recommendation based on click behavior. In: Proceedings of the 15th International Conference on Intelligent User Interfaces, pp. 31–40. ACM (2010)
19. Lommatzsch, A., Albayrak, S.: Real-time recommendations for user-item streams. In: Proceedings of the 30th Annual ACM Symposium on Applied Computing, pp. 1039–1046. ACM (2015)
20. Moro, A., Raganato, A., Navigli, R.: Entity linking meets Word Sense Disambiguation: a unified approach. Trans. Assoc. Comput. Linguist. (TACL) **2**, 231–244 (2014)
21. Ning, X., Karypis, G.: SLIM: sparse linear methods for top-n recommender systems. In: Proceedings of the 2011 IEEE 11th International Conference on Data Mining, pp. 497–506. IEEE (2011)
22. Ning, X., Karypis, G.: Sparse linear methods with side information for top-n recommendations. In: Proceedings of the Sixth ACM Conference on Recommender Systems, pp. 155–162. ACM (2012)
23. Noia, T.D., Ostuni, V.C., Tomeo, P., Sciascio, E.D.: SPrank: semantic path-based ranking for top-n recommendations using linked open data. ACM Trans. Intell. Syst. Technol. (TIST) **8**(1), 9 (2016)
24. Odijk, D., Schuth, A.: Online learning to rank for recommender systems. In: Proceedings of the 11th ACM Conference on Recommender Systems, pp. 348–348. ACM (2017)
25. Rendle, S.: Factorization machines. In: Proceedings of the 2010 IEEE International Conference on Data Mining, pp. 995–1000. IEEE (2010)
26. Rendle, S., Freudenthaler, C., Gantner, Z., Schmidt-Thieme, L.: BPR: Bayesian personalized ranking from implicit feedback. In: Proceedings of the 25th Conference on Uncertainty in Artificial Intelligence, pp. 452–461 (2009)
27. Salakhutdinov, R., Mnih, A.: Bayesian probabilistic matrix factorization using Markov chain Monte Carlo. In: Proceedings of the 25th International Conference on Machine Learning, pp. 880–887. ACM (2008)
28. Salton, G.: Automatic Text Processing: The Transformation, Analysis, and Retrieval of. Addison-Wesley, Reading (1989)
29. Santos, J., Peleja, F., Martins, F., Magalhães, J.: Improving cold-start recommendations with social-media trends and reputations. In: Adams, N., Tucker, A., Weston, D. (eds.) IDA 2017. LNCS, vol. 10584, pp. 297–309. Springer, Cham (2017). https://doi.org/10.1007/978-3-319-68765-0_25
30. Shams, B., Haratizadeh, S.: Graph-based collaborative ranking. Expert Syst. Appl. **67**, 59–70 (2017)
31. Steck, H.: Evaluation of recommendations: rating-prediction and ranking. In: Proceedings of the 7th ACM Conference on Recommender Systems, pp. 213–220. ACM (2013)

32. Wang, M.X., Wang, J.Q., Li, L.: New online personalized recommendation app-roach based on the perceived value of consumer characteristics. J. Intell. Fuzzy Syst. **33**(3), 1953–1968 (2017)

33. Weimer, M., Karatzoglou, A., Smola, A.: Improving maximum margin matrix fac-torization. Mach. Learn. **72**(3), 263–276 (2008)

34. Wu, L.Y., Chen, K.Y., Chen, P.Y., Cheng, S.L.: Perceived value, transaction cost, and repurchase-intention in online shopping: a relational exchange perspective. J. Bus. Res. **67**(1), 2768–2776 (2014)

35. Yu, X., et al.: Personalized entity recommendation: a heterogeneous information network approach. In: Proceedings of the 7th ACM International Conference on Web Search and Data Mining, pp. 283–292. ACM (2014)

36. Zhou, Z., Jin, X.L., Fang, Y.: Moderating role of gender in the relationships between perceived benefits and satisfaction in social virtual world continuance. Dec. Support Syst. **65**, 69–79 (2014)

Discovering Microservices in Enterprise Systems Using a Business Object Containment Heuristic

Adambarage Anuruddha Chathuranga De Alwis[1]([✉]), Alistair Barros[1],
Colin Fidge[1], and Artem Polyvyanyy[2]

[1] Queensland University of Technology, Brisbane, Australia
{adambarage.dealwis,alistair.barros,c.fidge}@qut.edu.au
[2] The University of Melbourne, Parkville, VIC 3010, Australia
artem.polyvyanyy@unimelb.edu.au

Abstract. The growing impact of IoT and Blockchain platforms on business applications has increased interest in leveraging large enterprise systems as Cloud-enabled microservices. However, large and monolithic enterprise systems are unsuitable for flexible integration with such platforms. This paper presents a technique to support the re-engineering of an enterprise system based on the fundamental mechanisms for structuring its architecture, i.e., business objects managed by software functions and their relationships which influence business object interactions via the functions. The technique relies on a heuristic for deriving business object exclusive containment relationships based on analysis of source code and system logs. Furthermore, the paper provides an analysis of distributing enterprise systems based on the business object containment relationships using the NSGA II software clustering and optimization technique. The heuristics and the software clustering and optimization techniques have been validated against two open-source enterprise systems: SugarCRM and ChurchCRM. The experiments demonstrate that the proposed approach can identify microservice designs which support multiple desired microservice characteristics, such as high cohesion, low coupling, high scalability, high availability, and processing efficiency.

Keywords: Microservice discovery · System reengineering
Cloud migration

1 Introduction

Microservices have been introduced to the software industry as the latest form of service-based software, allowing systems to be distributed through the Cloud as fine-grained components, containing individual operations, in contrast to services under a Service-Oriented Architecture (SOA) which includes all logically related operations [1]. Such loosely coupled, highly cohesive composition of the microservices enables scaling up and replication of specific parts of systems and

© Springer Nature Switzerland AG 2018
H. Panetto et al. (Eds.): OTM 2018 Conferences, LNCS 11230, pp. 60–79, 2018.
https://doi.org/10.1007/978-3-030-02671-4_4

business processes through the Cloud, and allows them to be flexibly composed in Web, mobile computing, and Internet-of-Things (IoT) applications.

Such benefits have led Netflix^{TM}, and now Twitter^{TM}, eBay^{TM} and Amazon^{TM} to develop novel architectures for software solutions as microservices. Nonetheless, microservices have so far not been adopted for the dominant form of software in businesses, namely enterprise systems, limiting such systems' evolution and their exploitation of the full benefits of cloud-enabled platforms such as Google Cloud and Amazon AWS. In particular, this limits the evolution of business applications involving IoT and blockchain [2].

Enterprise systems, such as enterprise resource planning (ERP), customer relationship management (CRM) and supply chain management (SCM), are large and complex and contain complex business processes encoded in application logic managing business objects, in typically many-to-many relationships [3]. Restructuring enterprise systems as microservices is technically cumbersome. It requires tedious search and identification of suitable parts of the system to restructure, program code rewrites, and the integration of the newly developed microservices with the remaining 'backend' enterprise systems. This is a costly and error-prone task for developers, mainly due to two reasons. Firstly, it is difficult to identify the functional dependencies between different functions and operations by examining millions of lines of code in the system. Secondly, it is challenging to figure out an optimal splitting of the system functionalities as fine-grained microservices while minimizing the communication cost (i.e. service calls) between them in order to provide better availability and processing efficiency.

Automated software re-engineering techniques have been proposed to improve the efficiency of transforming legacy applications, structures [4], specifically focusing on optimizing cohesion and coupling of software packages and components using static analysis techniques that focus on source code [5] and dynamic analysis techniques that focus on software execution patterns and system logs [6]. However, these techniques have, to date, not been applied to the re-engineering challenges of microservices, which are more fine-grained (i.e single operational functions) and distributed compared to Service-Oriented-Architecture (SOA) services in which multiple operations are combined within a single function.

Enterprise systems provide semantic insights, available through the business objects that they manage, which influence the software structure and the processes they support. For instance, an order-to-cash process in SAP ERP is supported through functions of software components: multiple sales orders, deliveries shared across different customers, shared containers in transportation carriers, and multiple invoices and payments. To support this process, multiple functions are invoked asynchronously, reflecting business object relationship types and cardinalities, and these can be seen through cross-service interactions, correlations, and data payloads [7]. Such insights provided by business object relationships are promising for improving the feasibility of automated system re-engineering, where modules correspond to single business objects. As examples, Pĕrez-Castillo *et al.* [8] used the transitive closure of strong business object dependencies derived from databases to recommend software function hierarchies, while Lu *et al.* [9] demonstrated process discovery using SAP ERP logs based on business objects.

This paper presents discovery techniques that support the identification of suitable consumer-oriented parts of enterprise systems which could be re-engineered as microservices based on the knowledge gained through business object relationships and their execution patterns. Specifically, the paper addresses two fundamental areas of microservice discovery, namely exclusive containment of business object relationships, while analysing the cost and complexity of functional calls between different microservices based on a heuristic rule by optimizing the Non-dominated Sorting Genetic Algorithm (NSGA) II. Experiments were conducted on SugarCRM[1] and ChurchCRM[2] to validate the presented methodology and showed that it can identify microservice designs which support multiple microservice characteristics, such as high cohesion, low coupling, high scalability, high availability, and processing efficiency while preserving coherent features of enterprise systems and minimizing the overall communication overhead of the system.

The remainder of the paper is structured as follows. Section 2 presents a containment heuristic, while Sect. 3 describes a microservice discovery process based on the heuristic. Section 4 discusses an implementation and validation of the proposed technique. Related work is summarized in Sect. 5. The paper closes with a conclusion.

2   Containment Relationships and Heuristic

Enterprise systems (ESs) use different Business Objects (BOs) to store the information related to their functionality, and these BOs have different relationships between them. For example, the creation of a 'purchase order' will result in the invocation of functions involved in the creation of 'line items' reflecting an exclusive containment of business objects. It is important to identify such relationships between BOs, since microservices (MSs) are functionally isolated and loosely-coupled parts connected to each other, much like components of a distributed system, and typically focus on individual BOs, locally managed through a database [10]. A better understanding of such BO relationships can be obtained through the following formal characterization.

Given an ES s, by OP_s, A_s, T_s, and B_s, we refer to the set of its all *operations, attributes, database tables,* and *business objects,* respectively. We will omit the subscripts where the context is clear. We define domination and exclusive containment relationships over business objects as follows.

---

[1] https://www.sugarcrm.com/.
[2] http://churchcrm.io/.

Definition 2.1 (Domination [11] and exclusive containment [12] relationships)
Given two business objects $b, b' \in B$, of an ES we say that:

- b *dominates* b' iff for every create or delete operation $op \in OP$ that either uses some attribute of b' as one of its input parameters or writes its result into some attribute of b', it holds that op uses some attribute of b as one of its input parameters or writes its result into some attribute of b;
- b' is *exclusively contained* in b iff $b' \neq b$, and b dominates b', and there exists no $b'' \in B$, $b'' \neq b$, $b'' \neq b'$, such that b'' dominates b'. ⌟

By $\gamma : B \to \mathcal{P}(B)$, we denote the function that relates every business object to the corresponding set of business objects it exclusively contains.

The behaviour of an ES, or a MS system, is based on the invocation of operations which consist of well-defined processing sequences governed by BO relationships. Such sequences illustrate a particular execution pattern based on the structure and behaviour of an organization. Therefore, we argue that a proper analysis of such process sequences and BO relationships will help to derive prominent microserviceable components. This assumption leads us to derive an exclusive containment heuristic which assists in MS discovery that aligns with Definition 2.1. As an example, assume that an ES induces a pattern of CRUD operation dependencies depicted in Fig. 1; in the figure, each node represents a CRUD operation. These operations further relate to the BOs on which they are performed, see BO1, BO2, and BO3 in the figure. If BO2 is exclusively contained in BO3, every time an operation that involves BO2 gets executed, it also processes BO3, i.e. BO3 does not have an independent life-cycle and depends on BO2. If we decouple software corresponding to the CRUD management of different BOs the communication overhead between the software components will increase and will result in a lower level of the system availability and efficiency. This understanding leads us to Heuristic 2.2.

Heuristic 2.2 (Exclusive containment)
A MS composed of a business object $b \in B$, a non-empty set of business objects $C \subset \gamma(b)$, and a non-empty set of operations $D \subseteq OP$, each performed over at least one business object in $\{b\} \cup C$ (i.e., each operation in D either uses an attribute of some business object in $\{b\} \cup C$ as an input parameter or writes its result into an attribute of some business object in $\{b\} \cup C$), when used as part of an MS system, leads to higher levels of the system's availability and scalability, and processing efficiency. ⌟

An ES can consist of BOs which do not participate in the exclusive containment relationships with other BOs. A better understanding for a possible function splitting in the presence of such BOs can be achieved through the knowledge of execution calls and their frequencies, since the number of executions between

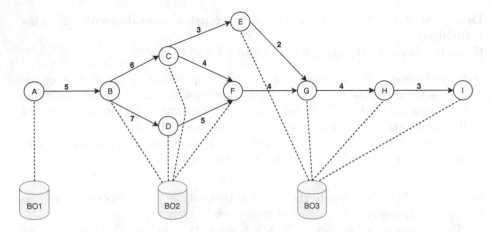

Fig. 1. A pattern of CRUD operations and BO relationships.

different BOs plays a major role in achieving processing efficiency and system availability. In general, if the number of communications between microservices increases, the number of network hops between the microservices also increases, which inevitably results in lower availability of the corresponding MS system and, consequently, long waiting times [1]. Hence, a proper microservice discovery and recommendation technique should consider both BO relationships, like exclusive containment, and execution frequencies of the operations over different BOs. Taking this understanding further, we developed an automated microservice discovery process, which is described in the next section.

3 Automated Microservice Discovery

To perform microservice discovery, we developed a five-step approach, which is illustrated in Fig. 2. Since MSs are focused on accessing operations of BOs, or partitions of BOs, in the system [13], we propose to start microservice discovery with the identification of the BOs used by a given ES, refer to step 1 in the figure. To derive the BOs, we evaluate all the SQL queries of the given ES and identify the relationships between database tables, which are then used to derive the BOs according to the approach described by Nooijen *et al.* [14]. In the second step, the operations performed by the system are analysed using static analysis techniques and classified into different categories based on their relationships and types, such as association create, association delete, create and delete. The BOs derived from step one and the operations extracted and categorised using step two are provided as the input to the third step, in which we identify the containment relationships between different BOs as described in Sect. 3.1.

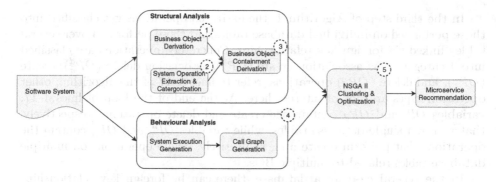

Fig. 2. Overview of the microservice discovery approach.

After performing the steps related to structural (i.e. static) analysis, behavioural (i.e. dynamic) analysis is performed as the fourth step to generate the call graphs related to the system execution. In this step, we use scripts to automate the system to generate system execution logs based on user behaviours and then use those execution logs to generate the call graphs. Finally, as the fifth step, all the structural and behavioural details generated are provided to an optimization algorithm in order to discover an optimal system splitting for MSs. The optimization algorithm analyses the BO relationships and operation calls to provide a microservice recommendation, as described in Sect. 3.2.

3.1   Containment Derivation

As depicted in Fig. 2, in order to derive a satisfactory splitting of system operations and BOs into MSs, the clustering and optimization algorithm needs two inputs, one from structural analysis and the other from the behavioural analysis. To perform the structural analysis to derive the BOs and the exclusive containment relationships among the BOs, we have developed Algorithm 1 which is composed of five steps.

In an ES, the information related to a BO is often stored in several database tables. Thus, one can define a BO $b \in B$ as a collection of database tables which it is scattered across, i.e. $b \subseteq T$. To identify the BOs, in the first step, the *BOS* function is performed by Algorithm 1, which derives the BOs, B, of the system through the analysis of the database table relationships and their data similarities, as described by Nooijen *et al.* [14]. In the second step of the algorithm, function *OPS* performs static analysis of the system and extracts all the operations *OP* of the system.

In the third step of Algorithm 1, the extracted operations get classified into those performed on individual database tables and those performed over several tables linked via foreign key relationships. Concretely, operations are classified into 4 categories, as association create (OP_a^c), association delete (OP_a^d), create (OP_c), and delete (OP_d) operations, refer to lines 4–17 of the algorithm; other operation types are not of interest here. At the end of the loop of lines 4–17, variables OP_c and OP_d contain the create and delete operations, respectively, that run over single database tables, while variables OP_a^c and OP_a^d contain the operations that perform create and, respectively, delete operations on multiple database tables related to multiple BOs.

In the general case, in a database, there can be foreign key relationships among the tables that relate to the same BO $b \in B$. Such relationships are not important for the exclusive containment derivation. Therefore, in Algorithm 1, filtration is done in order to identify the create and delete association operations related to multiple BOs, in lines 5–13. To achieve this filtration, first, the *TBLS* function extracts the tables T_k related to each association operation op_k. Next, after confirming that the tables in T_k do not relate to the same BO b, the algorithm adds the association operation to the respective set, either OP_a^c or OP_a^d.

In the fourth step, Algorithm 1 identifies the BOs which are related by a create (OP_a^c) or delete (OP_a^d) association operation, and stores them for further processing, in lines 18–22. Since association operations which occur within the same BO are not considered, at this step the algorithm analyses the operations in OP_a^c and OP_a^d to identify related BOs and stores them into pairs of BOs, $B_r \subseteq B \times B$.

Finally, in the fifth step, the algorithm evaluates whether any of the BOs related through an association operation and stored in B_r has its own create OP_c or delete OP_d operation (i.e. an operation performed over all the tables of the BOs), and verifies that at least one of the associated BOs is not associated with any other BOs of the system, in lines 25–26. Given two BOs $b, b' \in B$, if b' does not have its own create OP_c or delete OP_d operation, and if b' does not participate in further exclusive containment relationships with other BOs, except for the one it has with b, then we identify that b' is exclusively contained in b, as b' does not have its own independent life-cycle apart from b (i.e. b' is created and destroyed together with b). In the last line of the algorithm, the identified exclusive containment relationships γ and the BOs of the system get returned.

Algorithm 1. Computing exclusive containment relationship over business objects

---

Input: Source code SC and database schema DB of an ES s.
Output: A function γ that captures exclusive containment relationships over the
  business objects of s, and the set of all business objects B of s.

1 $B = \{b_1, \ldots, b_n\} := BOS(SC, DB)$;   // Identify BOs
2 $OP = \langle op_1, \ldots, op_m \rangle := OPS(SC)$;   // Identify operations
3 $OP_a^c := OP_a^d := OP_c := OP_d := B_r := \emptyset$;
   /* Classify operations in OP */
4 **for** *each* $k \in [1 \mathbin{..} m]$ **do**
5 $\quad$ **if** op_k *is an association create operation* **then**
6 $\quad\quad$ $T_k := TBLS(op_k)$;
7 $\quad\quad$ **if** $\nexists\, b \in B \,.\, T_k \subseteq b$ **then**
8 $\quad\quad\quad$ $OP_a^c := OP_a^c \cup \{op_k\}$; // Identify an association create operation
9 $\quad$ **else if** op_k *is an association delete operation* **then**
10 $\quad\quad$ $T_k := TBLS(op_k)$;
11 $\quad\quad$ **if** $\nexists\, b \in B \,.\, T_k \subseteq b$ **then**
12 $\quad\quad\quad$ $OP_a^d := OP_a^d \cup \{op_k\}$; // Identify an association delete operation
13 $\quad$ **else if** op_k *is a create operation* **then**
14 $\quad\quad$ $OP_c := OP_c \cup \{op_k\}$;   // Identify a create operation
15 $\quad$ **else if** op_k *is a delete operation* **then**
16 $\quad\quad$ $OP_d := OP_d \cup \{op_k\}$;   // Identify a delete operation
17 **end**
18 **for** *each* $b_i \in B$ **do**
19 $\quad$ **for** *each* $b_j \in B,\ b_i \neq b_j,$ **do**
20 $\quad\quad$ **if** $\exists\, op \in OP_a^c \cup OP_a^d \,.\, (b_i \cap TBLS(op) \neq \emptyset) \wedge (b_j \cap TBLS(op) \neq \emptyset)$ **then**
21 $\quad\quad\quad$ $B_r := B_r \cup \{(b_i, b_j)\}$;
22 $\quad$ **end**
23 **end**
24 **for** *each* $(b, b') \in B_r$ **do**
25 $\quad$ **if** $(\nexists\, op \in OP_c \cup OP_d \,.\, b \cup b' \subseteq TBLS(op)) \wedge$
   $\quad\quad (\{b'' \in B \setminus \{b\} \mid (b', b'') \in B_r\} = \emptyset)$ **then**
26 $\quad\quad$ Record in γ that b' is exclusively contained in b, i.e., $b' \in \gamma(b)$;
27 **end**
28 **return** γ, B

In addition to the identification of exclusive containment relationships over the BOs of the system through structural analysis, behavioural analysis should be performed to generate the call graphs to extract the details such as the graph nodes, execution calls between the nodes and the number of calls between the nodes. These structural data and behavioural analysis details are provided to the multi-objective optimization algorithm for further processing, as described in Sect. 3.2.

3.2   NSGA II Clustering and Optimization

The Non-dominated Sorting Genetic Algorithm II (NSGA II) is a multi-objective optimization algorithm which provides an optimal set of solutions while achieving global optima, when there are multiple conflicting objectives to be considered [15]. It has been evaluated as one of the best algorithms to cluster software packages and classes while achieving multiple objectives such as high cohesion and low coupling [5].

Since MS discovery should evaluate two major objectives to extract an optimal set of MSs, NSGA II was chosen to guide the extraction. The first objective is to minimize the number of communications between different nodes in the execution call graphs (i.e. the cost of calls between different MSs). The second objective is to minimize the clustering distance of operations and the BOs (i.e. the cost of clustering BOs). A better understanding of the two objectives can be achieved by referring to Fig. 1. When considering the nodes in the figure, one can decide to split the operations related to BO2 and BO3 into two groups in several ways. For example, a possible pair of groups can be 'B, C, D, F, E, G' and 'H, I', whereas 'B, C, D, F' and 'E, G, H, I' would be another such pair of groups. If two MSs get implemented based on the first splitting of the operations, then BO3 gets shared between the two MSs, which one may argue is not optimal. However, one can also argue that the splitting which ensures that each of the two BOs, i.e., BO2 and BO3, gets managed by a dedicated MS leads to a higher communication cost. In the figure, edge weights denote the numbers of calls between operations. Thus, the communication cost of the MSs according to the first splitting is equal to four, while according to the second splitting it is equal to seven.

For real system executions with thousands and millions of nodes and calls, deriving an optimal function splitting of the system with related BOs is a complicated task. Therefore, the NSGA II algorithm was modified to provide a set of optimal solutions as described in Algorithm 2.

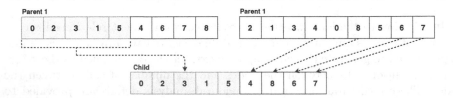

Fig. 3. Crossover to generate child population.

In order to derive optimal solutions, Algorithm 2 follows 3 steps and requires the population size (n), number of generations (Gen), chromosome length (C_Len), crossover probability (Cr_Prob) and mutation probability (Mut_Prob) as input data. Apart from the above standard parameters, our algorithm requires further input, such as the exclusively contained BO relationships (γ), BOs of the system (B) which were derived from Algorithm 1, and execution graph nodes (N) and their relationships (R) extracted from the execution graphs. In the algorithm, the population size (n) defines how many chromosomes are populated in a single generation, while the number of generations (Gen) defines the number of times the algorithm generates different populations before it stops. The crossover probability (Cr_Prob) and mutation probability (Mut_Prob) define the probability for performing crossover and mutation on chromosomes. Interested readers can find further details about NSGA II in A fast and elitist multiobjective genetic algorithm: NSGA-II by Deb *et al.* [15].

In the first step of Algorithm 2, the *SYNTHESIZEPOP* function synthesizes a parent population of the given size n (see line 1). *SYNTHESIZEPOP* uses a random number generator to generate chromosomes of length C_Len, where a chromosome is a sequence of numbers each representing a node in the execution graph. A chromosome generated for the execution graph in Fig. 1 can be represented as a sequence of numbers '0, 1, 2, 3, 4, 5, 6, 7, 8', as depicted in Fig. 3, in which the numbers refer to the nodes in 'A, B, C, D, E, F, G, H, I', such that 0 refers to A, 1 refers to B, etc. Apart from generating the parent population, *SYNTHESIZEPOP* calculates and stores the fitness for each parent. The fitness calculation is preformed in two steps. First, the algorithm calculates the maximum cost for a chromosome as $\sum_{i=0}^{C\_Len} 2^i$. Then, the algorithm calculates the cost of clustering as the cost of BO splittings and calls between the clusters. The node clustering cost represents to which extent the nodes related to the same BO have been grouped together. The information about the relationships between the nodes and BOs can be obtained through B (BOs) and N (operation nodes), as depicted in Fig. 4. For example, using the information provided in Fig. 4, it is clear that node '4' (or node 'E' in Fig. 1) is associated with BO3, and node '5' (or node 'F' in Fig. 1) is associated with BO2; refer to the directed arcs in Fig. 4. If there is an exclusive containment relationship between two BOs, they are combined and supplied as a single BO to the algorithm. For example, if BO1 and BO2 are in the exclusive containment relationship, then B in Fig. 4 must be replaced with $\langle 1, 1, 1, 1, 2, 1, 2, 2, 2 \rangle$, where 1 stands for the combination of BO1 and BO2, and 2 represents BO3.

N: <0, 1, 2, 3, 4, 5, 6, 7, 8>

B: <1, 2, 2, 2, 3, 2, 3, 3, 3>

R: <0-1-5, 1-2-6, 1-3-7, 2-4-3, 2-5-4, 3-5-5, 4-6-2, 5-6-4, 6-7-4, 7-8-3>

Fig. 4. Example data provided to NSGA II for the execution graph in Fig. 1.

Given the B and N information for the graph in Fig. 1, the best BO clustering would be 'A', 'B, C, D, F', 'E, G, H, I', which leads to the chromosome '0, 1,

---

Algorithm 2. NSGA II Algorithm

Input: $n, Gen, C\_Len, Cr\_Prob, Mut\_Prob, \gamma, B, N, R$
Output: A list of optimized clustering of BOs and OPs for MSs

1 $Pop^p = \langle pop_1, \ldots, pop_n \rangle := SYNTHESIZEPOP(n, C\_Len, \gamma, B, N, R);$
2 $Pop^c := Rank^f := \langle \rangle;$
   /* Perform crossover and mutation to generate child population   */
3 **while** $Pop^c.length() < n$ **do**
4 | **if** $RANDOM(0, 1) < Cr\_Prob$ **then**
5 | | $Pop^c := CROSSOVER(Pop^p, Pop^c);$
6 | **if** $RANDOM(0, 1) < Mut\_Prob$ **then**
7 | | $Pop^c := MUTATION(Pop^p, Pop^c);$
8 **end**
9 **for** $each\ i \in [1 .. Gen]$ **do**
10 | $Pop^t := Pop^p + Pop^c;$
11 | $Rank^f = \left\langle rank_1^f, \ldots, rank_m^f \right\rangle := FASTNONDOMINATEDSORT(Pop^t);$
12 | **if** $i == Gen$ **then**
13 | | $break;$
   | /* Identify the Pareto front of the generated population and rank them
   | */
14 | $Pop^c := \langle \rangle;$
15 | **for** $k \in [1 .. m]$ **do**
16 | | **if** $rank_k^f.length() < (n - Pop^c.length())$ **then**
17 | | | $Pop^c := Pop^c + rank_k^f;$
18 | | **else**
19 | | | $Pop^c := Pop^c + CROWDCOMPARISONSORT(rank_k^f);$
20 | **end**
21 | $Pop^p := Pop^c;$ // Initialize new parent population
22 | $Pop^c = \langle pop_1^c, \ldots, pop_n^c \rangle := SYNTHESIZECHILD(Pop^p);$
23 **end**
24 **return** $(Rank^f)$

2, 3, 5, 4, 6, 7, 8'. For each chromosome, the clustering cost is calculated as $\sum_{i=0}^{C\_Len} 2^d$, where d is the distance from the first occurrence of a node related to a particular BO to the next occurrence of the node related to the same BO within the chromosome. For example, if we calculate the clustering cost for the three clusters '0', '1, 2, 3, 5', and '4, 6, 7, 8', the first cluster contains only one node and, thus, contributes 2^0 to the clustering cost. The second cluster contains four nodes, i.e. '1, 2, 3, 5'. Node '1' is the first node that relates to BO2, which contributes the cost of 2^0, as the first node of the second cluster. However, subsequent nodes '2', '3', and '5', which are also associated with BO2, contribute the costs of $2^1, 2^2, 2^3$, respectively. Hence, if we generate the costs associated with each node '0, 1, 2, 3, 5, 4, 6, 7, 8', i.e. including the nodes that relate to BO3, these will be $2^0, 2^0, 2^1, 2^2, 2^3, 2^0, 2^1, 2^2, 2^3$, which leads the total clustering cost of '31'.

The cost of execution calls between clusters is computed as the sum of inter-cluster calls between the different clusters. For the running example, i.e. the chromosome '0, 1, 2, 3, 5, 4, 6, 7, 8', this sum would be $5 + 3 + 4 = 12$, because the costs of calls between the pairs of clusters in '0', '1, 2, 3, 5', '4, 6, 7, 8', are '5', '3' and '4'. The information on the costs of the calls between the nodes is extracted from the R relation, depicted in Fig. 4. For example, the number of calls between node 'A' (i.e. node '0') and node 'B' (i.e. node '1') is 5; this is given as 0-1-5 in R, refer to Fig. 4. Note that R is constructed based on the edge weights in Fig. 1. The cost of execution calls is often by far smaller than the cost of clustering. As this may create a bias in the optimization results, in order to minimize such effects, the total cost of calls is multiplied by a fixed number y. Afterwards, the *fitness* of the chromosome is calculated by subtracting the sum of all the cluster costs and the sum of the cost of inter-cluster calls from the maximum possible cost of the chromosome $\sum_{i=0}^{C\_Len} 2^i$.

The second step of the algorithm generates the child population by performing crossover operations and mutation operations on the parent chromosomes (see lines 3–8). In order to perform the crossover operation, the algorithm selects two parents using binary tournament selection [15]. This is performed by randomly identifying two parent chromosomes and extracting the chromosome with the highest fitness value out of them. After identifying two parent chromosomes for crossover, the algorithm splits the first parent chromosome from a predefined position (normally half of the chromosome length) and includes it as the first part of the child chromosome. In general, as the next step, a regular genetic algorithm would extract the other part from the second parent chromosome. However, in this situation, the child chromosome should not contain repeating node values. As such, the rest of the child chromosome is generated by extracting values from the other parent which are not in the first part of the child chromosome as depicted in Fig. 3. Mutation is achieved by changing the position of two genes (i.e. positions of two nodes) in the parent chromosome.

After generating the first child population, the algorithm generates Gen new populations, refer to lines 9–23 in Algorithm 2; which constitutes the third (and last) step of the algorithm. First, the current total population Pop^t is computed at line 10 by concatenating the parent population Pop^p and the child population Pop^c. Next, the algorithm calculates the non-dominated fronts, or the Pareto fronts, of the total population. A non-dominated front contains the chromosomes which have the optimal values for the two objectives that were defined above, namely the cost of node clustering and the cost of calls. The chromosome's optimization of node clustering is calculated as the difference between the maximum possible cost of the chromosome and cost of its node clustering. Similarly, the chromosome's optimization of execution calls is calculated as the difference between the maximum possible cost of the chromosome and cost between its cluster calls. The non-dominated chromosomes in Pop^t are extracted as the first front using function $FASTNONDOMINATEDSORT$ (see line 11). After extracting the first non-dominated front, the algorithm evaluates the other chromosomes in Pop^t and identifies the second non-dominated front. This process is repeated until all the chromosomes are categorised into different fronts (2, ..., m), where each generated front may contain multiple non-dominated chromosomes.

Once the Pareto fronts are obtained, a new child population is created by concatenating the ranked fronts in several steps (see lines 14–20). First, the algorithm verifies that there is enough space in the child population to add all the chromosomes in each ranked front $rank_k^f$ by comparing the remaining space in the child population $(n - Pop^c.length())$ with the rank front size $rank_k^f.length()$ (see line 16). If there is enough space, the rank front is directly added to the child population (see line 17). If there is no space, then the algorithm identifies the most prominent chromosomes in the front using a crowd comparison sort [15] and assigns them to the child population (see line 19). Through the loop of lines 15–20, the algorithm filters out the chromosomes in the total population Pop^t with the highest objective fitness values. The new population is used as the next parent population and again synthesizes a new child population by performing crossover and mutation (see lines 21–22). Finally, the non-dominated front (the Pareto optimal solution) $Rank^f$ is returned to the user which constitutes a suggestion for the best clustering of BOs and operation nodes in the system to develop MSs, line 24.

4　Implementation and Validation

A proper MS system should provide high execution efficiency with desirable levels of scalability and availability. Furthermore the packages and components related to each MS should be highly cohesive and loosely coupled [1,16]. In order to validate that our MS discovery and recommendation process provides MSs with these desirable characteristics, while optimizing BO relationships and operation call costs, we developed a prototype[3] based on the algorithms presented in Sect. 3 and experimented with it on the SugarCRM and ChurchCRM Systems.

This section presents the details of the experiments that we conducted on both the SugarCRM and ChurchCRM customer relationship management systems. SugarCRM contains 8116 source files and 600 attributes divided between 101 tables, while ChurchCRM contains 8039 source files and 350 attributes divided between 55 tables. Execution sequences were generated for both systems covering all the major functionalities and user cases related to them[4]. The logs related to both systems were captured using the log generation functionality available in the systems. They were then analyzed using the process mining tool Disco[5] and call graphs were generated for SugarCRM with 178 unique nodes and for ChurchCRM with 58 unique nodes. Each of the nodes in call graph represents unique operation performed on database tables in the systems and the edges between each node represent the number of calls between the nodes.

Discovered MSs: Based on the provided data, the prototype managed to identify 13 different business objects related to SugarCRM such as 'action control

---

[3] https://github.com/AnuruddhaDeAlwis/NSGAII.git.

[4] http://support.sugarcrm.com/Documentation/Sugar_Versions/8.0/Pro/Application_ Guide/.

[5] https://fluxicon.com/disco/.

lists', 'calls', 'contacts', 'campaigns', 'meetings', 'users', 'prospects', 'accounts', 'documents', 'leads', 'emails', 'projects' and 'email management'. The 'calls' and 'meetings' BOs are exclusively contained in 'contacts' BO and 'documents' BO exclusively contained in 'users' BO. The system identified 12 BOs such as 'calendar', 'locations', 'deposits', 'emails', 'events', 'family', 'group', 'property', 'query', 'users' and 'kiosk' for ChurchCRM. The BOs identified and the call graphs with execution details were given to the optimization algorithm and it derived 8 MSs for ChurchCRM and 11 MSs for SugarCRM.

Validation Process: The validation process was conducted by implementing two MSs for each system in Google Cloud. Each MS was hosted in Google Cloud using a cluster of size 2 which has two virtual CPUs and a total memory of 7.5 GB. The hosted MSs were exposed through the Google Cloud kubernetes API[6], allowing third party computers to access them via API calls. In order to simulate the legacy systems we created services which contain all the functionalities related to both MSs. The read and write operations to the local database were simulated by reading and writing data to a file resides in the MSs, themselves.

In order to validate the performance of the ChurchCRM MS system, evaluation was conducted under two criteria. First we tested each MS system against a load of 150,000 and 300,000 requests generated by 10 machines simultaneously, simulating the customer requests, while recording their total execution time, average memory consumption and average disk consumption. Then, we tested the same load against the legacy ChurchCRM system. In this execution we directly call the functions related to each MS without creating any interactions between the MSs. The results obtain are recorded in Table 3. However, in the real environment MSs interact with each other through executions and service calls. As such, to evaluate the performance of the MS system when there are interactions between MSs in the system, we generated service calls between them and tested against a similar load as described previously. The results obtained for the interactive execution are recorded in Table 5. We followed a similar approach to test the MS system related to SugarCRM with a load of 50,000 requests and 100,000 requests generated by 10 machines simultaneously. The results for the SugarCRM MS system without interaction between them are recorded in Table 7, while Table 9 contains the results obtained when there are interactions between MSs in the MS system. Since we have identified several exclusive containment relationships in SugarCRM, it was important to evaluate the validity of our Heuristic. As such, we implemented two MS systems. The first MS system contained two MSs which are exclusively related, but deployed in separate containers. The second MS system contained operations of both exclusively related BOs and deployed in a single container. Both systems were tested against a load of 50,000 requests and 100,000 requests generated by 10 machines and the obtained results are summarized in Table 11.

---

[6] https://kubernetes.io/.

Based on the results detailed in Tables 3, 5, 7, 9 and 11 we calculated the scalability, availability and execution efficiency of different combinations and the results obtained are summarized in Tables 4, 6, 8, 10 and 12. Scalability was calculated according to the resources usage over time as described by Tsai *et al.* [18]. In order to determine availability, first we calculated the time taken to process 100 requests if a particular MS is not available. Then, we used the difference between the total up-time and total down-time as described by Bauer *et al.* [19]. Efficiency gain was calculated by dividing the total time taken by the legacy system to process all requests by the total time taken by the corresponding MS system. Furthermore, we calculated the structural cohesion and coupling of the packages in the legacy system and the new MS systems, as described by Candela *et al.* [5]. The results related to cohesion and coupling for the MSs and the legacy systems are summarized in Tables 1 and 2.

Experimental Results: According to Tsai *et al.* [18], the lower the number the better the scalability. Thus, it is evident that the ChurchCRM legacy system has better scalability, availability and efficiency than MS system when there are no interaction between modules (refer Table 4). However, when there are interactions, MS system perform better in all three criteria of scalability, availability and efficiency than the legacy system as depicted in Table 6. When there are no interactions between modules, the SugarCRM MS system achieved less scalability than the legacy system (refer Table 8). However, the SugarCRM MS system managed to attain higher availability and eight times better execution efficiency than the legacy system when there are no interactions between MSs in the MS system as depicted in Table 8. When there are interactions between modules in SugarCRM, MS system performed better in all criteria than the legacy system as depicted by Table 10. Apart from legacy system comparisons, it is evident from Table 12 that exclusively contained MSs attained a higher level of scalability, availability and efficiency gain when they were developed and deployed as single MSs without separating them into different containers.

According to Candela *et al.* [5], lack of cohesion and structural coupling are inversely related to the cohesion and coupling of the system. The lower the number the better the cohesion and coupling of the system [5]. When considering the cohesion and coupling values of ChurchCRM MSs in Table 1, it is evident that they have obtained better cohesion and coupling values than the legacy system. Even though Table 2, related to SugarCRM MSs, does not show a prominent gain in cohesion and coupling values related to all MSs, most of them manage to achieve either better cohesion or coupling values when compared with the legacy system.

The obtained results have affirmed that the MSs extracted based on the optimization algorithm and the recommendation of the prototype can provide the same services to users while preserving overall system behaviour and achieving higher scalability, availability, efficiency, high cohesion and low coupling while aligning with BO relationships and containment heuristics.

5 Related Work

Microservices have emerged as the latest style of service-based software allowing systems to be distributed through the cloud as fine-grained components, typically with individual operations, in contrast to services under SOA which include all logically related operations [1]. Even though microservices can support the evolution of ERP systems by providing exploitation in cloud-enabled platforms such as the IoT [2], the research conducted in this particular area is limited. To the best of our knowledge there is no research related to the automation of MS discovery in legacy systems, apart from the manual migrations achieved by Balalaie et al. [20]. They have described the complexity associated with the system reengineering process while pointing out the importance of considering BOs and their relationships in the system migration process. Martin Fowler emphasizes the importance of adapting BO relationships in microservices [16] by mentioning the Domain Driven Design (DDD) principles [17].

However, existing software re-engineering techniques do not consider the complex relationship of BOs along with their behaviours in the re-engineering process. Furthermore, studies show that the success rate of existing software re-modularisation techniques, especially for large systems, remains low [5]. A key stumbling block is the limited insights available from syntactic structures of software code for profiling software dependencies and evaluating their measurements for coupling and cohesion metrics [4]. As such, to derive successful re-engineering techniques, a methodology should consider the enriched semantic insights available through the BOs and functions in an ES.

In such a process the first challenge would be identifying the BOs which are distributed among several database tables in an ES system, while identifying the relationships among them. Nooijen et al. [14] and Lu et al. [9] have proposed methodologies and heuristics to identify BOs based on the database schema and information in database tables. However, according to Lu et al. these derived BOs might not be perfect and they have to be re-clustered with the help of human expertise.

Table 1. Comparison of lack of cohesion and structural coupling in ChurchCRM.

Measure	Legacy	MS1	MS2	MS3	MS4	MS5	MS6	M7S	MS8
Lack of cohesion	122	32.5	0.0	0.5	0.5	0.0	0.0	0.5	1.0
Structural coupling	58	45.5	9.5	11.0	11.5	9.5	10.0	12.0	13.0

Table 2. Comparison of lack of cohesion and structural coupling in SugarCRM.

Measure	Legacy	MS1	MS2	MS3	MS4	MS5	MS6	M7S	MS8	MS9	MS10	MS11
Lack of cohesion	0.428	0.0	2.0	0.25	0.0	0.5	0.2	0.0	0.0	0.0	1.0	0.11
Structural coupling	7.857	3.0	17.33	12.0	9.0	20.0	11.8	15.7	5.0	24.0	14.67	8.1

Table 3. Legacy vs MS results without interactions between modules for ChurchCRM.

System type	No of requests	Ex. time (ms)	Avg mem (GB)	Avg disk (MB)
Legacy	150000	280800	3.0075	25.49
Legacy	300000	540000	3.084	45.719
MS system	150000	306000	2.915	25.094
MS system	300000	626400	3.018	46.369

Table 4. Legacy vs MS system characteristics comparison for ChurchCRM.

Campaign type	Scalability [mem]	Scalability [disk]	Availability [150000]	Availability [300000]	Efficiency [150000]	Efficiency [300000]
Legacy	1.896	3.3166	99.8754	99.940	1.00	1.00
MS system	2.169	3.8716	99.8642	99.930	0.92	0.86

Table 5. Legacy vs MS results with interactions between modules for ChurchCRM.

System type	No of requests	Ex. time (ms)	Avg mem (GB)	Avg disk (MB)
Legacy	150000	756000	3.043	25.225
Legacy	300000	1188000	3.1025	45.192
MS system	150000	709200	2.89	13.502
MS system	300000	954000	3.0043	24.239

Table 6. Legacy vs MS system characteristics comparison with interactions between modules for ChurchCRM.

Campaign type	Scalability [mem]	Scalability [disk]	Availability [150000]	Availability [300000]	Efficiency [150000]	Efficiency [300000]
Legacy	1.259	2.212	99.665	99.685	1.00	1.00
MS system	0.941	1.624	99.868	99.894	1.07	1.26

Table 7. Legacy vs MS results without interactions between modules for SugarCRM.

System type	No of requests	Ex. time (ms)	Avg mem (GB)	Avg disk (MB)
Legacy	50000	1101600	2.9325	25.36
Legacy	50000	2394000	2.94	25.48
MS system	100000	122400	2.953	25.20
MS system	100000	298800	3.0605	45.99

Table 8. Legacy vs MS system characteristics comparison for SugarCRM.

Campaign type	Scalability [mem]	Scalability [disk]	Availability [50000]	Availability [100000]	Efficiency [50000]	Efficiency [100000]
Legacy	2.367	2.372	95.779	97.662	1.000	1.000
MS system	3.088	5.438	99.512	99.702	9.000	8.012

Table 9. Legacy vs MS results with interactions between modules for SugarCRM.

System type	No of requests	Ex. time (ms)	Avg mem (GB)	Avg disk (MB)
Legacy	50000	72000	2.941	24.789
Legacy	100000	169200	3.119	48.866
MS System	50000	72000	2.898	19.712
MS System	100000	140400	4.088	43.174

Table 10. Legacy vs MS System characteristics comparison with interactions between modules for SugarCRM.

Campaign type	Scalability [mem]	Scalability [disk]	Availability [50000]	Availability [100000]	Efficiency [50000]	Efficiency [100000]
Legacy	2.929	5.443	99.713	99.831	1.000	1.000
MS System	2.682	4.164	99.713	99.859	1.000	1.21

Table 11. Exclusive MS vs separated MSs execution results for SugarCRM.

System type	No of requests	Ex. time (ms)	Avg mem (GB)	Avg disk (MB)
Exclusive MS system	50000	64800	2.9965	25.116
Exclusive MS system	100000	136800	3.0700	25.471
Separated MS system	50000	237600	3.0025	25.321
Separated MS system	100000	1252800	3.0218	36.009

Table 12. Exclusive MS vs separated MSs characteristics comparison for SugarCRM.

Campaign type	Scalability [mem]	Scalability [disk]	Availability [50000]	Availability [100000]	Efficiency [50000]	Efficiency [100000]
Exclusive MS system	2.283	2.260	99.971	99.984	3.67	5.27
Separated MS system	13.99	19.77	99.895	99.861	1.00	1.00

Furthermore, Wei *et al.* have derived BO relationships using the information available in WSDL files and have classified the BO relationships into exclusive containment, inclusive containment, sub-type and etc [12]. Apart from BO relationships, the number of execution calls between different microservices plays a major role in defining optimal MSs, because an excessive number of network calls can increase the response time while decreasing the availability of the service [1].

A proper identification of factors which fall under the behaviour of the system can be evaluated thorough dynamic analysis of the system [13]. However, there is still a gap in the area of correlating structural and behavioural analysis while considering the underlying BO semantics. As such, it is important to consider optimization techniques such as genetic algorithms to incorporate multiple objectives (i.e. system structure and behaviour) [5] in the software re-engineering process while focusing on BO relationships and the execution calls between different operations.

6   Conclusion

This paper presented a technique that can support the re-engineering of enterprise systems into microservices based on business objects and their relationships and associated operations with the coherent features and minimum communication overhead. A prototype was developed based on the proposed heuristic and the NSGA II optimization algorithm, and a validation was conducted using the implemented MS systems recommended by the prototype for SugarCRM and ChurchCRM systems. The paper demonstrated that the analysis of functions, CRUD operations, and BO relationships of an ES supports the effective identification of a solution to migrate the system into the corresponding MS system that has high cohesion, low coupling, and achieves higher scalability, higher availability, and processing efficiency.

References

1. Newman, S.: Building MSs NGINX, 1st edn. O'Reilly, Sebastopol (2015)
2. 2017 Internet Of Things (IoT) Intelligence Update. https://www.forbes.com/sites/louiscolumbus/2017/11/12/2017-internet-of-things-iot-intelligence-update/#43aa6f4c7f31. Accessed 5 May 2018
3. Magal, S.R., Word, J.: Integrated Business Processes with ERP Systems, 1st edn. Wiley, Hoboken (2011)
4. Anquetil, N., Laval, J.: Legacy software restructuring: analyzing a concrete case. In: 15th European Conference on Software Maintenance and Reengineering (CSMR), pp. 279–286 (2011)
5. Candela, I., Bavota, G., Russo, B., Oliveto, R.: Using cohesion and coupling for software remodularization: is it enough? ACM Trans. Softw. Eng. Methodol. (TOSEM) **25**, 24 (2016)
6. Shatnawi, A., Seriai, A.D., Sahraoui, H., Alshara, Z.: Reverse engineering reusable software components from object-oriented APIs. J. Syst. Softw. **131**, 442–460 (2017)

7. Barros, A., Decker, G., Dumas, M., Weber, F.: Correlation patterns in service-oriented architectures. In: Dwyer, M.B., Lopes, A. (eds.) FASE 2007. LNCS, vol. 4422, pp. 245–259. Springer, Heidelberg (2007). https://doi.org/10.1007/978-3-540-71289-3_20

8. Pérez Castillo, R., García Rodríguez de Guzmán, I., Caballero, I., Piattini, M.: Software modernization by recovering web services from legacy databases. J. Softw.: Evol. Process 25, 507–533 (2013)

9. Lu, X., Nagelkerke, M., van de Wiel, D., Fahland, D.: Discovering interacting artifacts from ERP systems. IEEE Trans. Serv. Comput. 88, 861–873 (2015)

10. De Alwis, A., Barros, A., Polyvyanyy, A., Fidge, C.: Function-splitting heuristics for discovery of microservices in enterprise systems. In: International Conference on Service-Oriented Computing (2018). (accepted on 25 July 2018)

11. Kumaran, S., Liu, R., Wu, F.Y.: On the duality of information-centric and activity-centric models of business processes. In: Bellahsène, Z., Léonard, M. (eds.) CAiSE 2008. LNCS, vol. 5074, pp. 32–47. Springer, Heidelberg (2008). https://doi.org/10.1007/978-3-540-69534-9_3

12. Wei, F., Ouyang, C., Barros, A.: Discovering behavioural interfaces for overloaded web services. In: 2015 IEEE World Congress on Services (SERVICES), pp. 286–293 (2015)

13. Hull, R.: Artifact-centric business process models: brief survey of research results and challenges. In: Meersman, R., Tari, Z. (eds.) OTM 2008. LNCS, vol. 5332, pp. 1152–1163. Springer, Heidelberg (2008). https://doi.org/10.1007/978-3-540-88873-4_17

14. Nooijen, E.H.J., van Dongen, B.F., Fahland, D.: Automatic discovery of data-centric and artifact-centric processes. In: La Rosa, M., Soffer, P. (eds.) BPM 2012. LNBIP, vol. 132, pp. 316–327. Springer, Heidelberg (2013). https://doi.org/10.1007/978-3-642-36285-9_36

15. Deb, K., Pratap, A., Agarwal, S., Meyarivan, T.A.M.T.: A fast and elitist multiobjective genetic algorithm: NSGA-II. IEEE Trans. Evol. Comput. 6, 182–197 (2002)

16. Microservices a definition of this new architectural term. https://martinfowler.com/articles/microservices.html. Accessed 3 May 2018

17. Evans, E.: Domain-Driven Design: Tackling Complexity in the Heart of Software, 1st edn. Addison-Wesley Professional, Boston (2003)

18. Tsai, W.T., Huang, Y., Shao, Q.: Testing the scalability of SaaS applications. In: IEEE International Conference on Service-Oriented Computing and Applications (SOCA), pp. 1–4 (2011)

19. Bauer, E., Adams, R.: Reliability and Availability of Cloud Computing, 1st edn. Wiley, Hoboken (2012)

20. Balalaie, A., Heydarnoori, A., Jamshidi, P.: Migrating to cloud-native architectures using microservices: an experience report. In: Celesti, A., Leitner, P. (eds.) ESOCC Workshops 2015. CCIS, vol. 567, pp. 201–215. Springer, Cham (2016). https://doi.org/10.1007/978-3-319-33313-7_15

Engineering a Highly Scalable Object-Aware Process Management Engine Using Distributed Microservices

Kevin Andrews, Sebastian Steinau$^{(\boxtimes)}$, and Manfred Reichert

Institute of Databases and Information Systems, Ulm University, Ulm, Germany
{kevin.andrews,sebastian.steinau,manfred.reichert}@uni-ulm.de

Abstract. Scalability of information systems has been a research topic for many years and is as relevant as ever with the dramatic increases in digitization of business processes and data. This also applies to process-aware information systems, most of which are currently incapable of scaling horizontally, i.e., over multiple servers. This paper presents the design science artifact that resulted from engineering a highly scalable process management system relying on the object-aware process management paradigm. The latter allows for distributed process execution by conceptually encapsulating process logic and data into multiple interacting objects that may be processed concurrently. These objects, in turn, are represented by individual microservices at run-time, which can be hosted transparently across entire server clusters. We present measurement data that evaluates the scalability of the artifact on a compute cluster, demonstrating that the current prototypical implementation of the run-time engine can handle very large numbers of users and process instances concurrently in single-case mechanism experiments with large amounts of simulated user input. Finally, the development of scalable process execution engines will further the continued maturation of the data-centric business process management field.

1 Problem Definition

For decades, researchers have been examining parallelism, concurrency, and scalability in computer hard- and software. The topic of scalability also became instantly relevant to workflow management systems (WfMS) when they first showed up on the market, as they were explicitly built with large-scale applications in mind [16]. First attempts to create scalable WfMS applied existing scalable architecture principles. The resulting approaches, such as WIDE [7], OSIRIS [17], ADEPTdistribution [5], and Gridflow [6], focused on the system architecture point of view, largely ignoring other aspects, such as role assignments, permissions, and data flow. However, the process models these approaches, especially Gridflow, are meant to support, are typically high-performance production workflows, where these aspects merely play a secondary role [16].

Furthermore, with the increasing digitization of business processes and data in recent years, the scalability and speed of process management systems that

© Springer Nature Switzerland AG 2018
H. Panetto et al. (Eds.): OTM 2018 Conferences, LNCS 11230, pp. 80–97, 2018.
https://doi.org/10.1007/978-3-030-02671-4_5

focus on the execution of human-centric processes has become a relevant topic. This is most noticeable in the widespread availability of commercial cloud-based BPM solutions and even academic implementations [18]. Such cloud-based BPM solutions rely heavily on a highly scalable back end architecture to enable multi-tenancy without creating individual virtual machines for each customer. Currently, however, no truly hyperscale process execution engine exists that combines a highly scalable back end with a process execution concept that allows more users to work on the same process instance than is possible in traditional, activity-centric process management, where the number of concurrently working users is typically limited by the branches in the process model [4].

This paper presents our in-depth experiences and details of the artifact that shall fill this gap: the PHILharmonicFlows process engine, which is implemented based on the object-aware process management paradigm [13]. Section 3 presents the solution objectives, detailing what we set out to achieve. Before delving into the artifact design and development in Sect. 4, we establish the necessary fundamentals for object-aware process management in Sect. 2. The evaluation of the artifact can be found in Sect. 5. Section 6 gives a brief overview on related work. Finally, Sect. 7 summarizes the contribution and gives an outlook.

2   Fundamentals of Object-Aware Process Management

PHILharmonicFlows, the object-aware process management framework we are using as a test-bed for the concepts presented in this paper, has been under development for many years at Ulm University [3,4,13,14,20]. PHILharmonicFlows takes the idea of a data-driven and data-centric process management system, enhancing it with the concept of *objects*. One such object exists for each business object present in a real-world business process. As can be seen in Fig. 1, an object consists of data, in the form of *attributes*, and a state-based process model describing the *object lifecycle*.

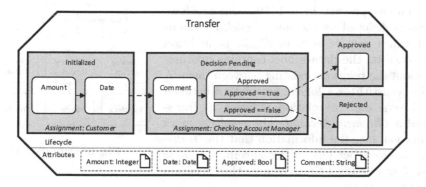

Fig. 1. "Transfer" object, with lifecycle process and attributes

The attributes of the *Transfer* object (cf. Fig. 1) include *Amount, Date, Comment,* and *Approved*. The *lifecycle process*, in turn, describes the different *states (Initialized, Decision Pending, Approved,* and *Rejected)*, a *Transfer* object may pass during process execution. In turn, a state contains one or more *steps*, each referencing exactly one of the object attributes, thereby forcing that attribute to be written at run-time. The steps are connected by *transitions*, allowing them to be arranged in a sequence. The state of the object changes when all steps in a state are completed. Finally, alternative paths are supported in the form of *decision steps*, an example of which is the *Approved* decision step.

As PHILharmonicFlows is *data-driven*, the lifecycle process for the *Transfer* object can be understood as follows: The initial state of a *Transfer* object is *Initialized*. Once a *Customer* has entered data for the *Amount* and *Date* attributes, the state changes to *Decision Pending*, which allows an *Account Manager* to input data for *Comment* and *Approved*. Based on the value of *Approved*, the state of the *Transfer* object changes to either *Approved* or *Rejected*. Obviously, this fine-grained approach to modeling business processes increases complexity compared to the activity-centric paradigm, where the minimum granularity of a user action is one atomic activity or task, instead of an individual data attribute.

Additionally, the object-aware approach allows for *automated form generation* at run-time. This is facilitated by the lifecycle process of an object, which dictates the attributes to be filled out before the object may switch to the next state, resulting in a personalized and dynamically created form. An example of such a form, derived from the lifecycle process in Fig. 1, is shown in Fig. 2.

Fig. 2. Example form

Note that a single object and its resulting form only constitutes one part of a PHILharmonicFlows process. To allow for complex executable business processes, many different objects may have to be involved [20]. The entire set of objects and relations present in a PHILharmonicFlows process is denoted as the *data model*, an example of which can be seen in Fig. 3. In addition to the objects, the data model contains information about the *relations* existing between them. A relation constitutes a logical association between two objects, e.g., a relation between a *Transfer* and a *Checking Account*. The resulting meta information, i.e., the information that the *Transfer* in question belongs to this specific *Checking Account*, can be used to coordinate the execution of the two objects.

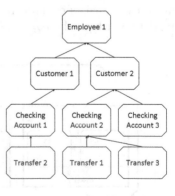

Fig. 3. Data model

Finally, complex object coordination, which is indispensable for processes with interacting business objects, is supported as well [19,20]. As objects publicly advertise their state information, the current state of an object is utilized as an abstraction to coordinate with other objects through a set of constraints, defined in a *coordination process*. As an example, consider the following constraint: "Only 4 *Transfer* objects that have a relation to the same *Checking Account* may be in the *Approved* state at the same time". A coordination process is always attached to one object, and can coordinate all objects related to that object.

In summary, *objects* each encapsulate data (i.e., the *attributes*) and logic (i.e., object behavior) which is based on attribute values (i.e., the *lifecycle process*). Therefore, objects are largely independent of each other, apart from the *relations* that exist between them, which are necessary for their orchestration by the *coordination processes*.

3   Solution Objectives

The artifact we present in this work is the distributed object-aware process execution engine PHILharmonicFlows. As stated in the problem definition, there are two main objectives we wish to achieve with this artifact: develop a highly scalable process management system, which uses an underlying process management concept that allows for a multitude of users to work concurrently on the same process instance (i.e., Objective 1) and is engineered in a way so that it scales out well when more hardware resources are added (i.e., Objective 2).

Objective 1 can be achieved by breaking with the traditional activity-centric process management approach, i.e., employing an approach such as artifact-centric [8], case handling [1], or object-aware process management [14]. Due to the fact that in such approaches the tasks users have to perform are not shoehorned into atomic activities, such as forms, which only one person at a time can view and edit, they are intrinsically more scalable from a user point of view as more users may execute parts of process instances concurrently [4].

Objective 2, engineering the process engine in a way such that it becomes highly scalable in regards to the hardware it runs on, requires a more precise explanation. First, it is necessary to clarify that the goal is not to create a system that scales up well, i.e. vertically with a more powerful processor, but scales out well horizontally with more computers added to a data center or computing cluster, as this is generally more desirable in cloud scenarios. In particular, we aim at achieving *ideal linear speedup*, i.e., increasing the amount of available processing power by factor p should speed up process execution by p [12].

Finally, while one can design an activity-centric process management engine in a way that allows it to scale well on the hardware side, the benefits of combining the necessary software architecture aspects with the conceptual aspects of object-aware process management are what make the artifact original.

4   Design and Development

The PHILharmonicFlows process engine has undergone many development cycles, starting with an extensive research phase concerning the conceptual foundations (cf. Sect. 2). The most important architectural iteration concerned the scalability aspects described in this paper.

4.1   Architectural Challenges

Initially, we had opted for a relational database to hold the process execution state, as it is common in many other process engines. However, during the testing phase of the development iteration, we noticed that the prototype was plagued by severe scalability issues when confronting it with large numbers of concurrent users and objects. Note that, as opposed to more traditional (i.e., activity-centric) process management technology, object-aware process management needs to react to very fine-grained user actions. Due to the nature of the lifecycle processes and the dynamically generated forms, the engine has to react to each data element input by users at run-time. In consequence, there is a much higher frequency at which small workloads have to be completed by the process engine. Note that this is the price one has to pay for the increase in flexibility compared to activity-centric systems, which use predefined forms and allow for far fewer possible execution variants.

As mentioned, a relational database is not ideally suited as the backbone for such a data-centric and data-driven system, as each of the actions a user completes on one object may have effects on multiple other objects, each represented by rows in database tables. As a consequence, a large number of rows (for various attributes, objects, and relations) have to be loaded into memory to determine the effects of a user action. In particular, if actions lead to large amounts of small changes to other objects, time is wasted on locking/unlocking rows and tables, slowing the system down considerably. Furthermore, the necessary communication between the individual objects is not predictable up front, as it depends on (1) the coordination process, (2) the structure of the data model, i.e., the relations that exist between the objects in question, and (3) the current state of each object. As these factors may change at any time during process execution, common techniques (e.g. relying on query optimization) are not ideal for our use case. In consequence, at least conceptually, object-aware process management has an unpredictable n-m-n communication pattern, a very simple depiction of which can be seen in Fig. 4. After carefully examining this unpredictable pattern we opted for a distributed approach to persisting the state of objects.

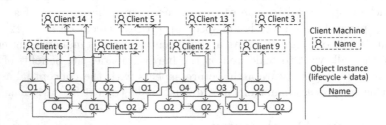

Fig. 4. Object communication pattern (simplified)

4.2   Design Methodology

After experimenting with highly distributed and lightweight document databases, such as RethinkDB and Couchbase, and not achieving satisfying performance results, we decided to not only distribute the persistence layer, but also the computation. To facilitate this, we applied *actor model theory*. The actor model is a well established theoretical foundation for concurrency in parallel systems in which the computation and persistence layer are split into largely independent primitives called *actors* [2]. Furthermore, it is supported by a number of frameworks for highly scalable applications and supports communication patterns such as the one present in object-aware process management (cf. Fig. 4).

Background on Actor Model Theory. The following gives an overview on the theory behind the *actor model*. In essence, an actor consists of a message queue and a store for arbitrary data. The actor can receive messages and handle them using the data from its store or by sending messages to other actors. An actor, however, may only complete exactly one task at a time, i.e., an actor currently servicing a request from its message queue may only work on answering that one message, whereas all others are ignored until the current message is removed from the queue. An actor system usually consists of a very large number of actors of different types, which each type having different functionality which can be completed by any instances of that type.

An example of the communication between a set of actors of different types, A, B, and C, can be seen in Fig. 5. Note that actor A receives a request from an external source, depicted by the message in its message queue. As each actor represents a small unit of functionality and data, an actor of type A might not have all the information or functionality to service the request, which necessitates communication with the other actors, e.g., B and C. However, the part of the request redirected at actor B triggers communication between Actor B and actor C. Due to the single conceptual "thread", as well as the forced message queuing, most concurrency problems concerning persistence and computation, such as race conditions and dirty read/writes, cannot occur in an actor system.

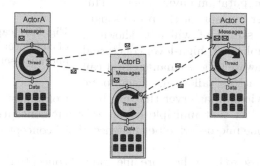

Fig. 5. Actor communication

Applying the Actor Model. While the actor model may not be fitting for systems with few, yet long-running, tasks, it is well suited to handle the challenges posed by a multitude of communicating and interacting objects present in an object-aware data model. While the actor model itself guarantees a highly scalable distributed system with few concurrency problems, the main challenge is to actually apply it to an existing concept or software system. In the context of our work, this means finding the correct mapping of the various conceptual elements of object-aware process management to individual actors. To this end, we elect to treat each object in a data model as an actor, which allows us to keep the conceptual elements contained in the object, i.e., the lifecycle process on the computation side, and the attributes on the persistence side, together as one unit. Note that this ensures that updates to individual objects, such as changes to attribute values (and the resulting updates to the lifecycle processes), can be handled independently from unrelated objects.

Note that the coordination processes (cf. Sect. 2) coordinate the various objects based on (1) their current state as well as (2) their relations to other objects. To enable (1), objects that advance to a different state after one of their attribute values is changed must inform their coordination process of the respective state change. We facilitate this by leveraging the actor message pattern described in Sect. 4.2. To enable (2), we encapsulate the relations themselves as actors. This allows the actor representing a new relation to send a message informing the coordination processes of its creation. Finally, to ensure that the coordination processes handle such messages in the same way as objects, i.e., ordered and race condition free, we redesigned them to be actors as well.

To be precise, all high-level conceptual elements present in object-aware processes, i.e., objects, relations, coordination processes, and the data model, are represented as actors in the PHILharmonicFlows engine. As the actor model allows for independent execution of logic, using only well-regulated message exchanges at certain points, actors can be hosted as individual *microservices* in computation environments. This results in a five layer concept for the process management engine, a sketch of which is shown in Fig. 6. As Fig. 6 implies, all high-level conceptual elements of object-aware process management can be interpreted as actors, allowing them to be hosted in microservices on a server that can be part of a cluster. Clearly, Fig. 6

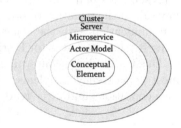

Fig. 6. Encapsulation diagram of conceptual elements, actors, and microservices

abstracts from the fact that multiple instances of any conceptual element may exist, resulting in one microservice per instance of the conceptual element existing at run-time.

Note that we chose to keep the more fine-grained conceptual elements, such as attributes, permissions, roles, and lifecycle states and steps as state information inside the actors representing the objects. Taking the checking of an attribute

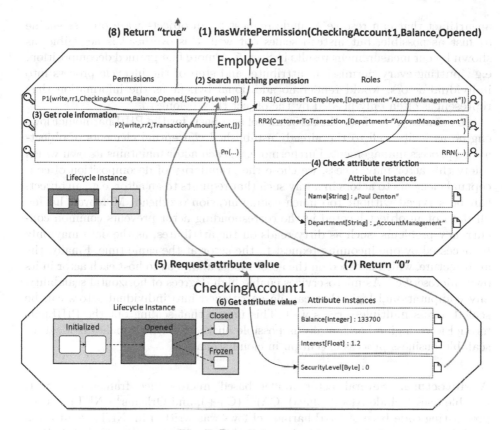

Fig. 7. Permission request

permission as an example, as shown in Fig. 7, it becomes evident why having the permissions and attributes as independent actors would make little sense.

In the example, two objects, *Employee1* and *CheckingAccount1*, each represented by an actor at run-time, are shown. Note that only markings **(1)**, **(5)**, **(7)**, and **(8)** constitute messages being passed between actors, all other markings are just operations that are completed using data local to the respective actor, the details of which are not relevant at this point, but can be found in previous work [3]. After the initial request **(1)** arrives in the message queue of *Employee1,* it has to complete a number of operations. Furthermore, this specific request causes the *Employee1* actor to communicate **(5)** with the *CheckingAccount1* actor. In particular, granting the permission depends on the value of the *SecurityLevel* attribute, which is only present in the actor for *CheckingAccount1*. Finally, after actor *CheckingAccount1* returns the value of the attribute **(7)**, actor *Employee1* can return the result of the request **(8)**.

Obviously, as the two actors for *Employee1* and *CheckingAccount1* may be located on different servers in the computing cluster, a request like this can introduce some communication overhead. However, as our goal is not to create an artifact that can resolve a single request to an object-aware process engine as fast as possible, but instead scales out well, this overhead is negligible, as shown by our measurement results in Sect. 5. A more fine-grained decomposition, e.g., putting every permission, attribute, and step of the lifecycle process into individual actors, would render no additional benefit as the information they represent is often only needed by the object they belong to.

In summary, we chose the actor model as a basis for the PHILharmonicFlows engine as it fits well to the already established conceptual elements of object-aware process management. Furthermore, as each actor maintains its own which solely this actor may access, we chose the granularity of decomposition of conceptual elements to actors in a way such that requests to an actor, e.g., an object, can be serviced without too much communication overhead. Moreover, having all data of an object located in the corresponding actor prevents common concurrency problems, such as dirty reads on the attributes, as the data may only be accessed by one incoming request to the actor at the same time. Finally, the architecture, which is based on the actor model allows us to host each actor in its own microservice. As microservices enable high degrees of horizontal scalability, any computational logic that can be partitioned into individual actors can be scaled across multiple servers well. This means that scaling out the PHILharmonicFlows engine horizontally is possible on the fly, which makes it ideal for scalable business process execution in cloud scenarios.

Architecture. Several actor model based microservice frameworks exist, notable ones include Akka[1] (Java), CAF[2] (C++), and Orleans[3] (.NET). As the preexisting code base of PHILharmonicFlows was written in .NET, we utilize a modified version of Orleans, which is part of the open source Service Fabric Reliable Actors SDK[4], for our prototype. Service Fabric allows us to run actor-based applications on development machines, on-premise research computing clusters, and in the cloud. This is enabled by a transparent placement of instantiated actors across all available servers. A diagram of the entire architecture of our engine is shown in Fig. 8. The "Actor Services" and "Framework Services" are hosted across all servers in the cluster, ensuring that they are all fully capable of instantiating actor microservices, such as those shown above "Instantiated Microservices". All depicted elements are implemented and working to the specifications of object-aware process management. Finally, note that the engine is still only considered a prototype for our artifact, as we have not yet conducted technical action research with real-world clients.

---

[1] https://github.com/akka.
[2] https://github.com/actor-framework.
[3] https://github.com/dotnet/orleans.
[4] https://github.com/Azure/service-fabric-services-and-actors-dotnet.

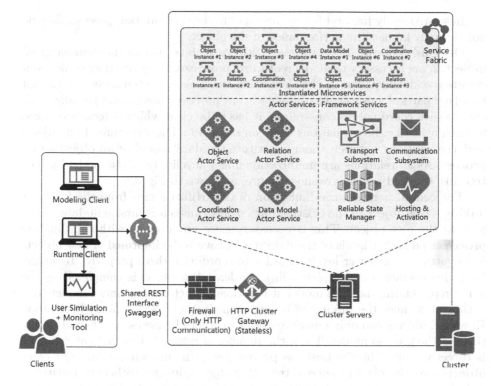

Fig. 8. Architecture overview

5 Evaluation and Demonstration

As other aspects of the PHILharmonicFlows process management system are still under development, both conceptually and from an implementation perspective, we have not completed technical action research to verify the solution objectives. Instead, we are currently conducing single-case mechanism experiments to evaluate the capabilities of the developed architecture, the results of which we present in this section. Before, however, we discuss conceptual performance limitations of object-aware processes as well as the measurement methodology.

5.1 Conceptual Performance Limitations

As each object in an object-aware data model can be interacted with individually, there are hardly any bottlenecks to be expected for the execution of the object lifecycle processes. However, there is the issue of coordinating the execution of inter-related objects that needs particular consideration. In general, coordination processes are informed by the objects when their states change due to the completion of steps in their lifecycle processes. How often this happens depends on the lifecycle process model of the object in question. In particular, as these are merely fire-and-forget messages to the coordination process, they do not actually impact the performance of the object.

Obviously, coordination processes with constraints, such as the example given in Sect. 2, are necessary to model real-world processes. However, they do not constitute a scalability issue in the computing sense, as it is often necessary to wait for other parts of a process to complete in any process management paradigm. To enable such coordination constraints, it has to be clear which objects are linked to each other, i.e. have relations between them [19]. The structure of all objects and the relations between them constitute the data model of an object-aware process. As all relations are unidirectional and acyclic, the data model forms a tree-like directed acyclic graph structure, as shown in Fig. 3.

The central performance limitation of the artifact stems from the fact that linking a new object to the existing data model causes a recursive update all the way to the root object. This is necessary since any objects with coordination processes on higher levels of the data model have to be informed of new objects being attached on lower levels in order to coordinate them properly. To ensure that this operation is completed in an ordered fashion, it is completed by the actor representing the data model at run-time. As actors may only complete one action at a time, the linking of objects constitutes a performance bottleneck. However, objects can only create relations to other objects as specified at design time in the process model. Thus, the number of relations creatable at run-time is directly limited by the business process itself. In summary, as in most cases objects are only related to one or two other objects directly (others transitively), only few relation creation operations are conducted for each object at run-time.

5.2   Experiment Scenario and Tooling

As our engine is an actor system running on Service Fabric (cf. Sect. 4.2), it can be deployed to a cluster with an arbitrary number of servers. For our single-case mechanism experiments, we employ an on-premise cluster with eight servers and a total of 64 logical processors (32 cores @ 2.4 GHz + hyper-threading). The data model used for the experiments is the Banking scenario presented in Sect. 2, an example of a typical object-aware process model.

Obviously, an object must be instantiated in a microservice before it can be linked to other objects or be manipulated through attribute value changes. However, the order in which the attributes of an object are set, or whether they are set before or after linking the object to others, has no influence on outcome after all actions are completed. This is due to the fact that object-aware execution is data-driven, which allows us to design the experiment as follows: (1) we instantiate all objects required for the scenario a predefined number of times, (2) we link the objects together using a predefined schema, and, finally, (3) we supply predefined attribute values to each object we instantiated, thereby executing their lifecycle processes. Our tooling simulates user interaction directly through the run-time client via REST, using the architecture shown in Fig. 8.

We can measure times for all three action types, i.e., instantiation (1), linking (2), and execution (3), as well as the total time for a run. This allows us to discuss the three distinct actions and to observe the impact of changing various parameters on the time they take in relation to the total time.

5.3   Statistical Measurement Methodology

The measurements follow the *guidelines for measuring the performance of parallel computing systems*, as defined in [12]. As a parallel computing system can render vastly different numbers for the same experiment scenario when run multiple times, it is hard to measure exact execution times.

Instead of simply measuring the mean or median execution times over a predefined arbitrary number of runs, we use the statistically exact method presented in [12] to determine the number of runs necessary to ensure high confidence in an adequately small confidence interval. As we are dealing with non-normally distributed data, the number of runs has to be determined dynamically i.e., there is no analytical method for predetermining it. As it can take several hundred minute long runs to get a narrow confidence interval, this exact calculation becomes necessary to not waste hours trying to find an adequate number of runs.

To this end, we run Algorithm 1 after every individual experiment run to ensure that after n runs the confidence interval is tight enough and the confidence in the interval is high enough. The inputs are the already completed experiment runs ($runs$), the maximum width of the confidence interval as a percentage of the confidence interval average ($\%_{CI}$), and the minimum confidence in the confidence interval $(1 - \alpha)_{min}$. The algorithm returns interval $[time_{lRank}, time_{uRank}]$, i.e., the total time of the runs at the lower and upper bounds of the confidence interval, as well as $(1 - \alpha)$, i.e., the exact confidence level of the returned interval. Note that Algorithm 1 uses the statistical method described in [15], Annex A, to determine which of the already measured runs constitute the bounds of the confidence interval with the required confidence $(1 - \alpha)_{min}$.

Algorithm 1. checkCIWidth

Require: $runs[], \%_{CI}, (1 - \alpha)_{min}$
Ensure: $n_{runs} \geq 6$ ▷ no confidence interval possible for $n \leq 5$
  $q \leftarrow 0.5$ ▷ quantile 0.5 = median
  $confidenceLevels[] \leftarrow [(lRank, uRank, (1 - \alpha)]$
  for $j = 1$ to n **do**
    for $k = 1$ to n **do**
      $confidenceLevels \leftarrow BinomialCDF(q, n, k - 1) - BinomialCDF(q, n, j - 1)$
    end for
  end for
  for all $(lRank, uRank, 1 - \alpha)$ in $confidenceLevels$ **do**
    $time_{lRank} \leftarrow runs[lRank].time$
    $time_{uRank} \leftarrow runs[uRank].time$
    $time_{mean} \leftarrow (time_{lRank} + time_{uRank})/2$
    $CIwidth_{max} \leftarrow time_{mean} \times \%_{CI}$
    if $time_{uRank} - time_{lRank} \leq CIwidth_{max}$ and $1 - \alpha \geq (1 - \alpha)_{min}$ **then**
      return $(time_{lRank}, time_{uRank}, 1 - \alpha)$
    end if
  end for

5.4   Results

We evaluated how well the artifact achieves the solution objectives (cf. Sect. 3) based on the measurement results from the single-case mechanism experiments presented in this section. The objective of the experiments was (1) to determine the limits of how many concurrent objects can be processes on the given eight server hardware setup, (2) find bottlenecks by simulating mass user interactions and (3) measure the impact of object lifecycle complexity on execution times.

To this end, we conducted the following series of single-case mechanism experiments with an example process model and simulated user input to the current PHILharmonicFlows engine prototype. While this is not technical action research in the real world, as explained in Sect. 5.2, the engine is interacted with exactly as if thousands of real users were executing the individual objects concurrently. We utilize these results to demonstrate the viability of a highly scalable actor model based microservice architecture for data-centric process management systems in general.

Each results table row represents an experiment series with a specific configuration and the following in- and outputs:

	Header	Description
Input	n_D	Number of data models created
	O	Object function, type and number of objects created per data model
	R	Relation function, A:B:100 indicates 100 relations between objects A and B
Output	n_O	Number of created objects across all data models
	n_R	Number of created relations across all data models
	$CI\,t_{inst}$	Confidence interval for total instantiation time
	$CI\,t_{link}$	Confidence interval for total linking time
	$CI\,t_{exec}$	Confidence interval for total lifecycle execution time
	$CI\,t_{total}$	Confidence interval for total run time of experiment
	$1 - \alpha$	Exact confidence in the $CI\,t_{total}$ confidence interval
	n	Number of runs completed to achieve $1 - \alpha$ confidence in $CI\,t_{total}$

All confidence intervals in all result tables are required to have a maximum width of 5% in respect to the median measured time, i.e., $\%_{CI} = 0.05$. Further, the confidence in each interval must be at least 95%, i.e., $1 - \alpha_{min} \geq 0.95$. As this means that a measurement with a suspected median time of 1000ms is required to have a confidence interval of $[975\,\text{ms}, 1025\,\text{ms}]$[5], and the confidence that the real median time lies in this interval must be at least 95%. Finally,

---

[5] 50 ms width, 5% of 1000 ms.

all time measurements are specified in the mm:ss.ms format. Table 1 shows the measurement results for a scenario in which we instantiate, link, and execute varying numbers of *Checking Accounts* (CA) and *Transfers* (TR).

Table 1. Simple data model: Checking Accounts (CA) and Transfers (TR)

n_D	O	R	n_O	n_R	$CI\,t_{inst}$	$CI\,t_{link}$	$CI\,t_{exec}$	$CI\,t_{total}$	$1-\alpha$	n
1	CA:100, TR:1000	TR:CA:1000	1100	1000	[00:00.960, 00:01.003]	[00:03.002, 00:03.190]	[00:00.422, 00:00.603]	[00:04.499, 00:04.969]	96.49	32
1	CA:500, TR:5000	TR:CA:5000	5500	5000	[00:04.452, 00:04.540]	[00:14.037, 00:14.984]	[00:01.898, 00:03.622]	[00:21.075, 00:23.272]	95.67	24
1	CA:1000, TR:10000	TR:CA:10000	11000	10000	[00:08.657, 00:08.993]	[00:29.127, 00:33.835]	[00:04.499, 00:06.333]	[00:42.898, 00:46.550]	96.14	11
2	CA:500, TR:5000	TR:CA:5000	11000	10000	[00:04.723, 00:04.979]	[00:16.713, 00:18.122]	[00:02.810, 00:04.482]	[00:24.648, 00:27.076]	95.67	25
4	CA:250, TR:2500	TR:CA:2500	11000	10000	[00:02.943, 00:03.307]	[00:11.161, 00:12.908]	[00:02.707, 00:04.004]	[00:17.742, 00:19.554]	95.86	20
8	CA:125, TR:1250	TR:CA:1250	11000	10000	[00:04.130, 00:04.516]	[00:10.109, 00:10.670]	[00:03.239, 00:05.202]	[00:18.493, 00:20.439]	95.3	37

A few things are noteworthy here. First, regarding the first four series, in which all objects and relations were part of a single data model, one can observe almost *ideal linear scaling* of the various median times with the respective workloads, as evidenced by Fig. 9. This demonstrates the capability of the microservices on the cluster to handle increasing concurrent workloads extremely well. Any below linear curve would indicate the system becoming congested.

Second, note the *super-linear scaling* of $CI\,t_{link}$ in the four series with 10.000 relations spread over an increasing number of data models (cf. Fig. 10). This indicates a conceptual bottleneck due to the fact that the linking operations must be ordered to ensure correct recursive updating of the entire data model, as explained in Sect. 5.1. To this end, each linking operation is queued and executed by the actor representing the data model in question, reducing concurrency.

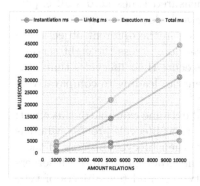

Fig. 9. Single data model

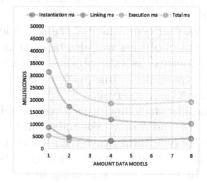

Fig. 10. Multiple data models

Table 2. Complex data model: Employees (EM), Customers (CU), Checking Accounts (CA), and Transfers (TR)

n_D	O	R	n_O	n_R	$CI\,t_{inst}$	$CI\,t_{link}$	$CI\,t_{exec}$	$CI\,t_{total}$	$1-\alpha$	n
1	EM:1, CU:10, CA:100, TR:1000	CU:EM:10, CA:CU:100, TR:CA:1000,	1111	1110	[00:00.926, 00:00.993]	[00:05.424, 00:06.160]	[00:00.418, 00:00.482]	[00:06.892, 00:07.573]	96.48	14
1	EM:5, CU:50, CA:500, TR:5000	CU:EM:50, CA:CU:500, TR:CA:5000,	5555	5550	[00:04.518, 00:04.754]	[00:27.701, 00:30.809]	[00:03.800, 00:05.538]	[00:37.184, 00:40.179]	96.09	9
1	EM:10, CU:100, CA:1000, TR:10000	CU:EM:100, CA:CU:1000, TR:CA:10000,	11110	11100	[00:09.110, 00:09.380]	[00:57.553, 01:02.829]	[00:06.504, 00:08.429]	[01:12.990, 01:19.123]	96.14	12

Table 2 shows the experiment results when creating a significantly more complex data model, with all objects and relations shown in Fig. 3. The objects involved are *Checking Account* (CA), *Employee* (EM), *Transfer* (TR), and *Customer* (CU). However, we adjusted the total amount of objects created to be almost identical to the experiment series shown in the first three rows of Table 1. Note the large increase in the $CI\,t_{total}$ interval when comparing Table 2 with Table 1. However, the increase clearly stems from the higher effort when linking new objects into the more complex data model, as evidenced by the higher $CI\,t_{link}$ values, as the average $CI\,t_{inst}$ and $CI\,t_{exec}$ values are similar.

Second, consider the wide $CI\,t_{exec}$ intervals in comparison to the very tight $CI\,t_{inst}$ intervals (only the $CI\,t_{total}$ interval width is fixed at 5%). This can be explained with the fact that, while both instantiation and execution are tied to the complexity of the respective lifecycle process, instantiation is done by the actor service, while execution is done by the thousands of object actors created during instantiation and spread across the cluster. As we only have four actor services active during the experiment series shown in Table 2, the actor framework will distribute them to four distinct servers for each experiment run. As every server is equal, this leads to almost identical measured times across all experiments. However, as the underlying actor framework does not have knowledge of the varying complexity of the lifecycles processes in the different objects, the thousands of objects will also be distributed at random across the eight servers. In consequence, as some objects take longer to execute their lifecycles than others, servers might be unequally tasked in this scenario, leading to comparatively wide confidence intervals.

Consider the following as a very simplified and extreme example of this effect: objects of type A may take one second to execute their lifecycle process, whereas objects of type B may take ten seconds to execute their lifecycle process. If there are two servers and ten objects of each type, in one experiment run both servers might be tasked with executing five objects of type A and five objects of type B, which would take 55 s in total. Another run might see all objects of type A executed by one server, taking ten seconds, and all objects of type B executed by the other server, taking 100 s.

To further examine these differences in execution times, we instantiated and executed each object type used in Table 2 10.000 times. The results of this experiment can be seen in Table 3. As there are no relations in this experiment, we instead included the number of attributes, steps, and states the objects possess, as they give an indication as to how complex their lifecycle processes are. The results show the clear correlations between lifecycle complexity and instantiation/execution time.

Table 3. Comparison of object performance: Employees (EM), Customers (CU), Checking Accounts (CA), and Transfers (TR)

n_D	O	Attributes	Steps	States	$CI\,t_{inst}$	$CI\,t_{exec}$	$CI\,t_{total}$	$1-\alpha$	n
1	CA:10000	1	3	3	[00:06.537, 00:06.757]	[00:04.076, 00:04.753]	[00:10.731, 00:11.529]	95.1	16
1	EM:10000	2	4	3	[00:08.158, 00:08.726]	[00:04.415, 00:05.857]	[00:12.804, 00:14.118]	96.87	6
1	TR:10000	4	6	4	[00:08.350, 00:08.723]	[00:06.095, 00:07.521]	[00:14.499, 00:15.929]	95.72	30
1	CU:10000	8	11	4	[00:11.974, 00:12.358]	[00:11.222, 00:13.784]	[00:23.576, 00:25.979]	95.64	41

6 Related Work

There is a large amount of literature concerning the scalability of software systems, little of which is concerned with process management systems. While the works mentioned in the introduction, WIDE [7], OSIRIS [17], ADEPTdistribution [5], and Gridflow [6] are fairly dated and do not take modern architectures into consideration, there is some newer research that does.

[9] and [11] present architectures for distributing business process workloads between a client-side engine and a cloud-based engine, taking into consideration that users might not want to store their business data in the cloud. Thus, the approaches suggest to primarily run compute-intensive workloads on the cloud-based engine and transfer business data only when necessary. [9] further presents a method for decomposing the process model into two complementary process models, one for the client engine, and one for the cloud engine.

[10] introduces a resource controller for cloud environments that monitors process execution and can predict how compute intensive future workloads will be depending on previous executions. This data is used for auto-scaling the virtual machines the process engine and external systems are running on.

[18] gives an in-depth overview of the state of the art concerning cloud business process architecture, revealing that most current approaches use virtual machine scaling, simply replicating process engines to achieve scalability.

7 Summary

In this work, we demonstrated the viability of creating a *hyperscale process management system* using a data-centric approach to process management on the conceptual side as well as actor model theory and microservices on the architecture side. Thus, we maximize the possible concurrent actions conducted by process participants at any given time during process execution, without simply relying on virtual machine scaling as most of the related work does. Our measurements show that the PHILharmonicFlows engine scales linearly with the number of objects created and executed (i.e., user-generated workload) in a single process instance. Furthermore, the measurements give insights into what the engine is capable of, with even this first prototype with no "professional" optimization executing the lifecycle processes of 11.000 objects in around five seconds. This is even more impressive considering the fact that these are full executions of the respective lifecycle processes. As the example objects have an average of 4–5 attributes and steps this equates to around 50.000 user interactions the engine is handling in the aforementioned five second time frame.

While the data from our single-case mechanism experiments shows that data-centric process engines have the potential to scale extremely well and to handle many users working on a single process instance at the same time, we identified a conceptual bottleneck in the linking of newly created objects to the existing data model. As this has to be handled centrally by the data model, it cannot be done concurrently. However, in a more real-world scenario with more running data models and less objects per data model, this is not much of an issue. This is especially true when considering that in general the ratio of object instantiations and linking to actual execution actions, such as form inputs by users, will be low.

In future work, we will work on optimizing the engine further and subjecting it to more real-world usage when conducing technical action research. Another important task is comparing the performance of PHILharmonicFlows to activity-centric process management systems, although finding a process scenario in which the two very different paradigms are scientifically comparable from a performance perspective will not be easy. Finally, as one of our stated goals is to increase the maturity and acceptance of data-centric process management, we are actively developing advanced capabilities, such as ad-hoc changes and variant support, on top of the presented artifact.

Acknowledgments. This work is part of the ZAFH Intralogistik, funded by the European Regional Development Fund and the Ministry of Science, Research and the Arts of Baden-Württemberg, Germany (F.No. 32-7545.24-17/3/1).

References

1. Van der Aalst, W.M.P., Weske, M., Grünbauer, D.: Case handling: a new paradigm for business process support. Data Knowl. Eng. **53**(2), 129–162 (2005)
2. Agha, G., Hewitt, C.: Concurrent programming using actors. In: Readings in Distributed Artificial Intelligence, pp. 398–407. Elsevier (1988)

3. Andrews, K., Steinau, S., Reichert, M.: Enabling fine-grained access control in object-aware process management systems. In: EDOC, pp. 143–152. IEEE (2017)
4. Andrews, K., Steinau, S., Reichert, M.: Towards hyperscale process management. In: Proceedings of EMISA, pp. 148–152 (2017)
5. Bauer, T., Reichert, M., Dadam, P.: Intra-subnet load balancing in distributed workflow management systems. Int. J. Coop. Inf. Syst. **12**(03), 295–323 (2003)
6. Cao, J., Jarvis, S.A., Saini, S., Nudd, G.R.: Gridflow: Workflow management for grid computing. In: International Symposium on Cluster Computing and the Grid, pp. 198–205 (2003)
7. Ceri, S., Grefen, P., Sanchez, G.: WIDE - a distributed architecture for workflow management. In: RIDE-WS, pp. 76–79. IEEE (1997)
8. Cohn, D., Hull, R.: Business artifacts: a data-centric approach to modeling business operations and processes. Bull. IEEE TCDE **32**(3), 3–9 (2009)
9. Duipmans, E.F., Pires, L.F., da Silva Santos, L.O.B.: Towards a BPM cloud architecture with data and activity distribution. In: 2012 IEEE 16th International Enterprise Distributed Object Computing Conference Workshops (EDOCW), pp. 165–171. IEEE (2012)
10. Euting, S., Janiesch, C., Fischer, R., Tai, S., Weber, I.: Scalable business process execution in the cloud. In: 2014 IEEE International Conference on Cloud Engineering (IC2E), pp. 175–184. IEEE (2014)
11. Han, Y.B., Sun, J.Y., Wang, G.L., Li, H.F.: A cloud-based BPM architecture with user-end distribution of non-compute-intensive activities and sensitive data. J. Comput. Sci. Technol. **25**(6), 1157–1167 (2010)
12. Hoefler, T., Belli, R.: Scientific benchmarking of parallel computing systems. In: IEEE SC 2015, p. 73. ACM (2015)
13. Künzle, V., Reichert, M.: PHILharmonicFlows: towards a framework for object-aware process management. JSME **23**(4), 205–244 (2011)
14. Künzle, V., Reichert, M.: Striving for object-aware process support: how existing approaches fit together. In: Aberer, K., Damiani, E., Dillon, T. (eds.) SIMPDA 2011. LNBIP, vol. 116, pp. 169–188. Springer, Heidelberg (2012). https://doi.org/10.1007/978-3-642-34044-4_10
15. Le Boudec, J.Y.: Performance Evaluation of Computer Systems. Epfl Press, Lausanne (2010)
16. Leymann, F., Roller, D.: Production Workflow: Concepts and Techniques. Prentice Hall PTR, Upper Saddle River (2000)
17. Schuler, C., Weber, R., Schuldt, H., Schek, H.J.: Scalable peer-to-peer process management - the OSIRIS approach. In: IEEE ICWS, pp. 26–34 (2004)
18. Schulte, S., Janiesch, C., Venugopal, S., Weber, I., Hoenisch, P.: Elastic business process management. FGCS **46**, 36–50 (2015)
19. Steinau, S., Andrews, K., Reichert, M.: The relational process structure. In: Krogstie, J., Reijers, H.A. (eds.) CAiSE 2018. LNCS, vol. 10816, pp. 53–67. Springer, Cham (2018). https://doi.org/10.1007/978-3-319-91563-0_4
20. Steinau, S., Künzle, V., Andrews, K., Reichert, M.: Coordinating business processes using semantic relationships. In: Proceedings of CBI, pp. 143–152 (2017)

Applying Sequence Mining for Outlier Detection in Process Mining

Mohammadreza Fani Sani[1]([✉]), Sebastiaan J. van Zelst[2],
and Wil M. P. van der Aalst[1,2]

[1] Process and Data Science Chair, RWTH Aachen University,
52056 Aachen, Germany
{fanisani,wvdaalst}@pads.rwth-aachen.de
[2] Fraunhofer FIT, Birlinghoven Castle, Sankt Augustin, Germany
s.j.v.zelst@pads.rwth-aachen.de

Abstract. One of the challenges in applying process mining algorithms on real event data, is the presence of outlier behavior. Such behaviour often leads to complex, incomprehensible, and, sometimes, even inaccurate process mining results. As a result, correct and/or important behaviour of the process may be concealed. In this paper, we exploit sequence mining techniques for the purpose of outlier detection in the process mining domain. Using the proposed approach, it is even possible to detect outliers in case of heavy parallelism and/or long-term dependencies between business process activities. Our method has been implemented in both the ProM- and the RapidProM framework. Using these implementations, we conducted a collection of experiments that show that we are able to detect and remove outlier behaviour in event data. Our evaluation clearly demonstrates that the proposed method accurately removes outlier behaviour and, indeed, improves process discovery results.

Keywords: Process mining · Sequence mining · Event log filtering
Event log preprocessing · Sequential rule mining · Outlier detection

1 Introduction

The main aim of process mining is to increase the overall knowledge of business processes. This is mainly achieved by (1) process discovery, i.e. discovering a descriptive model of the underlying process, (2) conformance checking, i.e. checking whether the execution of the process conforms to a reference model and (3) enhancement, i.e. the overall improvement of the view of the process, typically by enhancing a process model [1]. In each of these aspects, event data, stored during the execution of the process, is explicitly used to derive the corresponding results.

Many process mining algorithms assume that event data is stored correctly and completely describes the behavior of a process. However, real event data typically contains noisy and infrequent behaviour [2]. Usually, noise occurs rarely

© Springer Nature Switzerland AG 2018
H. Panetto et al. (Eds.): OTM 2018 Conferences, LNCS 11230, pp. 98–116, 2018.
https://doi.org/10.1007/978-3-030-02671-4_6

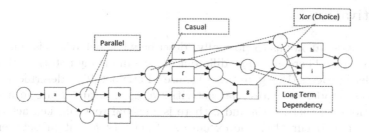

Fig. 1. An example of a process model with *Xor, parallel, long distance dependency* and *casual* behaviour.

in an event data, so, many researchers consider it as infrequent behaviour. Generally, noise relates to behaviour that does not conform to the process specification or its correct execution. However, infrequent behaviour refers to behaviour that is possible according to the process model, but, in exceptional cases of the process. Without having business knowledge, distinguishing between noise and infrequent behaviour is a challenging task. We, therefore, consider this as a separate research question and do not cover this in this paper. Here, we consider both noise and infrequent behaviour as **outliers**.

The presence of outlier behaviour makes many process mining algorithms, in particular, process discovery algorithms, result in complex, incomprehensible and even inaccurate results. Therefore, to reduce these negative effects, in process mining projects, often a preprocessing step is applied that aims to remove outlier behaviour and keep good behaviour. Such *preprocessing phase* increases the quality and comprehensiveness of possible future analyses. Usually, this step is done manually, which needs domain knowledge and it is costly and time-consuming.

In this paper, we focus on improving process discovery results by applying automated event data filtering, i.e., filtering the event log prior to apply any process discovery algorithm, without significant human interaction. Using sequential rules and patterns [3,4], the proposed filtering method is able to detect outlier behaviour even in event data with lot of concurrency, and long-term dependency behaviour. The presence of this type of patterns is shown to be hampering the applicability of automated existing general purpose filtering techniques [5,6]. By using the ProM [7] based extension of RapidMiner, i.e. RapidProM [8], we study the effectiveness of our approach, using synthetic and real event data. We show that our proposed filtering method more accurately detects outlier behaviour compared to existing event log filtering techniques in particular for event data with heavy parallel and long term dependences. Consequently, it increases more the overall quality of process discovery results.

The remainder of this paper is structured as follows. Section 2 motivates the need for applying filtering methods on event logs. In Sect. 3, we discuss related work, then after explaining some preliminaries in Sect. 4, in Sect. 5, we describe our proposed method. Details of the evaluation and corresponding results are given in Sect. 6. Finally, Sect. 7 concludes the paper and presents directions for future work in this domain.

2   Motivation

A process model allows us to (formally) describe what behaviour is (im)possible within a process. There are many different process modeling notations that allow us to model a process [1], e.g. in Fig. 1 we use a Petri net [9] to describe a process. This process model indicates that activities b, c, d, e, and f are in a parallel relation. However, between b and c there is a casual relation, i.e., activity c is only allowed to occur after the execution of activity b, but in between them other activities like d and e are allowed to be executed. Between e and f and also among h and i there are Xor (or exclusive choice) relations. Finally, the process model indicates that there are long term dependency relations between activities e and h and also between f and i. This means that, if in the middle of the process e happens, only activity h ends it.

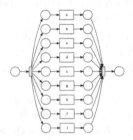

(a) Results of the Inductive Miner [10] on the raw event data.

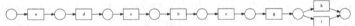

(b) Result of the Alpha Miner [11] on the event log that filtered beforehand with *AFA* [6].

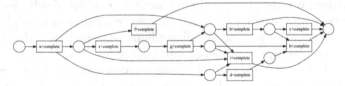

(c) Result of the Alpha Miner on the filtered event log using matrix filter [5] method (*SF*).

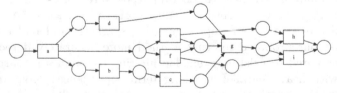

(d) Result of the Alpha Miner on the filtered event log using our proposed filtering method.

Fig. 2. Process models discovered on the noisy event log corresponding to Fig. 1.

Process discovery algorithms aim to discover process models, i.e. models such as Fig. 1, on the basis of event data. The interpretability of such process model largely depends on the (graph-theoretical) complexity of such a model. However, often process discovery algorithms because of the presence of outlier behaviour in the event data, return complicated and not understandable results on real data. To illustrate the problem we use two examples with synthetic and real event data. In the first example, we generate an event log based on the process model of Fig. 1. Thereafter, different types of noisy behaviour like removing or adding activities are added to these process instances.

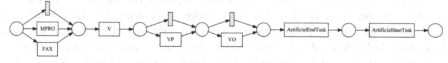

(a) Results of the Inductive Miner [10] on the whole event log.

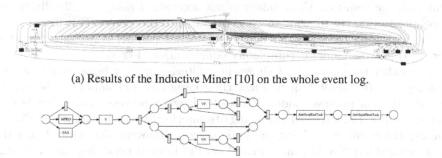

(b) Result of the Inductive Miner [12] on the event log that filtered beforehand with Matrix Filter [5]. The precision of this model is 0.88 and its fitness is 0.92.

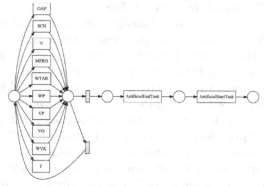

(c) Result of the Inductive Miner [12] on the event log that filtered beforehand with *AFA* [6]. The precision of this model is 0.96 and its fitness is 0.92.

(d) Result of the Inductive Miner [12] on the filtered event log using our proposed filtering method (*SF*).The precision of this model is 1.0 and its fitness is 0.92.

Fig. 3. Discovering process models by the Inductive Miner on the *ICP.anon* event log.

The process model that is discovered by the Inductive Miner [10] and its embedded noise filtering mechanism for this event log, is shown in Fig. 2a. This process model lets all activities happen all in parallel and it means the embedded noisy filtering algorithm in the Inductive Miner is not able to detect and remove all types of added outlier behaviour. We also try to first filter out outlier behaviour and after that apply the Alpha Miner [11] that is a noise sensitive process discovery algorithm on the cleaned event log. Figure 2b shows Anomaly Free Automaton*AFA* filtering method [6] removes many of correct behavoiur during filtering process. Also using *Matrix Filter* [5] that is a probabilistic filtering method in Fig. 2c because it does not detect and remove some outlier behaviour, the result of Alpha miner is not accurate. Finally, Fig. 2d illustrates the result of using the filtering method proposed in this paper. This filter is able to cope with long term dependency, casual - and parallel behaviour, then the discovered process model is completely equivalents to Fig. 1.

As another example, Fig. 3 shows how filtering outlier behaviour in a real event log, i.e. *ICP.anon* [13], reduces the complexity and improves the understandability of a process model. Figure 3a shows a process model that is discovered by the Inductive Miner using its filtering method. Moreover, Fig. 3d indicates the result of applying the same process discovery algorithm (but without its embedded filtering mechanism) on the filtered event log that contains 65% of the process instances of the original event log using our proposed filtering method. Note that, in the process model and also in the event data activity "*ArtificialEndTask*" comes before "*ArtificialStartTask*".

For the real event data, because usually there is not any reference process model, we use quality measures of the discovered process model. *Fitness* and *precision* are measures that are widely used to assess quality of process models [14]. Fitness computes how much behaviour in the event log is also described by the process model. The fitness value equals to 1 indicates that all behaviour in the event data is replayable with the process model. However, precision measures the amount of behaviour described by the process model that is also presented in the event log. The precision value equals to 1 shows that all behaviour in the event log is also presented in the event data. The fitness values of Fig. 3a and d are 1.0 and 0.92 whereas their precision values are 0.64 and 1.0 respectively. This means that the process model in Fig. 3a describes more behaviour that is also presented in the event log, however, in order to do this it is underfitting. Hence, it allows for much more behaviour compared to the model in Fig. 3a. As a consequence, the model in Fig. 3a is more inaccurate. In other words, by sacrificing a little in fitness we reach a more precise model that represent the main stream bahaviour of the event data. Note that, most of the activities in Fig. 3a are rarely present in the event data. Note, Fig. 3c and b also increase the precision by little sacrificing in fitness. However, some casual relations like *VO* eventually happens after *VP* are not detectable with these filtering methods, because they just consider the direct flow relation of activities.

3   Related Work

Early work in process discovery focused solely on the discovery of process models, however, more recently process discovery algorithms have been extended to be able to handle outliers as well [10,15]. However, the extended filtering methods are tailored towards the internal procedures of the corresponding algorithm and hence do not return a filtered event log. This hampers the applicability of these internal filtering techniques as general purpose event log filtering techniques. Some methods like [16,17] are specifically designed to cope with outlier behaviour. However, they do not result in process models with clear execution semantics and again suffer from the previous problem. Many of the commercial process mining tools use simple frequency based filtering methods that is not applicable for some real event data, and moreover, they are again tailored towards their process modeling notation.

Outlier detection for temporal and sequential data is also addressed in the data mining field. For example, [18] surveys on different methods of detecting outliers on discrete sequential data and [19] presents a similar study for temporal data. Also, there are some related techniques that are specifically proposed for the process mining domain. In [20,21], the authors propose filtering techniques that use additional information such as training event data or a reference process model. But, providing a set of training traces that cover all possible outliers or having a reference process model is impractical. In [6], by constructing an Anomaly Free Automaton (AFA) based on the whole event log and a given threshold, all non-fitting behaviour, w.r.t. the AFA, is removed from the event log. In [5], we propose a filtering method that detects outliers based on conditional probabilities of subsequences and their possible following activities. Also, [22] proposes an on-line adjustable probabilistic filtering method that detects outlier behaviour for streaming events. The AFA method is similar to a specific case of probabilistic method that the given subsequence has length 1. [23] presents an entropy-based method to filter chaotic activities i.e., activities that occur spontaneously at any point in the process. Finally, [24] presents a method that detects outliers based on frequent contexts, and subsequently repairs this behaviour instead of removing traces with outlier. In this method sometimes activities that do not happen in reality are added to the event log.

One key difference of process event logs with other general sequential data is the existence of parallel and long term behaviour between activities. All the mentioned previous filtering algorithms just consider the directly follow dependency of activities. However, considering just directly follow relations of activities is not enough to detect outlier behaviour in processes with *parallel, casual* and *long term dependency* relations.

For example, the *AFA* method [6] is not able to detect all outliers in such event logs. Moreover, if the subsequence length that is used in conditional probability based methods [5,22] is not enough, they are also not able to detect *parallel* and *long term dependency* relations. For example, if the length of the condition part is 2, $\langle a, f, b, d, f, g, h \rangle$ is accepted as normal behaviour in the event log that corresponds to the process model in Fig. 1. But, it is impossible to execute f two times or not executing c. Also, if f will execute, activity i have to happen at the end of the process. As another example, $\langle a, d, e, c, g, h \rangle$ also is accepted as a normal behaviour. However, according to Fig. 1, it is not possible to execute c without execution of b beforehand.

4   Preliminaries

This section briefly introduces the basic process mining terminology and notations like event log and multiset, and also discusses concepts such as sequential patterns and sequential rules. Given a set X, a multiset M over X is a function $M: X \rightarrow \mathbb{N}_{\geq 0}$, i.e. it allows certain elements of X to appear multiple times. We write a multiset as $M = [e_1^{k_1}, e_2^{k_2}, \ldots, e_n^{k_n}]$, where for $1 \leq i \leq n$ we have $M(e_i) = k_i$ with $k_i \in \mathbb{N}$. If $k_i = 1$, we omit its superscript, and if for some $e \in X$ we have $M(e) = 0$, we omit it from the multiset notation. Also, $M = [\,]$ denotes an empty multiset, i.e. $\forall e \in X$, $M(e) = 0$. We let $\overline{M} = \{e \in X \mid M(e) > 0\}$, i.e. $\overline{M} \subseteq X$. The set of all possible multisets over a set X is written as $\mathcal{M}(X)$.

Let $\mathcal{A}$ denotes the set of all possible activities and let $\mathcal{A}^*$ denote the set of all finite sequences over $\mathcal{A}$. A finite sequence σ of length n over $\mathcal{A}$ is a function $\sigma: \{1, 2, \ldots, n\} \rightarrow \mathcal{A}$, alternatively written as $\sigma = \langle a_1, a_2, \ldots, a_n \rangle$ where $a_i = \sigma(i)$ for $1 \leq i \leq n$. The empty sequence is written as ϵ. Concatenation of sequences σ and σ' is written as $\sigma \cdot \sigma'$. Moreover, sequence $\sigma' = \langle a_1', a_2', \ldots, a_k' \rangle$ is a subsequence of sequence $\sigma = \langle a_1, a_2, \ldots, a_l \rangle$ if we are able to write σ as $\sigma_1 \cdot \langle a_1', a_2', \ldots, a_k' \rangle \cdot \sigma_2$, where both σ_1 and σ_2 are allowed to be ϵ. Finally, $\sigma' = \langle a_1', \ldots, a_k' \rangle$ is an *interval subsequence* of $\sigma = \langle a_1, \ldots, a_l \rangle$, if and only if, we are able to write σ as $\sigma_1 \cdot \langle a_1' \rangle \cdot \sigma_2 \cdot \langle a_2' \rangle \cdot \ldots \cdot \sigma_k \cdot \langle a_k' \rangle \cdot \sigma_{k+1}$. If all $\sigma_2 \ldots \sigma_k$ are equal to ϵ, σ' is also subsequence of σ.

Event logs describe sequences of executed business process activities, typically in context of an instance of the process (referred to as a case), e.g., a customer or an order-id. The execution of an activity in context of a case is referred to an *event*. A sequence of events for a specific case is also referred to a *trace*. Thus, it is possible that multiple traces describe the same sequence of activities, yet, since events are unique, each trace itself contains different events. Each of these unique sequences is referred to as a *variant*. In context of this paper, we define event logs as a multiset of sequences of activities, rather than a set of traces describing sequences of unique events.

Definition 1 (Trace, Variant, Event Log). *Let $\mathcal{A}$ be a set of activities. An event log is a multiset of sequences over $\mathcal{A}$, i.e. $L \in \mathcal{M}(\mathcal{A}^*)$. Also, $\sigma \in \mathcal{A}^*$ is a trace in L and $\sigma \in \overline{L}$ is a variant.*

Observe that each $\sigma \in \overline{L}$ describes a *trace-variant* whereas $L(\sigma)$ describes how many traces of the form σ present in the event log. We also define sequential patterns as follows.

Definition 2 (Sequential pattern). *Let $\rho = \langle a_1, a_2, \ldots, a_k \rangle \in \mathcal{A}^*$ and $\sigma \in \mathcal{A}^*$ be two non-empty sequences of activities. ρ is a sequential pattern in σ if and only if $\exists \sigma_1', \ldots, \sigma_{k+1}' | \sigma = \sigma_1'.a_1.\sigma_2'. \ldots .a_k.\sigma_{k+1}'$ and show it by $\rho \sqsubseteq \sigma$.*

It is not required that all items in a sequential pattern happen directly after each others. But, it is mandatory that the order of the activities in both sequences is preserved. So, $\rho \sqsubseteq \sigma$ if ρ is an interval subsequence of σ. Also, $\sqsubseteq$ returns a binary value that will be true if the mentioned sequential pattern ρ happens one or more in the sequence σ. For example, $\langle a, b, c \rangle$ and $\langle e, e \rangle$ are two sequential patterns in $\langle a, b, d, a, e, f, c, e \rangle$. The support of a sequential pattern ρ in the event log L is computed as follows.

$$Support(\rho) = \frac{|[\sigma \in L | \rho \sqsubseteq \sigma]|}{|L|} \tag{1}$$

When a pattern ρ happens multiple times in a trace, in the general sense, we count it one time. Moreover, we define sequential rules according to the following definition.

Definition 3 (Sequential rule). *Let σ is a sequence of activities and $A \subseteq \{a \in \sigma\}$ and $C \subseteq \{a \in \sigma\}$ are two non-empty sets of activities in that sequence. We say that there is a sequential relation from A to C in σ and denote it with $A \xrightarrow{\sigma} C$, if and only if $\exists \sigma_1, \sigma_2 \in \mathcal{A}^* | (\sigma = \sigma_1 \cdot \sigma_2 \wedge A \subseteq \{a \in \sigma_1\} \wedge C \subseteq \{a \in \sigma_2\})$ where σ_1 and σ_2 are two subsequences of σ. A is the antecedent and C is the consequent of the sequential rule. Similarly, $C \xleftarrow{\sigma} A$, if and only if $\{\exists \sigma_1, \sigma_2 | \sigma = \sigma_1.\sigma_2 \wedge A \subseteq \{a \in \sigma_2\} \wedge C \subseteq \{a \in \sigma_1\}\}$.*

The order of activities among the antecedent and consequent elements of a rule is not important. However, all activities of the consequent set should at least happen one time after the antecedent activities. For example, in $\sigma = \langle a, b, c, a, b, d, e \rangle$, $\{a, c\} \xrightarrow{\sigma} \{e, b\}$, $\{b\} \xrightarrow{\sigma} \{a, e\}$, and $\{b, c\} \xleftarrow{\sigma} \{a\}$ are possible sequential rules. Also, in both $A \xrightarrow{\sigma} C$ and $C \xleftarrow{\sigma} A$, the A is the antecedent but direction of rules are different. Also, $\xrightarrow{\sigma}$ is a binary function that returns true if the sequential rule occurs at least one time in that sequence. We compute the *Support* and *Confidence* of a sequential rule as follows.

$$Support(A \to C) = \frac{|[\sigma \in \overline{L} | (A \xrightarrow{\sigma} C)]|}{|L|} \tag{2}$$

$$Confidence(A \to C) = \frac{Support(A \xrightarrow{\sigma} C)}{|[\sigma \in \overline{L} | A \subseteq \{a \in \sigma\}]|} \tag{3}$$

These measure return a value between 0 and 1. A higher support value means more traces in the event log contain $A \to C$. The higher confidence value indicates that after occurring the antecedence's activities in a trace, it is more probable that consequence's activities also are present in that trace. Note that, we just consider the existence of a rule and not the frequency of it in a trace, e.g., in the sequence $\sigma = \langle a, b, c, a, b, d, e \rangle$, $\{a\} \rightarrow \{b\}$ is counted one time even though it happens three times. In the confidence formula, $A \subseteq \sigma = \langle \sigma_1, \ldots, \sigma_n \rangle$ if and only if $\{\forall a \in A, \exists k | 1 \leq k \leq n \wedge \sigma_k = a\}$. We simply also define maximum size of antecedent and consequence as $|L_A|$ and $|L_C|$.

5   Filtering Outlier Behaviour Using Sequence Mining

The proposed filtering method requires an input event log and some parameters that are adjustable by the user and consists of three main steps. Firstly, we discover sequential rules and patterns from the event log. Secondly, based on discovered sequential rules and patterns for each trace we search if it contains of any outlier behaviour. Finally, we remove traces with outlier behaviour from the event log. Algorithm 1 shows the pseudo-code of the proposed algorithm.

In the first step, we discover sequential rules and patterns from the given event log. However, we just want to find odd (or low probable) sequential patterns and high probable sequential rules. P is an odd sequential pattern if $Support(P) \leq Sup_O$. The minimum support of sequential patterns or Sup_O is set by the user. So, any sequential pattern with the support value below than Sup_O, will be considered as an odd pattern. For discovering odd patterns, we first discover all possible patterns in the event log (with minimum support equal to 0). Then we remove all sequential patterns with the support value of higher than Sup_O (we call them normal sequential patterns). In an informal way we say $\{OddPatterns\} = \{Patterns_{MinSupport=0}\} - \{Patterns_{MinSupport=Sup_O}\}$.

We also need to discover high probable sequential rules. $A \rightarrow C$ is a high probable sequential rule if $Support(A \rightarrow C) \geq Sup_H$ and $Confidence(A \rightarrow C) \geq Conf_H$. Both Sup_H and $Conf_H$ are also parameters that possibly set by the user and refers to the minimum support and the minimum confidence of high probable rules respectively. We discover high probable sequential rules in both directions (i.e., $A \rightarrow C$ and $C \leftarrow A$). The user also sets the maximum length of sequential patterns (L_P) and size of antecedence (L_A) and consequent (L_C) of sequential rules. These parameters affect the computational complexity of the proposed method. The complexity of discovering sequential patterns (in an event log with m traces and n activities) is $O(m \times n^{L_P})$ and complexity of discovering sequential rules is $O(m \times n^{L_A + L_C})$.

After discovering odd sequential patterns and high probable sequential rules, in the second step, we will discover outlier behaviour in process instances based on them. To detect outlier behaviour, for all traces in the event log we apply the following rules:

- Traces with antecedence of a high probable sequential rule, should also contain the consequence of that rule.
- Existence of odd sequential patterns considered as outlier behaviour.

Algorithm 1. Filtering Event Log using Sequential Mining

procedure DISCOVERING SEQUENTIAL RULES AND PATTERNS $(L, S_O, S_H, C_H, L_P, L_A, L_C)$
    ProbableRules ← {All sequential rules according to S_H, C_H, L_A, L_C }
    AllPatterns ← {All sequential patterns with length L_P }
    NormalPatterns ← {All sequential patterns with length L_P and minimum support of S_O }
    OddPatterns = *AllPatterns* − *NormalPatterns*
    return (*ProbableRules, OddPatterns*)

procedure DISCOVERING AND REMOVING OUTLIER(*L, ProbableRules, OddPatterns*)
    FilteredLog ← {}
    OutlierFlag = 0
    for each Trace $T \in L$ **do**
        for each Rule $R \in$ *ProbableRules* **do**
            if (T contains Antecedence of R & does not hold R) **then**
                OutlierFlag= 1
        for each Pattern $P \in$ *OddPatterns* **do**
            if (T contains P) **then**
                OutlierFlag= 1
        if (*OutlierFlag* ! = 1) **then**
            FilteredLog ← T
    return (*FilteredLog*)

Note that if $A \xrightarrow{\sigma} C$ is false it is not necessary results in that there is outlier behaviour in the trace σ. But, if a trace contains an antecedence part of a high probable sequential rule (A), it should hold that sequential rule completely ($A \xrightarrow{\sigma} C$ equals true), otherwise, according to our definition, this trace contains outlier behaviour.

In general, odd sequential patterns are used to detect inserted or wrong ordered activities in traces. For example, in Fig. 1, for the trace $\langle a, e, b, d, c, f, g, h \rangle$, we have the odd pattern $\langle e, f \rangle$. So, the existence of both the e and f is not normal in this trace and it is detectable only when we consider long term follow relations. Moreover, high probable sequential rules are used to detect possible removed activities in traces. For example in Fig. 1, for the trace $\sigma = \langle a, b, d, f, g, i \rangle$ and having $\{a, b\} \xrightarrow{\sigma} \{c\}$, we find that the activity c does not occur after b in this trace. Therefore, we detect that this trace contains outlier behaviour.

Finally, in the last step, all traces that contain outlier behaviour will be separated from the event log. Therefore, in the filtered event log that will be returned back to the user, there is not any trace that contains outlier behaviour. There is also an option that we return only traces that contain outlier behaviour. This option is useful when we want to analyze infrequent and abnormal behaviour in the process instead of having the general view and the mainstream of the process.

Observe that, according to the definitions of sequential patterns and sequential rules, it is not required that activities in the rules and patterns are executed directly after each other. For example, an odd pattern $\langle e, i \rangle$ indicates that if activity e happens, activity i should not happen anywhere after e in that trace, otherwise we consider it as outlier behaviour. Such long distance (or indirect) follow relations that are not considered in previous filtering methods, are helpful to detect outlier behaviour in event logs with the heavy presence of *parallel* and *casual* relations.

Implementation. To be able to apply the proposed filtering method on event logs and to find its helpfulness, we implemented the *Sequential Filter* plug-in (*SF*) in the ProM framework[1] [7]. This plug-in takes an event log as an input with some parameters and outputs a filtered event log. In this implementation, for discovering high probable sequential rules we use the *rule growth* algorithm [4]. Also for discovering sequential patterns we use *prefixspan* [3] Both these sequential mining algorithms have been implemented in the SPMF tool [25].

To apply our proposed method on various event logs with different thresholds and applying different process mining algorithms with various parameters, we ported the *Sequential Filter* (*SF*) plug-in to RapidProM. RapidProM is an extension in the RapidMiner tool that combines scientific workflows with a range of (ProM-based) process mining algorithms [26].

6   Evaluation

To evaluate our proposed filtering method we applied it on real and synthetic event logs. The main goal of this evaluation is assessing the capability of the sequential filter (*SF*) compared to other existing general purpose filtering methods from two aspects:

- Improvement rate of discovered process models.
- Level of detectability of filtering methods.

For the first aspect, we consider the improvement of the discovered process model using both real and synthetic event data. However, for the second aspect, we just consider the synthetic event logs, because we need reference models as the ground truths that indicate which of the traces contain outlier and which ones are clean. Note that, the filtered event log is just used for discovering purpose and for measuring the quality of the discovered model, the original event log has been used. In Table 1, we present the event logs that are used in this evaluation with some characteristics of them. All of these real event logs are accessible via https://data.4tu.nl/repository/collection:event_logs_real and http://www.processmining.be/actitrac. The number of activities in these event logs are different from 6 to 70. For some event logs like *BPIC_2018_Inspection* there are few but frequent variants, however, in the *Hospital_Billing* event log each most of variants are unique or happen just one time. We select these event logs to check the feasibility of filtering methods and how they are able to improve process discovery algorithms results for event logs from different domains. For the synthetic event, we first designed the reference process models. As we claimed that previous filtering methods are not able to detect all outlier behaviour in event logs with a heavy presence of parallel and/or long term dependency behaviour, the process models are designed with this behaviour. The reference process models are presented in Fig. 5. After generating corresponding event logs from these reference process models, we injected different percentages

---

[1] Sequential filter plugin svn.win.tue.nl/repos/prom/Packages/LogFiltering.

of artificial outlier behaviour to the original event logs. In this regard, we insert, remove and change the order of activities. The reference models are used to determine which traces are clean and which one contain outlier behaviour.

Table 1. Some details about the event logs that are used in the experiment.

Event log	Real/Synthetic	Activity #	Event #	Trace #	Variant #
$BPIC\_2012\_Application$	Real	10	60,849	13,087	17
$BPIC\_2012\_Offer$	Real	7	31,244	5,015	168
$BPIC\_2012\_Work$	Real	6	72,413	9,658	2263
$BPIC\_2017\_Offer$	Real	8	193,849	42,995	16
$BPIC\_2018\_Department$	Real	6	46,669	29,297	349
$BPIC\_2018\_Financial$	Real	36	262,200	13,087	4,366
$BPIC\_2018\_Inspection$	Real	26	197,717	5,485	3,190
$BPIC\_2018\_Parcel$	Real	10	132,963	14,750	3,613
$Hospital\_Billing$	Real	18	451,359	100,000	1,020
$Road\_Fines$	Real	11	561,470	150,370	231
$Sepsis$	Real	16	15,214	1,050	846
$TSL.anon$	Real	40	83,286	17,812	2,551
$MCRM.anon$	Real	22	11,218	956	212
$ICP.anon$	Real	70	65,653	12,391	1,411
$KIM.anon$	Real	18	124,217	24,770	1,174
$High\_Variants$	Synthetic	20	75,915	5,000	4,668
$High\_Parallel$	Synthetic	19	95,000	5,000	5,000
$Long\_Term\_Dependency$	Synthetic	14	50,000	5,000	3

To evaluate the quality of discovered process models, we use *fitness* and *precision*. Fitness computes how much behaviour in the event log is also described by the process model. Precision measures how much behaviour that is described by the discovered model is also presented in the event log. Low precision means that the process model allows for much more behaviour compared to the event log. Note that, there is a trade-off between these measures [27]. Sometimes, putting aside a small amount of behaviour causes a slight decrease in fitness, whereas precision increases much more. Therefore, to evaluate improvement of discovered process models, we use the *F-Measures* metric that combines fitness and precision: $\frac{2 \times Precision \times Fitness}{Precision + Fitness}$. Moreover, to assess outlier detectability of filtering methods, we map the problem to a classification problem. In other words, we should detect whether a trace contains outlier behaviour or whether it is clean. Therefore, we use the well-known classification measure *F1-score* [28] that combines *Precision* and *Recall* of filtering methods' outlier detectability on noisy event logs. So to have a high F1-score the filtering method should detect outlier as much as possible (i.e., Recall) and at the same time, most of the removed traces indeed contain outlier behaviour (i.e., Precision).

Also because the proficiency of all current filtering methods depends on their adjusted parameters, for each of them a grid search method is used to find their best result. Therefore, just the best result for each filtering method is depicted. In this regard, we use *AFA* method with 50 different thresholds from 0 to 1 and 25 different thresholds for *MF* with subsequence length equals 2 to 4. For process discovery purpose, we applied the basic Inductive Miner [12] on filtered event logs, because it always returns sound process models that makes it feasible to compute *fitness* and *precision* for discovered process models. Also, we used the Inductive Miner [10] with its embedded filtering mechanism with 50 different thresholds from 0 to 1.

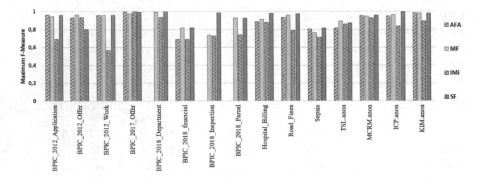

Fig. 4. The best F-Measure for using different filtering methods on some real event logs.

Figure 4, indicates the best F-Measures of discovered process models when different filtering methods are used to remove outlier behaviour. *AFA* and *MF* are consequently related to *Anomaly Free Automaton* [6] and *Matrix Filter* [5] methods and *SF* refers to the sequence mining based filtering method. We also compare these results with *IMi* that refers to using the Inductive Miner with its embedded filtering mechanism. Note that for the other filtering methods we just applied the basic *Inductive Miner* without its filtering mechanism. For most of the event logs, *SF* returns the best F-Measure. However, for the event log $BPIC\_2012\_Offer$ compare to other methods it does not perform well. It is because in this event log there is a long loop, i.e., that is a loop in the process model with more than 2 activities. In general, an existence of long loops in the given event log has negative effects on the outlier detectability of *SF*. Also, in the heavy presence of choice (*Xor*) behaviour it will be more probable that our proposed method is not able to detect all removed/missed activities. We will discuss limitations of the proposed method in Sect. 6. Observe, for some event logs like *Sepsis* even with filtering outliers we could not reach a process model with *F-Measure* value near 1. It is caused by characteristics of the event log. We found that if a rate of $1 - \frac{Variant\#}{Trace\#}$ be lower, then it would be harder to discover a process model with high precision and fitness at the same time.

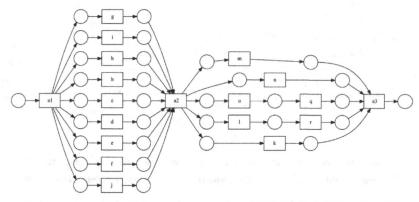

(a) A process model with heavy presence of parallel behaviour (*High_Parallel*)

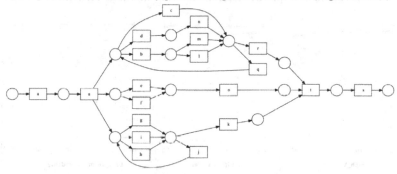

(b) A process model with all different types of behaviour and possibility of having high number of variants (*High_Variant*)

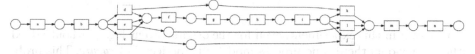

(c) A process model with long term dependency behaviour (*Long_Term_Dependency*)

Fig. 5. Synthetic process models with different types of behaviour.

Also, the *AFA* filtering method is not able to filter *BPIC_2018_Parcel* and *BPIC_2018_Inspection*. So, we have not corresponding results for them on Fig. 4.

We repeat this experiment for the synthetic logs. The best *F-Measure* discovered process models using different filtering methods on these synthesis event logs are given in Fig. 6. For *High_Parallel* event log with increasing the percentage of injected outlier behaviour just by using *SF* we are able to reach an acceptable process model. This is because except *SF*, other filtering methods use direct follow dependencies and it is not enough to detect all outliers when we have a heavy presence of parallel behaviour in an event log.

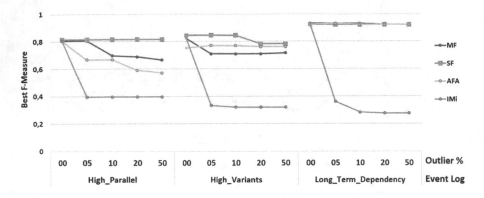

Fig. 6. The F-Measure of applying different filtering methods on synthetic event logs.

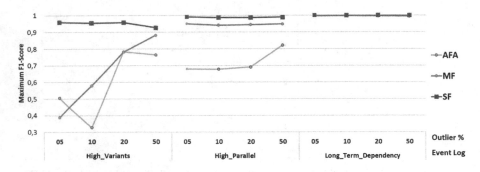

Fig. 7. The F1-Score of applying different filtering methods on synthetic event logs.

As shown in this experiment, even for the original event logs (without added outlier behaviour) there is no process model with perfect *F-Measure*. This problem is caused by process model discovery algorithm -here the *Inductive Miner*-that is not able to show long-term dependencies and also the definition of precision that does not return the value 1 even for the original process model and the original event log. As we use escaped edge definition [29] for computing precision, it is interesting to note that for complicated process models (with heavy presence of *parallel*, *loop* and *casual* relations), even the precision of the perfect process model will be lower than 1.

In the next experiment, using synthetic event logs we want to assess how different filtering methods are able to detect traces with injected outlier behaviour. The best *F1-Score* for detectability of different filtering methods are indicated in Fig. 7. For *Long_Term_Dependency* event log, the *F1-Score* for *SF* is 1 but for *AFA* and *MF* it equals to 0.993 and 0.998 respectively. As in Fig. 6, we used the Inductive Miner algorithm and it is not able to show long-term dependencies, there is no difference between the output of these filtering methods. However, if we use other algorithms like Alpha++ [30], we will discover a model exactly like Fig. 5c that its *F-Measure* value will be equal to 1.

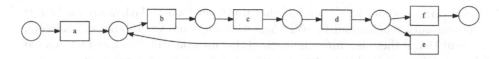

Fig. 8. A process model with loop behaviour.

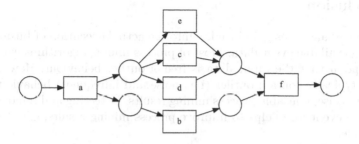

Fig. 9. A process model with *Xor* behaviour.

The experiment results show that all filtering methods improve the process discovery results. Also, results indicate that using sequential patterns and rules, we are able to detect outlier behaviour in process models with a heavy presence of parallel, long term-dependencies, and casual behaviour.

Limitations. Our proposed filtering method uses sequential patterns and rules that cause to consider indirectly (long term) follow relations. However, it has limitations because it does not benefit from directly follow relations. The first limitation is that when we have loop behaviour, the proposed method is not able to detect some outlier behaviour relates to activities that are participated in the *do* part of the loop. For example, in Fig. 8, activities *b*, *c* and *d* construct the *do* part and *e* is the *redo* part of the loop. In this process model, it is possible that the filtering method does not detect outlier behaviour in $\langle a, b, c, d, e, d, b, c, c, f \rangle$. Due to the existence of loop behaviour, it is more likely that we consider $\langle c, c \rangle$, $\langle c, d \rangle$, and $\langle d, b \rangle$ as normal sequential patterns. Therefore, it would be challenging to detect outlier behaviour that loop activities.

Another limitation of the proposed filtering method is that the presence of *Xor* behaviour has negative effects on the proficiency of it. For example, in Fig. 9 after the execution of activity *a*, one of activities *c*, *d*, and *e* execute (in parallel with activity *b*). The sequence filtering method is not able to detect *removed* activities that are participated in the *Xor* behaviour. But, added and misordered activities are detectable even with the heavy presence of *Xor* behaviour. Note that, by decreasing the minimum support of high probable sequential rules such outlier behaviour is detectable, but it causes to detect some of normal behaviour as outlier behaviour too. For example, in Fig. 9 to detect outlier behaviour of $\langle a, b, e \rangle$, we need to consider a sequential rule like $\{a\} \leftarrow \{c, f\}$ as a high probable rule that will cause to remove all traces that do not contain activity *c*.

Filtering methods like [5] and [6] that use direct follow relations are easily able to detect outlier behaviour in event logs with *loop* and *Xor* relations. Therefore, it seems that if there is a filtering method that uses both of direct and undirected follow relations it is able to detect outlier behaviour more accurately.

7   Conclusion

Process mining allows us gain insights into the actual execution of business processes using available event data. Most of process mining algorithms work under the assumption that the input data is free of outlier behaviour. However, real event logs typically contain outlier (i.e., noise and infrequent) behaviour which leads to imprecise/unusable process mining results. Detecting and removing such behaviour in event logs helps to improve process mining results, e.g. discovered process models.

To address this problem, we propose a method that takes an event log and returns a filtered event log. It exploits sequence mining algorithms to discover sequential patterns and rules. Using such information we able to discover flow relation of activities over long distances. By applying sequence mining methods, it does not just rely on the direct flow of activities and we are able to detect outlier behaviour in event logs with a heavy presence of *parallel, casual* or *long term dependency* behaviour.

To evaluate the proposed filtering method, we developed a plug-in in the ProM platform and the RapidProM. As presented, we have applied this method to several real event logs and compared it with other state-of-the-art process mining specific data filtering methods. Additionally, we applied the proposed method on synthetic event logs. The results indicate that the proposed filtering approach is able to detect outlier behaviour and consequently is able to help process discovery algorithms to return models that better balance between different behavioural quality measures. Furthermore, using these experiments we show that the sequence filter method outperforms other state-of-the-art process mining filtering techniques as well as the Inductive Miner algorithm with its embedded filtering mechanism for some real event logs.

As future work, we aim to conduct larger experiments to find out in which situations a particular filtering mechanism works better. We also aim to estimate the filtering parameters based on features of the given event log.

References

1. van der Aalst, W.M.P.: Process Mining - Data Science in Action, 2nd edn. Springer, Heidelberg (2016). https://doi.org/10.1007/978-3-662-49851-4
2. Maruster, L., Weijters, A.J.M.M., van der Aalst, W.M.P., van den Bosch, A.: A rule-based approach for process discovery: dealing with noise and imbalance in process logs. Data Min. Knowl. Discov. **13**(1), 67–87 (2006)
3. Han, J., et al.: PrefixSpan: mining sequential patterns efficiently by prefix-projected pattern growth. In: Proceedings of the 17th International Conference on Data Engineering, pp. 215–224 (2001)

4. Fournier-Viger, P., Wu, C.W., Tseng, V.S., Cao, L., Nkambou, R.: Mining partially-ordered sequential rules common to multiple sequences. IEEE Trans. Knowl. Data Eng. **27**(8), 2203–2216 (2015)
5. Sani, M.F., van Zelst, S.J., van der Aalst, W.M.P.: Improving process discovery results by filtering outliers using conditional behavioural probabilities. In: Teniente, E., Weidlich, M. (eds.) BPM 2017. LNBIP, vol. 308, pp. 216–229. Springer, Cham (2018). https://doi.org/10.1007/978-3-319-74030-0_16
6. Conforti, R., La Rosa, M., ter Hofstede, A.H.M.: Filtering out infrequent behavior from business process event logs. IEEE Trans. Knowl. Data Eng. **29**(2), 300–314 (2017)
7. van der Aalst, W., van Dongen, B.F., Günther, C.W., Rozinat, A., Verbeek, E., Weijters, T.: ProM: the process mining toolkit. BPM (Demos) **489**(31), 2 (2009)
8. van der Aalst, W.M.P., Bolt, A., van Zelst, S.J.: RapidProM: mine your processes and not just your data. CoRR abs/1703.03740 (2017)
9. Peterson, J.L.: Petri Net Theory and the Modeling of Systems. Prentice Hall Inc., Englewood Cliffs (1981)
10. Leemans, S.J.J., Fahland, D., van der Aalst, W.M.P.: Discovering block-structured process models from event logs containing infrequent behaviour. In: Lohmann, N., Song, M., Wohed, P. (eds.) BPM 2013. LNBIP, vol. 171, pp. 66–78. Springer, Cham (2014). https://doi.org/10.1007/978-3-319-06257-0_6
11. van der Aalst, W.M.P., Weijters, T., Maruster, L.: Workflow mining: discovering process models from event logs. IEEE Trans. Knowl. Data Eng. **16**(9), 1128–1142 (2004)
12. Leemans, S.J.J., Fahland, D., van der Aalst, W.M.P.: Discovering block-structured process models from event logs - a constructive approach. In: Colom, J.-M., Desel, J. (eds.) PETRI NETS 2013. LNCS, vol. 7927, pp. 311–329. Springer, Heidelberg (2013). https://doi.org/10.1007/978-3-642-38697-8_17
13. De Weerdt, J., vanden Broucke, S., Vanthienen, J., Baesens, B.: Active trace clustering for improved process discovery. IEEE Trans. Knowl. Data Eng. **25**(12), 2708–2720 (2013)
14. Buijs, J.C.A.M., van Dongen, B.F., van der Aalst, W.M.P.: On the role of fitness, precision, generalization and simplicity in process discovery. In: Meersman, R., et al. (eds.) OTM 2012. LNCS, vol. 7565, pp. 305–322. Springer, Heidelberg (2012). https://doi.org/10.1007/978-3-642-33606-5_19
15. van Zelst, S.J., van Dongen, B.F., van der Aalst, W.M.P.: Avoiding over-fitting in ILP-based process discovery. In: Motahari-Nezhad, H.R., Recker, J., Weidlich, M. (eds.) BPM 2015. LNCS, vol. 9253, pp. 163–171. Springer, Cham (2015). https://doi.org/10.1007/978-3-319-23063-4_10
16. Weijters, A.J.M.M., Ribeiro, J.T.S.: Flexible heuristics miner (FHM). In: CIDM (2011)
17. Günther, C.W., van der Aalst, W.M.P.: Fuzzy mining – adaptive process simplification based on multi-perspective metrics. In: Alonso, G., Dadam, P., Rosemann, M. (eds.) BPM 2007. LNCS, vol. 4714, pp. 328–343. Springer, Heidelberg (2007). https://doi.org/10.1007/978-3-540-75183-0_24
18. Chandola, V., Banerjee, A., Kumar, V.: Anomaly detection for discrete sequences: a survey. IEEE Trans. Knowl. Data Eng. **24**(5), 823–839 (2012)
19. Gupta, M., Gao, J., Aggarwal, C.C., Han, J.: Outlier detection for temporal data: a survey. IEEE Trans. Knowl. Data Eng. **26**(9), 2250–2267 (2014)
20. Wang, J., Song, S., Lin, X., Zhu, X., Pei, J.: Cleaning structured event logs: a graph repair approach. ICDE **2015**, 30–41 (2015)

21. Cheng, H.J., Kumar, A.: Process mining on noisy logs—can log sanitization help to improve performance? Decis. Support Syst. **79**, 138–149 (2015)
22. van Zelst, S.J., Fani Sani, M., Ostovar, A., Conforti, R., La Rosa, M.: Filtering spurious events from event streams of business processes. In: Krogstie, J., Reijers, H.A. (eds.) CAiSE 2018. LNCS, vol. 10816, pp. 35–52. Springer, Cham (2018). https://doi.org/10.1007/978-3-319-91563-0_3
23. Tax, N., Sidorova, N., van der Aalst, W.M.P.: Discovering more precise process models from event logs by filtering out chaotic activities. J. Intell. Inf. Syst. 1–33 (2018)
24. Fani Sani, M., van Zelst, S.J., van der Aalst, W.M.P.: Repairing outlier behaviour in event logs. In: Abramowicz, W., Paschke, A. (eds.) BIS 2018. LNBIP, vol. 320, pp. 115–131. Springer, Cham (2018). https://doi.org/10.1007/978-3-319-93931-5_9
25. Fournier-Viger, P., Gomariz, A., Gueniche, T., Soltani, A., Wu, C.W., Tseng, V.S.: SPMF: a Java open-source pattern mining library. J. Mach. Learn. Res. **15**(1), 3389–3393 (2014)
26. Bolt, A., de Leoni, M., van der Aalst, W.M.P.: Scientific workflows for process mining: building blocks, scenarios, and implementation. STTT **18**(6), 607–628 (2016)
27. Weerdt, J.D., Backer, M.D., Vanthienen, J., Baesens, B.: A robust F-measure for evaluating discovered process models. In: Proceedings of the CIDM, pp. 148–155 (2011)
28. Makhoul, J., Kubala, F., Schwartz, R., Weischedel, R., et al.: Performance measures for information extraction. In: Proceedings of DARPA Broadcast News Workshop, Herndon, VA, pp. 249–252 (1999)
29. Munoz-Gama, J., Carmona, J.: Enhancing precision in process conformance: stability, confidence and severity. In: 2011 IEEE Symposium on Computational Intelligence and Data Mining (CIDM), pp. 184–191. IEEE (2011)
30. Wen, L., van der Aalst, W.M.P., Wang, J., Sun, J.: Mining process models with non-free-choice constructs. Data Min. Knowl. Discov. **15**(2), 145–180 (2007)

Transparent Execution of Data Transformations in Data-Aware Service Choreographies

Michael Hahn[(✉)], Uwe Breitenbücher, Frank Leymann, and Vladimir Yussupov

Institute of Architecture of Application Systems (IAAS), University of Stuttgart,
Stuttgart, Germany
{michael.hahn,uwe.breitenbuecher,frank.leymann,
vladimir.yussupov}@iaas.uni-stuttgart.de

Abstract. Due to recent advances in data science, IoT, and Big Data, the importance of data is steadily increasing in the domain of business process management. Service choreographies provide means to model complex conversations between collaborating parties from a global viewpoint. However, the involved parties often rely on their own data formats. To still enable the interaction between them within choreographies, the underlying business data has to be transformed between the different data formats. The state of the art in modeling such data transformations as additional tasks in choreography models is error-prone, time consuming and pollutes the models with functionality that is not relevant from a business perspective but technically required. As a first step to tackle these issues, we introduced in previous works a data transformation modeling extension for defining data transformations on the level of choreography models independent of their control flow as well as concrete technologies or tools. However, this modeling extension is not executable yet. Therefore, this paper presents an approach and a supporting integration middleware which enable to provide and execute data transformation implementations based on various technologies or tools in a generic and technology-independent manner to realize an end-to-end support for modeling and execution of data transformations in service choreographies.

Keywords: Data-aware choreographies · Data transformation
TraDE

1 Introduction

With recent advances in data science the importance of data is increasing also in the domain of Business Process Management (BPM) [14,17]. The concept of Service-Oriented Architectures (SOA), i.e., composing units of functionality as services over the network, has found application in many research areas and application domains besides BPM [4,24], e.g., in Cloud Computing, the

© Springer Nature Switzerland AG 2018
H. Panetto et al. (Eds.): OTM 2018 Conferences, LNCS 11230, pp. 117–137, 2018.
https://doi.org/10.1007/978-3-030-02671-4_7

Internet of Things, or eScience. The composition of services can be realized in either an orchestration or choreography-based manner. *Service orchestrations*, or *processes/workflows*, are defined from the viewpoint of one party that acts as a central coordinator [13]. *Service choreographies* are defined from a global viewpoint with focus on the collaboration between multiple interacting parties, i.e., services, and their conversations without relying on a central coordinator [6]. Services taking part in such collaborations are represented as *participants* of a choreography and their conversations are defined through message exchanges.

Participants rely on their own internal data models on which their business logic is defined. Consequently, differences between the data formats of different participants have to be resolved to enable their interaction and definition of conversations between them. Therefore, *data transformations* have to be introduced to translate the underlying data to the different formats each participant requires. Such data transformations have to be defined within the participants of a choreography model, i.e., as part of their control flow, e.g., by adding corresponding transformation tasks that provide the required transformation logic. This approach is inflexible, time consuming and also pollutes the participants' control flow of choreography models with data transformation functionality that is not relevant from the perspective of individual participants but technically required to realize the conversations between them within a service choreography.

In Hahn et al. [10], we presented a first step to tackle these issues by introducing a modeling extension for defining data transformations in choreography models independently of participants control flow directly between the defined choreography data based on our concepts for *Transparent Data Exchange (TraDE)* [8]. However, execution support for the data transformations specified within a choreography model is missing, i.e., the actual implementations of defined data transformations need to be completely manually integrated into the execution environment to enable their automated execution during choreography run time. Although, this significantly eased the modeling of service choreographies with participants relying on different data formats, concepts for the automated integration and execution of modeled data transformations decoupled from participants' control flow are required to avoid error-prone and cumbersome manual integration steps which require significant technical expertise for integrating the required transformation software to a choreography execution environment.

In this paper, we tackle these issues by introducing concepts and a generic, technology-independent integration middleware which enable to provide, integrate and invoke data transformation implementations in an easy and automated manner to realize an end-to-end support for modeling and execution of data transformations in service choreographies. The contributions of this paper can be summarized as follows: (i) concepts for the specification and packaging of data transformation implementations, (ii) an architecture of a supporting integration middleware which enables the automatic integration of packaged transformation implementations into a choreography execution environment, (iii) concepts for the execution of data transformations in service choreographies decoupled from participants control flow in an automated and transparent manner based on our TraDE concepts, and (iv) the prototypical implementation of an integrated ecosystem for data-aware service choreographies with data transformation support.

The rest of this paper is structured as follows. Section 2 presents the problem statement of this work and introduces previous works on TraDE and our modeling extension for data transformations. In Sect. 3, the *TraDE Data Transformation* (TDT) approach is introduced. Section 4 presents how modeled data transformations can be executed in an automated and transparent manner, i.e., decoupled from the choreography control flow. The prototypical implementation of an integrated TraDE ecosystem is outlined in Sect. 5. Section 6 presents a case study from the eScience domain as an example for applying the TDT approach to an existing choreography model. Finally, the paper discusses related work (Sect. 7) and concludes with our findings and future work (Sect. 8).

2   Problem Statement and Background

Commonly, participants in service choreographies rely on their own, custom data formats. To enable the modeling of conversations among them, each participant must understand all involved data formats. This can be achieved by translating the data to the target formats required by individual participants. To define such format translations on the level of service choreographies, *data transformations* have to be specified as parts of the participants' control flow. One solution is to use a standardized choreography modeling language like BPMN [16], which allows modeling data transformations as explicit tasks. However, this approach is error-prone, time consuming and requires considerable amount of efforts. Firstly, modelers have to provide transformation implementations required by the underlying modeling language or execution environment, e.g., using XQuery or XSLT for XML-related data transformations. This requires an extensive level of expertise in transformation languages, technologies and underlying data modeling languages and formats. Moreover, such transformations, when modeled as tasks in possibly multiple participants, pollute the control flow of participants with data transformation functionality that is not relevant from a participants perspective but technically required to realize the communication between participants of a choreography. In addition, since the underlying transformation implementations become a part of the resulting choreography models, they are spread across multiple different models which hinders their reuse and makes it hard to maintain them. This is especially problematic when data formats of choreography participants change over time, as underlying choreography models and all affected transformation tasks have to be adapted to support these new data formats. While providing transformation implementations as services eases the reuse process, modelers must be able to wrap their transformation implementations as services to invoke them in choreography models.

To provide the background for this work, we first compare the state-of-the-art approach for data transformation modeling in choreographies and the TraDE modeling extensions introduced in our previous works [8,10]. Figure 1 depicts an example choreography modeled using these two approaches. Both choreographies are illustrated as Business Process Management Notation (BPMN) [16] collaboration models. The conversations among participants are defined using BPMN message intermediate events and message flows. Choreography data is modeled via BPMN data objects on the level of choreography participants and exchanged as part of messages through specified message flows, e.g., *mx1* in Fig. 1.

2.1   State-of-the-Art in Modeling Data Transformations

The left model in Fig. 1 demonstrates the state-of-the-art approach for data transformation modeling in choreographies. We call this standard way of modeling and exchanging data in choreographies *message-based data exchange* [8]. Whenever participant *P1* receives a request, modeled as BPMN message start event, the contained data are extracted from the message and stored in data objects *D* and *E*. These data is then wrapped and sent to participant *P2* in a message exchanged via message flow *mx1*. In a similar way, participant *P3* receives these data via message flow *mx2*. At participant *P3*, data object *E* has to be transformed and stored in data object *G*, which is used as an input for task *B*. Therefore, participant *P3* defines transformation task T_1 that executes required data transformation logic. The result of task *B* is stored in data object *H* and sent back to participant *P2* through message flow *mx3*. Similarly, transformation task T_2 is required for obtaining data object *K* which is used as input by task *C*. Upon completion of all tasks, a message to the initial requester with data object *H* is sent as the final result of the choreography execution.

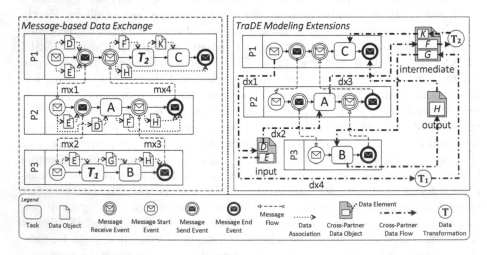

Fig. 1. Comparison of two modeling approaches, based on Hahn et al. [10].

This *message-based data exchange* approach has significant drawbacks [8,10]. First, the same data objects must be specified at each participant that uses the data, e.g., data objects E and H have to be specified in all participants. Moreover, the data flow within a participant can be seamlessly modeled through BPMN data associations, but data exchange across participants has to be modeled through a combination of message flows and related control flow modeling elements, e.g., BPMN *send* and *receive* tasks, and *message throw* or *message catch* events. Consequently, data cannot be exchanged across participants without introducing additional control flow constructs at the sender and receiver participants.

In addition, required data transformations have to be modeled manually through respective tasks and data associations on the level of choreography participants. For example, participant *P1* defines transformation task T_2 for translating the data produced by participant *P2* (data element F). Such tasks pollute the control flow of participants of choreography models with transformation functionality by mixing business and technical aspects together. Moreover, the underlying transformation implementations must be supported by the choreography modeling language and execution environment, i.e., as the task's implementation or as an invokable service. This approach lacks automation support and depends on the capabilities of the selected modeling language or execution environment. Furthermore, it still requires a significant amount of expertise on transformation languages, technologies and underlying data modeling languages and formats.

2.2   TraDE Data Transformation Modeling Extension

To improve and simplify the modeling of data transformations in service choreographies, we presented concepts for the specification of data as well as its exchange and transformation in service choreographies decoupled and independent from participants control flow [8,10]. The choreography model depicted on the right of Fig. 1 applies our TraDE concepts and modeling extensions, namely *cross-partner data objects*, *cross-partner data flows*, and *data transformations*, to substitute message-based data exchange and explicit definitions of transformation tasks. Choreography data can be modeled in a participant-independent manner using cross-partner data objects, e.g., *input* in Fig. 1, and the reading and writing of the cross-partner data objects from tasks and events is specified through cross-partner data flows, e.g., *dx1* or *dx3*. Explicitly modeled transformation tasks T_1 and T_2 can be substituted by TraDE data transformations linked to the data objects E and G (for T_1) as well as F and K (for T_2) through cross-partner data flows. These cross-partner data flows allow exchanging the data across participants independently of message flows and, therefore, decouple the exchange of data from the exchange of messages. Moreover, the transformation of data can be specified directly on the data itself, i.e., between cross-partner data objects, instead of introducing transformation tasks on the level of participants.

Each *cross-partner data object* has a unique identifier and contains one or more *data elements*. For example, cross-partner data object *input* in Fig. 1 contains data elements D and E. A data element has a name and contains a reference to a definition of its structure, e.g., a XML Schema Definition [20]. A *TraDE data transformation* (DT) allows to specify a reference to the software that provides the related data transformation logic, e.g., a web service, script, or executable, referred to as *DT Implementation* in the following. The inputs and outputs of a data transformation can be specified by adding cross-partner data flows between a data transformation and one or more cross-partner data objects. If a data transformation requires or produces several inputs or outputs, modelers are able to map the connected cross-partner data objects to respective inputs and outputs of the underlying DT Implementation through specifying a set of *Input/Output Mappings*. Furthermore, a TraDE data transformation allows to specify a set of *Input Parameters* which enables modelers to define input values for a DT Implementation that are not provided through cross-partner data objects. For example, to provide constant values, e.g., for the configuration or initialization of the underlying DT Implementation. In addition, an optional *Trigger Condition* and *Activation Mode* can be specified for each data transformation. A trigger condition allows to specify a boolean expression which is evaluated before the referenced DT Implementation is executed. The activation mode defines when a data transformation should be conducted: *on-read* or *on-write*.

The binding of modeled data transformations to concrete logic is not required during choreography modeling and can be deferred to choreography deployment. The main idea is to enable a separation of concerns, i.e., participants' business logic and choreography transformation logic is separated from each other, which introduces more flexibility since required transformations can be modeled within choreographies in an abstract manner and their actual binding to concrete DT Implementations can be done at a later point in time using the specified data transformations within a choreography model and their properties as a blueprint to identify or provide required DT Implementations. This allows modelers to focus on the modeling of participants and their conversations without taking care of how the differences of their data models can be solved.

As outlined in Hahn et al. [10], by supporting the definition of data transformations independent of choreography participants' control flow directly between cross-partner data objects, the main challenge is on how to provide, integrate and invoke the underlying data transformation implementations for modeled data transformations within service choreographies during choreography execution.

3   The TraDE Data Transformation Approach

In the following, the *TraDE Data Transformation* (TDT) approach is presented as the main contribution of this work. It combines our TraDE modeling extensions, an extended version of the TraDE Middleware [9], and introduces the new *Data Transformation* (DT) *Integration Middleware* to provide automatic integration and execution support for data transformations in service choreographies.

The presented TraDE data transformation modeling extension allows defining data transformations independent of choreography participants (see Sect. 2.2).

However, to support the execution of respective data transformations, referenced transformation implementations (DT Implementation) need to be integrated into the choreography execution environment. In addition, data transformations are often implemented in different programming languages or restricted to certain execution environments. To tackle such heterogeneity, in Sect. 3.1 we first present concepts for the technology-agnostic specification and packaging of DT Implementations in so-called *DT Bundles*. The goal is to abstract away any concrete technologies or tools while automating tedious integration processes to avoid manual wrapping of software. This allows modelers to easily create and provide their data transformation implementations as DT Bundles.

These DT Bundles can then be published to the DT Integration Middleware to make the contained DT Implementations available for use within choreographies. The architecture of the DT Integration Middleware and how it supports the fully automated provisioning and execution of DT Bundles is presented in Sect. 3.2. Finally, in Sect. 4, an integrated TraDE ecosystem is presented and the transparent execution of defined data transformations is described in more detail.

3.1 Specification and Packaging of DT Implementations

Based on the findings of related work discussed in Sect. 7 and lack of available and suitable standards, we introduce our own conceptual model for an easy and technology-agnostic specification and packaging of data transformation implementations that fully satisfies our requirements. The resulting model can be extended and adapted to support various required use cases and functionalities.

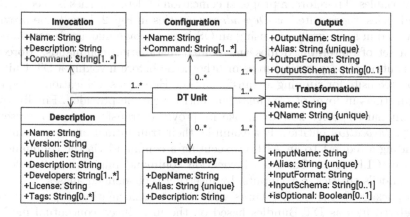

Fig. 2. A conceptual model for specifying DT Units.

The UML class diagram in Fig. 2 illustrates our proposed conceptual model for the specification of *data transformation units* (DT Units). In contrast to the already introduced DT Bundle, a DT Unit provides a specification of one or more DT Implementations, e.g., their inputs and outputs, required tools or execution environments. A DT Bundle represents a concrete materialization of a DT Unit by providing also the required concrete resources, e.g., data transformation implementations in form of executables or scripts, configuration files or installation scripts to setup required tools or frameworks for executing respective transformations. Since DT Implementations can vary in different dimensions, a black-box approach is employed for their specification and execution, i.e., considering DT Implementations as atomic reusable entities which have to remain immutable. Apart from general information such as name, version, or publisher specified as *Description* entity, a DT Unit has several more important characteristics. First, a DT Unit supports one or more transformations, e.g., transforming textual data into several different image formats. This definition is provided in *Transformation* entities representing DT Implementations. A Transformation has a name and an unique fully-qualified name (QName) which can be used, e.g., for searching transformations at the middleware or to reference them as transformation implementations in TraDE data transformations within choreography models. Each transformation is described by one or more inputs and outputs specified through *Input* and *Output* entities. Both entities have a name and must be uniquely identifiable by an alias, which can be used for referencing, e.g., to specify the invocation of a transformation of a DT Unit. Possible types of inputs or outputs can be messages, data streams, files, parameters, or data from databases. The inputs and outputs of a transformation might have a specific format and can therefore provide a schema file describing their data format.

DT Units can have a particular set of dependencies that have to be satisfied to execute their transformations. For example, a DT Unit can depend on certain software, libraries, (configuration) files or even operating system (OS) environment variables. Therefore, a proper specification of dependencies is needed. Such dependencies, represented as *Dependency* entities in Fig. 2, have to be provided or installed in some way, e.g., using an OS-level package manager's command or using a set of materialized files and related installation commands. Moreover, the execution of preparation steps or other logic before invoking a DT Unit can be a prerequisite for running a transformation. Hence, a specification of required configurations in form of *Configuration* entities can be provided. Finally, every DT Unit must specify how to invoke its provided transformations represented through *Invocation* entities. For example, their transformations can be invoked by sending a request to an API or executing a command via the command line interface (CLI) of an OS. Such invocation command might need to reference other model's entities, e.g., inputs, by inserting their defined aliases.

To package described DT Units with their transformation implementations and related files as DT Bundles based on the introduced conceptual model, a standardized packaging format is required. Introducing a predefined structure for packaging and storing DT Units is beneficial as no additional knowledge is needed to process the DT Bundles later. A packaged DT Unit, i.e., a DT Bundle, consists therefore of the following distinct parts: (i) *unit* part contains all DT Unit-related files, e.g., DT Implementation artifacts such as scripts or executables, (ii) *dependencies* part groups all required dependencies, (iii) *schemas* part contains optional schema files which define the structure of transformation inputs and outputs, (iv) *DT Unit specification* is an instance of the conceptual model for a concrete DT Unit materialized as a file, e.g., as JSON file.

3.2 Architecture of the DT Integration Middleware

Figure 3 presents the architecture of the DT Integration Middleware which allows modelers to publish DT Bundles to make their data transformation implementations available for use within choreographies. To allow a broad variety of potential implementations, the architecture is defined in a generic and technology-independent manner. Our focus is on the description of the logical building blocks and functionality which can be then combined with or implemented through well-established middleware solutions, e.g., such as Enterprise Service Buses (ESB) [5] know for their integration and transformation capabilities in the context of SOA.

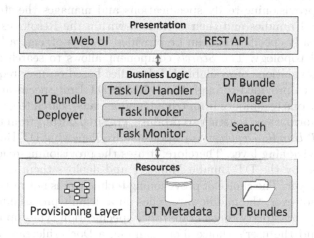

Fig. 3. Architecture of the DT Integration Middleware.

In the following, the architecture will be presented in a top-down manner followed by a more detailed description of its business logic components. The *Presentation* layer enables the communication of external clients with the middleware, e.g., through a *Web UI* or *REST API*. The *Business Logic* layer provides the core functionality of the middleware. Its components are responsible for the publishing, provisioning, and the execution of transformation implementations provided by DT Bundles in a task-based manner. The *Resources* layer provides and integrates actual technologies for storing and provisioning of DT Bundles to enable the execution of their contained transformation implementations. This comprises the storage of the actual files of a DT Bundle (see Sect. 3.1) in the file system (*DT Bundles* in Fig. 3). The related metadata of all managed DT Units and DT Bundles is persisted in a database (*DT Metadata* in Fig. 3) to simplify access and provide query support on the metadata. To support the provisioning of published DT Bundles as a prerequisite for their execution, the middleware relies on a *Provisioning Layer*, e.g., Docker or OpenTOSCA [3], to provide the specified run time environment and dependencies of a DT Bundle.

To make a published DT Bundle and its provided DT Implementations invokable, it has to be prepared for provisioning first. Since the specification of a DT Unit might contain references to remote resources, e.g., files or software dependencies, these references need to be materialized to preserve the state and behavior of the DT Bundle within the middleware, as referenced files can change over time leading to different bundle versions. For example, if a certain dependency is specified, exactly the specified version has to be present for a DT Bundle within the middleware. If materialization happens, the DT Unit specification has to reflect the changes affecting materialized references. Finally, a published DT Bundle needs to be stored, e.g., using a database, a file system, or a combination of both. The *DT Bundle Manager* shown in Fig. 3 provides the functionality for reference materialization, transforming DT Unit specifications of DT Bundles into provisioning-ready specifications and manages the storage of the resulting refined bundles and their metadata within the Resources layer. Such provisioning-ready specification can be provided in form of, e.g., a Dockerfile or a TOSCA [15] topology. The *Search* component allows to search and identify suitable transformations of available DT Bundles based on user requests utilizing the metadata provided through the available DT Unit specifications. Search can employ various techniques from trivial unique name search to composition of multiple transformations together to produce a desired output from the provided input. The *DT Bundle Deployer* is responsible for deploying DT Bundles to the supported provisioning layer. Therefore, it uses the provisioning-ready specifications generated by the DT Bundle Manager and deploys them to the selected Provisioning Layer. The choice of provisioning technology is not restricted by the architecture, however, the middleware relies on a default provisioning specification leaving the possibility to generate other specification types up to pluggable components and the user's choice. For example, a Dockerfile can be generated if Docker is the default provisioning specification type. As potentially multiple provisioning layers can be used together, the DT Bundle Deployer has to update the metadata of a DT Bundle, e.g., stored in a database, to reflect its deployment status at the Provision Layer, i.e., if it is available for executing its contained transformation implementations.

Another important part of the middleware is the task-based execution of transformations, i.e., the execution of a transformation implementation of a DT Bundle. Therefore, a new *transformation task* can be issued by sending a request to the REST API of the middleware. Such a request contains a reference to a DT Bundle, the fully-qualified name of a Transformation of the specified DT Bundle as well as required information about retrieving input and placing output data according to the DT Unit specification of the DT Bundle (see Sect. 3.1). The *Task I/O Handler* is responsible for preparing the specified inputs as a prerequisite to invoke a transformation as well as processing the resulting outputs. Therefore, inputs can be received in a pull or push-based manner. In the former case, inputs are provided as references within transformation task requests and need to be downloaded and prepared for the invocation. In the latter case, inputs are contained in the request itself. The actual invocation and execution of the specified transformation is managed by the *Task Invoker*. Therefore, it uses the prepared inputs to invoke the transformation based on the DT Unit specification (*Invocation* in Sect. 3.1). During the execution of the transformation, the *Task Monitor* component allows to monitor the state of the execution by sending corresponding requests to the REST API of the middleware. As soon as the transformation is completed, the *Task I/O Handler* component is responsible to process the resulting outputs and pass them back to the requester.

Since the DT Integration Middleware has to support various types of inputs and outputs (e.g., files, messages, or data streams), invocation mechanisms (e.g., CLI or HTTP), and monitoring concepts for different data transformation types, the middleware supports integration of several implementations of these three components in a pluggable manner. To automate the execution of data transformations in choreographies, the middleware is integrated with the TraDE Middleware as discussed in the following.

4   Transparent Execution of Data Transformations

Applying the TraDE Data Transformation (TDT) approach allows to specify and provide data transformation implementations as DT Bundles and execute them with the help of the DT Integration Middleware in a generic task-based manner. What is still missing is how DT Bundles can be used within choreographies to define data transformations and how the execution of a DT Bundle's transformation can be triggered during choreography execution. Therefore, Sect. 4.1 presents the integrated TraDE ecosystem and Sect. 4.2 outlines the execution of DT Bundle transformations through the TraDE Middleware in a transparent manner, i.e., independent of the choreography control flow during choreography run time.

4.1   Integrated TraDE Ecosystem

Figure 4 depicts the TraDE ecosystem which provides an end-to-end support for data transformations in service choreographies. Before we describe the execution of data transformations within the ecosystem, first the ecosystem itself is introduced and the resulting deployment artifacts of a data-aware choreography as well as their deployment to the components of the ecosystem are described.

As described in Sect. 3.1, data transformations are provided in form of *DT Bundles* which comprise one or more data transformation implementations and a DT Unit specification. They are published to the *DT Integration Middleware* to make them available to the overall TraDE ecosystem. As outlined in Sect. 2.2, the introduced TraDE data transformation modeling extension [10] allows to specify a reference to the software that provides the underlying data transformation

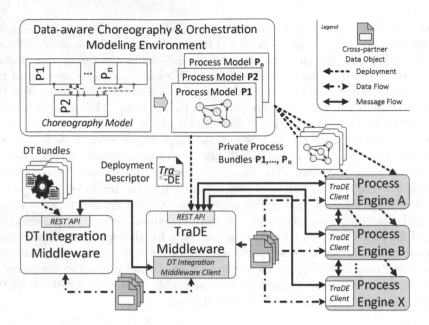

Fig. 4. Integrated system architecture and deployment artifacts of the TraDE ecosystem.

implementation. By following the TDT approach, such references to transformation software, i.e., transformation implementations can now be provided and integrated to choreography models by referencing corresponding DT Bundles with their fully-qualified name (QName) (see Sect. 3.1). This allows the TraDE Middleware to trigger a new transformation task at the DT Integration Middleware as means to conduct a modeled transformation by executing the referenced transformation implementation of a corresponding DT Bundle.

The *Data-aware Choreography & Orchestration Modeling Environment* enables modelers to specify data-aware service choreographies by modeling *cross-partner data objects*, *cross-partner data flows* and *data transformations*. Based on the fact that a lot of choreography modeling languages do not produce executable models, we follow the established approach of transforming choreography models into a collection of executable private process models which collectively implement the overall choreography [7] as shown in Fig. 4. The resulting private process models can then be manually refined by adding corresponding internal logic for each participant. The private process models are packaged together with related files, e.g., process engine deployment descriptors, or interface and schema definitions, as *Private Process Bundles* for their deployment on *Process Engines* as depicted in Fig. 4. Furthermore, all cross-partner data objects and their dependencies defined in a choreography model are exported to a *TraDE Deployment Descriptor* file. This file is uploaded to the *TraDE Middleware* where it is compiled into related internal representations to provide and expose all cross-partner data objects as resources through the middleware's REST API [9] as well as support the triggering of data transformations. Thus, the TraDE Deployment Descriptor contains information about all specified data transformations of a choreography. As introduced in Sect. 2.2, this comprises the reference to a data transformation implementation, Input/Output Mappings, Input Parameters, and an optional Trigger Condition and Activation Mode. The reference to a transformation implementation is specified by adding the fully-qualified name (QName) of a DT Bundle's transformation (see Sect. 3.1). This separation of concerns, i.e., participants' business logic is specified in private process models and transformation logic is specified/referenced in TraDE Deployment Descriptor, allows more flexibility since transformations can be provided and specified as DT Bundles independent of the choreography/private process models and therefore also be easily changed without affecting the private process models. This allows modelers to focus on the modeling of choreography participants and their conversations without taking care of how the differences of their data models can be solved. The actual binding of concrete transformation logic, i.e., transformation implementations being part of a DT Bundle, can be delayed to choreography deployment since this binding information is provided as part of the TraDE Deployment Descriptor and does not require any changes on the level of the private process models of a choreography.

The TraDE Middleware is integrated with the DT Integration Middleware as well as the respective process engines through clients. Therefore, the process engines are extended with a *TraDE Client* to communicate with the TraDE Middleware through its REST API. The TraDE Middleware contains a *DT Integration Middleware Client* to trigger the task-based execution of data transformations by sending *transformation task* requests to the DT Integration Middleware's REST API. As shown in Fig. 4, this enables the TraDE Middleware to act as a data hub between the private process models implementing choreography participants and referenced DT Bundles, i.e., defined data transformations. In the following, the execution of modeled data transformations within the ecosystem is described.

4.2 Automatic Triggering of Data Transformations

As outlined above, the TraDE Middleware comes with its own internal, choreography language independent metamodel as presented in Hahn et al. [9]. The middleware extracts all defined cross-partner data objects and data elements from the TraDE Deployment Descriptor and translates them to respective *CrossPartnerDataObject* and *DataElement* entities according to its metamodel. To represent the actual data of running choreography instances, i.e., collection of instances of the private process models implementing the choreography model, the metamodel defines further entities. For each choreography instance, *CrossPartnerDataObjectInstance* and *DataElementInstance* entities are created at the middleware with associated *CorrelationProperty* entities which enable to uniquely identify the choreography instance the data object and data element instances belong. The actual data of a choreography instance is represented through *DataValue* entities which are referenced by *DataElementInstance* entities. The TraDE Middleware provides an event model for each entity type, i.e., a life cycle with states and transitions. This allows firing an event whenever an entity changes its state, e.g., a DataValue is *initialized*. Based on these event models, the TraDE Middleware supports an event-based mechanism to trigger actions on respective events. This concept is used to transparently execute data transformations specified in choreography models by triggering the invocation of referenced transformations provided as DT Bundles at the DT Integration Middleware and handling the underlying data exchange.

For example, data transformation T_1 in Fig. 1 will be triggered as soon as data element E of cross-partner data object *input* is initialized or whenever it is modified. The invocation of the respective DT Bundle's transformation itself is straightforward. All required information is sent to the DT Integration Middleware within a request that triggers the task-based execution of a DT Bundle's transformation. This requires the resolution of DataValue entities for a specific choreography instance that hold the input data of the transformation. For the example depicted in Fig. 1, this means that the middleware has to first identify the DataElementInstance entity of data element E related to the running choreography instance. Next, the DataValue entity associated to the resulting data element instance can be resolved to get the actual data to transform. Instead of passing the input data within the invocation request to the DT Integration Middleware, a URL pointing to the respective resource exposing the required DataValue entity at the TraDE Middleware's REST API is added for each transformation input. The same applies for transformation outputs. Instead of retrieving output data in a response message, a DataValue resource URL is added to the invocation request for each transformation output. When the transformation is completed, the DT Integration Middleware uploads all results to the TraDE Middleware by pushing them to DataValue resources specified through URLs in the invocation request, making the data available for further use.

By default, a transformation is triggered whenever data is written to a DataValue associated to one of its input cross-partner data objects. The *trigger condition* and *activation mode* allow influencing the underlying behavior of the TraDE Middleware. In *on-write* activation mode, the TraDE Middleware first waits until all input data for a data transformation is available, i.e., the DataValue entities associated to cross-partner data objects specified as inputs are successfully initialized, and then invokes the DT Bundle's transformation. Furthermore, whenever one or more of the specified transformation inputs are modified, the TraDE Middleware invokes the DT Bundle's transformation again. Based on that, the specified outputs of a data transformation are always up-to-date. In *on-read* activation mode, the TraDE Middleware triggers a data transformation whenever one of its output cross-partner data objects or data elements are read. For example, data transformation T_1 in Fig. 1 will be triggered whenever data element G of cross-partner data object *intermediate* is read. Since reads and writes of cross-partner data objects are decoupled from choreography execution, the TraDE Middleware has to wait until all the required input cross-partner data objects are available before triggering the invocation of a DT Bundle's transformation. Further fine tuning of the data transformation triggering behavior at the TraDE Middleware is possible through the specification of a *trigger condition*. It allows to define a boolean expression that is evaluated by the TraDE Middleware to check if a data transformation should be triggered or not. For example, this can be used to trigger a transformation only if the value of an input cross-partner data object is within certain margins.

5 Prototype

To prove the technical feasibility of our approach, we describe the prototypical implementation of the TraDE ecosystem and its components in the following. For the modeling of data-aware choreographies with data transformations, the choreography modeling language BPEL4Chor [7] is used and extended. The underlying Data-aware Choreography & Orchestration Modeling Environment is built on existing tools, i.e., *Chor Designer* [21] and an extended version of the Eclipse *BPEL Designer*. As Process Engine an extended version of the open source BPEL engine Apache *Orchestration Director Engine* (ODE) is used. To enable the execution of cross-partner data flows, the implementation of Apache ODE is extended and integrated with the TraDE Middleware to enable the reading and writing of cross-partner data objects [9].

The TraDE Middleware itself is implemented as a Java-based web application which exposes its functionality through a REST API which is specified using Swagger and implemented with the *Jersey* RESTful Web Services framework. The TraDE internal representations and the actual data processed within the choreographies, can be persisted using MongoDB or the local file system. To support the event-based triggering of DT Bundles within the context of this work, the TraDE Middleware is extended with corresponding functionality implemented using Apache Camel to send requests to the REST API of the DT Integration Middleware. The TraDE Middleware open source code is available on GitHub[1].

The DT Integration Middleware is a web application implemented in Python Flask with its functionality exposed via a REST API. Swagger is used for the specification of the REST API. For storing DT Bundles a combination of MongoDB and a file system is used. The former stores metadata derived from the provided DT Unit specifications, whereas the latter is used for storing the files of DT Bundles. The prototype supports *file-based* DT Implementations which rely on files and parameters as input and output types and can be invoked through CLI commands. To provision DT Bundles, Docker is used as provisioning layer integrated to the middleware through a Docker SDK for Python. More complex DT Implementations and DT Bundles requiring other invocation mechanisms as well as input and output types will be supported using TOSCA [15] in future. The DT Integration Middleware open source code is available on GitHub[2].

---

[1] TraDE: https://github.com/traDE4chor/trade-core/releases/tag/v1.1.0.
[2] DT: https://github.com/traDE4chor/hdtapps-prototype/releases/tag/v1.0.0.

6 Case Study

As an example for applying the TDT approach, a case study from the eScience domain is presented in the following. Therefore, the naïve choreography model is presented where data transformations are defined by adding respective transformation tasks. Finally, the TDT approach is applied to the model as an example for easier modeling of data transformations and enabling their provisioning and execution in a technology-independent and transparent manner.

6.1 Naïve Modeling of Data Transformations

Figure 5 shows an excerpt of the choreography model of a Kinetic Monte Carlo (KMC) simulation using the custom-made simulation software *Ostwald ripening of Precipitates on an Atomic Lattice* (OPAL) [2]. OPAL simulates the formation of copper precipitates, i.e., the development of atom clusters, within a lattice due to thermal aging. The whole simulation consists of four major building blocks which are reflected as participants of the data-aware choreography depicted in Fig. 5. Following our TraDE concepts, all data relevant for the choreography model is specified independently of any participant and in a shared and reusable manner through cross-partner data objects (DO) and data elements (DE).

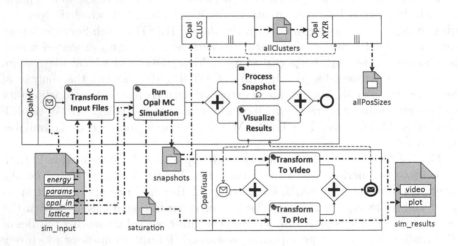

Fig. 5. Choreography conducting a thermal aging simulation from eScience [8].

Whenever the *OpalMC* participant receives a new request, a new instance of the KMC simulation is created. The initial request contains a set of inputs (*sim_input* DO), e.g., parameters such as the number of simulation snapshots to take (*params* DE), an initial energy configuration (*energy* DE), and a lattice (*lattice* DE). First, the *Transform Input Files* service task executes a data transformation to combine input parameters and energy configuration into the input format of the KMC simulation. The transformation result is stored in the *opal_in* DE. Next, the *Run Opal MC Simulation* service task invokes a service which conducts the KMC simulation based on the provided data. According to the specified number of snapshots in *opal_in* DE, the service saves the current state of the atom lattice at a particular point in time as a snapshot and replies all snapshots together (*snapshots* DO) as well as saturation data (*saturation* DO).

Based on the number of snapshots, the *Process Snapshots* send task is conducted multiple times to invoke the analysis of each snapshot individually at the *OpalCLUS* and *OpalXYZR* participants. First, all clusters within each snapshot are identified and stored in the *allClusters* DO through the *OpalCLUS* participant. This cluster information is then processed by the *OpalXYZR* participant to identify the position and size of each cluster. The respective results are stored in the *allPosSize* DO. Since the internal logic of the OpalCLUS and OpalXYZR participants do not provide further insights, they are depicted as a black box.

The *Visualize Results* service task triggers the visualization of snapshot and saturation data at the *OpalVisual* participant. The *Transform To Video* and *Transform To Plot* service tasks invoke related transformation services using the *snapshots* and *saturation* DO as input. The collection of snapshots is transformed into a video of animated 3D scatter plots and the saturation data is transformed to a 2D plot of the saturation function of the precipitation process as a final result which are stored in the respective data elements of the *sim_results* DO.

According to Sect. 2, the choreography model contains three transformation tasks that are not a relevant part of the simulation but technically required for pre-processing (sim_input DO) and post-processing (sim_results) of simulation data. Moreover, the simulation specific transformation implementations have to be manually wrapped as services to enable their integration and invocation in the choreography. This requires expertise and additional effort since the transformation implementations are provided as shell script (*Transform Input Files*) or Python (*Transform To Video*) and Gnuplot scripts (*Transform To Plot*).

6.2   Applying the TraDE Data Transformation Approach

Figure 6 depicts the OPAL choreography model with the introduced TDT approach applied. The definition of data transformations between cross-partner data objects allows to substitute the explicitly modeled transformations tasks: *Transform Input Files*, *Transform To Video* and *Transform To Plot*. Instead, TraDE data transformations t_1, t_2, t_3 are defined to transform the choreography data as required. This contributes to our goal of specifying data and its transformations independent of any participants in service choreographies directly between cross-partner data objects. Furthermore, the transformation implementations have no longer to be provided as services to enable their integration and invocation through tasks (e.g., *Transform Input Files*). Modelers are now able to specify and integrate their transformation implementations without manual wrapping effort, in form of DT Bundles to enable their transparent execution within the TraDE ecosystem. With the help of the TDT approach, the original scripts can be automatically wrapped and integrated into the TraDE ecosystem to enable their invocation. Only respective DT Unit specifications have to be created for each of the scripts to enable their packaging together with related files as DT Bundles and finally publish them to the DT Integration Middleware. To get an idea how a concrete DT Bundle looks like, a corresponding example for transformation t_2 (*Transform To Video*) is available on GitHub[3].

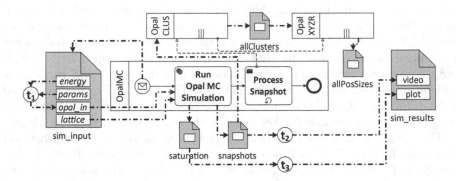

Fig. 6. Choreography model with TraDE data transformations applied.

7   Related Work

Since the focus of this work is on how to specify, integrate and execute heterogeneous data transformation implementations in an easy and automated manner in the context of data-aware service choreographies, this section presents related work regarding application reuse and wrapping techniques.

Zdun [23] introduces an approach for legacy application migration to the web. He describes a method with the following four steps: (i) providing an API using either wrapping or redevelopment approaches, (ii) implementation of a component responsible for mapping of requests to the legacy API, (iii) as well as implementation of a component responsible for response generation, and (iv) the integration of these components into a web server. Furthermore, a reference architecture supporting the introduced concepts and issues is presented.

Sneed et al. [18] introduce white-box wrapper generation approaches for wrapping functions in legacy applications based on XML descriptions. The presented tool supports, e.g., the transformation of PL/I and COBOL functions' into WSDL interfaces. Additionally, the transformation generates modules responsible for mediation of the input and output data between legacy and WSDL interfaces.

Afanasiev et al. [1] present a cloud platform called MathCloud which allows reusing scientific applications by exposing them as RESTful web services having a uniform interface for a task-based execution. Requests contain the task

---

[3] Opal snapshot-to-video transformation DT Bundle: https://github.com/traDE4 chor/hdtapps-prototype/tree/master/samples/opalVideo.

description, inputs specification and resulting output is returned when the task is completed. Sukhoroslov et al. [19] introduce Everest, a PaaS platform for reusing scientific applications based on the MathCloud platform [1]. The authors further improve the ideas of providing a uniform interface for task-based execution of applications.

Juhnke et al. [12] present the Legacy Code Description Language framework which allows wrapping legacy code. An extensible legacy code specification model is used as a basis for executable wrappers generation. The model stores the information necessary for wrapping binary and source code legacy applications.

Wettinger et al. [22] present an APIfication approach which allows generating API implementations for executable programs. The underlying assumption is that an executable is provided along with metadata describing its dependencies, inputs, outputs, and other required information. Additionally, the authors introduce *any2api* as a generic and extensible framework for reusing executable software.

Hosny et al. [11] introduce AlgoRun, a container template based on Docker suitable for wrapping CLI-based scientific algorithms and exposing them via a REST interface to simplify the reuse of scientific algorithms. Therefore, the algorithm has to be described using a predefined format. Moreover, a Dockerfile has to be created which wraps the algorithm's source code.

While some of the works are used as a basis for the TDT approach, none of them fit completely our needs. Since our focus is on data transformation software, data-related aspects and capabilities of such application reuse and wrapping techniques are of major relevance. The idea to create specifications for legacy applications similar to ones introduced by Juhnke et al. [12] and Hosny et al. [11] is used as an inspiration. However, we wanted to avoid any tight-coupling with a particular type of infrastructure or provisioning technology, since various provisioning specifications can be generated based on our introduced technology-agnostic DT Bundle specification. Our goal is to provide generic concepts and a supporting middleware for the specification, packaging, provisioning, and invocation of data transformation implementations as DT Bundles to enable their use within service choreographies.

8   Conclusion and Outlook

Data transformations are required on the level of choreographies to mediate between the different data formats of their collaborating participants. To support the execution of data transformations independent of choreography participants' control flow, the TDT approach is introduced to provide and invoke the underlying data transformation implementations for modeled data transformations within service choreographies. The main goal of the approach is to avoid the potentially tedious integration or even complete manual wrapping of required transformation software for its use within choreographies. Therefore, concepts for the specification and packaging of transformation implementations as DT Bundles and a supporting DT Integration Middleware enabling their execution are introduced. The resulting integrated TraDE ecosystem enables a seamless and transparent execution of data transformations within choreographies. Finally, we presented a prototypical implementation and a case study where we applied the TDT approach to an existing choreography model from the domain of eScience to show its feasibility.

In future, we plan to extend transformation capabilities for both modeling and execution of choreographies, e.g., by supporting the specification of trigger conditions for fine-grained control of triggering data transformations. Furthermore, an evaluation of the overall TraDE ecosystem is planned to compare and identify its behavior based on different scenarios, e.g., measure performance variations regarding the number of choreography participants and parallel reading/writing as well as transformation of shared cross-partner data objects.

Acknowledgments. This research was supported by the projects SmartOrchestra (01MD16001F) and SePiA.Pro (01MD16013F).

References

1. Afanasiev, A., Sukhoroslov, O., Voloshinov, V.: MathCloud: publication and reuse of scientific applications as RESTful web services. In: Malyshkin, V. (ed.) PaCT 2013. LNCS, vol. 7979, pp. 394–408. Springer, Heidelberg (2013). https://doi.org/10.1007/978-3-642-39958-9_36
2. Binkele, P., Schmauder, S.: An atomistic Monte Carlo simulation of precipitation in a binary system. Zeitschrift für Metallkunde **94**, 858–863 (2003)
3. Binz, T., et al.: OpenTOSCA – a runtime for TOSCA-based cloud applications. In: Basu, S., Pautasso, C., Zhang, L., Fu, X. (eds.) ICSOC 2013. LNCS, vol. 8274, pp. 692–695. Springer, Heidelberg (2013). https://doi.org/10.1007/978-3-642-45005-1_62
4. Bouguettaya, A., et al.: A service computing manifesto: the next 10 years. Commun. ACM (2017). https://doi.org/10.1145/2983528. Accessed 18 Sept 2018
5. Chappell, D.: Enterprise Service Bus. O'Reilly Media, Inc., Sebastopol (2004)
6. Decker, G., et al.: An introduction to service choreographies. Inf. Technol. **50**, 122–127 (2008)
7. Decker, G., et al.: Interacting services: from specification to execution. Data Knowl. Eng. **68**, 946–972 (2009)
8. Hahn, M., et al.: Modeling and execution of data-aware choreographies: an overview. Comput. Sci. - Res. Dev. **33**, 329–340 (2017)
9. Hahn, M., Breitenbücher, U., Leymann, F., Weiß, A.: TraDE - a transparent data exchange middleware for service choreographies. In: Panetto, H. (ed.) OTM 2017. LNCS, vol. 10573, pp. 252–270. Springer, Cham (2017). https://doi.org/10.1007/978-3-319-69462-7_16
10. Hahn, M., et al.: Modeling data transformations in data-aware service choreographies. In: EDOC (2018)
11. Hosny, A.: AlgoRun: a Docker-based packaging system for platform-agnostic implemented algorithms. Bioinformatics **32**, 2396–2398 (2016)
12. Juhnke, E., et al.: LCDL: an extensible framework for wrapping legacy code. In: iiWAS (2009)

13. Leymann, F., Roller, D.: Production Workflow - Concepts and Techniques. PTR Prentice Hall, Upper Saddle River (2000)
14. Meyer, S., et al.: Towards modeling real-world aware business processes. In: WoT (2011)
15. OASIS: Topology and Orchestration Specification for Cloud Applications (TOSCA) Version 1.0 (2013)
16. OMG: Business Process Model and Notation (BPMN) Version 2.0, January 2011
17. Schmidt, R., Möhring, M., Maier, S., Pietsch, J., Härting, R.-C.: Big data as strategic enabler - insights from central European enterprises. In: Abramowicz, W., Kokkinaki, A. (eds.) BIS 2014. LNBIP, vol. 176, pp. 50–60. Springer, Cham (2014). https://doi.org/10.1007/978-3-319-06695-0_5
18. Sneed, H.M.: Integrating legacy software into a service oriented architecture. In: Software Maintenance and Reengineering (2006)
19. Sukhoroslov, O., Afanasiev, A.: Everest: a cloud platform for computational web services. In: CLOSER (2014)
20. W3C: XML Schema Definition Language (XSD) 1.1 Part 1: Structures (2012)
21. Weiß, A., et al.: Modeling choreographies using the BPEL4Chor designer. Technical report 2013/03, University of Stuttgart (2013)
22. Wettinger, J., Breitenbücher, U., Leymann, F.: Streamlining APIfication by generating APIs for diverse executables using Any2API. In: Helfert, M., Méndez Muñoz, V., Ferguson, D. (eds.) CLOSER 2015. CCIS, vol. 581, pp. 216–238. Springer, Cham (2016). https://doi.org/10.1007/978-3-319-29582-4_12
23. Zdun, U.: Reengineering to the web: a reference architecture. In: Software Maintenance and Reengineering (2002)
24. Zimmermann, O.: Microservices tenets. Comput. Sci. - Res. Dev 32, 301–310 (2016)

In the Search of Quality Influence on a Small Scale – Micro-influencers Discovery

Monika Ewa Rakoczy[1(✉)], Amel Bouzeghoub[1], Alda Lopes Gancarski[1], and Katarzyna Wegrzyn-Wolska[2]

[1] SAMOVAR, CNRS, Telecom SudParis, Evry, France
monika.ewa.rakoczy@gmail.com,
{amel.bouzeghoub,alda.gancarski}@telecom-sudparis.eu
[2] AlliansTIC, Efrei Paris, Villejuif, France
katarzyna.wegrzyn@efrei.fr

Abstract. Discovery and detection of different social behaviors, such as influence in on-line social networks, have drawn much focus in the current research. While there are many methods tackling the issue of influence evaluation, most of them base on the underline assumption that a large audience is indispensable for an influencer to have much impact. However, in many cases, users with smaller but highly involved audience still are highly impactful. In this work, we target a novel problem of finding micro-influencers – exactly those users that have much influence on others despite of a limited range of followers. Therefore, we propose a new concept of micro-influencers in the context of Social Network Analysis, define the notion and present a flexible method aiming to discover them. The approach is tested on two real-world datasets of Facebook [24] and Pinterest [31]. The established results are promising and demonstrate the usefulness of the micro-influencer-oriented approach for potential applications.

Keywords: Micro-influence · Influence · Social scoring
Social Network Analysis

1 Introduction

The massive amount of users on on-line social networks and the induced enormous volume of data obtained, containing users' activities and preferences have led to a quick development of disciplines dedicated to the analysis of the connections they form, structures and groups they share, and others. The applications of such studies resulted in amelioration and expansion of Recommender Systems, Social Network Analysis and others. One of the most interesting and important, but still not fully explored part of the abovementioned studies involving on-line social networks is the research connected to investigation, discovery and evaluation of the influence between users in social networks.

H. Panetto et al. (Eds.): OTM 2018 Conferences, LNCS 11230, pp. 138–153, 2018.
https://doi.org/10.1007/978-3-030-02671-4_8

Currently, there are several issues tackled by the research connected to the subject. Influence Maximization [12] deals with the best way of spreading the information in the network where the connections between nodes indicate the existence of the influence and the possible canal for conveying the information. Consequently, the works rooted in Influence Maximization are based on the assumption that the network already possesses the knowledge about the established influence throughout all users. However, the discovery of such influence relations between the users, as well as evaluating and comparing the influence strength is a separate Social Network Analysis topic of research by itself.

Numerous works, such as [13,18,19,29], focused on an issue of evaluating influence using different features, e.g. the network topology (e.g. PageRank [19], centrality methods [29]) or a nature of the interactions between users [13]. Particularly, most of influence discovery algorithms focus on finding the influencers – users having overall highest ability of impacting others (e.g. [9,20,30]). Such ranking systems are already used by marketing companies, that utilize them for finding users to target advertisements, political and social campaigns, and others.

However, while many big companies with vast amounts of resources can afford collaboration with well-known people – influential and known on-line – in order to promote their brands, it is rarely the case for smaller businesses. Moreover, while very known Youtuber with a broad audience can advertise a variety of different products, from cosmetics to clothes [8], many enterprises want to be connected to a specific audience that is particularly interested in the discipline of enterprise focus, rather than to just vast group of any people. Furthermore, from the perspective of both quality and the number of responses to the posted content, users that have a big audience (e.g. high number of followers) can actually have the same impact on the audience as users with a vastly smaller audience, when we consider its value normalized by the size of audience. Hence, in many cases, the focus of the influence discovery methods should be placed not on the overall most influential users, but on users with influence of the same quality and strength, that have limited size of audience.

Some advertising companies [2–4] already realized the need for targeting such users, calling them **micro-influencers**. The advantages of using micro-influencers instead of top influencers for enterprise campaigns are twofold: not only companies can get recognition within the group of possible clients, but also they do not need to invest in expensive (Internet) celebrity collaboration. While some marketing research [1,14] made an attempt at briefly mentioning the role of micro-influencers, within Social Network Analysis the problem of micro-influencers discovery is still widely unknown and not dealt with. In fact, to best of our knowledge, our work is the first one addressing the formalization, discovery and evaluation of micro-influencers.

Our contributions are as follows:

– We define and distinguish the notion of a *micro-influencer* in the scope of Social Network Analysis (Sect. 3).

- We propose the formalization aiming to select micro-influencers based on a selected criteria (Sect. 3).
- We experiment and verify the proposed approach using two real-world datasets and utilizing an existing influence evaluation framework [20] (Sect. 4).

2   Related Works

As previously mentioned, the subject of influence in social networks has gained much attention over recent years. Different studies focused on diverse aspects and usages of the notion of influence.

It is very important to notice that influence, while being a well-known, intuitive concept taken from social sciences, does not have one accepted definition and is actually rarely precisely defined in the scope of Social Network Analysis [21]. This conceptual problem of who the influencer really is, caused works to use general, dictionary-based influence definitions, for example definition by [22]: *"changes in an individual's thoughts, feelings, attitudes, or behaviors that result from interaction with another individual or a group"* (used in e.g. [10,11,21]).

The premiere methods for influence discovery and evaluation were purely centered around the structure of the network graph, basing on the number of outgoing and incoming edges and connecting influence with the user's central position within the network. Approaches such as betweenness centrality, degree centrality, HITS [29] or widely-known PageRank [19] made the basis for more complex influence methods. Further approaches incorporated different factors in order to evaluate influence, considering tie strength between users [30], dynamicity of the network [18,25], or influencers' local or global environment [16]. Although including other factors, these approaches still base and partially identify the notion of influence with a very broad audience, which can be seen in methods basing on PageRank [7,9] or popularity[1] [5,17]. The underline assumption is that the larger number of people an influencer can impact, the better influencer he or she is. Such assumption means that *popularity* – the notion connected exactly with the audience (high popularity equals high number of followers) – got tangled with influence [21]. While one's central position in social network might indeed be one of the indicators of being an influencer, that is not the only factor that should be taken into consideration. This was already observed and presented in some of the previous works, e.g. [20], which showed a model that incorporated the notion of audience engagement into the influence computation, however, still not considering micro-influencers.

In this article, we argue that, while methods targeting top influencers with a broad number of followers are definitely useful, there is also a need of approaches that target finding users less broadly known but still influential in the niche they operate in. Therefore, this contribution should be regarded as a complementary work and an extension to other works dealing with determining the influence

---

[1] As it is not the main subject of this article, we refer curious readers to a great survey by Riquelme et al. [23] on influence methods in Twitter.

within social networks. In particular, we want to show the applicability of the term *influence* to users that have very high impact despite not having an enormous audience.

Micro-influencers are starting to be a topic of a very recent research. For instance work of Lin et al. [14], while focused in business domain, has mentioned micro-influencers as one of the important roles in a social network. To-date, the term is mainly used in marketing, where service sites are using the micro-influencer concept in order to engage the companies and the micro-influencers together for advertising purposes. While they focus on the application of the term, their definitions are similar and non-specific, e.g. [26] describes micro-influencers on Instagram platform as *"creators on social media platforms who typically have between 1,000 and 100,000 followers"*, and the exact boundaries of the audience size vary: article [15] limits the followers number to 5 000 followers, [27] gives limits of 10,000 and 500,000 followers. Furthermore, a recent study [1] investigating the usefullness of micro-influencers has shown much higher engagement rate (likes, comments) for users with less than 10 000 followers: *"1,000 followers generally received likes on their posts 8% of the time. Users with 10 million+ followers only received likes 1.6% of the time"*. Interestingly, a very recent publication of Côté and Darling [6] dealt with related subject of scientists' on Twitter reach of audience, especially small audiences and the property of those audiences. This study characterizes the possible audiences and discusses different prospects for scientists from different disciplines using Twitter, showing the vast differences of the properties depending on the audience size. While not exactly connected to our study, this article also stresses the recent interest in users with smaller, less broad public. Having said that, still there is a lack of clarification and thorough description of the micro-influencer notion.

All of the above clearly shows the need to define the term *micro-influencer* and develop the methods accustomed to finding micro-influencers, which is the aim of this article.

3   Micro-influencers

In this section, we first give the necessary basic definitions needed afterwards. Then, using them as a basis, we discuss and define the notion of *micro-influencer*. Finally, we introduce a framework for influence calculation that we later use in the experiments.

3.1   Preliminary Definitions

As discussed in Sect. 2, the term *influence* tends to be not only vaguely defined in Social Network Analysis, but also tightly associated with *popularity*, which implies that the influencer must have a lot of followers. However, as we aim to focus on those users that are still impactful yet are not the most popular, we will incorporate definitions from [20] in order to specify the necessary notions:

Definition 1 *Action: An entity $e \in E$ such as a person (user), a group of people (e.g. company) or an object (content, conference, etc.) performs an action $a \in A$ by creating new content (such as posting, photo-sharing etc.) and broadcasting or sharing existing ones. Activity performing entity is active or prominent in the social network meaning that he/she has many ties.*

Definition 2 *Reaction: An entity $e_1 \in E$ can react to an action $a \in A$ performed by other entity $e_2 \in E$ by giving a feedback (posting a comment, replying, following) or a reward (positive or negative likes).*

Definition 3 *Social Network: A social network SN is a triple $SN{<}E, A, R{>}$ where E is a set of entities, A is a set of actions performed by entities from E, and R is a set of reactions of entities from E.*

Definition 4 *Influencer: An entity $e_1 \in E$ is an Influencer iff:*

1. e_1 *performs actions $A' \subseteq A$ observable in SN*
2. *Actions from A' are recognized by other entities $e_{i \geq 2}$ using reactions from R*
3. *Actions from A' have an impact on the behavior or structure of SN.*

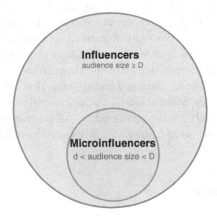

Fig. 1. Visualization of the placement of micro-influencers within a social network, where D and d are audience size limits (see Formalization 1)

To illustrate above definitions, let us consider YouTube platform. In such scenario a *social network* is created from different users, and an *influencer* is a user, who performs an *action*, e.g. posts a video, and receives multiple *reactions*, e.g. many up-votes and comments.

3.2   Micro-influence

From the above definitions, it is clear that an influencer is a user that is actively recognized by others in a social network, not only passively followed as it is in the case of many metrics, e.g. PageRank based. Importantly, for the many current applications of influence systems, this is exactly the targeted goal – to find users whose content is not only passively *viewed* but also actively *seen*. That is why we focus on the engagement of the audience which can be observed by their reactions.

Considering this context, we can finally define the notion of micro-influencer as follows:

Definition 5 *Micro-influencer: an entity $e \in E$ with:*

1. *high engagement from other entities $e' \neq e \in E$ manifested through high number of reactions from R*
2. *limited audience size, i.e. the number of reactive entities (audience) greatly smaller than the maximal audience size observed in the SN.*

The first crucial aspect of this definition is the high engagement (strength of the influence), that will apply to those of the followers of the user that are already active (through reactions). This notion is also completely independent from the structure of the network.

Secondly, the limitation of the audience size is a direct implication of our focus on the impactful yet not popular users. Obviously, the exact value setting the bounds for the size of the audience is a subject of arbitrary decision. The value will be highly dependent on the properties of the analyzed social network such as size of the network, density and average of users' followers, etc. Therefore, the value cannot be set as an absolute, but has to be relative to both the maximal and minimal observed size of the audience. Moreover, depending on the application, some additional boundaries and restrictions might be appropriate, e.g. targeting users that have no more than 1 000 followers, as we want to maintain a personal contact (via messages) with all the followers.

The problem of boundaries specification connects with the issue of inreach and outreach of audiences [6]. Particularly, depending on a use case, the interest can be put on users with outreaching audiences, that can attract users that are not directly connected to the specific subject or on the users with their followers being very dedicated to this particular niche. A good example of this can be seen on YouTube. Some users (both with bigger and smaller audiences), who brand themselves with some particular topics (e.g. gaming), are still more appealing to a various spectrum of users (not necessary video games enthusiasts). On the contrary, many of the users' channels are much more in-depth and will only be alluring to users with high interest in the subject. Therefore, there can be two separate cases of an advertiser searching either for highly dedicated focus group (inreach), in which case the boundaries will be smaller, or for less dedicated, more versatile group, in which case the limits can be set larger.

Due to the above, we propose a general formalization of the micro-influencer, complementary to Definition 5:

Formalization 1. *For any entity $e \in E$ for social network $SN = \,<E, A, R>$ the audience of this entity is symbolized as audience(e), the influence of the* *entity is written as* $influence(e)$ *and the maximal size of audience observed in* SN *is* $max\_audience$. *Then, the micro-influencer* m *can be formally described using the following formula:*

$$m \in E : \{max(influence(m)) \wedge d < audience(m) < D\} \tag{1}$$

where d and D are the adopted limits of the audience size that $0 < d < D$ and $D \ll max\_audience$ (much less than).

As mentioned, the exact boundary was deliberately left to be specified precisely according to the particular social network properties. Figure 1 illustrates the way micro-influencers place within a social network.

3.3 Influence Framework

In this section, we will briefly describe the model for influence evaluation, called ARIM, which we used as a base in order to obtain the influence values for discovered micro-influencers.

The model utilized here can be obviously changed to any other model that aims to evaluate and compute influence for each user in s social network, compliant with the definitions given in previous sections, and evaluates influence using quality measures. The choice of ARIM model is motivated by several reasons: (1) it bases on direct exchange of information between influencer and influencee (e.g. the act of posting content by influencer and reaction of influencee), which is easy to both observe and analyze, (2) it considers multiple possible types reactions on the content (post) such as upvotes or comments, hence it is flexible from the point of view of required data, (3) calculation of influence includes both influence quality (audience *engagement*) and quantity (*spread*). In order to fit the model for our purposes, we limited the calculation of influence solely to the quality aspect.

In order to introduce the model, let us assume that we want to calculate the influence for user u in a social network, who has performed multiple actions A (e.g. posting posts), and has a group of users RU that were reacting to these actions using different reactions types (e.g. upvoting and commenting posts). Without losing the generality, in this paper we assume three kinds of reactions: upvotes, comments and shares. We also limit the framework from [20] in order for the calculation of influence to be including engagement only (in comparison to original work that incorporates the audience size into the influence calculation as well). *Influence* for user u can be described using the formula:

$$Influence(u) = Engagement(u) \times fc(u) \tag{2}$$

where $Engagement(u)$ establishes the overall strength of users' involvement, which implies the influence strength. *Engagement* is defined as:

$$Engagement(u) = \frac{\sum_{i=1}^{|A|} PRI(u,i)}{|A|} \tag{3}$$

where A is the set of actions performed by user u and PRI is a metric which specifies how much, on average, appraisal (in the form of reactions) a post received, formally defined as:

$$PRI(u,a) = \frac{\sum_{ru=1}^{|RU(a)|} Strength(u,a,ru)}{|RU(a)|} \tag{4}$$

$RU(a)$ is the set of Reacting Users on the particular action a $(a \in A)$ and $Strength(u,a,ru)$ is described by the formula:

$$\begin{aligned}
Strength(u,a,ru) = w_1 * upvotes + w_2 * comments \\
+ w_3 * shares + w_4 * upvotes * comments \\
+ w_5 * upvotes * shares + w_6 * comments * shares \\
+ w_7 * upvotes * comments * shares
\end{aligned} \tag{5}$$

where $upvotes, comments, shares$ are the number of each of the reactions for each actor respectively and $w_1, \ldots, w_7$ are the weights that introduce additional hierarchy of the reactions.

The influence formula (Eq. 2) includes also the component that favors lower frequency of performing actions, called fc (frequency component), defined as:

$$fc(u) = e^{\frac{1}{|A|}} \tag{6}$$

where A is the set of actions performed by user u. This component for two users with equal spread and engagement, would favor the user that posts less.

Applying the above formulas enables the computation of the influence that is especially focused on engagement, while being simple and considering different reaction types. Utilizing such method is indispensable for discovery of micro-influencers.

4   Evaluation

In this section, we describe the experiments conducted using the method for discovery of micro-influencers detailed in Sect. 3 and utilizing the framework described in Sect. 3.3.

4.1   Experiments

The experiments were conducted in order to validate the proposed definition of micro-influencer and formalization of the term. Moreover, by using the framework compliant with the above-mentioned characterization of micro-influencers, we also want to verify if both of the conditions included in them are really the necessary and crutial ones.

The experiments were performed using two real datasets. The first consists of data from Facebook [24] containing information about posts and their comments (without the text content) with precise information about the time of each of action/reaction. The second dataset includes data from Pinterest [31], that contains repins (shares) and likes (upvotes). Table 1 presents the basic statistics about the both used datasets. The implementation was done using PostgreSQL[2] version 9.6 and R language[3] version 3.3.1.

Table 1. Statistics about used Facebook [24] and Pinterest [31] datasets

	Parameter	Number
Facebook	Number of users	1 067 026
	Number of users that reacted	23 426 682
	Number of posts	25 937 525
	Number of comments	104 364 591
	Time span of data	15/10/14–11/02/15
Pinterest	Number of users	1 307 527
	Number of users that reacted	8 314 067
	Number of posts	2 362 006
	Number of shares	37 087 685
	Number of upvotes	19 332 254
	Time span of data	03/01/13–21/01/13

In the experiments, we have applied the definition and the formalization of the micro-influencer term presented in Sect. 3. Firstly, we calculated the influence value using the limited version of ARIM framework, which gave the ranking for all users in the database. Then, we utilized the micro-influencer equation Eq. 1 with the limits $(d, D) = (100, 500)$. Importantly, in the experiments, for each user we identify the audience as the group of active users (i.e. users that commented or upvoted one's content).

As this is the first work dealing with micro-influencers, there are no comparable metrics. However, we did utilize PageRank method in order to show the key differences between standard state-of-the-art method applied with limits in order to try identifying micro-influencers and the application of our idea. The choice of the PageRank is twofold: firstly, the method is one of the most popular approaches utilized for calculating influence [28], and secondly, as PageRank targets the nodes with large audience, it should be seen that the usage of only the limits (thus, only utilizing one part of definition about audience size) is not sufficient enough to find the actual micro-influencers. We used weighted PageRank method with the reactions (comments, upvotes) as edges, directed from the user that performed reaction, and utilizing number of reactions (in-degree) as weights for the algorithm.

---

[2] https://www.postgresql.org/.
[3] https://www.r-project.org/.

4.2   Results

Facebook Dataset. The application of the limits $(d, D) = (100, 500)$ has led to selection of 79 389 users that have the audience of that size. The results of the experiment performed on the Facebook dataset [24] are shown in Table 2. In this table we can see the top twenty users in the order given utilizing the ranking from ARIM framework. In order to compare the results with the PageRank ranking, the columns *PR pos* and *PR val* present the ranking position (*PR pos*) and normalized PageRank influence value (*PR val*). Furthermore, Table 3 presents the results of top twenty users using PageRank, similarly compared with ARIM ranking position (*ARIM pos* and *ARIM val*). Normalized values were calculated using the minimal and maximal value for the overall rankings (including all users, not only micro-influencers). Both Tables 2 and 3 include user ids in Base-32 in order to safe space. Moreover, the opposite is also true: the high positioned users in PageRank have very low positions in ARIM ranking.

Table 2. Top 20 micro-influencers using ARIM method, compared with top users' position from PageRank for Facebook dataset [24]

User ID	ARIM pos	ARIM val	PR pos	PR val	Engagement	Audience size
11jh44w613qww	1	1	48262	0.001614	5.779887	118
15rfcd2cgpdds	2	0.502126	57692	0.001432	3.085694	133
eaa43njsf6yo	3	0.49617	73208	0.001014	3.053465	150
1scz2cw2buku8	4	0.489723	13858	0.002791	5.879393	314
-1anjuucz0wiyo	5	0.489336	56051	0.001465	3.016482	110
-1dtof2rg2vcow	6	0.480393	8654	0.003296	7.751748	192
x1nb85o7nif4	7	0.477513	65560	0.001256	2.952504	153
5fb51yi0w2v4	8	0.471037	9354	0.003209	2.917462	223
6mji7114m3gg	9	0.457631	75872	0.000879	2.844917	110
-edpabk3i4q9s	10	0.456656	28941	0.002075	2.83964	119
-1raq7kohfmeww	11	0.453498	78787	0.000492	2.822553	124
cvaxiriqapds	12	0.444122	44884	0.00168	2.771816	157
-1dwoa9vr4y1hc	13	0.422427	49006	0.001599	2.654413	108
-g4gbjzx0jif4	14	0.421442	14041	0.002778	4.367602	164
10vj1m2yomneo	15	0.419198	31837	0.001987	2.636937	114
-388wc65lggao	16	0.415836	76994	0.000793	2.618747	144
j5pvdoei10cg	17	0.406018	60214	0.001379	2.565618	104
-1xx9hmnsegd1c	18	0.387517	5770	0.003745	2.465503	336
-wkei8jiqc7pc	19	0.384298	75435	0.000906	2.44808	144
-1r3rhn6jhzuo	20	0.3831	46190	0.001654	2.441597	141

It can be clearly observed that the top micro-influencers of ARIM have extremely low positions in the PageRank rank. All of the top twenty users have the PageRank positions placed at a couple of thousands. The reason for such vast differentiation lies in the different focus of the methods. It can be seen that PageRank chooses the users with high spread value (large audience), while ARIM targets engagement. This is exactly this key difference that causes that the resulting PageRank users will indeed have a lot of users that will see the content shared, but will be less prone to react on it in any way. The contrary is true in the case of ARIM – the reach of audience might be smaller, but those are the users much higher involved in the things shared to them. As mentioned in Sect. 3, the main purpose behind finding micro-influencers is to find such users that, while they do not have vast spread, they highly impact their audience. Moreover, having a smaller audience can be additionally beneficial as the micro-influencer does have more time for replying and getting feedback from the audience.

Table 3. PageRank results for users with limited audience compared with their position from ARIM method for Facebook dataset [24]

User ID	PR posit	PR val	ARIM posit	ARIM val	Engagement	Audience size
-1jy1nmhvcdgcg	1	0.008702	33383	0.056201	1.49695	496
-qsiiojecsyyo	2	0.008427	31415	0.060834	1.150296	495
-fswnrkmo4yrk	3	0.008318	32253	0.058863	1.132718	486
198c8091cpdds	4	0.008241	44963	0.033605	1.453853	484
2gli1lt588hs	5	0.008147	41057	0.039427	1.338818	484
-4kx0785szx4w	6	0.008138	40971	0.039569	1.134784	464
-scejupm7ff9c	7	0.008093	37984	0.045554	1.576255	473
5a14f85mzdds	8	0.008069	12971	0.151025	1.185753	497
yxrki09k2cjk	9	0.007982	55313	0.022991	1.31333	494
-aymifid4w54w	10	0.007972	77495	0.006454	1.077537	470
1h5n33mesf9xc	11	0.007952	52250	0.025658	1.167382	496
-736jrswr4xvk	12	0.007946	38421	0.044526	1.187037	474
-egv4x59mhmv4	13	0.0079	6852	0.168751	1.281674	468
-1smwnk9u4zy80	14	0.007896	44255	0.034481	1.350198	478
-mdvxfedsgt8g	15	0.007895	71799	0.011508	1.116505	486
-15roml73v2ebk	16	0.007882	17224	0.14159	1.134692	467
o2xfdybxnthc	17	0.007865	57608	0.021221	1.27784	458
42w2131oqk74	18	0.007857	32391	0.058528	1.129727	454
-tmrw5uucvfuo	19	0.007848	62329	0.017793	1.095211	486
cuxc0d30szcw	20	0.007843	21281	0.131461	1.079881	492

Pinterest Dataset. In the experiment utilizing Pinterest dataset [31] the data comprised of both shares and upvotes of users. As we wanted to treat both of the reactions equally, we used equal weights for them. The limit application led to the selection of 90 438 users that make the criteria of audience size.

The outcome of the experiment using the Pinterest dataset is presented in Table 4. Analogically to results from Facebook, the table comprises of the top twenty users from ARIM framework compared with their position in PageRank ranking. Furthermore, Table 5 shows the top twenty users according to PageRank method compared with their positions from ARIM.

Table 4. Top 20 micro-influencers using ARIM method, compared with top users' position from PageRank for Pinterest dataset [31]

User ID	ARIM pos	ARIM val	PR pos	PR val	Engagement	Audience size
4328149	1	1	24767	0.000922	4	279
6097768	2	0.816224	5767	0.000185	3.333333	123
4637141	3	0.724336	48712	0.000492	3	249
3335628	4	0.724336	43040	0.000557	3	138
791721	5	0.724336	49399	0.000486	3	108
46382	6	0.619321	31436	0.000745	2.619048	110
337355	7	0.586504	3629	0.00204	2.5	315
620508	8	0.586504	54127	0.000441	2.5	153
12913341	9	0.586504	70954	0.000319	2.5	138
2629262	10	0.586504	67553	0.000341	2.5	125
2594225	11	0.586504	910	0.00021	2.5	103
33209	12	0.586504	87241	0.000231	2.5	124
205024	13	0.586504	11101	0.000156	2.5	110
4307526	14	0.586504	82371	0.000256	2.5	156
213980	15	0.558938	71066	0.000319	2.4	145
863299	16	0.547124	35723	0.000665	2.357143	185
2729817	17	0.54056	24814	0.00092	2.333333	290
504295	18	0.54056	62105	0.000378	2.333333	289
559898	19	0.54056	56604	0.00042	2.333333	261

The results, similarly to the one from Facebook dataset, show the vast difference between the top twenty list from ARIM framework, that considers both limitation of audience and the high engagement properties included in definition from Sect. 3, and the outcome of PageRank that follows presented the definition only partially, by using the limited audience. All the micro-influencers that are selected by ARIM have very low positions in PageRank ranking. Similarly, the PageRank top users are at the end of the micro-influencers list from

ARIM. Again, this shows the incapability of PageRank to select users with higher engagement, as the method uses limits for audience size. In comparison, ARIM selects users lower in the audience size, but having involvement of much higher rate. This shows the importance of two key points of the definition proposed in previous section. While the limitation of the audience is definitely a necessary condition for finding micro-influencers, it is not sufficient. Indeed, the real micro-influencer can be found only with the second condition involving the high engagement rate, for a user with limited audience size.

Table 5. PageRank results for users with limited audience compared with their position from ARIM method for Pinterest dataset [31]

User ID	PR pos	PR value	ARIM pos	ARIM value	Engagement	Audience size
7055243	1	0.000215	27004	0.241924	1.25	108
14340460	2	0.000215	40098	0.173008	1	168
6729025	3	0.000215	68993	0.120276	1.333333	155
1671014	4	0.000215	85585	0.038875	1	113
25821272	5	0.000215	48618	0.173008	1	101
15596641	6	0.000215	85630	0.038875	1	111
133874	7	0.000215	20829	0.264896	1.333333	118
3313897	8	0.000215	46661	0.173008	1	110
2925429	9	0.000215	56691	0.173008	1	117
15852983	10	0.000215	48724	0.173008	1	101
1368298	11	0.000215	45805	0.173008	1	114
2370736	12	0.002224	35196	0.173008	1	468
8517079	13	0.000215	83280	0.057082	1.333333	128
7495086	14	0.000215	47968	0.173008	1	104
21421	15	0.002224	10147	0.303586	1.473684	223
299640	16	0.000215	68407	0.127243	1.375	104
188893	17	0.000215	65674	0.173008	1	140
48052601	18	0.000215	52579	0.173008	1	183
7114546	19	0.000215	61556	0.173008	1	138
8258324	20	0.000215	64424	0.173008	1	126

5 Conclusion

In this paper, we have dealt with the novel issue of finding micro-influencers. We have presented definition of the notion of micro-influencer within Social Network Analysis. We have also proposed the formalization of the term, specifying the conditions for the methods for micro-influencers discovery. The definition includes two necessary conditions for finding micro-influencers, namely limited audience (1) with high engagement (2). We have performed experiments on two real-world datasets including data from two well-known social network sites, namely Facebook and Pinterest. In those experiments, we have used the ARIM framework which was compliant to the conditions presented in the formalization and definition, and compared the obtained results with the state-of-the-art method PageRank. The results show the adequacy of the proposed approach for finding micro-influencers. They also affirm the necessity of the two above-mentioned conditions, that are essential in order to locate the real-value micro-influencers, that can be used for real life applications e.g. in advertisement.

As future work, we intend to investigate further the issue of micro-influencers, focusing on their trends. This could lead to the possibility of not only finding the micro-influencers in offline dataset, but also to predict the users that have the potential to develop. Such approach could possibly help to discover and target micro-influencers that have potential of being a much bigger influencer in the future.

References

1. How brands can reach new audiences with micro-influencers. http://markerly.com/blog/instagram-marketing-does-influencer-size-matter/. Accessed 13 July 2018
2. Influenster. https://hwww.influenster.com/disclosure. Accessed 12 July 2018
3. Takumi branded instagram creative at scale. https://takumi.com/. Accessed 12 July 2018
4. Tribe influencer marketing martekplace. https://www.tribegroup.co/. Accessed 12 July 2018
5. Aleahmad, A., Karisani, P., Rahgozar, M., Oroumchian, F.: OLFinder: finding opinion leaders in online social networks. J. Inf. Sci. **42**(5), 659–674 (2016)
6. Côté, I.M., Darling, E.S.: Scientists on Twitter: preaching to the choir or singing from the rooftops? FACETS **3**(1), 682–694 (2018). https://doi.org/10.1139/facets-2018-0002
7. Ding, Z.Y., Jia, Y., Zhou, B., Han, Y., He, L., Zhang, J.F.: Measuring the spreadability of users in microblogs. J. Zhejiang Univ. Sci. C **14**(9), 701–710 (2013)
8. Gee, R.: Top 20 celebrity endorsers: the rise of the influencer. Marketing Week. https://www.marketingweek.com/2017/01/24/top-20-endorsers-2016/. Accessed 12 July 2018
9. Ben Jabeur, L., Tamine, L., Boughanem, M.: Active microbloggers: identifying influencers, leaders and discussers in microblogging networks. In: Calderón-Benavides, L., González-Caro, C., Chávez, E., Ziviani, N. (eds.) SPIRE 2012. LNCS, vol. 7608, pp. 111–117. Springer, Heidelberg (2012). https://doi.org/10.1007/978-3-642-34109-0_12

10. Jendoubi, S., Martin, A., Liétard, L., Hadji, H.B., Yaghlane, B.B.: Two evidential data based models for influence maximization in Twitter. Knowl.-Based Syst. **121**, 58–70 (2017)
11. Jiang, W., Wang, G., Bhuiyan, M.Z.A., Wu, J.: Understanding graph-based trust evaluation in online social networks: methodologies and challenges. ACM Comput. Surv. (CSUR) **49**(1), 10 (2016)
12. Kempe, D., Kleinberg, J.M., Tardos, É.: Maximizing the spread of influence through a social network. Theor. Comput. **11**(4), 105–147 (2015)
13. Kitsak, M., et al.: Identification of influential spreaders in complex networks. arXiv preprint arXiv:1001.5285 (2010)
14. Lin, H.C., Bruning, P.F., Swarna, H.: Using online opinion leaders to promote the hedonic and utilitarian value of products and services. Bus. Horiz. **61**(3), 431–442 (2018)
15. Muuga, E.: How to find instagram influencers in your niche (by using data). https://www.magimetrics.com/guides.html/find-instagram-influencers/. Accessed 13 July 2018
16. Myers, S.A., Zhu, C., Leskovec, J.: Information diffusion and external influence in networks. In: Proceedings of the 18th ACM SIGKDD International Conference on Knowledge Discovery and Data Mining, pp. 33–41. ACM (2012)
17. Nagmoti, R., Teredesai, A., De Cock, M.: Ranking approaches for microblog search. In: Proceedings of the 2010 IEEE/WIC/ACM International Conference on Web Intelligence and Intelligent Agent Technology-Volume 01, pp. 153–157. IEEE Computer Society (2010)
18. Ohsaka, N., Akiba, T., Yoshida, Y., Kawarabayashi, K.I.: Dynamic influence analysis in evolving networks. Proc. VLDB Endow. **9**(12), 1077–1088 (2016)
19. Page, L., Brin, S., Motwani, R., Winograd, T.: The PageRank citation ranking: bringing order to the web. Technical report, Stanford InfoLab (1999)
20. Rakoczy, M., Bouzeghoub, A., Lopes, A.G., Wegrzyn-Wolska, K.: Technical Report: Influence Model Based on Actions and Reactions in Social Networks, August 2018. https://hal.archives-ouvertes.fr/hal-01865770
21. Rakoczy, M., Bouzeghoub, A., Wegrzyn-Wolska, K., Gancarski Lopes, A.: Users views on others - analysis of confused relation-based terms in social network. In: Debruyne, C., et al. (eds.) OTM 2016. LNCS, vol. 10033, pp. 155–174. Springer, Cham (2016). https://doi.org/10.1007/978-3-319-48472-3_9
22. Rashotte, L.: Blackwell Encyclopedia of Sociology Online: Influence. http://www.sociologyencyclopedia.com/fragr_image/media/social. Accessed 27 Apr 2016
23. Riquelme, F., González-Cantergiani, P.: Measuring user influence on Twitter: a survey. Inf. Process. Manag. **52**(5), 949–975 (2016)
24. Spasojevic, N., Li, Z., Rao, A., Bhattacharyya, P.: When-to-post on social networks. In: Proceedings of the 21th ACM SIGKDD International Conference on Knowledge Discovery and Data Mining, pp. 2127–2136. ACM (2015)
25. Tantipathananandh, C., Berger-Wolf, T.Y.: Finding communities in dynamic social networks. In: 2011 IEEE 11th International Conference on Data Mining (ICDM), pp. 1236–1241. IEEE (2011)
26. Mediakix Team: What are "micro influencers"? definition & examples. http://mediakix.com/2017/07/what-are-micro-influencers/. Accessed 13 July 2018
27. Wissman, B.: Micro-influencers: the marketing force of the future? Forbes. https://www.forbes.com/sites/barrettwissman/2018/03/02/micro-influencers-the-marketing-force-of-the-future/. Accessed 13 July 2018
28. Wu, X., et al.: Top 10 algorithms in data mining. Knowl. Inf. Syst. **14**(1), 1–37 (2008)

29. Zafarani, R., Abbasi, M.A., Liu, H.: Social Media Mining: An Introduction. Cambridge University Press, Cambridge (2014)
30. Zhang, Y., Li, X., Wang, T.W.: Identifying influencers in online social networks: the role of tie strength. Int. J. Intell. Inf. Technol. (IJIIT) **9**(1), 1–20 (2013)
31. Zhong, C., Shah, S., Sundaravadivelan, K., Sastry, N.: Sharing the loves: understanding the how and why of online content curation. In: 7th International AAAI Conference on Weblogs and Social Media (ICWSM13), Boston, US, July 2013

Execution of Multi-perspective Declarative Process Models

Lars Ackermann, Stefan Schönig$^{(\boxtimes)}$, Sebastian Petter, Nicolai Schützenmeier, and Stefan Jablonski

University of Bayreuth, Bayreuth, Germany
{lars.ackermann,stefan.schoenig,sebastian.petter,
nicolai.schuetzenmeier,stefan.jablonski}@uni-bayreuth.de

Abstract. A Process-Aware Information System is a system that executes processes involving people, applications, and data on the basis of process models. At least two process modeling paradigms can be distinguished: procedural models define exactly the execution order of process steps. Declarative process models allow flexible process executions that are restricted by constraints. Execution engines for declarative process models have been extensively investigated in research with a strong focus on behavioral aspects. However, execution approaches for *multi-perspective* declarative models that involve constraints on data values and resource assignments are still not existing. In this paper, we present an approach for the execution of multi-perspective declarative process models in order to close this gap. The approach builds on a classification strategy for different constraint types evaluating their relevance in different execution contexts. For execution, all constraints are transformed into the execution language *Alloy* that is used to solve satisfiability (SAT) problems. We implemented a modeling tool including the transformation functionality and the process execution engine itself. The approach has been evaluated in terms of expressiveness and efficiency.

Keywords: Processes execution · Declarative modeling
Multi-perspective

1 Introduction

A Process-Aware Information System is a collaborative system that executes processes involving people, applications, and data on the basis of process models. Two different paradigms can be distinguished: *(i)* procedural models describe the execution paths in a graph-based structure, *(ii)* declarative models consist of temporal constraints that a process must satisfy. Declarative languages like Declare [1], DCR graphs [2] and Declarative Process Intermediate Language (DPIL) [3,4] have been proposed to define the latter.

Declarative models represent processes by restrictions over the permissible behaviour. The restricting rules are named constraints, which express those conditions that must be satisfied throughout process execution. Modelling languages

© Springer Nature Switzerland AG 2018
H. Panetto et al. (Eds.): OTM 2018 Conferences, LNCS 11230, pp. 154–172, 2018.
https://doi.org/10.1007/978-3-030-02671-4_9

like Declare [1] provide a repertoire of templates, i.e., constraints parametrised over activities. Execution engines for declarative process models have been extensively investigated in research with a strong focus on behavioral aspects.

A central shortcoming of languages like Declare is the fact that constraints are not capable of expressing the connection between the behaviour and other perspectives of the process. Behavior can be intertwined with dependencies upon value ranges of data parameters and resource characteristics [5,6]. Therefore, Declare has been extended towards Multi-Perspective Declare (*MP-Declare*) [7]. However, yet to date, an execution approach for MP-Declare models that involves constraints on data values and resource assignments has not yet been devised.

To overcome these issues, we introduce an approach for the execution of MP-Declare models that builds on a classification strategy for different constraint types evaluating their relevance in different execution contexts. For execution, all constraints are transformed into the execution language Alloy that is used to solve satisfiability (SAT) problems. We implemented a modeling tool including the transformation functionality and the process execution engine. The approach has been evaluated in terms of expressiveness and efficiency. Screencasts as well as the implementation itself are accessible online at http://mpd.kppq.de.

The remainder of this paper is structured as follows: Sect. 2 introduces fundamentals of multi-perspective declarative process modelling and execution as well as the Alloy language. In Sect. 3 we describe our approach for executing MP-Declare process models. In Sect. 4 we discuss the implementation of our approach as well as the evaluation. Sect. 5 gives an overview of related work and Sect. 6 concludes the paper.

2 Background

In this section, we describe fundamentals of declarative process modelling, process execution, and the Alloy language.

2.1 Multi-perspective, Declarative Process Modeling

Declarative constraints are strong in representing the permissible behavior of business processes. Modeling languages like Declare [8] describe a set of *constraints* that must be satisfied throughout the process execution. Constraints, in turn, are instances of predefined *templates*. Templates, in turn, are patterns that define parameterized classes of properties. Their semantics can be formalized using formal logics such as Linear Temporal Logic over finite traces (LTL$_f$) [9].

A central shortcoming of languages like Declare is the fact that templates are not directly capable of expressing the connection between the behavior and other perspectives of the process. Consider the example of a loan application process. The process modeller would like to define constraints such as the following:

1. Activation conditions: When a loan is requested and *account balance > 4,000 EUR*, the loan must subsequently be granted.

2. Correlation conditions: When a loan is requested, the loan must subsequently be granted and *amount requested = amount granted*.
3. Target conditions: When a loan is requested, the loan must subsequently be granted by a specific member of the financial board.
4. Temporal conditions: When a loan is requested, the loan must subsequently be granted *within the next 30 days*

Standard Declare only supports constraints that relates activities without considering other process perspectives. Here, the **F**, **X**, **G**, and **U** LTL$_f$ future operators have the following meanings: formula $\mathbf{F}\psi_1$ means that ψ_1 holds sometime in the future, $\mathbf{X}\psi_1$ means that ψ_1 holds in the next position, $\mathbf{G}\psi_1$ says that ψ_1 holds forever in the future, and, lastly, $\psi_1\mathbf{U}\psi_2$ means that sometime in the future ψ_2 will hold and until that moment ψ_1 holds (with ψ_1 and ψ_2 LTL$_f$ formulas). The **O**, **Y** and **S** LTL$_f$ past operators have the following meaning: $\mathbf{O}\psi_1$ means that ψ_1 holds sometime in the past, $\mathbf{Y}\psi_1$ means that ψ_1 holds in the previous position, and $\psi_1\mathbf{S}\psi_2$ means that ψ_1 has held sometime in the past and since that moment ψ_2 holds.

Consider, e.g., the *response* constraint $\mathbf{G}(A \rightarrow \mathbf{F}B)$. It indicates that if A *occurs*, B must eventually *follow*. Therefore, this constraint is fully satisfied in traces such as $\mathbf{t}_1 = \langle A, A, B, C \rangle$, $\mathbf{t}_2 = \langle B, B, C, D \rangle$, and $\mathbf{t}_3 = \langle A, B, C, B \rangle$, but not for $\mathbf{t}_4 = \langle A, B, A, C \rangle$ because the second occurrence of A is not followed by a B. In $\mathbf{t}_2$, it is *vacuously satisfied* [10], in a trivial way, because A never occurs.

An *activation activity* of a constraint in a trace is an activity whose execution imposes, because of that constraint, some obligations on the execution of other activities (target activities) in the same trace (see Table 1). For example, A is an activation activity for the *response* constraint $\mathbf{G}(A \rightarrow \mathbf{F}B)$ and B is a target, because the execution of A forces B to be executed, eventually. An activation of a constraint leads to a *fulfillment* or to a *violation*. Consider, again, $\mathbf{G}(A \rightarrow \mathbf{F}B)$. In trace $\mathbf{t}_1$, the constraint is activated and fulfilled twice, whereas, in trace $\mathbf{t}_3$, it is activated and fulfilled only once. In trace $\mathbf{t}_4$, it is activated twice and the second activation leads to a violation (B does not occur subsequently).

The importance of multi-perspective dependencies led to the definition of a multi-perspective version of Declare (MP-Declare) [7]. Its semantics build on the notion of *payload* of an event. $e(activity)$ identifies the occurrence of an event in order to distinguish it from the activity name. At the time of a certain event e, its attributes $x_1, \ldots, x_m$ have certain values. $p^e_{activity} = (val_{x1}, \ldots, val_{xn})$ represents its payload. To denote the projection of the payload $p^e_A = (x_1, \ldots, x_n)$ over attributes $x_1, \ldots, x_m$ with $m \leqslant n$, the notation $p^e_A[x_1, \ldots, x_m]$ is used. For instance, $p^e_{ApplyForTrip}[Resource] = \mathrm{SS}$ is the projection of the attribute *Resource* in the event description. Furthermore, the n-ples of attributes x_i are represented as $\boldsymbol{x}$. Therefore, the templates in MP-Declare extend standard Declare with additional conditions on event attributes. Specifically, given the events $e(A)$ and $e(B)$ with payloads $p^e_A = (x_1, \ldots, x_n)$ and $p^e_B = (y_1, \ldots, y_n)$, the *activation condition* φ_a, the *correlation condition* φ_c, and the *target condition* φ_t are defined. The activation condition is part of the activation ϕ_a, whilst the correlation and target conditions are part of the target ϕ_t, according to their respective time of

Table 1. Semantics for MP-Declare constraints in LTL$_f$.

Bin	Template	LTL$_f$ Semantics
II	existence	$\top \rightarrow \mathbf{F}(e(A) \wedge \varphi_a(x)) \vee \mathbf{O}(e(A) \wedge \varphi_a(x))$
II	responded existence	$\mathbf{G}((A \wedge \varphi_a(x)) \rightarrow (\mathbf{O}(B \wedge \varphi_c(x,y) \wedge \varphi_t(y)) \vee \mathbf{F}(B \wedge \varphi_c(x,y) \wedge \varphi_t(y))))$
II	response	$\mathbf{G}((A \wedge \varphi_a(x)) \rightarrow \mathbf{F}(B \wedge \varphi_c(x,y) \wedge \varphi_t(y)))$
I	alternate response	$\mathbf{G}((A \wedge \varphi_a(x)) \rightarrow \mathbf{X}(\neg(A \wedge \varphi_a(x)) \mathbf{U}(B \wedge \varphi_c(x,y) \wedge \varphi_t(y)))$
I	chain response	$\mathbf{G}((A \wedge \varphi_a(x)) \rightarrow \mathbf{X}(B \wedge \varphi_c(x,y) \wedge \varphi_t(y)))$
III	precedence	$\mathbf{G}((B \wedge \varphi_a(x)) \rightarrow \mathbf{O}(A \wedge \varphi_c(x,y) \wedge \varphi_t(y)))$
III	alternate precedence	$\mathbf{G}((B \wedge \varphi_a(x)) \rightarrow \mathbf{Y}(\neg(B \wedge \varphi_a(x)) \mathbf{S}(A \wedge \varphi_c(x,y) \wedge \varphi_t(y)))$
III	chain precedence	$\mathbf{G}((B \wedge \varphi_a(x)) \rightarrow \mathbf{Y}(A \wedge \varphi_c(x,y) \wedge \varphi_t(y)))$
III	not responded existence	$\mathbf{G}((A \wedge \varphi_a(x)) \rightarrow \neg(\mathbf{O}(B \wedge \varphi_c(x,y) \wedge \varphi_t(y)) \vee \mathbf{F}(B \wedge \varphi_c(x,y) \wedge \varphi_t(y))))$
III	not response	$\mathbf{G}((A \wedge \varphi_a(x)) \rightarrow \neg \mathbf{F}(B \wedge \varphi_c(x,y) \wedge \varphi_t(y)))$
III	not precedence	$\mathbf{G}((B \wedge \varphi_a(x)) \rightarrow \neg \mathbf{O}(A \wedge \varphi_c(x,y) \wedge \varphi_t(y)))$
III	not chain response	$\mathbf{G}((A \wedge \varphi_a(x)) \rightarrow \neg \mathbf{X}(B \wedge \varphi_c(x,y) \wedge \varphi_t(y)))$
III	not chain precedence	$\mathbf{G}((B \wedge \varphi_a(x)) \rightarrow \neg \mathbf{Y}(A \wedge \varphi_c(x,y) \wedge \varphi_t(y)))$

evaluation. The *activation* condition is a statement that must be valid when the activation occurs. In the case of the *response* template, the activation condition has the form $\varphi_a(x_1, \ldots, x_n)$, meaning that the proposition φ_a over $(x_1, \ldots, x_n)$ must hold true. The *correlation* condition is a statement that must be valid when the target occurs, and it relates the values of the attributes in the payloads of the activation and the target event. It has the form $\varphi_c(x_1, \ldots, x_m, y_1, \ldots, y_m)$ with $m \leqslant n$, where φ_c is a propositional formula on the variables of both the payload of $e(A)$ and the payload of $e(B)$. *Target* conditions exert limitations on the values of the attributes that are registered at the moment wherein the target activity occurs. They have the form $\varphi_t(y_1, \ldots, y_m)$ with $m \leqslant n$, where φ_t is a propositional formula involving variables in the payload of $e(B)$.

2.2   Process Execution

Process models are, among others, a valuable resource for the configuration of enterprises' *information systems* in order to align information flows with the underlying business process and to control the latter. Controlling a process involves the management of process entities (e.g. resources, activities, data) according to the determinations contained in the process model. Thus, *process-aware* information systems are built upon a *process execution engine* which is in charge of interpreting the process model to distinguish valid from invalid process actions and states. By performing a process activity the current state of a process is transformed into a new state. However, performing an activity usually takes time and, therefore, is considered a subprocess called *activity life-cycle*. For the paper at hand we assume a simplified activity life-cycle model shown in Fig. 1 (blue parts). However, the execution principle discussed in Sect. 3.1 is also able to support additional process states and actions (gray parts).

Independently from any particular activity life-cycle it is essential that a process execution engine is aware of whether the whole process instance can be terminated. In Fig. 1 this action is called *case completion*. Regarding the

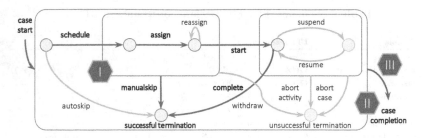

Fig. 1. Activity life-cycle model (based on [11]) (Color figure online)

activity life-cycle (Fig. 1) *scheduling* an activity means planning its execution. Afterwards the activity is *assigned* to a resource which means that it is added to its work list. Later the particular resource *starts* the activity. After some time the started activity completes. Activities that are scheduled but never assigned are considered *manually skipped*. Additionally the execution principle proposed in Sect. 3.1 is based on three assumptions: *(i)* An activity is *automatically* scheduled if the process model currently allows its execution, *(ii)* activities are assigned to resources by themselves through a claiming step, and *(iii)* a process instance is completed manually. Consequently, an execution system has to be able to answer the following questions for an arbitrary process state:

Q1. Can the current process instance be completed *(case completion)*?
Q2. Which activities can proceed in their individual life-cycle *(schedule, assign, start, complete)*?

In order to answer these questions a process execution engine needs access to the current process execution state – called *trace* from now on – and has to be able to evaluate a process model with respect to this state. For reasons of conciseness we introduce the definition of a trace only informally. According to the literature (e.g. [11, pp. 134–137]) a trace is a sequence of *events* whereby each event is an unordered set of key-value pairs that are called attributes and one pair uniquely identifies the event within one trace. Some further default attributes are the activity name, the life-cycle action that triggered the event and a timestamp stating when the event happened. This means that an event always refers to a particular activity. Potential additional attributes are the performing resource and a snapshot of all process variables and their current value allocation.

Imperative process models describe possible traces explicitly by means of step-by-step flow descriptions. Hence, for process execution it is possible to "navigate" through an imperative process model to the next possible process actions and states. However, this principle cannot be applied to declarative process models since they do not encode traces explicitly. Instead *all* traces are treated as valid unless they violate any rule contained in the process model. Thus, this enables us to transform the execution task for declarative process models into a *conformance checking* task that evaluates whether a given trace conforms to the declarative process model that is executed. However, this checking task still has to be aligned with the activity life-cycle that assumes an existing execution semantics for each process rule. Since current descriptions of MP-Declare lack a definition of its execution semantics the paper at hand suggests a possible solution based on a logic language and evaluation engine called *Alloy*.

2.3 Alloy

Alloy is a declarative language for building models that describe structures with respect to desired restrictions. It is used as a process execution language for the approach discussed in Sect. 3.1 and, thus, we have to summarize Alloy's basic language features. Signatures (*sig*) are similar to classes in object-oriented programming languages (OOPLs). They can be abstract and quantified. A *fact* is comparable to *invariants* in the *Object Constraint Language (OCL)* [12] and allows for specifying non-structural constraints like mutual exclusion. A function (*fun*) is a parameterizable snippet of re-usable code, that has a return type and performs computations based on the given parameter values. A predicate (*pred*) is a function with a boolean return value. A major difference to functions is that Alloy is able to *run* a predicate, which means that a SAT solving algorithm searches for instances of the Alloy specification for which the particular predicate holds. For further information about the Alloy syntax we would like to refer to the dedicated literature [13] as well as the included vivid tutorials.

For the approach discussed in Sect. 3.1 the Alloy framework is used threefold: *(i)* Its capabilities for modeling structures is used to define a trace meta-model, *(ii)* MP-Declare models are translated into a set of signatures (process entities), predicates (rule templates) and facts (process rules) and *(iii)* allowed actions during process execution are determined by applying the SAT solving functionality on the combination a given trace and the translated process model.

3   Execution Approach for MP-Declare Models

Our main contribution section starts by formulating a set of challenges an execution engine for multi-perspective declarative process models has to deal with (Sect. 3.1). Afterwards an execution principle based on rule binning is described that solves a portion of these challenges. Afterwards we describe an Alloy-based meta-model for process execution *traces* that can be used to represent process execution *states* (Sect. 3.2). By introducing a mapping from MP-Declare and user-system interactions to Alloy (Sects. 3.3 and 3.4) we enable the latter's deduction capabilities to answer the two central questions introduced in Sect. 2.2.

3.1   Execution Principle

Executing declarative process models can be treated as a conformance checking task (Sect. 2.2) leading to the insight whether a trace conforms to the given process model or not. However, in order to answer the two central questions

(Sect. 2.2) whether a process instance can be completed (Q1) or which activities may continue regarding their individual life-cycle (Q2) the trace has to be treated differently. Evaluating declarative process models in order to answer question Q1 means treating the current trace as completed and checking if all rules are fulfilled. Question Q2 requires extending the current trace with candidates for a subsequent event that represents the next life-cycle-dependent action and checking whether this action conforms to all rules. In the following the major challenges for both evaluation contexts are emphasized.

Challenges. The main challenge in checking the conformance of a partial trace regarding some model are *temporarily invalid traces*. Let us assume an exemplary model only consisting of three activities (A, B and C) and a rule without any activation, target or correlation condition response(A,B) (Table 1). Furthermore, a current process state showing that only activity A has been executed so far. Based on this example it would be valid to execute C within the next step. However, running any conformance checking function (the trace is now $\langle A, C \rangle$) leads to the false result that executing C is invalid since it violates the given response rule. The reason is that at this point in time just checking the conformance between the trace and the single rule ignores the fact that the process instance is still running and, thus, the trace is incomplete. The response rule only demands that after A was executed *eventually* B has to be executed, too. Thus, a trace like $\langle A, C, B \rangle$ would be valid and, consequently, an incomplete trace – like $\langle A, C \rangle$ has to be treated as *temporarily valid* and must not block any subsequent actions except the *termination* of the current process instance. On the other hand side it is never necessary to check rules like precedence in order to determine whether the process instance can be completed. The reason is that this constraint – and others too – only formulate *pre-conditions* for further events in the trace but since events always refer to activity-life-cycle actions (Sect. 2.2) this rule type does not have any impact on issue of process instance completion. This suggests the development of a rule binning and execution strategy.

A second challenge refers to particular rules, namely chainResponse and chainPrecedence (Table 1). According to the corresponding LTL_f formulae these rule templates restrict two immediately adjacent events. chainResponse (A,B) requires that after A was executed B has to be executed "immediately" afterwards. However, due to the original definition of MP-Declare A and B are activity life-cycle events instead of atomic activities. This leads to the issue that the notion of the mentioned two rule templates has to be refined regarding their usage in the modeling phase. chainResponse(complete(A),complete(B) is – though an intuitive approach – a trivially false rule since before completing activity B it has to be scheduled, assigned, and started. Consequently, in order to consider the activity life-cycle the rule template has to be extended. We suggest the following form: $\mathbf{G}((A \wedge \varphi_a(x)) \rightarrow \mathbf{X}(\neg event(\neg B)\mathbf{U}complete(B) \wedge \varphi_c(x, y) \wedge \varphi_t(y)))$. Here *event* is a placeholder for any life-cycle action that expresses the desired meaning which we cannot determine universally. Hence, this challenge must not be treated by the approach discussed below but rather by the modeling expert. However, for the prototypical implementation we assume a conjunction of all life-cycle events according to the original meaning of chainResponse to block all actions except the execution of a particular subsequent activity.

Rule Binning and Execution Strategy. The challenge of temporarily invalid traces can be solved using a *rule binning strategy* which constitutes one of the major conceptual contributions of the paper at hand. This strategy is based on the idea that MP-Declare rule templates can be classified regarding their *impact* on the life-cycle actions of process activities (Fig. 1). Considering the example above the response rule template is, for instance, irrelevant with respect to activity scheduling. Consequently, this rule template belongs to the "bin" that is ignored when determining the activities that can be scheduled for execution. Other rule types are irrelevant for activity assignment, start, complete or the termination of the whole process instance. Hence, the challenge is to determine criteria for evaluating the rule relevance for each of these actions.

For our *execution strategy* we define three bins which are already included in Table 1. The first bin (I) contains all the constraints that have to be checked during the activity life-cycle as well as at the completion of the process. One representative of this bin is the chainResponse constraint because it restricts the next event and, thus, has to be checked if we want to complete the process and if we desire to proceed with a particular activity. The second bin (II) contains all the constraints which must solely be checked when the instance is to be completed. One constraint that belongs to this bin is the existence constraint. It does not have any influence on other activities that might be running at the moment but it covers restrictions for finalized traces. The third bin (III) contains all the rules that only have to be checked during the activity life-cycle. For example all the constraints that start with a negation (¬) on the right hand side of the implication arrow belong to this bin because these constraints solely exclude particular activity-related events based on the current trace. The formal bin determination for all constraints is shown in Fig. 2.

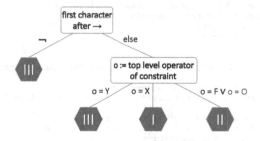

Fig. 2. Binning strategy for MP-Declare rule templates

3.2   Representing Execution Traces in Alloy

As discussed in the previous section we describe the state of a running process execution by means of a process execution trace. Since Alloy is utilized as the execution language, it is necessary to be able to represent a trace in Alloy. Hence, the subsequent sections describe an Alloy-based trace meta-model (Listing 1.1) and its usage in the execution context described in Sect. 3.1.

The trace meta-model shown in Listing 1.1 has been adapted from a previous version [14]. Concerning this the differences are a simplified set of constraints to organize traces as gapless chains of events and an extension of the Alloy representation for data objects and values. Furthermore it has been extended (Listing 1.2) in order to support the activity life-cycle (Fig. 1).

In order to keep the meta-model concise and reusable, the trace meta-model first imports three general modules: commons, orgMM and util/integer. The first only consists of a single signature called AssociatedElement that is used in the remaining two modules. To be able to model organizational structures, we make use of the Alloy representation of the organizational meta-model already proposed in [15] that has already been proposed in [14]. It adds the ability to assign resources (Identity) to events, to build arbitrary organizational structures and to formulate rules that consider properties and relations of organizational units. The module util/integer provides basic arithmetic operations like addition (sum) and some constants, especially the lowest and the highest available integer (integer/min and integer/max).

The meta-model itself consists of three parts, i.e. signatures that describe the events, facts that arrange the events in a gapless chain and a set of utility functions that are mainly queries to retrieve trace contents.

```
   open commons
2  open orgMM
   open util/integer
4
   // Signatures: Events and event contents
6  abstract sig PEvent { pos: disj Int }
   abstract sig TaskEvent extends PEvent{
8      assoEl: some AssociatedElement
   }{ #(Task ∩ assoEl) = 1 }
10 sig HumanTaskEvent extends TaskEvent {}{
       #(Identity ∩ assoEl) = 1 }
12
   abstract sig Task extends AssociatedElement{}
14 abstract sig DataObject {}
   abstract sig VariableObject extends DataObject{}
16 abstract sig WriteAccess extends AssociatedElement{
       data: one VariableObject,
18     value: one (Int + String)
   }
20
   // Facts/Invariants: Trace structure, non-structural constraints
22 fact{
       one te: TaskEvent | te.pos = integer/min
24     ∀ te: TaskEvent | te.pos = integer/min or sub[te.pos,1] in TaskEvent.pos
   }
26 fact { ∀ da: WriteAccess | da in TaskEvent.assoEl }
   fact { ∀ te: TaskEvent, wa1, wa2: WriteAccess |  wa1 ≠ wa2 and #(te.assoEl ∩ wa1 ∩
       wa2) > 1 → wa1.data ≠ wa2.data }
28
   // Utility Functions
30 fun inBefore(currentEvent: TaskEvent, asso: AssociatedElement) : set TaskEvent {
       { hte: TaskEvent | hte.pos < currentEvent.pos and asso in hte.assoEl }
32 }
   // further utility functions: inAfter, inBetween, any, atPos, vAtPos
```

Listing 1.1: Meta-model for traces

An event can, for instance, be the execution of an activity by a human performer. In order to represent these information in Alloy, the abstract signatures `PEvent` and `TaskEvent` as well as the signature `HumanTaskEvent` are introduced. `PEvent` just contains its unique position within the trace. `TaskEvent` inherits this property and adds at least one instance of the `AssociatedElement` signature. This must be a `Task`, a signature that is used to represent process activities. `HumanTaskEvent` extends `TaskEvent` and adds a human performer to each of its instances. In order to keep the description of the meta-model concise, we omit further event types since they do not add any conceptual value to the approach. The signatures `DataObject`, `VariableObject` and `WriteAccess` provide the functionality for representing value assignments to variables within events. A data object can be, for instance, a document that can be named by extending it or variables (`VariableObject`) that form the payload discussed in Sect. 2.1. A `WriteAccess` that contains a field which refers to a variable and a field for its assigned value that can be either an integer or a character sequence.

The first fact in Listing 1.1 restricts possible solutions to a gapless chain of events through restricting their indexes to consecutive numbers. The two subsequent facts stipulate that variable values are observed only as snapshots within events (`WriteAccess`) which conforms to the MP-Declare semantics (Sect. 2.1).

As we know from Sect. 2.1 most of the MP-Declare rule templates focus either on restricting previous or future occurrences based on a given trace. Consequently, we define some Alloy functions to provide a reusable set of trace query templates that keep the transformed MP-Declare rules concise. The function `any` selects all events with a given attribute key-value combination. The same holds for the functions `inBefore` and `inAfter` but the selected set of events is reduced to those that occur *before* or *after* a given event. All subsequently mentioned functions[1] complement the set of event selectors to cover all possible event locations within a trace. As an exception `vAtPos` determines a write action of a specific variable, with a given value and within an event at a specific position.

```
    one sig LC {
2       assigned: set TaskEvent,
        started: set TaskEvent,
4       completed: set TaskEvent
    }
6   fact {
        #(LC.assigned + LC.started + LC.completed) = #TaskEvent
8       #(LC.assigned ∩ LC.started) = 0 and #(LC.started ∩ LC.completed) = 0 and #(LC.
            assigned ∩ LC.completed) = 0
        ∀ te: TaskEvent | te in LC.started → #(inBefore[te,(te.assoEl ∩ Task)] ∩ LC.
            assigned) > #(inBefore[te,(te.assoEl ∩ Task)] ∩ LC.started)
10      ∀ te: TaskEvent | te in LC.completed → #(inBefore[te,(te.assoEl ∩ Task)] ∩ LC.
            started) > #(inBefore[te,(te.assoEl ∩ Task)] ∩ LC.completed)
    }
12  fun assign(t: one Task):  set TaskEvent {
        { te: Lifecycle.assigned | #(te.assoEl ∩ assoEls) ≥ #assoEls  }
14  }
    // further utility functions: start, complete
```

Listing 1.2: Extension of activity-life-cycle

---

[1] The complete meta models including also the utility functions just mentioned in the comments at the bottom line are available at http://mpd.kppq.de.

In order to distinguish between different activity-life-cycle actions the signature LC in Listing 1.2 extends the trace meta-model (Listing 1.1). The subsequent fact requires that all activity-related events are uniquely classified regarding these life-cycle actions. Furthermore the fact requires that any start action for a particular activity occurs iff a corresponding assign action precedes. The same holds for actions of type complete. The utility functions (See footnote 1) at the bottom are used to retrieve or determine life-cycle events (e.g. assigned) for a given task.

3.3   Translating MP-Declare Models into Alloy Language

This section covers the essential procedure of translating MP-Declare models into a representation that conforms to both Alloy and the meta-model provided in Sect. 3.2. The procedure comprises three major steps: *(i)* process entities *(ii)* rule templates and *(iii)* rule template instances, i.e. process rules.

Process Entities. For the focus of the current paper, we consider tasks (T), performers (I) and data objects (D) as entities. The corresponding transformation rules π_T, π_I and π_D are then defined as follows:

- $\forall t \in T | \pi_T(t) =$ one sig t extends Task{}
- $\forall i \in I | \pi_I(i) =$ one sig i extends Identity{}
- $\forall d \in D | \pi_D(d) =$ one sig d extends VariableObject{}

Each entity is transformed into a unique and eponymous signature, extending the meta-model signature that corresponds to the particular entity type.

Rule Templates. Since in literature MP-Declare is always considered as a basic set of constraint templates, we rely on this set (Table 1), too. Hence, it is possible to provide a one-to-one mapping from MP-Declare rule templates to Alloy predicates (Table 2). This mapping can and must be extended for each additional rule template. The Alloy predicates are mainly based on two conceptual ideas. First, temporal relationships between events are mapped to positional relationships within one trace. Second, each additional attribute condition is mapped to a constraint that selects a subset of all existing events based on their attributes.

According to Table 1 the parameters of each mapped Alloy predicate consist of one or two activity-life-cycle events and additional restrictions, i.e. activation, target and correlation conditions. Depending on whether the predicate represents a unary or a binary rule the first or the first two parameters are of type Task. The additional conditions can be integrated by adding up to three additional parameters, namely act, tar, and cor. The activation and target conditions contain a set of TaskEvents which fulfill the respective condition, e.g. contain a specific value for a VariableObject. The correlation condition refers to both, the activation activity as well as the target activity. To integrate it into the predicate, the attribute is a set of tuples of TaskEvents. A template without an activation activity does neither get an activation nor a correlation condition. A template without a target activity, such as existence, can only be parameterized with an activation condition. Thus, we consider three possible attribute combinations:

Table 2. Translating MP-Declare rule templates into Alloy formulae

Template	Alloy Formulae
| existence | ```
pred existence[μₐ] {
  #(te1 ∩ act) > 0
}
``` |
| responded existence | ```
pred respondedExistence[μₐₜc] {
  ∀ hte: te1 ∩ act | #(inAfter[hte,te2.assoEl ∩ Task] ∩ te2 ∩
  tar ∩ cor.hte) > 0 ∨ #(inBefore[hte, te2.assoEl ∩ Task] ∩ te2
  ∩ tar ∩ cor.hte) > 0
}
``` |
| response | ```
pred response[μₐₜc] {
  ∀ hte: te1 ∩ act | #inAfter[hte, te2.assoEl ∩ Task] ∩ te2 ∩
  tar ∩ cor.hte > 0
}
``` |
| alternate response | ```
pred alternateResponse[μₐₜc] {
  (∀ hte1, hte2: te1 ∩ act | (hte2.pos > hte1.pos) →
  #(inBetween[hte1, hte2, te2.assoEl ∩ Task] ∩ te2 ∩ tar ∩
  cor.hte2) > 0) and response[te1, te2, act, tar, cor]
}
``` |
| chain response | ```
pred chainResponse[μₐₜc] {
  (∀ start: te1 ∩ act, end: te2 ∩ tar ∩cor.start | start.pos
  < end.pos and #notInBetween[start, end, (te2.assoEl ∩ Task)]
  = 0) and response[te1, te2, act, tar, cor]
}
``` |
| precedence | ```
pred precedence[μₐₜc] {
  ∀ hte: te2 ∩ act | #(inBefore[hte, te1.assoEl ∩ Task] ∩ te1 ∩
  tar ∩ cor.hte) > 0
}
``` |
| alternate precedence | ```
pred alternatePrecedence[μₐₜc] {
  precedence[te1, te2, act, tar, cor] and ∀ hte1, hte2: te2 ∩
  act |(hte1.pos > hte2.pos) →#(inBetween[hte2, hte1,
  te1.assoEl ∩ Task] ∩ te1 ∩ tar ∩ cor.hte1) > 0
}
``` |
| chain precedence | ```
pred chainPrecedence[μₐₜc] {
  (∀ start: te1 ∩ act, end: te2 ∩ tar ∩ cor.start | start.pos
  < end.pos and #notInBetween[start, end, (te2.assoEl ∩ Task)]
  = 0) and precedence[te1, te2, act, tar, cor]
}
``` |
| not responded existence | ```
pred notRespondedExistence[μₐₜc] {
  ∀ hte: te1 ∩ act | #(inAfter[hte, te2.assoEl ∩ Task] ∩ te2 ∩
  tar ∩ cor.hte) = 0 and #(inBefore[hte, te2.assoEl ∩ Task] ∩
  te2 ∩ tar ∩ cor.hte) = 0
}
``` |
| not response | ```
pred notResponse[μₐₜc] {
  ∀ hte: te1 ∩ act | #(inAfter[hte, te2.assoEl ∩ Task] ∩ te2 ∩
  tar ∩ cor.hte) = 0
}
``` |
| not precedence | ```
pred notPrecedence[μₐₜc] {
  ∀ hte: te2 ∩ act | #(inBefore[hte, te1.assoEl ∩ Task] ∩ te2 ∩
  tar ∩ cor.hte) = 0
}
``` |
| not chain response | ```
pred notChainResponse[μₐₜc] {
  ∀ hte: te1 ∩ act | #(atPos[te2.assoEl ∩ Task, add[hte.pos, 1]]
  ∩ te2 ∩ tar ∩ cor.hte) = 0
}
``` |
| not chain precedence | ```
pred notChainPresedence[μₐₜc] {
  ∀ hte: te2 ∩ act | #(atPos[te1.assoEl ∩ Task, sub[hte.pos, 1]]
  ∩ te1 ∩ tar ∩ cor.hte) = 0
}
``` |
```

- μ_{atc} = te1, te2, act, tar: TaskEvent, cor: TaskEvent $\rightarrow$ TaskEvent
- μ_a = te1, act: TaskEvent
- μ_t = te1, tar: TaskEvent

Process Rules. After introducing the transformation rules for activation, target and correlation conditions it is now straightforward to translate whole MP-Declare rules into Alloy. Since each such rule is assumed to be an instance of a MP-Declare rule template the corresponding constraint in Alloy is formed by different parameterizations of a predefined predicate (Table 2). To call e.g. the response-template we write `response[assign[A],assign[B],(e: TaskEvent|vAtPos[e.pos,Temp, Int],value>10),TaskEvent,TaskEvent->TaskEvent]`. This means whenever the TaskEvent assign[A] (activation activity) appears in the trace and has an attribute Temp with an value bigger than 10 (activation condition) it has to be followed by a TaskEvent assign[B] (target activity). To form the conjunction of these constraints they simply would have to be listed in an Alloy `fact` (Sect. 2.3). However, since we have to separate the set of rules according to the previously discussed binning algorithm (Sect. 3.1) we define three predicates whereby each represent one of these bins. Consequently, we add all translated rules to their corresponding bins.

3.4 Alloy-Based Process Execution

According to Sect. 2.2 the execution engine has to answer the two basic questions whether a process instance can be terminated (Question Q1) and which activities can proceed (Q2). To answer any of these questions the current execution state of the process instance has to be translated into Alloy. This is achieved by describing the properties of each past event by means of further Alloy constraints. Listing 1.3 shows an exemplary trace for a loan redemption payment that consists of a single event. The first constraint (line 2) defines the activity, the performing resource and the life-cycle action for the first event in the trace[2] whereas the second describes the remaining payload of the event, i.e. two process variables.

```
  fact {
2      #(atPos[pay_installment,pos[0]] ∩ atPos[CUST-BT-e3748,pos[0]] ∩ LC.assigned)>0
       #(vAtPos[pos[0],Debt,25000] ∩ vAtPos[pos[0],Req_ID,20160602])>0
4  }
```

Listing 1.3: Alloy representation of process execution state

After specifying the current process execution state it is now possible to answer question Q1, whether the process instance can be terminated. Since by means of Alloy we transformed the process execution problem into a SAT problem, we now can apply Alloy's SAT solving capabilities. This is done using the Alloy `run` command that can be configured regarding the predicates that have to be evaluated. According to (Sect. 3.1) only the predicates that represent the two rule bins I and II have impact on process instance termination. Hence, if the

---

[2] The position is calculated based on a utility function `pos` that relates the desired position to the configured integer range.

evaluation of these two predicates successfully determines a valid instance this means that the whole process instance can be completed. Otherwise terminating the instance is currently prohibited.

In order to answer the question which activities may proceed in their life-cycle (Question Q2) the run command is modified through replacing bin II with bin III. Additionally the trace that only consists of past events so far has to be extended with a new event *candidate* that describes a hypothetical next action. Hence, assigning, starting and completing[3] an activity, requires to extend the fact statement in Listing 1.3 by additional constraints that are analogous to those already contained. According to the exemplary trace only the activity pay_installment might be started and all other activities can be assigned only (Fig. 1). In contrast to the procedure of answering Question Q1 the engine now checks a potential next execution state for each process activity and life-cycle action. Each activity the engine is able to identify a solution for may proceed.

4   Implementation and Evaluation

To assess our approach, we have implemented a modeling and execution pro-totype and executed a diverse set of constraints in different process models. A performance evaluation shows the practical applicability of the approach.

4.1   Prototypical Implementation and Expressiveness

Since there is currently no modeling language for MP-Declare the modeling tool is implemented as a web-based *configurator* to be able to easily create multi-perspective, executable, declarative process models. After creating activi-ties and attributes the templates as well as the activation and target activity can be selected with help of drop-down-menus. If the selected template got activa-tion, correlation or target conditions, the user is able to create them afterwards. The tool automatically translates the user input into an Alloy model. Custom MP-Declare templates can be also defined, but the user has to provide the cor-responding mapping to Alloy, too.

In order to support collaborative process execution, the execution system is prototypically implemented as a web application. Screencasts as well as the prototype can be accessed and tested at http://mpd.kppq.de. Back-end and front-end are decoupled through a REST API providing the opportunity to reuse the former with a different front-end.

---

[3] Scheduling an activity is not recorded in the trace since this would *spam* the trace with events just describing that an activity *might have been processed*.

For showing the capabilities of our execution approach, we provide Alloy templates for commonly known MP-Declare process constraints (cf. Table 2) referencing different perspectives and tested them in different process models.

4.2   Efficiency

SAT solving for propositional logic is known to be NP-complete (Cook-Levin theorem). Hence, it is important to evaluate the practical applicability of a process execution engine that is based on this principle in terms of its runtime performance. This section discusses a performance study that is based on a set of artificial but, thus, fully determined MP-Declare models that have been translated into Alloy. The Alloy representations are deterministically enriched with initial traces that represent likewise artificial process execution states. The crucial result is that the main influence factor is the length of the trace that describes the currently running process instance.

For the experiment we used a RapidMiner integration[4] of the execution engine. The desired insight of the performance study is to determine the major influence factors on the computation time. In terms of Alloy this primarily means the number of signatures (number process entities) and rules (number of process rules and events in the initial trace) the model contains. Consequently, we evaluate the engine's runtime dependent on varying numbers of process entities (5 to 20), process rules (0 to 20) and initial trace lengths (0 to 30). All results are cleaned from outliers and averaged over ten repetitions. The runtime measurement is based on a Dell Latitude E6430 (Core i7-3720QM, 8×2.6 GHz, 16 GB memory, SSD drive and Windows 8 64 Bit).

The minimum runtime was lower than 20 ms and a first crucial insight is that this minimum time occurred for arbitrary numbers of process entities and rules whereby the initial trace length was always 0. This suggests that the trace lengths have a significant impact on the overall performance. This is confirmed by Fig. 3[5]: The two sub-figures (a) and (b) are based on a constant initial trace length (T), respectively, and show only slight runtime variations with different amounts of entities and rules. In contrast, the sub-figures (c) and (d) – show far higher variations for a constant number of rules (R) or a constant number of entities (E). Finally, sub-figure (e) shows that the reaction time of the system in a process scenario with up to 10 past events is lower than five seconds. Afterwards the runtime increases rapidly leading to the experimental maximum runtime of about 3 min (20 entities, 20 rules, 30 past events). Thus, the execution engine is currently limited to rather small application scenarios. Since the current trace length is as a major runtime influencing factor, our future work will focus on an extensive time and space complexity analysis to quantify this dependency.

---

[4] Download the RapidMiner process and all measurements: http://mpd.kppq.de.

[5] The time dimension for sub-figures (a)–(d) is represented in a logarithmic scale.

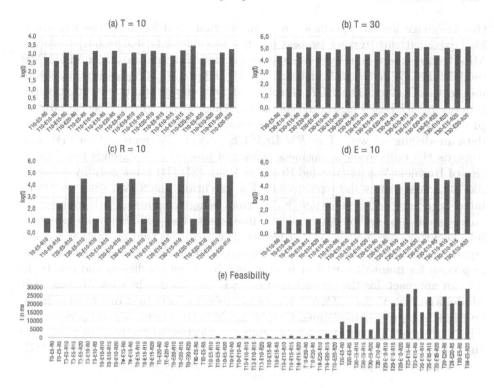

Fig. 3. Runtime dependency on number of entities, rules, and past events

5   Related Work

This work relates to the stream of research on (multi-perspective) declarative process management. The *Declare* framework was designed for modelling and executing declarative business processes. In its most publicized variant, a Declare process model is built from a set of rule templates each of which is mapped to an expression in Linear Temporal Logic (LTL). The resulting LTL formula is then converted to an automaton for execution [1]. Declare only constrains the starts of activities and interrelates them temporally. Data oriented aspects and the organizational perspective are completely missing in traditional Declare. The approaches proposed in [16,17] allow for the specification of constraints that go beyond the traditional Declare templates. In [18], the authors define *Timed Declare*, an extension of Declare that relies on timed automata. In [19], the authors introduce for the first time a data aware semantics for Declare. In [7] a general multi perspective LTL semantics for Declare (*MP-Declare*) has been presented. Here, Declare is extented with elements of first order logic to refer to data values in constraints. Data aware as well as generalized MP-Declare models are currently only supported in the context of conformance checking [7], process discovery [20] and trace generation [14,21]. A system supported modelling and execution is currently not possible. *CLIMB* [22] is a first-order logic declarative language for the specification of interaction models. Here, the Declare is also extented with further process perspectives like data and resources. As for MP-Declare, there is no system support for modelling and execution of CLIMB models. The *DCR Graph* framework [23,24] and graphical representation is similar to the Declare. The DCR Graph model directly supports execution of the process model based on the notion of markings of the graph. The declarative process modelling and execution framework *DPIL* [3,4] covers resource and data modelling as well. The *EM-BrA²CE* project [25] represents a first step towards the unification of business rules and processes. It extends the Semantics of Business Vocabulary and Business Rules (SBVR) framework by concepts like activities, states and participants. For execution, the SBVR rules are translated to event-condition-action (ECA) rules using templates. Both frameworks lack system support for data and resource oriented aspects. Several approaches for executing case models and artifact-centric processes that are similar but not equal to declarative processes have been proposed. In [26] the authors present an approach for managing artifact interactions based on conditions and events. In [27] an approach for the execution of cases is described. The Case Management Model and Notation (*CMMN*)[6] represents recent efforts to standardize declarative business process modelling. CMMN neglects the organizational perspective. The performer of a human task can only be selected on the basis of a role and the perspective is completely missing in the graphical representation of CMMN models. System support for data in CMMN is still not available.

6   Conclusion and Future Work

In this paper, we introduced an approach for the execution of MP-Declare models. The execution engine builds on a classification strategy for different constraint types and a transformation component into the execution language Alloy that is used to solve SAT problems. We implemented a modeling tool and the process execution engine. The evaluation shows the practical applicability of the declarative workflow engine. The approach still has some weaknesses and limitations that we will tackle in future work, e.g., a reduced set of possible attribute condition contents in terms of operational aspects and complex organizational relations. Furthermore, the system is still local optimizing, i.e., process execution might reach states where an instance is not able to terminate anymore.

References

1. Pesic, M., Schonenberg, H., van der Aalst, W.M.P.: Declare: full support for loosely-structured processes. In: IEEE International EDOC Conference 2007, pp. 287–300 (2007)
2. Hildebrandt, T.T., Mukkamala, R.R., Slaats, T., Zanitti, F.: Contracts for cross-organizational workflows as timed dynamic condition response graphs. J. Log. Algebr. Program. **82**(5–7), 164–185 (2013)

---

[6] http://www.omg.org/spec/CMMN/.

3. Zeising, M., Schönig, S., Jablonski, S.: Towards a common platform for the support of routine and agile business processes. In: Collaborative Computing: Networking, Applications and Worksharing (2014)
4. Schönig, S., Ackermann, L., Jablonski, S.: Towards an implementation of data and resource patterns in constraint-based process models. In: Proceedings of the 6th International Conference on Model-Driven Engineering and Software Development, pp. 271–278. SciTePress (2018)
5. Rozinat, A., Mans, R.S., Song, M., van der Aalst, W.M.P.: Discovering simulation models. Inf. Syst. **34**(3), 305–327 (2009)
6. de Leoni, M., van der Aalst, W.M.P., Dees, M.: A general process mining framework for correlating, predicting and clustering dynamic behavior based on event logs. Inf. Syst. **56**, 235–257 (2016)
7. Burattin, A., Maggi, F.M., Sperduti, A.: Conformance checking based on multi-perspective declarative process models. Expert Syst. Appl. **65**, 194–211 (2016)
8. van der Aalst, W., Pesic, M., Schonenberg, H.: Declarative workflows: balancing between flexibility and support. CSRD **23**, 99–113 (2009)
9. Montali, M., Pesic, M., van der Aalst, W.M.P., Chesani, F., Mello, P., Storari, S.: Declarative specification and verification of service choreographies. ACM Trans. Web **4**(1), 3 (2010)
10. Burattin, A., Maggi, F.M., van der Aalst, W.M., Sperduti, A.: Techniques for a posteriori analysis of declarative processes. In: EDOC, Beijing, pp. 41–50. IEEE, September 2012
11. van der Aalst, W.: Process Mining: Data Science in Action. Springer, Heidelberg (2016). https://doi.org/10.1007/978-3-662-49851-4
12. Warmer, J.B., Kleppe, A.G.: The Object Constraint Language: Precise Modeling With UML (Addison-Wesley OTS). Addison-Wesley Professional, Boston (1998)
13. Jackson, D.: Software Abstractions: Logic, Language, and Analysis. MIT Press, Cambridge (2012)
14. Ackermann, L., Schönig, S., Jablonski, S.: Simulation of multi-perspective declarative process models. In: Dumas, M., Fantinato, M. (eds.) BPM 2016. LNBIP, vol. 281, pp. 61–73. Springer, Cham (2017). https://doi.org/10.1007/978-3-319-58457-7_5
15. Bussler, C.: Analysis of the organization modeling capability of workflow-management-systems. In: PRIISM 1996 Conference Proceedings, pp. 438–455 (1996)
16. Lamma, E., Mello, P., Riguzzi, F., Storari, S.: Applying inductive logic programming to process mining. In: Blockeel, H., Ramon, J., Shavlik, J., Tadepalli, P. (eds.) ILP 2007. LNCS (LNAI), vol. 4894, pp. 132–146. Springer, Heidelberg (2008). https://doi.org/10.1007/978-3-540-78469-2_16
17. Chesani, F., Lamma, E., Mello, P., Montali, M., Riguzzi, F., Storari, S.: Exploiting inductive logic programming techniques for declarative process mining. In: Jensen, K., van der Aalst, W.M.P. (eds.) Transactions on Petri Nets and Other Models of Concurrency II. LNCS, vol. 5460, pp. 278–295. Springer, Heidelberg (2009). https://doi.org/10.1007/978-3-642-00899-3_16
18. Westergaard, M., Maggi, F.M.: Looking into the future: using timed automata to provide a priori advice about timed declarative process models. In: Meersman, R., et al. (eds.) OTM 2012. LNCS, vol. 7565, pp. 250–267. Springer, Heidelberg (2012). https://doi.org/10.1007/978-3-642-33606-5_16
19. Montali, M., Chesani, F., Mello, P., Maggi, F.M.: Towards data-aware constraints in declare. In: SAC, pp. 1391–1396. ACM (2013)

20. Schönig, S., Di Ciccio, C., Maggi, F.M., Mendling, J.: Discovery of multi-perspective declarative process models. In: Sheng, Q.Z., Stroulia, E., Tata, S., Bhiri, S. (eds.) ICSOC 2016. LNCS, vol. 9936, pp. 87–103. Springer, Cham (2016). https://doi.org/10.1007/978-3-319-46295-0_6

21. Skydanienko, V., Francescomarino, C.D., Maggi, F.: A tool for generating event logs from multi-perspective declare models. In: BPM (Demos) (2018)

22. Montali, M.: Specification and Verification of Declarative Open Interaction Models: A Logic-Based Approach, vol. 56. Springer, Heidelberg (2010). https://doi.org/10.1007/978-3-642-14538-4

23. Hildebrandt, T., Mukkamala, R.R., Slaats, T., Zanitti, F.: Contracts for cross-organizational workflows as timed dynamic condition response graphs. J. Log. Algebr. Program. **82**(5), 164–185 (2013)

24. Slaats, T., Mukkamala, R.R., Hildebrandt, T., Marquard, M.: Exformatics declarative case management workflows as DCR graphs. In: Daniel, F., Wang, J., Weber, B. (eds.) BPM 2013. LNCS, vol. 8094, pp. 339–354. Springer, Heidelberg (2013). https://doi.org/10.1007/978-3-642-40176-3_28

25. Goedertier, S., Haesen, R., Vanthienen, J.: Rule-based business process modelling and enactment. Int. J. Bus. Process Integr. Manag. **3**(3), 194–207 (2008)

26. Hull, R., Damaggio, E., et al.: Business artifacts with guard-stage-milestone life-cycles: managing artifact interactions with conditions and events. In: International Conference on Distributed Event-Based System (2011)

27. Hewelt, M., Weske, M.: A hybrid approach for flexible case modeling and execution. In: La Rosa, M., Loos, P., Pastor, O. (eds.) BPM 2016. LNBIP, vol. 260, pp. 38–54. Springer, Cham (2016). https://doi.org/10.1007/978-3-319-45468-9_3

Combining Model- and Example-Driven Classification to Detect Security Breaches in Activity-Unaware Logs

Bettina Fazzinga[1], Francesco Folino[1], Filippo Furfaro[2], and Luigi Pontieri[1](✉)

[1] ICAR-CNR, Rende, Italy
{bettina.fazzinga,francesco.folino,luigi.pontieri}@icar.cnr.it
[2] DIMES, University of Calabria, Rende, Italy
furfaro@dimes.unical.it

Abstract. Current approaches to the security-oriented classification of process log traces can be split into two categories: (*i*) *example-driven methods*, that induce a classifier from annotated example traces; (*ii*) *model-driven methods*, based on checking the conformance of each test trace to *security-breach* models defined by experts. These categories are orthogonal and use separate information sources (i.e. annotated traces and a-priori breach models). However, as these sources often coexist in real applications, both kinds of methods could be exploited synergistically. Unfortunately, when the log traces consist of (low-level) events with no reference to the activities of the breach models, combining (*i*) and (*ii*) is not straightforward. In this setting, to complement the partial views of insecure process-execution patterns that an example-driven and a model-driven methods capture separately, we devise an abstract classification framework where the predictions provided by these methods separately are combined, according to a meta-classification scheme, into an overall one that benefits from all the background information available. The reasonability of this solution is backed by experiments performed on a case study, showing that the accuracy of the example-driven (resp., model-driven) classifier decreases appreciably when the given example data (resp., breach models) do not describe exhaustively insecure process behaviors.

1 Introduction

Increasing attention has been paid in recent years to the problem of detecting and analyzing "insecure" process instances (i.e., instances that involved some kind of *security breaches*, e.g., frauds, attacks, misuses), based on log data. In fact, the occurrence of such breaches may cause severe damages to enterprises/organizations in terms of extra-costs (e.g., penalties) or reputation loss. This explains recent attempts [3,6] of exploiting process mining techniques (such as process discovery and conformance checking) as a support to such a security-oriented analysis.

© Springer Nature Switzerland AG 2018
H. Panetto et al. (Eds.): OTM 2018 Conferences, LNCS 11230, pp. 173–190, 2018.
https://doi.org/10.1007/978-3-030-02671-4_10

In the literature, there are several approaches for classifying process instances as *"secure"* or *"insecure"* on the basis of the "post-mortem" data collected in the form of log *traces*. These approaches can be divided into two categories:

(i) *example-driven methods* [6,8,9,13,15]: they exploit a set $\mathcal{L}^{AET}$ of *Annotated Example Traces*, where the annotation of each trace says whether the corresponding process instance contained a security breach or not. From these traces, they induce a mechanism for deciding whether a process instance encoded by a "new" trace contains a security breach;

(ii) *model-driven methods* [10]: they exploit *security-breach* models, encoding some knowledge of the behaviors symptomatic of security risks. The process instances are classified according to the result of the conformance checking to these models.

These two kinds of methods are clearly orthogonal, but their respective sources of knowledge/information (i.e., models and annotated data) often co-exist. Thus, the core idea of this work is that of exploiting them synergistically, in order to complement the partial views of insecure process-execution patterns that they provide separately. In particular, we address the security-classification problem in the challenging setting that the traces are made of low-level events with no reference to the high-level activities that caused them. This scenario often occurs in practice (and several process-mining works dealt with it [2,4,10]), as many enactment and tracing systems keep track of the executions of basic "low-level" operations, and not of their translation to the high-level activities the analysts are familiar with.

Example of the Scenario. *Consider an issue management process that logically consists of the following high-level activities:* Create *a ticket,* Reply *to the customer,* Assign *a ticket to a solver, write a* Report*, contact the customer through a private channel (*Contact Privately*), and* Close *a ticket. If the process is not enacted over a structured process-aware system (e.g., a WfMS), it may happen that the events traced in the process' log just capture low-level generic operations, which cannot be mapped univocally to the above activities. For example, different communication-like activities (e.g.,* Reply *and* Contact Privately*), may be simply stored in the log as occurrences of a low-level event (e.g., "Message sent") representing a generic messaging operation. As a form of security-oriented analysis, one might want to check whether a private communication occurred without a need, e.g., after the closure of the ticket. Clearly, this requires each trace to be properly interpreted, by mapping each event "Message sent" to one of the activities* Reply *or* Contact Privately*, and check whether the events mapped to* Contact Privately *occurred after the event mapped to* Close *in the trace.* □

In this setting, combining methods of the two types (*i*) and (*ii*) is not straightforward, since exploiting the behavioral models in (*ii*) requires reasoning at the high abstraction level of activities, while exploiting annotated event traces in (*i*) requires reasoning at the lower abstraction level of events. Unfortunately, moving to one abstraction level to the other is a complex issue, since the mapping between activity types and events is many-to-many, due to the presence of shared functionalities (i.e., events that can correspond to the executions of different activities) and of "polymorphic" activities, whose distinct executions can cause different events. This means that the same trace (i.e., event sequence) can have multiple interpretations (i.e., it can be the result of different sequences of activity instances). Hence, combining classifiers that use information/knowledge at different abstraction levels requires some mechanism for "reconciling" these standpoints.

It is worth noting that the scenario described so far, where the correspondence between the types of activities, in terms of which the process models are defined, and the types of events, recorded in the log traces, is not one-to-one, also describes real-life situations other than those where the events recorded in the log are low-level operations. For instance, it can happen that each symbol reported in the log traces has a clear reference to a high-level activity, but the alphabet of the activities explicitly referred to by the trace symbols is different from the alphabet used to define the process models. This situation happens when the experts who defined the process models tend to interpret/describe the actions performed during the process enactments differently from the experts who assisted the design of the tracing system and defined the alphabet of activities used by the tracing system to encode the actions performed during the process enactments. The different perspectives underlying the encodings of the actions in the process models and in the log traces can be either due to the different background knowledge characterizing the two typologies of experts, or can be somehow enforced by the fact that the business process is very complex, and the set of high-level activities that are performed within it is very large. In this case, in order to enhance the readability and compactness of the process models, a coarser granularity in the description of the activities is often used, so that process models using fewer activities than those recorded by the tracing system are obtained.

Our Contribution: A Novel Classification Framework. We investigate the problem of classifying low-level event traces as either *insecure* or *secure* in the presence of the following main kinds of information/background knowledge:

(1) an annotated log $\mathcal{L}^{AET}$, where each trace ϕ is a sequence of low-level events and is associated with its correct (or *ground-truth*) interpretation $I^*(\phi)$ (i.e., the sequence of high-level activities that really generated it) and a *security flag* $SF(\phi)$, certifying the corresponding process instance as either *secure* or *insecure*;
(2) a set of *process models* and a set of *security-breach models*, describing what is known about the behaviors of the processes and the behaviors symptomatic of security breaches, respectively. In particular, we consider declarative behavioral models expressed via presence/absence and/or precedence/causality constraints over the activities, like those in [1].

In order to investigate new solutions to the security-classification task capable of exploiting the three sources of knowledge/information listed above, we first review the solutions in the literature providing example-driven and model-driven methods, and then discuss the possibility of making them synergistically work. In this regard, we devise an abstract framework, where the results of the classification tasks performed by example-driven and model-driven techniques are assembled into a unique measure. In particular, we start from the availability of an example-driven classifier C^E and a model-driven classifier C^M, where[1]: (1) C^E is induced from the event traces, by leveraging standard learning methods [17], and (2) C^M is the classifier introduced in [10], that is able to exploit the knowledge of process and security-breach models to provide a security classification of event log traces. The possibility of integrating C^E and C^M by means of a meta-classifier is discussed, and the reasonability of this solution is backed by the results of our experimental analysis. Therein, we show that C^E and C^M are accurate only if the labeled data and the models, respectively, are quite exhaustive in describing the secure/insecure behaviors. This makes an approach based on a meta-classifier a promising solution, as it is likely to be effective in enhancing the accuracy of the classification by exploiting the complementarity of the sources of knowledge onto which C^E and C^M are based.

2   Related Work

Model-Driven Approaches. These approaches rely on the assumption that a precise and complete enough description of insecure execution patterns is available, provided by domain experts in the form of behavioral models, such as the declarative breach models used in [10] (expressed via the same kind of composition rules as in our setting) or the procedural "misuse" models adopted in [16]. Based on such a-priori models, it is possible to classify any trace by simply checking its compliance to these models, provided that both the models and trace's events refer to the same set of activities. Clearly, the same approach can also applied, in a "complementary" way, in settings where the a-priori models describe the space of secure/normal process instances (as in [3]), and insecure/deviant traces are those that do not comply with these models. This compliance checking task, however, gets harder when the mapping between trace events and the activities in the reference models is unknown. A simple solution for circumventing this issue consists in using semi-automated supervised abstraction approaches, like those proposed in [4], which help the analyst define an "optimal" deterministic event-activity mapping, so that each log trace can be converted deterministically into a sequence of activities, in order to eventually check whether this sequence complies to some of the reference models. Since such a strategy (relying on converting a trace τ into a single activity sequence) may well lead to misleading results in settings where the event-activity mapping is inherently uncertain, probabilistic methods have been proposed recently to evaluate the compliance of a trace against either all its possible interpretations [2] or a representative subset of them [10]. In particular, based on given security-breach models, the approach

---

[1] Superscripts E and M stand for *event* and *model*. The reason for using the superscript E for the data-driven classifier is that it performs the classification by looking at the low-level events reported in the traces.

defined in [10] allows the analyst to probabilistically classify a novel activity-unaware trace ϕ as secure/insecure by generating a sample of ϕ's interpretations (via Montecarlo simulation) and comparing them with the models.

Example-Driven Classification Approaches. A recent stream of Process Mining research, known as "Deviance Mining" has approached the problem of classifying log traces as either deviant/insecure or normal as an inductive learning task [6,8,9,13,15]. The only kind of information exploited by these approaches in the classification of a trace consists of historical log traces, equipped each with a binary class label. These example traces are used to train a classifier (with some induction method) to discriminate between the two classes. All of the example-driven trace classification approaches proposed so far rely on preliminary encoding the training log into a propositional form. This preliminary task can be accomplished by constructing a bag-of-activity representation of the example traces, or by projecting them onto the space of sequence patterns (such as tandem/maximal repeats [7] and frequent discriminative sub-sequences [14]), or by resorting to ad-hoc encodings defined for complex event sequences [9,13].

Combining multiple encoding and learning methods was considered in [8], which proposed an ensemble-based approach to the discovery of a multi-view deviance classifier, which includes different base classifiers, discovered each by applying one of the learning method to the log view yielded by one of the encoding methods.

Limitations of Current Solutions. The two families of approaches described above have been conceived as orthogonal solutions, and none of them can exploit both the sources of information that are assumed to be available in our problem setting: annotated (activity-unaware) log traces and (partial) background knowledge including known security-breach models. This implies that, if the a-priori breach models defined by the experts (resp., whenever the annotated example traces) just cover a rather limited part of all the relevant kinds of security breaches that should be detected, any model-driven (resp., example-driven) approach is likely to yield poorly accurate classification results, even when a rich collection of annotated example traces (resp., of a-priori security-breach models) is available that captures information useful for improving such results. This limitation also affects the ensemble-based approach of [8], where any base classifier can only reason on event sequences and cannot exploit known security-breach patterns described at the level of (hidden) process activities. Thus, to the best of our knowledge, this work is the first attempt in the literature to exploit both these heterogenous sources of information in order to classify activity-unaware traces.

3 Preliminaries

Logs, Traces, Processes, Activities and Events. A log is a set of *traces*. Each trace ϕ describes a process instance at the abstraction level of basic *events*, each generated by the execution of an activity. That is, an instance w of a *process* consists of a sequence $a_1, \ldots, a_n$ of *activity* instances; in turn, each activity instance a_i generates an event e_i; hence, the trace ϕ describing w consists of the sequence $e_1, \ldots, e_n$.

Observe that with the term "event" we mean a type of low-level operation. Hence, different executions of the same type of low-level operation result are described by the same event and, thus, they are encoded by the same symbol in the log traces. For instance, consider the type of operation e: "*E-mail sent from X to Y*", and assume that a process instance w consists in performing two activities in a row: the first yields the operation of sending a mail from Matthew to Sarah, and the other the operation of sending a mail from Sarah to Anthony. Then, the trace ϕ describing the execution of w is $\phi = ee$. This means that we disregard every piece of information reported in the log traces but the type of low-level operation, thus making different instances of the same low-level operation indistinguishable. Obviously, log traces can contain a richer description of the operations performed within process executions. For instance, the trace ϕ above could contain, for each occurrence of e, the specification of the sender X and the recipient Y of the mail, as well as the time when the mail was sent and received, respectively. However, considering these further attributes could make the discussion of the problem that we address and the presentation of our research more complex, thus we disregard their presence for the sake of simplicity. For the same reason, we focus on the case that activities are simple, i.e., the execution of an activity results in exactly one event (however, as it will be clearer later, we consider the challenging case that the mapping between activity types and events is many-to-many, meaning that two different executions of the same activity can lead to different events, and, vice versa, two occurrences of the same event can have been caused by different activities). The case where each activity is composite (i.e., it results in a sequence of events, rather than a single event) is discussed in Sect. 6.

We assume given the set $\mathcal{W}$ of known process models, the set $\mathcal{A}$ of (types of) activities, and the set $\mathcal{E}$ of the types of events that can occur in the log. We denote the elements of $\mathcal{W}$ and $\mathcal{A}$ with upper-case alphabetical symbols (such as W, A), and the instances of processes, activities and events with lower-case symbols (such as w, a, e). Observe that we are assuming $\mathcal{W}$ to be a set, as a log may store traces coming from different processes (or different process variants).

Process Models. We assume that each process model $W \in \mathcal{W}$ encodes a-priori knowledge on the behavior of a process in terms of activity constraints, and defines the sequences of <u>activities</u> that the process' executions can yield. This reflects what typically happens in practice: even when the log report low-level events, process models are at the abstraction level of activities, i.e., the level with which analysts are familiar.

Specifically, following declarative modelling approaches [1], we assume that any process model simply is a set of *composition rules* of the forms: (1) $A\bullet\!\!\rightarrow B$; (2) $A\bullet\!\!\rightarrow\neg B$; (3) $A\!\rightarrow\!\bullet B$; (4) $\neg A\!\rightarrow\!\bullet B$; where $A, B \in \mathcal{A}$. Herein, $A\bullet\!\!\rightarrow B$ (resp., $A\bullet\!\!\rightarrow\neg B$) is a "*response relationship*" meaning that every instance of activity A must be (resp., must not be) followed by an instance of B. Analogously,

$A\!\rightarrow\!\bullet B$ (resp., $\neg A\!\rightarrow\!\bullet B$) encodes the *"precedence relationship"* imposing that any instance of B must (resp., must not) be *preceded* by an instance of A. The rules *true* $\bullet\!\rightarrow\!A$ and *true* $\bullet\!\rightarrow\!\neg A$ are special cases of rules imposing the presence and the absence of instances of activity A, respectively. The reason for using such rules is that they allow us to specify the structure of a process (or of a security-breach) even partially/loosely—see Sect. 6 for how it can be adapted to other forms of models.

Example 1. Let W be a process model such that $W = \{A\bullet\!\rightarrow\!\neg B; C\!\rightarrow\!\bullet A\}$. Then, the sequence $a\,b\,d\,c$, whose elements are instances of the activities A, B, D, C, cannot be an instance of (the process modeled by) W, as it violates both its composition rules. By contrast, the sequence $c\,d\,a$ conforms to W and can be viewed as an instance of W. □

Mapping Between Activities and Events. We consider the general case that the mapping between the types of activities and events is *many to many*, that is: (1) for every activity $A \in \mathcal{A}$, different executions of A can generate different events; (2) conversely, an occurrence of an event e in a trace cannot be univocally interpreted as the result of an execution of an activity A, since there can be another activity $B \in \mathcal{A}$ whose execution may have generated e. We assume that the mapping of each event $e \in \mathcal{E}$ onto the activities is probabilistically modelled by a pdf $p_e(A) : \mathcal{A} \rightarrow [0,1]$, where A is a random variable ranging over $\mathcal{A}$. Basically, $p_e(A)$ encodes the probability that a generic occurrence of the event e was caused by an execution of activity A. The "mapping" set $\mu = \{p_e(A) \mid e \in \mathcal{E}\}$ of such pdfs represents the knowledge available on event-activity mappings, which can be derived from the given annotated log data as explained at the end of this section.

Interpretations and Their Probabilities. An activity instance a of A is said an *interpretation* of e if $p_e(A) > 0$ (meaning that e can be plausibly viewed as the result of executing A). An *interpretation* of a trace $\phi = e_1 \ldots e_n$ is a sequence of activity instances $a_1 \ldots a_n$ such that, $\forall i \in [1..n]$, a_i is an interpretation of e_i. The set of ϕ's interpretations is denoted as $\mathcal{I}(\phi)$.

The given pdfs $p_e(A)$ can be used for defining a pdf over $\mathcal{I}(\phi)$: assuming independence between the events, each $I = a_1 \ldots a_n$ in $\mathcal{I}(\phi)$ is assigned $p(I) = \Pi_1^n p_{e_i}(A_i)$ as the probability of being the activity sequence that generated ϕ.

When process models are taken into account, not all the interpretations in $\mathcal{I}(\phi)$ are equally reasonable: if an interpretation I satisfies no process model, it can be discarded. Interpretations satisfying some process model are called *valid interpretations*, and their set is denoted as $\mathcal{I}^V(\phi)$. Correspondingly, the probabilities of the interpretations can be revised by performing probabilistic conditioning w.r.t. the property of being valid, thus obtaining the pdf p^V defined as follows: $p^V(I) = 0$, if $I \in \mathcal{I}(\phi) \setminus \mathcal{I}^V(\phi)$; and: $p^V(I) = p(I)/\sum_{I \in \mathcal{I}^V(\phi)} p(I)$, if $I \in \mathcal{I}^V(\phi)$. Thus, p^V assigns 0 probability to invalid interpretations, while the probabilities of the other ones are implied by the probabilities of their single steps of being the true interpretations of the corresponding events.

Example 2. Let $\mathcal{A} = \{A, B, C\}$, $\mathcal{E} = \{e_1, e_2\}$, and consider the log $\mathcal{L} = \{\phi\}$ with $\phi = e_1 e_2$. Assume that $p_{e_1}(A) = 0.4$, $p_{e_1}(B) = 0.6$, $p_{e_2}(A) = 0.3$ and $p_{e_2}(C) = 0.7$. Denoting as a, b, c the generic instances of A, B and C, respectively, we can interpret ϕ as one of the following sequences of activity instances: $I_1 = a\,a$, $I_2 = b\,a$, $I_3 = a\,c$, or $I_4 = b\,c$, with probabilities $p(I_1) = p_{e_1}(A) \cdot p_{e_2}(A) = 0.12$, $p(I_2) = p_{e_1}(B) \cdot p_{e_2}(A) = 0.18$, $p(I_3) = p_{e_1}(A) \cdot p_{e_2}(C) = 0.28$, and $p(I_4) = p_{e_1}(B) \cdot p_{e_2}(C) = 0.42$.

If $\mathcal{W} = \{W\}$ and $W = \{B{\rightarrow}C, B{\rightarrow}A\}$, the only valid interpretations are I_2 and I_4, and their revised probabilities are: $p^V(I_2) = p(I_2)/(p(I_2) + p(I_4)) = 0.18/0.60 = 0.3$, and $p^V(I_4) = p(I_4)/(p(I_2) + p(I_4)) = 0.42/0.60 = 0.7$. □

Security-Breach Models and Annotated Example Traces. Besides the process models discussed above, we assume the presence of further knowledge about process behaviors and security issues, encoded as *security-breach models* and *labeled example traces.* Security-breach models are analogous to process models, but describe behaviors that are symptomatic of security breaches. In the following, we denote as $\mathcal{SBM}$ the set of security-breach models.

Example 3. Let $SBM = \{\neg A{\rightarrow}B\}$ be a security breach model, where A is the activity *"Detection of critical trouble"* and B is *"Communication with the customer via private channel"*. The composition rule of SBM means that a security breach is supposed to happen when a customer is contacted privately not after a critical trouble. □

On the other hand, a log $\mathcal{L}^{AET}$ of *Annotated Example Traces* can be given, which provides examples of process behaviors and of security breaches at the abstraction levels of both activities and events. There, each trace $\phi = e_1, \ldots, e_n$ is equipped with: (1) the true interpretation $I^*(\phi) = a_1 \ldots a_n$ of ϕ, i.e., the actual sequence of activity instances that have caused the sequence of events ϕ; (2) the security flag $SF(\phi)$, that is a boolean value telling whether a security breach is known to have occurred during the process instance represented by ϕ (in this case, it is $SF(\phi) = 1$) or not ($SF(\phi) = 0$)).

Where do models, $\mathcal{L}^{AET}$ and $p_e(A)$ come from?

- Process and security-breach models are typically provided by domain experts (in some cases, they can be derived from manuals and documentation describing normal behaviors and security issues, if available).
- The correct interpretations of the example traces can be obtained by asking the executors of the activities to label the generated event with the activity name. Clearly, an expert analyst can participate to this task (or do it all by her/him-self) especially for events produced by activities that were not supervised by humans.
- The security flag $SF(\phi)$ of each example trace ϕ in $\mathcal{L}^{AET}$ can be set by a domain expert or by exploiting existing security-oriented evaluation/feedback facilities, which are available in several real-life settings. Consider, e.g., process instances where a fraud is committed (by some of the workers involved)

and uncovered post-mortem with the help of extemporary auditing activities or of inquiries/denunciations.

- The probabilistic event-activity mapping $\mu = \{p_e(A) \mid e \in \mathcal{E}\}$ can be easily obtained by extracting statistics from $\mathcal{L}^{AET}$. In fact, for each $e \in \mathcal{E}, A \in \mathcal{A}$, $p_e(A)$ can be set equal to the percentage of times that an occurrence of the event e in $\mathcal{L}^{AET}$ is associated with the activity A in the true interpretation of the trace containing e. Obviously, domain experts may check/refine the so obtained probabilistic mapping.

4   An Abstract Framework for the Security-Classification Problem

The following security-oriented (probabilistic) classification problem is addressed in our work: given a low-level activity-unaware log trace ϕ, we want to estimate the probability $p_{ins}(\phi)$ that ϕ belongs to the class of *insecure* traces, i.e., that the process instance that generated ϕ involved a security breach. To do this, we exploit both a log $\mathcal{L}^{AET}$ of annotated example traces and explicit background knowledge, including process models $\mathcal{W}$ and security-breach models $\mathcal{SBM}$ (describing known kinds of breaches).

As discussed above, the knowledge of security breaches encoded in the given security-breach models has a different origin from that implicitly captured by the annotated traces. As such, security-breach models and annotated example traces are both partial views of insecure behaviors. Thus, it may happen that a trace annotated as "insecure" in $\mathcal{L}^{AET}$ does not conform to any security-breach model. Analogously, a trace whose correct interpretation conforms to a security-breach model may be associated in $\mathcal{L}^{AET}$ with a *false* (i.e., 0) security flag.

Our research aims at investigating the effectiveness of the solutions that perform the security classification by exploiting only one of the above-mentioned partial views (i.e., solutions belonging to the classes of *model-driven* and *example-driven* approaches), and then devising an abstract framework where these approaches are integrated to exploit the complementarity of the two views. The inspiration is that, this way, more accurate classifications than those obtainable by considering security-breach models and annotated traces separately can be provided. What makes this challenging is the inherent uncertainty that must be faced when trying to interpret the trace ϕ to be classified: since the event-activity mapping $p_e(A)$ is many-to-many, ϕ can have many "candidate" interpretations, that may give different indications on the presence of a security breach in the process instance encoded by ϕ (Fig. 1).

To circumvent the difficulty of combining the two kinds of knowledge mentioned above, our research goes into the direction of adopting an ensemble classification approach (as sketched in Fig. 2), where two different base classifiers are used and integrated in a "black-box" way: a *model-driven classifier* C^M, which simply relies on checking the conformance to the given breach models in $\mathcal{SBM}$; and an *example-driven classifiers*, denoted as C^E, induced automatically from the annotated example traces in $\mathcal{L}^{AET}$.

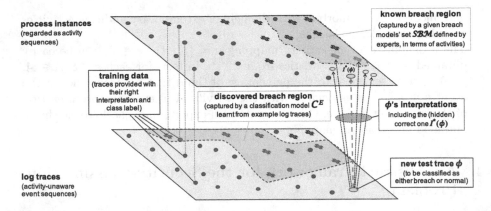

Fig. 1. The problem: classify a new test trace (shown in the bottom right part, as an instance of the lower-abstraction space of log traces) as insecure/secure. Two main kinds of information are given, besides the test trace: (i) a-priori process knowledge including a set $\mathcal{SBM}$ of known breach models expressed at the higher abstraction level of process instances/activities; (ii) training log data, providing information on past process executions in terms of both log traces (bottom) and their originating process instances (ground-truth interpretations), labelled each as either breach/insecure (red-cross symbol) or normal (blue-oval symbol). (Color figure online)

Following the approach of existing example-driven methods (like those discussed in Sect. 2, the classifier C^E can be induced from annotated log traces, by leveraging standard learning methods [17], combined with suitable sequence encoding mechanisms. On the other hand, we propose to exploit the method defined in [10] to implement a model-driven classifier C^M that can provide a security classification for low-level log traces, based on high-level process and security-breach models.

For the sake of generality and uniformity, let us regard both C^E and C^M as functions returning a value in $[0, 1]$ that represents an "estimate" of the probability that the given trace (in the case of C^E) or interpretation (in the case of C^M) is insecure. In fact, C^M simply returns 1 (resp., 0) if I conforms to some (resp., none) of the security-breach models in $\mathcal{SBM}$.

These two classifiers are used to obtain two different estimates, denoted as $\tilde{p}_{ins}^M(\phi)$ and $\tilde{p}_{ins}^E(\phi)$, respectively, for $p_{ins}(\phi)$. Now, while $\tilde{p}_{ins}^E(\phi)$ can be naturally defined as $C^E(\phi)$ (i.e., the result of applying C^E to ϕ), the estimate $\tilde{p}_{ins}^M(\phi)$ cannot be defined as $C^M(\phi)$, since C^M can take as input only activity sequences. A sensible way to define $\tilde{p}_{ins}^M(\phi)$ based on C^M is that of taking the set $\mathcal{I}^V(\phi)$ of valid interpretations of ϕ and return the cumulative conditioned probability of the valid interpretations that C^M classifies as insecure, i.e.,

$$\tilde{p}_{ins}^M(\phi) = \sum_{I \mid I \in \mathcal{I}^V(\phi) \land C^M(I) > 0.5} p^V(I) \qquad (1)$$

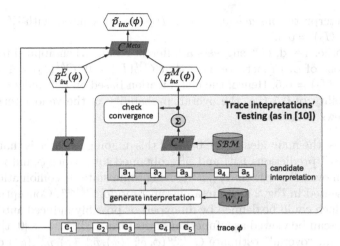

Fig. 2. Proposed approach to the probabilistic classification of a trace ϕ.

Despite this way of defining $\tilde{p}_{ins}^M(\phi)$ is sound, its computation may be unfeasible, due to the possibly huge number of candidate interpretations. For instance, a trace of length 50, where each event can be produced by 2 distinct activities on the average, admits $2^{50} \cong 10^{15}$ interpretations. Hence, instead of considering the whole set $\mathcal{I}^V(\phi)$ of valid interpretations, one could just focus on a representative subset S of $\mathcal{I}^V(\phi)$, and compute the estimate $\tilde{p}_{ins}^M(\phi)$ using only the values returned by C^M over the interpretations in S.

Following the approach proposed of [10], such a subset S can be generated through an iterative Montecarlo sampling scheme, by using the process models in $\mathcal{W}$ and the mapping $\mu = \{p_e(A)\}$ (preliminary extracted from $\mathcal{L}^{AET}$) to guide the generation of interpretations, and some suitable convergence-check criterion (such as the Agresti-Coull interval). More specifically, the models in $\mathcal{W}$ can be exploited to discard generated interpretations that are not valid, while the pdfs $p_e(A)$ can be used to drive the sampler, so that the probability that an interpretation $I \in \mathcal{I}^V(\phi)$ is generated (and put into S) is proportional to $p^V(I)$. This allows the probability $\tilde{p}_{ins}^M(\phi)$ in Eq. (1) to be evaluated as the fraction of interpretations in S that C^M classify as insecure—the computation of this fraction is symbolized by Σ in Fig. 2.

Example 4. Consider a scenario with one process model $W = \{A\bullet\!\!\rightarrow\!B, \neg C\!\rightarrow\!\bullet B\}$, one breach model $SBM = \{B\bullet\!\!\rightarrow\!C\}$, and $\mathcal{E} = \{e_1, e_2\}$, $\mathcal{A} = \{A, B, C\}$. Assume that, based on annotated traces, we extracted the mapping probabilities $p_{e_1}(A) = 1$, and $p_{e_2}(B) = p_{e_2}(C) = 0.5$, and a classifier C^E that classifies a (low-level) trace as insecure iff it ends with an occurrence of event e_2.

Now, a novel trace $\overline{\phi} = e_1 e_2 e_2$ must be classified. According to C^E only, $\overline{\phi}$ would be definitely classified as *insecure*: $\tilde{p}_{ins}^E(\overline{\phi}) = C^E(\overline{\phi}) = 1$. Denoting the generic instances of activities A, B, C as a, b, c, respectively, it is easily seen that the only valid interpretations for $\overline{\phi}$ are $I_1 = abb$ and $I_2 = abc$ (indeed, the remaining interpretations acb and acc in $I(\overline{\phi})$ do not comply with W), and that $p^V(I_1) = p^V(I_2) = 0.5$.

On the other hand, C^M suggests a different result, when applied to the valid interpretations of $\overline{\phi}$. In fact, we have that $C^M(I_1) = 0$, $C^M(I_2) = 1$ and, thus, $\tilde{p}^M_{ins}(\overline{\phi}) = p^V(I_2) = 0.5$. Hence, the classification based on C^M judges $\overline{\phi}$ insecure with probability of 0.5 (i.e. the overall probability of the valid interpretations that C^M views as insecure). $\qquad\square$

Given this, the main idea at the basis of this ongoing research is that of taking the two "base" predictions $\tilde{p}^M_{ins}$ and $\tilde{p}^E_{ins}$ obtained for a trace ϕ and integrating them into an overall prediction $\tilde{p}_{ins}$ by using some suitable combination mechanism, represented in Fig. 2 as a meta-classifier model C^{Meta}. Conceptually, such a model—which could be defined by an expert or possibly induced automatically from $\mathcal{L}^{AET}$—can be viewed as a function of the form $C^{Meta} : \mathcal{E}^* \times [0,1]^2 \to [0,1]$, that returns an "overall" estimate $C^{Meta}(\phi, \tilde{p}^E_{ins}(\phi), \tilde{p}^A_{ins}(\phi), \tilde{p}^M_{ins}(\phi))$ of $p_{ins}(\phi)$.

The first parameter of C^{Meta} is meant to possibly allow the meta-classifier to combine the base predictions differently, depending on the value of such "context" features (as in [5]).

Using a meta-classifier C^{Meta} can help overcome the limitations of its underlying base classifiers C^E and C^M, which, as confirmed by our experimental analysis, are expected to provide accurate classifications only when the labeled data and the a-priori security-breach models, respectively, describe insecure process behaviors in an exhaustive way. In fact, since the sources of knowledge onto which C^E and C^M are based usually do not provide fully overlapping pieces of information, the ensemble consisting of these two base classifiers is likely to exhibit a sufficient level of diversity and complementarity.

This makes an approach based on a meta-classifier a promising solution for enhancing the accuracy of current security-classification solutions.

5   Case Study

The empirical analysis was carried out on synthetic real-like data, generated according to the guidelines of the administrative unit of a service agency. In this scenario, a process instance consists of activities performed by the unit's staff, in response to a customer's request, such as: creating a new folder, preparing new documents and putting them into a folder, updating existing documents, contacting the customer, etc. Folders are of different types, and folders of the same type can be regarded as instances of the same business process. We specifically focused on 2 such processes, whose executions were ensured to obey to certain "activity-level" constraints, and defined a subset W of 2 process models (i.e., sets of composition rules) to represent their behaviors, respectively. Based on the descriptions of 8 known types of security breaches, we analogously built a set $\mathcal{SBM}^{full}$ of 8 security-breach models. Processes' and security-breaches' models contained 2.5 and 3.4 composition rules in the average, respectively. Table 1 reports the setting of major parameters used to generate the log.

Table 1. Log's statistics and setting of the parameters used to generate it.

No. of different processes	2	Min, Max activities per event	1, 8
Num. of different breach models	8	Avg. candidate activities per event	$\sim$2.3
No. of different activities	14	Avg. no. of events per trace	$\sim$48
No. of different events	20	No. of example log traces/interpretations	10^4

Besides the composition rules, we were given 40 real traces describing different process instances at the level of events, along with their ground-truth interpretations. We used these traces and interpretations to generate both the set μ of pdfs of the form $p_e(A)$ and a wider collection of annotated example traces, which we used for the tests. To this end, starting from each ground-truth interpretation I, we produced a set $perturb(I)$ of 300 sequences of activity instances by randomly perturbing I similarly to what done in [10]—roughly speaking, we iteratively tried to generate new valid interpretations by exchanging elements of I or by replacing an activities appearing in I with another activity chosen at random. Then, we turned each I' in $perturb(I)$ into a trace (i.e., event sequence) by randomly replacing each activity of I' with one of its associated events (chosen according to the pdfs in P), and put it in the log.

At the end of this procedure, we obtained $10K$ annotated example traces (consisting of about $480K$ events in total), collectively called hereinafter the *log* and denoted as $\mathcal{L}^{full}$. The ground-truth class of each trace ϕ in $\mathcal{L}^{full}$ was determined by simply checking whether its correct $I^*(\phi)$ was compliant with at least one of the 8 models in $\mathcal{SBM}^{full}$ (in this case ϕ belongs to the class of insecure traces) or not. This resulted in a little unbalanced class distribution: 67% normal traces vs. 33% insecure ones.

5.1   Test Procedure and Evaluation Measures

We regarded $\mathcal{SBM}^{full}$ as a complete and precise high-level description of all the different security-breach types that our approach should be able to learn, and to exploit in the classification of new traces. In our experimentation, we tried to simulate realistic scenarios where the given collection of known security-breach models and that of annotated example traces only provide, in their own, partial information on insecure behaviors that just covers a subset of the reference security-breach types defined in $\mathcal{SBM}^{full}$.

To this end, we split $\mathcal{SBM}^{full}$ into two (possibly overlapping) sets of models: *(i)* a subset $bkModels$ of "disclosed" models, representing the explicit background knowledge on security breaches that is available; and *(ii)* a subset $hdModels$ of "hidden" models, including at least all the security-breach models in $\mathcal{SBM}^{full} \setminus bkModels$ (but, possibly, also models from $bkModels$), which we only employed to set the security flags of the annotated traces used to discover an example-driven classifier. In other words, the models in $bkModels$ let us simulate the explicit description of known security breaches (encoded by security experts) that can be used for the security-classification task, while $hdModels$ only played as an "oracle" for labelling the given traces. Thus, the models in $bkModels$ and the example traces, annotated according to $hdModels$, represents the two different sources of information on the behavior of insecure process instances that are considered in our setting.

In order to allow the study of the sensitivity of the accuracy to the "amounts" of information encoded in the sources of knowledge over which the considered classifiers are studied, we used two ad-hoc parameters in the experiments: the fraction $bK\%$ of ("disclosed") breach models in $bkModels$, and the fraction $oP\%$ of models in $bkModels$ that also appear in $hdModels$ (as an indicator of the degree of overlap between the given breach models and the given examples of insecure process instances). We made $bK\%$ and $oP\%$ range over $\{0.0, 0.25, 0.50, 0.75, 1.0\}$ and $\{0.0, 0.50, 1.0\}$, respectively. In the special cases where $bK\% = 0.0$, it is $hdModels = \mathcal{SBM}^{full}$, i.e., the log contains examples of all the reference breach types, and we only set $oP\% = 0.0$. Moreover, in the "extreme" configurations with $bK\% = 1.0$ (resp., $oP\% = 1.0$), the information encoded by $bkModels$ (resp., by the example traces) is complete, as it describes all the reference breach models in $\mathcal{SBM}^{full}$. In particular, when $bK\% = 1.0$, the breach types covered by the example traces are a subset of those described by $bkModels$. The other combinations of $bK\%$ and $oP\%$ represent typical cases where the given breach models and the example traces provide incomplete, and mutually complementary, pieces of information on insecure behaviors.

Precisely, the tests were performed according to the following *hold-out* scheme, for each configuration of $bK\%$ and $oP\%$:

1. we first produced 6 random splits of $\mathcal{L}^{full}$ into two parts: a training log $\mathcal{L}^{train}$ containing 80% of the example triples of $\mathcal{L}^{full}$, and a test log $\mathcal{L}^{test}$ containing the remaining ones;
2. for each pair $(\mathcal{L}^{train}, \mathcal{L}^{test})$ generated this way, we randomly extracted 3 different pairs $(bkModels, hdModels)$ from $\mathcal{SBM}^{full}$, and modified the security flags of each triple in $\mathcal{L}^{train}$ according to the models in $hdModels$;
3. for each pair $(bkModels, hdModels)$ we built up a classifier H by using some suitable example-driven or model-driven security-classification method (see Subsect. 5.2 for more details on this respect);
4. the quality of each model H obtained this way was assessed by comparing, for each test trace ϕ in $\mathcal{L}^{test}$, the real class of ϕ (decided on the basis of $\mathcal{SBM}^{full}$) with the most probable class that H predicted for ϕ (namely, insecure iff the probability returned by the model for ϕ is higher than 0.5).

The following classic metrics were computed over these pairs of real and predicted classes: *Accuracy* (i.e., fraction of test examples classified correctly), the "imbalance-aware" measure *G-mean* [12] (*geometric mean*) and the micro-averaged *Precision* and *Recall* and *F1* measures for the (minority) class of insecure traces.

5.2   Base Model/Example-Driven Classification Approaches Tested

We empirically studied the behavior (and limitations) of the two categories of approaches that have been devised so far for the classification of security-breaches, i.e., model-driven and example-driven—which we are proposing to employ as two of the complementary base classifiers of our probabilistic classification framework.

Specifically, we built up a model-driven classifier C^M that just checks the conformance to the "disclosed" breach model in $bkModels$, by implementing the Montecarlo-based method proposed in [10] and summarized in Sect. 4 (while setting set $\epsilon = 0.15$ and $1 - \alpha = 95\%$). This method constitutes indeed the sole model-driven breach classification approach in the literature that can deal with "activity-unaware" log traces (if excluding the former preliminary conference version of the same work, published in [11]).

By contrast, as discussed in Sect. 4, the discovery of the example-driven trace classifier C^E could be accomplished by resorting to a vast variety of inductive learning methods, after suitably abstracting the given collection of annotated traces into a propositional vectorial form. For the sake of simplicity and of concreteness, we next present only the results obtained when applying the rule-based learning algorithm Ripper [17] (more specifically, the Java implementation of this algorithm provided by the Weka's plugins $JRip$) to the propositional dataset obtained by transforming each of given example trace s into a tuple containing two kinds of boolean attributes: (i) an attribute f^x for any event type x, indicating whether x appears in s, and (ii) an attribute $f^{x,y}$ for any pair of event types x, y, indicating whether s contains an occurrence of x before one of y.

It is worth noticing that we observed similar results and trends when evaluating the accuracy of the classifiers discovered by using other learning methods (including the Weka's plugins for the induction of SVM, decision-tree, MLP, Gaussian-Process, and Random-Forest classifiers) as well as other sequence encoding methods.

5.3   Test Results

Figure 3 shows the scores achieved by the base classification methods considered, for different combinations of $bK\%$ and $oP\%$. For each combination, the averages of the results obtained in 18 different trials (performed as explained in Sect. 5.1) are reported.

Let us first study the behavior of the methods in terms of Recall, based on Fig. 3(c). Clearly, when keeping fixed $bk\%$ (whatever its value) and making $oP\%$ increase, C^E improves their Recall score, differently from the model-driven classification scheme C^M, the recall of which only depend on the amount of background knowledge (set through $bk\%$) it can exploit. This can be explained by observing that, with $bk\%$ fixed, increasing $oP\%$ leads to an increase for the amount of hidden models in $hdModels$ that can be used to label the example traces, so that the classifier C^E can be trained with more kinds of breaches and have a higher chance to correctly classify an insecure process instance as such. An opposite Recall's trend happens when increasing $bK\%$ and keeping $oP\%$ fixed, which corresponds to both shrinking the amount of breach examples used for training C^E and providing C^M with more breach models. Indeed, this causes a progressive increase (resp. decrease) of the Recall of C^M (resp. of C^E).

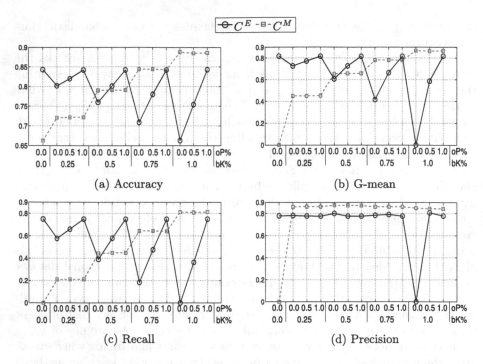

Fig. 3. Average effectiveness scores obtained by the two base classification methods described in Sect. 5.1 when varying $bk\%$ and $oP\%$.

In terms of Precision results, shown in Fig. 3(d), all the baseline methods look pretty stable, irrespectively of $bK\%$ and $oP\%$. The only exceptions concern C^E in the special configuration $bk\% = 1.0 - oP\% = 1.0$, where $hdModels = \emptyset$ and all the example traces were labelled as secure. In this case, indeed, the baselines classified all the test traces as secure, so getting Precision of $\frac{0}{0}$, which we eventually evaluated as 0, as usual in the literature—in fact, in this extreme configuration both classifiers also got a Recall of 0.

The trends of the Accuracy and G-mean scores in Fig. 3(a), (b) resemble the Recall's ones, modulo the fact that the Accuracy curves never go down to 0, and settle on 0.67 in the configurations where the other metrics are zeroed. This descends from the fact that 67% of the log traces belong to the secure class, and even a "dumb" majority classifier that assigns any trace to this class (hence missing every insecure one) can reach this accuracy level.

Further final remarks on the results obtained in the experimentation are provided in the next section.

6 Discussion and Extensions

The empirical analysis illustrated in the previous section proves that there is no ultimate winner among the two different kinds of methods that have been developed so far in the literature for the security-oriented classification of process traces. Indeed, it is clear that the effectiveness of either kind of methods strongly depends on the quality of the background information it is provided with. In principle, one should prefer a model-driven (resp. an example-driven) classifier when there is a guarantee that the security-breach models defined by the experts (resp., the example annotated traces available) suffice to cover well enough all the different types of insecure instances of the process under analysis. However, in real application scenarios, it is not reasonable to have such a guarantee, so that the idea of relying on only one of these orthogonal approaches leads to the risk of incurring in poor classification results, even in settings where just one of the two information sources is not complete enough. This confirms the soundness of our proposal to exploit both kinds of classification methods in an integrated manner, adopting a meta-classification approach.

Currently, we are working on testing and tuning different concrete instantiations of the classification framework proposed here, which is indeed parametric to several core methodological parts of it, which include primarily (i) the language to be adopted for the specification of process/breach models, and (ii) the encoding and learning methods to be employed for inducing the base example-driven classifier (and possibly the meta-classifier).

In fact, for the sake of readability, in the presentation of our framework we have just adopted simplistic solutions. However, the framework can be easily extended by replacing these solutions with more advanced ones. In particular, the rules used to represent process/breach models (which suit well the case of flexible processes and breach patterns) may be imprecise in modelling highly-structured processes. In such a case, however, it is easy to make the framework use more precise behavioral models. For example, allowing it use expressive composition rules (e.g., where a rule's tail is augmented with conditions describing the "context" that activates the rule), or even automata or Petri nets, just requires to exploit more refined (but existing) compliance checking mechanisms.

On the other hand, it is possible to also consider a wider range of attributes for both events and activities (including, e.g., their durations and executors) and extend the composition rules to allow the specification of conditions over such attributes. In particular, using information on both the start and end time of the activities can help describe the behavior of a process/breach more precisely, possibly stating constraints on the way two activities may/must overlap over the time (e.g., strict precedence, temporal inclusion).

References

1. van der Aalst, W.M.P., Pesic, M., Schonenberg, H.: Declarative workflows: balancing between flexibility and support. Comput. Sci. - R&D **23**(2), 99–113 (2009)
2. van der Aa, H., Leopold, H., Reijers, H.A.: Checking process compliance on the basis of uncertain event-to-activity mappings. In: Dubois, E., Pohl, K. (eds.) CAiSE 2017. LNCS, vol. 10253, pp. 79–93. Springer, Cham (2017). https://doi.org/10.1007/978-3-319-59536-8_6

3. Accorsi, R., Stocker, T.: On the exploitation of process mining for security audits: the conformance checking case. In: ACM SAC 2012, pp. 1709–1716 (2012)
4. Baier, T., Mendling, J., Weske, M.: Bridging abstraction layers in process mining. Inf. Syst. **46**, 123–139 (2014)
5. Bennett, P.N., Dumais, S.T., Horvitz, E.: Probabilistic combination of text classifiers using reliability indicators: models and results. In: ACM SIGIR 2002, pp. 207–214 (2002)
6. Bose, R., van der Aalst, W.: Discovering signature patterns from event logs. In: CIDM 2013, pp. 111–118 (2013)
7. Jagadeesh Chandra Bose, R.P., van der Aalst, W.M.P.: Abstractions in process mining: a taxonomy of patterns. In: Dayal, U., Eder, J., Koehler, J., Reijers, H.A. (eds.) BPM 2009. LNCS, vol. 5701, pp. 159–175. Springer, Heidelberg (2009). https://doi.org/10.1007/978-3-642-03848-8_12
8. Cuzzocrea, A., et al.: A robust and versatile multi-view learning framework for the detection of deviant business process instances. Int. J. Coop. Inf. Syst. **25**(04), 1–56 (2016)
9. Cuzzocrea, A., Folino, F., Guarascio, M., Pontieri, L.: A multi-view multi-dimensional ensemble learning approach to mining business process deviances. In: 2016 International Joint Conference on Neural Networks (IJCNN), pp. 3809–3816. IEEE (2016)
10. Fazzinga, B.: Online and offline classification of traces of event logs on the basis of security risks. J. Intell. Inf. Syst. **50**(1), 195–230 (2018)
11. Fazzinga, B., Flesca, S., Furfaro, F., Pontieri, L.: Classifying traces of event logs on the basis of security risks. In: Ceci, M., Loglisci, C., Manco, G., Masciari, E., Ras, Z.W. (eds.) NFMCP 2015. LNCS (LNAI), vol. 9607, pp. 108–124. Springer, Cham (2016). https://doi.org/10.1007/978-3-319-39315-5_8
12. Kubat, M., Holte, R., Matwin, S.: Learning when negative examples abound. In: van Someren, M., Widmer, G. (eds.) ECML 1997. LNCS, vol. 1224, pp. 146–153. Springer, Heidelberg (1997). https://doi.org/10.1007/3-540-62858-4_79
13. Leontjeva, A., Conforti, R., Di Francescomarino, C., Dumas, M., Maggi, F.M.: Complex symbolic sequence encodings for predictive monitoring of business processes. In: Motahari-Nezhad, H.R., Recker, J., Weidlich, M. (eds.) BPM 2015. LNCS, vol. 9253, pp. 297–313. Springer, Cham (2015). https://doi.org/10.1007/978-3-319-23063-4_21
14. Lo, D., Cheng, H., Han, J., Khoo, S.C., Sun, C.: Classification of software behaviors for failure detection: a discriminative pattern mining approach. In: Proceedings of the 15th ACM SIGKDD International Conference on Knowledge Discovery and Data Mining. pp. 557–566. ACM (2009)
15. Nguyen, H., Dumas, M., La Rosa, M., Maggi, F.M., Suriadi, S.: Mining business process deviance: a quest for accuracy. In: Meersman, R., et al. (eds.) OTM 2014. LNCS, vol. 8841, pp. 436–445. Springer, Heidelberg (2014). https://doi.org/10.1007/978-3-662-45563-0_25
16. Sauer, T., Minor, M., Bergmann, R.: Inverse workflows for supporting agile business process management. In: Wissensmanagement, pp. 204–213 (2011)
17. Witten, I.H., et al.: Data Mining: Practical Machine Learning Tools and Techniques. Morgan Kaufmann, Burlington (2016)

CMMI-DEV v1.3 Reference Model in ArchiMate

Luís Valverde[1][✉], Miguel Mira da Silva[1][✉],
and Margarida Rolão Gonçalves[2][✉]

[1] Instituto Superior Técnico, Universidade de Lisboa, Lisbon, Portugal
{luis.valverde,mms}@tecnico.ulisboa.pt
[2] QuasInfalível, Lda, Lisboa, Portugal
margarida.goncalves@quasinfalivel.pt
https://tecnico.ulisboa.pt/en/, http://www.quasinfalivel.pt/

Abstract. Reference models allow the verification of existing concepts of a model and how these concepts relate to each other, giving an idea of how a model works. The purpose of this paper is to address the problem of the perceived complexity of Capability Maturity Model Integration (CMMI) by proposing a graphical reference model using ArchiMate as the chosen Enterprise Architecture (EA) modeling language. This paper will focus on the part of CMMI related to the development of both products and services, more known as CMMI-DEV in the version 1.3. With ArchiMate as the EA modeling language, we develop using the Design Science Research Methodology (DSRM) the CMMI-DEV v1.3 reference model to reduce the perceived complexity of the framework by representing their concepts and relationships with graphical concepts of ArchiMate. In this paper, we demonstrate our proposed reference model (artifact) with the use of an EA of an organization and evaluate it with well know techniques to evaluate design science artifacts. The paper concludes with some findings and future work on this topic.

Keywords: Reference models
Capability Maturity Model Integration · Enterprise Architecture
ArchiMate · Design Science Research Methodology · Artifact

1 Introduction

Nowadays, organizations are increasingly focusing on the quality and functionality of the software they develop, much of which involves redesigning their software process to follow the best practices known in the industry so that the software they developed becomes trustworthy, reliable, of a high quality, fit its purpose and is consistently delivered on time to their customers [1].

A software process can be seen as the glue that connects people, tools and equipments, and procedures and methods in a consistent way through a set of interrelated activities that, together, interact to develop and maintain software and the associated work products and may include tools, methods, material,

© Springer Nature Switzerland AG 2018
H. Panetto et al. (Eds.): OTM 2018 Conferences, LNCS 11230, pp. 191–208, 2018.
https://doi.org/10.1007/978-3-030-02671-4_11

and people [1, 2]. The Software Engineering Institute (SEI) that is an American research, development and training center involved in computer software and network security and many other quality experts believe that there is a close relationship between the quality of the delivered software and the quality and maturity of the software processes [1]. To achieve mature processes with improved quality and effectiveness, the steps that organizations take are not so intuitive as they can not do it without a certain type of guidance, therefore there was a need to create initiatives that lead to a focus on software processes and on ways to improve them [3].

Software Process Improvement (SPI) initiatives define and measure best practices and processes for improving the existing processes in organizations, intending to help them develop higher quality software and products, and achieve their business goals more efficiently, where the business goals can be: faster delivery of software and products to the market on time and budget; improved customer satisfaction; improved quality of software and products; and cost reduction of development. In other words, SPI helps organizations to work smarter, as they build software and products, better, faster and cheaper than the competitors, providing a faster Return On Investment (ROI) [1].

There are international standards, frameworks, and models that define different programs for SPI, these are a set of best practices that are aligned with the business goals and play a key role in helping organizations to achieve their strategic goals. From all the models used for SPI, the one that is more related to software development (practices for processes in software and systems engineering) is Capability Maturity Model Integration (CMMI). CMMI contains a set of best practices from several areas, each of them to achieve a given purpose, that can include tools, methods, materials, and people. Organizations follow these practices to improve their software processes and meet their business needs more efficiently, as well as allowing them to do continuous improvement, adapt to technological innovations, and to prevent defects, to face future challenges [4–6].

Currently, the CMMI framework addresses three constellations, that are known as collections of CMMI components for a specific area of interest. The focus of this work is in the development constellation also known as CMMI-DEV [2] in the version 1.3.

Due to the complexity of CMMI-DEV v1.3, many organizations struggle to understand the model as they get lost in the various concepts of model and their relationship. To reduce the perceived complexity of the model, we propose to represent CMMI-DE v1.3 with an EA using for that matter, the ArchiMate modelling language to represent both concepts and relationships of the framework and test if the reading of model in ArchiMate can be easier for the users of the model as well as analyze potential benefits of representing it with an EA.

In this paper, we are going to use the Design Science Research Methodology (DSRM), so the structure of this document is strongly influenced by its phases: in Sect. 2 we describe the problem and motivation as well as the methodology used in the paper; in Sect. 3 we have the definition of the fundamental concepts and other author's researches related to our own; in Sect. 4 we describe our proposal; in Sect. 5 we demonstrate our proposal with the EA of an organization;

in Sect. 6 we do a critical evaluation of our proposal using well-known techniques to evaluate design science artifacts and constructs; finally, in Sect. 7 we have the conclusions of this paper as limitations and future work.

2   Problem

The main benefits of adopting CMMI for process improvement are the reduction of the overall costs, project schedule (improvements in schedule predictability and reductions in the time required to do the work), quality improvement (reductions in the number of defects), customer satisfaction and ROI. These benefits have been proven by many case studies of organizations that adopted CMMI from around the world and from different areas [4]. Despite this, only a little fraction of the software developing organizations adopt CMMI, so it is important to find why organizations do not adopt CMMI.

The authors from [7] studied why organizations do not adopt CMMI by collecting and analyzing two months of sales data from an Australian company that sells CMMI appraisals and improvement services. Their findings show that most organizations do not adopt CMMI because the CMMI program is expensive, it requires time that many organizations do not have, organizations do not understand the benefits of using it and many organizations think they are too small to adopt it [this being a direct influence from not understanding the benefits of CMMI and resources constraints (budget and time)].

Two years later the authors from [8] replicated the previous study in another country, Malaysia, by using data collected from three consulting companies that sell a CMMI Level 2 program subsidized by the Malaysian government. This study supports the study conducted by [7] and identifies the same adoption problems as well as the problem of organizations having other priorities than process improvement.

Another study [9], now related to organizations who have already adopted CMMI, was done through a study conducted in China with the purpose to investigate the adoption of CMMI. The authors inquired most of the organizations who have been rated in a certain CMMI assessment to find the reasons, success factors, benefits and problems in the adoption of CMMI. Through the survey's data, they identified the following problems: organizations think that CMMI is an over-complex and dogmatic process, the costs are high when adopting it and that there is a lack of automated supporting tools for CMMI.

Some of the problems previously mentioned regarding the low adoption and the adoption of CMMI are directly related to its complexity and difficulty to be understood. The existing textual reference model of CMMI-DEV v1.3 [2] has so much information that users tend to get lost as there are a total of twenty-two process areas and near two hundred practices in the model with various relationships between them, increasing the effort of users in reading this representation of the reference model. This, allied to the fact that CMMI tells what to do and not how to do it for process improvement increases its complexity.

Summarizing, the problem that this paper will tackle is the perceived complexity of CMMI-DEV v1.3 by its users. To tackle this problem we are going to propose a different way to represent the model, by using models with graphical elements which usually are more appellative to people and easier to understand.

To develop and evaluate our reference model to address this problem, we will use the DSRM. The DSRM is an iterative methodology that incorporates principles, practices, and procedures to carry out a Design Science research in the Information Systems (IS) area by creating and validating artifacts to address the research problem. These artifacts are broadly defined as constructs (vocabulary and symbols), models (abstractions and representations), methods (algorithms and practices), and instantiations (implemented and prototype systems) [10,11].

In this research, the artifacts that we are going to create and evaluate are going to be models and constructs, by models we are referring to the reference model of CMMI-DEV v1.3 and by constructs the mapping we chose between the CMMI-DEV v1.3 and ArchiMate.

3   Related Work

3.1   Capability Maturity Model Integration

CMMI was developed by a group of expert professionals from industry, government, and the Software Engineering Institute at Carnegie Mellon University and it is used to guide organizations to improve their processes and, consequently, improve software quality, time and costs of development and productivity by describing an evolutionary improvement path from ad hoc, immature processes to disciplined, mature processes with improved quality and effectiveness [5,6].

In our research, we are going to focus on the Development constellation also known as CMMI-DEV, that is used by organizations from different industries to cover activities for developing both products and services. CMMI-DEV is composed of practices that cover project management, process management, systems engineering, hardware engineering, software engineering, and other supporting processes used in the development and maintenance of projects. The version 1.3 is constituted by twenty-two process areas divided into four categories: Process Management, Engineering, Project Management and Support [5,6].

CMMI can be also used for assessment, with the SCAMPI appraisal methods, that can be used for evaluating the maturity of the organizations (staged representation) and capability of the processes (continuous representation), the maturity levels enables organizations to improve a set of related processes and the capability levels enable organizations to improve an individual process area or group of process areas chosen by the organizations. In both approaches to reach a particular level, an organization must satisfy all the goals of the process areas or set of process areas that are selected for improvement [5,6].

3.2   Enterprise Architecture

Currently, to manage the complexity of any large organization or system, an architecture is needed. Architecture can be described as the properties and concepts that are fundamental to a system in their environment, incorporated into its elements, relationships and in the principles required for its analysis, design and evolution [12].

The use of architecture in an organization gave form to the EA term which is defined by Lankhorst [12] as *"a coherent whole of principles, methods, and models that are used in the design and realization of an enterprise's organizational structure, business processes, information systems, and infrastructure"*.

Nowadays, business performance increasingly depends on a balanced and integrated EA, involving stakeholders, their competencies, organization structures, business processes, Information Technologies, finances, products, and services, as well as its environment. EA is seen as a holistic view of the representation of an organization and helps design the various layers of the EA in an organization [13].

One of the advantages of using EA models to describe these types of IS standards, frameworks and models is the fact that EA models are more readable and understandable than textual descriptions, lowering the user's perceived complexity and therefore facilitates the learning of this type of frameworks.

3.3   ArchiMate

ArchiMate is an EA modeling language developed by The Open Group, with focus, mainly in enterprise modeling, allowing to describe, analyze and visualize business architectures, using for this purpose graphical concepts for the entities and relations. ArchiMate provides uniform representations of EAs by the form of models, that contain well-defined relationships allowing to connect concepts from different domains of the business architectures. In order to do this, it defines several layers in the EA, relating and distinguishing each of them with a service-oriented approach, that is, the layers expose their functionality as a form of services to the layers above [14].

ArchiMate also defined a core set of generic relationships that can be used to connect the generic concepts and give a meaning to the way we look at the models. These relationships are *"overload"*, which means that the exact meaning of the connection between two concepts differs, depending on the source and destination concept [14].

3.4   CMMI Ontologies

There is no proposal on how to model CMMI in ArchiMate, but there are authors that propose other CMMI ontologies and metamodels using different modeling languages.

In the paper [15], the authors propose a CMMI-DEV v1.3 ontology based on Web Ontology Language (OWL), a primary language for the Semantic Web. The authors followed the same approach used in this language, first they formalize an ontology for the CMMI-DEV v1.3 that captures the main concepts and then they use a generic OWL reasoner to check the consistency of the representation of the CMMI-DEV 1.3 ontology to derive the classification of the level of maturity of the organization's development process. This will allow to determine the maturity levels of organizations through their data on the practices performed.

In the paper [16], following the paradigm Model Driven Development (MDD), the authors proposed a tool that supports the automatic generation of a language that can be used to specify practices of process areas. This generation is performed through a CMMI metamodel in Unified Modeling Language (UML) that they propose as well.

These researches were an important contribution to our work, as they will be used as a starting point for developing the proposed CMMI-DEV v1.3 metamodel in ArchiMate that contains the main concepts of CMMI-DEV v1.3 and their relationships.

3.5   ArchiMate and Information Systems Frameworks

The use of the ArchiMate modeling language to model frameworks related to the IS area and to enable the mapping with a standard-based EA representation it is well documented. We will highlight some of the researches conducted on this topic:

Lourinho [17] proposes in ArchiMate a metamodel for the ISO 27001 standard extended with the concepts of ISO TS 33052 and 33072, with the purpose of reducing the perceived complexity of implementing these IT frameworks and maps this metamodel with COBIT 5 metamodel proposed by Almeida [22] to show a complementary way of integrating the two. The same COBIT 5 metamodel, is used in another research by Percheiro [21], that proposes a metamodel in ArchiMate on how to integrate COBIT 5 with ITIL.

In other researchers, Vicente [18,19] proposes in ArchiMate a business motivation model for ITIL and a business-specific architecture using the principles of ITIL and the EA approach.

And finally, Silva [20] proposes in ArchiMate a model for TIPA, a framework specifically used for assessing maturity for those who use ITIL and demonstrates how the model in ArchiMate allows alignment between service management and the organization's concepts and artifacts in a standardized way.

These researches were an important contribution to our work, as they will be used as a starting point when mapping ArchiMate with CMMI, these frameworks have concepts that have similar meanings to the CMMI concepts, and the ArchiMate concepts that these authors chose to represent them can be used in our research.

4   Proposal

The purpose of the CMMI-DEV v1.3 reference model is to facilitate the learning of the CMMI-DEV v1.3 framework (reduce the perceived complexity), as well as understand what are the main components and their relationships. To solve the problem previously identified in Sect. 2, we propose a metamodel of CMMI-DEV v1.3 developed in ArchiMate (ontology), containing the main components and relationships between them, and further ahead a model more detailed that we named CMMI-DEV v1.3 reference model.

The metamodel has the main concepts of the CMMI-DEV v1.3 and their relations, giving an overview with focus on the metaclasses that represent the components and their relationships. The reference model is a more detailed model that has all the instantiations of the metaclasses identified in the metamodel.

To create our models in ArchiMate, we first chose which concepts of ArchiMate could represent the CMMI concepts. In order to do this, we did the mapping shown in Table 1 based on the previous studies in using ArchiMate with IS frameworks [17–22]. Then we chose which ArchiMate relationships to use and witch are the existing relationships between the CMMI concepts using the textual reference model of CMMI [2] and other studies of CMMI ontologies [15–17].

Table 1. Mapping CMMI concepts with ArchiMate

CMMI	ArchiMate	Justification [5, 14]
Process Area Category	Grouping	A Process Area Category represents a group of Process Areas from the same area of interest and can be represented by the Grouping concept which in turn can represent an element that composes concepts that belong together based on some common characteristic
Process Area	Grouping	A Process Area in CMMI is defined as a cluster of related practices and can be represented by the Grouping concept which in turn can represent an element that composes concepts that belong together based on some common characteristic
Purpose	Goals	A Purpose statement in CMMI describes the purpose of the process area and can be represented by the Goal concept which in turn can represent a high-level statement of intent, direction, or desired. In this case, it is due to the purpose represent the intention of satisfying the process area
Specific Goal	Goal	A Specific goal in CMMI describes the unique characteristics that must be present to satisfy the process area and can be represented by the Goal concept which in turn can represent a high-level statement of intent, direction, or desired. In this case, it is due to the fact that the goals represent the desired characteristic to implement a process area
Generic Goal	Goal	A Generic Goal in CMMI is called "generic" because the same goal statement applies to multiple process areas, and can be represented by the Goal concept for the same reason as in the Specific Goal
Specific Practice	Business Process	A Specific Practice in CMMI is the description of an activity that is considered important in achieving the associated specific goal and can be represented by the Business Process concept which in turn can represent a human activity
Generic Practice	Business Process	Generic practices are called "generic" because the same practice applies to multiple process areas and can be represented by the Business Process concept for the same reason as in the Specific Practice
Subpractice	Business Process	A subpractice in CMMI is defined as a detailed description that provides guidance for interpreting and implementing a specific or generic practice and can be represented by the Business Process concept for the same reason as in the Specific and Generic Practice
Example Work Products	Business Object	The Example Work Products in CMMI defines section lists of sample outputs from a specific practice and can be represented by the Business Object concept which in turn can represent information produced and consumed by an activity
Generic Practice Elaborations	Deliverable	Generic practice elaborations appear after generic practices to provide guidance on how the generic practices can be applied uniquely to process areas and can be represented by the Deliverable concept, which in turn can represent a support concept

For the relationships, we chose the composition to represent that a concept of CMMI its constituted by others CMMI concepts. We use this relationship instead of the aggregation because the concepts that constitute a concept only exist if that concept exists. We use the serving relationship when a concept of CMMI provides something to another concept of CMMI, the realization relationship it's used when a concept of CMMI helps to achieve another CMMI concept, the access relationship is used when referring that a concept of CMMI accesses (create) another CMMI concept and finally, for the association relationship, we use it when there are CMMI concepts that have some type of association that can not be represented by other ArchiMate relationship.

Based on the ArchiMate concepts and relationships that we chose to represent CMMI, we propose the CMMI-DEV v1.3 Metamodel as its shown in Fig. 1.

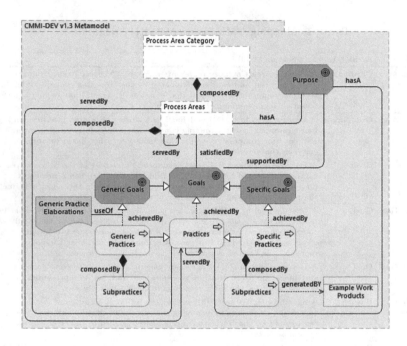

Fig. 1. CMMI metamodel in ArchiMate

So, we can read the metamodel in following way: a process area category is composed of a set of process areas, each process area has a purpose and each process area is composed of practices (specific and generic) that also have a purpose. To satisfy a process area all of the goals (specific and generic) have to be achieved\satisfied, and this can be done by performing all the practices (specific and generic) related to each goal, the achievement of all the goals also support the purpose of the process area. To achieve the generic goals in a particular process area the generic practice elaborations are used to provide guidance on how the generic practices can be applied. The practices are composed by subpractices, in the case of the subpractices of specific practices to verify if it is being implemented, there are example work products that are sample outputs of these subpractices. Each process area can be supported by other process areas as well as each practice can be supported by other practices and process areas.

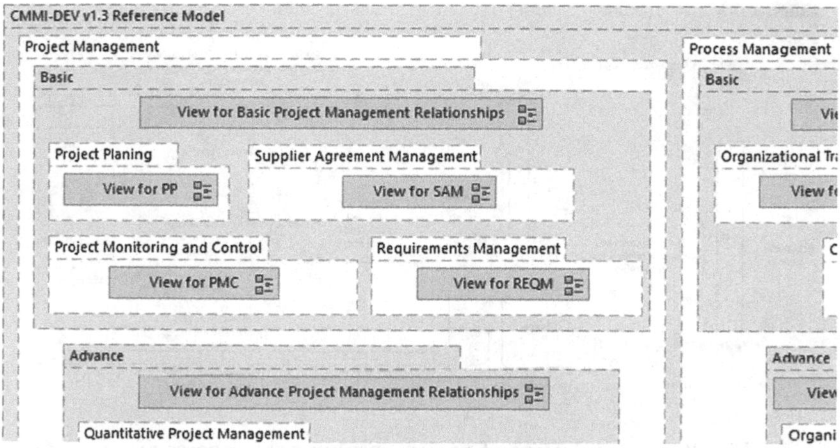

Fig. 2. Part of CMMI-DEV v1.3 reference model

The reference model shows all the instantiations of the metaclasses identified in the metamodel, showing all the concepts of CMMI-DEV v1.3 and their relations in a more detailed way. In Fig. 2 we have part of the reference model. As we can see in this part of the model, the first level of abstraction contains the process areas categories divided by basic and advanced, each of them containing a set of process areas [5].

To navigate to other parts of the reference model we have the views concepts, that are used as links to other parts of the model and if clicked on, will give a more detailed model of the concept they are referring to. For instance, if we click on the View for Basic Project Management Relationships we navigate to a detailed model of the interactions among the basic project management process areas and with other process area categories as shown in the Fig. 3. From this model, we can read as an example that the process area Project Monitoring and Control (PMC) provides corrective actions to the process area Supplier Agreement Management (SAM).

Returning to the first level of abstraction of our reference model, we can navigate to other parts of the model, for instance to navigate to a process area we click on the view related to that area, for example, if we click on the View for REQM it will show a detailed model of the process area Requirements Management (REQM) as it is shown in Fig. 4. This model contains all of the concepts of the process area, the purpose of the area, all the practices that compose the area, divided in specific and generic as well as all the high-level relationships with related process areas. From this model, we can see that the process area Risk Management (RSKM) provides the identification and analysis of risks to this area. For each type of practices, we a have view, to give in more detail the practices that are necessary to achieve the goals and satisfy the process area.

As an example, for the specific practices of this process area, we have the View for REQM Specific Practices that allows us to navigate to a detailed model

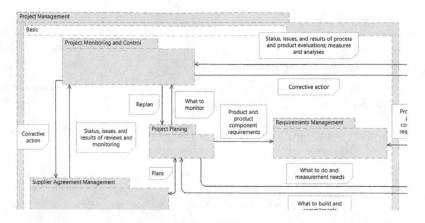

Fig. 3. Basic relations of project management process areas

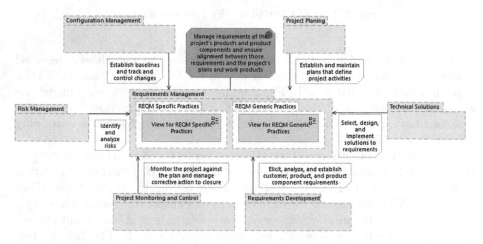

Fig. 4. REQM process area

of the specific practices of this process area. Figure 5 shows two models, one containing all the specific practices of these process area and other with a detailed model of one of these specific practices (REQM SP 1.2 - Obtain Commitment to Requirements). So, in the part of Fig. 5 containing all the specific practices we can see that this process area is satisfied by achieving the specific goal Manage Requirements, that can be accomplished by performing the five specific practices that compose the area. In the part of the specific practice 1.2 of these process area, we can see what the goal that this specific practice helps achieve, the subpractices that compose this specific practice, the example of work products of each subpractice and the process areas that support this specific practice. So we can see in the model for instance, that the subpractice Assess the impact of requirements on existing commitments has as output the Requirements impact

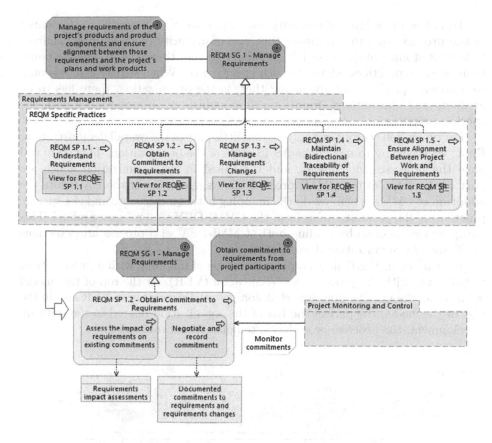

Fig. 5. REQM specific practices and specific practice 1.2

assessments as well as see that the process area PMC provides the monitor of commitments to this specific practice.

The full CMMI-DEV v1.3 reference model has twenty-two process areas divided by the four process area categories. We then, have a view for each process area, for types of practices in each process area and for each practice of the process area. The model contains as well for each process area views for the generic goals and practices and for each generic practice. In total the proposed reference model as more than 450 views.

5 Demonstration

To demonstrate the utility of representing CMMI-DEV v1.3 with a reference model developed using the EA modeling language ArchiMate, we are going to use as an example one of the biggest technological Portuguese organizations. One of their departments is adopting CMMI, more precisely, trying to achieve level 3 of maturity to became CMMI-DEV v1.3 Level 3 certified\rated.

To achieve this level of maturity they must satisfy all specific goals related to the process areas that compose this level of maturity (eighteen process areas in level 3 of maturity). To satisfy each specific goal they have to give response to all specific practices related to each specific goal. When we say give response to a specific practice, we are saying that, in the organization, there has to be artifacts and affirmations (from interviews) which are in accordance with the specific practices.

For dimension reasons, we only show a little part of the overall demonstration. First, we are going to model the AS-IS state of the organization. This state will have the processes, documents, and tools used in the organization which are part of the scope of the CMMI project, that is, the state of the EA before the adoption of CMMI. Then, we do the mapping between this state and the specific practices of the processes areas from the CMMI-DEV v1.3 reference model. This mapping can be done by reading both, CMMI-DEV v1.3 process areas sections in [2] and the organization documentation.

We can see in Fig. 6 an example of this type of mapping with a process area, in this case, with the process area Verification (VER). At the top of this model we have all the specific practices that compose the process area VER and in the rest of the model, the part of the EA of the organization related to the software development, the process, procedures, templates, and tools used.

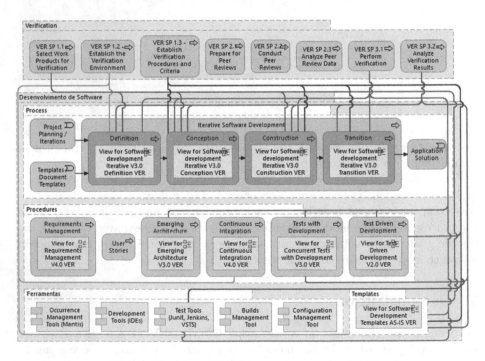

Fig. 6. Mapping of VER process area with AS-IS

We then have the relationships we found between this process area and this part of the EA, that identify the activities and documents that give response to the VER specific practices. For instance, we can see in this mapping that three of the specific practices related with peer reviewing of the process area VER (VER SP 2.1-2.3) are not mapped with any part of the organization EA.

In this model we have again the view elements, that lets us navigate to more specific model for each element of the model, specifying in a more detail the relationships between the element and the specific practices. For instance, we can see, that the specific practices VER 1.1, 1.2, 3.1 and 3.2 maps with the Software Development Iterative/Incremental Definition phase, to see in more detail what parts of this phase gives response to these practices, we have the View for Software development Iterative/Incremental V3.0 Definition in Fig. 7 that have the activities of the phase, the roles involved in the activities, and the documents which are represented with concepts from the Business Layer of ArchiMate and the tools used in the activities which are represented with concepts of the Application Layer of ArchiMare mapped with the specific practices.

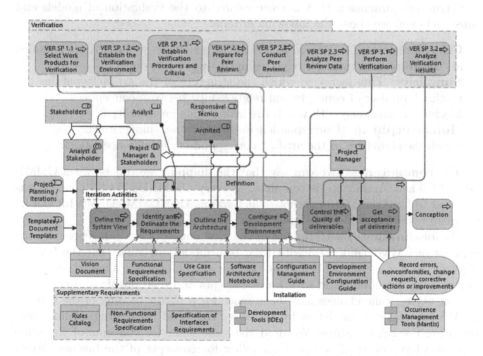

Fig. 7. View for Software development Iterative/Incremental V3.0 Definition VER

We use the association relationship to identify that an element of the EA gives response to a specific practice. These relationships have different colors to facilitate the reading of this mapping, for each specific practice we have a different color to represent the relationships associated with it, for instance, we use the green color to specify the elements of the EA that give response to the specific practice VER SP 1.2.

With this demonstration we can show that our reference model can be mapped with a EA of an organization before adopting CMMI and use this map to represent a different way of showing a gap analysis as well as be used to identify parts of the AS-IS that can be reused when developing the TO-BE state (EA state after adopting CMMI, that is, in conformity with CMMI).

6   Evaluation

In this paper we will do a critical evaluation of our proposal, to support this we will use the criteria identified by Prat [23] that identified the main criteria for artifact evaluation used in papers that follow the DSRM.

These authors concluded that DSRM artifacts can be viewed as systems and divided the identified criteria by five systems dimensions: Goal; Environment; Structure; Activity and Evolution. The ones we found most relevant belong to the structure dimension that is more related to the evaluation of models and constructs and we chose the following criteria:

- **Completeness**: The degree to which the structure of the artifact contains all necessary concepts and relationships between concepts;
- **Simplicity**: The degree to which the structure of the artifact contains the minimal number of concepts and relationships between concepts;
- **Style**: The elegance with which the artifact has been built;
- **Homomorphism** (Correspondence with another model): The degree to which the structure of the artifact corresponds to a reference model.

For **completeness**, we can say that the mapping we did between CMMI-DEV v1.3 and ArchiMate is complete, as every CMMI-DEV v1.3 concept was mapped to an ArchiMate concept, which means that CMMI-DEV v1.3 can be completely represented using ArchiMate.

As for **simplicity**, with the use of the view concepts, we can represent each concept of CMMI-DEV v1.3 with their own model, avoiding that the CMMI-DEV v1.3 reference model is only one big complex model but a model composed of less complex models and with fewer concepts and relationships.

For **style**, some choices have been made for a better reading of the CMMI-DEV v1.3 reference model as for instance: We avoid the overlap of lines representing the relationships; We used the same color for concepts of the same type and layer of architecture (e.g., yellow for concepts of the business layer) and changed the tone of the color when a concept is overlapping other (composition); As for the textual description of all concepts to be visible, we resize the graphic concepts of ArchiMate; For the names of the concepts, the views start always with "View for", for the Specific and Generic Goals and Practices the names have the sequential number given in [5], in the case of the specific goal and practice the name starts with the prefix of the process area (e.g., REQM SG 1 for the first specific goal of the process area REQM and REQM SP 1.1

for the first specific practice associated with the first specific goal of the process area REQM).

As for **homomorphism**, it can be evaluated with the support of the Wand and Weber ontological analysis method [24], that let us compare two grammars and identify ontology deficiencies between them. Here we are going to evaluate the developed construct (mapping between CMMI and ArchiMate). There are four deficiencies that the method states (Fig. 8).

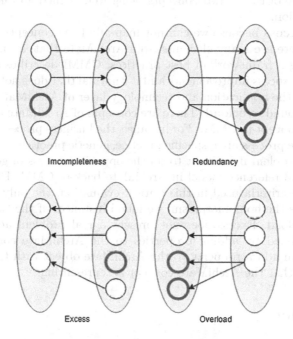

Fig. 8. Ontological deficiencies ([24])

- **Incompleteness**: can each concept of the set from the first grammar be mapped with a concept from the set of the second grammar? (the mapping is partial if it's not total);
- **Redundancy**: can each concept of the set from the first grammar be mapped with more than a single concept from the set of the second grammar? (the mapping is redundant if it is not ambiguous);
- **Excess**: can each concept of the set from the second grammar be mapped with a concept from the set of the first grammar? (the mapping is excessive if there are concepts of the second grammar without mapping);
- **Overload**: can each concept of the set from the second grammar be mapped to exactly one or more concept from the set of the first grammar? (the mapping is overloaded if at least one concept from the set of the second grammar is mapped to more than one concepts in the set of the first grammar).

Having the definitions of each deficiency, we can evaluate the mapping between the CMMI-DEV v1.3 (first grammar) with ArchiMate (second grammar).

We've already see that CMMI-DEV v1.3 can be completely represented with ArchiMate, so we did not find **incompleteness** in our mapping.

As for **redundancy**, we did not find it because there was no concept from CMMI that could be represented by more than one ArchiMate concept. This may be a consequence of the CMMI concepts being well defined and not ambiguous in their description.

We found **excess** because we can not map all of the concepts of ArchiMate with CMMI, there are many elements from ArchiMate that are not mentioned in CMMI. Being a framework of best practices, CMMI describes activities and motivations for process improvements and it's normal that does not mention concepts related to the application and technology layer of ArchiMate for instance.

Finally, we found **overload**. There are concepts of ArchiMate that represent more than one concept in CMMI. For instance, the business process of ArchiMate can represent the process area, specific practice, generic practice and subpractice. This can be a problem if we want to do the opposite process of going from the CMMI-DEV v1.3 reference model in ArchiMate back to CMMI-DEV v1.3.

From all the criteria used in this critical evaluation, the only one that was not satisfied was the homomorphism, we found instances of the two deficiencies excess and overload. Excess does not present a real problem and overload if occurs can be fixed by adding properties to the ArchiMate concepts. While modeling, we can add a property to the ArchiMate object with the type of the CMMI concept that the ArchiMate concept is representing.

7   Conclusion

This research was developed with the purpose of solving the problem of the perceived complexity that users have when reading the CMMI model, focusing on the version 1.3 of CMMI-DEV. There are already a few studies that approached some problems related to other IS frameworks using EA and ArchiMate to tackle them but there is little research about EA and ArchiMate with CMMI.

Thus, to solve this problem, we chose to use an EA approach and develop a reference model using the modeling language ArchiMate of the CMMI-DEV v1.3. With the visual representation of this reference model, we believe that we can lower the user's perceived complexity of CMMI and therefore turn CMMI easier to use, allowing users to read and understand the CMMI framework more easily and in a more interactive way.

Also, we can take advantage of using the approach of representing CMMI with the ArchiMate EA modeling language, for instance, we can represent the assessment in an organization with models, showing them a different way to see a gap analysis by mapping CMMI practices of the reference model with the present state of an organization (AS-IS) and show what parts of the organization EA give response to CMMI and what practices are not satisfied.

There are limitations to this work that are going to be tackled in future work. For instance, in the evaluation of our proposed models, we should validate the utility of our models using different techniques, by showing them to CMMI experts and practitioners and make some interviews and questionnaires to them to get feedback of our proposal.

Also, as future work, we want with the use of the modeling techniques to do the mapping between our CMMI-DEV v1.3 reference model and the TO-BE EA state of the same organization used in the demonstration section of this paper and show what where the changes in the EA of the organization after adopting CMMI (AS-IS vs TO-BE), underlying the changes they had to make to be CMMI compliant. Another interesting thing would be to apply the same approach to the new version of CMMI and then map the two reference models versions to show the differences in the new version in comparison to the older version.

References

1. O'Regan, G.: Concise Guide to Software Engineering: From Fundamentals to Application Methods. Springer, Heidelberg (2017). https://doi.org/10.1007/978-3-319-57750-0
2. CMMI Product team: CMMI for Development (CMMI-DEV). Version 1.3. Technical Report, CMU/SEI-2010-TR-033, Software Engineering Institute (2010)
3. Fantina, R.: Practical Software Process Improvement. Artech House Inc., Norwood (2005)
4. Goldenson, D., Gibson, D.L.: Demonstrating the impact and benefits of CMMI: an update and preliminary results. Special Report, CMU/SEI-2003-SR-009, Software Engineering Institute (2003)
5. Chrissis, M.B., Konrad, M., Shrum, S.: CMMI for Development: Guidelines for Process Integration and Product Improvement. Addison-Wesley Professional, Boston (2011)
6. Chaudhary, M., Chopra, A.: CMMI for Development: Implementation Guide. Apress (2017). https://doi.org/10.1007/978-1-4842-2529-5
7. Staples, M., Niazi, M., Jeffery, R., Abrahams, A., Byatt, P., Murphy, R.: An exploratory study of why organizations don't adopt CMMI. J. Syst. Softw. 80(6), 883–895 (2007). https://doi.org/10.1016/j.jss.2006.09.008
8. Khurshid, N., Bannerman, P.L., Staples, M.: Overcoming the first hurdle: why organizations do not adopt CMMI. In: Wang, Q., Garousi, V., Madachy, R., Pfahl, D. (eds.) ICSP 2009. LNCS, vol. 5543, pp. 38–49. Springer, Heidelberg (2009). https://doi.org/10.1007/978-3-642-01680-6_6
9. Wu, Z., Christensen, D., Li, M., Wang, Q.: A survey of CMM/CMMI implementation in China. In: Li, M., Boehm, B., Osterweil, L.J. (eds.) SPW 2005. LNCS, vol. 3840, pp. 507–520. Springer, Heidelberg (2005)
10. Von Alan, R.H., March, S.T., Park, J., Ram, S.: Design science in information systems research. MIS Q. 28(1), 75–105 (2004)
11. Peffers, K., Tuunanen, T., Rothenberger, M.A., Chatterjee, S.: A design science research methodology for information systems research. J. Manag. Inf. Syst. 24(3), 45–77 (2007). https://doi.org/10.2753/MIS0742-1222240302

12. Lankhorst, M.: Enterprise Architecture at Work: Modelling, Communication, and Analysis. Springer, Heidelberg (2017). https://doi.org/10.1007/978-3-662-53933-0
13. Greefhorst, D., Proper, E.: Architecture Principles: The Cornerstones of Enterprise Architecture. Springer, Heidelberg (2011). https://doi.org/10.1007/978-3-642-20279-7
14. ArchiMate® 3.0.1 Specification, an Open Group Standard. http://pubs.opengroup.org/architecture/archimate3-doc/
15. Soydan, G.H., Kokar, M.M.: A partial formalization of the CMMI-DEV-A capability maturity model for development. J. Softw. Eng. Appl. 5(10), 777–788 (2012)
16. Musat, D., Castaño, V., Calvo-Manzano, J.A., Garbajosa, J.: MATURE: a model driven based tool to automatically generate a language that supports CMMI process areas specification. In: Riel, A., O'Connor, R., Tichkiewitch, S., Messnarz, R. (eds.) EuroSPI 2010. CCIS, vol. 99, pp. 48–59. Springer, Heidelberg (2010). https://doi.org/10.1007/978-3-642-15666-3_5
17. Lourinho, R., Almeida, R., Mira da Silva, M., Pinto, P., Barafort, B.: Mapping of enterprise governance of IT practices metamodels. In: Themistocleous, M., Morabito, V. (eds.) EMCIS 2017. LNBIP, vol. 299, pp. 492–505. Springer, Cham (2017). https://doi.org/10.1007/978-3-319-65930-5_39
18. Vicente, M., Gama, N., da Silva, M.M.: Using ArchiMate to represent ITIL metamodel. In: IEEE 15th Conference on Business Informatics, Vienna, pp. 270–275. IEEE (2013). https://doi.org/10.1109/CBI.2013.45
19. Vicente, M., Gama, N., da Silva, M.M.: Modeling ITIL business motivation model in ArchiMate. In: Falcão e Cunha J., Snene, M., Nóvoa, H. (eds.) IESS 2013. LNCS, vol. 143, pp. 86-99, Springer, Heidelberg (2013). https://doi.org/10.1007/978-3-642-36356-6_7
20. Silva, N., da Silva, M.M., Barafort, B., Vicente, M., Sousa, P.: Using ArchiMate to model a process assessment framework. In: Proceedings of the 30th Annual ACM Symposium on Applied Computing, pp. 1189–1194. ACM (2015). https://doi.org/10.1145/2695664.2699486
21. Percheiro, I., Almeida, R., Pinto, P.L., da Silva, M.M.: Towards conceptual metamodeling of ITIL and COBIT 5. In: Themistocleous, M., Morabito, V. (eds.) EMCIS 2017. LNBIP, vol. 299, pp. 478–491. Springer, Cham (2017). https://doi.org/10.1007/978-3-319-65930-5_38
22. Almeida, R., Pinto, P.L., da Silva, M.M.: Using ArchiMate to integrate COBIT 5 and COSO metamodels. In: Proceedings of the 13th European Mediterranean and Middle Eastern Conference on Information Systems (EMCIS), Krakow, Poland (2016)
23. Prat, N., Comyn-Wattiau, I., Akoka, J.: A taxonomy of evaluation methods for information systems artifacts. J. Manag. Inf. Syst. 32(3), 229–267 (2015). https://doi.org/10.1080/07421222.2015.1099390
24. Wand, Y., Weber, R.: On the ontological expressiveness of information systems analysis and design grammars. Inf. Syst. J. 3(4), 217–237 (1993). https://doi.org/10.1111/j.1365-2575.1993.tb00127.x

Data Analytics Challenges in Industry 4.0: A Case-Based Approach

Manel Brichni[(⊠)] and Wided Guedria

Department of IT for Innovative Services (ITIS),
Luxembourg Institute of Science and Technology (LIST),
5, Avenue des Hauts-Fourneaux, 4362 Esch-sur-Alzette, Luxembourg
{manel.brichni,wided.guedria}@list.lu

Abstract. Creating business value with data analytics is a continuous process that requires to effectively consider the design and deployment of powerful analytics solutions. This requires a significant effort in understanding, customizing, assembling and adapting these solutions to the specific environment. However, this might be different from one context to another. The objective of this paper is to discuss the use of data analytics in Industry 4.0 by harvesting some challenges and lessons-learnt. A case-based approach is followed, as a research methodology to explore and understand complex and common issues related to data analytics. Scalability, interoperability and standardization are among the topics that are reviewed.

Keywords: Data analytics · Manufacturing
Case study research methodology

1 Introduction

Data Analytics is a recent phenomenon with the potential to transform and enhance the business value of products and services [32]. It is an interdisciplinary field that allows discovering hidden insights from massive amounts of structured and unstructured data, using methods such as statistics, machine learning, data mining, and predictive analytics in order to help companies in their decision making. One of the main industries that are taking advantage of data analytics capabilities is manufacturing [3,21,28].

With the need to strengthen the manufacturing companies' competitive position, the manufacturing industry has been continuously evolved to reach digitalization capabilities [4,15]. In most companies, different sensors implanted in different machines are able to communicate with each other and with humans in order to gather insights that could not be identified while being isolated. To this end, data from the entire production value chain [23], including products, customers, and orders data is networked in multiple systems to help capacity planning and production logistics, through production, all the way to quality

© Springer Nature Switzerland AG 2018
H. Panetto et al. (Eds.): OTM 2018 Conferences, LNCS 11230, pp. 209–221, 2018.
https://doi.org/10.1007/978-3-030-02671-4_12

control [12]. In this context, manufacturing will be transformed from single auto-mated cells to fully integrated, automated facilities that boost flexibility, speed, productivity and quality [23]. This phenomenon is known as Industry 4.0, as the next industrial revolution where data analytics is being part of [5].

However, manufacturing companies might face various and different chal-lenges to be able to take advantage of analytics capabilities. Literature inves-tigated this topic from both practical and research levels [11,15,19,20,24,35], in order to understand the challenges facing Industry 4.0 with the use of data analytics. However, to the best of our knowledge, literature does not provide a sufficient number of real case scenarios in manufacturing which limits the applicability of its findings. Consequently, the aim of this paper is to provide a real case scenario in manufacturing, in order to harvest some challenges and lessons-learnt and to contribute to the understanding of such a complex domain. To proceed, we came across with a real case scenario in collaboration with a steel making company, which has been digitizing essential functions along with its value chain, by continuously using growing and innovative technologies and data-based services.

The remainder of this paper is structured as follows. First, the research methodology and question are described in Sect. 2. Next, some preliminaries and related work are discussed in Sect. 3, followed by the presentation of the case-based scenario (Sect. 4). Then, the identified challenges in Industry 4.0 are analyzed in Sect. 5. Section 6 concludes the paper and brings forward some per-spectives.

2   Case-Based Research Methodology

For the purpose of this paper, an exploratory case study research methodology [10,27,31,33,34] is adapted to our objectives. Its strength is the ability to tackle the data analytics topic in real world settings, but also to open up the door for further examination of our findings. This helps to identify rigorous challenges and opportunities and to contribute to the state of the art with new applicable insights. As part of the case study research methodology, this paper is focused on the identification of the challenges with the use of analytics in the context of Industry 4.0.

According to [10], first, a case study research needs to be guided by the research question(s) in order to draw attention to the issues of the considered domain. Second, because the meaning of experience is also central in research, the literature that had the most relevance for the research question(s) needs to be reviewed. Third, a use case scenario needs to be undertaken to gain a deeper understanding of the domain. Finally, the findings based on the purpose and the research question(s) should be analyzed.

Indeed, the content of this paper falls into the steps of the case study research methodology, by defining in the following the research question, followed by some related work, the description of the use case scenario and the presentation of some challenges in Industry 4.0 with the use of data analytics.

Research Question

Developing and deploying data analytics solutions require a lot of understanding of the business needs, challenges and opportunities that might be different from one context to another. Particularly, in the context of Industry 4.0, manufacturing organizations need to involve powerful data analytics solutions that deal with digital technologies and data-driven services. Thus, our main research question is:

- What are the challenges facing a typical manufacturing company with the use of data analytics in Industry 4.0?

The next section presents some background and related work discussing the way literature has dealt with the challenges with the use of data analytics in the context of Industry 4.0.

3 Preliminaries and Related Work

The term Industry 4.0 was coined by the German federal government in the context of its high-tech strategy in 2011 [15]. It represents the fourth industrial revolution [12]. In the next sections, the life cycle of industrial manufacturing is described, followed by an introduction to Industry 4.0 and a discussion on some related work in the literature.

3.1 Life Cycle of Industrial Manufacturing

Industry 4.0, by its name, indicates that three industrial revolutions exist.

- **Industry 1.0:** Industry history started with the mechanization of production assets by the end of the 18th century. It is characterized by the introduction of mechanical manufacturing equipment that revolutionized the way products were made.
- **Industry 2.0:** The second industrial revolution began around the beginning of the 20th century. It is characterized by the use of the electrical energy for mass production based on the division of labor.
- **Industry 3.0:** The third industrial revolution began in the early 1970s and is still evolving nowadays. It has revolutionized manufacturing processes by introducing electronics and IT that support manual and brain work by bringing intelligence to machines.
- **Industry 4.0:** It is driven and enabled by networking and internet, through sensors communicating with each other and with humans in order to gather insights that could not be identified while being isolated.

Industry 4.0 as the phenomenon revolutionizing traditional manufacturing has become the focus and interest of most manufacturing industries. However, clear and exact definition is not provided, but it is usually defined by its design, scenarios and technological capabilities [11,15,25].

Industry 4.0 has been tackled by different manufacturing companies [7,12,23] that are seeking to transform their production processes, as well as by researchers [2,11,15,19,24,25,35] who are interested in studying the way such an evolving domain is applied. In the next section, some related work are discussed.

3.2   Related Work

Although investigating the topic of Industry 4.0 from a research perspective is difficult, it remains considered by researchers as an important and evolving topic [2,15,19,24,25,35]. In this section, literature is discussed from two points of view related to the challenges with the use of data analytics in the context of Industry 4.0: the considered case scenarios in manufacturing, and the categories of the identified lessons-learnt.

For example, six design principles have been identified in [11] from a literature review that companies should take into account when implementing and using data analytics in Industry 4.0: interoperability, virtualization, decentralization, real-time capability, service orientation and modularity. Actually, these are the main principles that define Industry 4.0 [17]. [35] describes worldwide movements in intelligent manufacturing, including governmental strategic plans from different countries and strategic plans from major international companies. As a result, a generic framework for intelligent manufacturing is given. [24] reviews some major EU industrial guidelines, roadmaps, and scientific literature that led to the depiction of the term Industry 4.0. This review sheds light on a new strategic perspective of the industrial evolution facing some fundamental changes and technological breakthroughs.

Despite the significant output of literature in defining the concept of Industry 4.0, describing initiatives and identifying opportunities and challenges, it still lack of real case scenarios in manufacturing, where most of the existing case studies in this domain are based on some literature review [2,15,19,24,25,35]. This is one reason why it still very difficult to tackle this domain from a research perspective.

However, despite this lack in real case scenarios, there still exist some meaningful papers that tackle analytics and industry 4.0 from a real perspective [6,17,30]. However, most of them describes the challenges from only a technical point of view, namely data acquisition, transformation, analysis, modeling and security.

Generally, to the best of our knowledge, one of the main domains that have been widely addressed by literature with the use of analytics is education [1,16,18]. Even though applying analytics for educational and learning purposes have shown important results and emphasized meaningful challenges and lessons-learnt, Industrial challenges remain different from education, because of its profitable and competitive strategy. For example, usability gaps that are facing students [18] should not be an issue in an industrial context using, applying or developing analytics solutions.

The aim of this paper is to contribute to the literature by discussing some important challenges facing a typical company in the context of Industry 4.0

from different points of view based on a specific manufacturing case scenario, as described in the following.

4   Case-Based Scenario

The considered case scenario has been conducted in collaboration with a leader in steel making. It explores predictive maintenance [22,29] based on data analytics techniques and infrastructure. For confidentiality reasons, the name of the company is omitted. For the purpose of this paper, we associate a fictive name to the company: ID4.

Steel making is a critical process in the manufacturing industry [13]. It follows very complex processes as it depends on several inputs, but also because it requires a lot of techniques and systems to manage and optimize the overall plant efficiency and stability. To this end, maintaining products distribution, such as oxygen enrichment, blast moisture, cold blast temperature, as stable as possible allows to consistently produce metal at a pre-established quality [22,29]. However, the process which takes place is highly complex to model and analyze which requires high digital capabilities. To this end, actively exploring data analytics solutions is needed, so that necessary control actions for thermal regulation can be quickly identified and applied.

For example, as part of the predictive maintenance, temperature prediction allows to seamlessly produce metal at a pre-established quality in order to keep the mix close to a target temperature. However, temperature prediction for steel making is a nonlinear and highly complex problem to model and analyze. New forms of process control could be identified and applied in actual production by exploring and deploying suitable analytics solutions.

Particularly, several facts have led ID4 company to proceed with its predictive maintenance by deploying data analytics solutions. First, the types of its data are becoming more complex. The produced data in ID4 is of both types structured and unstructured, which makes the analysis very challenging. In the current setup, the company records about 3000 to 5000 data points from its sensors for a typical process every minute such as temperature, pressure, heat losses, chemical analysis etc. Besides, data describing the chemical composition of raw materials is considered, in addition to operator controlled parameters. Second, the existing storage solutions, mainly Relational DataBase Management System (RDBMS), have become unable to deal with such a huge volume of data. Third, processing and exploring data with basic analytics techniques, in the case of temperature prediction, for example, do not provide satisfactory results and are not able to deal with a high number of complex parameters. For instance, the visualization tools that ID4 is using do not allow to visualize results in real-time while taking into account the changes that may happen inside the factory or by operators, basically every millisecond. In addition, data security has always been crucial in manufacturing and is continuously increasing with new needs, such as temperature prediction, where data needs to be extracted in real time, checked by operators, shared with data analysts and validated by business managers and other experts. Such a process involves several data exchanges, which requires ensuring its security and integration. Finally, making a multidisciplinary team with the required skills has been one concern of ID4. In fact, predictive maintenance subject has involved several experts in different domains involving business experts, data analysts and computer scientists.

To summarize, in the context of Industry 4.0, the predictive maintenance process would be positively impacted by the data analytics capabilities, but it is also facing several challenges that ID4 needs to deal with, as presented in the next section.

5   Challenges in Industry 4.0

Manufacturing companies, including ID4, are facing several challenges to be able to take advantage of analytics capabilities. The observed challenges are organized as follows: Technical, industrial and organizational. For the purpose of this paper, we focus mainly on the technical challenges.

5.1   Technical Challenges

Multiple Functionalities and Solutions

In manufacturing, a data analytics infrastructure requires varied components including data ingestion, storage, processing and visualization. Besides, each component involves more than one technique and/or solution.

For example, like other companies, ID4 is using traditional RDBMS for storing sensors data gathered from their sensors and equipments. As a result, multiple limitations have been observed mainly related to performance issues such as slow running queries, frequent pre-computing results and lack of scalability. To deal with such limitations, ID4 is frequently deleting its data, usually after few days. This is also observed in its customers' premises as ID4 is offering and providing the same storage solutions, so that they are facing the same issues in both locations.

Since in ID4 sensors data is always timestamped, monitored, down-sampled, and aggregated over time, it might be more suitable to use more advanced storage capabilities such as Time Series DataBases (TSDB), which offer parallel query performance, high concurrency, high volume random reads and writes, etc. To deal with the visualization problems that occur in ID4, we recommend more than one option with two levels of capabilities; one used locally and one used on its customers' premises. To this end, several commercial and open source tools have been evaluated and a heterogeneous solution for visualization have been deployed. Among others, Qlik Sense[1], Power BI[2] and Grafana[3] have been evaluated based on multiple criteria namely their flexibility to be integrated in ID4 ecosystem, their interoperability, their cost and their efficiency to deal with

---

[1] www.qlik.com.

[2] www.powerbi.microsoft.com.

[3] www.grafana.com.

advanced visualization options. As a result, a heterogeneous solution have been deployed, where Qlik Sense is used in ID4 for monitoring internal processes, such as overall equipment effectiveness, whereas Grafana is deployed in each ID4's client premises for monitoring their activities.

Design and Deployment

Building a data analytics solution requires a continuous design and deployment process [14]. The design component itself implies the assembly and/or the development of analytics solutions while the deployment part leads to a need of adapting to specific environment-related constraints. In ID4, the environment is also likely to run on top of multiple hosting targets that evolve over time, consequently requiring the deployed solutions to follow. This has been an important challenge in ID4, particularly for predictive maintenance.

For instance, automatically (re)deploying the predictive models into production requires enormous configuration efforts that are costly in terms of implementation, time-to-deploy and maintenance. In addition, because predictive maintenance models, such as temperature prediction, are essentially developed locally, they may not be stable for production-level deployment, they may not be compatible with the existing production components and they may not be easily transferable from one software environment to another in real production lines.

To this end, some capabilities to simplify the deployment of analytic models into production, throughout several systems in an efficient way, exist either from commercial or open sources solution, such as Predictive Model Markup Language (PMML)[4]. However, one of the main limitations of PMML is its failure in considering complex preprocessing steps like included in the predictive models developed by ID4. Consequently, this limits the applicability of the resulting PMML code substantially.

Consequently, it becomes mandatory for the analytics solutions and techniques, such as predictive models, to comply with such deployment standards and at the same time to be effectively integrated with the company's local tools while ensuring their effective functioning and preventing overhead. In general, a successful solution is expected to address on the one hand the design, development and evaluation of the analytics solution and on the other hand to ensure that the run-time deployed solutions encapsulate the desired functionalities and features that were developed earlier. As described in this section, important costly considerations need to be taken into account.

Big Data

In the context of Industry 4.0, manufacturing companies have been seeking to enlarge their portfolio to offer high value added knowledge-based services using data and advanced analytics. In the case of predictive maintenance for example, the data modeling task requires a huge amount of data of high quality in order to return accurate and meaningful results to substantially impact the decision-making process.

---

[4] http://dmg.org/pmml/v4-3/GeneralStructure.html.

On the one hand, many issues have been encountered in ID4 due to the data quality (incomplete, noisy, manually inserted, etc.). For instance, due to the frequent changes and evolution in the business processes and in the use of new materials and equipments, some data may still be missing. This can be as well due to the quality of the sensors that are not able to deal with extremely high temperature that may exceed 1500° C. Consequently, the quality of data may degrade the results of the data-driven models, in the case of the temperature prediction for example.

On the other hand, obviously, the effectiveness of the predictive modeling increases with the training amount of data. However, this might not be a rule. In ID4, predictive models have demonstrated that the data generated over 3 months has shown more accurate results than the data generated over 6 months. This is mainly due to the different changing states of the plant that have decreased the quality of the data. Consequently, coupling quantity and quality of data is mandatory to ensure accurate and meaningful analytics results.

Scalability and Decentralization
Providing decentralized infrastructure for manufacturing companies which are distributed in space (different plants, headquarters and R&D centers) helps to gain improvements from several angles.

For example, with many entities in over a dozen countries, ID4 would improve several capabilities including distributed storage, large-scale aggregations and data retrieval, high availability and scalability, access mechanisms and more. In the case of the temperature prediction, data can be automatically captured by sensors or manually entered by operators. It should be retrieved in real-time from each plant. It needs to be highly available and specific for each plant and it needs to be supported by scalable storage capacity and memory. To this end, a highly scalable, flexible and decentralized analytics infrastructure is a key concern in manufacturing senarios, such as temperature prediction.

5.2   Industrial Challenges

Interoperability
In Industry 4.0, one of the main challenges is the digital transformation. Indeed, companies such as ID4 try to align with new standards and embrace new related challenges. In this context, interoperability and communication between human beings, machines and resources [8,9,11,26] are paramount. This includes the connection and the coordination between legacy systems and new ones, as well as between human resources and this technology.

For example, in ID4, new technologies for storing, processing and visualizing sensors data need to effectively communicate with existing technologies such as the Process Rules System (PRS). In ID4, PRS is used to define, execute and monitor the decision logic within the company. In this case, one of the most challenging tasks is to apply the right rules and constraints that automate data analytics operations via the PRS. This becomes more challenging especially when the execution of such operations needs to run across many different and heterogeneous systems, including data ingestion, processing and visualizing. For example, in ID4, a typical process requires an operator to insert new values in the database that is storing real time sensors data. In such case, the operator inserts a new value in the visualization tool in the plant, that is then checked and validated by PRS, and finally the request is executed, so that the the new value is inserted in the database. This process requires the company to adopt interoperable infrastructure allowing heterogeneous systems to communicate in a secure and automated way.

One consequence of the process described above is the adaptability of operators and process engineers to the new digital capabilities and approaches. Usually, operators in manufacturing are used to enter data manually, which implies most of the time errors and missing values. As a result, since new trends in analytics and digital technologies have emerged, companies need to think and act like digital natives, willing to experiment with new technologies and learn new ways of operating. Throughout our use case, we noted the importance of establishing a digital culture, where training people, communicating, optimizing the use of interoperable resources may be required.

Standardization

In order to manage interoperability, standards are used to facilitate a key success factor for communication between systems. However, standards can be a barrier to new technologies, especially that the industry ecosystem lacks of digital standards, norms and certifications. As a result, promoting the communication between infrastructure systems and operators through standards and protocols need to deal with a lot of systems and requirements.

In ID4, new initiatives to standardize a unique specification for devices are adopted that ensure security of data gathering, for example, the Object Linking and Embedding for Process Control Unified Architecture (OPC-UA) and the Classical OPC developed by OPC Foundation[5]. They allow ensuring the communication between machines thorough IoT spans, and to interconnect devices while providing rules for their communication.

However, since manufacturing companies, such as ID4, use several and different solutions for data analytics, it becomes mandatory to integrate standards requirements in data analytics solutions. For example, the way data is shared between ID4's clients needs to comply with the way it is ingested from sensors based on OPC-UA protocols.

In addition, in the considered use case, not only sensors devices are considered, but also other sources, such as Manufacturing Execution Systems (MES) and Enterprise Resource Planning (ERP) systems including data about customers, suppliers, schedules, shifts etc. Consequently, even with a highly advanced solution for connecting devices, significant configuration efforts in terms of implementation, maintenance, administration and security are required.

---

[5] https://opcfoundation.org/about/opc-technologies.

5.3 Organizational Challenges

Expertise, Resources and Culture
The evolution of manufacturing from Industry 1.0 to 4.0 has shown a huge and rapid growth in automation, which makes it difficult to train or target people with the suitable skills, such as data analysts.

In ID4, making a multidisciplinary team with the required skills has been a challenging task. To this end, new initiatives, systems and tools have been implemented. Although they provide high capabilities, most of them are new and their uses need to be learned, adapted and regularly maintained. Thus, a lot of effort has been made. This is the case with new storage solutions used by ID4 that need to deal with time series data with specific format and way to query. To proceed, regular training sessions have been organized involving IT, data scientists and plants operators to learn and understand the use of the new technology. Besides, new execution processes have been added, such as using the PRS to monitor the decision logic with data analytics. Even though such processes are time consuming and require synchronization and collaboration, ultimately success or failure will depend not on the analytics technologies, but on the way they are used by people.

6 Conclusion and Perspectives

In this paper, we came across with a real case scenario from manufacturing in the context of Industry 4.0 that tackles predictive maintenance using data analytics. As a result, several challenges and lessons-learnt have been identified. Technical challenges include the need for a varied and heterogeneous infrastructure, standardization and scalability, whereas business challenges include the need for adequate quantity and quality of data, the interoperability between systems and with humans, as well as considering the cost of deployment.

Despite the care we took by adopting a case study as a research methodology, some limits have been identified. For example, due to confidentiality reasons, some information could not be shared or detailed. In addition, a common limitation of a case study method is the fact to be based on a single case exploration making it difficult to reach generalizable insights.

In terms of perspectives, we aim at expanding our case study not only to manufacturing but also to other domains where data analytics can be applied to deliver more generalized insights and to contribute to the understanding of this domain from multiple perspectives. In the long term, we aim at expand our results to design and develop a generalizable and adaptable data analytics solution that would deal with common business needs.

Acknowledgment. This work has been conducted in the context of the CoBALab project (Collaborative Business Analytics Laboratory), financed by the National Research Fund (FNR) of the Grand Duchy of Luxembourg (FNR). It involves the initiation of a joint laboratory between the Luxembourg Institute for Science and Technology (LIST) and the Business Analytics research centre at the National University of Singapore (NUS). It focuses on research activities in key areas, such as Industry 4.0, with the aim of achieving research with impact within the Business Analytics domain.

The second author has contributed to this work in the context of the PLATINE project (PLAnning Transformation Interoperability in Networked Enterprises), financed by the national fund of research of the Grand Duchy of Luxembourg (FNR), under the grant C14/IS/8329172.

References

1. Bakharia, A., Kitto, K., Pardo, A., Gašević, D., Dawson, S.: Recipe for success: lessons learnt from using xapi within the connected learning analytics toolkit. In: Proceedings of the Sixth International Conference on Learning Analytics & Knowledge, LAK 2016, pp. 378–382 (2016)
2. Bauernhansl, T.: Die vierte industrielle revolution. der weg in ein wertschaffendes produktionsparadigma. Industrie 4.0 in Produktion, Automatisierung und Logistik: Anwen-dung, Technologie, Migration, pp. 3–35 (2014)
3. Brichni, M., Dupuy-Chessa, S., Gzara, L., Mandran, N., Jeannet, C.: Business intelligence for business intelligence: a case study at stmicroelectronics. In: IEEE Ninth International Conference on Research Challenges in Information Science (RCIS), pp. 239–249 (2015)
4. Brichni, M., Dupuy-Chessa, S., Gzara, L., Mandran, N., Jeannet, C.: BI4BI: a continuous evaluation system for business intelligence systems. Expert Syst. Appl. **76**, 97–112 (2017)
5. Dassisti, M., et al.: Industry 4.0 paradigm: the viewpoint of the small and medium enterprises. In: 7th International Conference on Information Society and Technology, vol. 1, pp. 50–54 (2017)
6. Ferreira, L.L., et al.: A pilot for proactive maintenance in Industry 4.0. In: CISTER Conference 2016, pp. 1–9 (2017)
7. Griessbauer, R., Vedso, J., Schrauf, S.: Industry 4.0: building the digital enterprise. 2016 Global Industry 4.0 Survey (2016)
8. Guédria, W., Guerreiro, S.: Dynamic behavior control of interoperability: an ontological approach. In: Proceedings of the 9th International Joint Conference on Knowledge Discovery, Knowledge Engineering and Knowledge Management, vol. 2, pp. 261–268 (2017)
9. Guédria, W., Proper, H.A.: The need for second order interoperation - a view beyond traditional concepts. In: OTM Workshops, pp. 255–264 (2014)
10. Hamel, J., Dufour, S., Fortin, D.: Case Study Methods. Sage Publications, Newbury Park (1993)
11. Hermann, M., Pentek, T., Otto, B.: Design principles for Industrie 4.0 scenarios: a literature review. In: IEEE 49th Hawaii International Conference on System Sciences (HICSS), pp. 3928–3937 (2016)
12. HeynitzHarald, V., Bremicker, M., Amadori, D.M., Reschke, K.: Building the Factory of the Future. KPMG AG (2014)

13. Jiu-sun, Z., Xiang-guan, L., Chuan-hou, G., Shi-hua, L.: Subspace method for identification and control of blast furnace ironmaking process. In: American Control Conference, vol. 2, pp. 187–190 (2009)
14. Johnson, B.: Designing and deploying data and analytics-enabled business capabilities. Technical report, Department of Management Science and Engineering (2015)
15. Kagermann, H., Wahlster, W., Helbig, J.: Recommendations for implementing the strategic initiative Industrie 4.0. Technical report, Final report of the Industrie 4.0 Working Group (2013)
16. Kennedy, P.J.: Redesign of data analytics major: challenges and lessons learned. Proc. Soc. Behav. Sci. **116**, 1373–1377 (2014)
17. Khan, M., Wu, X., Xu, X., Dou, W.: Big data challenges and opportunities in the hype of Industry 4.0. In: International Conference on Communications (ICC), pp. 1–6 (2017)
18. Lonn, S., Aguilar, S., Teasley, S.D.: Issues, challenges, and lessons learned when scaling up a learning analytics intervention. In: Proceedings of the Third International Conference on Learning Analytics and Knowledge, LAK 2013, pp. 235–239 (2013)
19. Meissner, H., Ilsen, R., Aurich, J.C.: Analysis of control architectures in the context of Industry 4.0. Proc. CIRP **62**, 165–169 (2017)
20. Obitko, M., Jirkovský, V.: Big data semantics in Industry 4.0. In: Mařík, V., Schirrmann, A., Trentesaux, D., Vrba, P. (eds.) HoloMAS 2015. LNCS (LNAI), vol. 9266, pp. 217–229. Springer, Cham (2015). https://doi.org/10.1007/978-3-319-22867-9_19
21. Pang Yan, J.: Big data and business analytics: accelerating digital transformation in enterprises and industries [powerpoint slides]. In: European Data Science Conference (EDSC) Lecture (2016)
22. Qiu, D., Zhang, D., You, W., Zhang, N., Li, H.: An application of prediction model in blast furnace hot metal silicon content based on neural network. In: International Conference on Apperceiving Computing and Intelligence Analysis, pp. 61–64 (2009)
23. Rüßmann, M., et al.: Industry 4.0: the future of productivity and growth in manufacturing industries. Technical report, The Boston Consulting Group (2015)
24. Santos, C., Mehrsai, A., Barros, A., Araujo, M., Ares, E.: Towards Industry 4.0: an overview of European strategic roadmaps. Proc. Manuf. **13**, 972–979 (2017)
25. Schlick, J., Stephan, P., Loskyll, M., Lappe, D.: Industrie 4.0 in der praktischen anwendung. In: Industrie 4. 0 in Produktion, Automatisierung und Logistik, pp. 57–84 (2014)
26. Selway, M., Stumptner, M., Mayer, W., Jordan, A., Grossmann, G., Schrefl, M.: A conceptual framework for large-scale ecosystem interoperability and industrial product lifecycles. Data Knowl. Eng. **109**, 85–111 (2017)
27. Stake, R.E.: The Art of Case Study Research: Perspective in Practice. Sage, London (1995)
28. Tata, S., Mohamed, M., Megahed, A.: An optimization approach for adaptive monitoring in IoT environments. In: IEEE International Conference on Services Computing, vol. 116, pp. 378–385 (2017)
29. Tunckaya, Y., Koklukaya, E.: Comparative performance evaluation of blast furnace flame temperature prediction using artificial intelligence and statistical methods. Turkish J. Electr. Eng. Comput. Sci. **24**, 1163–1175 (2016)
30. Wang, S., Wan, J., Li, D., Zhang, C.: Implementing smart factory of industrie 4.0: an outlook. Int. J. Distrib. Sens. Netw. **12**, 1–10 (2016)

31. Widdowson, M.: Case study research methodology. Int. J. Trans. Anal. Res. **2**(1), 25–34 (2011)
32. Yang, X., Lu, R., Liang, H., Tang, X.: Big sensor data applications in urban environments. Big Data Res. **4**, 1–12 (2016)
33. Yin, R.K.: Case Study Research: Design and Methods. Sage Publications, Beverly Hills (1984)
34. Zainal, Z.: Case study as a research method. Jurnal Kemanusiaan bil **9**, 1–6 (2007)
35. Zhong, R.Y., Xu, X., Klotz, E., Newman, S.T.: Intelligent manufacturing in the context of industry 4.0: a review. Engineering **3**, 616–630 (2017)

Speech Acts Featuring Decisions in Knowledge-Intensive Processes

Tatiana Barboza[1], Pedro Richetti[1(✉)], Fernanda Baião[1],
Flavia Maria Santoro[1], João Carlos Gonçalves[1], Kate Revoredo[1],
and Anton Yeshchenko[2]

[1] Federal University of the State of Rio de Janeiro,
Avenida Pasteur 458, Rio de Janeiro, Brazil
{tatiana.barboza,pedro.richetti,fernanda.baiao,
flavia.santoro,joao.goncalves,
katerevoredo}@uniriotec.br
[2] Vienna University of Economics and Business (WU), Vienna, Austria
anton.yeshchenko@wu.ac.at

Abstract. A Knowledge-Intensive Process (KiP) is specified as a composition of a set of prospective activities (events) whose execution contributes to achieving a goal and whose control-flow, at the instance level, typically presents a high degree of variability among its several past executions. Variability is a consequence of a combination of decision points and informal interactions among participants on collaborative and innovative activities. These interactions may occur through message exchange, thus understanding the interplay of illocutionary acts within messages may bring insights on how participants make decisions. In this paper, we propose mechanisms that identify speech acts in the set of messages that mostly lead to decision points in a KiP providing an understanding of conversational patterns. We empirically evaluate our proposal considering data from a company that provides IT services to several customers.

Keywords: Knowledge-intensive process · Decision-making · Speech acts

1 Introduction

A Knowledge-Intensive Process (KiP) is specified as a composition of a set of prospective activities (events) whose execution contributes to achieving a goal and whose control-flow, at the instance level, presents a high degree of variability among its past executions. Variability is observed as a result of a combination of decision points and interactions among process participants on collaborative and innovative (i.e., unanticipated) activities [1, 2]. The management of KiPs is still a challenge; particularly, generating models through mining techniques proves difficult.

Santos França et al. [3] proposed KiPO, an ontology for the domain of KiP, which provides a semantically rich conceptualization, well-founded in UFO (Unified Foundational Ontology) [4], encompassing the 4 relevant perspectives to precisely understand and represent a KiP. Decision making is one of the most relevant perspectives. From another side, decision mining is a research area that has been improved in

© Springer Nature Switzerland AG 2018
H. Panetto et al. (Eds.): OTM 2018 Conferences, LNCS 11230, pp. 222–237, 2018.
https://doi.org/10.1007/978-3-030-02671-4_13

Business Process Management. Rozinat and Aalst [5] affirmed that decision mining is a way to detect and analyze decision points that affect the routine of a process. Decision discovery algorithms are generally applied to structured logs and aim to discover not only the points where there are deviations in the process, but the rules that guide those decisions [6, 7]. In structured process log, decision points mostly constitute a choice between possible branches. Nevertheless, Campos et al. [8] argued this type of discovery is not enough in the case of a KiP, since many decisions are not recorded in structured logs but, rather, occur in the interactions among process participants and proposes to apply Natural Language Processing and text mining techniques to discover decision-making records. Decision mining is the term crafted to discover decisions from process data. It is an active research field [9] that mostly relies on the discovery of branches in workflows and analysis of structured data. At the best of our knowledge, this current proposal is the first attempt to mine decisions in KiPs from message logs using natural language processing techniques.

Richetti et al. [10] proposed an automatic mechanism to discover speech acts representing Beliefs, Desires and Intentions of participants of a KiP from a message log and analyzed the process execution from the perspective of illocutionary points. In this paper we follow Richetti et al. approach for speech acts discovery, towards finding patterns of speech in KiP related to decisions made by participants. The goal of this paper is to propose mechanisms that identify speech acts that most characterize decision points in a KiP. An experiment was conducted on the dataset of the company that provides IT services to several customers.

The paper is organized as follows: Sect. 2 presents the research theoretical foundations; Sect. 3 describes the proposal; Sect. 4 presents an application scenario that preliminarily evaluations of the proposal; Sect. 5 discusses the results obtained; and Sect. 6 concludes the paper and presents future work directions.

2 Background Knowledge

The proposal of this paper is based in the concepts of Beliefs, Desires and Intentions as firstly proposed in the seminal BDI model [11], and its relation to Decision making elements as defined in KiPO (see Sect. 2.1). Moreover, the Speech Act Theory (see Sect. 2.2) supports the identification of decision patterns in conversation among the process participants.

2.1 Beliefs, Desires, Intentions and Decisions in KiPO

KiPO ontology [3] was developed to describe KiPs considering complementary perspectives, which were organized in sub-ontologies grouping relevant concepts of a KiP: (i) Collaboration Ontology (CO), knowledge exchange and collaboration between process participants; (ii) Business Process Ontology (BPO), traditional processes elements such as Activities, Flows and Data Objects; (iii) Decision Ontology (DO), representing the design rationale of the decisions made by the participants of the process; (iv) Business Rules Ontology (BRO), KiPs are typically more declarative than procedural by nature; (v) finally, the core concepts of a KiP, namely Core Ontology

(KiPCO), such as the beliefs, desires and intentions that drive the participant's decisions on the activities to execute, while also establishing relationships among all the perspectives. This paper is concerned with the concepts present in the Knowledge-Intensive Core Ontology and their relations to elements from the Decision Ontology.

KiPCO mainly deals with Agents and their Intentional modes and Knowledge Intensive Activities (KiA) they perform. An Agent is the one who intentionally commits to reach a Goal by executing an action (which is then named a Knowledge-intensive Activity). The Agent is motivated by her Desire and acts according to her Beliefs. An Agent may experience Feelings [3]. The intentional modes of agents follow the Belief-Desire-Intention Model (BDI) [11], that still an active research topic on modeling and simulation of agents' subject [12, 13].

BDI clarifies the human practical reasoning to explain future-directed intentions. It was applied in several areas (e.g. Psychology and Agent-based computing), and is especially relevant to KiP, since it aims to describe the human reasoning process that leads towards performing a specific activity. In this way, BDI concepts are fundamental mental attitudes of agents: beliefs have a 'mind-to-world' direction of fit (agents try to adapt their beliefs to the truths of the world), while intentions have a 'world-to-mind' direction of fit when agents try to make the world match their goals.

In a KiP, the activities executed by an agent are directed towards the realization of some specific state of the world. The anticipatory representation of such state is the agent's goal and the driving force behind her actions. Therefore, Goal is a very important concept, usually depicted in the sense of Process-level (complex action) Goals and Activity-level (atomic action) Goals. Moreover, the mechanism leading from desires to intentions is of key relevance in a KiP scenario, since decision-making is critical to the process, especially at the instance-level, where the actual "next step" of the activity flow is chosen.

In KiPO, an Agent intentionally commits to solving a Question by making a Decision. A Question is an unexpected event (a Contingency) defined by the Agent that is responsible for the execution of the KiA (the Impact Agent). A Decision is a specific subtype of a Knowledge-intensive Activity (KiA), which typically defines the subsequent activity that an Agent will execute. If a KiA executed by an Agent involves a Decision, then the KiA and the Decision involved in it are based on an Intention this Agent. An Intention represents the Desire of an Agent to accomplish a goal, in order to modify a domain situation to satisfy her needs. A Feeling is a mental moment belonging to an Agent. Feelings are motivated by Beliefs and Evidences generated by Facts in the universe of discourse that also influences on Agent's actions. Figure 1 is an excerpt of KiPO that highlights the intentional modes of an Agent (Belief, Desire, and Intention) and the relationships with KiA, Agent, and Decision.

2.2 Speech Acts Theory

A speech act is an illocutionary act, i.e., the act that one performs in emitting an utterance, such as an act of asserting a proposition, asking someone a question, or directing someone to do something. Searle and Vanderveken [15] describe the illocutionary act as the minimal unit of human conversation, e.g., statements, questions, and commands.

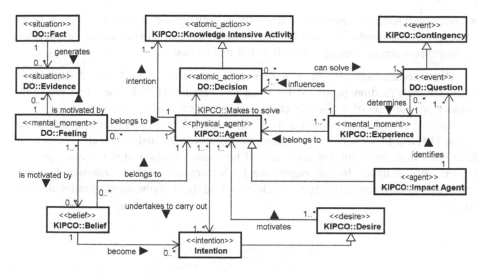

Fig. 1. Beliefs, desires, intentions and decisions in KiPO.

Whenever a speaker utters a sentence in a proper context, with certain intentions, she performs one or more illocutionary acts. Austin [16] decomposes the analysis of a speech act at three levels: the locutionary act (the performance of an utterance); the illocutionary act (the pragmatic 'illocutionary force' of the utterance); and the per-locutionary act (the actual effect of the act).

The Speech Act Theory can be applied to describe how the experience of an Intentional State is shared and communicated between individuals. Although the Intentional State itself is unique to each person, a number of externalizations can be expressed in several languages, in the form of speech acts. Yet, there is a clear distinction between Speech Acts and Intentional States: while the former are "acts" (actions, or intentional events) that depend on the production, presentation and/or usage of physical realizations (such as writing on paper or speaking), the latter are mental states, that is, they are independent of physical realization. Moreover, a speech act has a double level of intentionality: Intentional State expressed by it and the intention of properly emitting the speech act. For example, the speech act "John believes that Steve is bad" has the Intentional State of the belief "that Steve is bad" and the intention of emitting this speech act itself and conveying its associated Belief, both being distinct forms of Intentionality.

Bach and Harnish [14] proposed the Theory of Linguistic Communication and built a scheme for classifying speech acts as follows:

- Constatives: speech acts that express the speaker's beliefs, intentions and desires that the listener ends up understanding in a similar way;
- Directives: speech acts that express the speaker's attitudes towards some action, or the attitude or intention that the listener has expressed;
- Commissives: speech acts that express the intention and belief of the speaker and forces him to do something (perhaps under a certain condition);

- Acknowledgments: speech acts that express feelings considering the listener or the receiver. The speaker's intention, from what he speaks, satisfies a social expectation to express certain feelings and his belief that he does.

Those speech acts also have a number of different types. Figure 2 depicts the complete classification proposed by Bach and Harnish [14]. In the same work, the authors provide sets of verbs that characterize each class of the taxonomy.

Richetti et al. [10] proposed a method based on Theory of Linguistic Communication [14] and Process Mining to discover speech acts related to Beliefs, Desires and Intentions from an event log and showed how those relationships promotes process performance analysis. In this paper, we further argue that these intentional modes, expressed by their respective speech acts, may lead the decision-making rationale of an Agent.

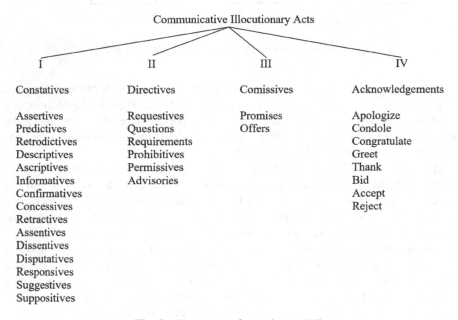

Fig. 2. Taxonomy of speech acts [14].

3   Communicative Interactions Within Decisions in KiP

We propose an automated mechanism to discover driving elements for decision-making from communicative interactions, using Natural Language Processing techniques [17] and the Theory of Speech Acts [14]. In this way, we aim to identify which speech acts stand out most in communicative interactions among agents and their association with agent's decisions.

To perform process analysis, it is fundamental to have data sources with sufficient information. Typically, business process execution systems logs have events, resources, timestamps and case ids recorded; they can also contain process data that changes while the process is executed [18]. From a knowledge-intensive perspective, other elements beyond the aforementioned ones are required to enrich the context of a process execution, such as decisions, collaboration and business rules. We argue that social media messages among agents are a rich source of contextual information that may be used in current environments; in fact, some BPM supporting systems allows participating agents to exchange message during the execution of their activities, and store this data associated to the execution log. This way, it is reasonable to consider message logs as a rich source of natural language communication exchanged among participants during process execution, that can be retrieved from email or similar forum-like threads. Any application that provides this kind of message log can be a target for this analysis.

Figure 3 shows the relation of speech acts with the Beliefs, Desires, Intentions and Feelings, as presented in the KiPO excerpt (Fig. 1), and how they participate in the communication process. Beliefs, Desires, Intentions and Feelings can be represented as Externalizations. These Externalizations are expressed in forms of specific subtypes of Speech Acts, e.g., a Constative Speech Act expresses the externalization of a Belief belonging to an Agent. A Sentence is the propositional content of one or more Speech Acts. An aggregation of sentences composes a Message that is the propositional content of a Communication. A Communication is a type of communicative act where an Agent sends information to one or more receivers. A Communicative Interaction aggregates the Communication among two or more Agents where information is exchanged. According to Guizzardi et al. [4], object-like entities have a causally active phase (e.g., an active enrollment, an ongoing troubleshooting). In this phase the particular properties of these entities are manifested through a number of events that accumulates and, at a specific point in time, represent their current life. These entities also have a causally inactive phase (e.g., a finished assignment, a solved troubleshooting) where, from this point, their properties become immutable. These two phases are specializations of their corresponding object, in a disjoint set composed by their active and inactive phases.

From a process analysis perspective, any log of a process execution keeps a representation of inactive phases of process related entities, such as events and messages. To define how to inspect communication-related elements from message logs, we consider the inactive phases of the objects, in which their immutable materialization is present in the event logs. Due to the lack of space, we omitted the active-phase classes from the diagram. This way, in a message log we have Performed Communicative Interactions that aggregate Performed Communications. Messages in the inactive phase are Exchanged Messages, composed by Uttered Sentences that are the propositional content of the Performed Speech Acts. In a Performed Communicative Interaction where Communications were performed among Agents, it is possible to observe occurrence of Speech Act Patterns. These Speech Act Patterns represent frequent dialogue behaviors among Agents that may influence process execution. For example, the constative-informative speech act present in "User Mary informs that she can't connect to the server" followed by a commissive-promise speech act "The L2 team will take action to re-establish the connection" characterizes a desired situation in the context of a troubleshooting process.

A Speech Act Pattern Occurrence is a manifestation of a Speech Act Pattern that can be measured, i.e. one can count these occurrences and compute metrics like frequency, confidence and coverage of the patterns within a message log [19]. Based on the diagram of Fig. 3, the following detailed definitions will be considered for message logs and their surrounding concepts in order to map them to event logs. This mapping allows message logs to be analyzed via process mining techniques, as proposed in [10].

Definition 1 (Uttered Sentence). An uttered sentence s is characterized by the tuple $s = (s_{id}, s_w, s_{ia})$, where s_{id} is the unique identifier of the uttered sentence, s_w is the sequence of words and punctuation that forms the uttered sentence and s_{ia} is a type of speech act associated with the s, $s_{ia} \in$ *{assertive, predictive, retrodictive, descriptive, ascriptive, informative, confirmative, concessive, retractive, assentive, dissentive, disputative, responsive, suggestive, suppositive, requestive, question, requirement, prohibitive, permissive, advisory, promise, offer, apologize, condole, congratulate, greet, thank, bid, accept, reject}.*

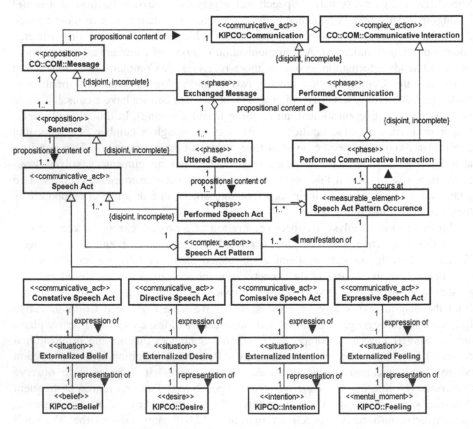

Fig. 3. BDIF and speech acts in inactive phase.

For instance, in the context of an ICT troubleshooting process, these are possible examples: s_1 = (258, "I advise you to restore the system.", "suggestive") and s_2 = (259, "Could you report me the situation after the system restoration?", "question").

Definition 2 (Decision Point). A decision point d is an uttered sentence s, in which the lemma of a word belonging to s matches a verb that expresses decisions according to a list of verbs proposed by Gunnarsson [20] and Campos [8], even though this decision point occur in a sentence together with a speech act type (Definition 1). Formally, a decision point d is characterized by the tuple $d = (d_{id}, d_w, "decision")$ where d_{id} is the unique identifier of an uttered sentence with a decision point, d_w is the sequence of words and punctuation that forms the uttered sentence with a decision point, having at least a word $w \in d_w$, $lemma(w) \in$ {"close", "complete", "normalize", "solve", "agree", "choose", "conclude", "determine", "elect", "end", "establish", "select", "set", "vote", "detail", "diagnose", "procedure"}. An example decision point should be d_1 = (214, "We completed the system restoration", "decision"). Note that in the same sentence we may have speech acts and decision points together. In this situation, the assumption is to consider them as parallel events, since they occurred in the same message with a single timestamp.

Definition 3 (Exchanged Message). An exchanged message m represents the propositional content of a Communication from a sender to one or more receivers, possibly comprising several exchanged messages. It is characterized by a tuple $m = (m_{id}, m_s, m_r, m_t, S)$, where m_{id} is the unique identifier of m, m_s is the single sender of m, m_r is the set of receivers of m, m_t is the timestamp of m occurrence and $S = S_{us} \cup S_d$ is the set of uttered sentences $s \in S_{us}$ and decision points $d \in S_d$ observed in m. In the ICT troubleshooting process scenario, a possible exchanged message would be m = (23, "manager",{"IT support"}, "12-03-2018 15:34", {s_1, s_2, d_1}) T.

Definition 4 (Performed Communicative Interaction). A performed communicative interaction c is characterized by the tuple $c = (c_{id}, M)$ where c_{id} is the unique identifier of the communicative interaction, and M is the set of all exchanged messages $m \in M$ observed during a performed communicative interaction.

Definition 5 (Message log). A message log L_M is characterized by the tuple $L_M = (S_M, C)$, where C is a set of performed communicative interactions selected for analysis, and S_M is the union of the sets of exchanged messages observed during each performed communicative interaction c_i, $c_j \in C$. Message Logs differ from Event logs in the sense that they mostly consist on plain text messages without a predefined structure that allows the direct identification of event attributes as in Event Logs. An example message log in an IT Support scenario may be the set of all communicative interactions between clients and technical staff about troubleshooting issues reported in a given time period.

4 Discovering Decisions in a KiP: Applying the Proposal

The chosen scenario to evaluate this proposal is an incident solution process of an ICT service provider company, in which customers open tickets with diverse maintenance requests. The process macro-steps are listed as follows:

1. The customer sends an e-mail to the Call Center of the company requesting maintenance in some equipment or software service in its environment;
2. The Call Center opens a ticket and forwards it to the responsible area;
3. This ticket can be further handled through message exchanges between different areas of the company, and the customer, every time more information is necessary; At each routing, a code is generated for the message. Thus, it is possible to record the history (log) of this ticket until its conclusion;
4. The ticket is only closed when the customer receives confirmation that his request was executed successfully.

So, in order to solve an incident, internal (between employees) and external (between employees and customers) messages are exchanged. All these messages are registered together with the respective ticket. The log period analyzed was from July 2015 to February 2016, with a total of 7,218 tickets (performed communicative interactions) and 33,397 exchanged messages. Each exchanged message was composed by the following fields: ticket identifier, message identifier, date and time of the sent message, name and origin email sender, name (s) and e-mail (s) of email destination, and the message itself (translated into English). Emails, addresses, special characters (%, #,...), dates, times, repeated data, and words expressing greetings were excluded from the message texts. Greetings ("Hi", "Hello", among others) were excluded because they are *Acknowledgment – Greet*, which is out of our scope. From the original event log, all traces containing only decisions and no speech acts were removed, since these cases do not contribute to revealing speech act patterns preceding decisions.

4.1   The Steps for Discovery

Natural Language Processing and text mining were applied to the message log using the resources available from Stanford NLP, a Natural Language Processing Java framework [17]. To perform the discovery of speech act patterns that lead to decisions, the mapping between message logs and event logs proposed by Richetti et al. [10] was considered. Once this mapping is done, the mapped message logs can be used as input for process mining. The procedure was composed by the following steps:

1. **Tokenization:** each message was reduced to a set of sentences, containing tokens (words, punctuations, etc.);
2. **POS-Tagging:** each token has been morphologically classified (verb, pronoun, etc.) using the modules POSTaggerME, POSModelLoader, POSModel;
3. **Lemmatization:** Verbs were reduced to their base form (e.g. had - have). The WordNet database was used in conjunction with the Morphology module (getBaseFormCandidates);
4. **Feature Selection:** The verbs of each sentence in the message log were compared with the verbs that indicate decision points, allowing to classify the corresponding messages as "Decision". We used the verbal structures pointed by Campos et al. [8] ("incident", "rule", "procedure", "solve") related to the domain, and the verbs that express decisions according to Gunnarsson [20];

5. **Discovery of predominant Speech Acts in the messages:** The messages prior to the decision points within the same performed communicative interaction were collected (i.e., the whole discussion before a Decision was made when handling a ticket), and the predominant speech act in each of those messages were identified.

The Theory of Linguistic Communication [14] proposes how to determine the predominant speech act in a message as follows: Given a speaker K, a hearer H, an expression (typically a sentence) in language L, and the context of utterance C, the main constituents of K's speech act can be schematically represented as follows:

- Utterance Act: K utters e from L to H in C;
- Locutionary Act: K says to H in C that so-and-so;
- Illocutionary Act: K does such-and-such in C;
- Perlocutionary Act: K affects H in a certain way.

The theory rules proposed by [14] for discovering the predominant speech act are:

- Assertive: In uttering e, K *asserts* that P if K expresses (i) the belief that P and (ii) the intention that H believe that P;
- Descriptive: In uttering e, K *describes* P as F if K expresses (i) the belief that P is F and (ii) the intention that H believe that P is F;
- Informative: In uttering e, K *informs* H that P if K expresses (i) the belief that P and (ii) the intention that H forms the belief that P;
- Requestive: In uttering e, K *requests* H to A if K expresses (i) the desire that H do A and (ii) the intention that H do A because (at least partly) of K's desire.

We implemented an algorithm in Java[1] to analyze the messages according to these rules and discover the predominant speech act.

4.2   Results Obtained

After computing the message log, 3,778 exchanged messages containing decision points were found. Table 1 shows examples of the messages found. From the tickets in which decision points were found, 20,896 exchanged messages preceding these points were collected and investigated for the discovery of speech acts.

Table 2 depicts the general results. The "Requestive" speech act prevails in this dataset, where a person requests something from another person because of his desire or intention to obtain this something. Thus, several requests (internal and external) were found, using the following verb structures: "ask", "request", "solicit", "urge". These verbs, according to [14], characterize "Requestive" speech acts.

Other speech acts that also occurred in this dataset were: (i) "Advisories" (advice given to someone through something they believe to be). The most common verbs that characterize this type are: "advise", "propose", "recommend", "suggest". (ii) "Informative" (report something they believe to be valid for the solution). The most common verbs that characterize this type are: "inform", "report", "tell", "testify". (iii) "Requirements" (by virtue of its authority, the speaker obliges the listener to

---

[1] The code is available at: https://github.com/tatianabarboza/speechactminer.

perform something that the speaker believes to be true). The most common verbs that characterize this type are: "demand", "require", "prescribe", "order", "direct". (iv) "Confirmative" (the speaker confirms something, based on the truth found from the experience he has already experienced). The most common verbs that characterize this type are: "appraise", "assess", "confirm", "find", "validate", "verify", "diagnose", "certify".

Table 1. Messages with decision points found in dataset.

Ticket ID	Message ID	Message text
164945	623915	Dear #, I inform you that your request about Problems in the scanner recorded in the call was completed by the FOT staff who took great pleasure in helping you. The problem in the user's station was the network cable, which was replaced, and this **solved** the problem. Please do not reply to this message unless you understand that your request should not be closed in our system. Thank you for your attention
165330	624707	Dear #, I am forwarding the call to our team of experts because the incident was more complex than expected. We will contact you as soon as possible for further testing or validation of the applied **solution**
165006	623994	Dear #, # informed that the request concerning WITHOUT SYSTEM recorded in the call was **completed** by CS GROUP SANTIAGO team who took great pleasure in helping you. Malware detectors were installed in the users' notebook where, after execution, 13 threats were found and removed. After running procedures, navigation tests have been successfully made. Please do not reply to this message unless you understand that your request should not be closed in our system

Due to the findings, we argue that the speech acts that most characterize a decision are: "Requestive", "Advisories", "Requirements", "Confirmative", "Informative". Even though they were manifested in different moments during the performed interactive communication, these four types of speech acts preceded the decisions made within the set of exchanged messages.

4.3 Evaluation

We collected a sample from the dataset to perform the analysis and validation of the results obtained. For this, we took 10% of the tickets that contained decision points, resulting in 1,010 related to them messages. By interpreting each of those messages, we checked if the predominant speech act determined by the algorithm was correct. The analysis and validation of the patterns found within the message log was carried out against the answers from an expert, who manually classified the dataset sample (over than 7,000 messages). After analyzing the results, we observed that more than 80%

were correct, since they presented single verbal structures and verbs related to only one speech act and, as so, they could be interpreted with no semantic confusion.

The remaining 20% of the classified messages contained verbal structures with more than one type of speech act, leading to ambiguous conclusions and some misunderstandings. As some rules of speech acts are very similar and deal with verbs with similar meanings, the application identified a particular act as predominant which was distinct from the expert's opinion. For example, the message "Please ask # to visit the # user station to validate if there is no error in the network interface" was automatically classified as Question, but for the expert it is a Requestive.

Table 2. Number of each type of speech acts found within the messages.

Category	Sub category	Total	%
Directive	Requestive	1288	38.63
Directive	Advisory	1181	38.63
Constative	Informative	619	35.42
Constative	Requirement	506	18.57
Directive	Confirmative	241	15.18
Constative	Permissive	206	7.23
Constative	Question	115	6.18
Constative	Responsive	89	3.45
Directive	Prohibitive	88	2.67
Constative	Retractive	76	2.28
Constative	Assertive	28	0.84
Constative	Concessive	24	0.72
Directive	Dissentive	18	0.54
Constative	Promise	7	0.21
Constative	Offer	6	0.18
Constative	Predictive	5	0.15
Constative	Assentive	4	0.12
Constative	Suggestive	2	0.06
Constative	Disputative	1	0.03

5   Discovered Patterns and Discussion

With an aim to discover specific speech act sequences, and patterns, that lead to a decision during communicative interactions registered in a message log, we applied the ProM framework[2]. ProM allows the analysis of time-based sequences of events and it provides a set of plugins to perform process mining tasks.

The first task was to filter only performed communicative interactions that ended up with a decision. This way we have a clear decision endpoint. By using ProM's Trace

---

[2] The tool is available at: http://processmining.org.

Variant Explorer, it was possible to find that there are 1,368 distinct variants in the log and the most frequent trace variant covers only 3.78% of the log, as shown in Fig. 4. Summing up the top five most frequent traces barely cover 16.53% of the message log. This behavior points to a high variability scenario, which confirms that human communication allows many possible dialogue combinations that may lead to decisions. Despite the high diversity, it is possible to observe that there are some recurring process fragments among trace variants. To precisely determine the support, confidence and coverage of these patterns, the semi-supervised pattern detection approach available in ProM's Log Pattern Explorer (LPE) tool [19] was applied. One example is the pattern is shown in Fig. 5 that shows a requestive act directly causing a descriptive act and both eventually causing a decision in 504 traces with a case coverage of 18.5% of the message log. It explains a general behavior where after a request (a desire of an agent), someone performed an explanation (a belief) by means of a descriptive speech act, and then a decision is made. Another example is the pattern *{descriptive, informative, responsive, requestive, question, requirement, requirement, permissive, advisories}*, directly causing a decision (Fig. 6) on 661 traces, and also is present in 4 of the top 10 most frequent trace variants. This pattern shows the interplay of desires (requestive, question, requirement, permissive, advisories) and beliefs (descriptive, informative, responsive) that implies on a decision.

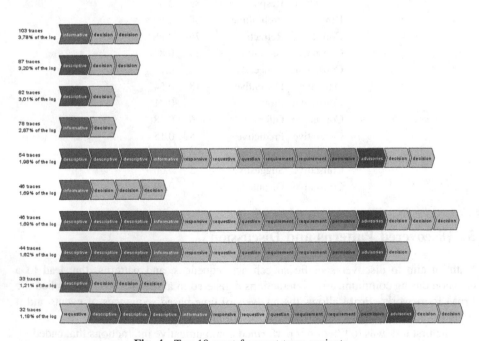

Fig. 4. Top 10 most frequent trace variants.

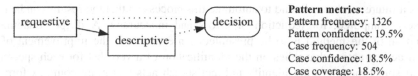

Fig. 5. Example of a discovered pattern with a case frequency of 504 traces.

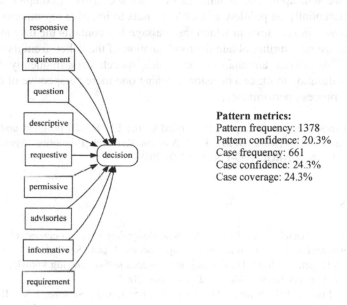

Fig. 6. Example of a discovered pattern with a case frequency of 661 traces.

6 Conclusions

This work brought contributions of the application of NLP to the discovery of elements that comprise Knowledge-intensive processes, improving research on conceptual modeling of such processes. From the decision discovery experiment and the types of speech acts found in the messages, it was possible to confirm the speech acts that most characterize a decision, such as requestives, advisories, requirements, confirmatives and informatives. As identified in the experiment, some speech act patterns that lead to decisions may be bound to specific domains. Kips scenarios demand networks of cooperating resources to work together in order to achieve a goal. Understanding how process agents make decisions can help to improve process and also to effectively design support systems. One limitation is that the analysis and verification of the results was performed by only one expert. The generalization of the analysis is limited by this example scenario, and the discovered patterns in other KiPs scenarios may be totally different.

As a future work, we intend to automate this process so that the results can be more precisely computed, for reduction of errors and inaccuracy. A deeper quantitative evaluation of the method is to be presented. An example is the improvement of the speech act extraction that relies on the identification of a verb list for each speech act type. It sometimes does not identify indirect speech acts and more complex forms of illocutionary acts [Searle and Vanderveken 1985], that can be improved by using fuzzy logic and machine learning techniques.

Besides, we will apply the techniques on other scenarios to compare the results obtained, preferentially on publicly available datasets to improve reproducibility of the results. Moreover, in scenarios in which the message log contains the date and time of each message, we may further obtain the total duration of the ticket, from its opening to completion. This allows an analysis on which speech acts frequently lead to a shorter/longer duration to make a decision, opening one more perspective of discussion related to the process performance.

Acknowledgments. This work is partially funded by the EU H2020 program under MSCA-RISE agreement 645751 (RISE BPM), FFG Austrian Research Promotion Agency (project number: 866270), and UNIRIO (PQ-UNIRIO N01/2018).

References

1. Di Ciccio, C., Marrella, A., Russo, A.: Knowledge-intensive processes: characteristics, requirements and analysis of contemporary approaches. J. Data Semant. **4**(1), 29–57 (2015)
2. Richter-von Hagen, C., Ratz, D., Povalej, R.: Towards self-organizing knowledge intensive processes. J. Univers Knowl. Manag. **2**, 148–169 (2005)
3. dos Santos França, J.B., Netto, J.M., do E. S. Carvalho, J., Santoro, F.M., Baião, F.A., Pimentel, M.: The knowledge-intensive process ontology. Softw. Syst. Model. **14**, 1127–1157 (2014)
4. Guizzardi, G., Guarino, N., Almeida, J.P.A.: Ontological considerations about the representation of events and endurants in business models. In: La Rosa, M., Loos, P., Pastor, O. (eds.) BPM 2016. LNCS, vol. 9850, pp. 20–36. Springer, Cham (2016). https://doi.org/10.1007/978-3-319-45348-4_2
5. Rozinat, A., van der Aalst, W.M.P.: Decision mining in ProM. In: Dustdar, S., Fiadeiro, J.L., Sheth, A.P. (eds.) BPM 2006. LNCS, vol. 4102, pp. 420–425. Springer, Heidelberg (2006). https://doi.org/10.1007/11841760_33
6. Bazhenova, E., Buelow, S., Weske, M.: Discovering decision models from event logs. In: Abramowicz, W., Alt, R., Franczyk, B. (eds.) BIS 2016. LNBIP, vol. 255, pp. 237–251. Springer, Cham (2016). https://doi.org/10.1007/978-3-319-39426-8_19
7. De Leoni, M., van der Aalst, W.M.P.: Data-aware process mining: discovering decisions in processes using alignments. In: Proceedings of the 28th Annual ACM Symposium on Applied Computing, pp. 1454–1461. ACM (2013)
8. Campos, J., Richetti, P., Baião, F.A., Santoro, F.M.: Discovering business rules in knowledge-intensive processes through decision mining: an experimental study. In: Teniente, E., Weidlich, M. (eds.) BPM 2017. LNBIP, vol. 308, pp. 556–567. Springer, Cham (2018). https://doi.org/10.1007/978-3-319-74030-0_44

9. De Smedt, J., Hasić, F., vanden Broucke, S.K.L.M., Vanthienen, J.: Towards a holistic discovery of decisions in process-aware information systems. In: Carmona, J., Engels, G., Kumar, A. (eds.) BPM 2017. LNCS, vol. 10445, pp. 183–199. Springer, Cham (2017). https://doi.org/10.1007/978-3-319-65000-5_11

10. Richetti, P.H.P., de A. R. Gonçalves, J.C., Baião, F.A., Santoro, F.M.: Analysis of knowledge-intensive processes focused on the communication perspective. In: Carmona, J., Engels, G., Kumar, A. (eds.) BPM 2017. LNCS, vol. 10445, pp. 269–285. Springer, Cham (2017). https://doi.org/10.1007/978-3-319-65000-5_16

11. Bratman, M.: Intention, plans, and practical reason. Harvard University Press, Cambridge (1987)

12. Adam, C., Gaudou, B.: BDI agents in social simulations: a survey. Knowl. Eng. Rev. **31**(3), 207–238 (2016)

13. Balke, T., Gilbert, N.: How do agents make decisions? A survey. J. Artif. Soc. Soc. Simul. **17**(4), 13 (2014)

14. Bach, K., Harnish, R.: Linguistic communication and speech acts (1979)

15. Searle, J.R., Vanderveken, D.: Foundations of Illocutionary Logic. Cambridge University Press, Cambridge (1985)

16. Austin, J.L.: How To Do Things With Words. Oxford University Press, Oxford (1975)

17. Reese, M.R.: Natural Language Processing with Java. Packt Publishing. Birmingham, Mumbai (2015). Open Source Community Experience Distilled

18. van der Aalst, W.: Process Mining: Discovery, Conformance and Enhancement of Business Processes. Springer, Heidelberg (2016). https://doi.org/10.1007/978-3-642-19345-3

19. Lu, X., et al.: Semi-supervised log pattern detection and exploration using event concurrence and contextual information. In: Panetto, H., et al. (eds.) OTM 2017. LNCS, vol. 10573, pp. 154–174. Springer, Cham (2017). https://doi.org/10.1007/978-3-319-69462-7_11

20. Gunnarsson, M.: Group decision making–Language and interaction. Ph.D. thesis, Department of Linguistics, Göteborg University (2006)

Cloud and Trusted Computing (C&TC) 2018

C&TC 2018 PC Co-chairs' Message

Welcome to the Cloud and Trusted Computing 2018 (C&TC2018), the 8th International Symposium on Secure Virtual Infrastructures, held in Valletta, Malta, as part of the OnTheMove Federated Conferences & Workshops 2018.

The conference solicited submissions from both academia and industry presenting novel research in the context of cloud and trusted computing. Theoretical and practical approaches for the following main areas have been called:

- Trust, security, privacy and risk management
- Data Management
- Computing infrastructures and architectures
- Applications

In this scope, a multitude of specific challenges have been addressed by our authors. These challenges included cloud security and acceptance, software compliance, evaluation of distributed ledger technologies, data storage integrity, and cloud-fog environment performance. All submitted papers passed through a rigorous selection process involving at least three reviews. In the end, we decided to accept 3 full papers and 3 short papers, reflecting a selection of the best among the excellent.

Organizing a conference like C&TC is a team effort, and many people need to be acknowledged. First, we would like to thank authors who submitted their contributions to this event for having chosen C&TC to present and discuss their work. Their contributions were the basis for the success of the conference.

Second, we would like to acknowledge the hard work of all our colleagues from the Program Committee, experts in the research domains of the conference, for performing the extremely valuable tasks of reviewing and discussing the many excellent contributions.

Finally, we would like to thank everyone at the OTM organizers team for their exceptional support and, in particular, the OTM Conferences & Workshops General Chairs Robert Meersman, Tharam Dillon, Hervé Panetto, and Ernesto Damiani, and the Publication Chair Christophe Debruyne.

All of these people contributed to the Proceedings of the 8th International Conference on Cloud and Trusted Computing, and all of them deserve our highest gratitude. Thank you!

October 2018

C. A. Ardagna
A. Belmonte
M. Conti
C&TC2018 Co-chairs

Latency-Aware Placement Heuristic in Fog Computing Environment

Amira Rayane Benamer[1](✉), Hana Teyeb[2](✉),
and Nejib Ben Hadj-Alouane[2](✉)

[1] Faculty of Sciences of Tunis, University of Tunis El Manar, Tunis, Tunisia
amira.rayane.benamer@gmail.com
[2] National Engineering School of Tunis, OASIS Research Lab,
University of Tunis El Manar, Tunis, Tunisia
hana.teyeb@gmail.com, nejib_bha@yahoo.com

Abstract. With the rise of IoT applications popularity, a new paradigm has emerged so-called Fog Computing. To facilitate their deployment on fog nodes, IoT applications are decomposed into a set of modules. These modules interact with each other in order to achieve a global goal. Placing these modules without a prior strategy may affect the overall performance of the application. Moreover, the restricted capacity of the fog nodes vis-a-vis the modules' requirements arises the problem of placement. In this paper, we focus on minimizing the overall latency of the application while placing modules on fog nodes. In order to address the module placement problem, we propose both exact and approximate solutions. Experiments were conducted using CPLEX and iFogSim-simulated Fog environment respectively. The results show the effectiveness of our final approach.

Keywords: Internet of things · Fog computing · Placement decision
Latency · Cloud

1 Introduction

Internet of Things (IoT) [1] is an infrastructure on which connected devices can communicate with one another via the internet [16]. With the fast growth of this technology and its high impact on several aspects of every-day life, many challenges have been raised. Some IoT applications still need more improvements [22] in terms of Quality of Service (QoS) such as response time, latency, location awareness, high throughput and decision making based on real-time analytics [3,4]. These requirements have a direct impact on the performance of the whole application. In this context, we distinguish several types of IoT applications such as video streaming, augmented reality, smart homes and e-health [2,3].

In spite of its unlimited resources capacities [18], its elasticity to respond to business demands, and its versatility [24], cloud computing [17] cannot scale

© Springer Nature Switzerland AG 2018
H. Panetto et al. (Eds.): OTM 2018 Conferences, LNCS 11230, pp. 241–257, 2018.
https://doi.org/10.1007/978-3-030-02671-4_14

to requirements of such an environment [8]. Due to its centralized architecture [14], cloud computing is still encountering severe challenges. It may cause unacceptable delays which are not efficient for delay-sensitive applications. In fact, this may lead to network faults and network congestion which in return will result in QoS degradation. Thus, researchers have explored other alternatives, for instance, Fog computing [14].

Fog computing extends the traditional cloud-based services to be closer to the users in order to satisfy their demands in real time with wide and dense geographical distribution. Fog computing has a distributed topology that aims to ensure low latency, high bandwidth connectivity for service applications requests, and the transfer of a huge amount of data over the network. In addition, fog computing supports mobility, heterogeneity, interoperability and scalability [3,8]. It is composed of different types of devices namely, set-top boxes, routers, proxy servers, base stations and switches [14]. Each of these is supplied with different resources in terms of computing units, storage, and memory. However, due to the restricted resource capacities of fog nodes, new placement challenges are raised.

In order to ease the deployment of the IoT applications on fog computing environment, applications are decomposed into a set of interdependent application modules that consequently promotes the concept of distributed application [10,21]. Hence, the placement of these different modules affects directly the performance of the whole application. This problem consists in achieving a trade-off between minimizing the overall latency of the application and ensuring the non-exceeding of fog nodes capacity as well.

Placement problems have attracted much attention in recent years. Many works have considered the inter-node latency and have optimized resources while minimizing the latency [15,25]. Whereas, other works have considered only the available capacity of resources for forwarding modules accordingly [21,23]. Nevertheless, the placement problem still needs additional investigations. Placing modules according to the resource capacities and regarding the nearest node is not enough. This is due to the limited vision of both strategies or even combining them together. The mapping of modules according to the resources may cause unacceptable delays between successive modules. As well, assigning modules to fog nodes which minimize the inter-node latency may not lead to the best combination of devices for the whole application modules. This placement policy lacks the efficiency and ignores the case where the placement of the module could be better for all modules already placed by minimizing the overall latency, but does not minimize the inter-node latency with it's previous. Therefore, the performance of the application will be impacted. In order to reduce the latency, we must optimize the placement scheme of the different application modules. This latter must not only consider latency between nodes but also, the latency of the overall application.

In this paper, we focus on the problem of placing application modules in cloud-fog environment. Our objective is to minimize the overall inter-node latency in order to ensure the QoS of the applications. Minimizing the overall latency leads to reduce network traffic and improves applications response time.

Table 1. Overview of related approaches.

Reference	Level	Inter node latency	Overall near-optimal latency	Prioritized placement	Resource optimization
[25]	MEC[a]	✓			✓
[21]	Fog-Cloud			✓	✓
[11]	Cloud	✓			
[15]	Fog-Cloud	✓		✓	✓
[23]	Fog-Cloud				✓
[19]	Fog			✓	✓
Our approach	Fog-Cloud	✓	✓	✓	✓

[a]Mobile Cloud Computing [12]

Hence, we propose both exact and heuristic approaches to solve the problem. In addition, we carry out extensive simulations using iFogSim simulator as well as CPLEX solver.

The remainder of this paper is organized as follows: Sect. 2 reviews relevant related works. In Sect. 3, we present the system model. As for Sect. 4, it describes the problem and presents the exact formulation and the proposed heuristic.

Section 5 details and illustrates the experiment results conducted on the proposed algorithms. Finally, we conclude in Sect. 6.

2   Related Work

Placement problems in fog computing environment have attracted much attention in recent years. In [25], the authors have integrated Blockchain as a decentralized public ledger to ensure the trust for an effective management of resources. Their aim was to provide services to users while ensuring minimum supply cost. The authors have considered the traffic between the services belonging to the same chain. The authors of [21] have proposed a mapping strategy for distributed applications in a fog-cloud environment. They aimed to ensure a good resource management of fog nodes while mapping application modules. The authors of this work have prioritized the modules per their requirements. An integer linear programming formulation (ILP) was proposed in [11]. It aims at minimizing latency, without any resource management. The authors have proposed also, an iterative sequential model to reduce the computation time of the ILP formulation. They have considered the time between the deployed modules, as well as the mobility with re-running the algorithm periodically. A large real-world latency data set has been used to conduct the experiments of deploying multiple cloud-based services. In [15], the authors have proposed a heuristic algorithm that solves the problem of module placement. This heuristic is aware of deliverance time, access delay, and inter-node communication delay. In order to optimize resources after the placement, a forwarding modules step is carried out. In [23], the authors have proposed a new platform as a service (PaaS) in a hybrid cloud-fog environment. The new platform aims to facilitate the development task through an automatic provisioning of applications. The authors have proposed a set of new modules for each layer in the architecture which perform a specific task. These modules coordinate between them in order to manage application components as well as the required resources to execute them. In order to meet the QoS requirements and to minimize the cost of execution in the fog layer, the authors of [19] have proposed an optimization model to ensure an optimal distribution of services on available fog resources. The approach is executed periodically in order to address any changes in the environment.

Despite the fact that the placement problem has been studied from different perspectives, it has converged towards more or less effective solutions, from which we distinguish the optimal and approximate ones. However, the aforementioned works do not consider the overall latency during the placement decision-making process. This will impact the performance of the application later.

Table 1 shows a summary of the most relevant works. Each work has studied the placement problem vis-a-vis some important points in a layer already mentioned. The main difference between our approach and the existent ones is the consideration of the overall latency of the application. In the previous works, minimizing latency was solved by focusing on the optimization of resources while mapping modules per nodes. Whereas, other ones aim to find the best decision placement for each module that minimizes the inter-node latency. In our work, the overall latency is not limited by a fixed threshold as we distinguish in some related works. Our approach continues until it obtains the minimum latency among all possible solutions. Moreover, our strategy could forward module from node to node in order to ensure the low latency and moving others to optimize resource allocation. In addition, we prioritize application with latency-sensitive modules.

In the next section, we present the system model and we illustrate a generic use case of an IoT application that we are studying.

3   System Model

In this section, we present an IoT application model as well as an overview of the fog architecture.

An IoT application consists of a set of modules that interact with each other to achieve a common goal as shown in the Fig. 1. In this context, a sense-process-actuate model is needed [10]. The example below is inspired from [21]. The sensor collects the data (blue color) and sends them as tuples to the application (a set of modules). The most important loops are those which transform the collected data into a valuable result displayed on the actuator (gray color).

The application modules connect to each other via an IoT data stream [10]. The delay response between these IoT services is crucial given its direct impact on the performance of the entire application and on the user satisfaction as well. For this reason, addressing a higher layer (Cloud) for a total management of all modules will infer an intolerable delay response. Therefore, the integration

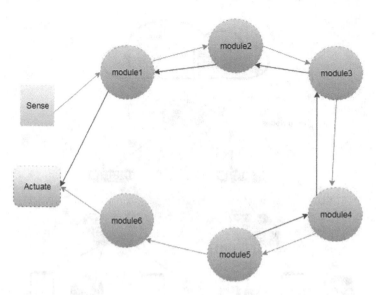

Fig. 1. Example of a direct acyclic graph of an IoT application. (Color figure online)

of an intermediate layer (Fog) to better manage these modules is necessary as illustrated in the Fig. 2.

Consequently, a fog architecture can be viewed as a three-tier network structure. We find at the lowest tier all sensors and devices which are responsible for sensing and collecting data in order to transmit it to an upper layer. The second tier includes all nodes that have a limited resource capacity. These nodes can process, run, and store the received data temporally. In the upper tier, we find the cloud which can process and store a huge amount of information [18, 20].

We assume that the second tier is divided into three levels. Each level contains nodes with different capacities compared to other levels. We consider the cloud as a standalone computational platform which could host modules tolerant to latency. The devices are connected vertically in the architecture, where each pair of devices from two different layers are linked via a latency link.

In this work, we have considered a vertical placement approach. The modules can be placed on the same device or on the next available within the path. The placement is based on both the capacity of the device in terms of CPU, RAM, Bandwidth and the latency which is our objective. In this work, we assume that the sensitivity of modules is defined according to their proximity to the sensors.

In the next section, we formally define the latency-aware module placement problem in Cloud-Fog environment.

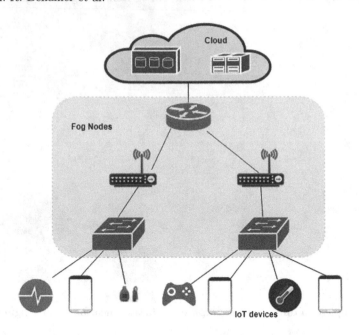

Fig. 2. Fog computing architecture.

4 Problem Formulation

In this section we present both exact and heuristic solutions for the Latency-Aware Module Placement Problem (LAMP) in Cloud-Fog environment.

4.1 Exact Solution

In this section, we formally define the Latency-Aware Module Placement Problem as an Integer Linear Programming model (ILP).

We are given a graph complete graph $G = (N; E)$, where N is the set of the nodes, constituted by fog nodes and the cloud. E is the set of edges. By considering a complete graph structure, we aim to estimate the inter-node latency. We denote by M the set of application modules that needs to be placed. The set of resources is defined by R. We denote by d_{hk} the latency between the node $h \in N$ and $k \in N$. Let us define the boolean matrix a_{ij}, which is equal to 1 if the module $i \in M$ is dependent on module $j \in M$, 0 otherwise. Let us define c_{hr} the capacity of the node $h \in N$ in terms of resources $r \in R$ (CPU, RAM, Storage, etc.) and u_{ir} the consumption of the module $i \in M$ in terms of resources $r \in R$.

In this formulation, we use the following decision variables:

- x_{ih} is equal to 1 if the module $i \in M$ is placed in the node $h \in N$, 0 otherwise.
- z_h is equal to 1 if the node $h \in N$ is used, 0 otherwise.

The LAMP is defined as follows:

$$\min \sum_{i \in M} \sum_{j \in M} \sum_{h \in N} \sum_{k \in N} a_{ij}.d_{hk}.x_{ih}.x_{jk} \tag{1}$$

$$\sum_{i \in M} u_{ir}.x_{ih} \leq c_{hr}.z_h \qquad\qquad \forall h \in N, r \in R \tag{2}$$

$$\sum_{k \in N} x_{ik} = 1 \qquad\qquad \forall i \in M \tag{3}$$

$$x_{ih} \leq z_k \qquad\qquad \forall k \in N, \forall r \in R \tag{4}$$

$$\sum_{k \in N} z_k \leq n \tag{5}$$

$$x_{ih} \in \{0,1\} \qquad\qquad \forall i \in M, \forall h \in N$$

$$z_h \in \{0,1\} \qquad\qquad \forall h \in N$$

The objective function (1) aims to minimize the overall latency. The first constraint (2) ensures that the set of application modules that will be placed in a certain node does not exceed its resource capacity. As for constraint (3), it ensures that every module is running exactly on one node. The constraint (4) stipulates that if a module is placed in a node, the latter is obviously used. The last constraint (5) ensures that the number of used nodes does not exceed the maximum number of nodes n.

However, this formulation presents non-linearity problems due to the quadratic objective function (1). In order to linearize the objective function, we introduce new decision variable $w_{ij}^{kh} = x_i^k.x_j^h$ which is equal to 1 when the module $i \in M$ is placed in node $k \in N$ and the module $j \in M, j \neq i$ is placed in node $h \in N$.

By replacing the variables we obtain the following formulation.

$$\min \sum_{i \in M} \sum_{j \in M} \sum_{h \in N} \sum_{k \in N} a_{ij}.d_{hk}.w_{ij}^{hk} \tag{6}$$

$$\sum_{i \in M} u_{ir}.x_{ih} \leq c_{hr}.z_h \qquad\qquad \forall h \in N, r \in R \tag{7}$$

$$w_{ij}^{hk} + 1 \geq x_{ih} + x_{jh} \tag{8}$$

$$\sum_{k \in N} x_{ik} = 1 \qquad\qquad \forall i \in M \tag{9}$$

$$x_{ih} \leq z_k \qquad\qquad \forall k \in N, \forall r \in R \tag{10}$$

$$\sum_{k \in N} z_k \leq n \tag{11}$$

$$x_{ih} \in \{0,1\} \qquad\qquad \forall i \in M, \forall h \in N$$

$$w_{ij}^{hk} \in \{0,1\} \qquad\qquad \forall i \in M, \forall h \in N$$

$$z_h \in \{0,1\} \qquad\qquad \forall h \in N$$

Algorithm 1. Latency Aware Placement Heuristic

  Input: listOfFogDevices, ListOfAppModules
  Output: List<moduleName,fogDevice> modulesMapping
1: Insert the most sensitive module on the first node connected to the sensor
2: **while** (!Empty(ListOfAppModules)) **do**
3:   temporal Overall Latency=0
4:   **if** (Module already Placed) **then**
5:     OptimizePlacement(module,device,modulesMapping)
6:   **else**
7:     **for** (device $\in$ listOfFogDevices) **do**
8:       **if** (Cpu $_{availdevice} \geq$ Cpu $_{reqmodule}$ and Ram $_{availdevice} \geq$ Ram $_{resmodule}$ and Bw $_{availdevice} \geq$ Bw$_{reqmodule}$) **then**
9:         Calculate Inter Latency between device and the latest one
10:         Calculate Overall Latency of the whole modules already placed plus the current module in the actual device
11:         **if** (Overall Latency calculated < temporal Overall Latency) || (It's the second module and the first device) **then**
12:           Save the current device
13:           temporal Overall Latency = Overall Latency calculated
14:         **end if**
15:       **end if**
16:     **end for**
17:   **end if**
18:   Save placement decision of the device with the low overall latency
19:   Affect module to *deviceSaved* and add them to *moduleMapping*
20:   Remove module
21: **end while**
22: **return** *modulesMapping*

The LAMP can be seen as a variant of the *Hub Location* problem where nodes are considered as hub nodes. This problem is known to be NP-Hard [7]. The above formulation turns out to be time and resource consuming as it presents a huge number of variables that is equal to $O|M|^2.|N|^2$, where N refers to the set of nodes and M refers to the set of modules. Therefore, we propose in the next section a heuristic solution aiming to provide the best placement scheme for the different application modules.

4.2   Heuristic Solution

In this section, we propose a heuristic solution to the latency-aware module placement problem.

The Latency Aware-Placement Heuristic (LAPH) aims to minimize the latency, while at the same time, optimize the resource allocation for the different IoT application modules.

The main idea of the algorithm is to provide an effective modules placement in order to maintain the overall latency as minimum as possible, especially for

---

Algorithm 2. OptimizePlacement Algorithm

Input: module,device List<moduleName,fogDevice> moduleMapping
Output: List<moduleName,fogDevice> modulesMapping

1: toBePlaced=module
2: **if** (there is at least one module on same device) **then**
3:    Calculate remaining capacity to be released
4:    **if** (space Calculated $\geq$ module $_{req}$) **then**
5:        toBePlaced = moduleToBeRemoved
6:        remove the selected module
7:        add module instance
8:        Update moduleMapping
9:    **end if**
10: **end if**
11: **while** (true) **do**
12:    getParent of the current device
13:    **if** (parent is the highest) **then**
14:        break
15:    **end if**
16:    **if** (There is modules already placed on parent) **then**
17:        **while** (Modules possible to be checked is not empty) **do**
18:            **if** (Remained capacity of the current device >= Module Requirement)
    then
19:                Move Module from deviceParent to current device
20:                Update moduleMapping
21:            **end if**
22:        **end while**
23:    **end if**
24:    **if** (deviceParent $_{cap_avail}$ $\geq$ toBePlaced $_{req}$) **then**
25:        Insert toBePlaced on deviceParent
26:        Update moduleMapping
27:        **return** *moduleMapping*
28:    **else**
29:        getParent of the current parent
30:    **end if**
31: **end while**
32: **return** *moduleMapping*

---

latency-sensitive IoT applications. Our aim is to ensure a near-optimal solution by checking all available devices and taking into account all cases where a node could host the module and ensure for it a good placement compared to the nodes already chosen for hosting modules already placed. Then, we save the best placement decision which minimizes the latency. The LAPH adjusts the placement decision of each module based on to the position of the latest placed module in order to minimize the inter-node latency. In addition, it takes into account the placement scheme of all modules that are already placed.

The modules mapping algorithm provides fog-cloud mapping decisions. As input, it takes the set of modules to be placed and the set of fog devices as well.

As output, it provides a near-optimal placement of modules with the lowest latency value while optimizing the resource allocation scheme. First, it defines the modules that should be placed in proximity to sensors in order to ensure high data transfer rates between IoT devices, IoT devices and potential end-users. Then it places them and it iterates through the modules that are yet to be placed. For each module, it goes through all the fog devices and, it tests the available capacity of each one, to avoid any capacity overload problem. The available capacity of each device must meet the module requirements in terms of CPU, RAM, and BandWidth (line 8). Note that, the proposed algorithm is scalable when adding more attributes for each node such as Geo-Location coordinates.

Once the module requirements are met, the inter-node latency will be calculated as well as the overall latency of the modules that are already placed (9 and 10 lines). The inter-node latency is equal to the end-to-end latency already specified between each two devices (the latest chosen device and the others ones), or even the sum of intermediate latency links. For the overall latency is equal to the sum of latency links between each two devices already chosen to host application modules already placed.

While going through devices the algorithm aims to find the best node that suits the current module. The placement decision of each module is affected both by the best placement decision of the device which optimizes inter-node latency. As well, the best placement decision compared to all modules already placed which optimizes the overall latency. When a module is already placed, an operation of optimization should be carried out (4 and 5 lines). The algorithm aims to adjust the placement of competing modules in order to ensure the best use of available resources which is the purpose of the OptimizePlacement Algorithm 2. In addition, it aims to keep the most sensitive modules ones as near as possible. Once all devices for one module have been checked, the placement scheme is executed.

As shown in Algorithm 2, if the number of instances of an application raises, the number of competing modules raises over access to resources that have a restricted capacity. For this reason, re-locating module from node to node must be carried out. This algorithm aims to optimize the usage of resources as well as reducing the network usage.

Algorithm 2 takes as input a module that have at least one module instance already placed on the current device as well as the list of modules, devices already placed and chosen respectively. As output, it provides the updated list of modules, devices. First, if there is at least one module tolerant to latency already placed on the current device, remaining capacity will be calculated. If this later fulfills module needs (CPU, RAM, BandWidth) the tolerant module will be saved and deleted from device to release place to another instance of the sensitive module (line 2–10).

In both cases, the algorithm continues checking the devices, if it is possible, in order to place the module *toBePlaced* (line 12–15). At the same time, the algorithm tries to relocate modules already upper placed to release the resource

Table 2. CPU, RAM, Bandwidth module's requirements

Module	CPU (MIPS)	Bandwidth (Mbps)	RAM (GB)
Module1	700	250	1
Module2	1500	500	4
Module3	2400	1000	2
Module4	1700	300	1.5
Module5	4000	2000	6
Module6	1700	5000	8

capacities to the current module (line 16–23). This operation aims to keep the latency as optimized as possible. In order to place the module, the algorithm will calculate the device remaining capacity and compare it with the module requirements (line 24–27). Otherwise, the algorithm gets the parent of the current device which is the parent of the previous one (line 27).

In the next section, we evaluate the proposed solutions in order to show their effectiveness to treat the latency aware-placement of IoT application modules.

5 Evaluation

In this section, we present the results of the experiments conducted on both the exact and the heuristic solutions.

In order to evaluate the performance of our heuristic, we have used iFogSim [10], which is a fog environment simulator developed upon the well-known framework of CloudSim [6,10]. This toolkit is dedicated to model and simulate fog and edge computing as well as cloud resources. We have implemented the algorithm using JAVA. For the exact model, we have used the OPL modeling language and the commercial solver CPLEX 12.8 [9].

The different experiments were executed on a machine that has an Intel Xeon 3.3 GHz CPU and 8 GB of RAM.

For each module, we have assigned CPU, RAM, Bandwidth requirements as shown in Table 2. Each device has a fixed resource capacity as it is represented in Table 3. These devices are distributed in different tiers. An end-to-end latency is specified between them as shown in Table 4. We have generated the values randomly as it has been done in previous articles [15,21].

In the evaluation, we have considered many configurations where the number of fog nodes in 2-tiers is specified with the corresponding workload-number of devices.

In order to compare the quality of the solution provided by both exact and heuristic solutions, we have generated randomly a multi-dimensional array of latency between nodes. A random number of modules, a random number of nodes and for each one a random requirements and capacities respectively.

In order to evaluate the effectiveness of the approximate solution with the exact model, we have calculated the optimality gap [5] between them.

Table 3. Fog nodes capacities

Fog node	Bandwidth (Mbps)	RAM (GB)	CPU (MIPS)
First level	250	2	4000
Second level	10000	6	8000
Third level	10000	8	15000
Cloud	10000	40	40000

Table 4. UpLink nodes latency

Node type	Latency (ms)
Sense to mobile	3
Mobile to gateway	5
Gateway to proxy	25
Proxy to cloud	220

Table 5. Average optimality gap and execution time.

Nbr of modules	Nbr of nodes	LAPH execution time (s)	LAMP execution time (s)	Gap %
10	10	0.041	1.49	0
20	15	0.161	52	5.892
25	18	0.27	357.5	14.6
30	17	0.399	937	12.881
50	30	1.160	-	-
100	70	7.33	-	-

We define by G the optimality gap, where S^* is the optimal solution and S is the approximate one.

$$G = \frac{|S^* - S|}{max\{S^*; S\}} * 100$$

The obtained results are expressed in %. If the gap is equal to 0, then the obtained solution is optimal. It becomes close to 100 when the obtained solution is very poor.

Table 5 shows the gap between the two solutions for a different number of modules. These results can be explained by the fact that the exact method explores all the possible branches till arriving at the optimal one. This, in turn, can make the exact solution slower for larger problems. On the other hand, the approximate solution doesn't guarantee the optimality in all cases but it gives a good quality of solution with a gap that does not exceed 15%. These results show how LAPH leverages the internet of things to release their potential. We note that the gap between the two solutions is small compared with the convergence time.

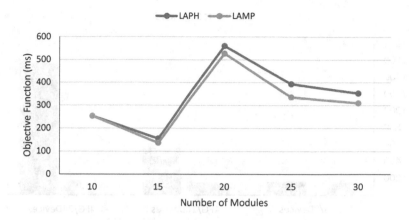

Fig. 3. Overall latency per module for LAMP and LAPH.

Note that the solver was not be able to find the optimal solution within 1 hour in the case of 50 modules and more. The problem as it has been defined previously is NP-Hard [7] and it becomes computationally expensive in terms of time and resources due to the Branch and Bound algorithm [13].

Figure 3 shows the comparison of the quality of solution between the exact model (LAMP) and the proposed heuristic (LAPH). We can say that the heuristic solution is much closer to the optimal in a very reduced time.

Then, we have compared our heuristic (LAPH) with a baseline algorithm known as Edge-ward module placement of iFogSim [10]. This latter places modules in nodes which meet their CPU requirements. In this set of experiments, we have focused on the number of devices per fog, to show how the heuristic will manage the mapping of all workloads with a restrict number of fogs in the second tier. The CPU fixed for the cloud is 6000 MIPS and 3000 MIPS for the third level in the fog layer with the same characteristics already mentioned in Table 3 for the others. The emission rate specified for this comparison is 5.1 ms.

As shown in Fig. 4, we note that there is a huge difference of the end-to-end delay between LAPH and Edge-ward module placement. For each configuration, our algorithm makes all modules close to the network edge with the management of modules priority that in turn decrease the congestion in the network.

Figure 5 depicts the network usage of our proposed algorithm and iFogSim's one. Increasing the number of devices leads to the increase of the number of workloads in the network. In the case of our algorithm LAPH (Latency Aware-Placement Heuristic), the modules are kept as near as possible from sensors on fog nodes. Hence, we notice a reduced network congestion. Whereas, in the case of iFogSim's algorithm, its concept pushes the modules up until using cloud resources which increases the congestion in the network and affects the response delay.

Next, we have compared our heuristic LAPH (Latency Aware-Placement Heuristic) with a *cloud-only* placement strategy. In this case, we have increased

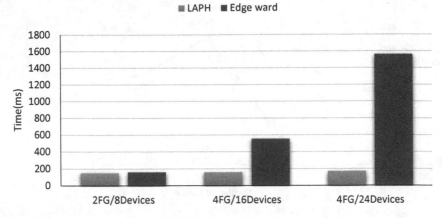

Fig. 4. End-to-end latency.

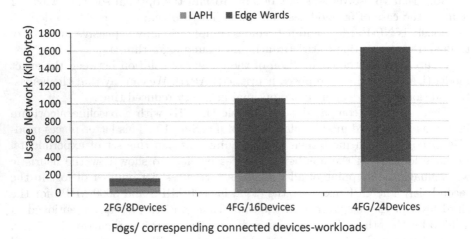

Fig. 5. Usage network.

the number of fog nodes with a fixed number of devices and we have plotted the end-to-end latency and the usage network for both approaches. The emission rate specified for this comparison is 10 ms. The results are depicted in Figs. 6 and 7.

As shown in the Fig. 6, our algorithm is able to keep the modules as near as possible from the sensor for local storage and immediate data processing compared to the *cloud-only* placement strategy. Therefore, LAPH helps to maintain low latency in all configurations with a reduced network congestion. On the other hand, putting all modules on cloud has caused a bottleneck in the network which has led to a significant increase of the latency. Increasing the number of

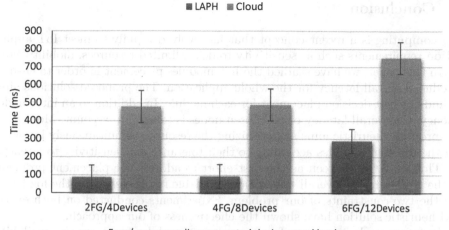

Fig. 6. End-to-end latency.

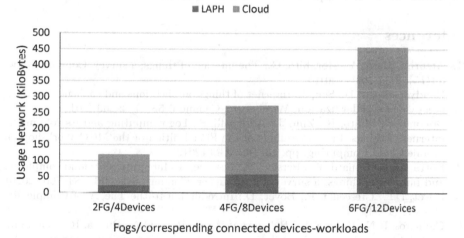

Fig. 7. Usage network.

workloads has led to multiple competing IoT applications. So the number of tuples increases significantly on the network. These applications have an impact on resource contention, therefore, processing latency will be increased.

In Fig. 7, we see the significant difference between the two placement strategies where cloud-based execution has led to network congestion because all data are processed in the cloud and to further degradation in the average delay. Note that the percent deducted compared to the processing latency of the two strategies (LAPH and cloud-only placement) is equal to 74,65. Whereas the percent deducted of (LAPH and iFogSim's algorithm) is equal to 55,41.

6   Conclusion

Fog computing is a recent concept that has evolved rapidly to meet IoT application requirements such as sensitivity to delay, limited resources, mobility, etc.

In this paper, we have studied the IoT modules placement in order to ensure a reduced overall latency for the whole application. The proposed solutions aim to find the best decision placement for each module. In addition to an inter-node latency, the overall latency of all chosen nodes is taken into account. Moreover, the proposed heuristic aims at optimizing the resources simultaneously by placing the different modules according to their tolerance and sensitivity to latency.

This work can be seen as the first effort to address the placement problem in the fog layer. The overall latency and available resources within the fog layer are the two constraints of our problem. Experiments conducted on both exact and heuristic solution have shown the effectiveness of our approach.

In future work, we aim to focus on placing modules to ensure the availability of the entire application while minimizing the overall latency. To resolve this shortcoming, we need to achieve a trade-off between latency and the high percentage of the IoT application modules availability.

References

1. Atzori, L., Iera, A., Morabito, G.: The internet of things: a survey. Comput. Netw. **54**(15), 2787–2805 (2010)
2. Bandyopadhyay, D., Sen, J.: Internet of things: applications and challenges in technology and standardization. Wirel. Pers. Commun. **58**(1), 49–69 (2011)
3. Bonomi, F., Milito, R., Zhu, J., Addepalli, S.: Fog computing and its role in the internet of things. In: Proceedings of the First Edition of the MCC Workshop on Mobile Cloud Computing, pp. 13–16. ACM (2012)
4. Botta, A., De Donato, W., Persico, V., Pescapé, A.: Integration of cloud computing and internet of things: a survey. Futur. Gener. Comput. Syst. **56**, 684–700 (2016)
5. Bovet, D.P., Crescenzi, P., Bovet, D.: Introduction to the Theory of Complexity. Citeseer (1994)
6. Calheiros, R.N., Ranjan, R., Beloglazov, A., De Rose, C.A., Buyya, R.: CloudSim: a toolkit for modeling and simulation of cloud computing environments and evaluation of resource provisioning algorithms. Softw.: Pract. Exp. **41**(1), 23–50 (2011)
7. Campbell, J.F.: Hub location and the p-hub median problem. Oper. Res. **44**(6), 923–935 (1996). https://doi.org/10.1287/opre.44.6.923
8. Dastjerdi, A.V., Gupta, H., Calheiros, R.N., Ghosh, S.K., Buyya, R.: Fog computing: principles, architectures, and applications. In: Internet of Things, pp. 61–75. Elsevier (2016)
9. Flatberg, T.: A short OPL tutorial (2009)
10. Gupta, H., Vahid Dastjerdi, A., Ghosh, S.K., Buyya, R.: iFogSim: a toolkit for modeling and simulation of resource management techniques in the internet of things, edge and fog computing environments. Softw.: Pract. Exp. **47**(9), 1275–1296 (2017)
11. Kang, Y., Zheng, Z., Lyu, M.R.: A latency-aware co-deployment mechanism for cloud-based services. In: 2012 IEEE 5th International Conference on Cloud Computing (CLOUD), pp. 630–637. IEEE (2012)

12. Kumar, L., Malik, N., Agghi, G., Anand, A.: Mobile cloud computing. IJRIT Int. J. Res. Inf. Technol. **2**(9), 787–792 (2014)
13. Lawler, E.L., Wood, D.E.: Branch-and-bound methods: a survey. Oper. Res. **14**(4), 699–719 (1966)
14. Mahmud, R., Kotagiri, R., Buyya, R.: Fog computing: a taxonomy, survey and future directions. In: Di Martino, B., Li, K.C., Yang, L.T., Esposito, A. (eds.) Internet of Everything. Internet of Things, pp. 103–130. Springer, Singapore (2018). https://doi.org/10.1007/978-981-10-5861-5_5
15. Mahmud, R., Ramamohanarao, K., Buyya, R.: Latency-aware application module management for fog computing environments. ACM Trans. Internet Technol. (TOIT) (2018)
16. Management Association, I.: The Internet of Things: Breakthroughs in Research and Practice. Critical explorations. IGI Global (2017). https://books.google.tn/books?id=7RshDgAAQBAJ
17. Rimal, B.P., Choi, E., Lumb, I.: A taxonomy and survey of cloud computing systems. In: 2009 Fifth International Joint Conference on INC, IMS and IDC. NCM 2009, pp. 44–51. IEEE (2009)
18. Sarkar, S., Misra, S.: Theoretical modelling of fog computing: a green computing paradigm to support IoT applications. IET Netw. **5**(2), 23–29 (2016)
19. Skarlat, O., Nardelli, M., Schulte, S., Dustdar, S.: Towards QoS-aware fog service placement. In: 2017 IEEE 1st International Conference on Fog and Edge Computing (ICFEC), pp. 89–96. IEEE (2017)
20. Stojmenovic, I.: Fog computing: a cloud to the ground support for smart things and machine-to-machine networks. In: 2014 Australasian Telecommunication Networks and Applications Conference (ATNAC), pp. 117–122. IEEE (2014)
21. Taneja, M., Davy, A.: Resource aware placement of IoT application modules in fog-cloud computing paradigm. In: 2017 IFIP/IEEE Symposium on Integrated Network and Service Management (IM), pp. 1222–1228. IEEE (2017)
22. Thaker, R., Khan, Y.F., Mughal, S.: Fog approach in internet of things: a review (2018)
23. Yangui, S., et al.: A platform as-a-service for hybrid cloud/fog environments. In: 2016 IEEE International Symposium on Local and Metropolitan Area Networks (LANMAN), pp. 1–7. IEEE (2016)
24. Zhang, S., Zhang, S., Chen, X., Huo, X.: Cloud computing research and development trend. In: 2010 Second International Conference on Future Networks. ICFN 2010, pp. 93–97. IEEE (2010)
25. Zhu, H., Huang, C., Zhou, J.: EdgeChain: blockchain-based multi-vendor mobile edge application placement. arXiv preprint arXiv:1801.04035 (2018)

Requirements for Legally Compliant Software Based on the GDPR

Sandra Domenique Ringmann[1,2,3(✉)], Hanno Langweg[2,4],
and Marcel Waldvogel[3]

[1] Siemens Postal, Parcel & Airport Logistics GmbH, Konstanz, Germany
[2] HTWG Konstanz University of Applied Sciences, Konstanz, Germany
{sandra.ringmann,hanno.langweg}@htwg-konstanz.de
[3] University of Konstanz, Konstanz, Germany
marcel.waldvogel@uni-konstanz.de
[4] Department of Information Security and Communication Technology,
Faculty of Information Technology and Electrical Engineering, NTNU,
Norwegian University of Science and Technology, Gjøvik, Norway

Abstract. We identify 74 generic, reusable technical requirements based on the GDPR that can be applied to software products which process personal data. The requirements can be traced to corresponding articles and recitals of the GDPR and fulfill the key principles of lawfulness and transparency. Therefore, we present an approach to requirements engineering with regard to developing legally compliant software that satisfies the principles of privacy by design, privacy by default as well as security by design.

Keywords: Requirements engineering · GDPR · Compliant software
Security by design · Privacy by design and by default

1 Introduction

The General Data Protection Regulation (GDPR) entered into force on 24th of May 2016 and the transition period ended on 25th of May 2018, making the rules applicable in all member states of the European Union. It has attracted attention world-wide, across all industries. As a result of the territorial scope defined in Article 3 of the GDPR, more companies must be compliant with the GDPR, e.g., especially referring to companies that process personal data which was acquired over the internet. Furthermore, the GDPR specifically requires that processing of personal data must comply with the GDPR and this compliance must be verifiable. This is postulated through the principles of lawfulness and transparency, for example, in Art. 5(1)(a).

Most data processing is done with the help of software – either with human interaction or fully automated. Therefore, it makes sense to have a look at the software development process in the context of the GDPR. At the beginning of each software development life cycle, requirements are gathered and defined by

© Springer Nature Switzerland AG 2018
H. Panetto et al. (Eds.): OTM 2018 Conferences, LNCS 11230, pp. 258–276, 2018.
https://doi.org/10.1007/978-3-030-02671-4_15

taking into account various stakeholders. According to [23], the government, i.e., by enforcing laws and regulations is one of the stakeholders to be considered. Applying the principles of lawfulness and transparency of the GDPR, it must be provable that the software which processes personal data is compliant with the rules laid down in the GDPR. However, the requirements defined in the articles and paragraphs of legislative texts are usually not serviceable for requirements engineering in software development.

In contemplation of being able to define reusable requirements for software development, we define the scope for which this research applies. The first limitation is that we keep the definition of technical requirements generic in order to be able to have reusable software requirements which can be applied to all kinds of software. Second, we do not specify any purpose for which software is developed, whether the software is developed by a potential data processor or controller, whether the personal data processed is that of an end-user of the software, or whether personal data is to be transferred to third countries or international organizations. Third, we do not consider special categories of personal data nor processing of personal data of children. Fourth, we leave out any additional or altered requirements that could result from taking into account national laws for data protection or any other laws that might need to be considered. The main goal of this research is to define technical requirements that need to be implemented to make software compliant with the GDPR and being able to trace which legal requirements from the GDPR are fulfilled with these technical requirements. A detailed application example that illustrates the various requirements is not in scope of this paper and will be part of future research.

The remainder of this paper is structured as follows. Section 2 provides an overview of the related work. Then, the methodology is described. Section 4 contains the technical requirements that were derived from the GDPR. In Sect. 5 we look at the impact of the identified requirements on stakeholder interests. Then, we discuss the findings in Sect. 6 and conclude with an outlook on future work in Sect. 7.

2   Related Work

Our work relates to the research areas requirements reuse and regulatory compliance in software systems. Furthermore, previous work on the methodology and with regard to the GDPR is considered.

2.1   Reusable Requirements

Reusing requirements for a software product is a beneficial strategy that leads to improved productivity and quality in the software development process and the product obtained [27]. The definition of security requirements is suited well for reusability because software often faces similar threats and mitigation techniques are quite standardized [7].

In [25,26], Toval et al. develop the requirements engineering method SIREN (SImple REuse of software requiremeNts) and specify templates for reusable requirements regarding security as well as data protection based on the Spanish implementation of the European Data Protection Directive 95/46/EC. Correspondingly, the work by [20] applies the Norwegian implementation of the EU Directive 95/46/EC to identify reusable security requirements for health-care applications. The work by [7] presents the methodology SQUARE (Security Quality Requirements Engineering) that contains a nine-step process for identifying, classifying, and prioritizing reusable security requirements. Our work proposes a different methodology for identifying reusable security and personal data protection requirements with regard to the GDPR which replaces the national implementations of the EU Directive 95/46/EC.

2.2 Regulatory Compliance

Continuing with the topic of requirements engineering, it is essential to verify that specified requirements are compliant with applicable laws and regulations. A research overview on how laws and regulations have been handled in the context of software development is given by [22]. Methodologies that deal with requirements engineering and regulatory compliance are proposed in [2,5,9]. In this paper, we identify technical requirements that can be traced back to the legal requirements from which the technical requirements were derived using the method KORA. Thus, verification of compliance is given if it can be demonstrated that an information system satisfies the technical requirements.

2.3 KORA

KORA is a method that was introduced by [14] and has been used in German legal research. KORA is the abbreviation for "Konkretisierung rechtlicher Anforderungen" (concretization of legal requirements). In [16,17], a short description and exemplary applications are provided. KORA is used to derive requirements for information systems. [4,24] are further works where KORA is applied in the context of the *Common Criteria*. KORA is the method that is used in this research to derive technical requirements from legal requirements.

2.4 GDPR-Specific Research

The report by the European Union Agency for Network and Information Security (ENISA) [10] on privacy and data protection by design focuses on the implementation of the privacy properties transparency, unlinkability, data minimization and intervenability. It provides an overview of existing approaches regarding privacy design strategies and the utilization of privacy-enhancing techniques. Security and privacy properties have been investigated by [21] in the cloud context, not yet referring to the GDPR. The Standard Data Protection Model (SDM) [1] takes into account all data protection goals defined in the GDPR and can be applied as a tool for identifying and assessing technical and organizational measures (TOMs) as well as performing a risk analysis.

The process of when which articles from the GDPR apply, can be mapped by petri nets (visualization technique). This is suggested by [11] where petri nets are utilized to model the legal process and the software process in order to achieve privacy by design and compliance with the GDPR. Legal requirements that result from the GDPR are investigated by [6]. The work is similar to our proposal. However, the research by [6] is limited to listing legal requirements in the security context related to big data. Furthermore, we identify legal requirements and generic technical requirements with regard to developing a software product.

3 Methodology

KORA is a method that bridges the gap between abstract legal requirements and concrete technical requirements. We use KORA to identify software requirements from the GDPR. We decided to use this method because it fits the purpose best: it is well established, it can be used with little knowledge in the legal area, it is straightforward to use and it matches the abstraction level of requirements engineering. The method consists of four steps:

1. definition of legal requirements through selection of relevant articles from applicable laws
2. determination of legal criteria for IT systems based on identified legal requirements
3. derivation of technical requirements from legal criteria, yielding functional and non-functional characteristics of an IT system
4. creation of technical design proposals based on the technical requirements.

First, from applicable laws the relevant articles and paragraphs are selected as legal requirements. In the context of this research, we only examine the 99 articles of GDPR [12]. Based on the legal requirements, we determine legal criteria by describing implications of the legal requirements with regard to an information system. The 173 recitals of the GDPR [13] guide the articles and can serve as a first basis to derive legal criteria. In the future, it could also be that court decisions will contribute further and more detailed legal criteria. From the legal criteria, we can identify technical requirements that will specify functional or non-functional characteristics of an information system. Some sentences of the articles in the GDPR are very specific and can directly serve as technical requirements. In other cases, the help of recitals and interpretations is necessary to identify technical requirements. We used the interpretations in [1,3,19] as well as our own expertise to define the technical requirements and also identify which parts of which articles and recitals were relevant for which categories of requirements. As a last step, technical design proposals would be made that fulfill the technical requirements and serve as a guideline to implement the technical requirements. We find that this last step is hard to generalize as it is depending on the utilized programming languages, frameworks and libraries. Therefore, we limit our goal to deriving reusable technical requirements from the GDPR.

The key principles relating to processing of personal data within the GDPR are: lawfulness, fairness, transparency, purpose limitation, data minimization, accuracy, storage limitation, integrity, confidentiality and accountability (Art. 5). To have a better overview of the kinds of requirements that can be derived from the GDPR, we classified the requirements into categories. The categories we defined are similar to the key principles but summarize some of the principles and add the categories availability and data transfer. As an orientation served [1] and [10]. Many paragraphs of articles refer to multiple categories, thus, creating redundancy issues. When requirements are present in other categories, references are made accordingly. All references to articles and recitals are from the GDPR.

4   Technical Requirements Based on Legal Requirements

4.1   Confidentiality

The data protection goal confidentiality arises particularly from Art. 5(1)(f), Art. 28(3)(b) and Art. 32(1)(b). Furthermore, Articles 25(2), 29 and 32(2) play a role in this context. Confidentiality is supposed to ensure that no unauthorized or unlawful processing of data takes place. A violation of confidentiality usually also violates the principle of lawfulness that is discussed in Sect. 4.9. [1, p. 18]

The content of Art. 5(1)(f) is enhanced by Recitals 39(12) and 49(1-2). We identify the following legal criteria:

- protection against unauthorized and unlawful processing (Art. 5(1)(f))
- protection against unauthorized access to or use of personal data in storage or transition as well as access to networks and services that process this data (Recital 39(12) and 49(1-2))
- protection against accidental loss (data disclosure) (Art. 5(1)(f))
- ensure network and information security (Recital 49(1))
- identify TOMs for ensuring confidentiality, thus, implementing an appropriate security of personal data (Art. 5(1)(f) and Recital 39(12)).

From the legal criteria, we deduce technical requirements as follows [1, p. 21]:

- secure authentication and authorization mechanisms for all components that allow access to personal data including access to networks, services, and systems
- definition of an access control policy on the basis of an identity management where access is limited to specific roles or attributes (who is allowed to do what with the personal data)
- depending on the location and accessibility of the data, it should be considered to encrypt all data at rest and/or in motion.

Art. 28(3)(b) refers to the processor's responsibility to ensure confidentiality of personal data. Along with Art. 29, requirements are of a contractual nature between controller and processor and should not be interpreted into technical requirements for a software product.

Art. 32(1)(b) along with Recital 83(2-3) require TOMs for state-of-the-art, ongoing confidentiality of processing systems and services. Moreover, a risk analysis is expected and in case the risk is found to be "high", a data protection impact assessment according to Art. 35 must be carried out. Risk in combination with confidentiality is also treated by Art. 32(2) in conjunction with Recital 75. Therefore, we can conclude that a threat and risk analysis must be conducted. In general, Recitals 84, 89, 90, 91 and 95 contain more information on the data protection impact assessment. In the context of confidentiality, risk assessment for unauthorized disclosure or access to personal data transmitted, stored or otherwise processed is of importance. Based on the results of the threat and risk analysis, further technical requirements will have to be defined.

From Art. 25(2) and the corresponding Recital 78, the necessity for authentication and access control can be deduced which is covered by Art. 5(1)(f). Furthermore, the article refers to the implementation of TOMs to ensure data protection by design and default.

It can be summarized that the following mechanisms are necessary for the fulfillment of the confidentiality data protection goal: authentication, authorization, access control and encryption of personal data. Further measures may result from risk analysis including the identification of TOMs.

4.2 Integrity

The goal to guarantee integrity of data is regulated primarily by Art. 5(1)(f) and 32. For Art. 5(1)(f), we identify some further legal criteria and technical requirements regarding the integrity of data. As already mapped out in the previous section, authorization and access control are essential. In the context of integrity, Art. 5(1)(f) along with Recital 49(1-2) expects protection against damage and unauthorized erasure or modification of data. Again, TOMs for ensuring integrity need to be defined. TOMs are always underpinned by Art. 25(1) in general and by Art. 32(1) regarding security and risk assessment. Therefore, Art. 32(1)(b) in combination with Recital 83(2) require TOMs for state-of-the-art, ongoing integrity. From Art. 32(2), an obligation for a risk assessment regarding accidental or unlawful destruction, alteration or loss is derived as a legal criterion. Results from the risk analysis will serve as additional technical requirements. From Art. 5(1)(f) we deduce further technical requirements [1, p. 21]:

- limitation of rights for writing or changing files that contain personal data
- check the integrity of data before, during and/or after processing the data, utilizing signatures, check-sums or electronic identifiers
- document which roles are authorized to read/write/create/modify which resources
- define and implement processes for maintenance and timeliness/up-to-dateness of data
- define the expected behavior of processes, make regular tests and document whether the full functionality is still available.

In summary, mechanisms for limiting access to data as well as ensuring the integrity of data and processes must be implemented. Further measures may result from risk analysis including the identification of TOMs.

4.3   Availability

The availability of a system and data within that system is postulated in Art. 32(1)(b,c,d) in the context of secure processing. In Art. 5(1)(e), the availability of data is a requirement for the identification of the data subject. However, availability of data is limited to the necessity/purpose of processing. Art. 13(2)(a), 15(1) and 20(1,2) deal with the controller's duty to inform about and provide access to a user's personal data [1, p. 18].

From Art. 32(1)(b) in combination with Recital 49, we can identify the legal criterion to apply TOMs for state-of-the-art, ongoing availability and resilience of processing systems. This includes "...ensuring network and information security, i.e., the ability of a network or an information system to resist, at a given level of confidence, accidental events or unlawful or malicious actions..." (Recital 49(1)). Technical requirements then include DoS protection, intrusion prevention, as well as input validation (prevent malfunctioning of the system). Prior to determining the technical requirements, a risk assessment regarding availability is necessary. The results of the risk assessment can alter or demand additional technical requirements. This is also the case for the following legal requirement.

Art. 32(1)(c) refers to incident handling. It requires "...the ability to restore the availability and access to personal data in a timely manner in the event of a physical or technical incident;". Along with Recital 83(3), it can be concluded that there is need for incident detection, a process for incident handling (to restore availability), backup & restore as well as disaster recovery.

Art. 32(1)(d) requires that security of processing is always assured. Thus, the TOMs implemented for system security must be regularly reviewed. Technical requirements in this context must be defined depending on the TOMs implemented for assuring security of processing. For example, a process that takes into account vulnerability and patch management as well as progress of the state-of-the-art could make this requirement compliant. Art. 32(1)(d) is also referenced in Sects. 4.6 and 4.9.

Art. 5(1)(e) calls for limited storage duration of personal data, see also Sects. 4.4 and 4.5. In the context of availability, this means that personal data must only be available for the time that it is needed for processing. Art. 5(1)(e) in accordance with Recital 39(10) demands that a time limit is defined after which data is either erased because it is no longer needed for processing or a review is made that assesses whether data is still needed for processing. A review would need to be repeated periodically after the defined time limit. If personal data is to be kept longer than needed for processing purposes as allowed in Art. 5(1)(e), e.g., for statistical, archiving, scientific, or historical purposes, it must be altered using, i.e., pseudonymization (see Art. 89(1), 25(1), 32(1)(a), 40(2)(d), 6(4)(f) as well as Recitals 28 and 78).

Art. 13(2)(a) builds upon Art. 5(1)(e) and further requires the controller to tell the data subject for how long the personal data will be stored (or be available) "... or if that is not possible, the criteria used to determine that period;". This last part of the sentence may alleviate the first part when companies would then just inform the data subject that storage of the personal data will be as long as some sort of processing for some sort of purpose is necessary. Thus, there is an "either-or" technical requirement to comply with this part of Art. 13. Either, there is a defined period after which data is deleted. Or, there are defined criteria that would determine when data must be deleted when no fix period can be determined.

Art. 15(1) and Art. 20(1,2) deal with providing access to a data subject's personal data. Art. 15(1) along with Recital 63 give the data subject the right to find out whether a controller is processing personal data concerning the data subject. Therefore, the technical requirement to be able to search for a potential data subject's identity can be deduced. Furthermore, if the inquiry of the data subject is positive, the controller would need to give the data subject access to its data. This can be accomplished as described in Art. 20. In case of a large amount of data, the software would also need to be able to filter for data categories (see Recital 63(7)). Art. 15(1)(a-h) moreover requires the controller to inform the data subject, e.g., for which purposes processing takes places, which categories of personal data are involved in the processing, for how long personal data is stored, whether processing includes automated decision making as well as how rectification or erasure of data or a complaint about the controller can be made.

Art. 20(1)(a,b) as well as Recital 68(3-6) specify under which processing conditions Article 20(1) applies. In case it applies to the way data is processed in the software, Recital 68 and, in addition, Art. 20(2) further describe the controller's responsibility to send a collection of the processed personal data to the data subject. Therefore, there exist the following technical requirements:

- export function for sending collection of personal data to a data subject (Art. 20(1), Recital 68(1))
- the format of the exported data must be commonly used, machine-readable and inter-operable (in order to move data to another controller) (Art. 20(1), Recital 68(1-2))
- if technically feasible: export function that sends collection of personal data to another controller (Art. 20(2), Recital 68(10)).

Measures for assuring availability are split into two categories. On the one hand, availability refers to the system and its corresponding components. On the other hand, the personal data of the data subject must be made available to him or her. Further measures may result from risk analysis including the identification of TOMs.

4.4   Unlinkability

The data protection goal unlinkability is requested particularly through Art. 5(1)(b) "purpose limitation". Unlinkability in this context refers to the obligation to process data only for the purposes that the data was collected for. This is also dealt with in points (c) and (e) of Art. 5(1). If further processing is wanted that goes beyond the initial purposes, Art. 6(4) must be applied. Any kind of automated individual decision-making (including profiling) that is used during processing of personal data is regulated by Art. 22. Pseudonymization is acknowledged as a suited method for assuring unlinkability (see previous section for article references) [1, p. 18].

Art. 5(1)(b) in accordance with Recital 39(6) and Art. 5(1)(e) demand an extended definition of the data life cycle (see Sect. 4.6) where it should be documented during each stage of the data life cycle that the purpose for which the data is processed, is specific, explicit and legitimate. Art. 5(1)(c) along with Recital 39(9) further require documentation that the "purpose of the processing could not reasonably be fulfilled by other means". Art. 5(1)(c,e) also refer to data minimization and are further covered in Sect. 4.5.

Art. 6(4) must only be considered if processing beyond the initially agreed-upon purposes that the data subject consented to (or any of the other grounds defined in Art. 6(1)(a-f) – see Sect. 4.9). Therefore, in addition to having defined the data life cycle, it would also be necessary to prove that data is following the defined life cycle and document that this life cycle is in accordance to the lawfulness of processing as defined in Art. 6(1)(a-f). If Art. 6(4) has to be applied, it would be required to document and assess that "processing is compatible with the purposes for which the personal data were initially collected" (Recital 50(1)). Points (a-e) of Art. 6(4) and Recital 50(6) define the scope of the assessment.

Art. 22 must be applied if data processing includes automated individual decision-making, including profiling. Paragraph 1 actually gives the data subject "the right not to be subject to a decision based solely on automated processing, including profiling, which produces legal effects concerning him or her or similarly significantly affects him or her". This is further interpreted in Recital 71(1-2). Exceptions to paragraph 1 of Art. 22 are defined in paragraph 2. In case points (a) or (c) from paragraph 2 apply, we can then derive the technical requirement from paragraph 3 along with Recital 71(4) to implement safeguards regarding automated processing by at least being able to intervene manually in the processing activities.

Art. 25(2) in accordance with Recital 71(6) and 60(3) in the context of possible profiling activities requests to use appropriate mathematical or statistical procedures for the profiling, use TOMs to prevent data inaccuracies, secure personal data, prevent that profiling activities have discriminatory effects and inform the data subject that profiling activities take place and which consequences they have.

It can be summarized that besides documentational requirements, further measures to satisfy the unlinkability data protection goal must only be taken if automated individual decision-making or profiling is involved.

4.5   Data Minimization

The goal of data minimization is closely linked to unlinkability. Similar articles apply. Art. 5(1)(c) in accordance with Recital 39(7-8) are the main contributors to data minimization. It is demanded that "the period for which the personal data are stored is limited to a strict minimum"(Recital 39(8)). Therefore, it can be deduced that personal data must be deleted – or, as postulated in Recital 39(10), periodically reviewed – after a defined amount of time. This should be provided as a function within a software product. Furthermore, as few data as needed should be collected and processed. Therefore, the documentation of the data life cycle should also include an assessment regarding data minimization. The requirement for Art. 5(1)(e) was already covered in the context of availability, see Sect. 4.3. Art. 25(2) along with Recital 78(2-3) refers to data minimization as a measure to show compliance to data protection by design and data protection by default.

4.6   Transparency

The principle of transparency is one of the main goals of the GDPR. Important Articles include Art. 5(1)(a) as well as the obligation to provide information stipulated in Articles 12 through 14. [1, p. 19] There is even a separate Recital for transparency (Recital 58). Transparency will mostly involve either documentation to prove law-fulness or providing information to the data subject or supervisory authority. This information is to be "concise, easily accessible and easy to understand, and that clear and plain language and, additionally, where appropriate, visualization be used."(Recital 58(1)) Therefore, requirements will be of a non-functional nature regarding documentation unless information is to be displayed through the software.

Art. 5(1)(a) deals with transparency regarding the processing of personal data. Recital 39(2-4) further describes how this can be done and which information must be provided. Two requirements can be deduced: transparent processing of personal data is to be documented in the data life cycle and a privacy notice must be defined. The second requirement is a document of a contractual nature and should only be included in the technical requirements if displaying the privacy notice and having the user consent to it before transferring any personal data is to be part of the software. Working out this document will be done by legal experts. Regarding the presentation, Recital 60(5-6) states: "That information may be provided in combination with standardized icons in order to give an easily visible, intelligible and clearly legible manner, a meaningful overview of the intended processing. Where the icons are presented electronically, they should be machine-readable." The requirement for a privacy notice and its content is clarified further in Art. 12, 13, 14 as well as Recitals 60, 61, 62.

Art. 15(1) was already covered in Sect. 4.3 and will be dealt with again in Sect. 4.7. Art. 19 requires the controller to notify the data subject about rectification, erasure or restriction of processing regarding his/her personal data. This will also be covered by Sect. 4.7.

Art. 25(1) and 25(2) refer to privacy by design and privacy by default. In the context of the transparency principle, it must be specified which requirements are defined to fulfill the demand for privacy by default and which requirements are defined to fulfill the demand for privacy by design. Furthermore, it should be checked whether the specified requirements are sufficient or whether more measures (e.g., TOMs) are necessary to reach compliance (Recital 78(2)).

Art. 30 in accordance with Recital 82 requires that processing activities are to be recorded by the controller and, where applicable, by the processor. Art. 30(3) states that the documentation must be in writing, including in electronic form. Paragraph 5 outlines exceptions for having to document all processing activities. The documentation stays internal unless, as stated in paragraph 4, the supervisory authority requests those records. Paragraphs 1 and 2 define the content of the records for the controller (paragraph 1) and the processor (paragraph 2). The information is similar to the one provided in the privacy notice and data life cycle. The records contain information from different stakeholders. Thus, the non-functional technical requirement would be to create those records. If records are to be created automatically by the software, a functional technical requirement would need to be defined further. According to Art. 30(1)(g) and 30(2)(d), one rather interesting part of the record is to document the implemented TOMs as referred to in Art. 32(1).

Art. 32(1)(d) along with Recital 74(1-3) require transparency and documentation regarding the assurance of the security of processing. Art. 32(1)(d) also relates to Sects. 4.9 and 4.3. Here, the GDPR basically states the technical requirement within the legal requirement. There must be "a process for regularly testing, assessing and evaluating the effectiveness of technical and organizational measures for ensuring the security of processing". The definition leaves quite some room for interpretation. Taking the perspective of a security professional, the requirement could include the following measures:

- continuous testing for software vulnerabilities
- regular installation of patches (software product as well as operating system)
- vulnerability management (which vulnerabilities exist, which new vulnerabilities are found, when are patches available, when are patches installed/implemented in which versions)
- re-testing all security requirements for new releases as well as re-evaluating whether new security requirements may have evolved through progress in, e.g., state-of-the-art.

Art. 33(5) and Recital 87 refer to data breaches. In case of a personal data breach, documentation must include: facts relating to the breach, its effects and the remedial action taken. Furthermore, the documentation serves as proof of compliance for the supervisory authority. This requirement is related to incident handling which was covered in Sect. 4.3. Therefore, the technical requirement would be to have the incident handling process as such that in case of a personal data breach, documentation of the incident is compliant with Art. 33.

In summary, satisfying the principle of transparency requires mostly appropriate documentation as well as providing information to the data subject or supervisory authority.

4.7 Intervenability

The data subject's right to intervene in the processing activities of the data controller/processor emerges mainly from the right to rectification (Art. 16), erasure (Art. 17), restriction of processing (Art. 18), object (Art. 21) as well as the right to data portability (Art. 20, has already been covered in Sect. 4.3). In this context, Art. 5(1)(d) requires the data processor/controller to create the necessary conditions for granting these rights to the data subject. [1, p. 19] According to Art. 5(1)(d), the data processor/controller must ensure that personal data is accurate. If personal data is found to be inaccurate, it must either be erased or rectified. This is also stipulated in Recital 39(11). Therefore, there are multiple requirements that can be deduced: data is to be kept up to date when necessary (thus, optional requirement); there ought to be some kind of process that checks regularly for erroneous data (without exceeding the purpose for which they are processed); if faulty data are found, there should be a way to either rectify or delete the data manually or automatically as soon as possible.

Art. 13(2)(c) and Art. 14(2)(d) require the controller to inform the data subject about the possibility to withdraw consent (only if processing is based on Art. 6(1)(a) or Art. 9(2)(a), see Sect. 4.9). This is usually part of the privacy notice (see Sect. 4.6). The difference between Art. 13 and 14 is that Art. 13 refers to data that has been directly obtained from the data subject while Art. 14 refers to data that has not been directly provided by the data subject.

Art. 15(1) was already covered in Sect. 4.6 and deals with the data subject's right to information on and access to personal data concerning him or her. In the context of intervenability, Art. 15(1)(e) gives the data subject the right to rectification (Art. 16), erasure (Art. 17), restriction of processing (Art. 18), as well as objection to processing (Art. 21) and access to the data (Art. 15(1)). The requirements resulting from the afore-mentioned articles all have the precondition that the data subject contacts the data controller with a certain request regarding his or her personal data. Therefore, the software product must be able to provide certain functionality upon request.

For Art. 15 through 21 (except Art. 20) and the corresponding Recitals, we can identify the following technical requirements:

- provide direct access to the data subject's personal access through a remote access to a secure system, if feasible (Art. 15(1), Recital 63(4))
- provide a copy of the personal data that is processed upon request by the data subject (Art. 15(3))
- correct faulty data and complete incomplete data upon request by the data subject (Art. 16, Recital 65(1))
- erase personal data upon request by the data subject (Art. 17(1), Recital 65(2))

- erase also any links to, copy or replication of personal data that was requested to be erased, including informing other controllers that are processing this data (Art. 17(2), Recital 66)
- have a process for erasing data as soon as one of the following occasions in Art. 17(1)(a-f) occur (also in Recital 65(2-4)); exceptions to those occasions are pointed out in Art. 17(3)
- restrict the processing of a data subject's personal data if requested or otherwise mandatory through application of Art. 18(1); Recital 67(1-3) provides proposals how to achieve the restriction of data processing – how this restriction is implemented is dependent on the software product and cannot be generalized
- inform the data subject about any activities regarding rectification, erasure or restriction of processing (Art. 18(3), 19)
- stop processing of a subject's personal data if the data subject objects to it (Art. 21(1) sentence 1) or prove and document that, as described in Art. 21(1) sentence 2 and Recital 69(1-2), there exist "compelling legitimate grounds for the [continuing] processing".

In summary, intervenability of the data subject requires that the controller or processor is able to erase, rectify or restrict the processing of personal data upon request by the data subject. Moreover, this category includes requirements regarding the handling of faulty data.

4.8 Data Transfer by the Controller

In contrast to the data subject moving his/her data, the controller may also have an interest in transferring data across territorial boundaries. This is, for example, an important topic for cloud deployments. Therefore, requirements in this section are to be seen as optional, applicable only if data is transferred to third countries or international organizations. Chapter 5 of the GDPR covers this topic mostly.

Art. 45(1) in accordance with Recital 103 allow data to be transferred without any specific authorization to third countries or international organizations if they have been approved of by the European Commission (i.e., such that an adequate level of protection of the data is ensured). Therefore, the (technical) requirement can be determined to check and document whether the country/organization is part of the approved ones by the European Commission.

If the country/organization has not been approved, Art. 46 must be applied and appropriate safeguards as described in Art. 46(2,3) as well as Recital 108 must be undertaken. Art. 15(2) gives the data subject the right to be informed about the safeguards that have been implemented in case of a data transfer across territorial boundaries. The technical requirement then to be fulfilled is to document, determine and implement safeguards necessary to assure compliance with data protection requirements (i.e., key principles regarding data processing and data protection by design and by default) as well as assuring that data subjects have appropriate rights with regard to processing in that third country or international organization.

Art. 30(1)(d,e) and 30(2)(c) demand documentation of any processing activities where data has been disclosed to recipients in third countries or international organizations. This relates to the recording of any processing activities covered in Sect. 4.6 and should be included in that requirement in case of data transfers to third countries or international organizations.

4.9 Lawfulness/Accountability/Fairness

Lawfulness is one of the basic principles for processing data. It is the main reason why we have started this research. Lawfulness referring to data processing is demanded throughout the entire GDPR, starting with Art. 5(1)(a). As soon as personal data is processed, the GDPR applies (Art. 1,2). Failure to comply with the basic principles for processing as demanded in Art. 5 may lead to substantial fines as defined in Art. 83(5)(a).

In Art. 6(1), the GDPR differentiates between the following lawful bases that can be selected for data processing: consent, contractual necessity, legal obligation, vital interests, public interest and legitimate interests [18]. Depending on the ground for processing personal data, various constellations of requirements resulting from the application of differing articles and recitals occur. We do not explore this topic further at this moment because it is very individual depending on the software product and type of personal data to be processed. In addition, more legal expertise in that specific domain is necessary. However, we can conclude one technical requirement from Art. 6(1): select and document the reasons for choosing a legal ground for processing personal data.

Art. 5(1)(a) in accordance with Recital 39(1) require processing to be lawful and fair. Fairness in this context means that data processing must not be done "in a way that is unduly detrimental, unexpected or misleading to the individuals concerned" [19, p. 18]. Further, taking into account Art. 5(2), which demands to be responsible and to be able to demonstrate compliance with the key principles for data processing, we can deduce the technical requirement to have auditable documentation of lawfulness for every legal requirement which applies. This is what we try to achieve in this research by selecting general legal requirements that would apply to most software products that process personal data and mapping these legal requirements to technical requirements.

Continuing with the principle of lawfulness, Art. 24(1) along with Recital 78 demand that TOMs are implemented in order to ensure compliant processing. Again, the demonstrability of these measures is required including further the review and update of TOMs. Therefore, a possible technical requirement that satisfies the legal requirement/criterion would be to demonstrate for each software version that compliance to current legislation is guaranteed.

Art. 24(2) requires the controller to have a data protection policy. The definition of a data protection policy is found in Art. 4(20) 'binding corporate rules'. However, this requirement is not a strict one as it applies only "where proportionate in relation to processing activities". Therefore, a non-functional technical requirement would include either the documentation of the data protection policy or the documentation of why it is not "proportionate" to have a data protection policy. Both requirements are of a contractual/legal nature. The requirement for the data protection policy can be of a functional nature if displaying it and having the user consent to it before transferring any personal data is to be part of the software.

According to Art. 24(3), compliance with a code of conduct or certification may be used to prove lawfulness of certain articles of the GDPR. Therefore, some of the previously identified requirements may be obsolete if they are fulfilled through adherence to a code of conduct or certification. Art. 33(5) deals with lawfulness in case of a data breach. It was already covered in Sect. 4.6 where the requirement already includes that compliance to the article must be verifiable. Art. 35(11) requires to review the data protection impact assessment which is part of a requirement in Sects. 4.1, 4.2 and 4.3. Art. 37(7) which demands to publish contact details of data protection officer was also covered in Sect. 4.6.

It can be summarized that the key principle of lawfulness requires documentation of regulatory compliance.

5 Stakeholder Requirements

For requirements engineering, it must be clear who the stakeholders are. The requirements identified in the preceding section can serve as a first basis for defining requirements with regard to the government as a stakeholder, taking the government as a representative for applicable laws and regulations. Software usually consists of multiple components that communicate over interfaces. Hence, in our previous work [23], we proposed a method to identify the stakeholders' interests for each software component/interface regarding the security properties confidentiality (C), integrity (I) and availability (A). While the matrix was generated with a specific software product and stakeholders in mind, the method can be applied to any requirements engineering process where stakeholders and their interests should be included. Having now a broader view on the legal requirements, we found it necessary to expand the matrix with the privacy properties transparency (T), unlinkability (U), data minimization (M) and intervenability by the data subject (V) with respect to personal data. An exemplary matrix is displayed in Table 1 where stakeholder interests of the vendor and the government (through laws) regarding the security and privacy properties are matched to processing of personal data in interfaces of a software product, for example, source code (as part of intellectual property) and identified personal data. No interest is represented by white cells, partial interest by grey cells and full interest by black cells.

The technical requirements that were identified in Sect. 4 must be broken down according to their applicability to system components and data that is to be processed. Based on this matrix, it should be determined which requirements must be fulfilled in the context of which component/interface. Hence, we need to sort out and match those technical requirements regarding the security and privacy properties for each system component. This is out of scope in the context of this paper and will be part of our future work.

Table 1. Stakeholder interests regarding confidentiality (C), integrity (I), availability (A), transparency (T), unlinkability (U), data minimization (M) and intervenability (V)

Stakeholder	Source Code							Identified personal data						
	C	I	A	T	U	M	V	C	I	A	T	U	M	V
Vendor	■		■						▨	■				
Government			■	■	■	■	■	■	■	■	■	■	■	■

6 Discussion

The scope of this paper is limited since we wanted to keep the requirements as universally applicable as possible. Neither data of children nor special categories of personal data were taken into account. Furthermore, the national laws were not considered. National laws will be important when it comes to data transfers, for example, when software processes personal data in the cloud in a different country than the data was collected in. The GDPR leaves room for national laws to be more restrictive or liberating in certain areas, thus, overruling articles stated in the GDPR.

Specific requirements resulting from a threat and risk analysis as well as identified technical and organizational measures (TOMs) in the context of privacy by design, privacy by default as well as security by design remain unclear. In Germany, as a result of and in addition to the application of the Standard Data Protection Model [1], there should have been a publication of measures and modules since the end of May 2018. These measures and modules could be an initial set of TOMs. However, no publication was made so far [15]. In the context of privacy by design and privacy by default, the works by [8,10,11] serve as a good starting point. This area will be explored in further research. Another topic to be discussed is how to interpret the legal requirements defined in the articles and recitals. Lawyers and court rulings will argument about certain formulations in the GDPR. Therefore, we advise to include legal experts in the requirements engineering process in order to check which requirements apply and whether further requirements from certain legal constellations (e.g., national laws) or changes emerge. Thus, another limitation of this work lies in the probable incompleteness of the list of requirements.

7 Conclusion and Future Work

We present a first proposal of generic reusable technical requirements for the software development process that satisfy the key principles of the GDPR. The requirements can be traced back to the corresponding articles and recitals, thus, making regulatory compliance demonstrable. Furthermore, we link those requirements to stakeholder interests. As a result, we need to consider stakeholder interests with regard to security properties as well as privacy properties in future research.

As indicated in the discussion, the impact of national laws on the requirements worked out in this research should be assessed as a next step. Furthermore, when considering data transfers to third countries or international organizations outside of the EU, national laws of these countries must be taken into account. This is an especially interesting topic for a cloud deployment of the software.

In order to demonstrate applicability of our findings, we will apply the requirements to a specific application context. Once all requirements for compliant software in a specific software product are identified, it should be investigated which measures can be implemented and verified using automated mechanisms. This requires, in particular, more research on TOMs and includes, for example, specifying requirements with regard to privacy by default and privacy by design – taking into account privacy-enhancing technologies – as well as security by design.

References

1. AK Technik der Konferenz der unabhängigen Datenschutzbehörden des Bundes und der Länder: Das Standard-Datenschutzmodell - Eine Methode zur Datenschutzberatung und -prüfung auf der Basis einheitlicher Gewährleistungsziele. von der 95. Konferenz der unabhängigen Datenschutzbehörden des Bundes und der Länder, April 2018. https://www.datenschutzzentrum.de/uploads/sdm/SDM-Methode_V1.1.pdf, v. 1.1. Accessed 13 July 2018
2. Beckers, K., Faßbender, S., Küster, J.-C., Schmidt, H.: A pattern-based method for identifying and analyzing laws. In: Regnell, B., Damian, D. (eds.) REFSQ 2012. LNCS, vol. 7195, pp. 256–262. Springer, Heidelberg (2012). https://doi.org/10.1007/978-3-642-28714-5_23
3. Boardman, R., Mullock, J., Mole, A.: Bird & bird & guide to the general data protection regulation, May 2017. https://www.twobirds.com/~/media/pdfs/gdpr-pdfs/bird-bird-guide-to-the-general-data-protection-regulation.pdf?la=en. Accessed 13 July 2018
4. Bräunlich, K., Richter, P., Grimm, R., Roßnagel, A.: Verbindung von CC-Schutzprofilen mit der Methode rechtlicher IT-Gestaltung KORA. Datenschutz und Datensicherheit-DuD **35**(2), 129–135 (2011)
5. Breaux, T.D.: Legal requirements acquisition for the specification of legally compliant information systems. Ph.D. thesis, North Carolina State University (2009). https://repository.lib.ncsu.edu/bitstream/handle/1840.16/3376/etd.pdf?sequence=1&isAllowed=y. Accessed 17 July 2018
6. Cesar, J., Debussche, J.: Novel EU legal requirements in big data security: big data-big security headaches. J. Intell. Prop. Info. Tech. Elec. Com. L. **8**, 79–88 (2017)
7. Christian, T.: Security requirements reusability and the square methodology. Technical report, Carnegie-Mellon University, September 2010. http://www.dtic.mil/dtic/tr/fulltext/u2/a532572.pdf. Accessed 17 July 2018

8. Colesky, M., Hoepman, J.H., Hillen, C.: A critical analysis of privacy design strategies. In: Security and Privacy Workshops (SPW), pp. 33–40. IEEE (2016)
9. Compagna, L., El Khoury, P., Krausová, A.: How to integrate legal requirements into a requirements engineering methodology for the development of security and privacy patterns. Artif. Intell. Law **17**(1), 1–30 (2009)
10. Danezis, G., Domingo-Ferrer, J., et al.: Privacy and data protection by design - from policy to engineering. Technical report, ENISA, December 2014. https://arxiv.org/ftp/arxiv/papers/1501/1501.03726.pdf. Accessed 13 July 2018
11. Diver, L., Schafer, B.: Opening the black box: petri nets and privacy by design. Int. Rev. Law Comput. Technol. **31**(1), 68–90 (2017)
12. European Union: General Data Protection Regulation (GDPR): Articles (2018). https://gdpr-info.eu/. Accessed 13 July 2018
13. European Union: General Data Protection Regulation (GDPR): Recitals (2018). https://gdpr-info.eu/recitals/. Accessed 13 July 2018
14. Hammer, V., Roßnagel, A., Pordesch, U.: KORA: Konkretisierung rechtlicher Anforderungen zu technischen Gestaltungsvorschlägen für IuK-Systeme. provet (1992)
15. Hansen, M.: SDM-Bausteine, July 2018. https://www.datenschutzzentrum.de/sdm/bausteine/. Accessed 13 July 2018
16. Hoffmann, A., Hoffmann, H., Leimeister, J.M.: Anforderungen an software requirement pattern in der Entwicklung sozio-technischer Systeme. In: Lecture Notes in Informatics, pp. 379–393. Ges. für Informatik (2012). Accessed 17 July 2018
17. Hoffmann, A., Schulz, T., Hoffmann, H., Jandt, S., Roßnagel, A., Leimeister, J.: Towards the use of software requirement patterns for legal requirements. In: 2nd International Requirements Engineering Efficiency Workshop (REEW) 2012 at REFSQ 2012, Essen, Germany. SSRN Journal (SSRN Electronic Journal) (2012)
18. i-SCOOP: GDPR: legal grounds for lawful processing of personal data, July 2018. https://www.i-scoop.cu/gdpr/legal-grounds-lawful-processing-personal-data/. Accessed 13 July 2018
19. ico.: Guide to the General Data Protection Regulation (GDPR), March 2018. https://ico.org.uk/media/for-organisations/guide-to-the-general-data-protection-regulation-gdpr-1-0.pdf, version 1.0.122. Accessed 13 July 2018
20. Jensen, J., Tøndel, I.A., Jaatun, M.G., Meland, P.H., Andresen, H.: Reusable security requirements for healthcare applications. In: International Conference on Availability, Reliability and Security, ARES 2009, pp. 380–385. IEEE (2009)
21. Kalloniatis, C., Mouratidis, H., Vassilis, M., Islam, S.: Towards the design of secure and privacy-oriented information systems in the cloud: identifying the major concepts. Comput. Stand. Interfaces **36**(4), 759–775 (2014)
22. Otto, P.N., Antón, A.I.: Addressing legal requirements in requirements engineering. In: 15th IEEE International Requirements Engineering Conference, RE 2007, pp. 5–14. IEEE (2007)
23. Ringmann, S.D., Langweg, H.: Determining security requirements for cloud-supported routing of physical goods. In: 2017 IEEE Conference on Communications and Network Security (CNS), pp. 514–521. IEEE (2017)
24. Simić-Draws, D., Neumann, S., et al.: Holistic and law compatible IT security evaluation: integration of common criteria, ISO 27001/IT-Grundschutz and KORA. Int. J. Inf. Secur. Privacy **7**(3), 16–35 (2013)
25. Toval, A., Olmos, A., Piattini, M.: Legal requirements reuse: a critical success factor for requirements quality and personal data protection. In: Proceedings IEEE Joint International Conference on Requirements Engineering, pp. 95–103 (2002)

26. Toval, A., Nicolás, J., Moros, B., García, F.: Requirements reuse for improving information systems security: a practitioner's approach. Requirements Eng. 6(4), 205–219 (2002)
27. Velasco, J.L., Valencia-García, R., Fernández-Breis, J.T., Toval, A.: Modelling reusable security requirements based on an ontology framework. J. Res. Practice Inf. Technol. 41(2), 119 (2009)

A Review of Distributed Ledger Technologies

Nabil El Ioini[✉] and Claus Pahl

Free University of Bolzano, Piazza Dominicani 3, 39100 Bolzano, Italy
{nabil.elioini,claus.pahl}@unibz.it

Abstract. Recently the race toward trusted distributed systems has attracted a huge interest, mostly due to the advances in crypto-currencies platforms such as Bitcoin. Currently, different Distributed Ledger Technologies (DLTs) are competing to demonstrate their capabilities and show how they can overcome the limitations faced by others. The common denominator among all distributed ledger technologies is their reliance on a distributed, decentralized peer-to-peer network and a set of modular mechanisms such as cryptographic hashes and consensuses mechanisms. However, their implementations vary substantially in terms of the used data structure, fault tolerance and consensus approaches. This divergence affects the nature of each instance of the DLT in terms of cost, security, latency and performance. In this paper, we present a snapshot of four existing implementations of DLTs. The particularities of each technology and an initial comparison between them is discussed.

Keywords: DLT · Blockchain · Tangle · Hashgraph

1 Introduction

DLT has attracted more attention with the introduction of blockchain and financial transactions. However, as the possible applications beyond the financial sector are rising, blockchain has been criticized for its cost and lack of scalability and therefore, new DLTs have been introduced. In this paper, we present a systematic comparison of four distributed ledger technologies and discuss their strengths and weaknesses. The contribution of this work is to initiate an effort to define the main properties and advantages of each of these technologies and help identify the possible applications domains for each one.

Based on our research, we have identified a set of quality criteria to evaluate and compare the different architectures based on SWOT analysis. Based on our analysis we found that a conceptual and theoretical comparison between the existing DLTs is possible, however, it is still difficult to compare them in practice, since they have not reached the required level of maturity in terms of implementation and adoption.

© Springer Nature Switzerland AG 2018
H. Panetto et al. (Eds.): OTM 2018 Conferences, LNCS 11230, pp. 277–288, 2018.
https://doi.org/10.1007/978-3-030-02671-4_16

The rest of the paper is structured as follows. Section 2 presents the different DLT technologies. Section 3 presents the comparison framework. Section 4 compares the four technologies and discusses the results before presenting the related work and the conclusions in Sects. 5 and 6.

2   Individual Technologies Review

One of the main goals of DLTs is to allow users who do not necessarily trust each other to interact without the need of a trusted third party [13]. In fact, an important scenario for DLT is a situation in which there is a degree of mistrust between the participating parties, such as business partners or anonymous entities [11]. By design, DLTs add a level of transparency, traceability, and security to this kind of environment [7]. At their core, DLTs are data structures to record transactions and set of functions to manipulate them. Each DLT differentiates itself using different data model and technologies, however, generally, all DLTs are based on three well-known technologies, *(i)* public key cryptography, *(ii)* distributed peer-to-peer networks, and *(iii)* consensus mechanisms, which have been blended in a unique and novel way. Since the goal is to operate in an untrusted environment, public key cryptography is used to establish a secure digital identity for every participant. Each participant is equipped with a pair of keys (one public, one private) to be able to record transactions in the Distributed Ledger (DL). This digital identity is used to enforce control of ownership over the objects managed by the DL. A peer-to-peer network is employed to be able to scale up the network, to avoid a single point of failure, and to prevent a single or small group of players to take over the network. A consensus protocol allows

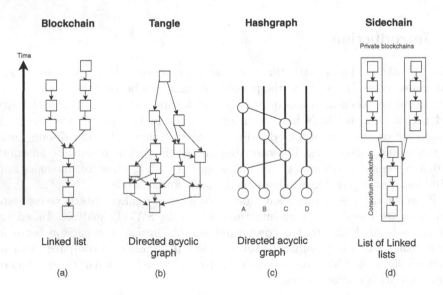

Fig. 1. An overview of the existing DLTs

all participants, i.e., all nodes of the DL, to agree on a single version of the truth, without the need of a trusted third party. In the following subsections, each of the four technologies is presented along with their strengths and limitations and unique features. Then the next section a comparison of the four technologies is discussed.

2.1   Blockchain

A blockchain is a distributed, decentralized and immutable ledger to store transactions history (Fig. 1(a)). The data is continuously appended and it can be accessed by all the network participants [3]. At its core, a blockchain is a linked list of blocks connected to each other using hash codes, where each block references the previous block in the chain. This has the advantage of making it hard for anyone to tamper with blocks content, since any change of a block will invalidate all the successor blocks. The main building blocks of a Blockchain are [6]:

- *Transactions*, which are signed pieces of information created by the participating nodes in the network then broadcast to the rest of the network;
- *Blocks*, are collections of transactions that are appended to the blockchain after being validated
- A *blockchain* is a ledger of all the created blocks that make up the network;
- The blockchain relies on *Public keys* to connect the different blocks together (similar to a linked list);
- A *consensus mechanism* is used to decide which blocks are added to the blockchain.

In general there are three classes of blockchain platforms (i) permissionless (ii) permissioned, and (iii) private. Permissionless blockchains are open platforms that allow everyone to access and submit transactions (e.g., Bitcoin and Ethereum). Permissioned blockchains are platforms managed by multiple organizations where the network participants are known and a degree of control is in place. Private blockchains are platforms managed by one organization with full control over the network. In the context of our comparison, we mainly consider the properties of permissionless platforms as they represent the baseline configuration.

Unique Features: Blockchain provides a set of features that differentiate it from the other DLTs

- *Number of implementations:* For the time being, one of the main advantages of blockchain over the other technologies is the increasing number of implementations, which suggests that the community has seen the potential it can bring to all application domains. The existing implementations address different issues and target different application domains. However, their main goal is to build a distributed ledger that allows all the participants to share the same truth.

– Smart contracts: They are pieces of executable code residing on the blockchain, which get executed if specific conditions are met. Smart contracts are not processed until their invoking transactions are included in a new block
– *Miners:* In blockchain, mining can been seen as an advantage for miners who can benefit financially from the mining activities.

Miners. In blockchain, mining can been seen as an advantage for miners who can benefit financially from the mining activities.

2.2 Tangle

As the interest in DLT increases, new models are being developed and tested. One of the recent platforms that poses itself as a blockchain alternative especially when it comes to Internet of Things (IoT) is the *Tangle* [12]. Developed by IOTA, Tangle is a decentralized data storage architecture and a consensus protocol, based on a Directed Acyclic Graph (DAG) data structure (Fig. 1(b)). Each node in the DAG (called site) represents a transaction, and the connections (direct edges) between transactions represent the validations of transactions.

One of the original goals of IOTA is to reduce or eliminate the transaction fees. This is especially critical in an IoT environment where M2M microtransactions are the norm. Another important idea that IOTA brought is the removal of the dichotomy between transaction makers and validators, this allows all users who are making transactions contribute to the network by validating other transactions. Additionally, the network does not put any design limit on the transaction rate, since there is no concept of blocks. Every transaction is treated separately (the concept of blocks is considered to be a bottleneck for the blockchain technology).

Figure 1(b) shows what a typical tangle looks like. In a tangle network, in order to add a new transaction, the user needs to choose and validate two existing transactions. Since there are no miners in a Tangle, the same users who make transactions are the ones who validate other transactions. In other words, if Alice wants to transact with Bob, Alice needs to perform a POW computation to validate two previous transactions. IOTA uses Hashcash as the POW algorithm with lower difficulty to allow devices with low computation power to be able to perform the computation. The main reason of using the concept of POW is to eliminate spam transactions [12]. The main advantages of tangle are

Unique Features: Tangle targets unique scalability, security and cost features

– *Scalability:* As the Tangle relies on all the network users to validate the submitted transactions, as the number of users increase it results in faster validation time. Additionally, as the network requires lower computation power to compute the POW, this gives users more incentive to join the network (e.g., smartphones and IoT devices).

- *Quantum-computation:* IOTA relies on the Winternitz One-Time signature scheme to generate the public addresses [5]. This method is believed to be quantum resistant. As quantum computing is becoming reality, using stronger encryption algorithms increases trust in the platform. In IOTA documentation, it is advised to use each generated address only one time, as every time it is used fragments of the private key could be leaked.
- *Transactions fees or Micro-transactions:* As IOTA merges the two roles (transaction makes and miners) into one role, there is no need to transaction fees. The incentive for supporting the network is to be able to submit transactions. This means that the participants of the network use their own computing power to trade assets instead of paying a miner to do that for them (when we say that the miner does it on their behalf, we refer to the fact that a miner adds the transaction to the chain).

2.3 Hashgraph

By many, hashgraph is considered a continuation of where the idea of blockchain begins [4]. As explained by Mance Harmon, Co-founder of Wirdls and Hedera "Hashgraph is an alternative to blockchain - a first generation tech with severe constraints in terms of speed, fairness, cost, and security" [1]. Hashgraph uses a DAG as data structure for storing transactions, and a voting algorithm combined with gossip protocol to quickly reach consensus among nodes (Fig. 1(c)).

The breakthrough of hashgraph is in its consensus protocol. It is mathematically proven to help replicate data in a much faster fashion compared to blockchain. At an abstract level a hashgraph is composed of columns and vertices (Fig. 2. Each column represents a user in the network and vertices are events. The users can basically perform two actions in the hashgraph.

- Submit a transaction: users can submit an event that contains a new transaction (Fig. 2 red vertex)
- Gossip about a transaction: users can randomly choose other users and tell them what they know. For instance, in Fig. 2 the user C has submitted an event, then it gossips to user D about it. This process allows for an exponential diffusion of information about newly submitted transactions.

Each event contains four pieces of information. Hash 1 is the hash of the previous event created by user receiving the gossip and hash 2 is the hash of the previous event of the user sending the gossip. The transaction contains any transactions submitted by the user sending the gossip and a timestamps field is used to keep track of when the event was submitted. We note that even if a user tries to forge the timestamps, the voting algorithm used to find consensus will detect it.

One of the main ideas that hashgraph has brought, is the idea of ordering and fairness, since it allows events to be ordered and they are validated based on their order. This means that if two users are competing to get access to some resources, the one who submitted the transaction first will be considered first (in blockchain the reverse order can happen depending on the transactions selected by the miners).

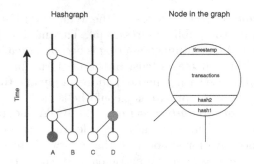

Fig. 2. Hashgraph data structure (Color figure online)

Unique Features: The concept of fairness has been one of the main new concepts that hashgraph brought to the DLTs

- *Fair network:* The timestamped consensus mechanism used guarantees the correct order of handling and recording transactions
- *Virtual voting:* Since every node has a full copy of the hashgraph, no node is required to send their votes across the network, rather they can all calculate the votes of the other nodes. The consensus algorithm takes also in consideration the cases when the network is not fully synchronized (not all nodes have the exact same copy of the hashgraph)
- *Efficiency:* No event becomes stale or get discarded as it is the case of blocks in the blockchain. The efficiency can also be seen in the bandwidth usage since only information about the transactions are transmitted
- *High transaction rate:* Hashgraph is a fast network due to the gossip protocol which reduces the communication overhead. However, till now hashgraph has been tested only in private environments.

2.4 Sidechain

Although blockchain is used as the backend technology, the novelty of sidechain is combining two blockchain architectures to overcome exiting limitations in terms of security, privacy and performance [2]. The architecture uses a central consortium blockchain to manage access requests of all the participants then a set of sidechain (private blockchain) to manage local transactions (Fig. 1(d)). This allows each local chain to seclude its information and share only selected pieces of information.

In a blockchain network transactions require consensus from the network nodes. This could pose a problem for network scalability. Sidechain breaks the network into sub-nets and each sub-net needs to validate only the transactions submitted to it. Each sub-net can be used by a group of partners that share some business interest (e.g., sensor data collectors and data consumers). At the same time, sidechains can be used to hide parts of the data from competitors.

Each sidechain contains a special set of nodes called validators that are also connected with the consortium network. Their role is to validate the local transactions and mitigate access to the logs from the consortium network.

Unique Features: Although sidechain inherits all blockchain features, its main unique feature is increased privacy. The architecture creates private channels with more control over who can access the blockchain data.

3   Extraction of a Conceptual Comparison Framework

To compare the four technologies, we used the SWOT analysis to show the strengths and weaknesses of each one of them [8]. Table 2 shows the results of the analysis. As it can be seen, each technology targets a set of properties to differentiate itself from the others. By looking at their white papers, the three technologies (sidechain, tangle and hashgraph) compare many of their strengths to blockchain. While it is clear that all the technologies target security and transparency they differ in terms of performance and privacy. Improving machine economy and machine to machine communication are among the main opportunities for implementing the discussed technologies, while regulatory barriers could hinder their adoption.

From the SWOT analysis we identified a set of quality criteria to compare the four technologies. Table 1 lists the quality criteria considered.

Table 1. DLT comparison quality criteria

Quality criteria	Description
Data structure	What type of data structure has been used and for what purpose i.e., what information is stored in it
Transactions	How transactions are represented
Consensus	The consensus mechanism used to accept transactions into the network
Fee	What is the cost of submitting transactions
Tps	How many transactions can be handled by the network (transactions per second)
Typology	How has access to the network and do users have different roles
Copyright	What copyright that the platform adopt
Privacy	How does the network deal with privacy
Security	The level of security guaranteed by the network
Validation time	Time needed for transactions validation
Maturity	How mature is the technology

Table 2. SWOT analysis of DLTs

SWOT	Blockchain	Sidechain	Tangle	Hashgraph
Strengths	- Transparency - Many implementations - It is commercially in use	- High privacy - Performance	- No mining needed - No transaction fee - Quantum security	- High number of transactions - Fairness - Scale in the number of transactions
Weaknesses	- Small block size - Low processing speed - Low scalability - Lack of interoperability - Transactions fees	- Permissioned and private	- Managed by single organization	- Gossiping overhead - employs coin toss to terminate consensus - Permissioned network
Opportunities	- Automation - Traceability - M2M interaction - world wild fast transactions	- M2M interaction	- Machine economy	- Innovation In Almost Every Industry Especially payment
Threats	- Regulation might be a problem - legal compliance - Gov. Willingness to adopt	- Interoperability between platforms - still experimental	- More research is needed - still experimental	- Patented technology - More research is needed - Works in a permissioned setting - making sure that each node is connected to at least one honest node is and open issue - Governing Council

4 Comparative Evaluation of Technologies Based on the Framework

Based on the quality criteria identified in the previous section, Table 3 presents the comparison results.

Table 3. DLTs comparison

	Blockchain	Sidechain	Tangle	Hashgraph
Data structure	Linked list	List of linked lists	DAG	DAG
Concensus	PoW: SHA256-Hash	PoW: Ethash	PoW: hashcash	Virtual voting
Transactions	Grouped into blocks	Two chains of blocks	Single transactions	Gossip events contains transactions
Fees	Yes	Yes for the public chain	No fee	No fee
Tps	4 to 7	Limited by consortium chain	500 to 800	>200,000
Validation time	Order of minutes	Order of minutes	Order of seconds	Order of seconds
Privacy	Low	High	Low	Low
Security	High	High	High	High
Maturity	Many implementation	Experimental	Experimental	Experimental
Platforms	Bitcoin, Ethereum	Ethereum and Monax	IOTA	Hedra
Copyright	Open source	Open source	Open source	Patented
Typologies	Public	Public and private	Private	Private

4.1 Data Structure

One of the main differences is the type of data structure used and what data they store. Blockchain relies on a linked list data structure where each element of the list is a block of transactions. Sidechain extends this design by having multiple connected linked lists. One main linked list represents the consortium blockchain and a set of linked lists represented by the private sidechains. On the other hand tangle and hashgraph use a DAG as the underlying data structure. In tangle, each node of the DAG is a transaction while in hashgraph a node represents an event, which can contain multiple transactions within.

4.2 Participants

Comparing the four technologies in terms of the participants in the network we find that:

- Blockchain: has two distinct parties (transaction issuers and miners), transition issuers are users of the blockchain network, while miners are maintainers of the network.
- Sidechain introduces a coordinator node in each of the private chains

- Tangle: in the current implementation a coordinator managed by IOTA is used to validate the submitted transactions. Other users are known entities and can submit transactions in a private setting.
- Hashgraph: Since the network is controlled by Swirlds, all participants are known and can submit transactions in a private setting.

4.3   Consensus

Consensus refers to fact that the whole network reaches agreement on the current state of the network. Blockchain relies on PoW used by miners to generate new blocks. The new blocks are then broadcast to reach consensus. Sidechain uses the same mechanism, however, since it is a permissioned network, the PoW difficulty can be reduced. Hashgraph consensus mechanism is based on gossip about gossip (sending information about gossip) and virtual voting. In tangle, the current implementation relies on a coordinator controlled by the IOTA foundation that issues zero-valued transaction periodically. All the transactions referenced by the coordinator transactions are considered confirmed.

4.4   Discussion

While some consider tangle and hashgraph to be superior technologies compared to blockchain, there are still no real evidence to support these claims. Based on the theoretical analysis, this claim might be true, however, we need to take in consideration the very active research going on by the different blockchain platforms to overcome many of the discussed limitations. We note that in our analysis we have considered the main two blockchain platforms as representatives for blockchain technology (Bitcoin and Ethereum), however, there are other blockchain platforms that can be even comparable in terms of performance to tangle and hashgraph. For instance, hyperledger fabric [6], which is a permissioned blockhain, can reach up to 700 tps, which is at the same level as tangle. Based on our analysis performance is definitely the biggest issue with blockchain technology. To increase security and remove spam transactions, most blockchain platforms adopt some type of Proof of Work, which affects the performance of the network as a whole. When discussing blockchain performance a number of properties need to be considered. For instance, the number of transactions per second (tps), the number of transactions per block (i.e., how many transactions can fit in one block), which is related to the block size. The validation time (i.e., how many blocks need to be added to the blockchain to be sure that the transaction will definitely persist). This problem rises in cases there are forks in the blockchain. Another issue is transaction fees or more precisely micro-transactions which result in having the cost of transactions higher than the value of the transactions themselves (e.g., sending 1 euro and paying 2 euros for the transaction). This is the case because miners need to be paid to maintain the integrity and security of the network. Tangle and hashgraph use different mechanisms to overcome these limitations. For instance, tangle removes the mining process and requires all participants to validates other transactions to be able to submit new transactions. This way transaction fees are removed (this can be argued because transactions validation requires performing some computation, which can be considered as a transaction fee). Hashgraph on the other hand uses the virtual voting to increase efficiency and transactions rate, however, the network that has been tested so far is private and the consensus mechanism is patented, which leaves some open question regarding its adoption by the community. When it comes to Sidechain, we found that it provides some advantages over the public blockchain in terms of performance, however, it presents also some limitations *(i)* the network overhead generated by the sidechain network, which is due to the platform used (Monax), *(ii)* difficult to generalize the approach using other blockchain platforms, and *(iii)* limited to consortium and private settings.

5 Related Work

To overcome the limitations of blockchain many initiatives took place to address specific issues. Some of the solutions focused on improving the current blockchain architecture by introducing alternative implementation of existing mechanisms such the consensus and communication protocols. Other solutions instead target the underlying infrastructure by introducing new models for modeling and managing transactions and their respective consensus protocols. Permissioned blockchains [11] have given more weight to performance and speed while putting more control in the network. In the literature most of the studies compare existing blockchain based DLTs. In [14] a taxonomy for the different blockchain platforms is presented along their advantages and limitations. Security and privacy have received higher interest in comparing the blockchain frameworks. [9] and [15] survey blockchain challenges and opportunities with a focus on security. In [10] a comparison of blockchain platforms in the context of IoT is discussed. The study identifies the main blockchain properties on interest for IoT.

To the best of our knowledge, no studies comparing the DLT by looking at technologies other than blockchain exist so far. To this end, our work can be a starting point to investigate this research field.

6 Conclusions

Distributed ledger technologies have shown a great potential that could revolutionize many industries. Decentralization, security, trust and low cost of operations are among the properties brought by DLTs. In this paper, we have presented a comprehensive overview of four technologies, then we compared them based on a set of quality criteria. As it can be seen from the comparison above, there are some critical shortcomings in each of the presented technologies, however, the research field itself is still in its infancy. Additionally, the rapid development in the blockchain community suggests that many of the open issues mentioned are being investigated. Furthermore, we used SOWT analysis and listed some strengths, weaknesses, opportunities and threats of each of the considered technology. For years blockchain has been used as a synonym for distributed ledger technology, however, now the situation is changing. The new technologies are starting to be used in prototypes to proof their claims, and be to provide more concrete benchmark results.

References

1. Hashgraph is new competitor for blockchain. https://bit.ly/2LAMNdN. Accessed 19 July 2018
2. Ali, M.S., Dolui, K., Antonelli, F.: IoT data privacy via blockchains and IPFS. In: Proceedings of the Seventh International Conference on the Internet of Things, p. 14. ACM (2017)
3. Antonopoulos, A.M.: Mastering Bitcoin: Unlocking Digital Cryptocurrencies. O'Reilly Media, Inc., Sebastopol (2014)
4. Baird, L.: The swirlds hashgraph consensus algorithm: fair, fast, byzantine fault tolerance. Swirlds, Inc., Technical report SWIRLDS-TR-2016 1 (2016)
5. Buchmann, J., Dahmen, E., Ereth, S., Hülsing, A., Rückert, M.: On the security of the Winternitz one-time signature scheme. In: Nitaj, A., Pointcheval, D. (eds.) AFRICACRYPT 2011. LNCS, vol. 6737, pp. 363–378. Springer, Heidelberg (2011). https://doi.org/10.1007/978-3-642-21969-6_23
6. Cachin, C.: Architecture of the hyperledger blockchain fabric. In: Workshop on Distributed Cryptocurrencies and Consensus Ledgers (2016)
7. El Ioini, N., Pahl, C.: Trustworthy orchestration of container based edge computing using permissioned blockchain. In: International Conference on Internet of Things: Systems, Management and Security (2018)
8. Hill, T., Westbrook, R.: SWOT analysis: it's time for a product recall. Long Range Plann. **30**(1), 46–52 (1997)
9. Lin, I.C., Liao, T.C.: A survey of blockchain security issues and challenges. IJ Netw. Secur. **19**(5), 653–659 (2017)
10. Pahl, C., El Ioini, N., Helmer, S.: A decision framework for blockchain platforms for IoT and edge computing. In: International Conference on Internet of Things, Big Data and Security (2018)
11. Pahl, C., El Ioini, N., Helmer, S., Lee, B.: An architecture pattern for trusted orchestration in IoT edge clouds. In: 2018 Third International Conference on Fog and Mobile Edge Computing (FMEC), pp. 63–70. IEEE (2018)
12. Popov, S.: Iota: The tangle. https://iota.org/IOTA_Whitepaper.pdf (2016). Accessed 19 July 2018
13. Walport, M.: Distributed ledger technology: beyond blockchain. UK Government Office for Science (2016)
14. Xu, X., et al.: A taxonomy of blockchain-based systems for architecture design. In: 2017 IEEE International Conference on Software Architecture (ICSA), pp. 243–252. IEEE (2017)
15. Zheng, Z., Xie, S., Dai, H.N., Wang, H.: Blockchain challenges and opportunities: a survey. Work Pap.-2016 (2016)

A Complete Evaluation of the TAM3 Model for Cloud Computing Technology Acceptance

Fotios Nikolopoulos[(⊠)] and Spiridon Likothanassis

University of Patras, University Campus, Rion, 265 04 Patras, Greece
{nikolopoulos,likothan}@ceid.upatras.gr

Abstract. In this work, we examine the technology acceptance of Cloud computing by using the third iteration of the technology acceptance model, from now on referred to as TAM3. TAM is a well established methodology widely used for the acceptance of technology. Empirical data was analyzed from 138 Cloud developers, IT professionals and managers using factor analysis. The results indicate that user acceptance of Cloud computing can be explained and predicted by variables concerning Perceived Usefulness, Perceived Ease of Use, Subjective Norm, Job Relevance, Image, Output quality, Result Demonstrability, Experience, Computer Self-Efficacy, Perception of external control, Cloud Anxiety, Perceived Enjoyment, Voluntariness, Intention to Use. These results further advance the theory and add to the bases for further research targeted at enhancing our knowledge of technology adoption for Cloud computing. They also provide a first base for companies and governments on how to adopt and successfully integrate Cloud technologies and specifically how users adopt Cloud technologies according to organization size, type and employee job role.

Keywords: Cloud computing · Technology adoption · TAM3

1 Introduction

Cloud computing is a technology field that has drawn the interest of every company related to it in the last few years. Companies such as Microsoft, Amazon Google and IBM [1] have invested enormous resources and research efforts into implementing and promoting Cloud technologies. Cloud computing has also garnered the attention of Computer Science researchers [2]. Although many models that predict technology acceptance do exist they do not specifically cater to the intricacies and continued evolution of Cloud Computing. The fact that investing in new technologies or migrating to them presents a substantial risk of failure a need for an accurate technology model that can predict the acceptance of Cloud technologies is necessary. The main question that we have to answer is "which factors determine the acceptance of Cloud computing?" To answer that question we are going to use the factors available by the third iteration of the TAM model and evaluate their ability to determine the acceptance of Cloud computing. Before we delve into the analysis of our main question we have to give a background to the technology of Cloud Computing and present the birth and evolution of the TAM model beginning from its first iteration to the third version.

H. Panetto et al. (Eds.): OTM 2018 Conferences, LNCS 11230, pp. 289–296, 2018.
https://doi.org/10.1007/978-3-030-02671-4_17

1.1   What Is Cloud Computing?

Some people even today question what Cloud computing is and we see that there is no simple answer. The views on the types are differentiated, both in IaaS, PaaS or SaaS and in the deployment difference between Private, Dedicated or Public Cloud. Also there are a few people who would associate it with Utility Computing and Virtualization. According to Mell and Grance [3] "Cloud computing is a model for enabling ubiquitous, convenient, on-demand network access to a shared pool of configurable computing resources (e.g., networks, servers, storage, applications, and services) that can be rapidly provisioned and released with minimal management effort or service provider interaction. This is possible though its inherit features, which are auto-recovery, self-monitoring, self-management, high scalability auto-reconfiguration, and the possibility of forming SLAs". Judging from this we can conclude that Cloud computing is a larger and more diverse technology than utility computing and virtualization. Adding the substantial cost/value benefits that can be achieved though Cloud computing it can safely be acknowledged as a new vibrant era for computing.

1.2   The Technology Acceptance Model 3

Davis [4] developed the Technology Acceptance Model (TAM) as means to determine the factors that influence technology adoption by users. TAM is a widely accepted model for defining user technology acceptance backed by substantial empirical research. The TAM model has included and tested two specific factors: Perceived Usefulness and Perceived Ease of Use. Perceived Usefulness is defined as the potential user's subjective likelihood that the use of a certain system will improve their action and Perceived Ease of Use refers to the effort that the user expects to put in the use of a certain technology. The potential for a user to adopt a technology is also influenced by external variables. TAM explains around 40% [5] of the variance of users behavior in adopting technologies and Google Scholar lists thousands of citations on the original article. TAM2, an extension of the TAM was developed due to the limitations of the TAM in terms of explanatory power. The goal for the TAM2 was to keep the original TAM constructs intact and include additional key determinants of TAM's perceived usefulness and usage intention constructs, and to understand how the effect of these determinants changed with increasing users experience over time with the target system [6]. Because TAM2 only focused on the determinants of TAM's perceived usefulness and usage intention constructs, TAM3 by Venkatesh and Bala [7] added the determinants of TAM's perceived ease of use and usage intention constructs for robustness. Therefore, TAM3 presented a complete nomological network of the determinants that predict user information technology adoption. Following the presentation of the TAM model the research methodology is going to be described, which will include an overview of the survey design, data collection and data analysis. Next the results of the survey are going to be presented which will include a presentation of the survey demographics. Moreover a reliability analysis and the model evaluation of the TAM3 model are going to be presented that show how user are influenced to use Cloud technologies. Finally there is going to be a discussion presenting the limitations of this work, the theoretical and practical implications, conclusion and the available opportunities for future research.

2 Methodology

2.1 Survey Design

The TAM3 model was evaluated by the conduction of a survey. The survey was divided into three sections. In the first section participants were asked to provide demographic and organization data, information about age, gender, educational background, location, job role, years of experience and organization size/type. The second part contained the TAM3 investigation. In order to determine the validity of the TAM3 questionnaire an exploratory factor analysis was conducted. The implementation of the exploratory factor analysis was performed by using the principal component analysis since it is considered a more robust process and less complex conceptually [8]. The size of the sample was 138 participants and it is considered sufficient [9]. The survey was conducted in the English language worldwide as it is the language that is commonly known throughout the world and especially in IT. A seven point Likert scale ranging from "strongly disagree" to "strongly agree" was mainly used. The tool used to analyze the results was SPSS v21.

2.2 Data Collection

The survey was conducted through web link sent by email via the Surveymonkey service acknowledging that no personal information will be divulged without the participants authorization. The survey was open for two months from May 1st, 2017. Another two month extension was given to reach the necessary number of answers. The email was sent to 500 Cloud developers, IT professionals, managers and other staff responsible for IT decisions from companies and government organizations worldwide. The survey was also posted on the linkedin.com social business network via ad web link for the same amount of time and dates. At the end of August we received a total number of 125 replies, amounting to a response rate of $125 \div 500 = 25\%$. This response rate is consistent with rates in similar surveys in information technology research. In addition, we received thirteen questionnaires via the linkedin.com ad, making it a total sample of N = 138.

3 Results

3.1 Sample Profile

In this section the descriptive and inferential statistics are being presented. Table 1 depicts the demographics of the survey.

Table 1. Demographics

		N	%
What is your gender?	Female	30	2.7%
	Male	108	78.3%
Which category below includes your age?	18–25	18	13.0%
	26–35	72	52.2%
	36–45	30	21.7%
	46–55	12	8.7%
	56–65	6	4.3%
What is the highest level of education you have completed?	High school	12	8.7%
	Master's or equivalent	48	34.8%
	PhD	6	4.3%
	University-college	72	52.2%
Geolocation	Africa	18	13.0%
	Asia	48	34.8%
	Australia	6	4.3%
	Europe	18	13.0%
	North America	48	34.8%

Table 2 depicts the job role of each participant along with the type of organization they work in and the its size according to employee number according to the Eurostat enterprise glossary.

Table 2. Job role, organization type and size

		N	%
What is your job role?	Cloud developer	13	9.4%
	IT professional	63	45.7%
	Manager	62	44.9%
Organization type	Education	12	8.7%
	Financial services	34	24.6%
	Health care	12	8.7%
	ICT technologies	26	18.8%
	Manufacturing	36	26.1%
	Media services	6	4.3%
	Public sector	12	8.7%
Organization size	1–9	12	8.6%
	10–49	30	21.7%
	50–249	22	15.9%
	<250	74	53.5%

3.2   Reliability Analysis and Model Evaluation

In this sections the reliability analysis and model evaluation are being presented. The relationship between the dependant variable (intention to use) and the independent variables is going to be analyzed. In Table 3 a multiple linear regression model is been presented with dependent variable "the intention to use" and independent variables "the perception of usefulness", "perceived ease of use", "subjective norm", "job relevance", "image", "output quality", "result demonstrability", "experience", "computer self–efficacy", "perception of external control", "cloud anxiety", "perceived enjoyment", "Voluntariness". The model was statistical significant $F(13, 124) = 20.802$, $p = .000$, $R2 = .686$. The model did not have any multicollinearity issues (all VIF less than 10) or a heteroscedasticity. Also, there was not any autocorrelation problem since Durbin Watson = 1.855. The analysis resulted that perceived usefulness (Beta = 0.205, $p = 0.044$), perceived ease of use (Beta = 0.206, $p = 0.036$), subjective norm (Beta = 0.427, $p = 0.001$), job relevance (Beta = -0.272, $p = 0.023$), image (Beta = -0.565, $p = 0.000$), experience (Beta = 0.378, $p = 0.000$), computer self effi-cacy (Beta = 0.571, $p = 0.000$), perceived enjoyment (Beta = 0.309, $p = 0.007$) and voluntariness (Beta = -0.322, $p = 0.001$) were statistical significant predictors of the intention to use. All predictors had positive effect on intention of use with the exception of the job relevance, image and voluntariness. For one unit improvement either in job relevance or image or voluntariness there was a reduction of -0.272 or -0.565 or -0.322 respectively. In order to find the influence of each factor on the intention to use we use the absolute value of BETA coefficients for the statistical significant factors, perceived usefulness (0.205), perceived ease of use (0.206), subjective norm (0.427), job relevance (0.272), image (0.565), experience (0.378), computer self efficacy (0.571), perceived enjoyment (0.309) and voluntariness (0.322). The sum of these values is $0.205 + 0.206 + 0.427 + 0.272 + 0.565 + 0.378 + 0.571 + 0.309 + 0.322 = 3.255$. Now, each value is been divided by 3.881 and we have 6.29%, 6.32%, 13.11%, 8.35%, 17.35%, 11.61%, 17.54%, 9.49%, and 9.89%. Therefore, the approximately contribu-tion of each factor in the intention to use is the following: perceived usefulness (6%), perceived ease of use (6%), subjective norm (13%), job relevance (8%), image (17%), experience (12%), computer self efficacy (18%), perceived enjoyment (10%) and vol-untariness (10%).

Table 3. Regression analysis for TAM3

Model		Unstandardized coefficients		Standardized coefficients	t	Sig.	Collinearity statistics	
		B	Std. error	Beta			Tolerance	VIF
1	(Constant)	−0.974	0.447		−2.180	0.031		
	Perceived usefulness	0.234	0.115	0.205	2.037	0.044	0.246	4.072
	Perceived ease of use	0.264	0.124	0.206	2.120	0.036	0.265	3.780

(*continued*)

Table 3. (*continued*)

Model	Unstandardized coefficients		Standardized coefficients	t	Sig.	Collinearity statistics	
	B	Std. error	Beta			Tolerance	VIF
Subjective norm	0.488	0.148	0.427	3.296	0.001	0.149	6.714
Job relevance	−0.322	0.140	−0.272	−2.308	0.023	0.180	5.563
Image	−0.572	0.143	−0.565	−4.010	0.000	0.126	7.958
Experience	0.460	0.089	0.378	5.164	0.000	0.467	2.143
Computer self-efficacy	0.780	0.157	0.571	4.966	0.000	0.189	5.300
Perceived enjoyment	0.369	0.134	0.309	2.765	0.007	0.200	4.991
Voluntariness	−0.392	0.115	−0.322	−3.424	0.001	0.283	3.536

a. Dependent variable: Intention to use

4 Discussion

4.1 Limitations

The fact that this is a worldwide survey with participation from all continents presents some limits to the final results. Trying to extrapolate a global view of technology acceptance behavior is challenging. The areas that are keener to respond are the ones with a more advanced technological background like Europe and America. Moreover different regional laws, social influences and economic regulations were not taken into account and would be even more difficult to extract useful results in such an attempt. Regional analysis would have to be restricted in the occasion of a survey that would include any of the factors above.

4.2 Implications

From this research we can extrapolate both theoretical and practical results. Cloud computing is continually gaining momentum in its adoption in all areas of technology use. Companies use cloud technologies for some years now but there still leys a need for an effective implementation that will result to the maximum gains that they can provide. The theoretical contribution is to provide additional insight as to how Cloud technology is adopted by users thought the analysis of one of the most influential technology acceptance models. The practical implications begin with giving additional knowledge, after the analysis done on the UTAUT2 [10] model, to managers and IT professionals as to how to approach and implement Cloud technologies in their workplace. Furthermore it will give them a better understanding to the challenges that the adoption of cloud technologies entail. Moreover this work has given an extensive analysis of Cloud computing usage and the conditions under which the users adopt Cloud technologies. In addition this investigation has provided and analysis as to how user experience influences Cloud technology acceptance. The TAM3 model has been validated as an accurate tool to describe the technology acceptance of Cloud computing although not all factors are significant enough to the intention to use and adjustments have to be made. The use of this model is only the second step after the analysis done on the UTAUT2 model in giving a more comprehensive answer to which factors determine Cloud adoption. The analysis of the UTAUT2 and TAM3 models will help in the creation of a definitive model for Cloud technology adoption.

4.3 Conclusion

These survey results combined with the UTAUT2 survey results have given us useful data as to how to move forward to the creation of a comprehensive technology acceptance model that will be specific to the adoption of Cloud. Our initial research question "Which factors determine the acceptance of Cloud computing?" can be answered as follows: Intention to use Cloud computing is primarily influenced by the factor of Computer Self Efficacy. Computer self-efficacy is the belief in one's ability to successfully perform a technologically sophisticated new task. It would seem that users in the last few years have become more accustomed to cloud technology use and feel confident to use it effectively. The Image factor was the second most influential factor in the TAM3 model. In the age of social media Image has taken a significant role as to how users think the adoption of a technology will reflect on them. Furthermore the factors of perceived usefulness, perceived ease of use, subjective norm, job relevance, experience, perceived enjoyment and voluntariness played a positive role in the Intention to Use Cloud technologies. Output quality, perception of external control, cloud anxiety and result demonstrability had a negative impact on the adoption of Cloud technologies and can be excluded.

4.4 Future Research

This research paper represents the final results of a broad survey for the TAM3 model. This paper is a continuation of the research for a complete technology acceptance model which started with a research paper on the UTAUT2 model [11]. The valuable conclusions and data drawn from the surveys done on the TAM3 and UTAUT2 models in being compiled into a model that will appropriately explain the technology adoption of cloud computing doing away with unnecessary factors used in the above models Further research will include a survey on the new model so as to validate it as a comprehensive technology acceptance model for Cloud Computing and answering the final research question.

References

1. Lohr, S.: Google and I.B.M. Join in 'Cloud Computing' Research. New York Times, October 2007
2. Armbrust, M., et al.: Above the clouds: a Berkeley view of cloud computing. Technical report, UC Berkeley Reliable Adaptive Distributed Systems Laboratory (2009)

3. Mell, P., Grance, T: The NIST definition of cloud computing. Technical report, U.S. Department of Commerce, National Institute of Standards and Technology, September 2011
4. Davis, F.D.: A technology acceptance model for empirically testing new end-user information systems: theory and results. Doctoral dissertation, MIT Sloan School of Management, Cambridge (1986)
5. Legris, P., Ingham, J., Collerette, P.: Why do people use information technology? A critical review of the technology acceptance model. Inf. Manag. **40**, 191–204 (2003). https://doi.org/10.1016/S0378-7206(01)00143-4
6. Venkatesh, V., Davis, F.D.: A theoretical extension of the technology acceptance model: four longitudinal field studies. Manag. Sci. **46**(2), 186–204 (2000). https://doi.org/10.1287/mnsc.46.2.186.11926
7. Venkatesh, V., Bala, H.: Technology acceptance model 3 and a research agenda on intervention's. Decis. Sci. **39**(2), 273–315 (2008)
8. Field, A.: Discovering Statistics Using SPSS, 2nd edn. Sage, London (2005)
9. Comrey, A.L., Lee, H.B.: A First Course in Factor Analysis. Erlbaum, Hillsdale (1992)
10. Venkatesh, V., Thong, J., Xu, X.: Consumer acceptance and use of information technology: extending the unified theory of acceptance and use of technology. MIS Q. **36**(1), 157–178 (2012)
11. Nikolopoulos, F., Likothanassis, S.: Using UTAUT2 for cloud computing technology acceptance modeling. In: Second International Conference on Internet of Things, Data and Cloud Computing, ICC 2017 (2017)

Towards the Blockchain Technology for Ensuring the Integrity of Data Storage and Transmission

Michał Pawlak, Jakub Guziur, and Aneta Poniszewska-Marańda[✉][ID]

Institute of Information Technology, Lodz University of Technology, Łódź, Poland
{michal.pawlak,jakub.guziur}@edu.p.lodz.pl,
aneta.poniszewska-maranda@p.lodz.pl

Abstract. Ensuring the security and integrity of data storage and transmission is a big challenge. One of the methods of its provision is the use of cryptographic techniques, which unfortunately require an additional time associated with the need for data encryption. The paper presents the solutions that ensure the data integrity, using blockchain technology. It describes two cases – an end-to-end verifiable blockchain-based electronic voting system with the ability to follow and verify votes and election results and a lightweight blockchain based protocol for secure data transfer to ensure the integrity of transferred data with a minimal cryptographic overhead.

Keywords: Blockchain technology · Data security · E-voting system
Verification · Data integrity · Data storage and transmission

1 Introduction

The development of the global market and a significant acceleration of information exchange through network increased the importance of data quality. As a result, development of secure network communication systems became priority for many organizations. Such systems are designed to protect data from threats from within and without the systems' environment.

Blockchain technology was introduced in 2008 by a person under a pseudonym Nakamoto [1]. In simple terms, blockchain technology is a distributed system of ledgers stored in a chain-like structure of connected blocks, which content is collectively negotiated and validated in a peer-to-peer network via dedicated algorithm [3,4]. The technology gained a lot of attention in recent years due to its potential to revolutionize many IT fields and new applications are constantly researched [2,5]. Two of such applications are presented in this paper – one in a field of electronic voting (e-voting) and the second in data transfer protocol to ensure the integrity of this data.

The voting systems used today are still not ideal and have many different issues with authentication, privacy, data integrity and transparency [6,8]. However, blockchain technology may be a solution to e-voting problems. Blockchain

© Springer Nature Switzerland AG 2018
H. Panetto et al. (Eds.): OTM 2018 Conferences, LNCS 11230, pp. 297–304, 2018.
https://doi.org/10.1007/978-3-030-02671-4_18

can be used for a creation of platforms allowing for public verification of the data stored inside, which in turn would allow the voters to audit and verify the results without dedicated institutions and officials. Some countries already started researching and implementing e-voting systems based on blockchain technology [10,11].

Transferring data through an open internet network is often a big security risk for users. The data may be intercepted, distorted or modified by malicious users. The most common threats include: loss of confidentiality, violation of data integrity, user impersonation. Blockchain technology consists of a chain-like data structure of blocks connected by hash references and an algorithm that ensures validity and integrity of the blockchain in a peer-to-peer network. It makes to be ideal for application requiring data integrity assurance.

The paper presents the application of blockchain concept in two exemplary cases – it describe an end-to-end verifiable blockchain-based electronic voting system with the ability to follow and verify votes and election results and a lightweight blockchain based protocol for secure data transfer to ensure the integrity of transferred data with a minimal cryptographic overhead.

The paper is organized as follows: Sect. 2 provides the overview of blockchain technology. Section 3 presents the original e-voting systems with related works concerning it while Sect. 4 deals with the lightweight blockchain communication protocol and its generals concept.

2   Blockchain Technology

The blockchain technology refers to a fully distributed system of ordered, immutable and append-only ledgers connected in a chain-like structure. It is composed of two main elements [3,17]: blockchain data structure, blockchain system or network.

Blockchain data structure is an ordered list of connected data units called blocks. Each block is composed of block header and transaction data. The block header contains block metadata, which contains information about block itself, for example, index and creation timestamp. Most important field in the header is hash representation of the previous block. This value is generated from the contents of the previous block and is used to connect block to each other. The transaction data contains a list of transaction and their respective data.

The *blockchain system* is a distributed peer-to-peer network of connected nodes which store and negotiate the information content of the blockchain. Each node validates incoming transactions and, if they are valid, propagates them to other nodes which continue this process until all nodes of the system are aware of the new transactions. In order to provide authentication and authorization, the blockchain systems use asymmetric cryptography. This approach utilizes public and private keys, which can be used to encrypt and decrypt messages. It is important that a messages encrypted with one key can only be decrypted with the other.

Blockchain technology is constantly developed and there exist many different implementations and applications. The best-known is Bitcoin virtual currency, from which the technology originates. It is fully distributed, public and permissionless system using proof-of-work algorithm. Second popular system is Ethereum Platform created by Ethereum Foundation [13]. It is blockchain platform which uses both proof-of-work and smart contracts. It provides a platform for creation of blockchain-based applications. Lastly, Multichain platform allows creation of private blockchain systems utilizing consensus protocol similar to practical-byzantine-fault-tolerance algorithm [12,14].

3   E-Voting System with the Use of Blockchain Technology

Electronic voting, also known as e-voting, is defined as any type of election or referendum that utilizes electronic means facilitating voting procedures (at minimum for casting votes) [7,9,15]. E-voting systems provide many benefits, for example, due to reduction of human factor in tallying process they can increase result's accuracy and minimize potential of frauds. Furthermore, they can improve voting accessibility with multilingual interfaces or with dedicated interfaces for disabled people. Finally, e-voting can reduce time and costs of the voting procedure due to reduction of spoiled ballots and removal of distribution and shipment of ballots.

Similarly to traditional voting systems, electronic voting consists of six phases: (i) voter registration, done personally or by an authority; (ii) authentication, that is confirming voter identity; (iii) authorization, that is allowing identified voters to vote; (iv) vote casting; (v) vote counting; (vi) vote verification, which is checking if the vote was conducted correctly and without frauds. In addition, all electronic voting solutions must have the following properties [6,16]: voter authentication and authorization, voter privacy, correctness, transparency, verifiability, integrity, availability, fairness.

Auditable Blockchain Voting System (ABVS) is a public and permissioned blockchain-based electronic voting system. It is designed as a non-remote and supervised voting system that uses blockchain system to store and verify the voting procedure. It is made of six components (Fig. 1): client applications (polling stations), system of trusted nodes, Vote Identification Tokens, voter-verified paper audit trail (VVPAT), vote error notification module, counting application.

The voting process of the ABVS system is divided into three subsequent stages (Fig. 2): election setup, voting, counting and verification.

Election setup is the first stage of the process. It starts with a selection of trusted public institutions which will act as nodes in the blockchain system of ABVS, by providing computing power and storage capabilities. The next step is to generate unique Vote Identification Tokens (VITs) for voters, which are used for identification and verification of votes in later stages. The VITs are split and assigned to polling stations.

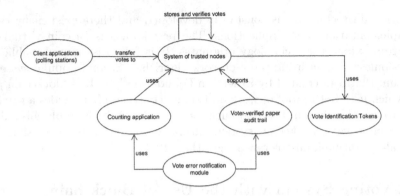

Fig. 1. Model of relations between Auditable Blockchain Voting System components

The *Voting* stage begins right before the actual voting and ends with the closing of the polling stations. The election officials at each of the polling stations launch the ABVS hardware and software. The trusted nodes will only accept votes from the signed and certified equipment and locations. When the actual election begins, voters identify themselves with the election officials. Next, each voter selects a random identification token containing a unique numeric code (VIT). Having completed these steps, voters proceed to voting stations which are equipped with printers and computers connected to the Internet. The voters cast their votes through application interface and confirm their choices using the codes form the VITs. The votes are sent through secured and encrypted communication channel to the trusted nodes where they are verified and processed by the blockchain algorithm. Approved blocks are added to a vote blockchain. At the same time, voters receive VVPATs and depose them into ballot boxes. Each VVPAT is mapped to a corresponding block in the blockchain via VIT present in both of them. The voters leave the polling stations with their VITs. Using the number that is provided on them, the voters can follow their vote and find it in the blockchain.

Counting and verification stage starts after a defined time of the election elapses. The election officials at each polling station deactivate the system and open containers with unused VITs. A list of the remaining tokens is sent to the national electoral central authorities for vote verification. Moreover, the election staff at each node creates a backup of the blockchain stored at their nodes. From that moment, each of the voters can verify not only presence and correctness of their votes (assuming they still possess their VITs) but can also examine the whole chain. This, with the addition of VVPATs, allows vote audition and verification. Using the vote tokens it is possible to compare votes in the blockchain with their corresponding paper trail.

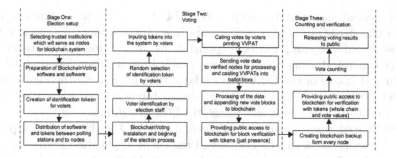

Fig. 2. Schema of Auditable Blockchain Voting System process

4 Integrity Communication Protocol with Blockchain Technology

As mentioned previously, securing data integrity is a major concern of many companies. There exist many solutions that are designed to enforce this property. One of the methods of keeping the data integrity intact is utilization of secure communication protocols. Their main objective is to ensure that the data exchanged over a network is kept confidential but also to keep data completeness and accuracy. Most of such methods are based on Public Key Infrastructure, which adds a significant overhead. It is a result of encryption-decryption process, which must be conducted on the exchanged data. Furthermore, third parties are often necessary for identification and authorization of both involved parties.

The blockchain technology consists of a chain-like data structure of blocks connected by hash references and an algorithm that ensures validity and integrity of the blockchain in a peer-to-peer network. Blockchain data structure is very expensive to modify as a result of two design properties: (i) each block stores a hash reference to the previous block, which is calculated from the content of the block; (ii) blockchain data structure is append-only, which means data can be only added to it but not changed, modified or removed [3]. These characteristics make it ideal for application requiring data integrity assurance.

Light Blockchain Communication Protocol (LBCP) is a data transfer protocol utilizing SHA-3 based seeds and blockchain technology for ensuring the integrity of a data transfer. It is a request-response protocol for data transfer between a client application and a server. A communication process with LBCP is composed of the following subsequent steps:

1. seed generation,
2. client's seed transmission,
3. data partition,
4. blockchain creation,
5. data transfer,
6. blockchain verification,
7. data fragments merging.

Seed generation is the first step of the LBCP communication process. When the data transfer is initiated, the client application generates a unique seed value which is one of the components responsible for data integrity assurance. The seeds are generated using SHA-3 cryptographic hash function based on BLAKE algorithm. It is one of the SHA-3 candidates that made it to the final round of the NIST competition. The algorithm uses 64 bit words, so it's works best on 64-bit platforms. The digest size using in LBCP is 256 bits.

Client's seed transmission is the second step of the data transfer process. Before the actual data can be exchanged the client application sends the generated in the previous step seed value to the server. The transmission is conducted using a standard communication procedure based on asymmetric cryptography. The process of seed transmission in conducted only once, which further reduces the overhead of the whole data transfer process. Data partition is the third step of LBCP communication process. When the client application is provided with data for transfer (e.g. text, image, sound, etc.) the received data is partitioned by the application into equal-sized fragments of a fixed size equal to 64 kB.

Blockchain creation is the fourth step of LBCP communication process and the last before the actual transfer of the data. Data fragments obtained in the previous step are transformed into connected data blocks. Each of the LBCP blocks is made of one of the data fragments and a block header containing a block index, a creation *timestamp*, a hash reference to the data fragment and a hash reference to the previous block header, which is calculated from the content of the whole header (Fig. 3).

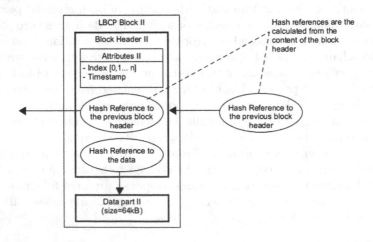

Fig. 3. Model of Light Blockchain Communication Protocol block

The creation of a blockchain starts with formation of a "genesis block" which is a block without hash reference to the previous block (as it is the first in the chain) and indexed with "0". Moreover, its data consist of the client's name. However, the hash reference to the previous block is not removed. Instead, it is replaced with a hash value of the whole blockchain calculated from hash values of all blocks of the blockchain and unique seed of the client application. Finally, the whole blockchain data structure is obtained (Fig. 4). The length of it is equal to the number of data fragments plus genesis block.

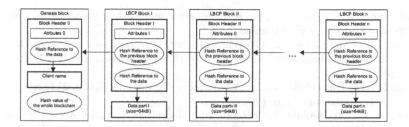

Fig. 4. Model of Light Blockchain Communication Protocol blockchain

Data transfer is the fifth step of the LBCP communication process. It consists of transmitting of the prepared blockchain to the destined recipient application on the server. *Blockchain verification* is the sixth step of the LBCP communication and consists of the server verifying the correctness and integrity of the received blockchain. Firstly, the server checks the format and attributes of the blockchain to ensure it is structurally correct. Secondly, all hash references are recalculated and compared to the originals. Finally, the hash of the whole blockchain is calculated using the seed transmitted in the first step. The obtained value is compared to the one stored in the genesis block. *Data fragments merging* is the last step of the LBCP data transfer process. Assuming the received blockchain is correct the data contained within is extracted and merged to recreate the initial file.

5   Conclusions

Development of the global market and corresponding acceleration of information exchange created a need for reliable methods of securing transferred data. There are many threats that must be taken into account before data can be safely exchanged. One of such threats is violation of data integrity, which is property of data that describes its compactness and accuracy.

Auditable Blockchain Voting System is a non-remote supervised internet voting system, which utilizes blockchain technology. It is intended as an end-to-end verifiable electronic voting system, allowing the common voters to follow their votes and verify the final results. To achieve this, ABVS utilizes voter-verified paper audit trails to provide point of reference for blockchain verification and Vote Identification Tokens allowing the voters to identify their votes without providing any personal information.

Light Blockchain Communication Protocol is a protocol utilizing blockchain technology for conducting relatively lightweight exchanges of data which does not need to be strictly confidential. LBCP can be applied in industrial networks, devices using the Internet of Things, applications based on client-server architecture, such as chats or video conferences.

References

1. Nakamoto, S.: Bitcoin: a peer-to-peer electronic cash system (2008). https://bitcoin.org/bitcoin.pdf. Accessed 2018
2. Zhao, J.L., Fan, S., Yan, J.: Overview of business innovations and research opportunities in blockchain and introduction to the special issue. Financ. Innov. **2**, 28 (2016)
3. Drescher, D.: Blockchain Basics: A Non-technical Introduction in 25 Steps, 1st edn. Apress, Frankfurt am Main (2017)
4. Karame, G., Audroulaki, E.: Bitcoin and Blockchain Security. Artech House Inc., Norwood (2016)
5. Risius, M., Spohrer, K.: A blockchain research framework - what we (don't) know, where we go from here, and how we will get there. Bus. Inf. Syst. Eng. **59**(6), 385–409 (2017)
6. De Faveri, C., Moreira, A., Araújo, J.: Towards security modeling of e-voting systems. In: Proceedings of IEEE 24th International Requirements Engineering Conference Workshops (REW), Beijing, China (2016)
7. Qi, R., Feng, C., Liu, Z., Mrad, N.: Blockchain-powered Internet of Things, E-governance and E-democracy. In: Vinod Kumar, T.M. (ed.) E-Democracy for Smart Cities. ACHS, pp. 509–520. Springer, Singapore (2017). https://doi.org/10.1007/978-981-10-4035-1_17
8. Willemson, J.: Bits or paper: which should get to carry your vote? J. Inf. Secur. Appl. **38**, 124–131 (2018)
9. Braun Binder, N., Driza, A., Krimmer, R., Serdült, U., Vinkel, P.: Focus on E-Voting. ACE Electoral Knowledge Network (2014). http://aceproject.org/ace-en/focus/e-voting/about. Accessed 22 Jan 2018
10. Ojo, A., Adebayo, S.: Blockchain as a next generation government information infrastructure: a review of initiatives in D5 countries. In: Ojo, A., Millard, J. (eds.) Government 3.0 - Next Generation Government Technology Infrastructure and Services. Public Administration and Information Technology, vol. 32, pp. 283–298. Springer, Cham (2017). https://doi.org/10.1007/978-3-319-63743-3_11
11. Enterprise Estonia: Factsheet on Estonian blockchain technology (2012). https://e-estonia.com/wp-content/uploads/facts-a4-v03-blockchain.pdf
12. Zheng, Z., Xie, S., Dai, H., Chen, X., Wang, H.: An overview of blockchain technology: architecture, consensus, and future trends. In: Proceedings of IEEE International Congress on Big Data (BigData Congress), Honolulu, HI, USA (2017)
13. Ethereum Foundation: Ethereum Project. Ethereum Foundation, August 2014. https://www.ethereum.org/. Accessed 20 Apr 2018
14. Coin Sciences: MultiChain. Coin Sciences (2015). https://www.multichain.com/. Accessed 20 Apr 2018
15. Naidu, P.S., Kharat, R., Tekade, R., Mendhe, P., Magade, V.: E-voting system using visual cryptography & secure multi-party computation. In: Proceedings of ICCUBEA, Pune, India (2016)
16. Zhou, Y., Zhou, Y., Chen, S., Wu, S.S.: MVP: an efficient anonymous E-voting protocol. In: Proceedings of GGLOBECOM, USA (2016)
17. Xu, X., et al.: A taxonomy of blockchain-based systems for architecture design. In: Proceedings of IEEE ICSA, Gothenburg, Sweden (2017)

A Taxonomy of Security as a Service

Marwa Elsayed[(✉)] and Mohammad Zulkernine

School of Computing, Queen's University, Kingston, ON K7L 2N8, Canada
{marwa,mzulker}@cs.queensu.ca

Abstract. With the evolving expansion of threat landscape (i.e., internal and external) and the growing shortage of cybersecurity resources (i.e., tools and skills), Security as a Service (SecaaS) is gaining a momentum to fill this pressing gap. In this paper, we propose a taxonomy of existing research work in SecaaS. The taxonomy explores the current state-of-the-art in SecaaS to reason about SecaaS work with respect to three main dimensions: service operation, security solution, and threat. This taxonomy enables the SecaaS consumers and researchers to better differentiate among existing approaches and assess if they meet their security needs.

Keywords: Security as a Service · Cloud computing

1 Introduction

On the heels of the evolving expansion of cybersecurity threat landscape (i.e., internal and external) and the growing shortage of cybersecurity resources (i.e., tools and skills) [1], Security as a Service (SecaaS) rises as a promising model to fill this pressing gap. SecaaS simply revolves around provisioning delivered, maintained, and managed security solutions as services over the cloud through subscription or on-demand basis to protect the security of cloud or on-premise systems [2]. Inheriting the cloud's gains, the SecaaS model promises cost, time, and maintenance effort reduction while providing a high-level of protection.

Despite the growing attention of the research community in the importance of SecaaS, there is a lack of studies providing a taxonomy of existing SecaaS work to draw deep and comprehensive insights of these offerings as well as understand their common characteristics and limitations. Wang and Yongchareon [29] address surveying the SecaaS work from a high-level perspective. The survey mainly maps the SecaaS categories identified by Cloud Security Alliance (CSA) [2] into three main categories: protective, detective, and reactive. However, it is still a crucial defy for SecaaS consumers, who are overwhelmed by the diversity of these offerings, to assess and select the proper solution which fulfill their security requirements.

Towards addressing these limitations, this paper aims to propose a taxonomy of SecaaS research work. The taxonomy allows for understanding the evolution and trends in this research area as well as reasoning about existing work with respect to three main dimensions: service operation, security solution, and threat.

In this sense, the proposed taxonomy reinforces the SecaaS consumers and researchers to gain clear and comprehensive insight about the operation and design of

© Springer Nature Switzerland AG 2018
H. Panetto et al. (Eds.): OTM 2018 Conferences, LNCS 11230, pp. 305–312, 2018.
https://doi.org/10.1007/978-3-030-02671-4_19

each work which include its delivery model, deployment model, and the responsible entities to operate the proposed service. It also helps consumers to perceive the security mechanism and the defense plan employed by each approach to achieve certain security requirements. Last but not least, the taxonomy also identifies the attack surface and methods of the security threats targeted to be mitigated by each work.

The paper is organized as follows: Sect. 2 presents our taxonomy of SecaaS research work and some observations about the trends in this research area. Finally, concluding remarks are outlined in Sect. 3.

2   Taxonomy of SecaaS

This section explains the taxonomy details and the current trends in this research area. Figure 1 portrays our taxonomy that aims to explore and identify each addressed SecaaS work through a three-dimensional perspective: the operational features of the security service, the security solution involved in the service, and the security threat to be mitigated. These three main dimensions seem orthogonal, albeit correlated, to reason about the addressed approaches. As depicted in the figure, each dimension comprises of different aspects which are further classified into finer categories representing the lower-levels of the taxonomy.

2.1   Service Operation

This dimension covers the aspects related to the service operation which include the service delivery model, the deployment model, and the responsible entity as defined below:

The Delivery Model. It identifies the IT resources utilized to deploy and deliver the SecaaS solution in the cloud. A SecaaS solution can be delivered in the form of cloud application (i.e., Software as a Service "SaaS") or as an add-on security service in cloud infrastructure (e.g., Infrastructure as a Service "IaaS", Data Storage as a Service "DaaS", or Communication as a Service "CaaS"), platform (i.e., Platform as a Service), or virtualization (e.g., Virtual Machine Monitor "VMM" a.k.a. hypervisor).

The Deployment Model. It represents the cloud datacenter used to deploy and run the SecaaS solution ranging from public, private, or hybrid which is a combination of the earlier two. A SecaaS solution may support multiple deployment models.

The Responsible Entity. It refers to the main entity responsible to deliver, maintain, and manage the SecaaS solution. This entity can have either a solo or shared responsibility. In case of a solo responsibility, the responsible entity can be one of three actors: the cloud/service provider offering the cloud resources/IT service, the cloud consumer utilizing cloud resources/IT service, or dedicated trusted third party offering the SecaaS solution. IFCaaS [27] is an example where the trusted party is in charge to provide the security service. In case of a shared responsibility, the responsible entity can be any combination of the aforementioned three actors such as SMaaS [28] where the responsibility is held by both the cloud analytic provider as well as the trusted party.

2.2 Security Solution

This dimension includes the aspects related to the employed security solution which are the security mechanism, the defense tactic, and the targeted security requirements.

The Security Mechanism. The SecaaS solutions expand the horizon by employing various security mechanisms that can be categorized according to their core functionalities. In our taxonomy, we utilize the twelve categories of SecaaS recently defined by the Cloud Security Alliance (CSA) [2]. These categories are explained in depth in the CSA study [2]. A SecaaS solution can adopt one of the following mechanisms: Identity and Access Management (IAM); Data Loss Prevention (DLP); Security Information and Event Management (SIEM); Business Continuity and Disaster Recovery (BCDR); encryption; web security; email security; network security; vulnerability scanning; security assessments; intrusion management; and continuous monitoring.

The Defense Tactic. It denotes the defense plan undertaken by the security mechanism employed through the SecaaS solution. This mechanism can be proactive (acting before the threat occurrence), detective (acting during the threat occurrence), or reactive (acting after the threat occurrence). A SecaaS solution can also employ a combination of these tactics.

The Security Requirements. It identifies the security requirements safeguarded by the SecaaS solution which include integrity, confidentiality, availability, privacy, authentication/non-repudiation, and authorization/access control. A SecaaS solution can target protecting a combination of these requirements.

2.3 Threat

This dimension constitutes the aspects related to the security threat as regards the attack surface and method.

Attack Surface. It refers to the combination of weak points in the target system that the SecaaS solution aims to protect ranging from data, application, infrastructure, network, virtualization, to physical layer.

Threat Method. It recognizes the combination of threat methods targeted by the SecaaS solution to mitigate. In our study, we consider the top twelve treacherous threats identified by the CSA [1]. They include, ordered by severity, data breaches, weak identity & access management, insecure interfaces and APIs, system and application vulnerabilities, account hijacking, malicious insiders, advanced persistent threat, data loss, insufficient due diligence, abuse of service/system, denial of service, and shared technology vulnerabilities.

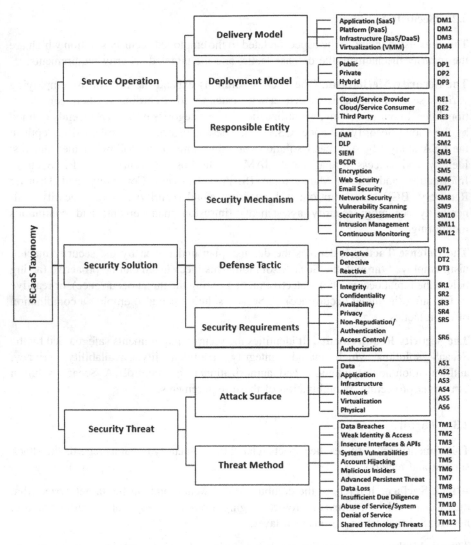

Fig. 1. Taxonomy of security as a service in the cloud. The category acronyms in the rightmost box will be used as the column headings in Table 1 and Fig. 2.

2.4   Some Observed Trends

In this section, we study the trends of the existing research in SECaaS with respect to two aspects: (a) the threat methods they target to mitigate and (b) the security mechanisms they adopt. These aspects are the most important to help security researchers in identifying the gaps in this research area. They are also crucial to differentiate between SecaaS solutions as well as assess if these solutions meet the security needs.

Table 1. Categorization of the existing Secaas work according to our taxonomy.

REF	DM1	DM2	DM3	DM4	DP1	DP2	DP3	RE1	RE2	RE3	SM1	SM2	SM3	SM4	SM5	SM6	SM7	SM8	SM9	SM10	SM11	SM12	DT1	DT2	DT3	SR1	SR2	SR3	SR4	SR5	SR6	AS1	AS2	AS3	AS4	AS5	AS6	TM1	TM2	TM3	TM4	TM5	TM6	TM7	TM8	TM9	TM10	TM11	TM12
[3]	•					•	•		•	•														•			•	•		•	•	•	•						•	•			•	•						
[4]	•			•				•						•										•		•						•						•	•			•							
[5]	•				•				•									•						•			•					•																		•
[6]	•		•	•		•	•											•						•	•						•	•	•							•	•				•	•	•		
[7]	•				•		•	•										•						•			•						•	•															•	
[8]	•				•		•											•						•			•						•	•															•	
[9]	•				•			•									•							•					•										•			•								
[10]		•			•		•	•											•					•				•		•									•											
[11]	•		•												•									•				•		•																			•	
[12]		•	•			•	•									•								•				•		•								•		•									
[13]	•		•							•														•			•			•								•							•	•				
[14]		•			•																		•		•	•		•										•	•				•	•						
[15]		•	•			•													•			•		•			•			•	•																			
[16]	•				•		•	•																•		•	•	•	•																	•				
[17]	•				•											•									•					•			•						•											
[18]		•		•	•	•	•	•	•									•						•			•		•					•																
[19]	•				•																	•			•			•			•														•	•				•
[20]		•	•			•													•					•	•	•					•	•													•	•				•
[21]	•					•			•	•			•												•				•	•	•								•	•										
[22]	•					•				•			•											•		•			•				•	•																
[23]	•					•																		•	•		•			•		•																		
[24]	•				•												•							•	•					•																				
[25]	•				•											•							•			•	•	•																			•			
[26]	•				•		•	•								•											•																							
[27]	•				•														•					•	•					•	•								•		•	•						•	
[28]	•			•		•														•			•	•	•	•				•	•								•			•		•					•

Table 1 presents the categorization of the existing SecaaS research work according to our taxonomy presented earlier in this section. Each existing work in our study is denoted in the "REF" column as regards its reference number in this paper. As mentioned earlier, the other column headings of the table represent the category acronyms listed in the rightmost box of Fig. 1. From the table, we derive the following observations about the evolution and trends of the current research in SecaaS:

The Top-Addressed Threats: They are data breaches, weak identity & access management, advanced persistent threat, malicious insiders, denial-of-service, and shared technology vulnerabilities, as depicted in Fig. 2, part (a). However, more prevalent and sever threats such as insecure interfaces & APIs, system & application vulnerabilities, and account hijacking did not receive the same attention.

The Top-Adopted Security Mechanisms: They are identity and access management (IAM), intrusion management, network security, and security assessment, as illustrated in Fig. 2, part (b). However, the least-adopted mechanisms are security information and event management (SIEM), business continuity and disaster recovery (BCDR), encryption, and email security.

We infer that there is still necessity to call for new SecaaS initiatives investigating other mechanisms and resolving unaddressed security threats.

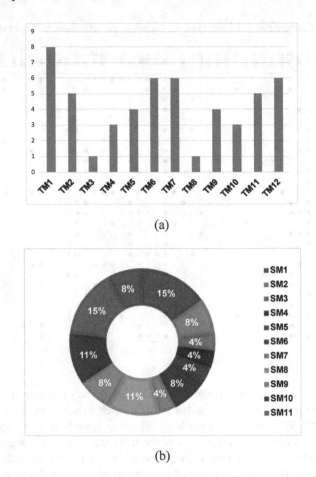

(a)

(b)

Fig. 2. The trends in the existing SecaaS research work with respect to two aspects: (a) the threat methods and (b) the security mechanisms, respectively.

3   Conclusion

The SecaaS model leverages the great advantages of the cloud like low-cost and high-scalability to meet the growing cybersecurity demands. This paper explores SecaaS based on our proposed tri-dimensional taxonomy: service operation, security solution, and threat.

The main contributions of this work can be identified as follows: (i) it discusses the necessity of a comprehensive taxonomy of SecaaS in the cloud; (ii) it proposes a taxonomy of the existing SecaaS work from a tri-dimensional perspective: service operation, security solution, and threat; and (iii) it sheds lights over the trends in the SecaaS research.

Acknowledgment. This research is partially supported by the Natural Sciences & Engineering Research Council of Canada (NSERC). Marwa Elsayed thanks the Schlumberger Foundation for supporting her Ph.D. study in Canada.

References

1. Cloud Security Alliance: The Treacherous 12 - Cloud Computing Top Threats in 2016 (2016)
2. Cloud Security Alliance: Defining Categories of Security as a service (2016)
3. Carvalho, C.A.B., Castro, M.F., Castro, R.M.: Secure cloud storage service for detection of security violations. In: Proceedings of the 17th IEEE/ACM International Symposium on Cluster, Cloud and Grid Computing. IEEE Press (2017)
4. Thomas, K., Grier, C., Ma, J., Paxson, V., Song, D.: Design and evaluation of a real-time URL spam filtering service. In: Proceedings of 2011 IEEE Symposium on Security and Privacy (SP), pp. 447–462. IEEE (2011)
5. Alharkan, T., Martin, P.: IDSaaS: intrusion detection system as a service in public clouds. In: Proceedings of the 12th IEEE/ACM International Symposium on Cluster, Cloud and Grid Computing (CCGRID), pp. 686–687 (2012)
6. Varadharajan, V., Tupakula, U.: Security as a service model for cloud environment. IEEE Trans. Netw. Serv. Manag. **11**(1), 60–75 (2014)
7. Hawed, M., Talhi, C., Boucheneb, H.: Security as a service for public cloud tenants (SaaS). Procedia Comput. Sci. **130**, 1025–1030 (2018)
8. Meng, Y., Li, W., Xiang, Y.: Towards designing privacy-preserving signature-based IDS as a service: a study and practice. In: Proceedings of 5th International Conference on Intelligent Networking and Collaborative Systems (INCoS), pp. 181–188. IEEE (2013)
9. Wu, R., Zhang, X., Ahn, G.J., Sharifi, H., Xie, H.: ACaaS: access control as a service for IaaS cloud. In: Proceedings of 2013 International Conference on Social Computing (SocialCom), pp. 423–428. IEEE (2013)
10. Lang, U.: OpenPMF SCaaS: authorization as a service for cloud & SOA applications. In: Proceedings of IEEE Second International Conference on Cloud Computing Technology and Science (CloudCom), pp. 634–643. IEEE (2010)
11. Guenane, F., Nogueira, M., Serhrouchni, A.: DDoS mitigation cloud-based service. In: Proceedings of 2015 IEEE Trustcom/BigDataSE/ISPA, vol. 1, pp. 1363–1368. IEEE (2015)
12. Pappas, V., Kemerlis, V.P., Zavou, A., Polychronakis, M., Keromytis, A.D.: CloudFence: data flow tracking as a cloud service. In: Stolfo, S.J., Stavrou, A., Wright, C.V. (eds.) RAID 2013. LNCS, vol. 8145, pp. 411–431. Springer, Heidelberg (2013). https://doi.org/10.1007/978-3-642-41284-4_21
13. Wood, T., Cecchet, E., Ramakrishnan, K.K., Shenoy, P.J., van der Merwe, J.E., Venkataramani, A.: Disaster recovery as a cloud service: economic benefits & deployment challenges. In: Proceedings of HotCloud, vol. 10, pp. 8–15 (2010)
14. Ghazi, Y., Masood, R., Rauf, A., Shibli, M. A., Hassan, Q.: DB-SecaaS: a cloud-based protection system for document-oriented NoSQL databases. EURASIP J. Inf. Secur. (1), 16 (2016)
15. Zhou, H., et al.: Agentless and uniform introspection for various security services in IaaS cloud. In: Proceedings of 2017 4th International Conference on Information Science and Control Engineering (ICISCE), pp. 140–144. IEEE (2017)
16. Kaliski Jr, B.S., Pauley, W.: Toward risk assessment as a service in cloud environments. In: Proceedings of HotCloud (2010)

17. Mahalakshmi, J., Kuppusamy, K.: Security-as-a-service for files in cloud computing—a novel application model. In: Proceedings of 2016 10th International Conference on Intelligent Systems and Control (ISCO), pp. 1–5. IEEE (2016)
18. Rak, M., Suri, N., Luna, J., Petcu, D., Casola, V., Villano, U.: Security as a service using an SLA-based approach via SPECS. In: Proceedings of IEEE 5th International Conference on Cloud Computing Technology and Science (CloudCom), vol. 2, pp. 1–6. IEEE (2013)
19. Sun, Y., Nanda, S., Jaeger, T.: Security-as-a-service for microservices-based cloud applications. In: 2015 IEEE 7th International Conference on Cloud Computing Technology and Science (CloudCom), pp. 50–57. IEEE (2015)
20. Tupakula, U., Varadharajan, V., Karmakar, K.: SDN-based dynamic policy specification and enforcement for provisioning SECaaS in cloud. In: Bouguettaya, A., et al. (eds.) WISE 2017. LNCS, vol. 10570, pp. 550–561. Springer, Cham (2017). https://doi.org/10.1007/978-3-319-68786-5_44
21. Zhang, Y., Chen, J.L.: Access control as a service for public cloud storage. In: Proceedings of 32nd International Conference on Distributed Computing Systems Workshops (ICDCSW), pp. 526–536. IEEE (2012)
22. Roundy, K.A., et al.: Smoke detector: cross-product intrusion detection with weak indicators. In: Proceedings of the 33rd Annual Computer Security Applications Conference, pp. 200–211. ACM (2017)
23. Shu, X., Yao, D.: Data leak detection as a service. In: Keromytis, A.D., Di Pietro, R. (eds.) SecureComm 2012. LNICST, vol. 106, pp. 222–240. Springer, Heidelberg (2013). https://doi.org/10.1007/978-3-642-36883-7_14
24. Zawoad, S., Hasan, R., Haque, M.M., Warner, G.: CURLA: cloud-based spam URL analyzer for very large datasets. In: Proceedings of 2014 IEEE 7th International Conference on Cloud Computing (CLOUD), pp. 729–736. IEEE (2014)
25. Gonzales, D., Kaplan, J.M., Saltzman, E., Winkelman, Z., Woods, D.: Cloud-trust—a security assessment model for infrastructure as a service (IaaS) clouds. Proc. IEEE Trans. Cloud Comput. 5(3), 523–536 (2015)
26. Poon, H.T., Miri, A.: Scanning for viruses on encrypted cloud storage. In: Proceedings of 2016 International IEEE Conferences on Ubiquitous Intelligence and Computing, Advanced and Trusted Computing, Scalable Computing and Communications, Cloud and Big Data Computing, Internet of People, and Smart World Congress, pp. 954–959. IEEE (2016)
27. Elsayed, M., Zulkernine, M.: IFCaaS: information flow control as a service for cloud security. In: Proceedings of the 2016 11th International Conference on Availability, Reliability and Security, (ARES), Salzburg, Austria, pp. 211–216. IEEE (2016)
28. Elsayed, M., Zulkernine, M.: Towards security monitoring for cloud analytic applications. In: Proceedings of the 4th IEEE International Conference on Big Data Security on Cloud, BigDataSecurity 2018, Omaha, NE, USA. IEEE (2018). (Best student paper award)
29. Wang, W., Yongchareon, S.: A survey on security as a service. In: Proceedings of International Conference of Web Information Systems Engineering (WISE) (2017)

International Conference on Ontologies, DataBases, and Applications of Semantics (ODBASE) 2018

ODBASE 2018 PC Co-chairs' Message

We are delighted to present the proceedings of the 17th International Conference on Ontologies, DataBases, and Applications of Semantics (ODBASE) which was held in Valletta, Malta 23–24 October 2018. The ODBASE Conference series provides a forum for research and practitioners on the use of ontologies and data semantics in novel applications, and continues to draw a highly diverse body of researchers and practitioners. ODBASE is part of the OnTheMove (OTM 2018) federated event composed of three interrelated yet complementary scientific conferences that together attempt to span a relevant range of the advanced research on, and cutting-edge development and application of, information handling and systems in the wider current context of ubiquitous distributed computing. The other two co-located conferences are CoopIS'18 (Cooperative Information Systems) and C&TC'18 (Cloud and Trusted Computing). Of particular relevance to ODBASE 2018 were topics that bridge traditional boundaries between disciplines such as artificial intelligence and Semantic Web, databases, data analytics and machine learning, social networks, distributed and mobile systems, information retrieval, knowledge discovery, and computational linguistics.

This year, we received 36 paper submissions and had a program committee of dedicated researchers and practitioners from diverse research areas. Special arrangements were made during the review process to ensure that each paper was reviewed by approx. 3–4 members of different research areas. The result of this effort is the selection of high quality papers: nine regular research papers, three experience papers, and seven short papers. Their themes included studies and solutions to a number of modern challenges such as data governance, semantic enrichment, ontology engineering, data transformation, semantic querying and search, rule technologies, linked data, and semantics-based applications to various domains, such as health and tourism.

We would like to thank all the members of the Program Committee for their hard work in selecting the papers and for helping to make this conference a success. We would also like to thank all the researchers who submitted their work. Last but not least, special thanks go to the members of the OTM team for their support and guidance.

We hope that you enjoy ODBASE 2018 and have a wonderful time in Valletta!

September 2018

Dumitru Roman
Elena Simperl
Ahmet Soylu
Marko Grobelnik

Learning Structured Video Descriptions: Automated Video Knowledge Extraction for Video Understanding Tasks

Daniel Vasile[✉] and Thomas Lukasiewicz

Department of Computer Science, University of Oxford, Oxford, UK
danielionut.vasile@gmail.com, thomas.lukasiewicz@cs.ox.ac.uk

Abstract. Vision to language problems, such as video annotation, or visual question answering, stand out from the perceptual video understanding tasks (e.g., classification) through their cognitive nature and their tight connection to the field of natural language processing. While most of the current solutions to vision-to-language problems are inspired from machine translation methods, aiming to directly map visual features to text, several recent results on image and video understanding have proven the importance of specifically and formally representing the semantic content of a visual scene, before reasoning over it and mapping it to natural language. This paper proposes a deep learning solution to the problem of generating structured descriptions for videos, and evaluates it on a dataset of formally annotated videos, which has been automatically generated as part of this work. The recorded results confirm the potential of the solution, indicating that it manages to describe the semantic content in a video scene with a similar accuracy to the one of state-of-the-art natural language captioning models.

Keywords: Structured video captioning · Video understanding

1 Introduction

Video understanding represents one of the central problems in computer vision, and can be described as the task of automatically detecting and naming the objects in a scene, listing their attributes, and describing the relations between them. Several sub-problems are gathered under this generic task, such as *video classification*, *video captioning*, or *visual question answering*, the last two being part of the sub-category of *vision to language* problems. While *video classification* focuses on labelling videos based on their semantic content, *video captioning* aims to capture a video's semantics by generating a summarizing natural language sentence, and *visual question answering* involves reasoning over the semantic content of a video to answer a question formulated in natural language.

Recently, significant progress has been made towards understanding videos, with the current state-of-the-art models being able to classify and caption videos

© Springer Nature Switzerland AG 2018
H. Panetto et al. (Eds.): OTM 2018 Conferences, LNCS 11230, pp. 315–332, 2018.
https://doi.org/10.1007/978-3-030-02671-4_20

with natural language descriptions at close to human-level precision on certain datasets [22]. However, these models are still unable to logically reason about the semantics of a scene. A benchmark study on the current solutions for visual question answering identified that these performed poorly in situations requiring short-term memory (e.g., attribute comparisons), and that they struggled with long reasoning chains (such as count or existence questions) [8].

In a response to this, recent research in computer vision has been advocating for modelling the interactions and relationships between the objects in a scene using a *formalized representation* of these components [9]. This is based on the observation that reasoning using natural language is still a major open problem, while the task of reasoning in a formal setting (e.g., using ontology languages) has been extensively studied and is more approachable.

This paper tackles the general problem of video understanding by proposing three different models for learning structured descriptions that capture the semantic content of a video. These descriptions, formulated as RDF graphs, can be further expanded by leveraging commonsense and topic-specific knowledge available in Linked Data ontologies, and used to perform logical reasoning over the semantics of a video. We evaluate the proposed models on a semantically parsed video captioning dataset, and discuss the improvements that learning structured descriptions could bring to solving various video understanding tasks.

The motivation for our work on automatically describing videos in a structured manner stems from the very promising and impactful possible applications of such a solution. On the one hand, there is the potential of improving the reasoning abilities of the present state-of-the-art visual models, by abstracting away from the natural language currently used to describe video semantics. On the other hand, the wide availability of background information collected in the last decade in comprehensive knowledge bases such as DBpedia [2] and linguistic linked data graphs such as Framester [6], motivates devising general, domain-independent, and scalable video understanding solutions that harvest it. Lastly, the accelerated increase in the amount of video data across the internet, along with the potential of devising methods to structure and organise the information contained in it for later use in retrieval or question answering tasks, represents one more driving factor for this work.

Recent research indicates that explicitly extracting the semantics in a visual scene represents a promising direction to follow when solving vision to language problems. In [21], image captioning is addressed by first describing the image through a set of high-level concepts identified in it, and then using this representation to generate a summarizing sentence, to ultimately outperform the models that attempted to directly map image features to text. Moreover, being able to extract formal representations of the information inside videos would open the way towards mining commonsense and ontological knowledge from video data.

A natural step to take, once one is able to identify the semantic components in a visual scene, is to link them to entries in external knowledge-bases, in order to enrich the semantics extracted. To prove the usefulness of such a step, [19] presents a video captioning solution that detects the most relevant five objects in a scene, queries a knowledge base to obtain the semantic features describing these objects, and then maps this information to a summarizing natural language sentence. Their solution outperforms the more widely adopted video captioning models that only capture the knowledge present in their training datasets, highlighting the value of leveraging external knowledge. Furthermore, links to background information could also significantly impact the video semantics extraction phase, by giving the option of ranking and refining the automatically generated annotations through reasoning.

Finally, it is worth pointing out that devising a solution to comprehensively and formally annotate video content would significantly impact video understanding. From captioning, visual query answering, and action detection to video retrieval and learning from video input through knowledge extraction, all major fields of video understanding can benefit from such a solution.

The main contributions of this paper are summarized as follows:

- We provide a dataset[1] of formally annotated videos. Since at the time of writing, no dataset of videos annotated in a formal language was publicly available, we first automatically devise such a dataset by semantically parsing to RDF graphs the natural language annotations in MSVD [3], a widely used video captioning dataset. The new dataset contains 1,970 video clips annotated by multiple RDF graphs composed of 4.3 triples on average (linked to entities in Framester [6]) and post-processed such that each represents a collection of facts formulated in the same underlying ontology.
- We develop a model based on deep neural networks to formally annotate videos. The main aim of this paper is the development of a machine learning model to produce formal descriptions for videos, structured as RDF graphs. We formulate the problem as multi-label classification, and address it using recent advances in deep neural video processing. We propose three learning models that map videos to structured annotations formulated as RDF graphs. The final test results, obtained by validating the proposed models on the newly devised dataset, indicate that they are able to describe the semantic content in a video scene with a similar accuracy to the one of state-of-the-art natural language captioning models.

To our knowledge, we are the first to provide a dataset of formally annotated videos and to develop a neural model to formally annotate videos.

The rest of this paper is organized as follows. Section 2 gives some preliminaries required to understand and contextualise our approach. Section 3 discusses the method used to devise datasets of formally annotated videos, and Sect. 4 presents the learning models employed to generate structured annotations. Section 5 describes the methodology used for validating and evaluating the proposed solution, and presents the annotation performance results recorded. Lastly, Sect. 6 concludes the paper, ending by setting possible directions for future work.

---

[1] The dataset can be accessed on the authors' web pages.

2 Preliminaries

We now briefly recall the basics of vision-to-language problems, deep-learning vision-to-language approaches, structured visual annotations, evaluating vision-to-language performance, and evaluating structured annotation performance.

2.1 Vision-to-Language Problems

Vision-to-language problems stand at the intersection of video understanding and natural language processing, and have been the main focus of the recent work on automatically processing video content due to their impactful applications.

One of the central vision-to-language problems is *video captioning*, which aims to produce natural language sentences for describing video scenes. This goes beyond detecting the objects in the scene, or classifying it according to a set of labels, since it requires that the relationships between the participating entities are captured by the output description. Recently, there has been significant progress made on *image* captioning, most of the proposed solutions being based on deep-learning algorithms. When compared to image/frame captioning, describing videos poses the supplementary challenge of modelling spatio-temporal dynamics and relations. The task of *visual query answering* adds a reasoning component to video captioning, by requiring that the output sentence generated is the answer to an input query formulated in natural language.

2.2 Deep-Learning Vision-to-Language Approaches

The current state-of-the-art solutions to vision-to-language problems are based on deep neural architectures, taking advantage of recent breakthroughs in image analysis and machine translation. Most approaches in this category fit a common general setup described in Fig. 1, aiming to project the semantics of both the textual query input $\mathbf{Q}$ (in the case of query answering tasks), and the video input $\mathbf{V}$ to a vector encoding $\mathbf{E}$ residing in a common space, to then decode these into a natural language sequence $\mathbf{S}$.

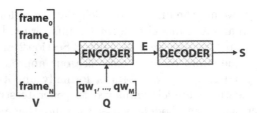

Fig. 1. General setup of a deep-learning vision-to-language model

The core of this type of systems, originally introduced for captioning images in [18], is an encoder-decoder setup inspired from machine translation. The input image is *encoded* using a CNN that is pre-trained on an image classification task; the fixed-length vector of the activations in the last hidden layer of the network is chosen as the image encoding. The *decoding* of this representation is achieved by passing it to an RNN that is trained to generate the captioning sequence of words one by one, at each step seeing the encoded image, as well as remembering the preceding generated words.

The main challenges of adapting such solutions to video annotation are handling variable-sized inputs, and addressing the temporal dynamics specific to sequences of frames. Figure 2 depicts the general structure of a deep-learning video encoder using LSTMs for capturing the frame-to-frame temporal variation. The role of the LSTM network is to provide a *soft location attention* [14] by focusing each encoding e_i onto the relevant parts of **frame**$_i$. The encoding of an optional query input is omitted in the diagram.

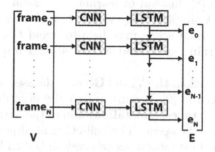

Fig. 2. General setup of a deep-learning video encoder

Due to the nature of video clips being of variable length, the generative RNN language model used for decoding cannot directly input **E**. Instead, the decoder for video captioning is augmented with an attention mechanism, which focuses on only a part of the encoding at each decoding step, producing fixed-length inputs for the language model. Figure 3 describes the approach to video captioning presented in [5].

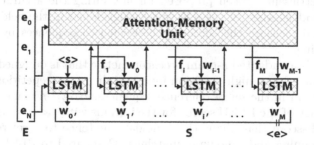

Fig. 3. Attention-memory deep-learning video decoder presented in [5]

The *Attention-Memory Unit* depicted in Fig. 3 and introduced in [5] is an iterative memorized attention between the encoding **E** of an input video and the generated description **S**, which learns where to attend in the video. It remembers encoded versions of the video and of the corresponding generated language (depicted by the **f** vectors in the diagram), allowing the decoding language model to selectively access the relevant information about the entire video and the previously generated words at each decoding step.

2.3 Structured Visual Annotations

As highlighted in the introduction, the current state-of-the-art vision-to-language models struggle to perform even simple logical reasoning, although they manage to achieve relatively high scores on visual question answering tasks. This might indicate that these models learn to exploit language biases in the benchmarking datasets [8], instead of learning to reason using visual and natural language inputs. A simpler, more abstract, and structured representation of the semantics in a visual scene may help to avoid the complexity of natural language when learning such models, and should improve their reasoning abilities.

Based on this observation, the Visual Genome dataset of formal dense image annotations is introduced in [9]. It aims to formally describe the components of each image, providing detailed annotations about the attributes and relations of each of the objects in the scene. The collection of objects in an image, their attributes, and relationships form a *scene graph* linked to WordNet synsets.

The annotations' density comes from the high average number of objects (35), attributes (26), and pairwise relationships between objects (21) per image, which significantly surpass the semantic complexity of the summary-level natural language captions in the standard image captioning datasets. The set of formal image annotations has been collected by employing an Amazon Mechanical Turk pipeline. To our knowledge, no similar dataset of structured *video* annotations was freely available at the time of writing.

2.4 Evaluating Vision-to-Language Performance

A series of metrics have been proposed for measuring the accuracy of vision-to-language models. Most of these have been developed in the field of machine translation, and measure the similarity between two sequences by performing n-gram matching.

BLEU [12] is an adapted n-gram precision metric that is designed to penalize predictions that achieve high precision by containing more repetitions of particular n-grams than in the set of reference sequences. *BLEU-n* is measured as an weighted average of the BLEU scores for the i-grams with $i <= n$. *METEOR* [4] is a unigram F-score that aligns the candidate sentence to a reference one by leveraging stemming and synonym matching. Compared to BLEU, METEOR is evaluated for each reference in a corpus; the scores are aggregated by selecting the highest one.

CIDEr [17] has been specifically proposed for measuring image captioning performance. It is designed to estimate the similarity between a predicted caption and a corpus of reference sentences by the sum of cosine similarities across n-grams, weighted by their term frequency-inverse document frequency (tf-idf) to reflect their *informativeness*.

While the metrics above have been shown to correlate well with human judgement on specific datasets (especially METEOR and CIDEr) [17], it is expected that only focusing on *n-gram overlap* (even when performing stemming and synonymy matching) is not enough to measure the *semantic overlap* between a predicted sequence and a corpus of reference ones.

SPICE [1]is a recent alternative metric focusing on measuring the semantic overlap and has been shown to correlate with human judgements better than BLEU, METEOR, and CIDEr. To measure the SPICE score, both the predicted and the reference captions are first semantically parsed into *scene graphs* using an adaptation of the rule-based Stanford Scene Graph Parser [13].

2.5   Evaluating Structured Annotation Performance

Measuring similarities between graphs of linked entities is usually achieved by comparing their structure and the semantic distance between entities given an underlying ontology. The authors of SPICE propose evaluating it as a specific F-score described below, in which entities are matched at WordNet synset level.

First, let $G(c)$ denote the scene graph obtained by parsing a predicted caption (or question answer) c, and let $G(S)$ be the union of the scene graphs $G(s_i)$ obtained by parsing the reference sequences $s_i \in S$. Next, define $T(G)$ to be the function that returns the union between the set of triples and the set of mentioned subjects and objects in the scene graph G. Finally, define precision P, recall R, and the SPICE F-score as follows:

$$P(c,S) = \frac{|T(G(c)) \otimes T(G(S))|}{|T(G(c))|}, \tag{1}$$

$$R(c,S) = \frac{|T(G(c)) \otimes T(G(S))|}{|T(G(S))|}, \tag{2}$$

$$SPICE(c,S) = \frac{2P(c,S)R(c,S)}{P(c,S) + R(c,S)}, \tag{3}$$

where $\otimes$ performs the intersection of two sets of tuples by matching entities at WordNet synset level.

3   Devising Datasets of Formally Annotated Videos

In the absence of free datasets of formally annotated videos, and considering the significant cost of manually building a new dataset, we present a way of automatically devising collections of formally annotated videos by semantically parsing the natural language annotations in existing video captioning datasets.

3.1   Semantically Parsing Natural Language Annotations

We used the FRED machine reading service [7] to parse natural language annotations into linked knowledge graphs. For each sentence, a call is made to the FRED service, and an RDF response is received. The requests made specify the flag *wsd* in order to indicate FRED to perform word sense disambiguation, and thus to provide alignments to entities in the Framester linked lexical knowledge base [6] whenever possible.

Figure 4 shows three frames extracted from a video in the MSVD dataset, together with the FRED output graph for its captioning sentence.

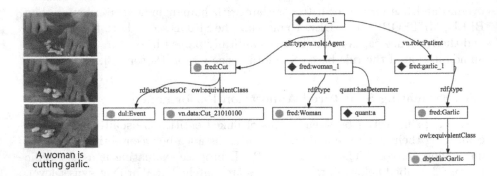

Fig. 4. FRED parsed video annotation example

3.2   Post-processing the Devised Formal Annotations

Each knowledge graph output by FRED contains edges that define relationships between individuals (e.g., (*fred:cut_1, vn.role:Agent, fred:woman_1*)), type predicates (e.g., (*fred:garlic_1, rdf:type, fred:Garlic*)), and ontological rules (e.g., (*fred:Garlic, owl:equivalentClass, dbpedia:Garlic*)). Due to the way the graphs are generated by FRED, a certain amount of redundant information is contained in each of them (e.g., every graph that contains the individual *fred:garlic_1* will also contain the type predicate (*fred:garlic_1, rdf:type, fred:Garlic*)).

In order to simplify the task of learning to map videos to such graphs, we post-process the formal annotations output by FRED. This involves isolating the type predicates and the ontological rules from each RDF annotation, in order to extract an underlying linked ontology for the entire dataset. The extracted facts can be inferred at a later stage by reasoning in the resulting underlying ontology.

Merging Identical Entities and Isolating the Ontological Rules. The main source of redundant background information in the generated graphs is represented by the ontological rules inserted by FRED in order to align the entities identified to entries in Framester. Equivalent concepts linked by the *owl:equivalentClass* predicate, as well as equivalent individuals linked by the *owl:sameAs* relation are merged together. The other ontological rules (e.g., *rdf:subClassOf* rules) are isolated in an external ontology. Figure 5 describes the result of performing this processing step on the annotation graph given in Fig. 4. Notice that at this point, every edge in the graph has at least one individual at one of its ends.

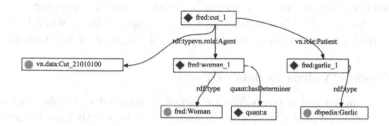

Fig. 5. Example result of isolating the ontological rules

Isolating the Type Predicates. The type specifications for each individual are part of the background ontological knowledge applicable to the entire dataset, and should thus be extracted to reduce the complexity of the annotation graphs. The result of isolating the type predicates on the example graph is given in Fig. 6.

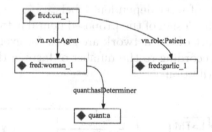

Fig. 6. Example result of isolating the type predicates

Dealing with Type Conflicts. Due to the particular way in which FRED performs Skolemization on the first-order predicate variables that it identifies along its parsing steps [7], it might be the case that the same individual is typed differently in two different formal annotations. An immediate example scenario is the one of using a homonym, such as *"lie"*, to name an individual; the extracted individual *fred:lie_1* could then be typed as a WordNet noun synset, or as an unrelated VerbNet class. Since the convention made earlier is that types are extracted as background knowledge (and are hence not to be handled by the video annotation models), there is a need to solve these conflicts, in order to avoid distorting the semantics of a video when later expanding a compressed annotation. This is achieved by extending the set of individuals in the ontology to distinguish between those with conflicting types.

4   Formal Video Captioning Models

In this section, we present three neural network models for learning structured video descriptions. The first one maps videos to sets of facts, while the second and the third one are based on adapting natural language annotation models.

4.1   Mapping Videos to Sets of Facts

There is a one-to-one correspondence between knowledge graphs and sets of facts, and hence, learning to formally annotate videos with knowledge graphs is equivalent to learning to map videos to such sets of facts, i.e., solving *multi-label classification* for videos, where the possible labels are the facts used in the training annotations.

The first formal annotation model explored by this work attempts to map sequences of frames to sets of facts by using a neural network architecture formed of a CNN-RNN temporal encoder, followed by a multi-label classifier network. Considering the high semantic dependency between the facts in an annotation that would need to be modelled, this solution involves training a single classifier instead of one for each label. The approach is motivated by the results presented in [10], which highlight the superiority of single classifiers when mapping documents to large sets of inter-dependent labels.

Figure 7 describes the design of the proposed neural network model. The layer sizes in the labelling part of the network are given for exemplification purposes and need to be tuned according to the number of facts in the training data, and to their frequency distribution.

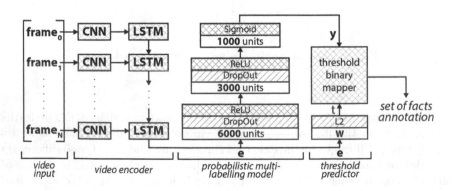

Fig. 7. Video to set-of-facts mapping model

Video Temporal Encoder. For processing the frame level information, the model uses an encoder of the type depicted in Fig. 2, taking the LSTM state at time N as the video encoding (as suggested in [11]). Each frame is initially passed through a pretrained version of the VGG-19 image recognition model [15], and at each time step, the activations in the last hidden layer of the CNN are input by a 2-layer standard LSTM RNN using 1500 units.

Multi-label Classification Network. For solving the multi-label classification problem of mapping the encoded video to a set of facts, the model employs a 2-stage solution originally suggested in [10]. First, it learns a probabilistic model that outputs a distribution $y_i \in [0,1]^L$ over the set of labelling facts (where L is the number of distinct facts used to label training videos). This is achieved by employing a standard feed-forward neural network composed of two hidden layers using ReLU activations, and an output layer made of Sigmoid units. Dropout [16] is employed at the hidden layers for regularisation. Given M training video encodings e_i and ground labellings $\bar{y}_i \in \{0,1\}^L$, the model aims to minimize the cross-entropy loss

$$c \equiv -\sum_{i=1}^{M}(\bar{y}_i \log y_i + (1 - \bar{y}_i) \log(1 - y_i)). \qquad (4)$$

Transforming the obtained probability distribution to a binary vector encoding of a set is done via learning a threshold t_i for each video, sorting the set of labels by the output probabilities y_i, and then mapping the values above t to 1, and the ones below to 0. The thresholds are learned using an L2-regularised linear regression model $t_i = \theta^T e_i$ with loss

$$l \equiv \frac{1}{2M}\sum_{i=1}^{M}(\theta^T e_i - \bar{t}_i)^2 + \frac{\lambda}{2}||\theta||^2. \qquad (5)$$

The ground threshold values $\bar{t}_i$ are obtained by using the generated probability distributions y_i for the training data, and for each data-point i, searching for the value $\bar{t}_i$ that maximises the F score of the generated set when mapping the distribution to a binary vector.

The probabilistic labelling model is trained end-to-end, together with the encoding RNN. The threshold predictor is learned in isolation in a second phase, using the already trained video encoder and probabilistic multi-labeller.

4.2   Adapting a Natural Language Annotation Model

As indicated in Sect. 2.2, there has been significant work done towards solving the problem of video captioning. Naturally, captioning models could be adapted to map videos to sequences of arbitrary entities, and doing so would mean benefiting from the important progresses made towards modelling and incorporating memory and attention into them.

Inspired by [20], which proposes a solution for performing multi-label image classification using RNNs in order to model the semantic dependence between labels, we attempt to encode the annotating knowledge graphs as sequences and then train standard video captioning models over the obtained encodings. The next two models proposed use the same neural network architecture as the one introduced for natural language video captioning in [5] and briefly discussed in Sect. 2.2, up to a set of fine-tuned hyper-parameters. While this approach may seem counter-intuitive at first sight, since sequences are intrinsically ordered, while graphs are not, we explore a few variants for mapping knowledge graphs to ordered representations.

Knowledge Graphs as Sequences of Facts. The first encoding explored follows from the one based on binary vectors for representing subsets of facts used in the multi-label classifier model. The set of L facts mentioned in the training annotations is turned into a vocabulary, and the graphs are then represented as ordered sequences of elements in this vocabulary.

The two orderings between facts that we experiment with are the lexicographic one, and the one of the frequency of a fact inside the corpus of training formal annotations. Comparing the two orderings, there is a very negligible performance between them (this matches the experimental results reported in [20] for multi-label image classification). However, both orderings significantly outperform randomly shuffling the sequences; in the latter case, the captioning model is virtually not trainable.

Knowledge Graphs as Sequences of Entities. Using sequences of facts as encodings has the disadvantage of a very large vocabulary to cover the large set of facts in the training corpus. At the cost of modelling longer sequences, but benefiting from a compressed vocabulary, the second proposal for encoding knowledge graphs is as sequences of separated, explicitly represented triples of entities. An example encoding for the set of facts

$$\{(man, sitsOn, bench), (woman, sitsOn, bench)\}$$

would be "*man sitsOn bench | woman sitsOn bench*". In this variant, a vocabulary is extracted from the set of entities mentioned in the training annotations.

Similarly to the previous encoding, there is a need for inserting order into the sequences. For this encoding, we have chosen to format each triple of entities using the template "*subject predicate object*", and then lexicographically sort the triples of entities in the sequence.

5   Experimental Evaluation

In this section, we experimentally evaluate the three devised neural architectures for learning structured video descriptions. We first describe the evaluation methodology and then provide quantitative and qualitative evaluations. We highlight the potential of the devised models, indicating that they manage to capture the semantic content in a video scene with an accuracy that is similar to the one of a state-of-the-art natural language captioning model.

5.1   Evaluation Methodology

The three formal video annotation models suggested in Sect. 4 are evaluated by employing the same precision, recall, and F-score equations as the ones used by SPICE to measure the similarity between a predicted annotation graph and a corpus of reference ones. Since the graphs in the dataset of formally annotated videos (referred to as *MSVD-f* below) have been post-processed, the semantically equivalent entities have already been merged; thus, when measuring the semantic overlap, the entities in the graphs are aligned using exact matching.

By using the same scoring strategy as SPICE (up to the parsing mechanisms employed), the semantic capturing performance of the models proposed can be comparatively evaluated against the natural language captioning baselines. This is essential, considering the absence in the literature of other structured annotation algorithms and datasets to compare the recorded results against.

The results presented below have been computed by analyzing the predicted annotation graphs directly, before expanding them using the extracted background knowledge, to focus the analysis on the models' performance. The recorded scores have all been scaled to the 0–100 domain in order to allow for cross-comparisons. All the models analyzed below have been trained for 24 hours using a single Tesla P100 16 GB GPU on the JADE Tier-2 high-performance computing facility. In order to obtain test scores that can be compared to the other approaches in the literature on video captioning, we have followed the same training/validation/test split as the one used in [5] for both MSVD and MSVD-f.

5.2   Benchmarking Results

Natural Language Baselines. Before evaluating the formal annotation models, a baseline is set by training and evaluating the video captioning model proposed and open-sourced in [5] on MSVD. The test scores are listed in Table 1 and have been checked to be in line with the ones reported in [5].

It is noticeable that *the SPICE score is an order of magnitude lower than the other reported metrics.* This is due to the reference sets of captions being semantically diverse, which, in combination with the design choice made for SPICE to evaluate the recall by considering the union of all reference scene graphs $(G(S))$, leads to lower scores. *To better contextualise the results, the average SPICE score for picking one of the reference annotations as a prediction on the test fold of MSVD is 12.63.*

As expected, the evaluation results of the structured video annotation models on MSVD-f show a comparably low recall as well (and hence, a low F-score), as described below.

Multi-Label Classifier (MLC). The first formal annotation model evaluated is the multi-label video classifier introduced in Sect. 4.1. The model has been trained after choosing the hyper-parameter L and restricting the training labelling sets to subsets of the most frequent L facts. Iteratively increasing L gave the best

Table 1. Natural language captioning baseline performance

BLEU-1	BLEU-4	METEOR	CIDEr	SPICE
75.43	43.03	30.21	59.85	5.03

validation results for $L = 1000$ in the case of both datasets. Table 2 lists the test scores recorded for this model.

It is noticeable that the precision score is an order of magnitude higher than the recall score. This is expected considering the semantic diversity of the natural language annotations in MSVD, as discussed before.

Table 2. Multi-label classifier F-score

Precision	Recall	F-score
25.6	1.96	3.68

Video to Sequence Models (Vid2Facts and Vid2Ents). Moving on to the video to sequence models introduced in Sect. 4.2, Table 3 presents the test scores for the models trained on annotation graphs encoded as sequences of facts (*Vid2Facts*), and on the ones encoded as sequences of entities (*Vid2Ents*).

For *Vid2Facts*, although BLEU-1 records a 23% facts overlap, and the average precision recorded is 34.95% (the precision formula used awards partial credit for facts that correctly identify the objects in a scene, even when they are wrongly related), the SPICE score is brought down by a low average recall of only 3.10%.

For *Vid2Ents*, the high n-gram overlap scores, together with a relatively high average precision of 41.41% indicate that the model is able to capture a significant part of the combined semantics of the reference annotation graphs. Again, the F-score is brought down by a low corpus-level average recall of 3.36%.

Table 3. Video to sequence-of-facts test performance

Model	BLEU-1	BLEU-4	METEOR	CIDEr	Pre.	Rec.	F-score
Vid2Facts	23.00	12.10	9.40	20.80	34.98	3.10	5.58
Vid2Ents	65.60	35.40	29.50	80.80	41.41	3.36	6.11

Summary of the Recorded Results. The results presented above indicate that the formal annotation models proposed manage to partially capture video semantic content in a structured manner. It has also been shown that their performance, measured by the proposed F-score, is in line with the SPICE performance of a state-of-the-art natural language baseline model.

Comparing the three proposed methods, it is apparent that the adapted natural language models (Vid2Facts and Vid2Ents) outperform MLC on both datasets. Table 4 gives one insight into why this might be the case, showing that the MLC model outputs smaller graphs, further affecting its recall scores. This suggests that the threshold predictor used for mapping probability distributions to sets could be a potential bottleneck, and future attempts to improve performance could focus on better modelling it.

Table 4. Average annotation graph sizes

Ground	MLC	Vid2Ents	Vid2Facts
3.61	2.60	3.27	3.68

5.3   Qualitative Analysis

To complete the evaluation of the models proposed by this report, Fig. 8 presents four test scenarios extracted from the MSVD dataset, each containing a selection of three reference natural language annotations, together with the predictions made by the baseline natural language model, and by the three formal annotation models discussed (in the form of knowledge graphs); each prediction has attached its SPICE/F score.

The given examples reveal the discussed semantic diversity of the reference annotations in MSVD, with the recorded F scores being biased towards the larger annotations that overlap more with the union of the reference graphs (e.g., the annotation that describes both a man cooking, and the fact that chicken is being cooked, receives a higher score than the one that describes the more specific action of a man putting seasoning in a plastic container).

The last example highlights the impact on performance of the machine reader used to semantically parse datasets: the term *rodent* is consistently incorrectly parsed by FRED as a "*VeryShortRodeoRide animal*" in the training dataset.

Finally, the selection of examples in Fig. 8 highlights the similar ability of the four annotation models to capture the semantic content of the reference corpora. Both the natural language and the formal annotation models usually output well-structured captions that are semantically close to the references.

6   Summary and Outlook

This paper was focused on developing a solution for automated video knowledge extraction in the form of linked graphs. In the absence of existing public formal video annotation datasets at the time of writing, we first introduced MSVD-f, a formal video annotation dataset obtained by semantically parsing and post-processing a natural language video captioning corpus. The main presented contribution was then designing three formal video captioning models

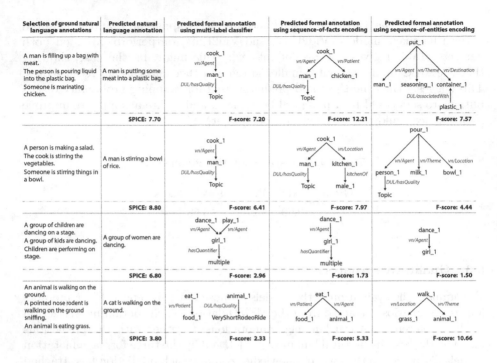

Fig. 8. Qualitative analysis

and evaluating them on the devised dataset. The best performing two of them were shown to be able to describe the semantic content of the test videos with a similar degree of accuracy to the one of state-of-the-art natural language captioning models. To our knowledge, no formal video captioning solution had been publicly presented and evaluated at the time of writing. Some interesting directions for future research are summarized below.

The semantic parsing mechanism used to devise MSVD-f has been chosen to provide alignments to linked background knowledge bases, to enable reasoning on top of the predicted annotation graphs, once these are generated. However, the models proposed by this report do not input these alignments. A promising direction towards improving the video knowledge extraction performance would be to leverage the background information in the annotation prediction phase. Reasoning over partially generated graphs or over a set of candidate graphs, while employing commonsense knowledge may increase the annotation performance by iteratively expanding the set of observed facts at each prediction step, and by early detecting and isolating potential semantic anomalies.

The performance metrics for the proposed models (see Sect. 5.2) are interpreted assuming that the reference formal annotations in the two automatically devised datasets are correct. While making such an assumption is reasonable when comparing the designed models against each other, assessing their real-world performance requires that the accuracy of the reference annotations used for training is factored in. Future work on video knowledge extraction could consider exploring more accurate semantic parsers, and ultimately employing human judgement, in order to improve the evaluation accuracy and the relevance of the obtained models.

The devised dataset is composed of small, summarizing annotation graphs (4.3 triples on average) that fail to capture the complete semantics of most video scenes. A proof in this sense is the high semantic diversity of the reference annotation corpora in MSVD; as reference annotations, they are all valid, but describe disjoint semantics by focusing on different aspects in a video scene. One would expect video knowledge extraction models to generate *dense* structured descriptions that fully capture the semantics of video scenes, similarly to how the dense structured annotations in the Visual Genome dataset [9] capture *image/frame* semantics. An immediate step towards training such models would be to automatically generate datasets of dense formal video annotations by joining the reference captions of each video into single annotation graphs.

Acknowledgements. This work was supported by The Alan Turing Institute under the UK EPSRC grant EP/N510129/1, and by the EPSRC grants EP/R013667/1, EP/L012138/1, and EP/M025268/1.

We are grateful to the authors of [5] for open-sourcing and documenting a very powerful video captioning model. We thank the STLAB team for making the FRED machine reader [7] publicly available, and acknowledge the use of the Microsoft Video Description (MSVD) dataset [3]. Finally, we thank Oana Tifrea-Marciuska, Patrick Hohenecker, and Ruomei Yan for insightful discussions on semantic parsing, encoding knowledge graphs, and deep neural video captioning.

All the computation required for carrying out this work has been performed using the JADE Tier-2 high-performance computing facility.

References

1. Anderson, P., Fernando, B., Johnson, M., Gould, S.: SPICE: semantic propositional image caption evaluation. In: Leibe, B., Matas, J., Sebe, N., Welling, M. (eds.) ECCV 2016. LNCS, vol. 9909, pp. 382–398. Springer, Cham (2016). https://doi.org/10.1007/978-3-319-46454-1_24

2. Auer, S., Bizer, C., Kobilarov, G., Lehmann, J., Cyganiak, R., Ives, Z.: DBpedia: a nucleus for a web of open data. In: Aberer, K., et al. (eds.) ASWC/ISWC -2007. LNCS, vol. 4825, pp. 722–735. Springer, Heidelberg (2007). https://doi.org/10.1007/978-3-540-76298-0_52

3. Chen, D.L., Dolan, W.B.: Collecting highly parallel data for paraphrase evaluation. In: Proceedings of ACL, vol. 1, pp. 190–200 (2011)

4. Denkowski, M., Lavie, A.: Meteor universal: language specific translation evaluation for any target language. In: Proceedings of WMT, pp. 376–380 (2014)

5. Fakoor, R., Mohamed, A.R., Mitchell, M., Kang, S.B., Kohli, P.: Memory-augmented attention modelling for videos. arXiv:1611.02261 (2016)

6. Gangemi, A., Alam, M., Asprino, L., Presutti, V., Recupero, D.R.: Framester: a wide coverage linguistic linked data hub. In: Blomqvist, E., Ciancarini, P., Poggi, F., Vitali, F. (eds.) EKAW 2016. LNCS (LNAI), vol. 10024, pp. 239–254. Springer, Cham (2016). https://doi.org/10.1007/978-3-319-49004-5_16

7. Gangemi, A., Presutti, V., Reforgiato Recupero, D., Nuzzolese, A.G., Draicchio, F., Mongiovì, M.: Semantic web machine reading with FRED. Semant. Web **8**(6), 873–893 (2017)
8. Johnson, J., Hariharan, B., van der Maaten, L., Fei-Fei, L., Zitnick, C.L., Girshick, R.: CLEVR: a diagnostic dataset for compositional language and elementary visual reasoning. In: Proceedings of IEEE CVPR, pp. 1988–1997 (2017)
9. Krishna, R., et al.: Visual Genome: Connecting language and vision using crowd-sourced dense image annotations. arXiv:1602.07332 (2016)
10. Nam, J., Kim, J., Loza Mencía, E., Gurevych, I., Fürnkranz, J.: Large-scale multi-label text classification — revisiting neural networks. In: Calders, T., Esposito, F., Hüllermeier, E., Meo, R. (eds.) ECML PKDD 2014. LNCS (LNAI), vol. 8725, pp. 437–452. Springer, Heidelberg (2014). https://doi.org/10.1007/978-3-662-44851-9_28
11. Ng, J.Y.H., Hausknecht, M., Vijayanarasimhan, S., Vinyals, O., Monga, R., Toderici, G.: Beyond short snippets: deep networks for video classification. In: Proceedings of IEEE CVPR, pp. 4694–4702 (2015)
12. Papineni, K., Roukos, S., Ward, T., Zhu, W.J.: BLEU: a method for automatic evaluation of machine translation. In: Proceedings of ACL, pp. 311–318 (2002)
13. Schuster, S., Krishna, R., Chang, A., Fei-Fei, L., Manning, C.D.: Generating semantically precise scene graphs from textual descriptions for improved image retrieval. In: Proceedings of VL, pp. 70–80 (2015)
14. Sharma, S., Kiros, R., Salakhutdinov, R.: Action recognition using visual attention. arXiv:1511.04119 (2015)
15. Simonyan, K., Zisserman, A.: Very deep convolutional networks for large-scale image recognition. arXiv:1409.1556 (2014)
16. Srivastava, N., Hinton, G., Krizhevsky, A., Sutskever, I., Salakhutdinov, R.: Dropout: a simple way to prevent neural networks from overfitting. JMLR **15**(1), 1929–1958 (2014)
17. Vedantam, R., Lawrence Zitnick, C., Parikh, D.: CIDEr: Consensus-based image description evaluation. In: Proceedings of IEEE CVPR, pp. 4566–4575 (2015)
18. Vinyals, O., Toshev, A., Bengio, S., Erhan, D.: Show and tell: a neural image caption generator. In: Proceedings of IEE CVPR, pp. 3156–3164 (2015)
19. Wang, D., Song, D.: Video captioning with semantic information from the knowledge base. In: Proceedings of IEEE ICBK, pp. 224–229 (2017)
20. Wang, J., Yang, Y., Mao, J., Huang, Z., Huang, C., Xu, W.: CNN-RNN: a unified framework for multi-label image classification. In: Proceedings of IEEE CVPR, pp. 2285–2294 (2016)
21. Wu, Q., Shen, C., Liu, L., Dick, A., van den Hengel, A.: What value do explicit high level concepts have in vision to language problems? In: Proceedings of IEEE CVPR, pp. 203–212 (2016)
22. Wu, Z., Yao, T., Fu, Y., Jiang, Y.G.: Deep learning for video classification and captioning. arXiv:1609.06782 (2016)

Generating Executable Mappings from RDF Data Cube Data Structure Definitions

Christophe Debruyne(✉) ⓘ, Dave Lewis ⓘ, and Declan O'Sullivan ⓘ

ADAPT Centre, Trinity College Dublin, Dublin 2, Ireland
{christophe.debruyne,dave.lewis,
declan.osullivan}@adaptcentre.ie

Abstract. Data processing is increasingly the subject of various internal and external regulations, such as GDPR which has recently come into effect. Instead of assuming that such processes avail of data sources (such as files and relational databases), we approach the problem in a more abstract manner and view these processes as taking datasets as input. These datasets are then created by pulling data from various data sources. Taking a W3C Recommendation for prescribing the structure of and for describing datasets, we investigate an extension of that vocabulary for the generation of executable R2RML mappings. This results in a top-down approach where one prescribes the dataset to be used by a data process and where to find the data, and where that prescription is subsequently used to retrieve the data for the creation of the dataset "just in time". We argue that this approach to the generation of an R2RML mapping from a dataset description is the first step towards policy-aware mappings, where the generation takes into account regulations to generate mappings that are compliant. In this paper, we describe how one can obtain an R2RML mapping from a data structure definition in a declarative manner using SPARQL CONSTRUCT queries, and demonstrate it using a running example. Some of the more technical aspects are also described.

Keywords: Data cube · R2RML · Data transformation

1 Introduction

The Resource Description Format [18] (RDF) provides us a flexible data model for semantic interoperability and data integration, especially in scenarios where data from various heterogeneous sources need to be processed for a particular purpose. Organizations have become increasingly sensitive to data processing policies, both organizational and especially those put forward by legislation (such as GDPR). Scholars rightfully argue that compliance should be treated in the early phases of information systems design [4]. In cases where data needs to be integrated or when a particular data processing activity was not yet foreseen, one is faced with additional challenges, such as:

- Are we allowed to process the data in a particular way?
- Are we allowed to use all the data?
- Have people given their consent for their data to be processed?

© Springer Nature Switzerland AG 2018
H. Panetto et al. (Eds.): OTM 2018 Conferences, LNCS 11230, pp. 333–350, 2018.
https://doi.org/10.1007/978-3-030-02671-4_21

The data that is needed are often stored in different files or databases, which means they have to be retrieved and integrated. The integration of heterogenous resources can be facilitated with the Resource Description Framework (RDF), a W3C Recommendation. Mapping languages such as R2RML [6] have been used to map relational (or tabular) data to RDF datasets. R2RML can thus be used to retrieve and integrate data for the creation of a dataset for a particular data processing activity. The use of RDF allows our work to be integrated with post-hoc analysis methods reported in [16].

While the vocabularies, representations, or even formats for these datasets may be bespoke, we will adopt a standardized RDF vocabulary for representing datasets and their structure. The RDF Data Cube Vocabulary [19] is an ontology[1] for describing multi-dimensional datasets on the Semantic Web where the structure of a *dataset* can be prescribed via so-called *Data Structure Definitions* (DSDs) where *observations* are identified by their *dimensions*, capture one or more observed values via *measures*, and observed values can be annotated with *attributes*. Linked Data principles allow all these entities to be linked with other Linked Data datasets, providing one with the means to interpret or correctly process the data. Such datasets are thus curated with particular (types of) data processing in mind.

Using RDF Data Cube and R2RML[2], the steps to create a dataset would look as follows:

1. Declare a data structure definition for an application;
2. Declare a dataset which will contain the observations from a database;
3. Create a mapping from a relational database (table or query) to that dataset;
4. Execute the mapping for creating the dataset; and
5. Validate the resulting dataset.

While databases are typically used by various applications within an organizational context, particular processes often need only a subset of the data (often retrieved with a query). Similarly, the data contained in a dataset will only contain those fit for a particular purpose; e.g., the number of sales per product and week. If (parts) of the data were to be subject of a particular policy, one needs to be cautious. Since datasets are curated for a particular purpose, and those datasets may be subject to policies, it makes sense to attach such policy information to the dataset or DSDs (rather than the mapping). Mappings are only concerned with retrieving and transforming the information. The problem, however, is that one tends to create a mapping manually.

---

[1] While RDF provides us the data model, data is usually integrated using a common model captured in a so-called ontology. Ontologies – being commonly defined as "a [formal] explicit specification of a [shared] conceptualization" [10] – are also developed for a particular purpose, but the ontologies (or vocabularies) we observe on the Linked Data Web are often lightweight and meant for information exchange. Applications that consume such Linked Data are not (necessarily) known beforehand and are often published with very accessible licenses such as Creative Commons.

[2] Even if we were not to use RDF Data Cube and R2RML, similar steps would be necessary for capturing the schema or structure of the dataset, and the creation and execution of a mapping to populate that schema.

The research question we aim to answer in this paper is: "Can we generate an R2RML mapping from a data structure definition?" An algorithm generating such a mapping could subsequently be extended to take into account policies so as to generate mapping that is compliant. In other words, the algorithm for generating R2RML mappings would then be "policy-aware".

The remainder of this paper is organized as follows: Sect. 2 presents some related work on generating datasets from relational data; Sect. 3 presents our approach using a running example and describes our declarative approach using SPARQL CON-STRUCT queries to generate an R2RML mapping from a DSD; Sect. 4 elaborates on some of the more technical aspects of our approach; Sect. 5 discusses some aspects of our approach; Sect. 6 then discusses the rationale of annotating DSDs with policy information and to extend our approach for generating customized mappings (which is part of our future work); and finally, in Sect. 6, we conclude our paper.

2 Related Work

To the best of our knowledge, related work in generating (R2RML) mappings from other representations is quite limited. The authors in [23] – who proposed a declarative language for ontology-based data access where a single description results in an ontology, mappings and rules for transforming queries – mentioned adopting R2RML because of its increasing uptake.

TabLinker, mentioned in [14], transforms Excel documents into Data Cube datasets by mapping the markup of cells in a Microsoft Excel's XML file to elements to a Data Cube dataset (and structure). In other words, users have to manually format the Excel file and that formatting is then used to generate the RDF dataset. OLAP2DataCube and CSV2DataCube are two tools proposed in [22] for extracting statistical data and the creation of data cube datasets. When using OLAP2DataCube, queries are mapped onto datasets, dimensions, and measures.

The Open Cube Toolkit [12] provides a D2RQ [3] extension for generating an RDF graph – according to the RDF Data Cube Vocabulary – using D2RQ's R2RML support. The D2RQ data provider requires a mapping relating a table to a dataset using a bespoke XML mapping language. The XML file – of which an example is shown in **Listing 1** – is then used to generate an R2RML mapping which is then executed by D2RQ's engine. Their approach is thus similar in that it generates an executable R2RML file from the mapping. The limitations of their approach are brought forward by their mapping language; it is bespoke, not in RDF and has not been declared in a particular namespace.

```
1   <?xml version="1.0" encoding="UTF-8"?>
2   <mapping>
3      <dataset>
4         <table-name>OBSERVATIONS</table-name>
5         <label>people age in Ireland</label>
6         <uri>people-in-ireland</uri>
7         <pattern>{"ID"}</pattern>
8      </dataset>
9      <dimensions>
10        <dimension>
11           <column>D1</column>
12           <label>Age group</label>
13           <uri>age-group</uri>
14           <property>age-group</property>
15        </dimension>
16     </dimensions>
17     <measures>
18        <measure>
19           <column>MEASURE</column>
20           <label>Have a personal computer</label>
21           <uri>have-a-personal-computer</uri>
22           <property>have-a-computer</property>
23           <datatype>xsd:int</datatype>
24        </measure>
25     </measures>
26  </mapping>
```

Listing 1. Example of the Open Cube Toolkit's mapping declaring where the various elements of a dataset can be found in a relational database table, which came out of the toolkit's box.

Wigham et al. highlighted some of the problems with the RDF Data Cube Vocabulary and proposed their own model for capturing (relational) datasets [25]. Capturing multiple observation values, for instance, is not straightforward, and they thus propose vocabulary for relational data where "cells" can be added to record tables and where records can be nested. The authors also presented a Microsoft Excel plugin for generating RDF graphs using their Record Table schema in [20]. Similar to TabLinker, the mapping from the spreadsheet to the RDF is a built-in plugin.

In [1], the author presented a tool that generated diagrams based on TURTLE. The tool is aimed to facilitate modelling by guaranteeing consistency between statements and visualization; "what you see is what you mean". In [1], the author furthermore criticizes the complexity and verbosity of R2RML, and presented an extension of the tool. By embedding SQL queries and fieldnames in the examples (in TURTLE), the tool is able to generate a complete and executable R2RML mapping.

3   R2DQB – Approach Demonstration

In this section we present R2DQB, pronounced R-2-D-cube, which is a contraction of **R2**RML and **D**ata **QB** (short for "cube").

The approach we adopt is to avail of RDF's data model to annotate data structure definitions (DSDs) (and dimensions, measures, and attributes) in such a way that DSDs are reusable, and R2RML mappings can be generated that will create a dataset "populating" the DSD. The different steps in our approach are depicted in Fig. 1 and will be described in this section. The generated Data Cube Datasets should refer to its DSD with a `qb:structure` statement (from `qb:DataSet` to `qb:DataStruc-tureDefintion`), which basically informs agents that this dataset is structured according to that DSD. To exemplify our approach, we will first introduce our running example.

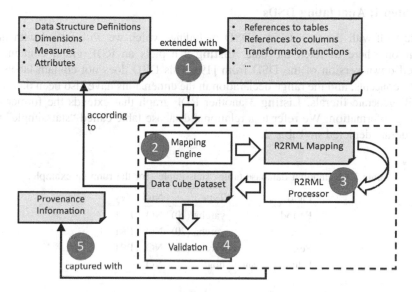

Fig. 1. The various steps in generating and executing an R2RML mapping from a DSD for the creation of a data cube dataset.

3.1 Running Example

We have chosen to adopt the example from the RDF Data Cube Vocabulary's specification [19], shown in Table 1. In this table, we have examples of life expectancy (in number of years) broken down by region, age and time. There are thus three dimensions (region, time period, and gender) and one measure (life expectancy). One can also model attributes of the measure, e.g. the unit is to be interpreted as a number of years.

Table 1. Excerpt from the statswales report number 003311 which describes life expectancy broken down by region, age and time (from [19])

	2004–2006		2005–2007		2006–2008	
	Male	Female	Male	Female	Male	Female
Newport	76.7	80.7	77.1	80.9	77.0	81.5
Cardiff	78.7	83.3	78.6	83.7	78.7	83.4
Monmouthshire	76.6	81.3	76.5	81.5	76.6	81.7
Merthyr tydfil	75.5	79.1	75.5	79.4	74.9	79.6

The example (re)uses resources (URIs) for the dimension. Albeit possible in our approach, we will first describe the steps using the values (i.e., literals) for each of the dimension. We note that according to [19], dimensions may either be a resource or a literal. We will demonstrate the use of URIs, as well as other technicalities of our approach, in a subsequent section.

3.2   Step 1: Annotating DSDs

We start off with the (re)use of a DSD including, which we will extend with information on where to fetch the data. **Listing 2** depicts an RDF graph containing a stripped-down version of the DSD from [19]. This DSD does not contain labels and links to concepts, and the range declaration in the dimensions have also been omitted as we will generate literals. **Listing 3** another RDF graph that extends the former with mapping information. We refer to a relational database table called "statssimple" with the structure depicted in Table 2.

Table 2. Relational database table "statssimple" for the running example.

Field	Type	Null	Key
Period	varchar(20)	NO	PRI
Area	varchar(20)	NO	PRI
Sex	varchar(20)	NO	PRI
Life expectancy	float	NO	

```
1   @base <http://www.example.org/>
2   <#refPeriod> a rdf:Property, qb:DimensionProperty;
3   rdfs:subPropertyOf sdmx-dimension:refPeriod .
4
5   <#refArea> a rdf:Property, qb:DimensionProperty;
6   rdfs:subPropertyOf sdmx-dimension:refArea .
7
8   <#lifeExpectancy> a rdf:Property, qb:MeasureProperty;
9   rdfs:subPropertyOf sdmx-measure:obsValue;
10  rdfs:range xsd:decimal .
11
12  sdmx-dimension:sex a rdf:Property, qb:DimensionProperty .
13
14  <#dsd-le> a qb:DataStructureDefinition;
15  # The dimensions
16  qb:component [ qb:dimension <#refArea> ];
17  qb:component [ qb:dimension <#refPeriod> ];
18  qb:component [ qb:dimension sdmx-dimension:sex ];
19  # The measure(s)
20  qb:component [ qb:measure <#lifeExpectancy> ] .
```

Listing 2. And RDF graph describing a DSD.

```
1    @base <http://www.example.org/>
2    <#refPeriod> rr:column "period";
3    <#refArea> rr:column "area";
4    <#lifeExpectancy> rr:column "lifeexpectancy";
5    sdmx-dimension:sex rr:column "sex" .
6    <#dsd-le> rr:tableName "statssimple";
```

Listing 3. Extending the DSD of **Listing 2** with mapping information.

For this study, and to prove the feasibility of our approach, we have chosen to reuse R2RML predicates. R2RML provides us with the necessary predicates to annotate DSDs and their components with instruction on where to find the information in a relational database. As a consequence, the graph in **Listing 3** does not constitute a valid R2RML document. A more generic approach will be considered as future work.

3.3 Step 2: The Generation of an R2RML Mapping

We have chosen to adopt a declarative approach to generating the R2RML mapping via a sequence of SPARQL CONSTRUCT queries. The various queries can be summarized as follows: (1) Create the triples maps (for mapping tables, views or queries to RDF); (2) Use the dimensions to create subject maps; and (3) Create predicate object maps for the measures, and dimensions.

We obtain an executable R2RML mapping by merging the models of each SPARQL CONSTRUCT query. This model is not meant to be merged with the prior RDF graphs from **Listing 2** and **Listing 3**, as it is meant to generate RDF that will be a dataset, which can be regarded as an instance of the DSD captured in **Listing 2**. In a wider governance narrative, the resulting mapping may be stored to inform stakeholders of the provenance of the datasets.

We now begin with the description of each query. We have omitted prefixes and base declarations from the queries for brevity.

The generation of a logical table for each DSD related to a table is shown in **Listing 4**. Note that views are also referred to with `rr:tableName`. A similar CONSTRUCT query is used for DSD's related to a query with the `rr:query` predicate. The namespace pam refers to our vocabulary developed for this study. In this listing, we create a link between triples maps and their DSDs. This will come in handy to attach the different components of the R2RML mapping (described later on). The resulting triples map is a blank node. The query can be changed to assign it an IRI, either with the IRI function or as a parameter provided by a user.

```
1    CONSTRUCT {
2      [] rr:logicalTable [ rr:tableName ?t ] ;
3         pam:correspondsWith ?x .
4    } WHERE {
5      ?x a qb:DataStructureDefinition ;
6         rr:tableName ?t .
7    }
```

Listing 4. Generating an R2RML triples map for each data structure definition

The CONSTRUCT query for generating the subject map is shown in **Listing 5**. Dimensions are used to identify each observation. We use that information to generate the subject map of a triples map. The columns used by the dimensions are used for creating a template that will identify each observation in the dataset. An R2RML processor will use the template, which will generate values, to keep information of each observation in an appropriate data structure (e.g., a dictionary). Next to a subject map, this mapping also creates a predicate object map that will relate individual observations to a particular dataset.

```
1    CONSTRUCT {
2      ?tm rr:subjectMap [
3        rr:class qb:Observation ;
4        rr:termType rr:BlankNode ;
5        rr:template ?x ;
6      ] .
7      ?tm rr:predicateObjectMap [
8        rr:predicate qb:dataSet ;
9        rr:object ?ds;
10     ] .
11   } WHERE {
12     ?tm pam:correspondsWith ?dsd ;
13       rr:logicalTable [ rr:tableName ?t ] ;
14     BIND(IRI(?t) AS ?ds)
15     {
16     SELECT
17       (CONCAT("{", GROUP_CONCAT(?c; SEPARATOR="}-{"), "}") as ?x) {
18       ?dsd qb:component ?component .
19       { ?component qb:dimension [ rr:column ?c ] }
20       UNION
21       { ?component qb:dimension [
22                       rrf:functionCall [
23                          rrf:parameterBindings ( [ rr:column ?c ] )
24                       ]
25                    ] }
26     } GROUP BY ?dsd
27     }
28   }
```

Listing 5. Generating an R2RML triples map for each data structure definition

Notice that we cover two cases in **Listing 5**; dimensions based on column values, and dimensions based on function calls. Function calls are used to relate column values to literals or URIs – simulating an association. We will later describe why the use of such functions is desirable.

Listing 6 provides the CONSTRUCT queries for adding object predicate maps to the triples maps based on measures. The CONSTRUCT query for a similar mapping based on dimensions is similar; one of the main differences is the predicate (highlighted in yellow). If a dimension or a measure has been declared a range, we will add that range declaration to the R2RML mapping only if that range is declared in the XSD namespace. The predicates used for dimensions and measures may both be used for literals and resources. The `rr:datatype` predicate of R2RML is only used for data types (literals). If we were to remove the filter, we could end up with predicate object maps that generate resources *and* are provided a datatype. The R2RML specification states that this is erroneous.

A current limitation is that we can only deal with XSD datatypes. Mappings using datatypes outside of XSD, such as `geo:wktLiteral` for polygons for geospatial data in GeoSPARQL [15], cannot yet be generated. A naïve approach would be to keep track of an exhaustive list of datatypes in the query, but more elegant approaches will be investigated as part of our future work.

```
1   CONSTRUCT {
2     ?tm rr:predicateObjectMap [
3       rr:predicate ?measure ;
4       rr:objectMap [
5         ?p ?c ; rr:termType ?type ; rr:datatype ?range ;
6       ] ;
7     ]
8   } WHERE {
9     ?tm pam:correspondsWith ?dsd .
10    ?dsd qb:component ?component .
11    ?component qb:measure ?measure .
12    ?measure ?p ?c .
13    ?measure rr:column|rr:template|rr:constant|rrf:functionCall ?c .
14    OPTIONAL { ?measure rr:termType ?type }
15    OPTIONAL {
16      ?measure rdfs:range ?range .
17      FILTER(
18        CONTAINS(STR(?range), "http://www.w3.org/2001/XMLSchema#")
19      )
20    }
21  }
```

Listing 6. Generating predicate object maps from measures

Finally, the generated dataset also needs to be connected to its DSD. This is straightforward with the following CONSTRUCT query (in **Listing 7**). The IRI of the dataset is based on the table's name (or query). Some relational databases allow spaces (or other special characters) to be used in table names. The function `ENCODE_-FOR_URI` ensures that characters in table names (such as spaces in some databases) are correctly encoded.[3]

---

[3] We thank the anonymous reviewer for spotting this issue.

```
1   CONSTRUCT {
2     ?ds a qb:DataSet ; qb:structure ?x .
3   } WHERE {
4     ?x a qb:DataStructureDefinition ;
5        rr:tableName ?t .
6     BIND(IRI(ENCODE_FOR_URI(?t)) AS ?ds)
7   }
```

Listing 7. Creating an instance of a dataset based on an annotated DSD

With these mappings – which are declarative and implemented as SPARQL CONSTRUCT queries – we are able to generate an executable R2RML mapping. Given our table "statssimple" (see Table 2) and the snippets from **Listing 2**, the R2RML in **Listing 8** is generated. While it is not explicit that the resource is a `rr:TriplesMap`, it will be inferred by the R2RML engine as such due to the domain of `rr:logicalTable` being `rr:TriplesMap`.

```
1   [ pam:correspondsWith    <http://www.example.org/#dsd-le> ;
2     rr:logicalTable        [ rr:tableName  "statssimple" ] ;
3     rr:predicateObjectMap  [
4       rr:objectMap  [ rr:column  "area" ] ;
5       rr:predicate  <http://www.example.org/#refArea>
6     ] ;
7     rr:predicateObjectMap  [
8       rr:objectMap  [ rr:column  "period" ] ;
9       rr:predicate  <http://www.example.org/#refPeriod>
10    ] ;
11    rr:predicateObjectMap  [
12      rr:objectMap  [ rr:column  "sex" ] ;
13      rr:predicate  sdmx-dimension:sex
14    ] ;
15    rr:predicateObjectMap  [
16      rr:objectMap  [
17        rr:column    "lifeexpectancy" ;
18        rr:datatype  xsd:decimal
19      ] ;
20      rr:predicate  <http://www.example.org/#lifeExpectancy>
21    ] ;
22    rr:predicateObjectMap  [
23      rr:object      <statssimple> ;
24      rr:predicate  qb:dataSet
25    ] ;
26    rr:subjectMap  [
27      rr:class      qb:Observation ;
28      rr:template   "{area}-{period}-{sex}" ;
29      rr:termType   rr:BlankNode
30    ]
31  ] .
```

Listing 8. Generated R2RML

3.4   Step 3: Execution of the R2RML Mapping

For the execution of our mapping, we rely on an implementation of the R2RML implementation developed by the ADAPT Centre.[4] This implementation complies with the
R2RML implementation as it is used to demonstrate minimal extensions of the mapping
language (such as functions written in JavaScript [7]). The mapping in **Listing 8** contains
no statements that fall outside R2RML's scope and should work with other implementation of the specification. This mapping execution generated 144 triples; 6 triples for each
of the 24 observations. An example of such an observation is shown in **Listing 9**.

```
1    [ a                                      qb:Observation ;
2    qb:dataSet                               <statssimple> ;
3    sdmx-dimension:sex                       "Male" ;
4    <http://www.example.org/#lifeExpectancy> 78.6 ;
5    <http://www.example.org/#refArea>        "Cardiff" ;
6    <http://www.example.org/#refPeriod>      "2005-2007"        ] .
```

Listing 9. An observation generated with the R2RML mapping of **Listing 8**

In the case of an XSD datatype, our R2RML processor checks whether a value that
is generated by an object map corresponds with that datatype and reports when this is
not the case. When a datatype is not part of the XSD namespace is used for an object
map, such as `ex:myInteger` for instance, the literal is merely typed with that
datatype. If no datatype is provided, the datatype of the literal depends on the datatype
of the column (see Sect. 10.2 "10.2 Natural Mapping of SQL Values" of [6]).

3.5   Step 4: Validating the Generated RDF

We validate the generated RDF by checking the integrity constraints put forward by the
RDF Data Cube Vocabulary, presented as a set of so-called integrity constraints in the
specification [19]. This is necessary as the execution of the R2RML mapping does not
guarantee a well-formed cube. R2RML prescribes, for instance, that a triple is not
added to the model if any of the columns used for a predicate, object or subject contains
a NULL value. If a cell for a dimension were to have a NULL value, then no triple is
generated, but an observation must be related to all dimensions.

3.6   Step 5: Provenance Information

We note that Step 5 is not really a step per se, but that the process captures provenance
information during all aforementioned steps. Provenance information provides insights
on a resource's origin, such as who created that resource, when it was modified or how
it was created [26]. PROV-O [21], which we have adopted for this study, is a W3C
Recommendation for representing and exchanging provenance information as RDF.
PROV-O's core concepts and relations (shown in Fig. 2) provide a good starting point
for describing the activities and intermediate artifacts that lead to the realization of an
ontology mapping.

---

[4] https://github.com/chrdebru/r2rml.

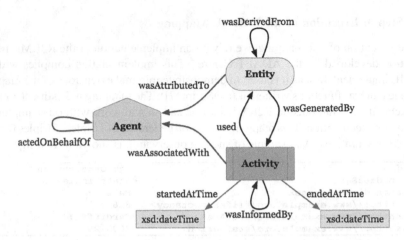

Fig. 2. Core concepts and relations in PROV-O from [21], Copyright © 2011–2013 W3C® (MIT, ERCIM, Keio, Beihang).

Rather than providing a snippet of the generated RDF, we will describe how we extended PROV-O and how the entities are used an interrelated. The classes we have declared in our namespace and which PROV-O concepts they specialize are shown in Table 3. Our proof-of-concept relies on R2RML-F, which will be an instance of `pam: R2RML_Processor`. Our `pam:Mapping_Generator` is our implementation of D2RQB. We also developed an instance of `pam:Validator`, which currently implements the integrity constraints prescribed by [19].

Table 3. Classes that extend PROV-O

Classes extending `prov:Entity`	
`PAM:DSD_DOCUMENT`	Used to represent RDF documents/graphs containing our annotated data structure definitions
`pam:R2RML_Mapping`	Used to represent the generated R2RML mappings
`pam:Dataset`	Used to represent the generated Data Cube datasets
`pam: Validation_Report`	Used to represent the validation reports
Classes extending `prov:Activity`	
`pam: Generate_Mapping`	Represents the activity of generating an R2RML mapping from an annotated DSD
`pam: Execute_Mapping`	Represents the activity of executing the R2RML mapping
`pam: Validate_Dataset`	Represents the activity of validating a mapping
Classes extending `prov:(Software)Agent`	
`pam: Mapping_Generator`	Represents the software agent that generates an R2RML mapping as per approach
`pam: R2RML_Processor`	Represents the software agent executing the mapping
`pam:Validator`	Represents the software agent validating the dataset

Figure 2 clearly depicts how the main entities of PROV-O are interrelated. The relations between our entities are as follows:

- A pam:Generate_Mapping uses (prov:uses) a pam:DSD_Document to generate a pam:R2RML_Mapping. A mapping is thus generated by (prov: wasGeneratedBy) such an activity. This activity was performed (prov: wasAssociatedWith) by our implementation of our approach (pam:Mapping_Generator). The mapping is also derived from the pam:DSD_Document, so we also assert a prov:wasDerivedFrom between the two entities.
- A pam:Execute_Mapping uses (prov:uses) a pam:R2RML_Mapping to generate a pam:Dataset. That dataset was thus generated by (prov: wasGeneratedBy) that activity. This activity was performed by (prov: wasAssociatedWith) by the pam:R2RML_Processor we adopted.
- A pam:Validator uses (prov:uses) both a generated dataset (pam:Dataset) and DSD document (pam:DSD_Document) for validating the dataset and producing a report (pam:Validation_Report). It relies on an implementation (prov:wasAssociatedWith a pam:Validator) of at least the integrity constraints prescribed by [19].

We also store timestamps (start and end-time) of each activity. The adoption of PROV-O in this study allows us to create traceable data flows where a DSD can be used to generate an executable R2RML document multiple times. This helps us fulfill some of the requirements put forward by policies.

4 Extended Demonstration

In the previous section we demonstrated our approach using a running example. In this section, we demonstrate more advanced aspects of our approach starting from the same example.

4.1 Mapping Values onto URIs

A common mapping problem is relating column values to a corresponding set of "values" (IRIs or literals); for instance "blauw" corresponds with dbpedia:Blue, "rood" with dbpedia:Red. R2RML provides no support for capturing such correspondences as part of the mapping. One can create a mapping from an SQL query in which an SQL CASE function is used to relate column values to, for instance, IRIs, but these then become quite cumbersome to maintain. The D2R mapping language [2] provided a convenient way to relate these correspondences via a so-called "translation table". In our approach, we adopted a minimal extension of R2RML called R2RML-F with support [7] for functions. R2RML-F allows us to create a function that takes as input a column-value and returns the corresponding value. We then still are able to benefit from keeping the table or query to be mapped as simple as possible and — if need be — only change the function to deal with changes in the ontology or source data. We provide more detail on how these functions look like in the next subsection.

4.2   Inclusion of Data Transformation Functions

The example of [19] proposes to use the data.gov.uk reference time service to represent the time period. The following URI represents a 3-year period starting from the 1st of January, 2004: http://reference.data.gov.uk/id/gregorian-interval/2004-01-01T00:00:00/P3Y We can use this knowledge to extract the start year from our period and fill in a template to generate such an IRI in our DSD, as shown in **Listing 10**. One can easily see how correspondences described in Sect. 4.1 can then be implemented using conditions.

```
<#refPeriod> a rdf:Property, qb:DimensionProperty;
  rrf:functionCall [
    rrf:function _:b0 ;
    rrf:parameterBindings ( [ rr:column "period" ] ) ;
  ]                                                          ;
  rr:termType rr:IRI ;
  rdfs:label "reference period"@en;
  rdfs:subPropertyOf sdmx-dimension:refPeriod;
  rdfs:range interval:Interval;
  qb:concept sdmx-concept:refPeriod
.
_:b0
  rrf:functionName "translateperiod" ;
  rrf:functionBody """
    function translateperiod(var1) {
      return "http://reference.data.gov.uk/id/gregorian-interval/" +
             var1.substring(0, 4) + "-01-01T00:00:00/P3Y"
    }
  """                                                        ;
.
```

Listing 10. Using functions in a DSD to transform data

The example in **Listing 10** only relies on string manipulation. While seemingly simple, the example serves to demonstrate a particular aspect of our approach. [17] argued why and when support for functions in mappings are desirable; e.g., when the underlying (database) technology provides no support for data transformation.

4.3   Interlinking Datasets

Both dimensions and measures may refer to either literals or resources. The use of resources (typically identified by a URI) are common for dimensions, but less so for measures. One measures values that you want to manipulate, compare, etc. In our approach, this is feasible by creating predicate object maps that generate resources (with a URI). By changing

```
<#refArea> rr:column "area";
sdmx-dimension:sex rr:column "sex";
```
   in **Listing 2** into
```
<#refArea> rr:template "http://example.org/area/{area}";
sdmx-dimension:sex rr:template "http://dbpedia.org/resource/{sex}";
```

we create resources for areas and gender. The first generates "local" resources as http://example.org/ is the namespace of our running example. The second generates DBpedia [13] URIs. If the second is used, not only does one create links across datasets, but also with other Linked Data datasets as well.

5 Discussion

While our approach adopted R2RML for the mapping, adoption of other R2RML dialects such as RML [8] and xR2RML [11] is feasible. These implementations provide native support for other formats such as CSV and JSON. The R2RML processor we have adopted allows us to approach non-relational data as such by either treating tabular data files as relational tables (without keys) or by formulating SQL queries for NoSQL databases by means of Apache Drill[5]. As long as the DSD is annotated with the names of tables, views and fields that appear in the database, an executable R2RML mapping can be produced. Verifying whether those annotations are correct (e.g., does the table exist) falls outside the scope of this paper. Similarly, verifying whether the resulting dataset complies with the DSD or the ontologies used by the DSD are up to the Data Cube validator and external tools respectively. The R2RML processor may be in charge of verifying whether values comply with datatypes, but the Recommendation does not require this functionality.

W3C has published Recommendations for representing the "schemas" of tabular data the Web [17] and how to generate RDF from those [24]. The goals of these initiatives were to standardize access to information in tabular form, to propose a schema language for tabular data, and to specify the conversion of such data into RDF (amongst others) as part of that initiative. Their goal was thus not to represent datasets in RDF. The advantage of [17] is that its schema language does provide straightforward value constraints and the investigation of this vocabulary and converters as an alternative might be worthwhile investigating.

This study focuses on the generation of an R2RML file for creating RDF Data Cube Datasets. We note that the RDF Data Cube Vocabulary allows one to publish multi-dimensional data *in general*. While the vocabulary's underlying model is indeed an ISO standard for representing statistical data and its metadata, the vocabulary is generic enough to represent even simple "relational" data and datasets fit for training Machine Learning models. As it is capable of representing a wide variety of datasets and is – unlike other vocabularies – standardized, we deemed it the most suitable for our study.

---

[5] https://drill.apache.org/.

6 Towards a Policy-Aware Mapping Engine

Now that we have demonstrated the feasibility of annotating a data structure definition such that an executable R2RML mapping can be generated, we can elaborate on our vision towards a policy-aware mapping engine.

We stated that datasets are created for a particular purpose. Those purposes are not necessarily known beforehand and have to be created. Regulations – both internal as well as external (such as GDPR) – may require that the data contained in datasets and data processing complies with these regulations. In the case of GDPR, for instance, users have to be informed how their data is used, and they also have to give their consent.

The next step in our research is thus to tackle the problem of generating datasets which ensure that compliance. Given a knowledge base containing formalized descriptions of regulations, informed consent, etc., how can we adapt our mapping engine (number 2 in Fig. 1) as to generate executable mappings that generate compliant datasets? In [9], the authors propose a semantic model for expressing consent leveraging existing semantic models of provenance, processes, permission and obligations. We may be able to use this as a basis for formalizing data processing purposes and the data used in that processing. Knowing the importance of regulatory compliance, such an approach renders compliance checking a flexible, adaptable top-down approach to data processing.

7 Conclusions and Future Work

The increasing pressure for organizations to be compliant with various regulations and policies provided the motivation for this study. As organizations need to demonstrate that their data processing activities (which evolve over time) are compliant (e.g., GDPR), they can benefit from semi-automated processes that facilitate compliance processes. In this study, we argued that data processing activities rely on datasets. A data process will rarely need all the data stored in one or more data sources. W3C put forward a Recommendation for describing the structure and capturing multi-dimensional datasets, called the RDF Data Cube vocabulary. This allows one to declare how a data set should look like for a particular data processing activity. In this study, we aimed to answer the following research question: "How can we generate an R2RML mapping from a data structure definition?" in order to create the datasets.

We have proposed a declarative approach to generating an R2RML mapping from a Data Set Structure definition by (1) annotating the DSD with some predicates based on R2RML, and (2) executing a sequence of SPARQL CONSTRUCT query that generates the R2RML mapping. The demonstration in our study shows that our approach is viable, and even highlighted some of the limitation of R2RML (data transformation functions and syntactic sugar for correspondences). Our approach is furthermore built on top of PROV-O, a provenance ontology, as to ensure the traceability of data processing activities. While this study limits itself to the generation of provenance information of our prototype, PROV-O can be immediately used to relate our generated datasets with data processing activities. This is for instance demonstrated in [16], where PROV-O is used to validate the informed consent for data processing activities.

The next step in our research is thus to tackle the problem of generating datasets which ensure that compliance. While studies like [17] investigate the use of PROV-O to check compliance "post-hoc" basis or based on a questionnaire, we will investigate a "policy-aware" mapping generator.

Acknowledgements. The ADAPT Centre for Digital Content Technology is funded under the SFI Research Centres Programme (Grant 13/RC/2106) and is co-funded under the European Regional Development Fund.

References

1. Alexiev, V.: RDF by example: rdfpuml for true RDF diagrams, rdf2rml for R2RML generation. In: Semantic Web in Libraries 2016 (2016). http://vladimiralexiev.github.io/pres/20161128-rdfpuml-rdf2rml/
2. Bizer, C.: D2R MAP - a database to RDF mapping language. In: King, I., Máray, T. (eds.) Proceedings of the Twelfth International World Wide Web Conference - Posters, WWW 2003, Budapest, Hungary, 20–24 May 2003 (2003)
3. Bizer, C., Seaborne, A.: D2RQ - treating non-RDF databases as virtual RDF graphs. In: ISWC 2004 (Posters), November 2004. http://sites.wiwiss.fu-berlin.de/suhl/bizer/pub/Bizer-D2RQ-ISWC2004-Poster.pdf
4. Bonazzi, R., Hussami, L., Pigneur, Y.: Compliance management is becoming a major issue in IS design, pp. 391–398. Physica-Verlag HD, Heidelberg (2010). https://doi.org/10.1007/978-3-7908-2148-2_45
5. Crotti Junior, A., Debruyne, C., Brennan, R., O'Sullivan, D.: An evaluation of uplift mapping languages. IJWIS **13**(4), 405–424 (2017)
6. Das, S., Cyganiak, R., Sundara, S.: R2RML: RDB to RDF mapping language. W3C recommendation, W3C, September 2012. http://www.w3.org/TR/2012/REC-r2rml-20120927/
7. Debruyne, C., O'Sullivan, D.: R2RML-F: towards sharing and executing domain logic in R2RML mappings. In: Auer, S., Berners-Lee, T., Bizer, C., Heath, T. (eds.) Proceedings of the Workshop on Linked Data on the Web, LDOW 2016, co-located with 25th International World Wide Web Conference (WWW 2016). CEUR Workshop Proceedings, vol. 1593. CEUR-WS.org (2016). http://ceur-ws.org/Vol-1593/article-13.pdf
8. Dimou, A., Vander Sande, M., Colpaert, P., Verborgh, R., Mannens, E., Van de Walle, R.: RML: a generic language for integrated RDF mappings of heterogeneous data. In: Bizer, C., Auer, S., Berners-Lee, T., Heath, T. (eds.) Proceedings of the Workshop on Linked Data on the Web, LDOW 2014, co-located with the 23rd International World Wide Web Conference (WWW 2014). CEUR Workshop Proceedings, vol. 1184. CEUR-WS.org (2014). http://ceur-ws.org/Vol-1184/ldow2014_paper_01.pdf
9. Fatema, K., Hadziselimovic, E., Pandit, H.J., Debruyne, C., Lewis, D., O'Sullivan, D.: Compliance through informed consent: semantic based consent permission and data management model. In: Brewster, C., Cheatham, M., d'Aquin, M., Decker, S., Kirrane, S. (eds.) Proceedings of the 5th Workshop on Society, Privacy and the Semantic Web - Policy and Technology (PrivOn 2017), co-located with 16th International Semantic Web Conference (ISWC 2017), Vienna, Austria, 22 October 2017. CEUR Workshop Proceedings, vol. 1951. CEUR-WS.org (2017). http://ceur-ws.org/Vol-1951/PrivOn2017_paper_5.pdf
10. Gruber, T.R.: Toward principles for the design of ontologies used for knowledge sharing? Int. J. Hum.-Comput. Stud. **43**(5–6), 907–928 (1995). https://doi.org/10.1006/ijhc.1995.1081

11. Michel, F., Djimenou, L., Faron-Zucker, C., Montagnat, J.: Translation of relational and non-relational databases into RDF with xR2RML. In: Monfort, V., Krempels, K.-H., Majchrzak, T.A., Turk, Z. (eds.) WEBIST 2015 - Proceedings of the 11th International Conference on Web Information Systems and Technologies, pp. 443–454. SciTePress (2015)

12. Kalampokis, E., et al.: Exploiting linked data cubes with opencube toolkit. In: Horridge, M., Rospocher, M., van Ossenbruggen, J. (eds.) Proceedings of the ISWC 2014 Posters & Demonstrations Track a Track within the 13th International Semantic Web Conference, ISWC 2014, Riva del Garda, Italy, 21 October 2014. CEUR Workshop Proceedings, vol. 1272, pp. 137–140. CEUR- WS.org (2014). http://ceur-ws.org/Vol-1272/paper109.pdf

13. Lehmann, J., et al.: DBpedia - a large-scale, multilingual knowledge base extracted from Wikipedia. Semant. Web 6(2), 167–195 (2015). https://doi.org/10.3233/SW-140134

14. Meroo-Peuela, A., Hoekstra, R., Guret, C., Schlobach, S.: Detecting and reporting extensional concept drift in statistical linked data. In: Capadisli, S., Cotton, F., Cyganiak, R., Haller, A., Hamilton, A., Troncy, R. (eds.) Proceedings of the 1st International Workshop on Semantic Statistics (SemStats), No. 1549 in CEUR Workshop Proceedings, Aachen (2013). http://ceur-ws.org/Vol-1549/#article-10

15. Open Geospatial Consortium: GeoSPARQL - a geographic query language for RDF data. OGC (2012). http://www.opengeospatial.org/standards/geosparql

16. Pandit, H.J., Lewis, D.: Modelling provenance for GDPR compliance using linked open data vocabularies. In: Brewster, C., Cheatham, M., d'Aquin, M., Decker, S., Kirrane, S. (eds.) Proceedings of the 5th Workshop on Society, Privacy and the Semantic Web - Policy and Technology (PrivOn 2017), co-located with 16th International Semantic Web Conference (ISWC 2017), Vienna, Austria, 22 October 2017. CEUR Workshop Proceedings, vol. 1951. CEUR-WS.org (2017). http://ceur-ws.org/Vol-1951/PrivOn2017paper6.pdf

17. Pollock, R., Tennison, J., Kellogg, G., Herman, I.: Metadata vocabulary for tabular data. W3C recommendation, W3C, December 2015. https://www.w3.org/TR/2015/REC-tabular-metadata-20151217/

18. Raimond, Y., Schreiber, G.: RDF 1.1 primer. W3C note, W3C, June 2014. http://www.w3.org/TR/2014/NOTE-rdf11-primer-20140624/

19. Reynolds, D., Cyganiak, R.: The RDF data cube vocabulary. W3C recommendation, W3C, January 2014. http://www.w3.org/TR/2014/REC-vocab-data-cube-20140116/

20. Rijgersberg, H., Wigham, M., Top, J.L.: How semantics can improve engineering processes: a case of units of measure and quantities. Adv. Eng. Inf. 25(2), 276–287 (2011). https://doi.org/10.1016/j.aei.2010.07.008

21. Sahoo, S., McGuinness, D., Lebo, T.: PROV-o: the PROV ontology. W3C recommendation, W3C, April 2013. http://www.w3.org/TR/2013/REC-prov-o- 20130430/

22. Salas, P.E.R., Mota, F.M.D., Breitman, K.K., Casanova, M.A., Martin, M., Auer, S.: Publishing statistical data on the web. Int. J. Semant. Comput. 6(4), 373–388 (2012). https://doi.org/10.1142/S1793351X12400119

23. Skjaeveland, M.G., Giese, M., Hovland, D., Lian, E.H., Waaler, A.: Engineering ontology-based access to real-world data sources. J. Web Semant. 33, 112–140 (2015). https://doi.org/10.1016/j.websem.2015.03.002

24. Tandy, J., Herman, I., Kellogg, G.: Generating RDF from tabular data on the web. W3C recommendation, W3C, December 2015. https://www.w3.org/TR/2015/REC-csv2rdf-20151217/

25. Wigham, M., Rijgersberg, H., de Vos, M., Top, J.: Semantic support for tables using RDF record table. Int. J. Adv. Intell. Syst. 8(1–2), 128–144 (2015)

26. Zhao, J., Hartig, O.: Towards interoperable provenance publication on the linked data web. In: Bizer, C., Heath, T., Berners-Lee, T., Hausenblas, M. (eds.) WWW 2012 Workshop on Linked Data on the Web, Lyon, France, 16 April 2012. CEUR Workshop Proceedings, vol. 937. CEUR-WS.org (2012). http://ceur-ws.org/Vol-937/ldow2012-paper-03.pdf

Optimization of Queries Based on Foundational Ontologies

Jana Ahmad[✉], Petr Křemen, and Martin Ledvinka

Czech Technical University, Prague, Czech Republic
{jana.ahmad,petr.kremen,martin.ledvinka}@fel.cvut.cz

Abstract. Using ontologies for enterprise data integration brings an opportunity to use them for efficient data query evaluation. The rationale is that ontologies represent common-sense structures that are reflected also in queries posed by data users and thus can be used for query optimization. This paper presents how proper foundational-ontology-based knowledge can be used to design a generic index, which can help in answering a wide range of queries compliant with the foundational ontology. We discuss several indexing techniques and evaluate our proposal for different UFO-based queries extracted from different query sets.

Keywords: Foundational ontologies · SPARQL · Indexing

1 Introduction

A conceptual model is a model of the world where we live in, created within a human mind. It can be understood as the result of an activity of formally describing some aspects of the physical and social world around us for purposes of understanding and communication [23]. The aim of a conceptual model is to express concepts' meaning which can be used to discuss problems in a specific domain and to find the correct relationships between different concepts. Therefore, the aspect of conceptual modeling has become widespread in the context of cognitive science [10,23]. Formal ontologies [10] produced by conceptual modeling activities represent shared common vocabularies of concepts together with formal relationships among them valid in the particular domain. As such, they are suitable abstractions for data access and integration.

In this paper, we will deal with RDF [17] data integration. Principles behind RDF have been adopted by technology leaders for collecting and accessing knowledge, like Facebook[1], Google[2], or Microsoft[3]. There are many RDF management and storage systems[4] e.g., Sesame and virtuoso. These systems are based on the

---

[1] http://ogp.me, accessed 2018-07-16.
[2] https://tinyurl.com/g-knowledge-graph, accessed 2018-07-16.
[3] https://tinyurl.com/ms-concept-graph, accessed 2018-07-16.
[4] E.g. http://rdf4j.org/, cit. 16.7.2018, or https://virtuoso.openlinksw.com/, cit. 16.7.2018, to list some.

© Springer Nature Switzerland AG 2018
H. Panetto et al. (Eds.): OTM 2018 Conferences, LNCS 11230, pp. 351–367, 2018.
https://doi.org/10.1007/978-3-030-02671-4_22

RDF model, using generic RDF indexing techniques for improving query performance. However, generic RDF indices do not take into account the semantics of
the data. Thus, ontological patterns which can be presented in data and reflected
in queries are not optimized in any way.

From previous points, this paper optimizes RDF query evaluation by means
of an index based on actual knowledge structure provided by the conceptual
model-based ontology. Since we use a *foundational ontology* [10], we defend that
such index is reusable for a wide range of queries, corresponding to *foundational
query patterns*, i.e., query patterns expressed in a foundational ontology and
compliant with many queries in the actual domain.

1.1   Contribution

The main contribution of this paper is foundational query patterns analysis
and foundational-ontology-based index design to make query evaluation more
efficient, tailored to RDF data, see Fig. 1.

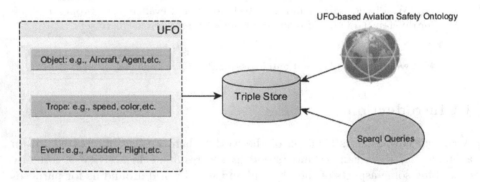

Fig. 1. UFO-based aviation safety domain queries architecture.

In particular, this paper proposes: (i) a new RDF indexing approach based
on Unified Foundational Ontology (UFO) which is top-level ontology, aimed at
answering queries compliant with common query patterns. (ii) Benchmark of
queries for evaluation (applied in aviation safety domain ontology as a use case).

The paper is organized as follows. Section 2 reviews the necessary background
of RDF and querying, in Sect. 2.2 we briefly define the notion of the Unified Foundational Ontology (UFO). Section 3 presents related work. UFO index design
is presented in Sect. 4 including motivating scenario, query patterns, analyzing
UFO query patterns in different data sources and UFO-based index tables. The
evaluation of UFO indexing techniques and query results are given in Sect. 5,
with the description of our use-case. Conclusion is in Sect. 6.

2   Background

First, we introduce a fragment of OWL 2-DL [1] in a simplified manner, as a knowledge-representation language together with simple conjunctive queries over this fragment. Next, we give an overview of UFO, as one of the foundational ontologies. Last, we show an example of RDF representation of an OWL-based UFO fragment and queries.

2.1   OWL 2-DL

An OWL 2-DL *ontology* $\mathcal{O} = \{\alpha_i\}, i \in \{1, \ldots, N_{\mathcal{O}}\}$, where α_i is an axiom is either

- a class assertion A(a), saying that "a is an instance of A", e.g. Person(Frank).
- a object property assertion P(a, b), saying that "a is related to b through P", e.g. hasFriend(Frank, John).
- a terminological axiom of the form $C_1 \sqsubseteq C_2$.

Where A is an OWL atomic class, $C_{(i)}$ are OWL class expressions (discussed later), a is an OWL individual and P is an OWL object property. Typical OWL class expressions could be constructed from atomic classes as follows

- each atomic class A is a class expression.
- boolean operators $(C_1 \sqcap C_2)$, $(C_1 \sqcup C_2)$, or $(\neg C_2)$, for class intersection/union and complement. For example, (Person $\sqcap$ Male) denotes the concept of men.
- existential restriction $(\exists P \cdot C)$, denoting a class, elements of which are related through P to at least one instance of C. For example, ($\exists$hasChild·Man) denotes a class of all individuals having at least one son.
- universal restriction $(\forall P \cdot C)$, denoting a class, elements of which are related through P only to instances of C. For example, ($\forall$hasChild · Man) denotes a class of all individuals having only sons as children, if any,
- qualified cardinality restrictions $(\leq n P \cdot C)$, or $(\geq n P \cdot C)$, $(= n P \cdot C)$, denoting a class, elements of which are related through P to at least/at most/exactly n individuals through P. For example, (≥ 4 hasChild · Man) denotes a class, elements of which have at least four sons (and possibly some other daughters).

We omitted parts of OWL 2-DL that we do not use in this paper, namely inverse properties, nominals, role chains and data types. Full OWL 2-DL syntax as well as its formal semantics can be found in [1].

Having an OWL 2-DL ontology $\mathcal{O}$, we define a *distinguished conjunctive query* as $Q(?x_1, \ldots, ?x_n) = \mu_1, \ldots, \mu_M$, where $?x_i$ is a variable occurring in some μ_i, μ_i is an atom of the form A(y) or P(y, z), where A is an atomic OWL class, P is an OWL object property and y, resp. z is either a variable $?x_i$, or an OWL individual. Intuitively, queries match the class/property assertion axioms, possibly extended by inferencing from other axioms. Let's show the notions on an example. Full query syntax and semantics of distinguished conjunctive queries can be found in [21].

Example. Having an OWL 2-DL ontology $\mathcal{O}$ = {Agent $\sqsubseteq$ Object, Agent(a), performs(a, b)}, the query $Q(?x_1, ?x_2)$ = Object($?x_1$), performs($?x_1, ?x_2$) asks for all object and actions they perform. In our case, the query returns a single result binding {$(?x_1, ?x_2)$ → (a, b)}, because a is inferred to be an object (Agent $\sqsubseteq$ Object).

2.2   Unified Foundational Ontology

Ontologies are used to specify the meaning of terms of some domain, categorizing it and setting relationships among these terms. They define basic concepts like objects, relations, events, processes, situations, and other high-level domain-independent categories. A *top-level ontology* is an ontology that describes general concepts that are common to multiple domains. There are many well-known foundational ontologies, like (DOLCE) [23], Unified Foundation Ontology (UFO) [10], and Basic Formal Ontology (BFO) [7].

For the purpose of this study, we have chosen to build our proposal on top of UFO. Because of (i) our experience in using UFO in various conceptual model-based domains [20], (ii) UFO addresses many essential aspects for conceptual modeling, which have not received a sufficiently detailed attention in other foundational ontologies [10], (iii) the availability of its formal translation to OWL [4], (iv) availability of OntoUML, an ontology modeling language based on UFO [10].

UFO is a top-level ontology. Its main concepts fundamental for this study are sketched in the UML class diagram[5] in Fig. 2. UFO describes static objects (UFO-A) [10], events (UFO-B) [13] and social agents (UFO-C) [12]. UFO splits entities into endurants and perdurants (Endurant $\sqsubseteq$ Individual) (Perdurant $\sqsubseteq$ Individual)[6]. Endurants can be observed as complete concepts in a given time snapshot. Endurants can be any object (an agent, an aircraft) (Object $\sqsubseteq$ Endurant), or its tropes (e.g. speed, location) (Trope $\sqsubseteq$ Endurant), that exist as long as an object they inhere in exists (Trope $\sqsubseteq$ (= 1 inheresIn·Object)).

Perdurants only partially exist in a given time snapshot. They involve events (Event $\sqsubseteq$ Perdurant), situations (Situation $\sqsubseteq$ Perdurant) and object snapshots (ObjectSnapshot $\sqsubseteq$ Perdurant).

Events can be either atomic or complex (Event $\sqsubseteq$ (AtomicEvent $\sqcup$ ComplexEvent)). Events occur in time, have participants (Event $\sqsubseteq$ ($\geq$ 1 hasParticipant · Object)). complex events have parts ($\exists$ hasEventPart · $\top$ $\sqsubseteq$ ComplexEvent). Events themselves can be temporally related, i.e. one happening before another, during another, etc. [13]. ObjectSnapshot: is an immutable state description of an object within a situation. Situation: is a snapshot of object states valid in the given temporal range.

---

[5] The figure is a straightforward visualization of a fragment of UFO axiomatization in OWL, e.g. Trope $\sqsubseteq$ $\forall$inheresIn · Individual $\sqcap$ $\exists$inheresIn · Individual denotes the edge from Trope to Individual. See [4] for details.

[6] We reuse Description Logic formalization of basic UFO concepts introduced in [4].

Additionally, UFO introduces the notion of agents (Agent ⊑ Object), i.e., proactive objects with an intention (e.g. a person, or a company), their intentions, commitments and actions they perform (∃ performs · ⊤ ⊑ Object), and services [20, 22].

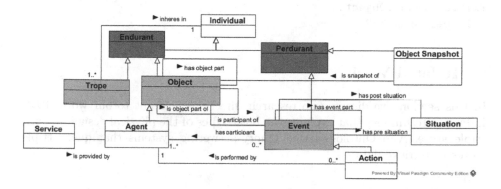

Fig. 2. Main concepts of UFO

2.3 RDF Representation of UFO Models

To use a wide-spread technology for UFO index representation, we will consider RDF triple stores. Indexing techniques over RDF are discussed in Sect. 3. At this point, we show how to represent common OWL axioms, representing an OWL ontology, in RDF and a distinguished conjunctive query over the ontology as basic graph patterns of SPARQL [15], a query language for RDF.

Consider a *triple pattern*, an ordered tuple $t^v = (s^v, p^v, o^v)$, where s^v is its *subject term*, p^v is its *predicate term* and o^v is its *object term*. Each subject is either a *variable V*, or a *constant*[7] C.

Having an OWL ontology $\mathcal{O}$, its RDF serialization is given directly by OWL specification [1]. For distinguished conjunctive queries, we translate each atom of the form A(y) into an RDF triple pattern (y rdf:type A)[8] and each atom of the form P(y, z) into an RDF triple pattern (y P z). Note that all constants (A, P) and possibly (y, z) are represented by the corresponding IRIs.

Example. Having an OWL 2-DL ontology $\mathcal{O}$ from example in Sect. 2.1, its RDF serialization would be[9]

---

[7] For the purpose of this paper, we consider constant to be URIs only.

[8] rdf:type is a special predicate of RDF denoting instantiation.

[9] We use the prefix ":" to denote the namespace <http://example.org/>, thus a translation of Agent into its RDF representation would be an IRI <http://example.org/Agent>.

```
:Agent rdfs:subClassOf :Object.
:a :performs :b.
```

and the SPARQL representation of the query Q would be a SPARQL basic graph pattern

```
?x1 rdf:type :Object.
?x1 :performs ?x2.
```

3   Related Work

In this section, we discuss two research directions relevant to our work. RDF Indexing Techniques that explains the basic types of the physical design for each triple store. And Ontology-based Query-answering systems that query triple stores to retrieve data.

3.1   RDF Indexing Approaches

There has been a significant amount of research done on developing systems for storing and managing RDF data. Triple stores use different physical organization techniques to store RDF data, such as a triple table, property table, vertical partitioning approaches [2,6,14,18].

In the *Triple Table* (TT) approach, each RDF statement of the form $(s\ \ p\ \ o)$ is stored as a triple in one table with three columns. Indexes are then added for each of the columns to make joins less expensive. Since all triples are stored in a single RDF table, very large data and complex queries cause the execution time to be prohibitive [2,6]. An example of a triple store that uses this approach is 3store [14].

When using the *Property Table* (PT) technique, each table contains a column for the subject of the triple and separate columns for several fixed properties. The main idea is to discover clusters of subjects often appearing with the same set of properties. However, the disadvantage of the property table technique is that it generates many NULL values since, for the given cluster, not all properties will match all subjects and multi-valued attributes. Another disadvantage of this approach is that adding properties requires also to add a new table [2,6]. This approach has been used in Jena 2 [25].

Using the *Vertical Partitioning* (VP) approach, each triple table includes n-two column tables where n is the number of unique properties in the data. In each of these tables, the first column contains the subjects that match property and the second column contains the object values for those subjects [2,3,14]. In this indexing technique, each table is sorted by subject, thus particular subjects can be located quickly. And this approach supports multi-valued attributes.

Compressed Indexes use six B+ tree indices to store RDF triples tables or quads of a subject, predicate, object, and a "context". In each B+ tree, the key is a concatenation of the subject, predicate, object, and context [18].

Relation to Our Approach. In our approach, we build on these existing techniques, extend them and use them together with UFO patterns to improve the efficiency of queries based on foundational ontologies (UFO-based query answering).

3.2 Ontology-Based Query-Answering Systems

Next research direction to mention are ontological query answering systems that use triple stores to query data.

Ontology-Based Data Access (ODA) [19] is a paradigm for accessing data through a conceptual layer. In the OBDA, an ontology defines a high-level global schema of data sources and provides a vocabulary for user queries. End-users formulate queries using the ontological terms and thus they are not required to understand the structure of the data sources, trading it for limitations in expressiveness [16].

In Ontoseek [9], queries are represented as conceptual graphs, then the query answering problem is reduced to ontology-driven graph matching where individual nodes and arcs match if one subsumes the other.

AQUA [24] is a question answering system which integrates NLP, logic, information retrieval and ontologies. It transfers the English question into logical queries, expressed in QLL language.

Ontology-mediated query answering (OMQA) [5] is a paradigm for accessing legacy data while taking into account knowledge expressed by a domain ontology.

Relation to Our Approach. Although each of the related works above presents a unique solution for data storage and query answering, none of them proposes a foundational Ontology as a solution for query processing. Thus, this paper discusses, how proper foundational-ontology-based index design can help to optimize query answering.

4   UFO Index

The meanings of the variety of words such: red, John, Jana, marriage, accident, ball, process, attend, happen, party, hot, warm, play, situation, tasks, etc. reflects the essential differences between things that happen and who performs these things, i.e., the distinction between behavioral elements and structural elements. UFO distinguishes between these two categories with the behavioral elements referred to as "events" and the structural referred to as "objects". The question words *("how")* versus *("what")* is often invoked to check the different nature of these elements [11].

For more comprehensive representation of any ontological domain, it is important to focus on the representation of endurants (e.g., objects, their parts, their properties, etc.) and perdurant (e.g., events, their parts, etc.), and that is exactly what UFO considers. Based on them, we constructed eight competency questions [8] shown in Table 1. The questions show foundational patterns that are used in real queries. Let's discuss the questions in more details and show their realistic exemplifications in two domains: the aviation safety domain and the social relation domain.

Table 1. Foundational query patterns and their DCQ representation.

	Question	DCQ formalization
Q_1	Who participates in an event?	$Q_1(?o, ?e) \rightarrow$ ufo:has-participant(?e, ?o)
Q_2	Which objects participate in a specific event e1 ?	$Q_2(?o) \rightarrow$ ufo:has-participant(e1, ?o)
Q_3	What are the properties of (inhere in) a certain object o1?	$Q_3(?t) \rightarrow$ ufo:inheres-in(?t, o1)
Q_4	what are object's parts ?	$Q_4(?o1, ?o2) \rightarrow$ ufo:has-object-part(?o1, ?o2)
Q_5	What are the snapshots of a specific object?	$Q_5(?s) \rightarrow$ ufo:is-snapshot-of(?s, o1)
Q_6	What caused an event?	$Q_6(?e1, ?e2) \rightarrow$ ufo:is-caused-by(?e1, ?e2)
Q_7	How is a particular process structured?	$Q_7(?e) \rightarrow$ ufo:has-event-part(e1, ?e)
Q_8	What are snapshots of any object?	$Q_8(?s, ?o) \rightarrow$ ufo:is-snapshot-of(?s, ?o)

Q_1 and Q_2 show the relation between an event and an object. Events are mapping of statements or occurrence in the reality, in which objects (things and people) participate playing certain tasks ((Event $\sqsubseteq$ (≥ 1 hasParticipant $\cdot$ Object)). E.g., who participates in Jana's birthday party?

Q_3 presents inherence relation between an object and its qualities that are existentially dependent on the object itself (Trope $\sqsubseteq$ ($= 1$ inheresIn $\cdot$ Object)) [10]. I.e., a trope is a property of some object or another trope that cannot exist without the object it inheres in. E.g., what are the tropes or properties vehicle-i has?

In UFO, endurants are entities that, whenever they exist, they exist with all their parts, while maintaining their identity (Object $\sqsubseteq$ ($= 1$ isObjectPartOf $\cdot$ Object)). This is what Q_4 presents. E.g., what are the parts of aircraft-i?

Q_5 and Q_8 present the notion of an object snapshot which is an immutable state description of an object within a situation. Regarding to UFO, object snapshot and object share the attribute types and relation types of their identifying objects (Object Snapshot $\sqsubseteq$ ($=1$ isSnapshotOf $\cdot$ Object)). Where the object serves only for identification purpose. E.g., What are all revisions of reports of specific occurrence? And What is the last snapshot of a specific aircraft just before take-off?

What are the changes from and to a certain situation in the world? An answer is an event, which is the answer of Q_6. E.g., How the accident-i happened? UFO defines full meaning of events, describing how events relate to their parts (ComplexEvent $\sqsubseteq$ (≥ 2 hasEventPart $\cdot$ Event). Moreover, it prescribes all temporal precedence involving events. This notion could translate to Q_7. E.g., what happened before the accident-i?

The previous questions motivate us to create UFO-based physical design index tables that store RDF data according to the main concepts of UFO, Perdurant and Endurant.

Use of the Questions in Enterprise Information Systems. The above-defined questions represent generic foundational query patterns that are inherent to all information systems. The advent of harmonization in enterprise data management gave rise to unified data models.

For example, *customer master data*[10] model customers (endurants), their properties like the name (trope). Particular writes into the master data base corresponding to the individual snapshots of the name, resp. customer. Thus, by instantiating Q_3, we can easily retrieve all properties a master data base contains about a customer.

Another example might be an information system for customer care[11]. It gathers activities (events), as well as their responsible organizations (event participants). Thus, by instantiating Q_1, we can get all organizations which are responsible for performing some activity.

Analyze UFO Queries in Different Data Sources. The question now is: how can we represent UFO query patterns in different data sources, e.g., Wikidata? How could different data source queries be analyzed with UFO? Or how data source queries could be translated to UFO?

For this purpose, in this section, we discuss the representation of UFO-based queries and how $Q_1 \ldots Q_8$ competence questions match different queries in two different data sources Wikidata[12] and Reporting Tool[13]. Reporting Tool is an ontology-based information system allowing to manage safety data in the aviation industry. Most of the queries in the Reporting Tool are centered around events, especially safety events, that can match Q_1, Q_6 and Q_7 of competence questions. Or around the snapshot of objects in specific time which match Q_5 and Q_8. *For example*: what is the last revision of specific occurrence reports? According to UFO we can map this query to Q_5 in competence questions (what is the last snapshot of a specific object), where the last version could be represented as the snapshot of occurrence report.

Wikidata which is a collaboratively edited knowledge base under development by the Wikimedia Foundation. There are different sets of queries: (i) simple questions: about objects, properties, and events which match $Q_1..Q_8$ (Such as Humans without children (Q_1, Q_2, Q_4), Recent Events (Q_5, Q_6), Popular eye colors (Q_3), etc.). (ii) Showcase Queries: that are centered around objects and their properties or tropes(such as: Whose birthday is today? that match Q_1) (iii)

[10] https://wiki.scn.sap.com/wiki/display/SD/Customer+master+data,   cit.   16.07. 2018.

[11] E.g. http://www.adrm.com/ba-customer-service.shtml, cit. 16.07.2018.

[12] https://www.wikidata.org/wiki/Wikidata:SPARQL-query-service/queries/examples Showcase-Queries, cit. 16-07.2018.

[13] https://github.com/kbss-cvut/reporting-tool, cit. 16.07.2018.

Samples with coordinates to illustrate maps queries: about objects and trope (such as Locations of universities in Germany that match Q_3) and others. So, we can noticed that the most queries of Wikidata about endurant (object and trope). Let's analyze a complete query: e.g., select people whose gender we know or we don't know?

With respect to UFO, Human is an Object that has tropes that inhere in it, which is here (gender) therefore, this query match Q_3 (Trope $\sqsubseteq$ ($= 1$ inheresIn $\cdot$ Object)) of competence questions.

4.1   UFO Index Tables Approaches Discussion

Due to the nature of RDF that represents data as triples (subject, predicate, object), the goal is to handle variant types of queries such as: triples having the same property, triples having the same subject and finally, list of subjects or properties related to a given object. Thus, there is a real need of efficient tools for storing and querying knowledge using the ontologies and the related resources.

In this section, we discuss technical challenges for the indexing and query processing regarding to our novel approach in designing index tables for top-level ontology concepts (namely UFO). We discussed the indexing techniques without UFO in Sect. 2.

Triple Tables. As we mentioned before UFO is divided mainly into two categories, Perdurant (event) and Endurant (object), ((Event $\sqcup$ Endurant) $\sqsubseteq$ $\top$). Applying triple table technique in UFO will store all instances of these two categories in one table which will lead not only to slow in query execution but also the insufficient use of the UFO conceptualization (see Table 2). Therefore, our proposal in this approach is to divide Table 2 physically into two tables; one for each category (Perdurant and Endurant). See Tables 3 and 4.

Table 2. Triples table

Subject	Predicate	Object
Event-i	has-participant	Agent-i
Person-i	is-participant-of	Event-i
Agent-i	performs	Action-i
Process-i	is-event-part-of	Event-i
Action-i	is-performed-by	Agent-i
E_n	P_n	O_n

Based on UFO-tables, we answer Q2: what objects participate in a specific event (e.g., Action-i?) ((Action $\sqsubseteq$ Event) $\rightarrow$ (Action $\sqsubseteq$ ($= 1$ hasParticipant $\cdot$ Object)). Instead of searching in the whole triple table, the query will be executed

Table 3. Perdurant table

Subject	Predicate	Object
Event-i	has-participant	Agent-i
Process-i	is-event-part-of	Event-i
Action-i	is-performed-by	Agent-i

Table 4. Endurant table

Subject	Predicate	Object
Person-i	is-participant-of	Event-i
Agent-i	performs	Action-i

in the endurant table. And this will be more efficient because we use the conceptualization of UFO, and faster because it searches only in endurant table (logically it needs half of TT time).

Property Table. UFO describes the relationship between two categories: behavioral elements (events) and structural elements (objects), by specifying conceptual properties that help to distinguish between event and object. For example, each event has an object participant who participates and performs a specific task in a particular event (e.g., What objects participate in a specific event? (Q_2)). Therefore, our proposal is also to build a UFO property table for endurant and another table for event and snapshot perdurant (see Tables 5 and 6), that will reduce Null values in each table, but we will still have them.

Table 5. Endurant property table

Subject	is-object-part-of	is-participant	Performs	has-trope
Object-i	Object-ii	Event-i	Event-i	Trope-i

Vertical Partitioning. Applying vertical partitioning (see Sect. 3) as UFO-indexing technique would gain the benefit from UFO predicates (i.e., Object Properties). For example: what are objects that are parts of another object (Q_4)? To answer this question, the query will be constructed such that: select all objects with property (has-object-part) of another object (Object $\sqsubseteq$ (=1 isObjectPartOf · Object)) see Table 7.

5   Evaluation

For evaluation, we constructed a benchmark of SPARQL queries on 30000 triples. Then analyzed these queries to evaluate our proposal when using one or more of

Table 6. Perdurant property table

Subject	is-event-part-of	has-participant	is-performed-by	is-snapshot-of
Event-i	Event-i	Person-i	Agent-i	
Object-Snapshot				Object-i

Table 7. Has-object-part predicate table

Object-i	Object-ii
Object-i	Object-iii

indexing techniques that any triple store uses for storing UFO-based ontological data. We use the aviation safety ontology as a use case.

5.1   Aviation Safety Ontology

We built our Aviation Safety Ontology on top of the Unified Foundational Ontology (UFO) [10,23]. We designed Aviation Safety Ontology for describing safety issues in aviation organizations, and to increase the awareness of analytical methods and tools in the aviation community for safety analysis in the aviation domain [20]. Our strategy is to analyze safety events that lead to incidents or accidents and explain factors, that contribute to these safety events. Thus, Aviation Safety Ontology consists of the common aviation domain concepts, such as objects (e.g., aircraft, crew, aerodrome) and events (e.g. flight, accident) [20]. Figure 3 depicts basic concepts in Aviation Safety Ontology that are represented in UFO.

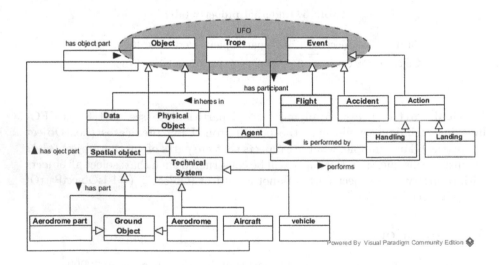

Fig. 3. Aviation safety ontology

5.2   Benchmark of Queries

To optimize the evaluation of UFO-based queries, consider a domain ontology (Aviation Safety Domain), we instantiated the queries $Q_1..Q_8$ in the aviation domain:

- Q_1': What objects participate in specific flight (flight-i)?
- Q_2': What are aircraft-i's parts?
- Q_3': What events are performed by Cabin-crew?
- Q_4': What are the tropes of a person in aviation safety domain?
- Q_5': What are the events that contribute in a specific flight (flight-i)?

These questions should be analyzed to evaluate the expressiveness of the ontology that is required to represent the competency questions and to characterize their solutions. Users in Aviation Safety Domain are interested in having answers to domain-specific questions like: knowing who is responsible for an aviation safety event. Who and what participate in aviation safety events (e.g. flight, process). And what are the properties (tropes) of the domain?

Thus, we transferred the previous constructed competence questions to formal representation (SPARQL queries[14]) with their conceptual models that may help to defend our suggestion of using UFO, then we discussed the answers of these queries in the UFO indexing techniques proposal. Finally, we tested one of the native triple stores (RDF4J[15]) that physically designed bases on B-Tree indexing triple tables with context, by comparing the execution time of these queries with and without UFO index tables. We use RDF4J context mechanism [15] to group all perdurant statements together through a single group identifier (Named Graph), i.e., in one perdurant table that contains around 15000 UFO-aviation safety data triples. And all endurant triples in another endurant table also around 15000 triples. This grouping process is executed automatically, by iterating all perdurants (events) from RDF and adding them to the perdurant table or objects to the endurant table.

Foundational Query Patterns Evaluation. To answer Q_1': Which is instantiated from Q_2 of competence questions, as shown in Fig. 4:

```
SELECT ?term FROM NAMED
<http://onto.fel.cvut.cz/ontologies/ufo/perdurant>
WHERE {GRAPH ?g
{ aviation-safety:flight-i ufo:has_participant ?term} }
```

---

[14] Common SPARQL prefixes include rdfs: to denote http://www.w3.org/2000/01/rdf-schema, rdf: to denote http://www.w3.org/1999/02/22-rdf-syntax-ns, ufo: to denote http://onto.fel.cvut.cz/ontologies/ufo/ and aviation-safety: to denote http://onto.fel.cvut.cz/ontologies/aviation-safety/.

[15] E.g. http://rdf4j.org/, cit. 16.7.2018.

– In *UFO Triple Table*: each event has objects as participants (Event $\sqsubseteq$ (= 1 hasParticipant · Object)), thus the query will be executed on perdurant table. In *Property Table*: the system will search for (has-participant) property in perdurant property table. By using UFO-based *Vertical Partitioning*: each table is built regarding to unique UFO-predicate, so that, the search process will look for has-participant UFO-predicate.

To evaluate Q_2' that is instantiated from Q_4, as shown in Fig. 4:

```
SELECT ?term
FROM NAMED <http://onto.fel.cvut.cz/ontologies/ufo/endurant>
where{ GRAPH ?g
{ ?term ufo:is_Object_part_of aviation-safety:aircraft-i.}}
```

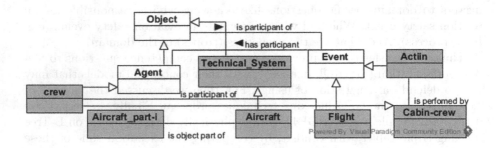

Fig. 4. Conceptual model for Q_1', Q_2' and Q_3'

– In *Triple Table*: this query looks for objects that are part of Aircraft-i which is also an object. Therefore, Q_2' will be executed on the endurant table. In *UFO-Property Table*: Aircraft-i has many parts, so the UFO-based system will search for (is-object-part-of) property in endurant property tables. In *Vertical Partitioning* Proposal: the search process will look for (is-object-part-of) UFO-predicate.

Q_3' that instantiated from Q_1 (where is-performed-by is sub-property of is-participant-of), this query selects in perdurant table all events or actions that are performed by Cabin-crew (Object), see Fig. 4. (Event $\sqsubseteq$ (= 1 isPerformedBy·Object)). Its SPARQL transcription would be

```
SELECT ?term
FROM NAMED <http://onto.fel.cvut.cz/ontologies/ufo/perdurant>
where { GRAPH ?g
{ ?term ufo:is_performod_by aviation-safety:Cabin-crew-i}}
```

– The same discussion for Q_4' that is instantiated from Q_3 and Q_5' is instantiated from Q_7.

Evaluation Results. So, based on our proposal the query will be executed either on the perdurant table (named graph) or on the endurant table. The average execution time results and standard deviation are in Table 8, where the given results are averages from executing each query ten times in RDF4J store. The experiments were performed on a Dell computer with Intel(R) core(TM)i7-2600 CPU (3.40 GHz). The machine was equipped with 16.0 GB installed memory and HDD 1000 GB, running on Windows 7 professional 64-bit. Java version 8 update 66. Storage RDF4J version 2.1.1.

Table 8. Execution query time, σ denotes standard deviation, ϕ denotes mean value, MD denotes difference of the means.

	ϕ UFO TT	ϕ without-UFO	σ UFO TT	σ without-UFO	MD
Q_1'	134.4 ms	152.7 ms	4.9 ms	7.7 ms	18.3 ms
Q_2'	130.7 ms	138.8 ms	7.2 ms	6.2 ms	8.1 ms
Q_3'	132.3 ms	184.5 ms	7.9 ms	17.7 ms	52.2 ms
Q_4'	128.2 ms	142 ms	5.6 ms	9.3 ms	13.8 ms
Q_5'	125.1 ms	141.2 ms	3.9 ms	5.8 ms	16.1 ms

In our experiment, we have shown a performance increase on a relatively small data sample for all foundational queries. The table shows that

- having a foundational ontology, we can design a few index tables. The index tables can be reused for all datasets compliant with the foundational ontology and bring performance boost of evaluation of many queries (represented by foundational query patterns Q_1 to Q_5).

Pragmatically, the performance boost can be easily achieved for existing RDF stores by proper conceptual analysis and modeling of the datasets and queries by means of a foundational ontology.

6 Conclusion and Future Work

In this paper, we presented our novel approach to improve the efficiency of SPARQL queries by using UFO-based indexing techniques, discussed the different techniques using UFO-based index tables, and evaluated benchmark of SPARQL queries regarding to our proposal to explain how UFO-indexing approaches make the search process easier. In the next step, we will evaluate our idea practically in different ontological domains, different triple stores and large data sets with respect to UFO indexing techniques. A limitation of our approach is that it might not work perfectly for noisy data.

Acknowledgments. This work was supported by grant No. GA 16-09713S Efficient Exploration of Linked Data Cloud of the Grant Agency of the Czech Republic and by grant No. SGS16/229/OHK3/3T/13 Supporting ontological data quality in information systems of the Czech Technical University in Prague.

References

1. OWL 2 web ontology language document overview. Technical report, W3C Consoritum (2012). http://www.w3.org/TR/owl2-overview. Accessed 30 Aug 2018
2. Abadi, D.J., Marcus, A., Madden, S.R., Hollenbach, K.: Scalable semantic web data management using vertical partitioning. In: Proceedings of the 33rd International Conference on Very Large Data Bases, VLDB 2007, pp. 411–422. VLDB Endowment (2007)
3. Abadi, D.J., Marcus, A., Madden, S.R., Hollenbach, K.: SW-Store: a vertically partitioned DBMS for semantic web data management. VLDB J. **18**(2), 385–406 (2009)
4. Benevides, A.B., Bourguet, J., Guizzardi, G., Peñaloza, R.: Representing the UFO-B foundational ontology of events in SROIQ. In: JOWO. CEUR Workshop Proceedings, vol. 2050. CEUR-WS.org (2017)
5. Bienvenu, M., Bourhis, P., Mugnier, M.L., Tison, S., Ulliana, F.: Ontology-mediated query answering for key-value stores. In: IJCAI International Joint Conference on Artificial Intelligence, pp. 844–851 (2017)
6. Faye, D.C., Cure, O., Blin, G.: A survey of RDF storage approaches. ARIMA J. **15**, 11–35 (2012)
7. Grenon, P., Smith, B.: SNAP and SPAN: towards dynamic spatial ontology. Spat. Cogn. Comput. **4**(1), 69–104 (2004)
8. Grüninger, M., Fox, M.: Methodology for the design and evaluation of ontologies. In: Workshop on Basic Ontological Issues in Knowledge Sharing, IJCAI 1995 (1995)
9. Guarino, N., Masolo, C., Vetere, G.: OntoSeek: content-based access to the web. IEEE Intell. Syst. Appl. **14**(3), 70–80 (1999)
10. Guizzardi, G.: Ontological foundations for structural conceptual model. Ph.D. thesis (2005)
11. Guizzardi, G., Guarino, N., Almeida, J.P.A.: Ontological considerations about the representation of events and endurants in business models. In: La Rosa, M., Loos, P., Pastor, O. (eds.) BPM 2016. LNCS, vol. 9850, pp. 20–36. Springer, Cham (2016). https://doi.org/10.1007/978-3-319-45348-4_2
12. Guizzardi, G., Wagner, G.: Using the unified foundational ontology (UFO) as a foundation for general conceptual modeling languages. In: Poli, R., Healy, M., Kameas, A. (eds.) Theory and Applications of Ontology: Computer Applications, pp. 175–196. Springer, Dordrecht (2010). https://doi.org/10.1007/978-90-481-8847-5_8
13. Guizzardi, G., Wagner, G., de Almeida Falbo, R., Guizzardi, R.S.S., Almeida, J.P.A.: Towards ontological foundations for the conceptual modeling of events. In: Ng, W., Storey, V.C., Trujillo, J.C. (eds.) ER 2013. LNCS, vol. 8217, pp. 327–341. Springer, Heidelberg (2013). https://doi.org/10.1007/978-3-642-41924-9_27
14. Harris, S., Shadbolt, N.: SPARQL query processing with conventional relational database systems. In: Dean, M., et al. (eds.) WISE 2005. LNCS, vol. 3807, pp. 235–244. Springer, Heidelberg (2005). https://doi.org/10.1007/11581116_25
15. Harris, S., Seaborne, A.: SPARQL 1.1 query language. Technical report, W3C Consoritum (2013)
16. Kharlamov, E., et al.: Optique: towards OBDA systems for industry. In: Cimiano, P., Fernández, M., Lopez, V., Schlobach, S., Völker, J. (eds.) ESWC 2013. LNCS, vol. 7955, pp. 125–140. Springer, Heidelberg (2013). https://doi.org/10.1007/978-3-642-41242-4_11

17. Klyne, G., Carroll, J.J.: Resource description framework (RDF): concepts and abstract syntax. Technical report, W3C Consoritum (2004)
18. Kolas, D., Emmons, I., Dean, M.: Efficient linked-list RDF indexing in parliament. In: CEUR Workshop Proceedings, vol. 517, pp. 17–32 (2009)
19. Kontchakov, R., Rodríguez-Muro, M., Zakharyaschev, M.: Ontology-based data access with databases: a short course. In: Rudolph, S., Gottlob, G., Horrocks, I., van Harmelen, F. (eds.) Reasoning Web 2013. LNCS, vol. 8067, pp. 194–229. Springer, Heidelberg (2013). https://doi.org/10.1007/978-3-642-39784-4_5
20. Kostov, B., Ahmad, J., Křemen, P.: Towards ontology-based safety information management in the aviation industry. In: Ciuciu, I., et al. (eds.) OTM 2016. LNCS, vol. 10034, pp. 242–251. Springer, Cham (2017). https://doi.org/10.1007/978-3-319-55961-2_25
21. Křemen, P., Kouba, Z.: Conjunctive query optimization in OWL2-DL. In: Hameurlain, A., Liddle, S.W., Schewe, K.-D., Zhou, X. (eds.) DEXA 2011. LNCS, vol. 6861, pp. 188–202. Springer, Heidelberg (2011). https://doi.org/10.1007/978-3-642-23091-2_18
22. Křemen, P., et al.: Ontological foundations of European coordination centre for accident and incident reporting systems. J. Aerosp. Inf. Sys. 14(5), 279–292 (2017)
23. Mylopoulos, J.: Conceptual modelling and Telos. In: Conceptual Modeling, Databases, and Case An integrated view of information systems development, pp. 49–68 (1992)
24. Vargas-Vera, M., Motta, E.: AQUA – ontology-based question answering system. In: Monroy, R., Arroyo-Figueroa, G., Sucar, L.E., Sossa, H. (eds.) MICAI 2004. LNCS (LNAI), vol. 2972, pp. 468–477. Springer, Heidelberg (2004). https://doi.org/10.1007/978-3-540-24694-7_48
25. Wilkinson, K., Sayers, C., Kuno, H., Reynolds, D.: Efficient RDF storage and retrieval in Jena2. In: Proceedings of the 1th International Workshop on Semantic Web and Databases, pp. 35–43 (2003)

Semantically Enhanced Interoperability in Health Emergency Management

Danai Vergeti[(⊠)], Dimitrios Ntalaperas, and Dimitrios Alexandrou

UBITECH Ltd., Thessalias 8, 15231 Chalandri, Athens, Greece
{vergetid, dntalaperas, dalexandrou}@ubitech.eu

Abstract. Health Emergency Management is a domain which involves a number of stakeholders operating under different protocols, rules, and languages forming a complex world where incident coordination and decision making is a vital requirement. The data that is used during a health emergency include heterogeneous datasets from various data sources. Thus, data harmonization techniques must be adopted against a common reference schema to assure data consistency. Moreover, the need for interoperability between the involved agencies at national and international level is strong. Currently, there is no reference schema which captures all the dimensions of the Health Emergency Management domain and also aligned with the common incident management interoperability protocols. The HERMES Semantic Model consists of an ontological representation of the conceptual model of the Health Emergency Management domain and aims at: (a) providing an integral conceptual model of Health Emergency Management covering all the involved knowledge domains and, (b) addressing the aforementioned interoperability and integration issues. HERMES reuses existing ontologies and offers a new upper model, a set of vertical models and a data facet. The model is used by a specific mechanism which imports data from the various resources in order to provide an integrated and homogenized view of the data. The final harmonized data may be used by various incident management platforms to assist in decision making during an emergency. Finally, the model and the data harmonization procedure are evaluated using open data from open data repositories. The results of the evaluation verify the correctness of the approach.

Keywords: Data harmonization · Semantic model
Health Emergency Management · Ontology · Open data · Interoperability

1 Introduction

Throughout the mankind history society struggles, and still does, with a large number of victims from natural and man-made disasters. Extreme weather conditions due to climate changes and human interventions to the natural environment, physical phenomena as well as technological disasters, man-made hazards and terrorist attacks are some of the hazardous events types that have increased the number of affected people the last years. These disastrous events have shown that health emergency operations involve a number of stakeholders operating under different protocols, rules, and languages forming a complex world where incident coordination and decision making is a

© Springer Nature Switzerland AG 2018
H. Panetto et al. (Eds.): OTM 2018 Conferences, LNCS 11230, pp. 368–385, 2018.
https://doi.org/10.1007/978-3-030-02671-4_23

vital requirement. Although dealing with the same incident or disaster, the information needed by different groups may be very diverse. Moreover, the collected information during these incidents includes heterogeneous datasets from various multidisciplinary data sources. Semantic heterogeneity of the emergency data is still one of the biggest challenges in emergency response [10]. Semantic interoperability refers to the data difference on meanings of a language, code, message or any other form of representation [36]. Thus, semantic interoperability in Health Emergency Management is a strong need in order to assist responsiveness and decision making. Data harmonization techniques must be adopted to assure data consistency. Based on the UN/CEFACT definition, **data harmonization** is an iterative process of capturing, defining, analyzing and reconciling information requirements [38]. The heterogeneous datasets can be reconciled by utilizing a common reference schema which will capture the corresponding knowledge domains, eliminating any issues of mismatches and data redundancy. Apart from the structure of the data, there are approaches which focus on the semantics of the data in order to resolve issues of data redundancy and semantic interpretation during the data integration process. An ontology describes a domain of interest in a formal manner [1] and is used to explicitly define schema terms and, among others, address any semantic conflicts in heterogeneous information systems. It also provides the accurate semantic interpretation of data from multiple sources and verifies the mappings used to integrate that data [39].

The paper presents HERMES (Health Emergency Management Semantic model), an ontology which is used to address semantic interoperability in Health Emergency Management. The model includes the main concepts and the relationships between the concepts of the Health Emergency Management domain. The ontology (1) defines a new generic upper model of emergency management, (2) imports a large set of domain ontologies related to Health Emergency Management, (3) is aligned with interoperability standards already used in emergency management. In this way it provides a holistic approach of the Health Emergency Management world which captures any type of health emergency event (everyday incidents to mass casualty disasters).

HERMES represents the disastrous events, the resources, the activities and the agencies that are involved in a health emergency, as well as the relationships among them. It also covers a number of other domains related to health emergency. The model comprises three layers: The Upper Model, the Vertical Modules and the Data Facet. Additionally, the technical approach of the data harmonization procedure against the HERMES model is described. Following, the model and the data harmonization procedure are evaluated using a set of data sources.

The paper is organized as follows: Sect. 2 provides the related work on the field where a number of studies have adopted an ontological model for emergency management. HERMES model is presented in Sect. 3. The working methodology, the scope and the high-level requirements are analyzed. The three layers of the conceptual model are presented. Section 4 describes the data harmonization process. Section 5 provides the evaluation of the semantic model using various datasets from open sources and simulated data while, Sect. 6 concludes the paper.

2 Related Work

A number of approaches have been implemented to provide semantic interoperability in Health Emergency Management based on a semantic model with different levels of semantic expressiveness and complexity.

Rauner et al. [34] developed a decision support system (DSS) to enhance interoperability of policy makers for disaster preparedness, response, and recovery. They established a skills taxonomy for a DSS Toolset to interlink key emergency interventions and tasks with main national emergency responders supported by international emergency responders with a special focus on the EU. An interoperability data model for chemical incident response is introduced in [4]. The model implementation is based on Activity Theory [2]. The model is an XML-based response data model that defines consistent data semantics and internal structures using documents generated from actual chemical incidents. Both aforementioned approaches provide a semantic model which achieves interoperability mostly based on interoperability standards and other classifications, without using the semantic expressiveness of an ontological model related to Health Emergency Management, as does HERMES.

Gençtürk et al. [13] propose an ontology based on the integration of interoperability standard schemas and the transformation of the exchanged messages. Common Data Elements (CDEs) is a common ontology which is used as the semantic dictionary of the interoperating applications which support the EDXL family of standards [23] and the Open Geospatial Consortium's (OGC) Sensor Web Enablement Initiative standards [24]. Our approach is not limited to these protocols. HERMES is aligned with interoperability protocols and at the same time includes a number of other domains related to health emergency.

Domain Ontology for Mass Gatherings (DO4MG) [14] is a domain ontology which focuses on medical emergency management. The ontology has been evaluated through the implementation of a case-based reasoning decision support system for emergency medical management in mass gatherings. HERMES covers a wider spectrum of emergency incidents and also aims at semantic interoperability among the various stakeholders, not only the medical actors.

Fan et al. [10] introduce the Emergency Management Ontology based on the analysis of a case study. The ontology interlinks a dynamic ontology and a static ontology. The dynamic data ontology consists of domain ontologies needed for specific purposes such as disaster, time ontology, hydrology, etc. and rules. The static data ontology is composed of various kinds of data ontologies related to the case. Also, a set of ontologies for actors are defined (police, fire brigade, municipalities, medical centers). HERMES approach is completely different since it defines a generic upper model for emergency response in order to be able to be applied to any incident (everyday and mass emergency). Moreover, HERMES is aligned with interoperability standards which are not foreseen in the Emergency Management Ontology.

Concerning data harmonization, the general approach of the ontology-driven mapping of structured and unstructured data into RDF and the subsequent use of that data by a Semantic Web application is via a SPARQL endpoint [15]. Relational databases (RDBs) are still one of the main sources of data. Data stored in relational systems can be extracted via queries, stored procedures, or any other process that will extract the data from the database. The transformation process changes the data from one format to another and/or cleans up data elements according to a configuration file, which can either be built automatically or semi-automatically. Table columns and rows will be mapped to concepts and attributes defined in that model. The D2RQ Platform [8] is a system for accessing relational databases as virtual, read-only RDF graphs. It offers RDF-based access to the content of relational databases without having to replicate it into an RDF store. D2RQ Platform provides a declarative language, the D2RQ Mapping Language, for mapping relational database schemas to RDF vocabularies and OWL ontologies. Ontop [27] is a platform to query databases as Virtual RDF Graphs using SPARQL. Ontop provides On-the-fly Ontology-based Data Access, SPARQL over RDFS/OWL mappings, Data Integration with DB federation. The mapping language that is used for the Ontop mappings is R2RML [33]. Virtuoso RDF Views [7] allows mapping arbitrary collections of relational tables, views, procedures, or web services into SPARQL accessible RDF. Virtuoso includes a declarative Meta Schema Language for defining the mapping of SQL data to RDF ontologies. The data harmonization approach that is proposed in the current paper uses D2RQ server.

3 The HERMES Ontology

HERMES is an ontology, implemented in OWL [42]. In the current section we will present the objectives of the semantic model, the working methodology, the different domains that the model needs to cover, as well as the relevant domain ontologies. Moreover, the core model of HERMES, the vertical models and finally, the data facet of the ontology are presented.

3.1 Working Methodology

HERMES focuses mainly on the Health Emergency Management, while capturing a wider area of knowledge, semantically related to Health Emergency Management. The approach used to develop this conceptual model follows the METHONTOLOGY, a methodology to build ontologies from scratch defined by Fernández-López et al. [11], with the ontology lifecycle being viewed as an evolving prototype. The methodology was chosen since it has its roots in the main activities identified by the IEEE software development process and in other knowledge engineering methodologies [5]. Adopting this method, the development of the HERMES ontology consists of the following steps: (1) Specification of the **purpose of the ontology** (see Sect. 3.2), (2) Specification of the **high-level requirements** of the semantic model. (see Sect. 3.2), (3) Definition of the **end users**: The end users of the ontology include the main stakeholders which are involved during a health emergency: first responders, public safety agencies, national, regional, local emergency operation centers, volunteer organizations, personnel in hospitals and critical infrastructures, civilians etc., (4) Definition of **simple use cases**: Simple use cases are used to provide a first instantiation of the conceptual model. The main use cases include surge capacity, logistics, supply and human resource in everyday health incident management as well as in mass public health emergency or health crisis (national or international cooperation). (5) Acquisition of knowledge through **literature review**, in parallel with requirements analysis. This stage also involved exploring and examining relevant existing ontologies that could be reused. (see Sect. 3.3) (6) Development of a **first draft** of the overall conceptual model to structure the domain knowledge, (7) Formalization of the **first definitions** through their implementation in Protégé [31], with the main classes and object and data properties specified, (8) **Validation** of the model defined in step 7., (9) Formalization of the **complete semantic model** in Protégé, (10) **Validation** of the model defined in step 9.

The next subsections analyze briefly the purpose and the objectives of the model, the high-level requirements as well as the main dimensions of the model.

3.2   HERMES Scope and High-Level Requirements

The main objectives of HERMES address the purpose and scope of the model. They include the following:

Semantic Interoperability: HERMES should provide an ontological model to enable the exchange of information through different agents during a health emergency. Thus, a representative model of the Health Emergency Management is provided in order to support internal and cross-border usage scenarios.

Data Harmonization: HERMES should be used for data harmonization. Thus, the Semantic Model needs to covers the domains of the requisite areas of the Health Emergency Management in order to conceptualize the data that are imported from the various data resources.

In order to address the aforementioned objectives, the model needs to meet the following **high-level requirements**: (1) Representation of the **main concepts** involved in the Health Emergency Management: (a) Stakeholders and agents, (b) Resources, (c) Emergency events, (d) Interactions among the involved entities (stakeholders and agents), (2) Representation of **other domains** related to Health Emergency Management, (3) Support for **interoperability** among international stakeholders and multiple agents, (4) Support and **compatibility** with emergency management and health standards, (5) Support and **reusability** of existing vocabularies, thesauri etc. (6) Support for **emergency management data**, such as health data and logistics data.

The aforementioned high-level requirements provide a first insight of the main domains of knowledge that HERMES needs to cover and the relevant imported domain ontologies, the upper model of the ontology, the classifications and the data of the ontology, which are analyzed in the following subsections.

3.3   Semantic Model Dimensions

The requirements of HERMES map to different domains of discourse which belong to the area of Health Emergency Management, crisis management, health status, disasters, etc. For the purposes of the HERMES model, we have studied the available bibliography [22] and incorporated classes that are of interest for this ontology, as well as performed the appropriate mappings to code systems such as the WHO family of

International Classifications [44], the EDXL family of Standards [23]. Liu et al. [22] define a wide list of domain and ontologies related to emergency management. In order to meet the requirements of the semantic model we have limited the main semantic layers of Health Emergency Management to the following list (Table 1):

Table 1. Layers mapping to different domains of the HERMES model

Layers	Ontologies/classifications
People and stakeholders	FOAF, WAI
Infrastructure	OTN
Geography	Geo ontology
Meteorology	WeatherOntology
Health status	ICD-10, ICF, ICECI, ICHI
Event	DOLCE + DnSUltralite (DUL)
Roles	WAI ontology
Activity	PROV-O
Disasters	EM-DAT

The selection of the relevant ontologies was based on the requirements that were described in Sect. 3.2. Thus, attention was made on the selection of models and classifications that enhance the interoperability and are implemented using international standards. In the next paragraphs we describe briefly each ontology and classification that is imported into HERMES.

Friend-Of-A-Friend (FOAF) [12] is a project devoted to linking people and information using the Web. FOAF Core provides a vocabulary for human resources and agents. FOAF is imported into HERMES and is used in order to describe human individuals, agents and groups of agents using the classes foaf:Agent, foaf: Group, foaf:Organization, foaf:Person. WAI [40] extends FOAF by introducing the concepts of roles and profiles. WAI is also imported to provide a conceptualization of the hermes:Responders as a list of roles that an individual may take during a health emergency.

For the purpose of describing geospatial facts about regions, we incorporate Geo Ontology [45]. Also, the longitude and latitude vocabularies can be used to describe the location of a place where an incident happens.

Weather refers to the state of the environment over a short period of time, of temperature, precipitation and wind activity while climate refers to the average weather conditions over a long period of time. The Weather Ontology [41] provides a formal conceptual model of the weather domain. This ontology consists of several properties and classes related to meteorological concepts: humidity, precipitation, atmospheric pressure, storm, visibility and wind. The Weather Ontology is imported into HERMES in order to use the properties in relation to temperature, humidity and other weather variables.

OTN (Ontology of Transportation Networks) [25] focuses on transportation infrastructure and is a formal description of the Geographic Data Files (GDF) ontology.

OTN is imported to describe the transportation classes as they are expressed by the hermes:Transportaion class.

ICD-10 [17] is the 10th revision of the International Statistical Classification of Diseases and Related Health Problems (ICD), a medical classification list by the World Health Organization (WHO) [43]. It contains codes for diseases, signs and symptoms, abnormal findings, complaints, social circumstances, and external causes of injury or diseases. ICF ([18] is a classification of health and health-related domains. As the functioning and disability of an individual occurs in a context, ICF also includes a list of environmental factors. ICF is the WHO framework for measuring health and disability at both individual and population levels. ICECI (International Classification of External Causes of Injury) [19] is a free practical tool for classifying the circumstances in which injuries occur. Thus, it can be used in surveillance and research to support injury and trauma prevention and control efforts throughout the world. ICHI [20] is a classification for health interventions. A health intervention is an act performed for, with or on behalf of a person or population whose purpose is to assess, improve, maintain, promote or modify health, functioning or health conditions. ICD-10, ICF and ICECI provide a taxonomy of states of the health status to HERMES. ICD10, ICHI and ICF are used to provide input about the code lists of diseases, parameters of health status, injuries etc. and interventions of the data facet of the HERMES Ontology.

DOLCE + DnS Ultralite (DUL) ontology [26] provides a set of upper level concepts under which the hermes:HEE and other classes of the upper layer are listed.

The PROV Ontology (PROV-O) [32] expresses the PROV Data Model using the OWL2 Web Ontology Language (OWL2) [28]. It is used to interchange provenance information generated in different systems, under different contexts. PROV-O is imported into the HERMES Ontology to describe the hermes:Activity class.

The EM-DAT [9] is a disaster database which provides a classification of disasters. It distinguishes two generic disaster groups: natural and technological disasters. Each group covers different disaster main types, each having different disaster sub-types. EM-DAT classification is used in HERMES, since it provides the basic classes of the hermes:Natural categorization of the Hermes:HEE. Its utilization is explained in the following sections.

The aforementioned ontologies have been imported into HERMES in order to express various concepts of the HERMES Ontology and reuse the already existing knowledge in order to assure a cost-effective implementation of a high-quality semantic model [3]. These concepts are more generic concepts which belong in the aforementioned domain areas. Additionally, HERMES defines a set of entities (classes and instances), properties and relations oriented to Health Emergency Management in order to provide an integral conceptual model which captures the main actors and operations taking place during a health emergency.

3.4 HERMES Upper Model

HERMES provides an upper model which defines the main entities of the Health Emergency Management domain and their properties. This upper model is extended with a set of classifications, the vertical models. Each vertical model defines an hierarchy of entities and instances which further analyzes each entity of the upper model.

Finally, the model provides a data facet which includes the data of the semantic model. These three layers are presented into the following sections.

The upper model of the HERMES ontology should include the main concepts of the Health Emergency Management (stakeholders and agents, resources, emergency events, interactions among the involved entities) and at the same time, be compatible with various health emergency interoperability standards, as already stated in Sect. 3.2.

The HERMES Upper Model consists of four main concepts:

HEE (Health Emergency Event): The concept refers to the emergency events and incidents that take place and require response. It includes a classification of natural disasters, technological disasters, emergency incidents, the structural damages etc.

Person: The concept refers to the human individual. It contains the basic categories that describe a person in the context of a health emergency (health status, roles etc.)

Resource: The concept refers to any artifact that can be used to support or help in the response during a health emergency.

Activity: The concept refers to any activity that takes place by a health agency, a stakeholder etc. in order to reduce the impact of an emergency event.

The aforementioned entities and their relationships are presented in the Fig. 1 below:

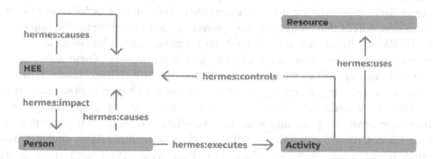

Fig. 1. HERMES upper model

HEE as Event. Health Emergency Management incidents include everyday incidents to disastrous situations. These incidents may require special arrangements, which may be qualitatively different than those of routine activities. Health Emergency Event (HEE) acts as a general concept, covering a wide variety of subcategories of events, based on different key defining properties (urgency, scale, extend, predictability etc.) The HEE entity is divided into Natural (which refers to natural disasters), and Human Factor (which refers to technological disasters which involve technology and the human factor). Both categorizations have adopted the EM-DAT classification. HERMES considers the HEE as an event, as it is met in real life. Thus, in order to describe efficiently the nature of the HEE entity, an upper class of the event entity is needed to interconnect with the HEE. As mentioned above, DUL provides a set of upper level concepts that can be the basis for easier interoperability among many middle and lower level ontologies. HERMES uses the dul:Event, as a superclass of hermes:HEE.

Person as Individual with a Role. The HERMES Person concept represents a single individual. A single individual may be affected by a HEE or/and may be involved in an activity in order to eliminate the impact of a HEE. Also, a Person may cause a HEE. Thus, this concept contains information concerning the health status of an individual as well as the roles that an individual may take during a health emergency. Based on these, a Person needs to be described as an individual who undertakes specific roles during an emergency and also maintains a specific health status. HERMES Ontology uses FOAF in order to describe Person as an individual. To model people and their groups, FOAF provides the classes `foaf:Agent`, `foaf:Person` and `foaf:Group`, which are used by the HERMES Ontology. WAI provides the class `wai:Role` to describe the role that a person may play. It refers only to human individuals and it is imported into HERMES. We also feature a data type property that associates a person/affected person with a numeric ID (not a name/surname) – it only identifies a person in an emergency event that has occurred. HERMES defines `hermes:Person` as equivalent class to `foaf:Agent` which describes an agent (e.g. person, group, software or physical artifact). Also, the `hermes:Human` which is a subclass of `hermes:Person` is defined as an equivalent class of `foaf:Person`, since both refer to human individuals

Resource. The HERMES Resource concept refers to anything that is used to support or help in the response during a health emergency. This concept includes any material and human resources that an agency may provide in order to eliminate the impact of a HEE. HERMES Resources are divided into various categories such as material equipment, human resources, infrastructure and organizations. These subcategories cover a wide area of entities which need to be described by various classes. HERMES Ontology uses `dul:Physical_artifact` in order to conceptualize material and `foaf:Group` in order to describe the human resources as a specific group of responders in emergency management i.e. Ambulance service, civil protection, etc. HERMRES describes the buildings with the class `otn:Building` and the transportation infrastructure with the class `otn:Feature`. `otn:Building` is also associated with `geo:SpatialThing` via `equivalentClass`. Organizations are described by the Organization ontology.

Activity. The HERMES Activity regards any action that takes place in order to reduce the impact of a HEE event. Activity is associated with the PROV-O. More specifically, `hermes:Activity` is associated `withprov:Activity` (via an equivalentClassobject) which describes an activity that occurs over a period of time and acts upon or with entities.

Upper Model Object Properties. `hermes:impact` (domain: HEE, range: HERMESPerson) defines the impact that a HEE may have on a group of people. A HEE has an effect and influences a Person in a specific way. Moreover, a `Person` may cause a HEE by a specific action. i.e. a `Person` may cause a wild fire. Also, a HEE may cause another HEE i.e. the collapse of a building may cause a fire in the building. This relation is captured by `hermes:causes` (domain: union of HERMESPerson and HEE, range: HEE). Also, a `Person` (or a group of people) under specific roles (i.e. rescue team coordinator) executes an `Activity` which controls the range of a HEE. This is represented by the property hermes:controls (domain: HEEActivity, range: HEE). hermes:uses (domain: HEEActivity, range: HEEResource) expresses the state where an Activity uses a Resource in order to control the range of a HEE. Finally, a Person (or a group of people) executes an Activity in order to respond to a HEE. This is represented by hermes:executes property (domain: HEEPerson, range: HEEActivity).

3.5   Reference Semantic Model Vertical Modules

The Vertical Modules of the HERMES model consist of a number of classifications which further analyze the concepts of the Upper Model. These classifications have been defined based on the study of state-of-the-art bibliography results and emergency management interoperability standards forming a taxonomy of classes using the rdfs:subClassOf property. In the current section, we present the main classifications which derive from the concepts of the Upper Model.

HEE Classification. The main subcategories of the HEE classification include natural and human factor disasters. The classification was based on the EM-DAT classification of disasters [9]. Natural disasters are disastrous incidents of Biological, Geophysical, Meteorological, Climatological, Biological, Hydrological nature. The main subcategories of the Human Factor disasters are divided in disasters happening in industry, in transportation, as well as in disastrous incidents that can take place in various domains and areas, such as an explosion, a fire etc.

Person Classification. The Person classification refers to the human individuals and classifies them based on their way that they are involved into a health emergency. This categorization results into two main categories: affected and responders. In order to express the state where a responder is simultaneously an affected person and vice versa the FOAF and WAI vocabulary are also used, besides the rdfs:subClassOf property that is used for the construction of the classifications.

Resources Classification. Resources classification includes the available resources that can be used during an activity executed by the responders. These resources include material equipment, as well as, human resources such as rescue organizations, stakeholders etc. The human resources can also be identified by the Person class as a group of individuals under a specific role. In HERMES, the human resources are treated as Resource since they are involved as resources in a specific activity to eliminate the consequences of a disaster. Moreover, they participate in an emergency under a specific activity which imposes their presence on the field. Further object properties can be utilized to express this additional relationship between the classes.

Activities Classification. The Activities classification includes any action that takes place in order to reduce the impact of a HEE event. These activities include communication activities, management of the survivors of a HEE, medical and rescue services. A representative example of the Activities in HERMES, is the Rescue services that can be provided by the qualified agents. Rescue services include triage, psychological support, victim retraction, transportation to medical facilities field etc.

3.6   HERMES Data Properties and Code Lists

In this section we describe the data facet of HERMES which includes the data properties and other code lists that are imported into the ontology or created from scratch. The data facet constitutes the most detailed layer of the ontology which includes various lists with specific values (apart from data type properties) such as resources (e.g. equipment, vehicles etc.) or lists with diseases etc. For our purposes these lists are considered as controlled vocabularies and are described by the SKOS [37].

The data facet of HERMES includes lists such as resources (e.g. equipment, vehicles etc.) or lists with diseases, symptoms, injuries, treatments, assets, health state indicators, weather data etc. In the next paragraphs we will present briefly some of the code lists of HERMES as well as some of the data properties.

Spatiotemporal Dimensions. For the purpose of describing geospatial facts about regions, we have decided to incorporate Geo Ontology [45]. The geographical vocabularies are useful for encoding geospatial data in crisis information systems. For example, the longitude latitude data type properties can be used to describe the position of a place where an incident happens.

Another important aspect of the ontology is the evolution of events and their temporal attributes. HERMES has decided to follow a simple approach by incorporating a class that associates an event with a timestamp reference (class TimeSlice). HERMESPerson can impact or cause an Event associated with a particular reference in time with the object property "hasTimeSlice". With this approach we achieve a number of goals – to begin with, we allow events and people to be associated with time. More importantly, by introducing the aspect of time to the main classes of the ontology we allow all actions and event occurred to be described as stories in a chronological manner.

EDXL Family Alignment. The data facet of the Semantic Model is extended to import data for the EDXL family of protocols. In this way, the model is aligned with a cross-domain interoperability standards in Incident Management. In the current section a sample of the representation of the EDXL data is provided. More specifically, the OWL version of the main aspects of the EDXL-HAVE and the EDXL-TEP is provided as class and properties definitions. The EDXL-HAVE support serves interoperability between the various external database systems and the incident management platforms for the exchange of information about the bed status in the hospitals. The EDXL-TEP support serves the exchange of information between the various agencies about the health status of the injured people on the field. The namespace of the HERMESEDXL owl ontology is defined as HERMESEDXL. The ontology also imports the SKOS vocabulary in order to represent the various codelists that are included into the EDXL-HAVE and EDXL-TEP.

The EDXL-HAVE OWL Schema and Datatype Properties. The core class of the EDXL-HAVE owl schema is the HERMESEDXL:HospitalStatus which is the top level container element for reporting status of any number of hospitals. The main information about the bed availability (the number of available beds in each unit in each hospital) is represented by the HERMESEDXL:HospitalBedCapacityStatus and especially the subclasses HERMESEDXL:BedType and HERMESEDXL:Capacity which are two codelists expressing the various bed types (pediatrics, nursery beds, beds in operating rooms etc.) and their current capacity (available, not available) respectively in SKOS vocabulary.

The EDXL-TEP OWL Schema and Datatype Properties. The core class of the EDXL-TEP owl schema is the HERMESEDXL:Patient which is the top level container element for reporting the health status of a patient. The schema contains classes which represent the symptoms of the patient on the field as well as his/her location and transportation, such as the HERMESEDXL:patientCare and HERMESEDXL:patientTransfer. These classes can be used for the interoperability with incident management platforms that are used on the field. Both classes are aligned with the EDXL-TEP message schema and also extended with classes from the ICD10 and ICF classifications.

4   Data Harmonization and Interoperability

As stated in Sect. 2, our data harmonization approach uses the HERMES model in order to provide a semantically homogenized view of the multidisciplinary data. It uses D2RQ server, since it supports a wide range of database management systems and supports RDF Virtual views of the data using external ontologies. Additionally, D2RQ server was chosen instead of Ontop. another top candidate for this implementation, since it supports SPARQL 1.1 while Ontop supports SPARQL 1.0. The initial mappings are extended with mappings based on the HERMES model in order to provide interoperability between the various databases of agencies and emergency management systems that participate during an emergency. The process includes the following steps: **(1)** Provide a real-time RDF view of the data stored in external databases and other data sources, based on a specific mapping file using the HERMES model, **(2)** Provide access to RDF data views via SPARQL endpoint, **(3)** Execute SPARQL queries to RDF data and process the results, if necessary, **(4)** Handle and serve the requests for data. The relevant architecture of the harmonization process is the following (Fig. 2):

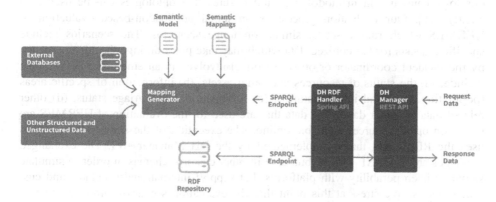

Fig. 2. Data harmonization process relevant architecture

The Mapping Generator is responsible for the mapping of data of various data sources (databases, files, rdf repositories etc.) to RDF classes, based on the HERMES model. Apart from relational data, data from other resources have been processed and cleaned (if needed) and stored as relational data. The mapping is implemented using D2RQ Mapping Language. An initial mapping is implemented using D2RQ while additional mappings are generated using a set of rules based on HERMES. These rules are periodically updated in case new data sources are imported or updates on the database schema take place. The result is a set of RDF triples which provides a harmonized view of the data. The data is stored into an RDF repository accessed through a SPARQL endpoint. Based on the fact that the Mapping Generator makes use of a D2RQ Server, a second SPARQL endpoint is provided by the D2RQ Server for the RDF triples of the relational data.

The DH RDF Handler (Data Harmonization RDF Handler) is an API which handles the requests for data. Upon data request, the component receives a set of parameters and generates a respective SPARQL query which is executed to the next layer (Mapping Generator and RDF repository). The RDF triples of the response are also processed by the DH RDF Handler and are forwarded to the DH Manager in order to be consumed by external applications (such as incident management platforms or other software platforms used during a health emergency).

The DH Manager (Data Harmonization Manager) is responsible for receiving, managing and sending data from and to external applications used in Health Emergency Management. The various requests for a harmonized view of data may include semantic queries such as: hospitals, resources, geographic areas, meteorological data, patient data etc. DH Manager also supports connection with message brokers and also provides a REST API for message exchange. Various formats of the response data are also supported for smooth integration with the external systems.

5   Evaluation and Future Work

Concerning ontology evaluation, a number of strategies are followed based on specific criteria. As stated in [6] application-based evaluation is widely adopted by a number of ontology construction methodologies and ensures that ontologies can be used efficiently [16]. Our evaluation process is an initial application-based evaluation of HERMES which runs a set of simulation usage scenarios. The scenarios include specific requests for harmonized data which may take place during a health emergency by the incident coordinator or other personnel involved in an emergency. These data include: (a) the status of resources and other assets, (b) information of specific areas (population & critical infrastructures), (c) information of the triage status, (d) other related data (weather data). The data that are used for the evaluation of HERMES are based on open resources available online. The execution of the simulation scenarios uses the REST API that is implemented by the DH Manager API. The exchanged messages are in EDXL format, but, also in other custom schemas in order to simulate semantic interoperability with platforms that support international standards and custom schemas. We stress at this point that the evaluation scenarios aim at evaluating

HERMES and the results of the harmonization process, and not to simulate a real emergency incident. The simulation scenarios are defined as follows:

S1. **Bed status:** The incident coordinator requests the current bed status in the various departments of nearby hospitals in order to decide the dispatching of the injured persons. The aforementioned scenario can take place for all the assets that are available in hospitals or ambulances for patient treatment and assist decision making. We assume that the information is gathered using the EDXL-HAVE message schema as well as other custom schemas.

S2. **Information of specific areas:** The incident coordinator highlights the affected area on a map provided from an incident management platform. Specific information of the highlighted area is provided for decision making. The information includes the population of the affected area and critical infrastructures of high priority.

S3. **Triage status:** The incident coordinator is updated with the current status of the injured people on the field and monitor their transfer to hospitals. We assume that the information is gathered from various incident management mobile units which exchange messages using EDXL-TEP and custom message schemas.

S4. **Other data:** The incident coordinator requests the current weather conditions and the forecasted weather conditions of an area for decision making. This scenario aims at simulating semantic interoperability for data semantically belonging to other generic domains yet related and complementary to Health Emergency Management.

The following table summarizes the aforementioned evaluation scenarios (Table 2).

The first results are optimistic about the correctness of the model. In all scenarios the imported data were smoothly harmonized and the response data were enriched as aimed. For example, in the case of scenarios S2 and S3 the incident data were extended with additional information that is not provided by the EDXL standard such as weather information, population and other information of specific areas. Nevertheless, adjustments of the semantic mappings that were used for the harmonization process took place. Also, the model needs to be improved, especially, on how the actors are related with a role. Performance improvements tasks need to take place either by optimizing the SPARQL queries or tuning the mapping between HERMES and the relational data. Also, indexing optimization techniques can be applied to the relational databases leading to better performance of the D2RQ Server.

Future steps about HERMES include the alignment of the model with more health emergency interoperability standards and the enrichment of the data facet with more code lists (vehicles, means of transport, assets, agencies per country). Moreover, the model could be improved by importing also other ontologies such as the Persona Data Model [29] and updating and fine tuning the relationships between the classes. The model will also be published as soon as it is considered final. Concerning the Data Harmonization Process, Linked Data [21] integration is also foreseen. More specifically, the RDF data provided by the Mapping Generator can be linked to other Linked Data resources based on specific criteria. Currently a set of Linked Data resources can be used related with more generic domains such as geographical data, POIs and population of areas. More study needs to be done in order to identify Linked Data

Table 2. Evaluation scenarios

Id	Data type	Data sources
S1	Open data	NHS England: bed availability and occupancy data – day only[a], bed availability and occupancy data – overnight[b] Eurostat: hospital beds[c] Open government data portal Austria: hospitals[d] Open data portal Ireland: acute hospital services[e], District/community extended hospitals and care[f]
S2	Open data, simulation data	Population data for UK, AT, IR, GR from geonames[g] and DBPedia[h]. For population per census blocks simulation data were used. Simulation data were created for critical infrastructure of specific areas
S3	Simulation data	A set of injured and patient profiles was created with different health status variables. The selection of the variables was based on the ICD-10 and ICF classification. The involved resources were also simulated
S4	Open data	Weather data were gathered from OpenWeatherMap[i] and were stored in a relational database for a number of regions

[a]https://www.england.nhs.uk/statistics/statistical-work-areas/bed-availability-and-occupancy/bed-data-day-only/
[b]https://www.england.nhs.uk/statistics/statistical-work-areas/bed-availability-and-occupancy/bed-data-overnight/
[c]https://data.europa.eu/euodp/data/dataset/sKm7xBoTFapXrD33EWRhcg
[d]https://www.europeandataportal.eu/data/en/dataset/stadt-linz_krankenanstalten
[e]https://www.europeandataportal.eu/data/en/dataset/acute-hospital-services
[f]https://www.europeandataportal.eu/data/en/dataset/districtcommunity-hospitals-and-extended-cares
[g]http://download.geonames.org/export/dump/
[h]http://downloads.dbpedia.org/2016-10/
[i]https://openweathermap.org/api

sources oriented to Health Emergency Management. Additionally, Ontop could be used instead of D2RQ in order to achieve better performance and use the R2RML W3C standard making the mappings more interoperable and reusable. Finally, a more extended evaluation will take place involving also ontology evaluation tools such as OOPS [30].

6   Conclusions

HERMES provides an ontological representation of the Health Emergency Management domain in order to provide a common reference schema for data harmonization and semantic interoperability between the various stakeholders during a health emergency. Currently, semantic models for Health Emergency Management rely mainly on interoperability standards which ensure compatibility of the exchanged messages between the various incident management platforms. HERMES provides an integral ontology which is aligned with the interoperability standards and in the same time covers the wide spectrum of the domain of health emergency extending entities such as the emergency event, health status, resources and their roles and importing entities such as meteorology, infrastructure, geography. The model provides a novel upper model and enhances each entity with a set of classifications and a data facet based on bibliography and other health standards. In this way semantic interoperability is achieved between the stakeholders regardless the schema of the data that they use. A data harmonization procedure is implemented using semantic mappings between the schema of the data and HERMES. In this way, all data is provided and queried under a common schema. The evaluation of HERMES focused on the efficient use of the model for data harmonization and semantic interoperability. The results of the evaluation process prove the correct approach of the model since all the simulation data were smoothly harmonized. Moreover, incident management data were extended with additional information that is not provided by the EDXL standard such as weather information, population and other information of specific areas. More research needs to take place for the extension of HERMES with health emergency interoperability standards and the enrichment of the data facet with more code lists. Concerning the Data Harmonization Process, the advantages of the Linked Data integration need to be taken under consideration.

References

1. Antoniou, G., Van Harmelen, F.: A Semantic Web Primer. MIT press, Cambridge (2004)
2. Bertelsen, O.W., Bodker, S.: Activity theory. In: Caroll, J.M. (ed.) HCI Models Theories, and Frameworks: Toward A Multidisciplinary Science, pp. 291–324. Morgan Kaufmann, San Francisco (2003)
3. Bontas, E.P., Mochol, M., Tolksdorf, R.: Case studies on ontology reuse. In: Proceedings of the IKNOW 2005, International Conference on Knowledge Management, vol. 74, p. 345 (2005)
4. Chen, R., Sharman, R., Chakravarti, N., Rao, H.R., Upadhyaya, S.J.: Emergency response information system interoperability: development of chemical incident response data model. J. Assoc. Inf. Syst. 9(3) (2008)
5. Corcho, O., Fernández-López, M., Gómez-Pérez, A., López-Cima, A.: Building legal ontologies with METHONTOLOGY and WebODE. In: Benjamins, V.R., Casanovas, P., Breuker, J., Gangemi, A. (eds.) Law and the Semantic Web. LNCS (LNAI), vol. 3369, pp. 142–157. Springer, Heidelberg (2005). https://doi.org/10.1007/978-3-540-32253-5_9
6. Degbelo, A.: A snapshot of ontology evaluation criteria and strategies. In: Proceedings of Semantics 2017, Amsterdam, Netherlands, September 2017
7. Declaring RDF Views of SQL Data. https://www.w3.org/2007/03/RdfRDB/papers/erling.html. Accessed 05 July 2018
8. D2RQ: Accessing Relational Databases as Virtual RDF Graphs. http://d2rq.org/. Accessed 05 July 2018
9. EM-DAT: The International Disaster Database. https://www.emdat.be/index.php. Accessed 01 July 2018
10. Fan, Z., Zlatanova, S.: Exploring ontology potential in emergency management. In: Proceedings of the Gi4DM Conference—Geomatics for Disaster Management, Torino, Italy (2010)

11. Fernández-López, M., Gómez-Pérez, A., Juristo, N.: Methontology: from ontological art towards ontological engineering. In: Proceedings of the Symposium on Ontological Engineering of AAAI (1997)
12. FOAF Vocabulary Specification 0.99. http://xmlns.com/foaf/spec/. Accessed 14 July 2018
13. Gençtürk, M., Evci, E., Guney, A., Kabak, Y., Erturkmen, G.B.L.: Achieving semantic interoperability in emergency management domain. In: Hřebíček, J., Denzer, R., Schimak, G., Pitner, T. (eds.) ISESS 2017. IAICT, vol. 507, pp. 279–289. Springer, Cham (2017). https://doi.org/10.1007/978-3-319-89935-0_23
14. Haghighi, P.D., Burstein, F., Zaslavsky, A., Arbon, P.: Development and evaluation of ontology for intelligent decision support in medical emergency management for mass gatherings. Dec. Supp. Syst. **54**, 1192–1204 (2013)
15. Health Care and Life Science (HCLS) Linked Data Guide. https://www.w3.org/2001/sw/hcls/notes/hcls-rdf-guide/. Accessed 05 July 2018
16. Hoehndorf, R., Dumontier, M., Gkoutos, G.: Evaluation of research in biomedical ontologies. Brief. Bioinform. **14**, 696–712 (2013)
17. ICD-10 classification browser, Version: 2016. http://apps.who.int/classifications/icd10/browse/2016/en
18. ICF classification browser. http://apps.who.int/classifications/icfbrowser/
19. ICECI. http://www.who.int/classifications/icd/adaptations/iceci/en/
20. ICHI classification browser. https://mitel.dimi.uniud.it/ichi/
21. Linked data – connect distributed data across the web. http://linkeddata.org/
22. Liu, S., Shaw, D., Brewster, C.: Ontologies for crisis management: a review of state of the art in ontology design and usability, networks. In: Proceedings of the Information Systems for Crisis Response and Management conference, ISCRAM 2013 (2013)
23. OASIS Emergency Management TC. https://www.oasis-open.org/committees/tc_home.php?wg_abbrev=emergency. Accessed 26 June 2018
24. OGC Sensor Web Enablement (SWE). http://www.opengeospatial.org/ogc/markets-technologies/swe. Accessed 12 July 2018
25. Ontology of Transportation Networks. https://pdfs.semanticscholar.org/889d/4f862729d17b1d89f6eb92d67828143de924.pdf
26. Ontology: DOLCE + DnS Ultralite. http://ontologydesignpatterns.org/wiki/Ontology:DOLCE+DnS_Ultralite. Accessed 01 June 2018
27. Ontop. http://ontop.inf.unibz.it/. Accessed 05 July 2018
28. OWL 2. https://www.w3.org/TR/owl2-overview/. Accessed 27 June 2018
29. Persona Data Model 2.0. https://wiki.eclipse.org/Persona_Data_Model_2.0. Accessed 28 August 2018
30. Poveda-Villalón, M., Gómez-Pérez, A., Suárez-Figueroa, M.C.: Oops!(ontology pitfall scanner!): an on-line tool for ontology evaluation. Int. J. Semant. Web Inf. Syst. (IJSWIS) **10** (2), 7–34 (2014)
31. Protégé. https://protege.stanford.edu/. Accessed 01 June 2018
32. PROV-O. https://www.w3.org/TR/prov-o/. Accessed 27 June 2018
33. R2RML: RDB to RDF Mapping Language. https://www.w3.org/TR/r2rml/. Accessed 05 July 2018
34. Rauner, M.S., et al.: An advanced decision support system for European disaster management: the feature of the skills taxonomy. Cent. Eur. J. Oper. Res. **26**(2), 485–530 (2018)
35. SIOC Core Ontology Specification. http://rdfs.org/sioc/spec/. Accessed 28 June 2018
36. Sheth, A.: Changing focus on interoperability in information systems: from system, syntax, structure to semantics. In: Goodchild, M., Egenhofer, M., Fegeas, R., Kottman, C. (eds.) Interoperating Geographic Information Systems. Kluwer (1998)

37. SKOS Simple Knowledge Organization System. https://www.w3.org/TR/2009/REC-skos-reference-20090818/. Accessed 04 July 2018
38. UNECE: Trade facilitation implementation guide, data harmonization. http://tfig.unece.org/contents/data-harmonization.htm
39. Wache, H., et al.: Ontology-based integration of information a survey of existing approaches. CiteSeerX:10.1.1.142.4390 (2001)
40. WAI Vocabulary Specification. http://vocab.ctic.es/wai/wai.html. Accessed 28 August 2018
41. WeatherOntology.   https://www.auto.tuwien.ac.at/downloads/thinkhome/ontology/WeatherOntology.owl. Accessed 04 July 2018
42. Web Ontology Language (OWL). https://www.w3.org/OWL/. Accessed 11 July 2018
43. World Health Organization. http://www.who.int/about-us. Accessed 04 July 2018
44. World Health Organization Classifications. http://www.who.int/classifications/en/. Accessed 04 July 2018
45. W3C Semantic Web Interest Group: Basic Geo (WGS84 lat/long) Vocabulary. https://www.w3.org/2003/01/geo/. Accessed 04 July 2018

Explanation of Action Plans Through Ontologies

Ivan Gocev[1,2]([✉]), Stephan Grimm[1], and Thomas A. Runkler[1,2]

[1] Siemens AG Corporate Technology, 81739 Munich, Germany
{ivan.gocev,stephan.grimm,thomas.runkler}@siemens.com
[2] Technical University of Munich, 85748 Garching, Germany

Abstract. In recent years, more and more AI systems have been
included in various aspects of human life, forming human-machine partnership and collaboration. The term Digital Companion can be referred
to the embodiment of AI as human's co-worker. Explanations why the
AI arrived at specific decisions will be highly beneficial in enabling AI
to operate more robustly, clarifying to the user why the AI brought certain choices, and significantly increase the trust between humans and AI.
A number of symbolic planners exist, which use heuristic search methods to come up with a sequence of actions to reach a certain goal. So
far the explanations to why a planner follows certain decision making
series are mostly embedded within the planner's operating style, composing so called glass box explanations. The integration of AI Planning
(using PDDL) and Ontologies (using OWL) gives the possibility to use
reasoning and generate explanations why, subsequently why-not, certain
actions were considered by the AI planner, without relying on the planner's functionality. An extended knowledge base is proportional to aiding
the construct of more precise clarifications of the decision making process of the planner. In this paper we present a general architecture for
black box plan explanations independent of the nature of the planner and
illustrate the approach of integrating PDDL and OWL, as well as using
justifications in ontologies to explain why a planner has taken certain
actions.

Keywords: PDDL · Ontologies · OWL · AI planning
Plan explanation

1 Introduction

In the application of Artificial Intelligence (AI) systems, explanation features
play a crucial role to establish trust and transparency in the human interaction
with increasingly autonomous computer systems. The phrase Explainable AI
points to AI systems that are capable of providing insights as to why they took
certain decisions, making their behavior transparent to a human user. Also for AI
planning, a goal-driven technique to derive an action plan for a planning problem
by means of symbolic knowledge representation, explanation is highly relevant:

© Springer Nature Switzerland AG 2018
H. Panetto et al. (Eds.): OTM 2018 Conferences, LNCS 11230, pp. 386–403, 2018.
https://doi.org/10.1007/978-3-030-02671-4_24

the user wants to know why an action has been included in a plan at a specific situation and why others have not. Modern planning systems are typically based on the planning domain definition language (PDDL), language for formulating planning problems in a logics-based formalism for action knowledge, which serves as a common ground for functionalities offered by specific planning systems. However, PDDL abstracts from a planner's specific features and provides no means for explanation mechanisms, even if an underlying planner would. On the other hand, ontologies provide a means to formalize domain vocabularies that are well suited for expressing explanations of system behavior well-understandable to users of that domain. In fact, for ontologies expressed in the Web Ontology Language (OWL), mechanisms for explanation are available that compute so called justifications for inferences drawn from domain ontologies by means of automated reasoning. It seems natural to combine AI planning with this form of ontology reasoning for deriving explanations for a planner's behavior in terms of logically formalized domain vocabularies familiar to the user.

A specific industrial application scenario that motivates this combination of technologies is the flexible manufacturing envisioned in Industry 4.0 smart factory environments. There, planning systems can be utilized to have autonomous production machines automatically derive sequences of production steps that are required to manufacture a previously unseen product, for which the production machinery has not been specifically programmed, as it would be in conventional factories. For example, imagine an assembly robot that derives the required sequence of assembly actions from the specification of a target product by means of goal-driven planning. Especially in such highly automated manufacturing scenarios, it is important to give a human operator the means to maintain trust and control over the system. At any point, the operators might want to know why the robot is taking a specific assembly action or includes a specific material and why not others, so that they have transparency over the production process and can possibly intervene.

To address transparency through AI explanation in such scenarios, we propose a (black-box) planning explanation approach that combines PDDL-based planner systems with OWL ontologies and justification reasoning. The idea behind the approach is to utilize an ontological domain vocabulary for formulating planning problems and for expressing resulting explanations in a user-understandable form. By means of a mapping between PDDL and OWL, we transform action planning knowledge expressed in OWL ontologies to PDDL as a target formalism for planning. After a planner came up with a solution in form of an action plan, we backward-transform the instantiated actions from the plan into the original vocabulary by means of the inverse mapping. Based on the resulting action plan ontology, we can then compute OWL justifications for the preconditions of actions being true in the plan, which give the user a rationale why a certain action could be applied at that point, and thus, why it has been included in the planner. We call this approach black-box because it does not rely on any internal computation of a specific planner but considers it as a black box, only using the OWL-PDDL mapping as a bridge between the two worlds. Thus, explanations can be provided for any planner that conforms to the PDDL language.

The contributions of the paper comprise:

- a mapping between OWL and PDDL that can be used for transforming action knowledge formalized in OWL into actual PDDL planning domain and problem specifications to be processed by a planner,
- a mechanism for evolving state representations in OWL ontologies to a desired target state for explanation, which mimics part of a planner's internal computation for applying actions as a basis for also providing explanations for intermediate states,
- a mechanism for deriving explanations for actions from any point in an action plan by means of computing OWL justifications for the respective action's pre-conditions being true, which give the user transparency on why the action has been applied at this stage in form of a relevant chain of reasoning.

This paper is organized in 6 Sections. After the introduction and preliminaries in Sects. 1 and 2 respectively, the overall black-box planning approach is introduced together with a use case scenario from the robotics assembly domain by means of a PDDL example in Sect. 3. Section 4 proposes the PDDL-OWL mapping to capture action knowledge in OWL domain ontologies. Continuing in Sect. 5, the mechanism for extracting explanations from transformed action plans by means of OWL justification reasoning is described. In the final Section a conclusing is given of the presented concept, as well as work in progress and future work.

2   Preliminaries

In this section some basic notions around PDDL and OWL are introduced, as well as related and state of the art work in this topic.

2.1   Planning Domain Definition Language

The Planning Domain Definition Language (PDDL) is a standard language for modeling a domain and problem of some nature. They are then parsed onto an AI planner to use the knowledge designed in that domain and generate a sequence of steps to reach a certain goal. PDDL is divided into two specifications:

- **Domain** - consists of the knowledge for the elements in the environment that the planner can interact with; concepts, roles,
- **Problem** - presents the initial (starting) conditions in which the objects in the environment are, and goal conditions the planner needs to reach.

Both, the domain and problem have specialized structures. The basic structures of the PDDL **domain** are:

- **Types** - concepts which can be recognized in the environment,
- **Predicates** - roles - n-ary statements that represent the condition in which an object is, and interaction with other concepts,

- **Actions** - functions which model a real fact or process of performing something. They are composed of three parts:
  - **Parameters** - these are resembling variables which an action is using to perform a task,
  - **Precondition** - an expression of predicates that are conditions of the action's parameters that need to be met in order to execute the action,
  - **Effect** - an expression of predicates that resemble the conditions of the action's parameters after the action has been applied.

The **problem** specifications consists of:

- **Objects** - individuals which instantiate the types of objects in the domain,
- **Initial conditions** - a conjunction of predicates characterizing the starting states of all individuals in the domain,
- **Goal conditions** - a conjunction of predicates characterizing the final states in which all of the individuals in the domain must be found at.

In Sect. 3 a more thorough explanation through a concrete example will be given of the separate parts of PDDL.

2.2 OWL and Description Logic

As mentioned in Sect. 1, the language used for representing the domain is the Web Ontology Language (OWL) [3]. The Web Ontology Language is based on Description Logic (DL) formalism [4], which defines an ontology as a set of axioms that describe either terminological (T-Box) or assertive (A-Box) knowledge.

Inference in OWL is built upon logical consequence following the axioms that define the ontology. The notation:

$$O \models \alpha \tag{1}$$

states that an axiom α is entailed by the ontology O, where

$$O \models \{\alpha_1, \alpha_2, \ldots, \alpha_n\} \tag{2}$$

entails a set of axioms.

The assertive (A-Box) knowledge of the ontology is extremely important for the methods presented in this paper. It is closely connected to PDDL, more specifically the initial/current state of the domain, and the evolution of the states in which the entities that exist in the environment are, and interact in the same settings where the planner operates. This will be discussed in more detail in Sect. 4, in which the integration between PDDL and OWL is described.

2.3 Justifications

A minimal subset of an ontology that supports a given entailment is defined as a **justification**, as given in [5].

Definition 1. *Given an ontology O and an axiom α with $O \models \alpha$, a set of axioms J is a justification for α in O if $J \subseteq O$, $J \models \alpha$ and there is no set J' such that $J' \subset J$ and $J' \models \alpha$.*

Justifications are the final component of the whole concept shown in Fig. 1. This method is used to generate explanations of why, subsequently why-not, the planner has chosen certain actions to execute or not. Note that the algorithms presented in Sect. 5 are constructed for why explanations. The why-not explanations are a part of future work.

2.4   Related Work

Recently in [6] several important questions are covered when it comes to explanation of action plans. Mainly, they ask about the causality of the processes and the preservation of said causality. These are the questions we focus answering, by means of the knowledge that the planner uses. They also tackle the generation of explanations as to why certain actions were not included in the plan, how would they alternate the plan, and the different outcomes from that. Questions such: "Why a certain action is not a part of the plan?", and "Why would I need to replan?" are a part of our future work, where a more concrete planner simulation is needed, also giving the possibility to consider different actions, and simulate different plans. In this paper we propose a different approach, in which the planner is seen as a black box, and the explanations are based only on the terminological and instantiated knowledge it uses.

Various works on connecting ontologies and AI planning base their mapping of the planner's knowledge domain to certain ontology concepts, as seen in [7] and [8]. Mostly these mappings are defined for a strict set of rules and implemented in different real world settings. The mapping of atomic concepts presented in this paper is similar to [8], with extension of the modeling of the representation of PDDL actions within ontologies, and the realization of the environment state and its usage in the methods presented in this paper.

In [9], an examination is carried on semantic reasoning supporting industrial tasks, as well as a comparative analysis is given on how state-of-the-art systems benefit from effective use of knowledge.

The combination of planning techniques with the expressiveness of knowledge representation is presented in [10]. The idea to connect describing planning knowledge in Description Logic, and reason about the logical definitions of the expressed concepts, is powerfull working in domains that are knowledge-rich.

3   Modeling of a Robot Assembly Planning Problem in PDDL

The general idea of the approach in this paper is shown in Fig. 1. The goal is to embed both languages and expand the potential to involve reasoning and generate explanations on any generated plan, by having the knowledge of the

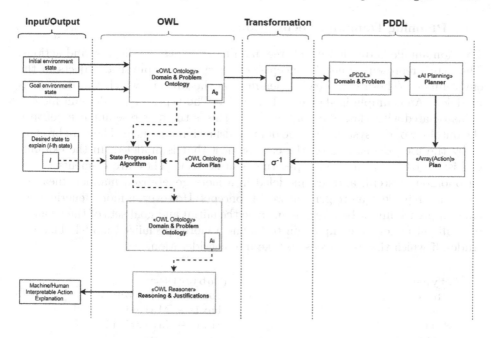

Fig. 1. Block scheme of the concept.

planner's domain modeled in the ontology. The concept consists of three basic parts: the representation of action knowledge in **OWL** ontologies, a mapping between OWL and PDDL used for **transformation** between these formalisms, and the representation of action knowledge in **PDDL**. The ontology part is responsible for representing and reasoning over the knowledge the planner uses. The transformation between OWL and PDDL is done for a finite set of methods and expressions in both languages. This is a mapping between concepts in both languages, which will be explained in detail in Sect. 4. Mainly, the approach orbits around the modeled knowledge that the AI planner uses and generates a sequence of actions that can be executed to reach a certain goal starting from a defined initial state (shown in the Input/Output part in Fig. 1), and then reason using the instantiated actions as an input to generate justifications as to why those actions are a part of the constructed plan.

The Planning Domain Definition Language (PDDL) is a form of programming language in Artificial Intelligence (AI) Systems suitable for solving decision-making problems. Having the right representation of the problem, and the tools that can be used, is crucial to successfully selecting a correct sequence of actions that the system needs to execute in order to reach a certain goal. The basic constituents of a planning specification in PDDL are the following:

- Domain - a set of requirements, types, predicates, and actions, all that are used for constructing a plan for reaching the goal,
- Problem - a set of environment objects, initial conditions, and an end goal.

3.1   Planning Domain Specifications

The domain file is divided into three main parts: types, predicates, and actions. The types represent general concepts, or more specific physical objects in the environment. These can vary, depending on the area in which the domain is modeled. An example is shown in Listing 1.1. The types in the domain file can be associated with classes in an Ontology. This is the first resemblance between the ontology of the system and the domain definition language. They are brought in by the user, depending on the environment that is modeled. In the example in Listing 1.1, there are six types that can be seen. They are elements of the autonomous system, and are modeled in a more generalized manner, meaning that they represent more general world concepts. However, a more generic modeling approach might be a problem, since the initial and goal sets of the problem file will get larger, in comparison to having a more specialized model. This is a trade-off which the user needs to take into consideration.

```
(: types                          (: objects
  Object                            robot1 − Resource
  Tool                              box1 − Material
  Part                              lid1 − Material)
  Material
  Resource
  Location )
```

Listing 1.1. Model of the hierarchical structure of PDDL types (left) and their instantiated versions (objects) (right).

The objects, also shown in Listing 1.1 in the environment are a specialized set of the types in the domain file. They are physical objects in the environment that are a subclass of their general type in the world. Listing 1.1 (right) shows how the objects are modeled in the problem file.

The second part of the domain file represents the predicates in the domain. The predicates resemble the connections between the objects in the domain. This can be linked to the object properties of the ontology classes, also known as **roles**. By definition the predicates represent relations between certain entities. Listing 1.2 shows how are the predicates modeled in the domain definition language.

```
(: predicates
  (isConnectedTo ?obj1 − Object ?obj2 − Object)
  (isAvailable ?obj1 − Object)
  (isPicked ?robot − Resourse ?lid − Material))
```

Listing 1.2. Example of PDDL predicates.

The **predicates** are closely related to the types (or objects) in the domain. They represent a certain state of an entity or combination of different ones in the domain. The parameters of the predicates are defined as certain types. Object states can be explained through one or more logical combinations of predicates.

The user can introduce any of them, and can connect the objects with certain predicates as he/she desires. This gives the freedom to model a wide set of problems and use the knowledge of the environment to represent real world scenarios. The predicates are not predefined keywords, and can be anything that the user sees fit. Such modeling leads to tool composition between machines and tools in this specific case, enriching the skill set of the Autonomous System, and giving the system the possibility to fulfill more requests.

Domain actions represent functions that entail a change of state in the environment where the system works. Interacting with one or more parameters (arguments), the action implements postconditions in the environment if certain preconditions are met, preserving the causality of actions. There are certain approaches that can be used to model an action in PDDL, that are dependent on the language itself. Some keywords that can be used are: **and**, **or**, **forall**, **exists**, and **then**. It is important to mention that the concept we introduce in this paper is tailored only for a conjunctive (**and** form) of the precondition and effect terms. Further research includes extending the OWL to PDDL mapping to a wider and more concrete foundation, as well as extending the explanation method.

Listing 1.3 shows one of the actions modeled in domain definition language.

```
(: action insertLid
 : parameters (? actor − Resource ?box − Material ? lid − Material)
 : precondition (and (not (exists ?x)(isConnectedTo ?box ?x))
                     (isConnectedTo ?lid ?actor))
 . effect (isConnectedTo ?lid ?box)
```

Listing 1.3. Representation of an action in the PDDL environment.

This specific function serves as a medium for relating a resource and a tool, therefore expanding the skills set of the resource. The parameters part of the action takes certain variables as inputs of the action. These variables represent the knowledge in the environment, necessary to perform a task. However, in order to execute a specific task, some conditions need to be met, therefore showing how the parameters of the action are connected and what impact they can have on the environment. This is a natural way of representing actions modeled through the preconditions and postconditions (effects) in the planning domain definition language, where the predicates vary as logical expressions. As mentioned before, the predicates can show a relation between certain objects and constructing logical expressions between them leads to the possibility of executing different tasks and changing the state of the environment. As a correlation to a human performing this action rather than a robot, to perform this action which represents wielding a certain tool, a human worker would also ask whether the resource to use is available (in that case is the worker's hand available for picking up the tool), whether the tool is available (if the tool is free, and not in use by another worker), and if it is possible to use the tool (a human hand is capable of grasping a tool). These are all conditions that need to be met, in order for the action to be executed. The execution itself will lead to a new state of the environment, which in the example in Listing 1.3 it says that the resource and tool are not available, since the tool is picked up by the resource.

3.2 Planning Problem Specifications

Defining the domain in which the system operates is only half of the modeling. To complete it, the problem needs to be modeled as well. The problem consists of the objects that exist in the environment, the initial state in the environment in which the system operates, and the goal state the system needs to reach.

```
(:init                          (:goal
(isAvailable  robot1)           (isConnectedTo  lid1  box1))
(isAvailable  box1)
(isAvailable  lid1))
```

Listing 1.4. Definition of the initial (left) and goal states (right) in the PDDL problem file.

The models of the initial and goal states are shown in Listing 1.4. As it can be seen in Listing 1.4, the initial state shows the relatedness between the objects (in this case the availability of resources, tools, and parts), how they can be linked with one another, and mode of being of the objects. The goal is constructed of one or more predicate/s which is/are not satisfied. Furthermore, a combination of actions is generated with the help of a planner, to reach a certain state in which the goal conditions are satisfied.

4   Modeling Action Knowledge in OWL

The main goal is to produce explanations of action plans, without relying on how the AI planner used in the process performs the search. We introduce the concept Black Box Action Plan Explanations (B^{2}APE), refering to the possibility to look at the planner as a black box, meaning that the explanations are only based on the knowledge in the domain and the instantiated actions in the plan, and not on the planner's functionality. This method provides the flexibility to use any type of a planner to come up with an action sequence, and then generate justifications as to why certain actions were chosen. The basic idea is to use ontological vocabularies to express explanations in a user-understandable way. In order to reason over the planner's knowledge, it needs to be represented in ontologies. That is the cause for proposing the modeling of PDDL actions in OWL, and capturing those representations of actions is a crucial part of the B^{2}APE algorithm, because of the aforementioned advantage the integration of both worlds give. To present the transformation, or in other words mapping, between OWL action and PDDL action, Table 1 shows both representations. In the right column the OWL form is represented, whereas in the left the PDDL. A specific class in the ontology is tagged as a PDDL action. This way classes that represent a skill are distinguished from other ones. The parameters of the action are modeled as named individuals. Further, the precondition and effect of the action are modeled as a class expression, with a key word inserted so they can be recognized as such. This mapping enables translating from an OWL to a PDDL action, and vice versa. Note that here we use a PDDL meta vocabulary (namespace abbrev. pddl:) for tagging OWL entities with their according PDDL elements; Exp_i are complex expressions in PDDL and Exp'_i are their counterpart OWL expressions (by some transformation not explicitly specified here); $<C>$ and $<p_i>$ are names used as OWL classes/individuals and PDDL actions/parameters, respectively.

Table 1. PDDL to OWL transformation.

PDDL	OWL
types	Classes (**Concepts**)
predicates	Object properties (**Roles**)
action	Class: $<C>$ Annotations: pddl:element pddl:Action
:parameters $(?<p_1>\ldots<p_n>)$	pddl:parameter $<p_1>$ $\ldots$ pddl:parameter $<p_n>$
:precondition (and $(<Exp_1> <Exp_n>))$	SubClassOf: $<Exp'_1>$ Annotations: pddl:element pddl:Precondition $\ldots$ SubClassOf: $<Exp'_n>$ Annotations: pddl:element pddl:Precondition
:effect (and $(<Exp_1> <Exp_n>))$	SubClassOf: $<Exp'_1>$ Annotations: pddl:element pddl:Precondition $\ldots$ SubClassOf: $<Exp'_n>$ Annotations: pddl:element pddl:Precondition
objects	Named individuals (**Instances**)

Starting from the OWL class concept, the classes in an ontology represent a hierarchy, and have properties similar to class-based inheritance, class instantiation etc. These classes can be correlated to PDDL types, since they have a number of similar or even identical properties as object-oriented programming classes and even ontology classes. Same as ontology **classes** represent world concepts, the **types** in PDDL represent the concepts in the environment which the planner can use. Therefore, the same concepts the PDDL types represent can be classified in the ontology as well. As shown before in Sect. 3 how PDDL types are modeled, they can be correlated constructing a class tree. An example showing this knowledge representation is shown in Fig. 2, labeled as OWL Ontology. However, it's misleading to think that all classes in the ontology will represent PDDL concepts. As we will see how the class actions are tagged, the same principle is applied on the specific classes for concept representations in PDDL.

Predicates characterize a state or a relation between two or more environmental objects. We relate this to OWL **object properties**, modeling the connections between domain entities. Although, they govern the same principle as object properties in ontologies, predicates can also be unary, whereas object properties not. This means that a restriction needs to be introduced in modeling predicates in an ontology, which will help to translate between both components. Therefore, all PDDL predicates, which are modeled in the ontology, must be modeled as binary predicates. Because of the OWL formalisms, it is also possible to model n-ary predicates, and show the relationship between more than two objects. In addition to the possibility of adding subproperties in an ontology, PDDL answers with the definition of **axioms**, that mimic the same behaviour as object properties and subproperties.

Another PDDL feature is the definition of specific objects in the environment. The class instances in the ontology describe the specific objects that exist in the PDDL problem description, and are the ones that instantiate the actions that the planner can apply. As an example of an instantiated objects is: $actor :=$ $robot1, lid := lid1, box := box1$. This states that in the environment, the concepts **actor**, **lid**, and **box** are existing in the form of **robot1**, **lid1**, and **box1**.

The most important part is to model PDDL actions in OWL. PDDL actions represent classes and are tagged with annotations, so they can easly be identified. As mentioned earlier, they are composed of three parts: parameters, precondition, and effect. The action parameters are similar to function arguments in any programming language. Particular types of objects that are needed for an action are parsed onto that action and used in the environment when that action is applied. Because the parameters are named individuals, they are already described in the ontology and can be extracted directly from the precondition and effect expressions of the action. Next type checking is required to see whether a specific individual is of the correct type in the expression. Moving to the precondition and effect of the actions, they are modeled as a class expression in OWL (see Fig. 2). To distinguish between a precondition and an effect, explicit **key words** are introduced which mark the statement. In continuation to the respective key word, the precondition's, or, effect's conjunctive expression is modeled in OWL. The mapping of PDDL actions in OWL is done in a specific way for conjunctive PDDL expressions only, as the form presented in Sect. 3, also seen in Table 1. From here, the expression after the key word, which is one precondition of the action, is extracted. After all preconditons, or effects, are extracted, an **and** statement is created to complete the collective PDDL term. Using the translation in Table 1, the mapping can be done automatically between both languages.

Figure 2 shows the PDDL and OWL models of an action. The ontology is modeled in Protege. The action in the example is Inserting, specifically inserting a lid on a box. The actor that performs the action is a robot. Note that the key words for precondition and effect are **involvesInitialMaterial** and **involves-ResultingMaterial**, respectively, for the robotic assembly line case. They can be different depending on the application area, or just left as **precondition** and **effect** to be generalized for any ontology. Each conditional term has a specific predicate connected to some of the parameters. For the represented simplified

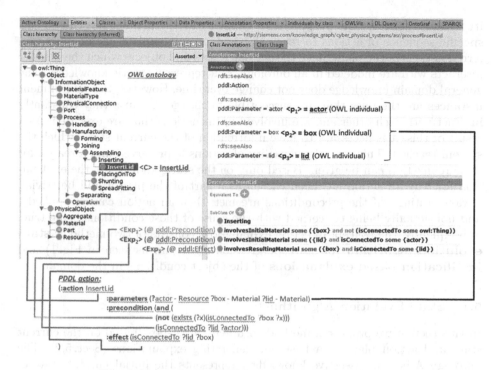

Fig. 2. Example of a PDDL action modeled in OWL.

inserting action in the example, the conditions that need to be met so that the action can be applied are the availability of the box, and the connection between the actor and the lid (or the actor holding the lid). They are modeled as Exp_1 and Exp_2 in Fig. 2. The separated modeling of the conditions, implies they are connected as a conjunctive term defining the complete precondition. The same modeling rules apply for the effect expression. As it can be seen from Fig. 2, there are other classes in the ontology that may or may not be related to the PDDL code. This depends on the problem the planner needs to solve and the set of entities it is allowed to use. This means that the skill set of the planner can be expanded, given the possibility of tagging other classes as actions and modeling their precondition and effect terms. Also, the richer the ontology is, the wider the skill set for the planner is.

5   Explanation of Actions

A generated action plan by an AI planner is a sequence of actions that are, or can be, applied to accomplish something. The range of the domain can be any area: industry, medicine etc. Through execution of the actions in the plan, the system reaches a certain desired state.

The actions are denoted with small letters, $plan\_sequence := a_1, a_2, a_3, a_4, a_5$. For example this plan has five actions in a distinct order, conserving the causality of those actions. The purpose is to explain why the planner has chosen this specific sequence of actions to reach the goal, or only explain one or more preferred actions in the plan. Since the actions it uses and objects which the planner interacts with are modeled in an ontology, that represents static knowledge. The general domain knowledge does not change over time. However, the environment instances are the ones that are susceptible to change, because they constantly interact with each other and are involved in the actions that are executed. As a result of this, it is necessary to have information of the current state, which the system reached. This way, the causality of actions is preserved and a reason for their realization can be given. Based only on the static knowledge, the explanation for why an action has been chosen as a part of the plan would be trivial, always stating: "if the preconditions are met, then an action can be applied", and not actually being concerned with the cause of those conditions being true. Subsequently, the concept of action explanations consists of two methods: **state evolution algorithm** (or state progression algorithm as seen in Fig. 1) and **justification based explanations** of the object conditions in the domain.

5.1   State Evolution Algorithm

In this section we propose a method to update an A-box, based on the current state and action plan, as a basis for generating explanations (Sect. 5.2). The ontology A-box, or assertive knowledge, represents the initial/current state of the environment in which the AI planner operates. The A-box shows the environment individuals and property assertions. As such, the A-box consists of all environment objects and their predicates. An example of that is:

$$A = \{lid1 := lid, box1 := box, robot1 := actor,$$
$$holds(actor, lid),$$
$$\neg \exists isConnectedTo.lid(box), \tag{3}$$
$$Manipulator(actor)\}$$

In the above A-box, the environment objects which the planner uses are **lid1**, **box1**, and **robot1**. Additionally, the environment is described by their relations, which in the example the property $holds(actor, lid)$ says that an actor is holding the lid, $\exists isConnectedTo.lid(box)$ states that the lid and the box in the setting are not connected, and $Manipulator(actor)$ declares the actor in the environment as a robotic manipulator. This is one state of the A-box, which can evolve by applying actions in the environment and changing the object's conditions or relations between them. This means that having the instantiated plan from the AI planner, we can use it to simulate the A-box evolution, and further explain at a specific moment why an action was chosen. Each action from the plan sequence can update the A-box to a new state if that action is applied.

    The state evolution algorithm is shown in Algorithm 1. As mentioned before, the A-box is the initial or current state of the domain. The evolution algorithm reads the initial A-box. The inputs to the State Evolution Algorithm are the

---

Algorithm 1. State Evolution Algorithm

1: **procedure** EVOLVESTATE($O, a_t, plan$)   ▷ Evolve system's state.
2:      // Get the current A-box from the ontology:
3:      $A_i \leftarrow O$
4:      // For each instantiated action in the plan, forward chain the state:
5:      **for each** a_i **in** $plan$ **do**
6:          // We have reached the targeted action to evolve to - stop evolution.
7:          **if** $a_i = a_t$ **then**
8:              **break**
9:          // Get the action's preconditions and effects, and update system's state:
10:         $p \leftarrow getPreconditionSetFromInstantiatedAction(a_i, A_i)$
11:         $e \leftarrow getEffectSetFromInstantiatedAction(a_i, A_i)$
12:         $A_i \leftarrow (A_i \setminus p) \cup e$
13:     // Return the updated state (A-box):
14:     $A^* \leftarrow A_i$
15:     **return** A^*

---

ontology, targeted action which we want to explain, and the plan sequence. The action plan is also input to the state evolution algorithm and the id number for the action we want to explain is assigned. Then, the method iterates through the action plan and updates the A-box in each step by applying the action at that moment, similar to forward chaining reasoning in production systems. First, each precondition and effect is extracted for that action. Next, the update is done by eliminating those preconditions from the A-box and adding the action's effects to it. This is done until the action that we want to explain is reached. As an example, let there be an action plan consisting of two actions:

$$P = \{pick(robot, lid1),$$
$$\qquad insertLid(actor, lid1, box1)\} \tag{4}$$

and let the initial A-box (A_0) for the corresponding example be the following:

$$A_0 = \{lid1 := lid, box1 := box, robot := actor,$$
$$\exists isConnectedTo.\bot(robot),$$
$$\exists isConnectedTo.\bot(lid1), \tag{5}$$
$$\neg \exists isConnectedTo.T(box1),$$
$$Manipulator(actor)\}$$

The **pick** and **insertLid** actions have simplified preconditions. The pick action preconditions state that nothing is to be connected to the robot and lid1 (meaning the robot and the lid are available). The preconditions for the pick action can be also seen in the initial A-box. Further, for the insertLid action, the lid needs to be already picked up by the robot and the box available to use. The state evolution algorithm first reads A_0 and updates the A-box to A_1, w.r.t.:

$$A^* = (A_i \setminus p) \cup e \tag{6}$$

where A_i is the current A-box (state), p and e are sets of precondition and effect axioms, respectively. A^* is the updated A-box. For the example, the updated A-box after one applying the pick action would be:

$$
\begin{aligned}
A_1 = \{ & lid1 := lid, box1 := box, robot := actor, \\
& \neg \exists isConnectedTo.T(box1), \\
& holds(actor, lid1), \\
& Manipulator(actor) \}
\end{aligned}
\tag{7}
$$

Further, explanations are generated for the action insertLid, or, as mentioned before, the action of interest to be explained.

5.2   Action Explanations

In this section we propose a method to generate explanations based on the updated A-box computed using the state evolution algorithm presented in the previous section. The algorithm for generating justifications as explanations for the causality of an action is shown as Algorithm 2. The inputs are the updated A-box (state of the environment) from the state evolution algorithm (A^*), and action of interest (to explain why it is a part of the plan) (a_t). What B^{2}APE does, through ontology reasoning, is checking whether a certain precondition is entailed in the current state (A-box), and justifying the conditional expression. This is done for all preconditions of the action of interest. The complete justification set for explaining why that action was applicable, represents a union of the justification sets of all entailed preconditions.

Algorithm 2. Explanation Algorithm

1: **procedure** GENERATEEXPLANATIONFORTARGETEDACTION(A^*, a_t)
2:     // Generate explanations for each precondition of the action of interest:
3:     **for each** p_i in a_t **do**
4:         **if** $isEntailed(A^*, p_i)$ **then**
5:             $J_i \leftarrow generateJustification(A_i \models p_i)$
6:             $J \leftarrow J \cup J_i$
7:     // Return the collective justification set:
8:     **return** J

The explanation method will be shown by the following example. Using the action plan from Eq. 4, as well as the evolved state from Eq. 7, the algorithm will check whether the second action from the plan (the action **insertLid**) is applicable, and also justify its applicability. The justification consists of three iterations.

The first entailment, along with the justification, is shown in Table 2. One of the preconditions to insert the Lid on the Box is the Box being free to use it in the operation. Also, the correct instance of the object must be used.

Table 2. Justification set of the first precondition of the insertLid action.

OWL		Interpretation
$A_1 \models \neg\exists isConnectedTo.T(box1)$		**Entailment 1:** There exists an object box1 and nothing is connected to it
$J_1 =$	$\{\forall isConnectedTo.\bot(box1)$	**Interpretation:** "box1 is connected to all things nothing = box1 is not connected to anything"
	$box1 := box\}$	**Interpretation:** "box1 is the specific box used in the action"

Justification meaning: There is a specified material2 in the environment, which is box1 (as it is the object that is used in the plan), and that specific object box1 is connected to nothing. This is the same as stating that there exists the box1 in the environment (as a specialized form of material), and this material2 is not connected to any thing

Moving on to the second precondition, in order for the Robot to insert the Lid, it needs to hold it. This has already been done with the **pick** action, making this condition true. Moreover, a Lid is a metalic material, which means it can be held only with a special tool (a magnet). Because of this, it is known that: **holds-Magnetically(actor, lid1)**. However, holding an object magnetically is a type of holding, which justifies the precondition of the **insertLid** action (Table 3).

Table 3. Justification set of the second precondition of the insertLid action.

OWL		Interpretation
$A_1 \models holds(actor, lid1)$		**Entailment 2:** An actor holds a material
$J_2 =$	$\{holdsMagnetically(actor, lid1),$	**Interpretation:** "robot1 holds lid1 with a magnet"
	$holdsMagnetically \sqsubseteq holds$	**Interpretation:** "any object that is held magnetically it is also a general form of holding that object"
	$lid1 := lid$	**Interpretation:** "lid1 is the specific lid used in the action"
	$actor := robot1\}$	**Interpretation:** "robot1 is the specific actor used in the action"

Justification meaning: robot1 holds lid1 with a magnet, which is a hold skill because holding magnetically is just a different version of holding, the object which is specifically holded is the lid1, which is the one that is needed

The last justification is checking whether the correct actor is used to apply the action. The instantiated actor, robot1, is a type of a robot. The precondition states that a manipulator is used to perform the action. However, a robot is a type of a manipulator, therefore justifying the correct operator of the action (Table 4).

Table 4. Justification set of the third precondition of the insertLid action.

OWL		Interpretation
$A_1 \models Manipulator(actor)$		**Entailment 3:** There exists an actor in the environment which performs the action, and that actory is of type Manipulator
$J_3 =$	$\{actor := robot1,$	**Interpretation:** "the specific actor for the action is robot1"
	$Robot(robot1),$	**Interpretation:** "robot1 is a type of Robot"
	$Robot \sqsubseteq Manipulator$	**Interpretation:** "any robot is a manipulator"

Justification meaning: As a precondition is also needed to identify the actor which performs the action. In this case, that actor is robot1, which is of a type robot, which represents a type of Manipulator, which justifies the entailment the actor is a type of a Manipulator

The final justification set for the action of interest, represents a union of all justification sets for the actions preconditions. For this specific action, the collective justification set is:

$$J = J_1 \cup J_2 \cup J_3 \tag{8}$$

In the case of several justifications they are all presented in a set of alternative explanatory texts. Having more justifications can be helpful to further clarify the autonomous actions of the systems, giving the user a better chance to understand the plan.

The approach foresees to use natural language annotations on axioms for generating exlpanatory texts that bear the structure of the OWL explanations. The concepts in the domain ontology have annotation properties that give a semantic meaning to them, and can additionally illustrate their purpose. This, combined with the justification axioms, gives an insight on which conditions are interacting and providing the necessary states for an action to be executed, as well as a context to what those conditions imply.

6   Conclusion and Future Work

We introduced a novel concept, Black Box Action Plan Explanations (B^2APE), for explanation of action plans based on an integration of the AI planning formalism PDDL with Ontologies expressed in OWL. The approach consists of three methods: a mapping for modeling PDDL directly in OWL ontologies, forming a bridge between both formalisms; a state evolution algortihm for simulating a planner like behaviour in order to derive an A-Box that captures the state of interest for the relevant action to be explained from the plan; the use of OWL justifications for generating explanations as to why actions were chosen as a part of the plan, explaining the preconditions that led to a certain state of the system and making it transparent. We have illustrated our methods through illustration in a simplified industrial robot assembly scenario.

There are various points of future work that we see as follow-up steps. The mapping between PDDL and OWL requires a more thorough investigation towards completeness of covering all possible PDDL expressions including open/closed-world discrepancies. In addition to the why-explanations presented here it is also interesting to investigate how respective why-not-explanations can be computed, e.g. by inducing hypothetical actions into the workflow that are not part of the plan. Moreover, we plan to apply this approach in a real industrial setting to test its feasibility in terms of performance and scalability of the AI methods applied, as well as acceptance and usability with human users.

References

1. Fikes, R., Nilsson, N.: STRIPS: a new approach to the application of theorem proving to problem solving. Artif. Intell. **2**, 189–208 (1971)
2. Nebel, B.: On the compilability and expressive power of propositional planning formalisms. J. Artif. Intell. Res. **12**, 271–315 (2000)
3. W3C OWL Working Group: OWL 2 web ontology language: document overview. W3C recommendation, 27 October 2009. https://www.w3.org/TR/owl2-overview/
4. Baader, F., Calvanese, D., McGuinness, D., Nardi, D., Patel-Schneider, P. (eds.): The Description Logic Handbook: Theory Implementation and Applications. Cambridge University Press, Cambridge (2007)
5. Kalyanpur, A., Parsia, B., Horridge, M., Sirin, E.: Finding all justifications of OWL DL entailments. In: Aberer, K., et al. (eds.) ASWC/ISWC -2007. LNCS, vol. 4825, pp. 267–280. Springer, Heidelberg (2007). https://doi.org/10.1007/978-3-540-76298-0_20
6. Fox, M., Long, D., Magazzeni, D.: Explainable planning, clinical orthopaedics and related research (CoRR) (2017)
7. Balakirsky, S., Kootbally, Z.: An ontology based approach to action verification for agile manufacturing. In: 2nd International Coonference on Robot Intelligence Technology and Application (2013)
8. Klusch, M., Gerber, A., Schmidt, M.: Semantic web service composition planning with OWLS-Xplan. In: 1st International AAAI Fall Symposium on Agents and the Semantic Web (2005)
9. Mehdi, G., Brandt, S., Roshchin, M., Runkler, T.: Towards semantic reasoning in knowledge management systems. In: Mercier-Laurent, E., Boulanger, D. (eds.) AI4KM 2016. IAICT, vol. 518, pp. 132–146. Springer, Cham (2018). https://doi.org/10.1007/978-3-319-92928-6_9
10. Gil, Y.: Description logics and planning. AI Mag. **26**(2), 73 (2005)
11. Steven, M.: LaValle: Planning Algorithms. Cambridge University Press, Cambridge (2006)

Rule Module Inheritance
with Modification Restrictions

Felix Burgstaller[1]($\boxtimes$), Bernd Neumayr[1], Emanuel Sallinger[2],
and Michael Schrefl[1]

[1] Johannes Kepler University Linz, Linz, Austria
{felix.burgstaller,bernd.neumayr,michael.schrefl}@jku.at
[2] University of Oxford, Oxford, UK
emanuel.sallinger@cs.ox.ac.uk

Abstract. Adapting rule sets to different settings, yet avoiding uncontrolled proliferation of variations, is a key challenge of rule management. One fundamental concept to foster reuse and simplify adaptation is inheritance. Building on rule modules, i.e., rule sets with input and output schema, we formally define inheritance of rule modules by incremental modification in single inheritance hierarchies. To avoid uncontrolled proliferation of modifications, we introduce formal modification restrictions which flexibly regulate the degree to which a child module may be modified in comparison to its parent. As concrete rule language, we employ Datalog$^\pm$ which can be regarded a common logical core of many rule languages. We evaluate the approach by a proof-of-concept prototype.

1 Introduction

In data- and knowledge-intensive systems it is good practice to separate explicit knowledge, elicited from domain experts and translated into declarative expressions by rule developers, from application code developed by application developers. Rule-based knowledge representation and reasoning build the core of systems for business rule engines [23], web data extraction [13], data wrangling [16], knowledge graph management [3], and information tailoring [8]. With the increasing number and complexity of rules, their maintenance and their adaptation to different settings and contexts become key challenges of rule developers. In this paper we present an approach employing rule modules and inheritance to cope with these challenges. In the following we sketch challenges and our approach along a self-contained business rule example which is used throughout the paper. Subsequently, we zoom out to give the big picture of potential application areas where the presented approach may serve as a central building block.

1.1 Challenges and Approach

In this paper, we present an approach which builds on *rule modules* – i.e., rule sets with interfaces describing the schema of input and output data – to provide a clear separation and interfaces between rule sets and data-intensive

© Springer Nature Switzerland AG 2018
H. Panetto et al. (Eds.): OTM 2018 Conferences, LNCS 11230, pp. 404–422, 2018.
https://doi.org/10.1007/978-3-030-02671-4_25

applications. These interfaces shield application developers from the intricacies of rule sets as well as rule developers from application code and clarify which knowledge and data schemata are internal to the module and which interface either as input or output.—For example, a bank clerk is responsible for processing a set of mortgage applications, i.e., assessing the applications' credit worthiness in order of their priority. Domain knowledge regarding assessment and prioritization of mortgage applications is encoded in a rule module MortgageApps. This rule module is employed by a data-intensive application collecting and managing mortgage applications and their assessment. Rule module MortgageApps takes as input a set of mortgage applications each described by the mortgage value and the estimated values of real estate securities. As output it produces a preliminary assessment of the credit worthiness, either good or bad, of each application together with a prioritization of the applications for detailed assessment. Any issues with applications, e.g., having a mortgage value below the specified minimum loan value, are also output.

Organizing business rules into rule modules entails the danger of *redundancy*: One and the same rule may be relevant in different settings and thus introduced and maintained separately in different modules. This duplicates human effort in developing and maintaining modules and makes it difficult to keep rules synchronized across modules.—For example, our bank decides to offer private loans as well, creating a rule module PrivateLoanApps. Some rules, such as the minimum loan value, apply in module MortgageApps as well as module PrivateLoanApps. Thus, any changes to this rule need to be performed in both rule modules.

In this paper we introduce *inheritance* of parent modules to child modules by incremental modification as one way to mitigate these problems without sacrificing flexibility. In child modules, rule developers may introduce additional rules, remove inherited rules, as well as extend and/or reduce the input and output interfaces. This reduces redundancy and thus should ease maintenance of modules adapted to different business settings.—For example, extracting common rules, such as the minimum loan value rule, into a parent module LoanApps we can remove redundancy. Any changes to a common rule are made in the parent module and by inheritance propagated to all child modules. Moreover, since we allow modifications to inherited rules, we can define default rules for loan application assessment and ranking in module LoanApps.

Allowing arbitrary modifications in child rule modules, however, would undermine the benefits of inheritance and would pave the way for *uncontrolled proliferation of variations*: a rule or application developer trying to get an overall picture of the interfaces and the behavior, i.e., the derived knowledge, encoded in a hierarchy of rule modules would still have to inspect all modules. Furthermore, undesired changes to inherited rules and interfaces would be possible.—For example, consider our minimum loan value rule in module LoanApps. Since arbitrary modifications are allowed we can simply remove this rule in child modules; any problematic loan applications would not be output anymore.

In this paper, we introduce a set of *modification restrictions* to flexibly regulate the degree to which a module's interfaces and behavior may be modified in comparison to its parent module's interfaces and behavior. Treating rule modules as black boxes, modification restrictions set boundaries within which a module may be modified. Thus, it should be sufficient to inspect the root module to get an abstract overview of the behavior implemented in a hierarchy of modules.

Structural restrictions restrain allowed modifications to the input and output schema of a module.—For example, module `LoanApps` specifies the basic input for loan application assessments. Child module `MortgageApps` requires further inputs like real estates provided as securities. Thus, we define `LoanApps`' inputs as non-omitable. Moreover, module `MortgageApps` fixes the output for all mortgage application modules. Thus, we define its output as non-extensible.

Behavioral restrictions constrain modifications changing the output at instance level (for a particular output schema element a behavioral modification may lead to different instances in the output).—For example, we want to prohibit child modules from deriving a subset of minimum loan value issues compared to module `loanApps`. Thus, we employ restriction non-shrinkable. Similarly, child modules must not have weaker requirements for good credit worthiness, i.e., must not derive good credit worthiness for a superset of loan applications compared to module `loanApps`. Thus, we employ restriction non-growable.

1.2   Potential Application Areas

Potential application areas, besides business rules as shown in the examples, are rule-based systems for information tailoring [8], web data extraction [13], and knowledge graph management [3], where rule modules encode knowledge for tasks such as data extraction, transformation, cleansing, and filtering and need to be adapted to different settings.

For example, in the DIADEM system for web data extraction [13], multiple rule modules, each responsible for a particular task such as web form understanding or form filling, are dynamically orchestrated in networks where one module's output is another module's input. Some of the encoded knowledge necessary for web form understanding is generic to 'all' web sites, while other encoded knowledge is specific to domains such as 'real estate' websites. Inheritance from the rule module for generic web form understanding to a rule module for web form understanding for 'real estate' websites should help to reduce redundancy and thus ease maintenance. Structural modification restrictions can be used to ensure that child rule modules remain orchestrable, similar to co- and contravariance in object-orientation which can be used to ensure type-safety and substitutability. Behavioral modification restrictions should help to keep the overall rule base understandable and thus maintainable, e.g., looking at a parent module and its behavioral restrictions gives an overview of possible behavior in child modules.

Regarding Web developments, e.g., Internet of Things, Semantic Web, or Smart Things, rules become a vital and integral part [30]. Due to the number of rules and their context-dependent applicability, efficient rule management is essential. Rule modules and module inheritance are means to manage such large rule sets and can be extended to manage contexts of application (c.f. [9]).

We expect our approach to be applicable and beneficial in these areas – an evaluation is yet to be performed. In this paper we focus on rule modules, their inheritance, and modification restrictions independent of specific applications.

1.3   Contributions and Overview

Currently, work on rule inheritance and related work on contextualized knowledge representation is fragmented and there exists no approach for inheritance of rule modules where modifications can be flexibly restricted.—In this paper we introduce an overall approach to rule module inheritance and specifically make the following contributions:

- formal definition of (1) downward rule and interface inheritance in single inheritance hierarchies of modules, and (2) modification restrictions and inheritance of modification restrictions
- discussion of conformance checks for detecting violations of defined structural and behavioral modification restrictions
- proof-of-concept prototype implementing formal definitions in Datalog, publicly available for further experimentation

The remainder of this paper is structured as follows: Sect. 2 presents our Datalog$^{\pm}$-based rule language and rule modules. In Sect. 3 we present our basic inheritance mechanism. Section 4 introduces modification restrictions and delineates inheritance of modification restrictions. In Sect. 5 we present a proof-of-concept prototype. Section 6 discusses related work. Section 7 concludes the paper.

2   Rule Modules

First, we discuss expressing rules with Datalog$^{\pm}$ where a rule is constructed from predicates and operators like logical conjunction. Subsequently, we introduce rule modules and discuss their structure and behavior.

2.1   Underlying Rule Language

This section delineates our notion of rules based on a formal language. In order to focus on rule module inheritance and modification restrictions, the underlying rule language and data model should be simple, i.e., have few constructs and operators, to avoid unnecessary complexity. A fitting family of formal languages is Datalog$^{\pm}$ [11] which has clearly defined formal semantics and employs a relational data model.

Datalog$^{\pm}$ extends plain Datalog by existentially quantified variables in rule heads, negative constraints, and equality-generating dependencies while restricting the language so as to achieve decidability and, more particularly, good performance. Vadalog [4] is a practical implementation of Datalog$^{\pm}$ that adds many features needed in commercial use, including a wide range of built-ins. Thus, Datalog$^{\pm}$/Vadalog is quite expressive, e.g., encompassing full Datalog with no restriction on recursion and SPARQL under the OWL 2 QL entailment regime, while still being efficient. Datalog$^{\pm}$/Vadalog is a versatile rule language family also employed for big data wrangling [16] and knowledge graph management [3].

A plain Datalog *rule* comprises a body (premise) and a head (conclusion) where the conclusion is derived if the premise holds. Both conclusion and premise are conjunctions of atoms (i.e., predicates with arguments). Datalog$^{\pm}$ allows use of existentially quantified variables in conclusions enabling value creation, truth value `false` in conclusions (negative constraints), and equality-generating dependencies, e.g., `Y=Z:- r1(X,Y), r2(X,Z)`.

Definition 1 (Rule Structure). *Predicates (a.k.a. relations) are taken from a universe of predicates P. Rules are taken from a universe of rules R. A rule $r \in R$ has body predicates $B_r \subseteq P$ and head predicates $H_r \subseteq P$.*

Example 1. Our bank deems mortgage loans of less than 10,000 Euro as not worth the organizational costs (rule `R0`). We translate this natural language rule to Datalog$^{\pm}$: `lowLValue(X,V) :- lValue(X,V), V < 10000`. The mortgage value applied for is represented by `lValue/2` (predicate `lValue` with arity two) relating loan applications with loan values while `lowLValue/2` annotates mortgage applications below the defined mortgage value threshold. Rule `R0` has body predicates $B_{\text{R0}} = \{\text{lValue/2}\}$ and head predicates $H_{\text{R0}} = \{\text{lowLValue/2}\}$.

2.2 Module Structure and Behavior

A collection of rules and facts (i.e., rules without variables and with premise true) in Datalog is called a Datalog program. In the following we extend Datalog programs with input schema and output schema to rule modules, where the Datalog program itself is the implementation of the rule module.

We derive *structural* aspects of rule modules from Datalog and Vadalog. Datalog splits the predicates of a program into extensional database (EDB) and intensional database (IDB). EDB contains predicates asserted in the knowledge base, IDB predicates defined by rules. A similar distinction is made in DMN's rule representation [22]. Vadalog [4] extends this idea to *inputs* provided by external sources (input predicates) and derived predicates *output* to external sinks (output predicates). These two sets are disjoint. Predicates derived and potentially used in rule bodies but not exported are auxiliary predicates.

Definition 2 (Rule Modules). *Rule modules are taken from a universe of rule modules M. A rule module $m \in M$ is defined by a set of rules R_m, a set of input predicates $I_m \subseteq P$, and a set of output predicates $O_m \subseteq P$. The sets of input and output predicates are disjoint. The predicates of a module m, P_m, are the union of its rule head, rule body, input, and output predicates.*

We now discuss the development of a rule module from an organizational perspective: Domain experts elicit and determine rules, often in natural language, and organize them into rule sets, e.g., a rule set may cover a specific business case. Furthermore, domain experts determine the necessary data input and derived output for the elicited set of rules. Once the domain experts consider a rule set and its inputs and outputs complete, rule developers translate the elicited rules and interfaces into a rule module with a Datalog$^{\pm}$ program as implementation.

module: MortgageApps
Input: loan/1, lValue/2, duration/2, customer/2, mProperty/2, pValue/2
[R0] lowLValue(X,V) :- lValue(X,V), V < 10000.
[R1] cwGood(X) :- loan(X), lValue(X,LV), A= #sum{SV: properties(X,S), sValue(S,SV)}, A > 0.8 x LV.
[R2] cwBad(X) :- not cwGood(X), loan(X).
[R3] priorityOver(X,Y) :- loan(X), loan(Y), lValue(X,VX), lValue(Y,VY), VX > VY.
[R4_1] ∃N property(N), properties(X,N), sValue(N,PV) :- loan(X), mProperty(X,P), pValue(P,PV).
[R4_2] mProperty(X,Y) :- loan(X), mProperty(X,Z), hasPart(Z,Y).
[R5_1] securities(X,P) :- properties(X,P).
[R5_2] security(X) :- property(X).
[R6] lowPropValue(X,P) :- properties(X,P), sValue(P,V), V < 30000.
Output: cwGood/1, cwBad/1, priorityOver/2, security/1, securities/2, properity/1, properties/2, sValue/2, lowLValue/2, lowPropValue/2

Fig. 1. Visual summary of module MortgageApps as described in Examples 1 and 2 comprising three compartments: the *input* and *output* compartments containing input and output declarations of predicate names and their arity and the *rules* compartment containing Datalog$^\pm$ rules with rule identifiers in brackets.

Example 2. We want to elicit for the process of assessing mortgage loan applications all relevant rules. In addition to rule R0 (see Example 1) we identified: Credit worthiness of a mortgage application is deemed good (predicate cwGood/1) if the value of provided properties exceeds 80 % of the mortgage's value (R1). In all other cases credit worthiness is deemed bad (R2 – output cwBad/1). Loan applications of higher loan values have priority over those with lower loan values (R3 – priorityOver/2). Each provided property and its value are associated with the corresponding loan application (R4 – property/1, properties/2, sValue/2). Associated properties are securities (R5 – securities/2, security/1). Properties of a value below 30,000 Euro are reported as problematic securities (R6 – lowPropValue/2). The predicates derived by rules R0-R6 form module MortgageApps's output predicates $O_{\text{MortgageApps}}$.

From these natural language rules our domain experts derive the necessary input. The rules employ information given with each mortgage application (loan/1). Such applications need to state the intended mortgage value (lValue/2), the duration (duration/2), the applying customer (customer/2), and any real estate properties which may be used as securities (mProperty/2) as well as their value (pValue/2). These predicates form the input predicates $I_{\text{MortgageApps}}$. Furthermore, properties may be hierarchically organized (hasPart/2), e.g., a property may consist of an area containing buildings. A visual summary including the Datalog$^\pm$ representation is given in Fig. 1.

Besides structure, a rule module exhibits behavior when executed. We regard rule module *behavior* as observable effects, i.e., derived facts, when applying the set of rules in a module to a dataset containing facts for its input predicates. Multiple facts for each predicate may be provided. A data set providing facts for all input predicates of a module is called applicable.

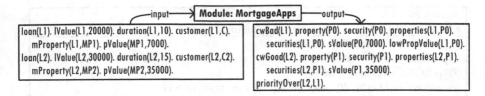

Fig. 2. Visualization of the execution of module `MortgageApps` on a dataset containing facts describing the two mortgage applications L1 and L2 and its output.

Definition 3 (Module Execution). *Data sets are taken from a universe of data sets D. A data set $d \in D$ with schema $P_d \subseteq P$ contains extensions, i.e., sets of facts, for all $p \in P_d$. A data set d is applicable input for module m if the module's input schema is a subset of the data set's schema, i.e., if $I_m \subseteq P_d$. The execution of a module m on applicable input data d results, for each output predicate $p \in O_m$, in a set of derived facts, denoted as p_m^d (p_m^d is the set of derived p-facts resulting from executing m on d).*

Example 3. Executing module `MortgageApps` on a dataset of two mortgage applications L1 and L2, its rules are evaluated and derived facts of output predicates (behavior) are returned (see Fig. 2).

3   Inheritance

In the following, we shortly summarize different aspects of inheritance in general. We describe the scope of our approach regarding the found aspects and subsequently define our notion of inheritance hierarchy for rule modules, rule inheritance therein, and abstract predicates and modules.

A common notion of inheritance is inheritance as incremental modification, that is, "reusing a conceptual or physical *entity* in constructing an incrementally similar one" [29, p. 55]. From related work we extracted various aspects and their options: All found inheritance mechanisms are transitive. Furthermore, inheritance is often discussed regarding certain *foci*, i.e., signatures (schema of inputs and outputs), behavior, or implementation [5,14,17,20,24,27,29]. Besides these aspects, inheritance is usually distinguished into single-inheritance and *multi-inheritance* [12,14,17,24,27,29], i.e., child entities inherit from a single or multiple parent entities respectively. *Direction* of inheritance is distinguished into downward [12,14], e.g., inheritance in Java, upward [12,14], e.g., an array inheriting properties from its entries, and lateral [12], e.g., a motorized trike is a motorcycle except that is has three wheels. *Granularity* [14,29] regards whether an inheritance mechanism is specified for groups of entities or single entities.

We restrict our investigation of rule module inheritance to the following inheritance options: *Focus* is on *signature* and *behavior* inheritance. *Multi-inheritance* is not investigated. *Direction* of inheritance is *downward*, from parent module to child module. *Granularity* is rule modules.

Definition 4 (Inheritance Hierarchy). *Rule modules are arranged in an inheritance hierarchy $H \subset M \times M$ which forms a forest (i.e., a set of trees). We say module m' inherits from m if $(m', m) \in H$, with m' playing the role of* child *and m playing the role of* parent.

Rules and sets of interface predicates (input and output predicates) are propagated from parent module to its child modules. A child module is modified by introducing additional rules or interface predicates and/or by deleting inherited rules or interface predicates. Thus, rules and interface predicates can only be overridden by deletion and addition. Modifying rules implies modification of a rule module's behavior.

Definition 5 (Inheritance by Incremental Modification). *When a module m' inherits from module m, $(m', m) \in H$, the child module m' inherits the parent's rule set R_m from which it may remove a set of rules $R_{m'}^{-} \subseteq R_m$ and to which it may add a set of rules $R_{m'}^{+} \subseteq R$, which results in the child module's rule set $R_{m'} \stackrel{\text{def}}{=} R_m \cup R_{m'}^{+} \backslash R_{m'}^{-}$. Inheritance and incremental modification of the sets of input and output predicates are defined analogously, i.e., $I_{m'} \stackrel{\text{def}}{=} I_m \cup I_{m'}^{+} \backslash I_{m'}^{-}$ and $O_{m'} \stackrel{\text{def}}{=} O_m \cup O_{m'}^{+} \backslash O_{m'}^{-}$.*

Often discussed, in particular regarding object-orientation, are *abstract entities*. For instance, an abstract method is a method for which the signature is defined but no implementation is available [20, 27, 29]. Methods fully defined and implemented are usually called *concrete*. Analogously, we distinguish predicates in a module into concrete and abstract. We define concrete predicates as the union of predicates which are in the input interface, truth value true (represented as a nullary predicate), and predicates which contain only concrete predicates in the body of any rule having them in the rule head. Abstract predicates are defined as predicates in a module which are not concrete. In object-oriented design, a class is abstract if it contains abstract elements. Analogously, we call a rule module abstract if it contains abstract predicates and concrete otherwise. Similar to abstract classes which cannot be instantiated, abstract modules should not be applied as their behavior is incomplete. Consequently, abstract predicates and modules should always be concreted in descendant modules. Leaf modules in the module hierarchy should always be concrete.

Definition 6 (Abstract Predicates and Modules). *A predicate p depends on a predicate p' in module m, denoted as $dep_m(p, p')$, if there is a rule r in R_m which has p in the head and p' in the body, i.e., $dep_m(p, p') \stackrel{\text{def}}{=} \exists r \in R_m : p \in H_r \wedge p' \in B_r$. A predicate p is concrete for a module m if it is nullary predicate* true *or an input predicate or depends on some and only concrete predicates, i.e., $concrete_m(p) \stackrel{\text{def}}{=} (p = \text{true}) \vee (p \in I_m) \vee ((\forall p' : dep_m(p, p') \to concrete_m(p')) \wedge (\exists p' : dep_m(p, p')))$. A predicate $p \in P_m$ is abstract for a module m if it is not concrete. A module is abstract if it has an abstract predicate.*

From an organizational viewpoint, inheritance of rule modules can be employed for rule elicitation, definition, and organization: (a) An existing module can be adapted to a more specific setting and context by constructing a child module. Therefore, rule developers have to know which rules and interface predicates are contained in a module. To this end, they look at resolved modules, i.e., modules for which all inheritance relations have been resolved. (b) A parent module can be constructed by extracting common/similar rules and interface predicates from child modules. Abstract modules are of importance to the latter approach allowing to extract common predicates although the rules defining those predicates are different in child modules. Hierarchical organization of modules eases management, in particular maintenance, as rule redundancy can be reduced and rule reuse is promoted.

Example 4. Recently, our bank decided to extend its services to private loan applications. Therefore, we elicited relevant rules for private loan applications. We uncovered overlaps with module MortgageApps, in particular rules R0-R3. Rule R0 overlaps with 'Private loan values must exceed 12,000' (for now RX), R1 with 'Credit worthiness of a private loan application is deemed good (predicate cwGood/1) if the value of provided securities exceeds 60 % of the loan's value' (for now RY), and rules R2 and R3 are identical. Non-overlapping are: Regarding income, private loans are reported if the customer earns less than 600 Euro per month (R7). The provided attachable income (attachableIncome/1) is calculated as 30% of the income earned over the loan's duration and associated with the loan application (R8 – incomes/2) as security (R9 – securities/2, security/1) allowing to reuse rule R1 for deriving credit worthiness. $O_{\text{PrivateLoanApps}}$ contains {cwGood/1, cwBad/1, attachableIncome/1, incomes/2, priorityOver/2, lowLValue/2, sValue/2, lowIncome/2}.

For these rules we identified the required inputs private loan application (loan/1), the intended loan value (lValue/2), the duration (duration/2), the applying customer (customer/2), and any incomes which may be used as securities (income/2). These predicates form the input predicates $I_{\text{PrivateLoanApps}}$ which considerably overlap with $I_{\text{MortgageApps}}$.

A subsequent discussion with domain experts revealed that rules R0, R2, R3, and RY are actually default rules applying to all existing and future loan types. We extract the default rules and MortgageApps's and PrivateLoanApps's common interface predicates into a parent module LoanApps. Rule RX is renamed to R0.1, R1 to R1.1, and RY to R1. Regarding interfaces we have $I_{\text{LoanApps}} =$ {loan/1, lValue/2, duration/2, customer/2} and $O_{\text{LoanApps}} = $ {cwGood/1, cwBad/1, priorityOver/2, lowLValue/1, sValue/2, securities/2, security/1}. Since predicates securities/2, security/1, and sValue/2 are not derived in LoanApps but in its child modules, module LoanApps is abstract. A visual summary of our use case including modification restrictions and Datalog$^{\pm}$ representations is given in Fig. 3. There, rule R0.1 overrides rule R0 and rule R1.1 rule R1, i.e., $R^{-}_{\text{PrivateLoanApps}} = \{\text{R0}\}$ and $R^{+}_{\text{PrivateLoanApps}} = \{\text{R0.1, R7, R8, R9\_1, R9\_2}\}$. Figure 4 depicts module PrivateLoanApps with inheritance resolved.

```
Module: LoanApps
Input: loan/1, IValue/2, duration/2, customer/2
¬omitable: loan, IValue, duration, customer
[R0] lowLValue(X,V) :- IValue(X,V), V < 10000.
[R1] cwGood(X) :- loan(X), IValue(X,LV), A = #sum{SV: securities(X,S), sValue(S,SV)}, A > 0.6 x LV.
[R2] cwBad(X) :- not cwGood(X), loan(X).
[R3] priorityOver(X,Y) :- loan(X), loan(Y), IValue(X,VX), IValue(Y,VY), VX > VY.
Output: cwGood/1, cwBad/1, priorityOver/2, lowLValue/2, sValue/2, securities/2, security/1
¬omitable: cwGood, cwBad, priorityOver, lowLValue, sValue
¬shrinkable: cwBad, priorityOver, lowLValue
¬growable: cwGood, priorityOver
```

```
Module: MortgageApps
Input: mProperty/2, pValue/2
¬omitable: mProperty, pValue
− ([R1]) [R1.1] cwGood(X) :- loan(X), IValue(X,LV),
    A = #sum{SV: properties(X,S), sValue(S,SV)}, A > 0.8 x LV.
[R4_1] ∃N property(N), properties(X,N), sValue(N,PV) :- loan(X),
    mProperty(X,P), pValue(P,PV).
[R4_2] mProperty(X,Y) :- loan(X), mProperty(X,Z), hasPart(Z,Y).
[R5_1] securities(X,P) :- properties(X,P).
[R5_2] security(X) :- property(X).
[R6] lowPropValue(X,P) :- properties(X,P), sValue(P,V), V < 30000.
Output (¬extensible): property/1, properties/2, lowPropValue/2
¬omitable: property, properties, lowPropValue
¬shrinkable: lowPropValue
```

```
Module: PrivateLoanApps
Input: income/2
¬omitable: income
− ([R0]) [R0.1] lowLValue(X,V) :- IValue(X,V), V < 12000.
[R7] lowIncome(X,I) :- income(X,I), I ≤ 600.
[R8] ∃N attachableIncome(N), incomes(X,N), sValue(N,I) :-
    loan(X), duration(X,D), income(X,S), I = 0.3 x S x D.
[R9_1] securities(X,P) :- incomes(X,P).
[R9_2] security(X) :- attachableIncome(X).
Output: attachableIncome/1, incomes/2, lowIncome/2,
    − (securities/2), − (security/1)
¬omitable: attachableIncome, incomes, lowIncome
¬shrinkable: lowIncome
¬growable: lowLValue, lowIncome
```

Fig. 3. Visual summary of the inheritance hierarchy of rule modules as described in Examples 4–7. Child modules MortgageApps and PrivateLoanApps (which may have their own child modules which are not depicted) incrementally modify parent module LoanApps by adding and removing (denoted by '−()') rules, input declarations, and output declarations. Input and output compartments further contain modification restrictions (denoted by ¬omitable and ¬extensible, ¬shrinkable, ¬growable) with child modules adding additional modification restrictions.

```
Module: PrivateLoanApps
Input: loan/1, IValue/2, duration/2, customer/2, income/2
¬omitable: loan, IValue, duration, customer, income
[R0.1] lowLValue(X,V) :- IValue(X,V), V < 5000.
[R1] cwGood(X) :- loan(X), IValue(X,LV), A = #sum{SV: securities(X,S), sValue(S,SV)}, A > 0.6 x LV.
[R2] cwBad(X) :- not cwGood(X), loan(X).
[R3] priorityOver(X,Y) :- loan(X), loan(Y), IValue(X,VX), IValue(Y,VY), VX > VY.
[R7] lowIncome(X,I) :- income(X,I), I ≤ 600.
[R8] ∃N attachableIncome(N), incomes(X,N), sValue(N,I) :- loan(X), duration(X,D), income(X,S), I = 0.3 x S x D.
[R9_1] securities(X,P) :- incomes(X,P).
[R9_2] security(X) :- attachableIncome(X).
Output: cwGood/1, cwBad/1, priorityOver/2, lowLValue/2, sValue/2, attachableIncome/1, incomes/2, lowIncome/2
¬omitable: cwGood, cwBad, priorityOver, lowLValue, sValue, attachableIncome, incomes, lowIncome
¬shrinkable: cwBad, priorityOver, lowLValue, lowIncome
¬growable: cwGood, priorityOver, lowLValue, lowIncome
```

Fig. 4. Visual summary of module PrivateLoanApps with inheritance of rules, input declarations, and output declarations resolved according to Definition 5 and inheritance of modification restrictions resolved according to Definition 10.

4   Modification Restrictions

Of particular interest to this paper are modification restrictions constraining the allowed modifications by child modules. We identified the following kinds of modifications: extension, elimination, and redefinition. Extension adds features to child entities [6,14,17,24,26,27,29]. The contrary modification is elimination (also called reduction) removing features [26,27,29]. Redefinition redefines inherited features but does not eliminate features [14,17,24,29].

In this paper, in order to keep the approach simple and compact, we focus on extension and elimination which can be used to simulate redefinition. We introduce restrictions for module structure prohibiting (a) to extend interfaces and (b) to remove specific predicates from interfaces. Regarding module behavior we introduce restrictions prohibiting: (c) to extend a module's behavior and (d) to reduce a module's behavior.

Definition 7 (Modification Restrictions). *A module m may define a set of modification restrictions S_m of the following forms:* no_additional_input, non_omitable_input(p) *with* $p \in I_m$, no_additional_output, non_omitable_output(p) *with* $p \in O_m$, non_growable(p) *with* $p \in O_m$, *and* non_shrinkable(p) *with* $p \in O_m$.

4.1   Structural Modification Restrictions

In order to regulate modification operations on module interfaces, we introduce four restrictions. The restrictions *no_additional_input* and *no_additional_output* prohibit the addition of predicates to the input and output interface respectively. The restrictions *non_omitable_input* and *non_omitable_output* prohibit to remove the specified predicate from the respective interface.

Definition 8 (Consistent Structural Modification). *Let module m' inherit from module m, $(m', m) \in H$. Structural modifications in child module m' are consistent with modification restrictions in parent module m if the following conditions hold:*

1. *if* no_additional_input $\in S_m$ *then* $I_{m'}^+ = \emptyset$,
2. *if* non_omitable_input(p) $\in S_m$ *then* $p \notin I_{m'}^-$,
3. *if* no_additional_output $\in S_m$ *then* $O_{m'}^+ = \emptyset$, *and*
4. *if* non_omitable_output(p) $\in S_m$ *then* $p \notin O_{m'}^-$.

Example 5. During the rule elicitation process our domain experts determined several modification restrictions regarding module LoanApps: Any application for a specific loan type must contain at least the same information as an application for a generic loan. Consequently, we define: *non_omitable_input*(loan), *non_omitable_input*(lValue), *non_omitable_input*(duration), *non_omitable_input*(customer). Furthermore, any loan application module must output at least the predicates for credit worthiness, priority, low loan values, and security values. Output securities may be replaced by more specific forms of outputs. Thus, we define cwGood, cwBad, priorityOver, lowLValue, and sValue as *non_omitable_output*. In Fig. 3 these restrictions are listed under ¬*omitable* in the respective interface.

Module MortgageApps finalizes the output for any rule module inheriting from it, i.e., such a module may employ more input predicates for determining securities and their value but may not output additional predicates. Therefore, we define *no_additional_output* for module MortgageApps. In Fig. 3 we denoted this as ¬*extensible* written next to the output of module MortgageApps.

From an organizational perspective, determining structural restrictions is part of rule elicitation, definition, and organization. Conformance checking of structural restrictions is necessary whenever an interface of a rule module is changed, a new rule module is added to the module hierarchy, or any structural restrictions of an existing module are modified. In the latter case, conformance of any child module of the modified module with the modified module's restrictions needs to be checked as well. A prerequisite for structural conformance checks is the identification of performed modifications. This is achieved by simple interface comparisons, e.g., parent's input schema with child's input schema.

4.2 Behavioral Modification Restrictions

Modifying rules contained in a rule module influences the module's behavior with respect to derived facts of output predicates. A child module, when applied on a dataset (see Definition 3), may return for a specific predicate the same, a superset, a subset, or a subset of a superset of derived facts compared to its parent module. To regulate behavioral modifications, we introduce the restrictions non_growable and non_shrinkable for output predicates. The restriction *non_growable* prohibits the derivation a superset of facts for a predicate in child modules whereas *non_shrinkable* prohibits child modules from deriving a subset of the facts derived by the parent module for a predicate.

Definition 9 (Consistent Behavioral Modification). *Let module m' inherit from module m, $(m', m) \in H$. Behavioral modifications in child module m' are consistent with modification restrictions in parent module m, if the following conditions hold for every data set $d \in D$ which is applicable to both m and m', as well as for every predicate p which is in the output of m and m':*

1. if $non\_growable(p) \in S_m$ then $p_{m'}^d \subseteq p_m^d$ and
2. if $non\_shrinkable(p) \in S_m$, then $p_{m'}^d \supseteq p_m^d$.

Example 6. Regarding behavior, domain experts reported several restrictions for module LoanApps: the basic rule for good credit worthiness (R1) is the minimum requirement, i.e., its condition may only be stricter. Thus, we define *non_growable*(cwGood) meaning that a loan application not deemed credit worthy according to the rules in parent module LoanApps may not be derived as credit worthy by child modules. Since every loan application is classified either cwGood/1 or cwBad/1 we state *non_shrinkable*(cwBad). Furthermore, the loan value in RO is the minimum threshold for loan values. Consequently, the value may only be increased when specializing module LoanApps, represented as $non\_shrinkable$(lowLValue). As every loan application must be prioritized, behavior regarding priorityOver/2 must not change, represented as $non\_growable$(priorityOver), $non\_shrinkable$(priorityOver).

From an organizational viewpoint, behavioral restrictions are determined during rule elicitation, definition, and organization. To perform *behavioral conformance checks*, performed behavioral modifications are compared with behavioral modification restrictions. This check can be performed during rule module testing or during execution: (a) Before modifications to a module are disseminated and deployed, they need to be thoroughly tested, i.e., the module, any parent module, and any child modules are tested with various input data sets. In addition to traditional testing, we then employ modification detection (see below) to check conformance to defined modification restrictions. (b) We can also compare the behavior of parent and child module at runtime when the child module is executed. Any violated behavioral restrictions are reported.

4.3   Detection of Behavioral Modifications

To determine performed behavioral modifications we propose: (a) asking responsible rule developer(s) to state his/her performed behavioral modifications manually, and (b) to automatically detect performed behavioral modification operations employing static or dynamic detection.

We expect complete static detection (by automatic reasoning over Datalog programs) of behavioral modification operations to be undecidable due to rule dependencies as well as references and predicates within input data. Nevertheless, partial detection is feasible by comparing a child module's with its parent module's rule dependency graph. A proof that this problem is undecidable as well as an algorithm for partial static detection are beyond this paper.

We now introduce dynamic detection of behavioral modifications which can be used as part of testing or during rule execution. Therefore, a child module and its parent module are executed on the same input data and their output facts compared. For a specific parent module m and child module m' we select a set of data sets from D applicable to both the child and the parent module. For each data set d, we execute both modules and compare the derived facts for concrete predicates; abstract predicates are not considered in conformance checks as their behavior is incomplete. For each predicate p concrete in the parent and child module, we compare $p_{m'}^d$ with p_m^d. If $p_{m'}^d \subset p_m^d$ the set of output facts has shrunk, if $p_{m'}^d \supset p_m^d$ the set of output facts has grown, if the sets of output facts has neither shrunk nor grown and $p_m^d \neq p_{m'}^d$ it has shrunk and grown, and lastly $p_m^d = p_{m'}^d$ implies no changes. The overall modification in behavior for a specific predicate is the union of all detected modifications in behavior. These detected behavioral modifications must not violate specified behavioral modification restrictions. The more data sets from D are employed, the more reliable the detected modification(s) in behavior is/are.

4.4   Inheritance of Modification Restrictions

In order to achieve transitive conformance to modification restrictions we need to introduce inheritance of modification restrictions. Basically, child rule modules must not remove any modification restrictions imposed on their ancestors.

Definition 10 (Inheritance of Modification Restrictions). *Let module m' inherit directly from module m, $(m', m) \in H$. The child module's set of modification restrictions $S_{m'}$ is the union of the set of modification restrictions S_m inherited from parent module m and the set of modification restrictions $S_{m'}^+$ added by the child module m', i.e., $S_{m'} \stackrel{def}{=} S_m \cup S_{m'}^+$.*

Example 7. Module `PrivateLoanApps` inherits from module `LoanApps`. Besides rules and interface predicates, the defined modification restrictions are inherited. Consequently, any modification restriction defined in module `LoanApps` must hold in module `PrivateLoanApps` as well. This is depicted in Fig. 4 where inheritance has been resolved for module `PrivateLoanApps`, e.g., *non_omitable*(`cwGood`) defined in module `LoanApps` must also hold in module `PrivateLoanApps`.

5   Proof-of-Concept Prototype

Our proof-of-concept prototype implements the presented formal definitions, structural and behavioral conformance checks, and proposed modification detections. To this end, we need meta-representations of rule modules including their interfaces, inheritance relations, modification operations, and modification restrictions. Therefore, we embed our prototype in an environment able to generate meta representations of Datalog$^\pm$ programs (e.g. Vadalog [4]).

To facilitate widespread experimentation we provide a download[1] containing a Datalog implementation of our prototype (`terms.datalog`) and Datalog meta-representations for the rule modules in our use case (`<module>Meta.datalog`). The meta-representations do not include built-ins. While Datalog code is, beyond this use case, in general severely limited in expressive power, it allows experimenting with our prototype independently of the concrete Datalog$^\pm$ engine.

Executing our prototype on meta-representations of rule modules resolves inheritance, i.e., determines rules, facts, and modification restrictions applying in each module, reports abstract predicates and modules, and detects violations of structural modification restrictions. In order to test dynamic behavioral modification detection, we provide meta-representations of the output facts resulting from executing module `LoanApps` and module `PrivateLoanApps` on the same input facts (`result<module>.datalog`).

Executing the prototype for our use case using DLV yields reasonable performance considering that the average times include DLV start-up and no performance optimizations have been carried out. Resolving inheritance, reporting abstract predicates and modules, detecting behavioral modification operations, and structural and behavioral conformance checking take on average 0.017 s (sd = 0.001 s) on a standard notebook (Intel Core i5-6200U, DDR4, 16 GB).

---

[1] http://files.dke.uni-linz.ac.at/publications/burgstaller/ODBASEPrototype.zip.

6   Related Work

In the following we discuss inheritance of single rules; rule sets, rule modules, and their inheritance; as well as contextual knowledge and its inheritance. Several researchers proposed inheritance of pre- and postconditions of operations (rule premises) where modifications to conditions are restricted to strengthening or weakening [20,21,27]. Other research regards inheritance of triggers (which can be considered event-condition-action rules) in object-oriented databases, where a trigger's premises may become weaker and trigger actions may be extended [5]. $\mathcal{FLORA}$-2 [14] combines rules and object-oriented features where methods are specified as rules and can be inherited.

6.1   Rule Sets, Modules, and Inheritance

Modularization is employed in many fields, e.g., software engineering or ontologies, enabling controlled and structured development of large systems [25]. Regarding knowledge, a knowledge base may either be partitioned into non-overlapping modules or relevant portions extracted into possibly overlapping modules [25]. The concrete modularization strategy depends on the use case.

Regarding ontologies, a triple containing an ontology, a query language, and a vocabulary can be considered a module, where the query language and the vocabulary serve as interface allowing interaction by querying [15]. A simple extension mechanism enabling addition of ontological statements is described [15].

Rule modules with relational schemas as interfaces are a simplified variant of relational transducers [1]. In the original proposal, relational transducers serve as "declarative specifications of business models, using an approach in the spirit of active databases" [1, p. 1]. Relational transducers transform sequences of input into sequences of output relations. In addition to input and output relations, a relational transducer specifies database, state, and log relations, where the log relations are the semantically relevant subset of input and output relations. Regarding inheritance, they discuss customization of relational transducers and with regard to restricted modification they discuss "containment and equivalence of relational transducers relative to a specified log" [1, p. 7].

Modular Web rule bases [2] separate interfaces, i.e., predicates used and predicates defined, from the logic program, i.e., rules. Each predicate in a module defines its reasoning mode, its scope, and its origin rule bases or rule bases it is visible to. Modular rule base extension is supported, allowing to add new rules to existing rule bases and to add new rule bases to the set of rule bases.

Inheritance of (business) rules is touched in [9,10] (see contextualized knowledge below) and discussed specific to situation-condition-actions rules in [17]. Inheritance of rule sets is discussed in [24]. Lang [17] identifies the rule of origin as prerequisite, i.e., a feature may only be defined in a single point. Moreover, he utilizes the abstract parent class rule. Situations, conditions, and actions may be specialized if the occurrence of a situation implies occurrence of its child situations and rule conditions are only weakened. Based on these conditions modification operations are proposed [17]: extension denotes addition of rules or redefining rules to fire more often, refinement denotes concreting abstract rules, i.e., concreting rule-triggering interval classes to event classes, and redefinition is constrained to specialized actions and events as well as weakened conditions. Pachet [24] describes rule set inheritance as inheriting all rules from parent rule sets and allows for unconstrained redefinition of rules.

A related field are business rule management systems (BRMSs) like IBM's JRules, JBoss Drools, FICO Blaze Advisor, or Oracle Business Rules, which organize business rules into rule sets. JRules supports inheritance of rules and rule sets where rules may be overridden. Drools and Blaze both support inheritance of rule conditions. Oracle does not report support for rule (set) inheritance.

Many of the above approaches support rule sets ([9,10,14,15,17,24,25], BRMSs) but only Abiteboul et al. [1], Analyti et al. [2], and Konev et al. [15] describe modules with explicit definition of input and output interfaces as supported by our approach. Rule set inheritance is supported by quite a few approaches, where some allow no or only predefined modification types ([1,9,15,17], Drools, Blaze) and others allow arbitrary modifications ([10,24], JRules). Nevertheless, none of them provides any means to assert fine-grained control over the allowed types of modifications to inherited rule sets as our approach does with the presented modification restrictions. By these modification restrictions, our approach allows, unlike the ones discussed above, to flexibly adapt the inheritance mechanism to the specific needs at hand.

6.2 Contextualized Knowledge Representation and Inheritance

A related field are contextual knowledge and its inheritance. Contextualized Knowledge repositories (CKR) [28] for the Semantic Web organize ontological concepts employing hierarchically ordered contexts. A context is defined by a set of values for various but fixed context dimensions. Allowed dimension values form a subsumption hierarchy from which the hierarchy of contexts is derived. Concepts propagate along this hierarchy from general contexts to more specific contexts. Concepts may assume different meanings in different contexts. A similar idea was proposed for knowledge organization in CYC [18] where it is explicitly allowed to contradict or override inherited knowledge. McCarthy [19] views contexts as generalizing collections of assumptions where a child context must have at least the same assumptions as its parent context. Knowledge from child contexts must be translatable into meaningful knowledge in the parent context, i.e., a root context would contain all knowledge in decontextualized form.

Building on these approaches, we introduced a contextualized (business) rule repository [10] allowing to organize rule sets into multi-dimensional context hierarchies. Regarding inheritance, we differentiate additive and most-specific inheritance of rule sets. With the former inheritance mechanism all rules of a parent rule set apply in its child rule sets as well. The latter approach allows redefinition of inherited rules. Previous work on contextualized rule repositories for the Semantic Web [9] employed an additive inheritance semantics only.

Since contexts can be considered modules, all of the above approaches support modules. Nevertheless, none of them explicitly defines clear input and output interfaces for modules as our approach does. Regarding module inheritance, all of the above approaches support inheritance of knowledge, some [10,18] allow redefinition of knowledge whereas others do not [9,19,28]. Compared to our approach, none of the above approaches supports modification restrictions, i.e., one cannot control modifications to the knowledge in a module.

7 Conclusion

We investigated inheritance of rule modules to foster reuse of rules, simplify adaptation, and ease maintenance. Therefore, we introduced rule modules and proposed a formal inheritance mechanism. We presented modification restrictions regulating modifications with corresponding conformance checks as mechanisms for keeping child modules aligned with parent modules.

In ongoing and future work we investigate:

- extending our proposed approach to multi-inheritance and integrating it into *context-aware business rule management* [7] and Vadalog [4].
- rule modules as part of derivation chains or module networks in *big data wrangling* [16] and *knowledge graph management* [3]. There, rule set adaptation is necessary to cope with the variety of relevant subject domains and the variety of integrated sources of data and knowledge. Furthermore, the interfaces of our rule modules support derivation chains and networks.

References

1. Abiteboul, S., Vianu, V., Fordham, B.S., Yesha, Y.: Relational transducers for electronic commerce. In: Proceedings of the Seventeenth ACM SIGACT-SIGMOD-SIGART Symposium on Principles of Database Systems, pp. 179–187 (1998)
2. Analyti, A., Antoniou, G., Damasio, C.V.: MWeb: a principled framework for modular web rule bases and its semantics. ACM Trans. Comput. Log. **12**(2), 17:1–17:46 (2011)
3. Bellomarini, L., Gottlob, G., Pieris, A., Sallinger, E.: Swift logic for big data and knowledge graphs. In: Proceedings of the Twenty-Sixth International Joint Conference on Artificial Intelligence, pp. 2–10 (2017)
4. Bellomarini, L., Sallinger, E., Gottlob, G.: The vadalog system: datalog-based reasoning for knowledge graphs. PVLDB **11**(9), 975–987 (2018)
5. Bertino, E., Guerrini, G., Merlo, I.: Trigger inheritance and overriding in an active object database system. IEEE Trans. Knowl. Data Eng. **12**(4), 588–608 (2000)
6. Bichler, P., Schrefl, M.: Inheritance of business rules. In: Hildesheimer Informatik-Berichte, 7. Workshop "Grundlagen von Datenbanken" (1995)
7. Burgstaller, F., Neumayr, B., Schuetz, C.G., Schrefl, M.: Modification operations for context-aware business rule management. In: 2017 IEEE 21st International Enterprise Distributed Object Computing Conference, pp. 194–203 (2017)
8. Burgstaller, F., Steiner, D., Schrefl, M., Gringinger, E., Wilson, S., van der Stricht, S.: AIRM-based, fine-grained semantic filtering of notices to airmen. In: Integrated Communication, Navigation, and Surveillance, pp. D3-1–D3-13 (2015)

9. Burgstaller, F., Schuetz, C., Neumayr, B., Schrefl, M.: Towards contextualized rule repositories for the semantic web. In: Joint Proceedings of the Web Stream Processing Workshop (WSP 2017) and the 2nd International Workshop on Ontology Modularity, Contextuality, and Evolution (WOMoCoE 2017), pp. 98–109 (2017). http://ceur-ws.org/Vol-1936/paper-09.pdf

10. Burgstaller, F., Steiner, D., Schrefl, M.: Modeling context for business rule management. In: IEEE 18th Conference on Business Informatics, pp. 262–271 (2016)

11. Calì, A., Gottlob, G., Lukasiewicz, T.: A general datalog-based framework for tractable query answering over ontologies. Web Semant. Sci. Serv. Agents World Wide Web **14**(Suppl. C), 57–83 (2012)

12. Carbonell, J.G.: Default reasoning and inheritance mechanisms on type hierarchies. SIGMOD Rec. **11**(2), 107–109 (1980)

13. Furche, T., et al.: DIADEM: thousands of websites to a single database. PVLDB **7**(14), 1845–1856 (2014)

14. Kifer, M., Yang, G., Wan, H., Zhao, C.: $\mathcal{E}RGO^L ite$ (a.k.a. $\mathcal{F}$LORA-2): user manual (2017). http://flora.sourceforge.net/docs/floraManual.pdf

15. Konev, B., Lutz, C., Walther, D., Wolter, F.: Formal properties of modularisation. In: Stuckenschmidt, H., Parent, C., Spaccapietra, S. (eds.) Modular Ontologies. LNCS, vol. 5445, pp. 25–66. Springer, Heidelberg (2009). https://doi.org/10.1007/978-3-642-01907-4_3

16. Konstantinou, N., et al.: The VADA architecture for cost-effective data wrangling. In: Proceedings of the 2017 ACM International Conference on Management of Data, pp. 1599–1602 (2017)

17. Lang, P.: Conceptual design of active object-oriented databases. Ph.D. thesis, Johannes Kepler University Linz (1997)

18. Lenat, D.: The dimensions of context-space (1998). http://www2.denizyuret.com/ref/lenat/context-space.pdf

19. McCarthy, J.: Notes on formalizing context. In: Proceedings of the 13th International Joint Conference on Artifical Intelligence, vol. 1, pp. 555–560 (1993)

20. Meyer, B.: Applying 'design by contract'. IEEE Comput. **25**(10), 40–51 (1992)

21. OMG: Object Constraint Language (2014). http://www.omg.org/spec/OCL

22. OMG: Decision Model and Notation (2016). http://www.omg.org/spec/DMN/

23. OMG: Semantics of Business Vocabulary and Business Rules (2017). http://www.omg.org/spec/SBVR

24. Pachet, F.: Rule base inheritance. In: Représentations par objets (1992)

25. Parent, C., Spaccapietra, S.: An overview of modularity. In: Stuckenschmidt, H., Parent, C., Spaccapietra, S. (eds.) Modular Ontologies. LNCS, vol. 5445, pp. 5–23. Springer, Heidelberg (2009). https://doi.org/10.1007/978-3-642-01907-4_2

26. Schrefl, M., Neumayr, B., Stumptner, M.: The decision-scope approach to specialization of business rules: application in business process modeling and data warehousing. In: 9th Asia-Pacific Conference on Conceptual Modelling, pp. 3–18 (2013)

27. Schrefl, M., Stumptner, M.: Behavior-consistent specialization of object life cycles. ACM Trans. Softw. Eng. Methodol. **11**(1), 92–148 (2002)

28. Serafini, L., Homola, M.: Contextualized knowledge repositories for the semantic web. Web Semant. Sci. Serv. Agents World Wide Web **12–13**, 64–87 (2012)

29. Wegner, P., Zdonik, S.B.: Inheritance as an incremental modification mechanism or what like is and isn't like. In: Gjessing, S., Nygaard, K. (eds.) ECOOP 1988. LNCS, vol. 322, pp. 55–77. Springer, Heidelberg (1988). https://doi.org/10.1007/3-540-45910-3_4

30. Weigand, H., Paschke, A.: The pragmatic web: putting rules in context. In: Bikakis, A., Giurca, A. (eds.) RuleML 2012. LNCS, vol. 7438, pp. 182–192. Springer, Heidelberg (2012). https://doi.org/10.1007/978-3-642-32689-9_14

Computing Exposition Coherence Across Learning Resources

Chaitali Diwan[1(✉)], Srinath Srinivasa[1], and Prasad Ram[2]

[1] IIIT Bangalore, 26/C, Electronics City, Bengaluru 560100, India
chaitali.diwan@iiitb.org, sri@iiitb.ac.in
[2] Gooru Inc, 350, Twin Dolphin Dr, Redwood City, CA 94065, USA
pram@gooru.org

Abstract. With increasing numbers of open learning resources on the web that are created and published independently by different sources, stringing together coherent learning pathways is a challenging task. Coherence in this context means the semantic "smoothness" of transition from one learning resource to the next, i.e., the change in topic distribution and exposition styles between consecutive resources is minimal, and the overall sequence of resources together provides a good learning experience. Towards this end, we present a model to compute exposition coherence between a pair of learning resources, based on representing exposition styles in the form of a random walk. It is based on an underlying hypothesis about exposition styles modelled as a sequence of topical entailments. Evaluation of the presented model on the dataset of learning pathways curated by the teachers of the educational platform *Gooru.org*, show promising results.

Keywords: Graph kernels · Co-occurrence graphs · Random walk
Word embedding · Technology enhanced learning
Semantic coherence · Open corpus educational resources

1 Introduction

The number of open learning resources on the web is increasing every year. Large numbers of educational resources are freely available covering various subjects and learning styles. In principle, it is possible for an interested learner to obtain significant levels of expertise in different subjects based on learning pathways created over disparate such resources. However, any meaningful learning experience requires a learning pathway that provides a *coherent* and *smooth* learning experience, maximizing comprehension and skill building. With open resources that are independently created, curating such learning pathways becomes a challenging problem [3]. We call the problem of curating a coherent learning pathway from independent resources, as the "Narrative arc" problem. A coherent narrative arc can aid learners in smoothly bridging conceptual gaps, thereby improving comprehension.

© Springer Nature Switzerland AG 2018
H. Panetto et al. (Eds.): OTM 2018 Conferences, LNCS 11230, pp. 423–440, 2018.
https://doi.org/10.1007/978-3-030-02671-4_26

Computing learning pathways has been pursued by researchers in various forms that include: rules based approaches, data mining techniques and swarm optimization [10,28,30]. Most of the approaches however, assume that the learning materials are created by a single source and hence implicitly assume coherence in exposition or presentation styles.

When the dataset contains learning resources created by independent third-party sources, the narrative arc problem is more challenging. Here, the style in which a topic is presented may vary across resources created by different parties. There is a need to not only compute the semantic smoothness of transition for creating a learning pathway, but we also need to account for smoothness in *exposition* – or style of presentation. This problem of curating learning pathways from open educational resources is a growing research field and is known as Open Corpus AEHS (Adaptive Educational Hypermedia Systems) [3,8].

Creating learning pathways requires some type of information or meta-data about the learning resources, like learning progressions, pre-requisite dependencies, instructional depth, etc. Building a narrative arc also requires specification of a starting point, a learning goal and a sequence of competencies or learning concepts (called route) that needs to be mastered by the learner to achieve the learning goal. To build a narrative arc, we need to associate different learning resources from the open corpus aligned with the route of selected competencies such that, a semantically coherent path is presented to the user.

To address the coherency problem, a narrative is first modelled as comprising of two components: its topical structure, and its style of presentation, or its "exposition". A coherent narrative arc should address coherency in both, the topical structure and the exposition. Coherency in the topical structure, pertains to how the semantic structure of the learning resources lead up to the learning goal. Coherency in exposition styles pertains to the way a concept is presented in a learning resource and is resonant with the way the next concept is presented in the next learning resource.

The exposition style of a learning resource is modelled as an unfolding distribution over topics. Typically there would be a main topic that is addressed by the resource and to explain the main topic, the resource may use other concepts or sub-topics to different extents. Building upon the ideas of discourse theory and cognitive load theory [1,17,22], we define the exposition coherence between two consecutive learning resources as semantic "smoothness" of transition from one learning resource to the next, i.e., the change in unfolding topic distribution between consecutive resources is minimal (but not zero), and the overall sequence of resources together provides a good learning experience.

A simple example of exposition coherence is as follows. When a learner wants to master a topic in combinatorics and he picks up the first resource, say Ramsey theory, which uses set theory to explain the concept and if the very next resource is about, say Dintz conjecture, that also uses set theory, then, it would be a smooth transition. But if the second resource would use graph theory and the third resource would use matrix theory for explanation, then due to different exposition styles, the continuity or engagement in learning would be low.

In this paper, we present a model for computing exposition coherence between a pair of learning resources by defining a graph kernel function. In the kernel function, an exposition is modelled as a random walk over a co-occurrence graph of topical terms.

We have also explored three different approaches for finding coherence between learning resources based on word and document embeddings. In first of these approaches, a random walk algorithm is implemented over a semantic space containing word embeddings [19] from the corpus. This approach is based on predicting the neighbourhood of a term, in contrast to the graph kernel model, that is based on counting co-occurrences. Other two approaches based on finding the cosine similarity of document embeddings [15] and word embeddings [19] are also explored, to test whether modelling of exposition styles can be obviated with just semantic embeddings.

The algorithms were evaluated over a dataset of independent learning resources, over which learning pathways were created by human curators as part of a web-enabled learning portal. The graph kernels, word embeddings and the document embeddings approaches returned a high coherency score for the resource pairs that were part of a human-identified pathway as compared to a random other resource pair. However, with the unfolding nature of a random walk based graph similarity measure, the graph kernel approach was able to discriminate between the consecutive learning resources in a pathway versus the non-consecutive resources of the same pathway, indicating the need for separate modelling of exposition styles.

2   Related Work

There is extensive literature on measuring semantic similarity between short texts, long texts and documents. Islam and Inkpen [9] propose a method that uses subsequence of strings, word semantic similarity and common word order similarity, to compare sentences. Mikolov et al. propose word embedding [19] and document embedding [15] models which map the words, phrases or sentences to vectors of real numbers that can be used to compare words, sentences or documents.

Yeh et al. [31] propose a personalised page rank approach to find semantic relatedness for words and texts using links between Wikipedia articles. An approach to semantic relatedness using conceptual graphs was proposed by Kongkachandra and Chamnongthai [12], which uses an effective but complex method for calculation based on word senses, parts of speech and syntactic relations. The model studied by Paul et al. [23] is based on the lexical knowledge graph WordNet and offers an efficient computational complexity of graph traversal. Huang et al. [7] propose a document similarity measure based on bag of words and bag of concepts, in which, concepts are derived from Wikipedia and WordNet.

Liu et al. [16] model semantic similarity using graph convolution networks. Ponza et al. [25] use textual context and knowledge graph structure around terms for computing semantic relatedness. Ni et al. [21] propose a semantic embedding model called Concept2Vec by measuring similarity between concept graphs. Mueller and Thyagarajan [20] propose a sentence similarity measure as an adaptation of Long Short-Term Memory (LSTM) neural network.

Semantic similarity studied in the above papers are framed in a general setting, without a distinction between topical structure and exposition. The proposed model in this paper is specifically directed towards expositional similarity, that can result in a smooth transition between one learning resource to another.

Apart from the distinction of the coherence from similarity, we look at two more aspects that our model offers in comparison to the approaches mentioned in the literature. First, while most of the sentence or document similarity approaches discussed above look at the static semantics, the random walk approach we propose, looks at the unfolding of topic distribution for comparison. Second, most of the above research require large general-knowledge training corpora. In contrast, our model is based solely on the provided dataset, and does not require training on larger, generic corpora. For educational resources in a niche area of study, or for a field that is emerging, our model would be a natural choice. Our model works well and gives accurate results even for a corpus of few thousand resources.

To the best of our knowledge, semantic comparison over learning resources or content has not been explored much in literature. Some approaches like that of Krieger et al. [13] create semantic fingerprint for a web based learning resource, which could be used to compute semantic relatedness, however it doesn't present a methodology for this comparison. An approach to computing concept coherence based on ontologies is proposed by Hsieh and Wang [6], however it measures semantic coherence between the learning resources, not exposition coherence. Similarity measures for pairs of educational items is studied by Pelánek et al. [24] using learners data. Even though this approach looks at similarity measure, it doesn't look at the content or semantic aspect of a learning resource.

Approaches to creating learning pathways are discussed in [10,28,30]. Most of the approaches however, assume that the learning materials are created by a single source and are in closed settings. Learning sequences studied as recommender system in [27,33] are also proposed in closed settings and have requirements of structured content. They are mostly based on learners profiles. Recommender system presented in [32] uses ontology to generate learning pathways and the semantic relatedness is calculated based on the depth of domain hierarchy. This model is also proposed in closed system of learning resources.

A genetic-based personalized e-learning system developed by Chen [5] is based on the difficulty of the course-ware and the results of pre-tests, but not on the content of learning resources. Some approaches for generating resource sequencing in open corpus are based on pre-requisites identification [4,18] and annotation (or generating meta data) [14]. However, as far as we know, generating learning pathways based on exposition coherence has not been pursued in the literature.

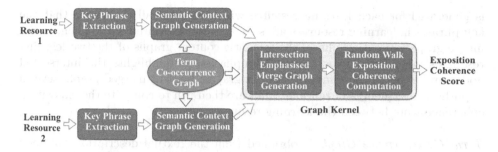

Fig. 1. Components of exposition coherence computation

3   The Proposed Model

The proposed model is presented in a setting, comprising of a large corpus of open learning resources, created by several authors independently. A learning resource is any kind of digital resource, that provides a tutorial introduction to a given topic. A learning resource could be in the form of a text document, a video, a set of slides, a podcast, etc. The only assumption about a learning resource is that the resource as a whole, addresses one central topic. The central topic may be presented using several other topics.

One of the first steps towards computing exposition coherence is to convert disparate kinds of learning resources into a canonical, text-based model. For this, we use several tools like transcript generators, OCR tools, etc., to convert every learning resource in the corpus, into a collection of sentences.

The exposition coherence problem is now defined as a function that measures consistency in exposition between any two learning resources. Exposition refers to the style in which a particular narrative is presented. To model this, we think of an exposition as an *unfolding sequence of topics*, that is used to present the primary topic addressed by the learning resource. The unfolding sequence of topics is in turn computationally modelled as a random walk.

The approach is based on *counting* co-occurrences, learning resources are represented as co-occurrence graphs and a kernel function is defined over the graphs to represent exposition coherence, based on the random walk.

3.1   Graph Kernel

A corpus-wide term co-occurrence graph is first built from all the learning resources in the corpus. Given a pair of learning resources, exposition coherence between them is computed by creating the semantic context graphs for each of the learning resources and passing them to a kernel function, that in turn computes the coherence on a combined co-occurrence graph.

Figure 1 outlines the overall approach. For each pair of learning resources that are compared, first the key-phrases are extracted from the textual description of the resource in the key-phrase extraction phase, then a semantic context graph is generated for each learning resource which includes all the words that the key-phrases in learning resources are semantically associated with. Then, in the merge-graph generation phase, the semantic context graphs of the two learning resources are merged in a way that emphasises or highlights the intersected nodes and edges of the semantic context graphs. On this merged graph, several hypothetical sequences of random walks are then run to compute the exposition coherence score between the learning resources.

Term Co-occurrence Graph is obtained from the textual description obtained either directly, or by a transcription of the given learning resource. This text is first pre-processed to extract the key-phrases. Pre-processing involves cleaning the data of unnecessary characters, removing numbers, punctuation and stop words, stemming and lemmatizing the words, and identifying phrases.

Two terms in a learning resource are said to co-occur if they appear in the same "occurrence context". Typically, a sentence is seen as an occurrence context. For learning resources with very short descriptions, the entire description is considered as an occurrence context.

A node is created for each of the key-phrases with name of the node same as the key-phrase. All the key-phrases that are present in a single occurrence context are considered to be pair-wise co-occurring with one another. Hence, each of them are connected to each other by an edge, forming a clique with an uniform edge weight of 1.

This clique is superimposed on the already available corpus-wide term co-occurrence graph, if any. Initially the corpus-wide co-occurrence graph is a null graph, and as learning resources are processed, the overall graph is built by merging of cliques obtained from occurrence contexts. The cliques are merged such that, if an edge that is in the clique is already present in the term co-occurrence graph, then edge weight in the term co-occurrence graph is increased by 1. Thus the edge weights between a pair of nodes represent the number of occurrence contexts in which they co-occur. Term co-occurrence graph is enhanced when new learning resources are added to the corpus.

Formally, the corpus-wide term co-occurrence graph is defined as a weighted, undirected graph: $G = (T, C, w)$ where T is a set of terms, $C \subseteq T^2$ depicts pair-wise co-occurrences of the terms, and weight $w : C \to \mathbb{R}$ is the frequency of co-occurrence of terms in the learning resources.

Semantic Context Graph. Given a learning resource represented by its set of extracted key-phrases k, the topical representation of the learning resource is computed from the corpus-wide co-occurrence graph in the form of a "semantic context" $\psi(k)$. The semantic context $\psi(k) \subseteq G$ is defined as:

$$\psi(k) = (T_k, C_k, w_k) \tag{1}$$

where T_k is the set of all terms that are either in k, or co-occurs with any term in k, C_k is the set of all co-occurrences between terms in T_k, and w_k is a subset of w representing co-occurrence weights between the co-occurring terms in T_k,

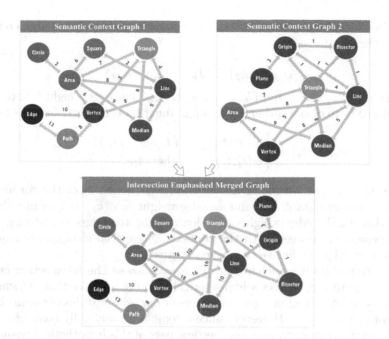

Fig. 2. Creating intersection emphasised merge graph from semantic context graphs

weights in w_k have the same edge weights as in w. In other words, a semantic context is the *induced subgraph* formed by taking all the terms in k and any terms that co-occur with any term in k.

Random Walk Graph Kernel. Given a pair of learning resources k_1 and k_2 represented by their set of terms respectively, semantic context graphs $\psi(k_1)$ and $\psi(k_2)$ are first created.

Exposition coherence is computed by comparing topical similarity between these semantic contexts. Similarity functions on numerical or vector valued data types are expressed in the form of a positive semi-definite *kernel* function. The concept of kernel functions have also been extended for graph-structured data [11, 29].

In our work, we develop a variant of the random walk kernel developed by Vishwanathan et al. [29] to compare semantic contexts. Semantic context graphs are sub-graphs of the same corpus-wide term co-occurrence graph and may have common terms and co-occurrences between them. The probability of a term following another term can be obtained by the relative co-occurrence weights. Overlap or common terms and edges between the contexts signify greater coherence.

To capture this, given a pair of semantic contexts $\psi(k_1)$ and $\psi(k_2)$, an *intersection emphasized merge graph* $\psi_M(k_1, k_2)$ is defined, that emphasizes intersection between the semantic context graphs. Figure 2 shows creation of *intersection emphasized merge graph* from its semantic context graphs. The merge creates a graph of the form:

$$\psi_M(k_1, k_2) = (T_{k_1 k_2}, C_{k_1 k_2}, w_M) \tag{2}$$

where $T_{k_1 k_2} = T_{k_1} \cup T_{k_2}$ and $C_{k_1 k_2} = C_{k_1} \cup C_{k_2}$. The edge weight function w_M is a modified form of the earlier edge weight function w and is defined as follows:

$$w_M(t_i, t_j) = \begin{cases} 2 * w(t_i, t_j) & \text{if } t_i \text{ and } t_j \in T_{k_1} \cap T_{k_2} \\ w(t_i, t_j) & \text{otherwise} \end{cases} \tag{3}$$

where $w(t_i, t_j)$ is the weight of an edge between t_i and t_j of the corpus wide term co-occurrence graph G (same as edge weight in $\psi(k_1)$ and/or in $\psi(k_2)$).

In other words, edge weights are doubled for the edges connecting nodes that are common between both the contexts. No special changes are made for co-occurrence edges exclusive to a given context.

The interpretation for such a graph is as follows. The intersection emphasized merge graph represents a hypothetical learning resource that is formed by stringing together common topic sequences or exposition styles between the two given learning resources. However, since a topic is semantically connected to all other topics in its vicinity, they too become part of this hypothetical resource. If the "noise" in the topic sequences is high, then despite emphasizing the common sequences, the probability of taking a non-common edge is high. It means that the exposition styles are not compatible.

The common nodes between both the graphs are distinguished by marking them with a commonality property. The commonality property c_{t_i} for a term $t_i \subseteq T_{k_1 k_2}$ in the merged graph is 1 if the node is common between both the semantic context graphs, else it is 0. It is defined formally as follows:

$$c_{t_i} = \begin{cases} 1, & \text{if } t_i \text{ is in } T_{k_1} \cap T_{k_2} \\ 0, & \text{otherwise} \end{cases} \tag{4}$$

To execute the random walks, a stochastic transition matrix T is created which represents the probabilities of walking from one node to another during the random walk sequence, for all the nodes in the graph. Let A be the weighted adjacency matrix of the merged graph ψ_M and $w_M(t_i, t_j)$ be the weight of an edge between t_i and t_j. The transition probability p_{ij} of moving from node t_i to node t_j is calculated as ratio of weight $w_M(t_i, t_j)$ to the sum of weights of all the columns of the ith row of the adjacency matrix and is denoted as follows:

$$p_{ij} = \frac{w_M(t_i, t_j)}{\sum_{j \in T} w_M(t_i, t_j)} \tag{5}$$

In the above, it should be noted that probabilities are calculated based on the corpus-wide distribution of co-occurrence weights and not just the co-occurrence weights that form a part of the merge graph. The function $w_M(\cdot, \cdot)$ defaults to the function $w(\cdot, \cdot)$ when node j represents a node that is not part of the merge graph.

The sum of all outgoing probabilities from a node in the merged graph need not add up to 1, since not all neighbours of a node may be part of the merged graph. As a result, such a transition graph is also called a "leaking" Markov chain [26]. Infinitely long random walks on such a graph eventually terminate, as every random walk has a non-zero probability of "escaping" the graph.

The transition matrix T has non-zero values for the nodes that have edges between them, and would have zero entries between the nodes that are not connected by an edge. But to get a random walk to reflect the stationary probability of a term being mentioned as a part of an exposition sequence, the graph should be irreducible and aperiodic. This means that the directed transition graph should be strongly connected, and have cycles of all possible values. In order to achieve this, we perform an additive "smoothing" by adding a very small value δ to each of the entries, i.e., there is a non-zero probability of going from one node to other even if there is no edge between the nodes in the term co-occurrence graph. The transition probability p_{ij} is now as follows:

$$p_{ij} = \frac{w_M(t_i, t_j) + \delta}{\sum\limits_{j \in T} (w_M(t_i, t_j) + \delta)} \tag{6}$$

Once the transition matrix T is calculated, numerous long random walks are performed on the *intersection emphasized merge graph*. A term representing the primary topic of either of the learning resources is randomly selected as the start node for a given random walk. The next node in the walk is selected randomly based on the transition probabilities in the transition matrix T. A walk is said to terminate or "escape" the *intersection emphasized merge graph*, if it chooses an edge that is not in it.

The result of a random walk process r_i is a "trace" $T_{r_i} \in T^*$ comprising a sequence of terms that characterised the random walk. For each such trace, an *intersection score* is calculated, which is the ratio of number of common nodes n_c divided by the total number of nodes n_n in the trace. The *intersection score* is formally represented as:

$$is(r_i) = \frac{n_c}{n_n} = \frac{\sum\limits_{t_i \in T_{r_i}} c_{t_i}}{n_n} \tag{7}$$

where t_i is the ith term occurring in the trace T_{r_i} and c_{t_i} is the commonality property of the term t_i as described above.

Several random walk traces are generated, after which, an average of the *intersection scores* is taken for all the random walk sequences which gives the *exposition coherence score* between the two learning resources. Let there be n number of random walk sequences, then the exposition coherence score ec between the two learning resources represented by k_1 and k_2 or semantic context graphs $\psi(k_1)$ and $\psi(k_2)$ is given by the following equation:

$$ec(k_1, k_2) = ec(\psi(k_1), \psi(k_2)) = \frac{\sum\limits_{i=1}^{n} is(r_i)}{n} \tag{8}$$

A running average is computed after every run, and the runs are terminated when the average score stabilises. We say that the running average is stable, if its value does not vary beyond a threshold θ over five consecutive runs.

The *exposition coherence score* is always between 0 to 1. If the semantic context graphs have no nodes in common, they have a *exposition coherence score* of 0. Larger values of $ec(k_1, k_2)$ indicate higher exposition coherence between the considered pair of learning resources.

4   Other Approaches

This section describes the different approaches we explored to compute coherence between learning resource pairs.

4.1   Random Walk over Word Embeddings

This method is based on co-occurrence *prediction*. A neural skip gram model is used to predict the neighbourhood of possible co-occurring terms, given a base term. This skip gram model is used to define a random walk. We use the seminal work of word embedding or word2vec [19] for this method.

The word2vec embedding model generates an m-dimensional vector for terms from a corpus, where semantically close terms are closer to one another in the vector space. The parameter m is a hyperparameter, to be specified during the training phase.

The embedding is performed by training a shallow neural network with one input layer, one output layer and one hidden layer. The hidden layer comprises of m neurons. The input and output layers comprise of $|V|$ neurons, where V is the vocabulary of all terms in the corpus.

The neural network is trained on a training dataset of the form (w, c_w) where w is an input term, and c_w is the k skip gram neighbourhood of w. That is, it is the set of all neighbouring terms that have a distance of at most k with w. The input is provided as a 1-hot vector representing w, and the output vector from the output layer, is compared against a $|c_w|$-hot vector representing the expected neighbourhood. A gradient-descent based backpropagation algorithm is then utilised to adjust the weights of the neurons.

Once the neural network is trained, all the rows of the weight matrix – that is, the set of all weights from the input layer to the hidden layer, forms the respective word vectors of all the terms in the input layer.

Training. In this work, an open-source, Java based deep-learning library $DL4J$[1] that implements word2vec was used. We trained the model with different training parameters for number of dimensions (m) and window size (k), to determine the most suitable model for the dataset. Finally, we used the dimensions of 100, and window size of 10 for training the model.

---

[1] https://deeplearning4j.org.

Semantic Context Set. Once word vectors are generated for every term in the corpus, the exposition style of a learning resource is simulated by a variant of the conventional random walk, on the m-dimensional vector space comprising of the embedded terms.

As with the previous model, we first define the semantic context of a learning resource, and the combined semantic context of a pair of learning resources.

For each learning resource, first the key words are extracted. The same keyphrase extraction module of the Graph Kernel method is used here. The semantic context of a given term is defined as the k nearest neighbours of the term, which is implemented in *DL4J* by a method called wordsNearest(). The semantic context set of a given learning resource is simply the union of nearest words or the context words of all the terms in the resource. And the combined semantic context of two learning resources is computed as the union of the semantic contexts of the two resources.

Random Walk based Exposition Coherence Computation. As with the earlier approach, a series of random walk computations are performed on the combined semantic context of two given learning resources k_1 and k_2. Each random walk starts with a term representing the primary topic from one of the learning resources.

Transition probabilities are computed by creating a k-dimensional simplex called *Transition Simplex* over the k nearest neighbours of a given term. This is done by normalising the cosine similarity score from the term to each of its neighbouring terms, by the sum of the total similarity scores. Let the current selected word be represented as c and the set of k nearest context-words of c be represented as cs, then the probability of transition $P_c(w_i)$ to the next context word w_i from c is computed as follows:

$$P_c(w_i) = \frac{cosine(c, w_i)}{\sum\limits_{w_i \in cs} cosine(c, w_i)} \tag{9}$$

Using the *Transition Simplex*, the next node in the random walk is chosen. At any step in the random walk, if the chosen node belongs to both the semantic context sets, a score of 2 is added to the overall score of the random walk trace. If the chosen node belongs to either but not both the semantic context sets, a score of 1 is added. The random walk is terminated if a node chosen from the nearest neighbour of the given context word does not belong to the either of the semantic context sets.

For a given random walk process r_i, comprising of n_i terms, suppose the overall accumulated score is x_i, then the exposition coherence score of r_i is computed as:

$$ec(r_i) = \frac{x_i}{2 \cdot n_i} \tag{10}$$

As with the earlier approach, a running average is computed after every run, and the runs are terminated when the average score stabilises. The scores obtained from several runs of random walks are averaged out to return the final coherence score which is also between 0 and 1.

4.2 Document Embedding Method

This approach is based on the concept of document embedding [15], as implemented in the *DL4J* paragraph vector library. Document embedding methods reduce an entire document into a single m-dimensional vector, that is typically a function of the word vectors of the words contained in them.

Document embedding can be used to compute semantic similarity between documents in a straightforward fashion, using vector algebraic techniques like cosine similarity or L_p norms.

We explored document embedding to test whether modelling exposition styles is necessary at all, and whether an existing method of document embedding comparison of learning resources would be enough to compute the exposition coherence.

In this approach, every learning resource was computed to its corresponding document vector. Coherence between the two learning resources was computed as the cosine similarity between their corresponding document vectors.

4.3 Word Embedding Method

Similar to Sect. 4.1, this approach is also based on the skip gram word embedding method introduced by Mikolov et al. [19]. Word embeddings are created for all the key words in the learning resources, which is implemented in the *DL4J* word2vec library. The word embeddings are then averaged for all the key words in the learning resources. The cosine similarity between these averaged word vectors gives the coherence score between the learning resources.

5 Experiments and Results

To evaluate our proposed models, we used the dataset of open learning resources aggregated by the educational platform *Gooru.org*[2]. The dataset comprised of about 4.2 million learning resources in total that were independently created by several authors, mostly obtained from the open educational resources. The data will be made available on request.

The learning pathways in the platform are created by teachers and contain a variety of resource formats, including questions, to differentiate learning and check for understanding. These collections and assessments have been successfully implemented in classrooms supporting innovative practices such as blended learning, flipped learning, and station-rotation models, and are maintained and updated by the educator authors [2]. They follow the instructional designs that aims to optimise the appeal, effectiveness and efficiency of instructional learning experiences. These learning pathways thus represent coherent sequences of learning resources that the students could use to achieve a learning goal, which we used as ground truth, for testing.

---

[2] https://gooru.org.

5.1   Experiment 1

We created a test sample of about 9000 learning resource pairs. The learning resource pairs were marked as *"Coherent"* or *"Incoherent"*. All the randomly created pairs of learning resources were considered *"Incoherent"* and the resources in a single learning pathway were considered to be *"Coherent"*. The learning resources pairs were classified using all the four approaches - Graph Kernel, Document Embedding, Word Embedding and Random Walk over Word Embeddings. The accuracy recorded for each of the methods are as follows: Graph Kernel classified with an accuracy of 96.08%, Document Embedding method with 98.4%, Word Embedding with 74.51% and Random Walk over Word Embeddings method classified with an accuracy of 98.04%. While all the approaches were able to classify the basic coherence with fairly high accuracy, for generating learning pathways, we need to make more specific classification. Hence we conducted one more experiment for multi-class classification as explained in the next subsection.

Table 1. Performance metrics comparing the models

Model	Accuracy	PPV	TPR	F1 score
Graph kernel	87.9%	79.0%	87.5%	83.20%
Document embedding	53.38%	54.198%	56.35%	55.25%
Word embedding	51.11%	60.9%	59.29%	60.09%
Random walk over word embeddings	44.6%	54.04%	50.98%	55.48%

5.2   Experiment 2

We used the same dataset of 9000 learning resource pairs and classified them into three classes - *"High"*, *"Medium"* and *"Low"* coherence, representing high exposition coherence, medium exposition coherence and low exposition coherence. All the resource pairs belonging to learning pathways were considered to be coherent and were divided into *"Medium"* and *"High"* coherence such that, the consecutive, near by resources in a sequence were considered or marked as having *"High"* coherence and the non-consecutive, far away resources (but from the same learning pathway) were considered as having *"Medium"* coherence. The resource pairs in the same learning pathway but far away in the sequence are *"coherent"* because they belong to the same learning pathway and are clubbed together to achieve a single learning goal, but do not have *"High"* coherence because they are many resources apart in the learning pathway. Whereas any pair of random resources from the corpus or the dataset were considered or marked as *"Low"* coherence.

The resource pairs were then classified by all the four approaches. We report the evaluation results for this experiment on Accuracy, PPV-Positive Predictive Value, TPR - True Positive Rate and F1 score. Confusion matrix is generated for this multi-class classification by first creating confusion matrix for each class and then by computing the average values for all the classes combined. From the confusion matrix entries, the performance metrics are calculated as follows:

$$\text{Accuracy} = \frac{\sum TruePostives + \sum FalsePositves}{\sum TotalPopulation}$$

$$\text{Positive Predictive Value (PPV)} = \frac{\sum TruePostives}{\sum TruePostives + \sum FalsePositves}$$

$$\text{True Positive Rate (TPR)} = \frac{\sum TruePostives}{\sum TruePostives + \sum FalseNegatives}$$

$$\text{F1 score} = \frac{2 * PPV * TPR}{PPV + TPR}$$

Table 1 shows the summary of performance of all the four models. We can see that the Graph Kernel model outperforms the other methods in all the performance measures.

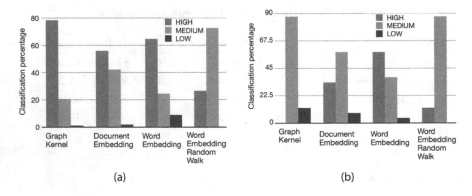

(a)   (b)

Fig. 3. Percentage of learning resources predicted for (a) consecutive or near-by learning resource pairs in a learning pathway that have *"High"* coherence. (b) learning resource pairs that are in the same learning pathway but far apart in the sequence that have *"Medium"* coherence.

We delved into each of the classes further, specifically the *"High"* and *"Medium"* coherence classes since the resource pairs with *"Low"* coherence were identified equally well by all the four models. Figure 3a shows the classification results for the resources that were *"High"* coherence and how they were classified by each of the models. We can observe that the Graph Kernel approach classifies most learning resource pairs as *"High"*, same as their true value, whereas Document Embedding, Word Embedding, and Random Walk over Word Embeddings approaches classified large number of *"High"* learning resource pairs as *"Medium"* coherence. Figure 3b shows the classification results for the resource pairs that were *"Medium"* coherence. We can observe that with Graph Kernel approach and Random Walk over Word Embeddings approach, the learning resource pairs were correctly classified as *"Medium"* coherence. But Word and Document Embedding methods classified most of the learning resource pairs as *"High"* coherence. However, if we observe the two graphs in Fig. 3a and b, Random Walk over Word Embeddings approach classified *"High"* coherence resource pairs also as *"Medium"* coherence. This can also be justified with low accuracy, PPV, TPR and F1 score for this method in Table 1.

As noted above, we can observe that, even though the embeddings models represented semantic similarity in a generic sense, it was not good enough to compute similarity in exposition styles. To illustrate this, we further analysed coherence scores obtained for non-consecutive, far away resources from a given collection. We used two approaches - Graph Kernel and Document Embedding, to test this. As we can see in Fig. 4, we computed the exposition coherence scores for far resource pairs, i.e., $ec(l_1, l_{14})$, $ec(l_1, l_{12})$, $ec(l_2, l_{13})$ and so on. We could see that Document Embedding method showed higher coherence scores between the resource pairs, despite the fact that the resources were far away in the collection. In contrast, Graph Kernel scores were much lower for far away resources in a collection, as compared to consecutive or near by resources.

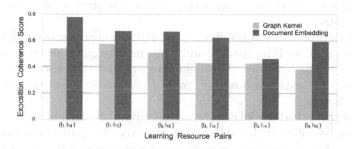

Fig. 4. Exposition coherence score for non-consecutive, far away resources in a single collection using Document Embedding and Graph Kernel methods.

Conclusions Drawn from Experiments. From the above results, we can argue that modelling exposition styles is a non-trivial augmentation over semantic models based on embeddings. This could be due to the fact that, the Graph Kernel model is based on modelling exposition styles as a random walk, while the Document and Word Embedding models were based on computing coherence directly from the embeddings.

5.3 Experiment 3 - Exposition Coherence Scores Within a Pathway

We performed yet another experiment to check how our model of exposition coherence fares when measured along a learning pathway. We considered a set of 8 human-identified learning pathways containing 12–15 resources each, for measurement. Let the human curated learning pathways or collections be denoted as $C_1, C_2, \ldots C_8$. For each of these collections, we computed exposition coherence $ec(l_i, l_j)$ for different resource pairs that are x resources apart starting

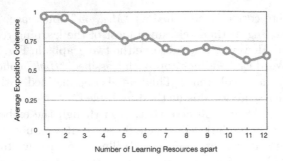

Fig. 5. Average exposition coherence score for different pairs of learning resources in learning pathways.

from $x = 1$ to $x = 12$ in the learning pathways, i.e., we computed coherence score for resource pairs one resource apart - $ec(l_i, l_{i+1})$, resource pairs two resources apart - $ec(l_i, l_{i+2})$ and so on up-to resource pairs being twelve resources apart - $ec(l_i, l_{i+12})$. Figure 5 shows the average exposition coherence scores (y-axis) for the learning resource pairs that were x resources apart in the learning pathways(x-axis).

We could conclude from the figure that exposition scores were high for consecutive resources, and dropped steadily, but not discontinuously, as we moved further away in the pathway. We would thus say that the exposition coherence is a first step towards reaching our goal of automatic generation of coherent learning pathways.

While the proposed model computes similarity in exposition styles, we do not claim this to be sufficient for solving the narrative arc problem. To compute a narrative arc, first an underlying sequence of competencies or the route is identified. Exposition coherence is then computed for all the open learning resources mapped to each of the competency to generate a knowledge graph of learning resources. This would be used to generate learning pathways. Several other factors like cognitive engagement, coherence with learning styles, etc., would then have to be applied to the candidate learning pathways identified using exposition style, to create effective learning pathways.

6   Conclusions

We proposed a model for computing exposition coherence between a pair of learning resources as a first step towards automatically curating learning pathways. Our model is an unsupervised method based on representing exposition styles using random walks on semantic context of a pair of learning resources. Evaluation of our model on interesting and effective learning pathways created by educators showed promising results. In future, we would use the exposition coherence score to automatically generate learning pathways from a set of learning resources. Once a generic set of learning pathways are generated automatically, we would work on a model to choose the best pathway among the generated pathways, personalising them to match student preferences, to enhance student learning and provide them good learning experience.

Acknowledgements. The authors would like to acknowledge and thank the contributions of the project associates P. Srinivasan, Karan Kumar Gupta, and Sanket Kutumbe.

References

1. Agrawal, R., Chakraborty, S., Gollapudi, S., Kannan, A., Kenthapadi, K.: Empowering authors to diagnose comprehension burden in textbooks. In: Proceedings of the 18th ACM SIGKDD International Cconference on Knowledge Discovery and Data Mining, pp. 967–975. ACM (2012)
2. Arnett, T.: Connecting ed & tech: partnering to drive student outcomes. Clayton Christensen Institute for Disruptive Innovation (2016)
3. Brusilovsky, P., Henze, N.: Open corpus adaptive educational hypermedia. In: Brusilovsky, P., Kobsa, A., Nejdl, W. (eds.) The Adaptive Web. LNCS, vol. 4321, pp. 671–696. Springer, Heidelberg (2007). https://doi.org/10.1007/978-3-540-72079-9_22
4. Changuel, S., Labroche, N., Bouchon-Meunier, B.: Resources sequencing using automatic prerequisite-outcome annotation. ACM Trans. Intell. Syst. Technol. (TIST) **6**(1), 6 (2015)
5. Chen, C.M.: Intelligent web-based learning system with personalized learning path guidance. Comput. Educ. **51**(2), 787–814 (2008)
6. Hsieh, T.C., Wang, T.I.: A mining-based approach on discovering courses pattern for constructing suitable learning path. Expert Syst. Appl. **37**(6), 4156–4167 (2010)
7. Huang, L., Milne, D., Frank, E., Witten, I.H.: Learning a concept-based document similarity measure. J. Assoc. Inf. Sci. Technol. **63**(8), 1593–1608 (2012)
8. Hummel, H.G., et al.: Combining social-based and information-based approaches for personalised recommendation on sequencing learning activities. Int. J. Learn. Technol. **3**(2), 152–168 (2007)
9. Islam, A., Inkpen, D.: Semantic text similarity using corpus-based word similarity and string similarity. ACM Trans. Knowl. Discov. Data (TKDD) **2**(2), 10 (2008)
10. Knauf, R., Sakurai, Y., Takada, K., Tsuruta, S.: Personalizing learning processes by data mining. In: 2010 IEEE 10th International Conference on Advanced Learning Technologies (ICALT), pp. 488–492. IEEE (2010)
11. Kondor, R.I., Lafferty, J.: Diffusion kernels on graphs and other discrete input spaces. ICML **2**, 315–322 (2002)
12. Kongkachandra, R., Chamnongthai, K.: Using linguistics information for improving the sentence-based semantic relatedness measurement. In: International Symposium on Communications and Information Technologies ISCIT 2007, pp. 1372–1376. IEEE (2007)
13. Krieger, K., Schneider, J., Nywelt, C., Rösner, D.: Creating semantic fingerprints for web documents. In: Proceedings of the 5th International Conference on Web Intelligence, Mining and Semantics, p. 11. ACM (2015)
14. Labutov, I., Lipson, H.: Web as a textbook: curating targeted learning paths through the heterogeneous learning resources on the web. In: EDM, pp. 110–118 (2016)
15. Le, Q., Mikolov, T.: Distributed representations of sentences and documents. In: International Conference on Machine Learning, pp. 1188–1196 (2014)

16. Liu, B., Zhang, T., Niu, D., Lin, J., Lai, K., Xu, Y.: Matching long text documents via graph convolutional networks. arXiv preprint arXiv:1802.07459 (2018)
17. Mann, W.C., Thompson, S.A.: Rhetorical structure theory: toward a functional theory of text organization. Text-Interdiscip. J. Stud. Discourse **8**(3), 243–281 (1988)
18. Manrique, R.: Towards automatic learning content sequence via linked open data. In: Proceedings of the International Conference on Web Intelligence, pp. 1230–1233. ACM (2017)
19. Mikolov, T., Sutskever, I., Chen, K., Corrado, G.S., Dean, J.: Distributed representations of words and phrases and their compositionality. In: Advances in Neural Information Processing Systems, pp. 3111–3119 (2013)
20. Mueller, J., Thyagarajan, A.: Siamese recurrent architectures for learning sentence similarity. In: AAAI, pp. 2786–2792 (2016)
21. Ni, Y., et al.: Semantic documents relatedness using concept graph representation. In: Proceedings of the Ninth ACM International Conference on Web Search and Data Mining, pp. 635–644. ACM (2016)
22. Paas, F., Renkl, A., Sweller, J.: Cognitive load theory and instructional design: recent developments. Educ. Psychol. **38**(1), 1–4 (2003)
23. Paul, C., Rettinger, A., Mogadala, A., Knoblock, C.A., Szekely, P.: Efficient graph-based document similarity. In: Sack, H., Blomqvist, E., d'Aquin, M., Ghidini, C., Ponzetto, S.P., Lange, C. (eds.) ESWC 2016. LNCS, vol. 9678, pp. 334–349. Springer, Cham (2016). https://doi.org/10.1007/978-3-319-34129-3_21
24. Pelánek, R.: Measuring similarity of educational items using data on learners' performance (2017)
25. Ponza, M., Ferragina, P., Chakrabarti, S.: A two-stage framework for computing entity relatedness in wikipedia. In: Proceedings of the 2017 ACM on Conference on Information and Knowledge Management, pp. 1867–1876. ACM (2017)
26. Rachakonda, A.R., Srinivasa, S., Kulkarni, S., Srinivasan, M.: A generic framework and methodology for extracting semantics from co-occurrences. Data Knowl. Eng. **92**, 39–59 (2014)
27. Shen, L., Shen, R.: Learning content recommendation service based-on simple sequencing specification. In: Liu, W., Shi, Y., Li, Q. (eds.) ICWL 2004. LNCS, vol. 3143, pp. 363–370. Springer, Heidelberg (2004). https://doi.org/10.1007/978-3-540-27859-7_47
28. Siehndel, P., Kawase, R., Nunes, B.P., Herder, E.: Towards automatic building of learning pathways. In: WEBIST, no. 2, pp. 270–277 (2014)
29. Vishwanathan, S.V.N., Schraudolph, N.N., Kondor, R., Borgwardt, K.M.: Graph kernels. J. Mach. Learn. Res. **11**(Apr), 1201–1242 (2010)
30. Wong, L.H., Looi, C.K.: Adaptable learning pathway generation with ant colony optimization. J. Educ. Technol. Soc. **12**(3), 309 (2009)
31. Yeh, E., Ramage, D., Manning, C.D., Agirre, E., Soroa, A.: WikiWalk: random walks on wikipedia for semantic relatedness. In: Proceedings of the 2009 Workshop on Graph-Based Methods for Natural Language Processing, pp. 41–49. Association for Computational Linguistics (2009)
32. Yu, Z., Nakamura, Y., Jang, S., Kajita, S., Mase, K.: Ontology-based semantic recommendation for context-aware e-learning. In: Indulska, J., Ma, J., Yang, L.T., Ungerer, T., Cao, J. (eds.) UIC 2007. LNCS, vol. 4611, pp. 898–907. Springer, Heidelberg (2007). https://doi.org/10.1007/978-3-540-73549-6_88
33. Yueh-Min, H., Tien-Chi, H., Wang, K.T., Hwang, W.Y.: A markov-based recommendation model for exploring the transfer of learning on the web. J. Educ. Technol. Soc. **12**(2), 144 (2009)

STypeS: Nonrecursive Datalog Rewriter for Linear TGDs and Conjunctive Queries

Stanislav Kikot[1], Roman Kontchakov[2(✉)], Salvatore Rapisarda[2],
and Michael Zakharyaschev[2]

[1] University of Oxford, UK
staskikotx@gmail.com
[2] Birkbeck, University of London, UK
{roman,srapis01,michael}@dcs.bbk.ac.uk

Abstract. We present STypeS, a system that rewrites ontology-mediated queries with linear tuple-generating dependencies and conjunctive queries to equivalent nonrecursive datalog (NDL) queries. The main feature of STypeS is that it produces polynomial-size rewritings whenever the treewidth of the input conjunctive queries and the size of the chases for the ontology atoms as well as their arity are bounded; moreover, the rewritings can be constructed and executed in LogCFL, indicating high parallelisability in theory. We show experimentally that Apache Flink on a cluster of machines with 20 virtual CPUs is indeed able to parallelise execution of a series of NDL-rewritings constructed by STypeS, with the time decreasing proportionally to the number of CPUs available.

1 Introduction

First-order (FO) query rewriting (or reformulation) lies in the core of ontology-based data access [24,28] and data integration [22]. An abstract formulation of the problem is as follows: given a set $\mathcal{O}$ of tuple-generating dependencies (tgds), called here an *ontology*, and a conjunctive query $q(x)$ with a tuple x of answer variables, construct an FO-formula $q'(x)$, called an *FO-rewriting* of the ontology-mediated query (OMQ) $(\mathcal{O}, q(x))$, such that, for any data instance $\mathcal{D}$ and any tuple a of constants in it,

$$q(a) \text{ holds in every model of } \mathcal{O} \cup \mathcal{D} \text{ iff } a \text{ is an answer to } q'(x) \text{ over } \mathcal{D}. \quad (1)$$

Thus, FO-rewriting is a reduction of the certain answer reasoning problem to database query evaluation, and so it can only be possible for OMQs given in carefully chosen languages. For ontology-based data access, the W3C standardised the *OWL 2 QL* profile of the Web Ontology Language *OWL 2* [23], which guarantees FO-rewritability of all OMQs with conjunctive queries (CQs) and ontologies in the *OWL 2 QL* profile [3]. Following the database tradition, more expressive, yet still ensuring FO-rewritability, languages have been suggested,

H. Panetto et al. (Eds.): OTM 2018 Conferences, LNCS 11230, pp. 441–460, 2018.
https://doi.org/10.1007/978-3-030-02671-4_27

including fragments of Datalog$^\pm$ such as linear tgds [11] (also known as atomic-body existential rules [5]) or sticky sets of tgds [12,13]. We remind the reader that a *tuple-generating dependency* (*tgd*) is an FO-sentence of the form

$$\forall \boldsymbol{X} \left(\gamma(\boldsymbol{X}) \to \exists \boldsymbol{Y} \, \gamma'(\boldsymbol{X}', \boldsymbol{Y}) \right), \tag{2}$$

where γ and γ' are conjunctions of atoms with variables $\boldsymbol{X}$ and $\boldsymbol{X}' \cup \boldsymbol{Y}$, respectively, and the variables of $\boldsymbol{X}'$ are contained in $\boldsymbol{X}$. A tgd is *linear* if $\gamma(\boldsymbol{X})$ is a single atom. As an illustration, we show how OMQs with linear tgds could be used in the system ETAP [10,27] designed to answer natural language questions by translating them into SPARQL and executing—along with background knowledge—over RDF data extracted from texts.

Example 1. Suppose we have a data instance with atoms *purchased(john, BD51SMR)* and *Car(BD51SMR)* representing the sentence 'John purchased car *BD51SMR*'. To answer the question 'Which cars have been sold?' ETAP utilises the ontology rules

$$\forall xy \left[purchased(x, y) \to \right.$$
$$\exists vz \left(Purchase(v) \land hasAgent_1(v, x) \land hasObject(v, y) \land hasAgent_2(v, z) \right) \right],$$
$$\forall vxyz \left[Purchase(v) \land hasAgent_1(v, x) \land hasObject(v, y) \land hasAgent_2(v, z) \to \right.$$
$$\exists v' \left(Sale(v') \land hasAgent_1(v', z) \land hasObject(v', y) \land hasAgent_2(v', x) \right) \right],$$

where v and v' represent the acts of purchase and sale, respectively. These rules are beyond the limitations of *OWL 2 QL*; however, the knowledge they represent can also be captured by means of linear tgds with ternary predicates:

$$\forall xy \left[purchased(x, y) \to \exists z \, Purchase(x, y, z) \right],$$
$$\forall xyz \left[Purchase(x, y, z) \to Sale(z, y, x) \right],$$

which are sufficient for answering the CQ $\boldsymbol{q}(y) = \exists xz \left(Car(y) \land Sale(x, y, z) \right)$ to obtain the answer *BD51SMR*. The resulting OMQ can be rewritten into the following FO-query (or equivalently, an SQL query), which can then be evaluated directly over the data:

$$\exists xz \left[Car(y) \land \left(Sale(x, y, z) \lor Purchase(z, y, x) \lor purchased(z, y) \right) \right].$$

FO-rewritability means, in particular, that OMQ answering is in the class AC^0 for *data complexity*, that is, as complex as standard database query evaluation. It has been discovered [19,21], however, that the shortest FO-rewritings can be of superpolynomial size compared to the given CQ, which makes reduction (1) impractical. Further investigations [7–9] revealed that, by restricting the class of linear tgds to those of bounded arity and bounded existential depth and the class of CQs to those of bounded treewidth, one can achieve polynomial-size rewritings in the form of *nonrecursive datalog* (NDL) queries (rather than FO-formulas). In the context of Example 1, the following is a rewriting in the form of an NDL query with the goal predicate G:

$$G(y) \leftarrow Car(y) \land Sale'(x, y, z), \qquad Sale'(x, y, z) \leftarrow Sale(x, y, z),$$
$$Sale'(x, y, z) \leftarrow Purchase(z, y, x), \quad Sale'(x, y, z) \leftarrow purchased(z, y).$$

(NDL queries can also be thought of as SQL queries with view definitions.) The NDL-rewritings obtained in [8,9] are *optimal* in the sense that the combined complexity of constructing and evaluating them is the same (LOGCFL) as the complexity of evaluating the underlying CQs [15,20,29]. (Note that the shortest rewritings into positive existential formulas in this case can still be of superpoly-nomial size, while polynomial-size FO-rewritings exist iff $\mathrm{LOGCFL}/\mathrm{poly} \subseteq \mathrm{NC}^1$, which is highly doubtful.) The experiments in [8] compared the size of the optimal NDL-rewritings constructed manually for a series of OMQs having the following fixed ontology:

$$\forall XY \left[P(X, Y) \rightarrow S(X, Y) \right], \qquad \forall X \left[A(X) \rightarrow \exists Y \, P(X, Y) \right],$$
$$\forall XY \left[P(X, Y) \rightarrow R(Y, X) \right], \qquad \forall X \left[B(X) \rightarrow \exists Y \, P(Y, X) \right],$$

with the rewritings produced by three known NDL-rewriters: Clipper [17], Presto [25] and Rapid [16], and established that, while the latter three grew exponentially, the former displayed linear growth.

The main distinguishing feature of the optimal NDL-rewritings from [9] is that, in theory, their evaluation can be performed by an efficient parallel algorithm because $\mathrm{LOGCFL} \subseteq \mathrm{NC}^2$ [26]. However, it has remained unclear whether such NDL-queries, which encode possibly exponentially large unions of CQs (UCQs), can be executed efficiently by a standard data management system, and whether the system can utilise the inherent parallelism of the NDL-rewritings.

The general aim of this paper is to give a positive answer to these questions. More specifically, we present a system STYPES that constructs an NDL-rewriting of any OMQ $(\mathcal{O}, q(x))$ with a set of linear tgds $\mathcal{O}$ and a CQ $q(x)$. The rewritings are of polynomial size if the treewidth of CQs and the arity and the size of the chase for ontology atoms are bounded. Moreover, in this case, they can be constructed and executed in LOGCFL. Our rewriting algorithm takes a tree decomposition of the CQ as input in order to generate a plan for constructing an NDL-rewriting. Another input of the algorithm is a set of chases for the ontology atoms that occur in the rule bodies. In STYPES, the chases are constructed by the Graal library [4]. We use STYPES to produce NDL-rewritings for the OMQs from [8] mentioned above and then execute the rewritings by means of Apache Flink on a cluster of machines with 20 virtual CPUs. The experiments show that Flink is indeed able to parallelise execution of these NDL-rewritings, with the execution time decreasing proportionally to the number of CPUs available.

The plan of the remaining part of the paper is as follows. Section 2 provides definitions of the main notions we use and illustrates them with examples.

Section 3 is the main technical contribution of this paper describing the NDL-rewriting algorithm implemented in STypeS. Section 4 presents and discusses our experimental results.

2   Preliminaries

Let Σ be a *relational schema*. By writing $P(\boldsymbol{x})$, for a predicate name P and an n-tuple $\boldsymbol{x}$ of variables (with possible repetitions), we mean that P is n-ary. Also, by writing $\gamma(\boldsymbol{x})$ we mean that $\boldsymbol{x}$ are the free variables of formula γ, where the tuple $\boldsymbol{x}$ contains no repetitions. When it is clear from the context, we use the set-theoretic notation for lists. In the series of examples below, we use relational schema Σ_0 with binary predicates R, S and T.

A *conjunctive query* (*CQ*) $\boldsymbol{q}(\boldsymbol{x})$ is an FO-formula of the form $\exists \boldsymbol{y}\, \varphi(\boldsymbol{x}, \boldsymbol{y})$, where φ is a conjunction of atoms $P(\boldsymbol{z})$ with predicate symbols from Σ and $\boldsymbol{z} \subseteq \boldsymbol{x} \cup \boldsymbol{y}$. The free variables, $\boldsymbol{x}$, are called the *answer variables* of the CQ, and a CQ without answer variables is called *Boolean*. We often regard CQs as *sets* of their atoms.

Example 2. For our running example, we use the Boolean CQ

$$q_0 \;=\; \exists xyz \,\big(R(x,y) \wedge T(y,z) \wedge R(z,v)\big), \tag{3}$$

which can be depicted as follows:

An *ontology* $\mathcal{O}$ is a finite set of *linear tuple-generating dependencies* (*linear tgds*), that is, sentences of the form

$$\forall \boldsymbol{X} \,\big(\gamma(\boldsymbol{X}) \to \exists \boldsymbol{Y}\, \gamma'(\boldsymbol{X}', \boldsymbol{Y})\big),$$

where γ is an atom and γ' a conjunction of atoms with predicate symbols from Σ and $\boldsymbol{X}' \subseteq \boldsymbol{X}$, for disjoint sets $\boldsymbol{X}$ and $\boldsymbol{Y}$ of variables ($\boldsymbol{Y}$ is possibly empty); as a convention, we will use capital letters for variables in tgds. When writing tgds, we omit both the universal and existential quantifiers. An *ontology-mediated query* (OMQ) $\boldsymbol{Q}(\boldsymbol{x})$ is a pair $(\mathcal{O}, \boldsymbol{q}(\boldsymbol{x}))$, where $\mathcal{O}$ is an ontology and $\boldsymbol{q}(\boldsymbol{x})$ a CQ. The variables $\boldsymbol{x}$ are called the *answer variables* of $\boldsymbol{Q}(\boldsymbol{x})$, and an OMQ without answer variables is called *Boolean*.

Example 3. For our running example, we use the Boolean OMQ $\boldsymbol{Q}_0 = (\mathcal{O}_0, \boldsymbol{q}_0)$, where the CQ $\boldsymbol{q}_0$ is given by (3) and $\mathcal{O}_0$ consists of the following linear tgds:

$$S(X, Z) \to R(X, Y) \wedge T(Y, Z), \tag{4}$$

$$T(X, Z) \to R(X, Y). \tag{5}$$

Note that X and Z are universally quantified and Y is existentially quantified in both tgds (4) and (5).

A *data instance* $\mathcal{D}$ over Σ is any finite set of ground atoms $P(\boldsymbol{a})$ with predicate symbols P from Σ. We denote by $\mathrm{ind}(\mathcal{D})$ the set of individual constants in $\mathcal{D}$. A tuple $\boldsymbol{a} \in \mathrm{ind}(\mathcal{D})^{|\boldsymbol{x}|}$ is a *certain answer* to an OMQ $\boldsymbol{Q}(\boldsymbol{x}) = (\mathcal{O}, q(\boldsymbol{x}))$ over $\mathcal{D}$ if

$$\mathfrak{M} \models q(\boldsymbol{a}), \qquad \text{for every model } \mathfrak{M} \text{ of } \mathcal{O} \cup \mathcal{D};$$

in this case we write $\mathcal{O}, \mathcal{D} \models q(\boldsymbol{a})$. If $\boldsymbol{Q}$ is Boolean, then the *certain answer* to $\boldsymbol{Q}$ over $\mathcal{D}$ is 'yes' if $\mathfrak{M} \models q$, for every model $\mathfrak{M}$ of $\mathcal{O} \cup \mathcal{D}$, and 'no' otherwise.

Canonical Models. An important property of tgds is the fact [1] that, for any $\mathcal{O}$ and $\mathcal{D}$, there is a (possibly infinite) *canonical* (or *universal*) *model* $\mathfrak{C}_{\mathcal{O},\mathcal{D}}$ such that

$$\mathcal{O}, \mathcal{D} \models q(\boldsymbol{a}) \quad \text{iff} \quad \mathfrak{C}_{\mathcal{O},\mathcal{D}} \models q(\boldsymbol{a}), \quad \text{for every CQ } q(\boldsymbol{x}) \text{ and } \boldsymbol{a} \in \mathrm{ind}(\mathcal{D})^{|\boldsymbol{x}|}. \quad (6)$$

Such a canonical model can be constructed by a *chase procedure* that, intuitively, 'repairs' $\mathcal{D}$ with respect to $\mathcal{O}$ by extending the data instance with fresh *anonymous individuals* (labelled nulls) to witness existential quantifiers in tgds (though not necessarily in the most economical way).

Remark 1. There are variants of the chase procedure with various termination conditions. In our running examples, we follow a particular variant called the *Skolem chase*. However, STYPES can employ any type of chase as a black box. Obviously, the class of OMQs for which STYPES terminates depends on this choice. In particular, it would terminate for *weakly-acyclic linear* tgds if it were supplied with a restricted chase engine. Note that the ontology from Example 3.8 in [18], serving there as the main motivating example for introducing weakly-acyclic tgds, falls into this class. Moreover, since linear tgds satisfy the polynomial witness property [19], for each fixed OMQ, one could construct the chases only up to the depth that guarantees completeness of answers for the particular CQ, rather than for all CQs; cf. (6). Therefore, such a modification of our NDL rewriting algorithm would terminate on *all* OMQs with linear tgds.

Example 4. In the context of Example 3, consider a data instance $\mathcal{D}_0 = \{ S(a,b) \}$. Then, tgd (4) is *applicable* to $\mathcal{D}_0$ because h with $h \colon X \mapsto a$ and $h \colon Z \mapsto b$ is a homomorphism from the body $S(X, Z)$ of the tgd to $\mathcal{D}_0$. An *application* of the tgd produces a fresh anonymous individual e_0 for its existential quantifier and results in

$$\mathcal{D}_1 = \mathcal{D}_0 \cup \{ R(a, e_0), T(e_0, b) \}.$$

Next, tgd (5) is applicable to $\mathcal{D}_1$ via a homomorphism h with $h \colon X \mapsto e_0$ and $h \colon Z \mapsto b$ from the body $T(X, Z)$ of the tgd to $\mathcal{D}_1$. So, its application produces another fresh anonymous individual, e_1, and results in

$$\mathcal{D}_2 = \mathcal{D}_1 \cup \{ R(e_0, e_1) \}.$$

In this example, the chase terminates at step 2 because all tgds are satisfied in $\mathcal{D}_2$ (and so there are no defects to repair). In general, however, the chase does not have to terminate.

NDL-Rewritings. A *datalog program*, Π, is a finite set of Horn clauses of the form

$$\forall z \, (\gamma_0 \leftarrow \gamma_1 \wedge \cdots \wedge \gamma_m),$$

where each γ_i is an atom $P(y)$ with $y \subseteq z$ or an equality $(z = z')$ with $z, z' \in z$. (As usual, we omit the universal quantifiers from clauses.) The atom γ_0 is the *head* of the clause, and $\gamma_1, \ldots, \gamma_m$ its *body*. All variables in the head must occur in the body, and $=$ can only occur in the body. The predicates in the heads of clauses in Π are *IDB predicates*, the rest (including $=$) *EDB predicates*. A predicate Q *depends* on P in Π if Π has a clause with Q in the head and P in the body. A program Π is a *nonrecursive datalog* (NDL) *program* if the (directed) *dependence graph* of the dependence relation is acyclic. The size $|\Pi|$ of Π is the number of symbols in it.

An *NDL query* is a pair $(\Pi, G(x))$, where Π is an NDL program and G a predicate. A tuple $a \in \mathsf{ind}(\mathcal{D})^{|x|}$ is an *answer to* $(\Pi, G(x))$ *over* a data instance $\mathcal{D}$ if $G(a)$ holds in the first-order structure with domain $\mathsf{ind}(\mathcal{D})$ obtained by closing $\mathcal{D}$ under the clauses in Π; in this case we write $\Pi, \mathcal{D} \models G(a)$. The problem of checking whether a is an answer to $(\Pi, G(x))$ over $\mathcal{D}$ is called the *query evaluation problem*. It is known to be P-complete for combined complexity provided that the arity of predicates is bounded.

An NDL query $(\Pi, G(x))$ is an *NDL-rewriting of an OMQ* $Q(x) = (\mathcal{O}, q(x))$ in case

$$\mathcal{O}, \mathcal{D} \models q(a) \quad \text{iff} \quad \Pi, \mathcal{D} \models G(a), \qquad \text{for any } \mathcal{D} \text{ and any } a \in \mathsf{ind}(\mathcal{D})^{|x|}.$$

Every OMQ is known to have an NDL-rewriting [6,11].

Example 5. For the OMQ Q_0 in Example 3, the following program with the nullary goal predicate P_1 is an NDL-rewriting:

$$P_1 \leftarrow R(x,y) \wedge T(y,z) \wedge P_2(z), \tag{7}$$
$$P_1 \leftarrow S(x,z) \wedge P_2(z), \tag{8}$$
$$P_2(z) \leftarrow R(z,v), \tag{9}$$
$$P_2(z) \leftarrow S(z,Z), \tag{10}$$
$$P_2(z) \leftarrow T(z,Z). \tag{11}$$

In Sect. 3, we describe an algorithm for computing such NDL-rewritings.

H-Completeness. A data instance $\mathcal{D}$ is said to be *H-complete* with respect to an ontology $\mathcal{O}$ if $\mathcal{D}$ validates all *full tgds* τ such that $\mathcal{O} \models \tau$ (full tgds have no existential variables). By default, STYPES produces an NDL-rewriting that is correct only for H-complete data instances (rather than over all data instances). An essentially NDL-rewriting that is correct for all data instances can be obtained by adding to it all full tgds τ with $\mathcal{O} \models \tau$. A proof of these statements is given in the extended version of [9].

3   NDL Rewriting

Our query rewriting algorithm takes two inputs, an ontology $\mathcal{O}$, which is a set of linear tgds, and a tree decomposition of a CQ $q(x)$.

Tree Decompositions. A *bag* β for a CQ $q(x)$ is a pair (ν, α), where ν is a subset of the variables in the CQ and α is a subset of query atoms with variables from ν; we refer to the two components as $\nu(\beta)$ and $\alpha(\beta)$, respectively.

A *tree decomposition* of a CQ $q(x)$ is a pair (T, λ) consisting of a (rooted directed) tree $T = (V, E)$ and a map λ associating a bag to each vertex in T such that the following conditions hold:

- for any atom $R(z)$ in q, there is a vertex $v \in V$ with $R(z) \in \alpha(\lambda(v))$;
- for any variable z in q, the set $\{v \in V \mid z \in \nu(\lambda(v))\}$ is connected in T.

The *width* of the tree decomposition (T, λ) is $\max_{v \in V} |\nu(\lambda(v))| - 1$. The *treewidth of* q is the minimum width over all tree decompositions of q. Tree decompositions can be computed by *htd* [2], which is an open-source application written in C++[1].

Example 6. A tree decomposition for q_0 in Example 2 can look as follows:

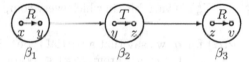

Atomic Canonical Models. The algorithm begins by extracting from the ontology $\mathcal{O}$ a set of atomic canonical models. Given a linear tgd $\gamma(X) \rightarrow \gamma'(X', Y)$, we call $\gamma(X)$ a *generating atom* and the canonical model $\mathfrak{C}_{\mathcal{O}, \mathcal{D}}$ for $\mathcal{D} = \{\gamma(X)\}$ an *atomic canonical model* for $\mathcal{O}$, where (somewhat abusing notation) we treat X as a tuple of individual constants. We assume that $\mathcal{O}$ is fixed and denote the atomic canonical model by $\mathfrak{C}_{\gamma(X)}$. The implementation of the algorithm in STYPES uses the *Graal* [4][2] library to construct the atomic canonical models for $\mathcal{O}$ by chasing its generating atoms.

Example 7. The ontology $\mathcal{O}_0$ in Example 3 has two generating atoms, $S(X, Z)$ and $T(X, Z)$, and the following atomic canonical models:

generating atom	atomic canonical model
$S(X, Z)$	$T(e_0, Z), R(e_0, e_1), R(X, e_0), S(X, Z)$
$T(X, Z)$	$R(X, e_0), T(X, Z)$

where e_0 and e_1 are the anonymous individuals; see Example 4.

---

[1] http://github.com/mabseher/htd.
[2] http://graphik-team.github.io/graal.

3.1   Bag Types

We use *term types* to indicate how query variables can be mapped into canonical models $\mathfrak{C}_{\mathcal{O},\mathcal{D}}$ for possible data instances $\mathcal{D}$. The *non-anonymous* term type ε is used when a variable is mapped to an individual constant from $\mathcal{D}$. An *anonymous* term type is a pair of the form $(\gamma(\boldsymbol{X}), e)$, where $\gamma(\boldsymbol{X})$ is a generating atom and e an anonymous individual from the atomic canonical model $\mathfrak{C}_{\gamma(\boldsymbol{X})}$ for $\gamma(\boldsymbol{X})$. For a given $\gamma(\boldsymbol{X})$, we denote by $\mathfrak{T}_{\gamma(\boldsymbol{X})}$ the set of all term types of the form $(\gamma(\boldsymbol{X}), e)$ and ε. In the sequel, we silently assume that term types of all answer variables are always ε.

Example 8. As follows from Example 7, $\mathcal{O}_0$ has four term types: ε, $(S(X,Z), e_0)$, $(S(X,Z), e_1)$ and $(T(X,Z), e_0)$.

A *partial type* $\boldsymbol{s}$ is a map that assigns term types to a subset of query variables. The domain of $\boldsymbol{s}$ is denoted by $\mathsf{dom}(\boldsymbol{s})$. Given a partial type $\boldsymbol{s}$, we denote by $var(\boldsymbol{s})$ the tuple of variables that contains, for $z \in \mathsf{dom}(\boldsymbol{s})$,

the variable z, if $\boldsymbol{s}(z) = \varepsilon$,   and   the variables $\boldsymbol{X}^z$, if $\boldsymbol{s}(z) \in \mathfrak{T}_{\gamma(\boldsymbol{X})} \setminus \{\varepsilon\}$,

where, for a tuple $\boldsymbol{X} = (X_1, \ldots, X_n)$ of variables and a decoration k, we denote by $\boldsymbol{X}^k$ the tuple $(X_1^k, \ldots, X_n^k)$ of variables in which every component is decorated by k.

Given a bag $\beta = (\boldsymbol{\nu}, \boldsymbol{\alpha})$ for q, we say that a partial type $\boldsymbol{s}$ is a *bag type for* β if $\boldsymbol{\nu}$ is the domain of $\boldsymbol{s}$ and, for every atom $R(\boldsymbol{z}) \in \boldsymbol{\alpha}$, one of the following applies:

(d) $\boldsymbol{s}(\boldsymbol{z}) \subseteq \{\varepsilon\}$ (in which case the variables of the atom are mapped to the individuals in the data instance, and the atom itself is in the data instance);

(b) $\boldsymbol{s}(\boldsymbol{z}) \subseteq \mathfrak{T}_{\gamma(\boldsymbol{X})}$, for some (uniquely determined) $\gamma(\boldsymbol{X})$, with $\boldsymbol{z}_\varepsilon \neq \emptyset$ and $\boldsymbol{z} \setminus \boldsymbol{z}_\varepsilon \neq \emptyset$, and there is a *grounding function* $g \colon \boldsymbol{z}_\varepsilon \to \boldsymbol{X}$ such that $R(\boldsymbol{c}) \in \mathfrak{C}_{\gamma(\boldsymbol{X})}$, where

$$\boldsymbol{z}_\varepsilon = \{\, z \in \boldsymbol{z} \mid \boldsymbol{s}(z) = \varepsilon \,\} \quad \text{and} \quad \boldsymbol{c}(z) = \begin{cases} g(z), & \text{if } \boldsymbol{s}(z) = \varepsilon, \\ e, & \text{if } \boldsymbol{s}(z) = (\gamma(\boldsymbol{X}), e) \end{cases}$$

(in which case the variables in $\boldsymbol{z}_\varepsilon$ are mapped to the individuals in the data instance, whereas $\boldsymbol{z} \setminus \boldsymbol{z}_\varepsilon$ are mapped to the anonymous individuals, that is, the atom is on the boundary of the data instance and the anonymous part of the chase);

(i) $\boldsymbol{s}(\boldsymbol{z}) \subseteq \mathfrak{T}_{\gamma(\boldsymbol{X})} \setminus \{\varepsilon\}$, for some (uniquely determined) $\gamma(\boldsymbol{X})$, and $R(\boldsymbol{c}) \in \mathfrak{C}_{\gamma(\boldsymbol{X})}$, where $\boldsymbol{c}(z) = e$ for z with $\boldsymbol{s}(z) = (\gamma(\boldsymbol{X}), e)$ (in which case all variables are mapped to the anonymous individuals, that is, the atom is in the interior of the anonymous part of the chase).

Given a bag type $\boldsymbol{s}$ for a bag $\beta = (\boldsymbol{\nu}, \boldsymbol{\alpha})$, we denote by $\equiv_\nu$ the smallest equivalence relation on $\boldsymbol{\nu}$ such that $z \equiv_\nu z'$ if $\boldsymbol{s}(z) \neq \varepsilon$, $\boldsymbol{s}(z') \neq \varepsilon$ and z and z'

occur in $R(z)$ and $R'(z')$, respectively, such that the two atoms share a variable z'' with $s(z'') \neq \varepsilon$. For a variable z, we denote by $[z]$ its $\equiv_\nu$-equivalence class; also, for a set z of variables occurring in an atom from α with $s(z) \subseteq \mathfrak{T}_{\gamma(X)} \setminus \{\varepsilon\}$, let $[z]$ be the $\equiv_\nu$-equivalence class of some (equivalently, any) $z \in z$.

The MakeAtoms function in the code of STYPES produces the formula $\text{At}^s(var(s))$ by mapping each atom $R(z)$ in α to

(d') $R(z)$ if $s(z) \subseteq \{\varepsilon\}$;

(b') $\gamma(X^{[z \setminus z_\varepsilon]}) \wedge \Big(\bigvee_{\substack{g:\, z_\varepsilon \to X \\ \text{is a grounding function}}} \Big[\bigwedge_{z \in z_\varepsilon \text{ and } g(z) = X} (z = X^{[z \setminus z_\varepsilon]}) \Big] \Big)$

if $s(z) \subseteq \mathfrak{T}_{\gamma(X)}$ but neither $s(z) \subseteq \mathfrak{T}_{\gamma(X)} \setminus \{\varepsilon\}$ nor $s(z) \subseteq \{\varepsilon\}$;

(i') $\gamma(X^{[z]})$ if $s(z) \subseteq \mathfrak{T}_{\gamma(X)} \setminus \{\varepsilon\}$.

We also add to the formula $\text{At}^s(var(s))$ the equalities $X^{[z]} = X^z$, for all $z \in \text{dom}(s)$ such that $s(z) \in \mathfrak{T}_{\gamma(X)} \setminus \{\varepsilon\}$ and $X \in X$.

Example 9. There are four possible bag types for $\beta_3 = (\{z, v\}, \{R(z, v)\})$. The bag type $t_3 = \{z \mapsto \varepsilon, v \mapsto \varepsilon\}$ trivially gives rise to the following At-formula, see (d'):

$$\text{At}^{t_3}(z, v) = R(z, v).$$

For the bag type $t_4 = \{z \mapsto \varepsilon, v \mapsto (T(X, Z), e_0)\}$, we have neither $t_4(z, v) \subseteq \{\varepsilon\}$ nor $t_4(z, v) \subseteq \mathfrak{T}_{T(X,Z)} \setminus \{\varepsilon\}$, and the only grounding function is $g: z \mapsto X$. Thus, by (b'), we obtain

$$\text{At}^{t_4}(X^v, Z^v, z) = T(X^{[v]}, Z^{[v]}) \wedge (z = X^{[v]}) \wedge (X^{[v]} = X^v) \wedge (Z^{[v]} = Z^v).$$

For the bag type $t_5 = \{z \mapsto \varepsilon, v \mapsto (S(X, Z), e_0)\}$, the At-formula is constructed similarly, with $S(X, Z)$ in place of $T(X, Z)$.

Finally, for the bag type $s = \{z \mapsto (S(X, Z), e_0), v \mapsto (S(X, Z), e_1)\}$, we have $s(z, v) \subseteq \mathfrak{T}_{S(X,Z)} \setminus \{\varepsilon\}$. So, by (i'), we obtain the following At-formula:

$$\text{At}^s(X^v, X^z, Z^v, Z^z) = S(X^{[v,z]}, Z^{[v,z]}) \wedge$$
$$(X^{[v,z]} = X^v) \wedge (X^{[v,z]} = X^z) \wedge (Z^{[v,z]} = Z^v) \wedge (Z^{[v,z]} = Z^z).$$

3.2   Splitters

A *splitter* S is a (rooted) directed tree and a map that associates a bag to each node of the tree, which is constructed by the following recursive algorithm. The constructor receives a tree decomposition (T, λ) of the given CQ and proceeds as follows. First, we find the splitting vertex of T by computing, for every vertex v of T, the size $|T_v|$ of the subtree at v, and then recursively moving from the root r of T to the child of the maximal size until we reach a vertex v with $|T_v| \leq |T_r|/2 + 1$. Then the root of S is associated with the bag $\lambda(v)$, which is called the *splitting bag* of S. The vertex v splits T into subtrees, whose induced tree decompositions are then used to recursively construct children in S. We will often refer to subtrees of S also as splitters.

For each splitter S, we define a set of its *boundary variables* $bv(S)$ by induction on the tree structure: for the root splitter, $bv(S)$ is the set of all answer variables of the given CQ, and, if S' is a child of S and β is the splitting bag of S, then $bv(S')$ is the restriction of $bv(S) \cup \boldsymbol{\nu}(\beta)$ to the set of all variables in the bags of the nodes of S'. A *boundary type* for a splitter S is a partial type defined on its boundary variables $bv(S)$.

Example 10. In our running example, we have the following root splitter S_1 with two children, S_2 and S_3:

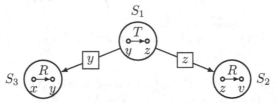

The sets of boundary variables for S_1, S_2 and S_3 are $\emptyset$, $\{y\}$ and $\{z\}$, respectively.

With any splitter S and a boundary type $\boldsymbol{w}$ for S, we associate a fresh IDB $P_{S,\boldsymbol{w}}$ with variables $var(\boldsymbol{w})$. In Example 10, we associate

- nullary predicate P_1 with S_1 and the empty boundary type $\{\}$;
- unary predicate $P_2(z)$ with S_2 and the boundary type $\{z \mapsto \varepsilon\}$;
- binary predicate $P_3(X^y, Z^y)$ with S_3 and the boundary type $\{y \mapsto (S(X, Z), e_0)\}$;
- and finally, unary predicate $P_4(y)$ with S_3 and the boundary type $\{y \mapsto \varepsilon\}$

(for simplicity, we use numerical subscripts rather than $S, \boldsymbol{w}$).

3.3 Bag Type Extender

A *splitting type* for a splitter S and its boundary type $\boldsymbol{w}$ is a type $\boldsymbol{s}$ for the splitting bag β of S that agrees with $\boldsymbol{w}$ on their common domain. `TypeExtender` produces all splitting types for a given bag $\beta = (\boldsymbol{\nu}, \boldsymbol{\alpha})$ and a given partial type $\boldsymbol{w}$ by constructing a rooted type extender tree with a labelling function ℓ that assigns to each node v a partial type $\ell(v)$ such that the root is labelled with $\boldsymbol{w}$, and $\ell(u)$ is an extension of $\ell(v)$ whenever u is a child of v. More precisely, the recursive algorithm maintains the following parameters when constructing the tree:

- the current node label, in other words, the partial type $\boldsymbol{w}'$ being extended (`currentType`);
- the subset $\boldsymbol{\alpha}'$ of atoms $\boldsymbol{\alpha}$ that are yet to be processed (`atomsToBeMapped`);
- the subset $\boldsymbol{\nu}'$ of variables $\boldsymbol{\nu}$ on which $\boldsymbol{w}'$ is yet to be defined (`varsToBeMapped`).

For the root of the type extender tree, we set $\boldsymbol{w}' = \boldsymbol{w}$, $\boldsymbol{\alpha}' = \boldsymbol{\alpha}$ and $\boldsymbol{\nu}' = \boldsymbol{\nu} \setminus dom(\boldsymbol{w}')$. Then, the constructor proceeds by recursion on decreasing sets $\boldsymbol{\alpha}'$ and $\boldsymbol{\nu}'$ using the following three rules in the given order:

(I) If ν' is empty, then, in function `filterThroughAtoms`, we check whether each atom in α' satisfies one of the three conditions, **(d)**, **(b)** or **(i)**, assuming that w' is a bag type for β. We mark the current leaf as *valid* if it is the case, and *invalid* otherwise.

(II) If α' contains an atom $R(z)$ such that w' is defined on some $z \in \boldsymbol{z}$ and $w'(z)$ is an anonymous individual from $\mathfrak{T}_{\gamma(X)}$, then we say that $R(\boldsymbol{z})$ *connected to* w' and, using $\mathfrak{C}_{\gamma(X)}$, extend w' to all variables $\boldsymbol{z}$ on which it is not defined. More precisely, in function `extendToAnAtom`, we use *Graal* to execute the query $R(\boldsymbol{z})$ on $\mathfrak{C}_{\gamma(X)}$ and then extract all possible extensions from its output.

(III) If a connected atom cannot be found, then we pick a variable from ν' and, in function `ExtendToATerm`, assign all possible term types to it.

Thus, the extension tree is constructed using the following procedure:

```
1   /* Receives a node of the type extender tree under construction
2       Returns a tuple (status, extensions), where
3       - status is the status of the node, and
4       - extensions is the children of the current node.
5   */
6
7   getExtensions(currentType, varsToBeMapped, atomsToBeMapped) {
8       if (varsToBeMapped is Empty) {
9           return (filterThroughAtoms(currentType, atomsToBeMapped),
10                      EmptyList)
11      }
12      else if (atomsToBeMapped contains
13                          an atom connected to the currentType) {
14          return (true, ExtendToAnAtom(currentType, atom))
15      }
16      else {
17          return (true,
18                      ExtendToATerm(currentType, varsToBeMapped.head))
19      }
20  }
```

When the type extender tree is fully constructed, all bag types s for β that extend w can be collected from the labels w' of valid tree leaves that satisfy $\mathrm{dom}(w') = \nu$.

Example 11. In the running example, initially, w' is empty, and so we apply rule **(III)** and create four children of the root for four possible term types for y. Then, we apply rule **(III)** to the node $\{y \mapsto \varepsilon\}$ and create four children for four possible term types for z. Then, by **(I)**, we apply the `FilterThroughAtoms` procedure to these four children and conclude that only $\{y \mapsto \varepsilon, z \mapsto \varepsilon\}$ is valid, while the other three siblings are not.

The three remaining children of the tree root have an atom $T(y, z)$ connected to its partial type, and so we apply rule **(II)** to them.

First, consider $\{y \mapsto (S(X, Z), e_0)\}$. We execute the query $T(y, z)$ on $\mathfrak{C}_{S(X,Z)}$, which yields $\{y \mapsto e_0, z \mapsto Z\}$. Since the obtained value for y matches the partial type $\{y \mapsto (S(X,Z), e_0)\}$, we create a single child $\{y \mapsto (S(X,Z), e_0), z \mapsto \varepsilon\}$, which is valid because α' is empty when FilterThroughAtoms is called.

Second, consider $\{y \mapsto (S(X,Z), e_1)\}$. The execution of the query $T(y,z)$ on $\mathfrak{C}_{S(X,Z)}$ gives the answer $\{y \mapsto e_0, z \mapsto Z\}$, which does not match the partial type, and so the node $\{y \mapsto (S(X,Z), e_1)\}$ has no children.

Third, the same happens with the remaining node $\{y \mapsto (T(X,Z), e_0)\}$.

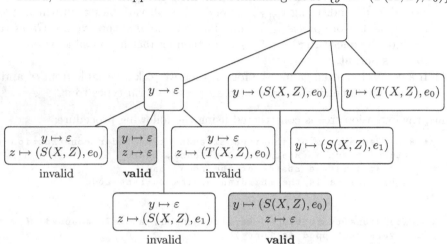

Finally, we collect the partial types from the valid leaves of the tree: note that the last two nodes considered do not give rise to any partial types because their labels w' do not satisfy $\mathrm{dom}(w') = \nu$. To sum up, there are two splitting types for S_1 and its empty boundary type that are compatible with $T(y,z)$:

$$t_1 = \{y \mapsto \varepsilon, \ z \mapsto \varepsilon\} \qquad \text{and} \qquad t_2 = \{y \mapsto (S(X,Z), e_0), \ z \mapsto \varepsilon\}.$$

3.4   Generating Rewriting

The GenerateRewriting(S, w) function in STYPES receives a splitter S and its boundary type w. It first calls TypeExtender to construct the splitting types for S and w. Then, for each splitting type s, the function creates a fresh IDB $P_{S,w}(var(w))$ for S and w (see Sect. 3.2) and produces a RuleTemplate, which describes clauses, whose head is $P_{S,w}(var(w))$ and whose body includes $\mathrm{At}^s(var(s))$ and the atoms $P_{S',w'}(var(w'))$ for children S' of S, where w' is the restriction of $w \cup s$ to the boundary variables $bv(S')$ of S'. The name RuleTemplate refers to the fact that the $\mathrm{At}^s(var(s))$ formulas in general contain disjunctions and therefore, each RuleTemplate may give rise to several clauses. Next, function GenerateRewriting(S', w') is called recursively for all children S' of S and their induced boundary types w'.

Example 12. We continue Example 11. For S_1 and its empty boundary type, the splitting types t_1 and t_2, give rise to the following:

$$P_1 \leftarrow T(y,z) \wedge P_2(z) \wedge P_4(y),$$
$$P_1 \leftarrow S(X^y, Z^y) \wedge P_2(z) \wedge P_3(X^y, Z^y) \wedge (z = Z^y).$$

For readability, we do not distinguish between variables V^u and $V^{[u]}$ and omit the respective equalities of the form $V^u = V^{[u]}$. Note that in these cases (and in the cases below) the $\mathsf{At}^s(var(s))$ formulas contain no disjunctions, and so we actually have clauses.

For S_2 and its boundary type $\{z \mapsto \varepsilon\}$, the splitting types t_3, t_4 and t_5 (see Example 9) give rise to the clauses

$$P_2(z) \leftarrow R(z, v),$$
$$P_2(z) \leftarrow T(X^v, Z^v) \wedge (z = X^v),$$
$$P_2(z) \leftarrow S(X^v, Z^v) \wedge (z = X^v).$$

Next, for the splitter S_3 and its boundary type $\{y \mapsto (S(X, Z), e_0)\}$, the only splitting type $\{y \mapsto (S(X, Z), e_0), \ x \mapsto \varepsilon\}$ yields the clause

$$P_3(X^y, Z^y) \leftarrow S(X^y, Z^y) \wedge (x = X^y).$$

Finally, for S_3 and its other boundary type, $\{y \mapsto \varepsilon\}$, the only possible splitting type $\{y \mapsto \varepsilon, \ x \mapsto \varepsilon\}$ gives

$$P_4(y) \leftarrow R(x, y).$$

The produced list of `RuleTemplates` is passed to the `generateDatalog` function, which converts them into clauses and simplifies the resulting NDL program in the following way. First, it recursively removes predicates of the form $P_{S,w}(var(w))$ that are guaranteed to be empty because they do not occur in the head of any clause. Then, it recursively eliminates predicates with a single definition: each $P_{S,w}(var(w))$ that has a single clause with $P_{S,w}(var(w))$ in the head is replaced by the body of the clause (with the existentially quantified variables appropriately renamed). Finally, all equalities are removed from the program by repeatedly replacing one of the terms of an equality for all terms that are equivalent to it in the clause.

Example 13. In Example 12, P_3 and P_4 have single definitions, and so, they can be eliminated. This gives us the following NDL program:

$$P_1 \leftarrow T(y, z) \wedge P_2(z) \wedge R(x, y),$$
$$P_1 \leftarrow S(X^y, Z^y) \wedge P_2(z) \wedge (z = Z^y) \wedge (x = X),$$
$$P_2(z) \leftarrow R(z, v),$$
$$P_2(z) \leftarrow T(X^v, Z^v) \wedge (z = X^v),$$
$$P_2(z) \leftarrow S(X^v, Z^v) \wedge (z = X^v).$$

After removing equalities and replacing variables accordingly, we obtain the final NDL-rewriting given in Example 5.

4   Experiments

To understand whether the NDL-rewritings computed by STYPES are efficient in practice and whether a standard data management system is capable of taking advantage of their inherent parallelism, we conducted a few experiments with the ontology and CQs designed in [8]. The ontology was given in the introduction and the CQs are path queries with up to 15 atoms that correspond to words in the language $\{R, S\}^*$. For example, the CQ $q(x_0, x_7)$ for the word $RSRRSRR$ is shown below (with black nodes representing answer variables):

$$\bullet \xrightarrow{R} \circ \xrightarrow{S} \circ \xrightarrow{R} \circ \xrightarrow{R} \circ \xrightarrow{S} \circ \xrightarrow{R} \circ \xrightarrow{R} \bullet$$
$$x_0 \qquad x_1 \qquad x_2 \qquad x_3 \qquad x_4 \qquad x_5 \qquad x_6 \qquad x_7$$

We used STYPES to compute NDL-rewritings for OMQ Q_{15} with a CQ of 15 atoms, Q_{22} with 7 atoms, and Q_{45} with 15 atoms. The queries are available at http://github.com/srapisarda/stypes/tree/master/src/test/resources/ODBASE.

Their NDL-rewritings have, respectively, 25, 5 and 30 clauses. Thus, for Q_{15}, the constructed NDL-rewriting looks as follows, where p1 is the goal predicate:

```
1   p1(x0,x15) :- p35(x0,x7), r(x7,x8), p2(x8,x15).
2   p1(x0,x15) :- p3(x0,x8), a(x8), p2(x8,x15).
3   p3(x0,X) :- p19(x0,x3), r(x3,x4), p28(x4,X).
4   p3(x0,x2) :- r(x0,x1), r(x1,x2), a(x2), p28(x2,x2).
5   p3(x0,x6) :- p19(x0,x6), b(x6), a(x6), r(x6,x6).
6   p28(x4,x4) :- a(x4).
7   p28(x4,x6) :- s(x4,x5), r(x5,x6), a(x6).
8   p2(x8,x15) :- p5(x10,x8), r(x10,x11), p14(x11,x15).
9   p2(x8,x15) :- r(x8,x9), a(x9), p14(x9,x15).
10  p14(x11,x15) :- r(x11,x12), s(x12,x13), p7(x13,x15).
11  p14(x11,x15) :- b(x11), p7(x11,x15).
12  p7(x15,x15) :- a(x15).
13  p7(x13,x15) :- s(x13,x14), r(x14,x15).
14  p5(x8,x8) :- b(x8).
15  p5(x10,x8) :- s(x9,x10), r(x8,x9).
16  p35(x0,x7) :- p43(x7,x2), r(x0,x1), r(x1,x2), a(x2).
17  p35(x0,x7) :- p19(x0,x3), r(x3,x4), p43(x7,x4).
18  p35(x0,x7) :- p40(x7,x3), p19(x0,x3), b(x3).
19  p19(x0,x3) :- r(x0,x3), b(x3).
20  p19(x0,x3) :- r(x0,x1), r(x1,x2), s(x2,x3).
21  p43(x7,x4) :- s(x4,x5), r(x5,x6), s(x6,x7).
22  p43(x7,x4) :- a(x4), s(x4,x7).
23  p43(x7,x4) :- s(x4,x7), b(x7).
24  p40(x7,x5) :- b(x5), r(x5,x6), s(x6,x7).
25  p40(x5,x5) :- b(x5).
```

It is to be noted [8] that UCQ-rewritings of these OMQs are very large. STYPES encodes these UCQs as 'deep' yet polynomial-size NDL-queries. Thus, in the example above, p1 depends on p2, which depends on p14, which in turn depends on p7, with each of these predicates having at least two defining clauses. This makes STYPES different from all other existing rewriters. Neither Rapid nor Clipper terminate on this OMQ within 15 min, while Presto (in the NDL mode) produces an NDL-rewriting with 2723 clauses (see [8] for details). The aim of our experiments was to understand whether the optimal NDL-rewritings computed by STypeS are (*i*) executable and (*ii*) efficiently parallelisable.

We executed the NDL-rewritings on Apache Flink [14], a highly scalable modern tool for parallel streaming and batch processing based on estimated cost-based choice of the optimal physical execution plan.

For our experiments, we created a Hadoop cluster with six nodes, where each virtual machine had four Intel(R) Xeon(R) E5-2640 v3 CPUs @ 2.60 GHz and 16 GB RAM. Each machine served as a data node equipped with Hadoop HDFS of 250 GB on SDD. For Flink, we used a stand-alone cluster configuration.

We represented clauses of NDL-rewritings using the `join-where-equalTo-map` sequences of standard Flink functions. For example, for the clause

$$p(x,z) \ :- \ w(x,y), \ v(z,x,y).$$

we produced the following Flink script:

```
val p = w.join(v).where(0,1).equalTo(1,2).map(t => (t._1._1, t._2._1))
```

In Flink, the `join` of two relations consists of all composite tuples (w, v) constructed from their tuples w and v. In the example above, `w.join(v)` consists of all composite tuples $((w_0, w_1), (v_0, v_1, v_2))$ for tuples (w_0, w_1) in `w` and tuples (v_0, v_1, v_2) in `v`. The arguments of the `where` function specify the positions in the first relation that must have the values equal to the values in the respective positions in the second relation specified by the arguments of `equalTo` (the positions start from 0). In the example above, the `where(0,1)` selects the first and second components of tuples in `w` (i.e., the components at positions 0 and 1), which are then matched by `equalsTo(1,2)` with the second and third components of tuples in `v` (which are at positions 1 and 2). Finally, we use function `map` to keep only the positions occurring in the clause head: for instance, `t => (t._1._1, t._2._1)` maps each composite tuple `t` to the first component of its first half and the first component of its second half.

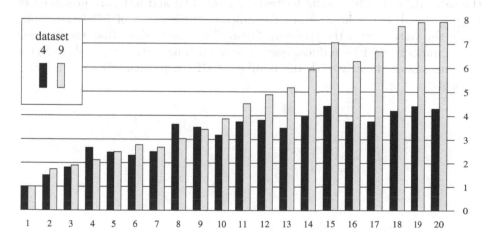

Fig. 1. Speed-up factor due to parallelisation for Q_{15}.

We used the following randomly generated datasets for the binary relation R and unary relations A and B:

dataset	$|V|$	p	q	avg. degree	#atoms	ttl size	csv size
1.ttl	1 000	0.050	0.050	50	61K	1 MB	0.5 MB
2.ttl	5 000	0.002	0.004	10	64K	1.2 MB	0.7 MB
3.ttl	10 000	0.002	0.004	20	257K	5 MB	3 MB
4.ttl	20 000	0.002	0.010	40	1M	20 MB	12 MB
5.ttl	30 000	0.002	0.010	60	2M	47 MB	28 MB
6.ttl	40 000	0.002	0.010	80	5M	84 MB	51 MB
7.ttl	50 000	0.002	0.010	100	6M	130 MB	70 MB
8.ttl	60 000	0.002	0.010	120	9M	190 MB	100 MB
9.ttl	70 000	0.002	0.010	140	13M	260 MB	140 MB

The parameter p is the probability of an R-edge between two points from V; q is the density of unary concepts A and B. The first four datasets come from [8], the last five were generated to create a significant load on the system. We intentionally decided to make the relation S empty in order to leave some margin for optimisation for the NDL-query planner, and also because empty relations are typical in the OBDA scenario.

We executed the constructed NDL-rewritings of the OMQs Q_{15}, Q_{22} and Q_{45} over the datasets 1.ttl–9.ttl on our cluster using Flink with the number of available virtual CPUs varying from 1 to 20. The run-times ranged from 3.91 s to 1797 s for Q_{15}, from 1.85 s to 1398 s for Q_{22}, and from 3.47 s to 1769 s for Q_{45}. Our main concern was the degree of parallelisability, which can be measured as the speed-up factor t_1/t_n, where t_i is the run-time on i-many CPUs over the same dataset. The results for two datasets, 4.ttl and 9.ttl, are presented in Figs. 1, 2 and 3: the horizontal axis indicates the number of CPUs available, while the vertical axis the speed-up factor. The charts show that the increase in the number of CPUs reduces query execution time, with the speed-up factor growing almost linearly with the number of CPUs, particularly on the larger dataset.

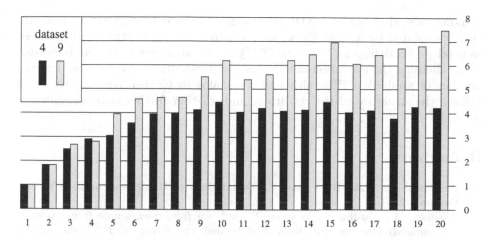

Fig. 2. Speed-up factor due to parallelisation for Q_{22}.

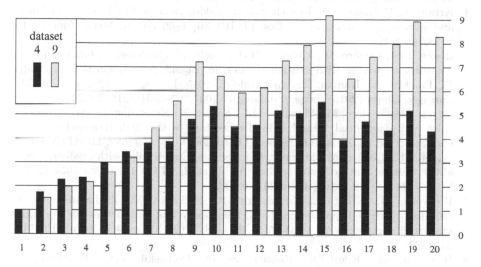

Fig. 3. Speed-up factor due to parallelisation for Q_{45}.

5   Conclusion

The contribution of this paper is twofold. First, it presents an OMQ rewriter STYPES that transforms conjunctive queries mediated by ontologies given as sets of linear tgds (in particular, $OWL\,2\,QL$ concept and role inclusions) into equivalent nonrecursive datalog queries over the data. A distinctive feature of STYPES is that, if the treewidth of the input conjunctive queries and the size of the chases for the ontology atoms as well as their arity are bounded, then the resulting rewritings are theoretically optimal in the sense that they can be constructed and executed in LOGCFL. Second, the paper experimentally demonstrates that optimal NDL-rewritings computed by STYPES can be efficiently executed by Apache Flink, whereas other existing rewriters struggle even to produce rewritings for the same OMQs. It is also shown that Fink is capable of parallelising the execution of STYPES's NDL-rewritings proportionally to the number of available CPUs, although it remains to be seen how exactly Flink utilises the structure of the rewritings and whether further improvements are possible.

References

1. Abiteboul, S., Hull, R., Vianu, V.: Foundations of Databases. Addison-Wesley, Boston (1995)
2. Abseher, M., Musliu, N., Woltran, S.: htd – a free, open-source framework for (customized) tree decompositions and beyond. In: Salvagnin, D., Lombardi, M. (eds.) CPAIOR 2017. LNCS, vol. 10335, pp. 376–386. Springer, Cham (2017). https://doi.org/10.1007/978-3-319-59776-8_30
3. Artale, A., Calvanese, D., Kontchakov, R., Zakharyaschev, M.: The DL-Lite family and relations. J. Artif. Intell. Res. (JAIR) **36**, 1–69 (2009). https://doi.org/10.1613/jair.2820
4. Baget, J.-F., Leclère, M., Mugnier, M.-L., Rocher, S., Sipieter, C.: Graal: a toolkit for query answering with existential rules. In: Bassiliades, N., Gottlob, G., Sadri, F., Paschke, A., Roman, D. (eds.) RuleML 2015. LNCS, vol. 9202, pp. 328–344. Springer, Cham (2015). https://doi.org/10.1007/978-3-319-21542-6_21
5. Baget, J.F., Leclère, M., Mugnier, M.L., Salvat, E.: Extending decidable cases for rules with existential variables. In: Proceedings of the 21th International Joint Conference on Artificial Intelligence (IJCAI 2009), pp. 677–682. IJCAI (2009)
6. Baget, J.F., Leclère, M., Mugnier, M.L., Salvat, E.: On rules with existential variables: walking the decidability line. Artif. Intell. **175**(9–10), 1620–1654 (2011). https://doi.org/10.1016/j.artint.2011.03.002
7. Bienvenu, M., Kikot, S., Kontchakov, R., Podolskii, V., Zakharyaschev, M.: Ontology-mediated queries: combined complexity and succinctness of rewritings via circuit complexity. J. ACM **65**(5), 28:1–28:51 (2018). https://doi.org/10.1145/3191832
8. Bienvenu, M., Kikot, S., Kontchakov, R., Podolskii, V.V., Ryzhikov, V., Zakharyaschev, M.: The complexity of ontology-based data access with OWL 2 QL and bounded treewidth queries. In: Proceedings of the 36th ACM SIGMOD-SIGACT-SIGAI Symposium on Principles of Database Systems, PODS 2017, pp. 201–216. ACM (2017). https://doi.org/10.1145/3034786.3034791
9. Bienvenu, M., Kikot, S., Kontchakov, R., Ryzhikov, V., Zakharyaschev, M.: Optimal nonrecursive datalog rewritings of linear TGDs and bounded (hyper)tree-width queries. In: Proceedings of the 30th International Workshop on Description Logics, DL 2017. CEUR Workshop Proceedings, vol. 1879. CEUR-WS.org (2017)
10. Boguslavsky, I., Dikonov, V., Iomdin, L., Lazursky, A., Sizov, V., Timoshenko, S.: Semantic analysis and question answering: a system under development. In: Computational Linguistics and Intellectual Technologies (Papers from the Annual International Conference Dialogue 2015), vol. 1, pp. 62–79. RSUH (2015)
11. Calì, A., Gottlob, G., Lukasiewicz, T.: A general datalog-based framework for tractable query answering over ontologies. J. Web Semant. **14**, 57–83 (2012). https://doi.org/10.1016/j.websem.2012.03.001

12. Calì, A., Gottlob, G., Pieris, A.: Advanced processing for ontological queries. PVLDB **3**(1), 554–565 (2010). https://doi.org/10.14778/1920841.1920912
13. Calì, A., Gottlob, G., Pieris, A.: Towards more expressive ontology languages: the query answering problem. Artif. Intell. **193**, 87–128 (2012). https://doi.org/10.1016/j.artint.2012.08.002
14. Carbone, P., Katsifodimos, A., Ewen, S., Markl, V., Haridi, S., Tzoumas, K.: Apache flink™: stream and batch processing in a single engine. IEEE Data Eng. Bull. **38**(4), 28–38 (2015)
15. Chekuri, C., Rajaraman, A.: Conjunctive query containment revisited. Theor. Comput. Sci. **239**(2), 211–229 (2000). https://doi.org/10.1016/S0304-3975(99)00220-0
16. Chortaras, A., Trivela, D., Stamou, G.: Optimized query rewriting for OWL 2 QL. In: Bjørner, N., Sofronie-Stokkermans, V. (eds.) CADE 2011. LNCS (LNAI), vol. 6803, pp. 192–206. Springer, Heidelberg (2011). https://doi.org/10.1007/978-3-642-22438-6_16
17. Eiter, T., Ortiz, M., Šimkus, M., Tran, T.K., Xiao, G.: Query rewriting for Horn-SHIQ plus rules. In: Proceedings of the 26th AAAI Conference on Artificial Intelligence, AAAI 2012, pp. 726–733. AAAI Press (2012)
18. Fagin, R., Kolaitis, P.G., Miller, R.J., Popa, L.: Data exchange: semantics and query answering. Theor. Comput. Sci. **336**(1), 89–124 (2005). https://doi.org/10.1016/J.tcs.2004.10.033
19. Gottlob, G., Kikot, S., Kontchakov, R., Podolskii, V.V., Schwentick, T., Zakharyaschev, M.: The price of query rewriting in ontology-based data access. Artif. Intell. **213**, 42–59 (2014). https://doi.org/10.1016/j.artint.2014.04.004
20. Gottlob, G., Leone, N., Scarcello, F.: Computing LOGCFL certificates. In: Wiedermann, J., van Emde Boas, P., Nielsen, M. (eds.) ICALP 1999. LNCS, vol. 1644, pp. 361–371. Springer, Heidelberg (1999). https://doi.org/10.1007/3-540-48523-6_33
21. Kikot, S., Kontchakov, R., Podolskii, V., Zakharyaschev, M.: Exponential lower bounds and separation for query rewriting. In: Czumaj, A., Mehlhorn, K., Pitts, A., Wattenhofer, R. (eds.) ICALP 2012 Part II. LNCS, vol. 7392, pp. 263–274. Springer, Heidelberg (2012). https://doi.org/10.1007/978-3-642-31585-5_26
22. Lenzerini, M.: Data integration: a theoretical perspective. In: Proceedings of the 21st ACM SIGACT-SIGMOD-SIGART Symposium on Principles of Database Systems, PODS 2002, pp. 233–246. ACM (2002). https://doi.org/10.1145/543613.543644
23. Motik, B., Cuenca Grau, B., Horrocks, I., Wu, Z., Fokoue, A., Lutz, C.: OWL 2 Web Ontology Language Profiles. W3C Recommendation (2012). http://www.w3.org/TR/owl2-profiles
24. Poggi, A., Lembo, D., Calvanese, D., De Giacomo, G., Lenzerini, M., Rosati, R.: Linking data to ontologies. J. Data Semant. **10**, 133–173 (2008). https://doi.org/10.1007/978-3-540-77688-8_5
25. Rosati, R., Almatelli, A.: Improving query answering over DL-Lite ontologies. In: Proceedings of the 12th International Conference on Principles of Knowledge Representation and Reasoning, KR 2010, pp. 290–300. AAAI Press (2010)
26. Ruzzo, W.L.: Tree-size bounded alternation. J. Comput. Syst. Sci. **21**(2), 218–235 (1980). https://doi.org/10.1016/0022-0000(80)90036-7
27. Rygaev, I.: Rule-based reasoning in semantic text analysis. In: Proceedings of the Doctoral Consortium, Challenge, Industry Track, Tutorials and Posters @ RuleML+RR 2017. CEUR Workshop Proceedings, vol. 1875. CEUR-WS.org (2017)

28. Xiao, G., Calvanese, D., Kontchakov, R., Lembo, D., Poggi, A., Rosati, R., Zakharyaschev, M.: Ontology-based data access: a survey. In: Proceedings of the 27th International Joint Conference on Artificial Intelligence, IJCAI-ECAI 2018, pp. 5511–5519. IJCAI/AAAI (2018). https://doi.org/10.24963/ijcai.2018/777
29. Yannakakis, M.: Algorithms for acyclic database schemes. In: Proceedings of the 7th International Conference on Very Large Data Bases, VLDB81, pp. 82–94. IEEE Computer Society (1981)

Knowledge Authoring for Rule-Based Reasoning

Tiantian Gao[✉], Paul Fodor, and Michael Kifer

Department of Computer Science, Stony Brook University,
Stony Brook, NY, USA
{tiagao,pfodor,kifer}@cs.stonybrook.edu

Abstract. Modern knowledge bases have matured to the extent of being capable of complex reasoning at scale. Unfortunately, wide deployment of this technology is still hindered by the fact that specifying the requisite knowledge requires skills that most domain experts do not have, and skilled knowledge engineers are in short supply. A way around this problem could be to acquire knowledge from text. However, the current knowledge acquisition technologies for information extraction are not up to the task because logic reasoning systems are extremely sensitive to errors in the acquired knowledge, and existing techniques lack the required accuracy by too large of a margin. Because of the enormous complexity of the problem, *controlled natural languages* (CNLs) were proposed in the past, but even they lack high enough accuracy. Instead of tackling the general problem of text understanding, our interest is in a related, but different, area of *knowledge authoring*—a technology designed to enable domain experts to *manually create* formalized knowledge using CNL. Our approach adopts and formalizes the FrameNet methodology for representing the meaning, enables incrementally-learnable and explainable semantic parsing, and harnesses rich knowledge graphs like BabelNet in the quest to obtain unique, disambiguated meaning of CNL sentences. Our experiments show that this approach is 95.6% accurate in standardizing the semantic relations extracted from CNL sentences—far superior to alternative systems.

1 Introduction

Much of human knowledge can be represented as facts and logical rules and then fed into state of the art rule-based systems, such as XSB [22], Flora-2 [11,27], or Clingo [8], to perform formal logical reasoning in order to answer questions, derive new conclusions and explain the validity of statements. However, human knowledge can be very complex and domain experts typically do not have the training needed to express their knowledge as logical rules, while trained knowledge engineers are, unfortunately, in short supply.

Ideally, one could try to extract the requisite knowledge from text, but this is an extremely complex task. Although impressive advances have been made in text understanding and information extraction (e.g., [2,9,15]) the technology is

H. Panetto et al. (Eds.): OTM 2018 Conferences, LNCS 11230, pp. 461–480, 2018.
https://doi.org/10.1007/978-3-030-02671-4_28

still very far from approaching the accuracy required for logic knowledge bases, which are extremely sensitive to errors (both wrong and missing data).

Controlled natural languages (CNLs) [12]—languages with restricted, yet fairly rich, grammars and unambiguous interpretations—were proposed as a technology that might help bridge the gap. CNL systems allows domain experts who lack the experience in logic to specify knowledge that can be cast into logical statements suitable for reasoning. Such systems include Attempto Controlled English (*ACE*) [6], Processable English (PENG) [24], and BioQuery-CNL [5]. However, CNL systems perform rather limited semantic analysis of English sentences and do not provide for accurate authoring of knowledge. Specifically, they fail to recognize when sentences have the same meaning but are expressed in different syntactical forms or using different language constructs. For instance, the state of the art system ACE translates the sentences *Mary buys a car*, *Mary is the purchaser of a car*, *Mary makes a purchase of a car*, and many other equivalent sentences into very different logical representations. As a result, if any of these sentences is entered into the knowledge base, the reasoner would fail to answer questions like *Who purchases a car?* or *Who is the buyer of a car?* because ACE and others would translate these questions into logical sentences that are very different from the logical formulas used for the data. Clearly, this is a serious obstacle to using CNL as input to logical reasoning systems. The typically proposed "solution" is to manually specify bridge rules between equivalent forms, but this requires a huge number of such rules and is impractical.

Aim of this Work. This work is *not* about text understanding or information extraction from general prose or even from technical manuals. Instead, we propose an approach to *knowledge authoring* with the aim of providing domain experts with tools that would allow them to translate their knowledge into logic by means of CNL. The difference between knowledge authoring and information extraction or knowledge acquisition is quite significant: whereas information extraction aims to enable machines to understand what humans write, knowledge authoring aims to enable humans to write in natural language so that machines could understand. At present, knowledge authoring technology (compared to knowledge acquisition and extraction) is in an embryonic state. Knowledge authoring was, in fact, the target that CNLs were eyeing, but failed to reach because not enough attention was paid to semantics. We believe that our work fills in much of the void left unfilled by CNLs, which will turn the latter into a widely accepted technology for creation of formalized knowledge.

Contributions. The contributions of this paper are four-fold:

(a) A formal, FrameNet-inspired [10] ontology *FrameOnt* that formalizes FrameNet frames and integrates linguistic resources from BabelNet [19] to represent the meaning of English sentences.

(b) An *incrementally-learned* semantic parser that disambiguates CNL sentences by mapping semantically equivalent sentences into the same *Frame-Ont* frames and gives them *unique logical representation* (ULR). The parser is layered over the Attempto Parsing Engine (*APE*),[1] and utilizes *FrameOnt*, BabelNet, and our novel algorithms for frame-based parsing and ontology-driven role-filler disambiguation.

(c) Explainability: the approach makes it possible to explain both why particular meanings are assigned to sentences and why mistakes were made (so they can be fixed).

(d) We developed the Knowledge Authoring Logic Machine (*KALM*)[2] to enable subject matter experts, who need not be proficient in knowledge representation, to formulate actionable logic via CNL. KALM achieves unmatched accuracy of 95.6% in standardizing the semantic relations extracted from CNL sentences—far superior to alternative systems.

Organization. Section 2 gives background information on APE (the Attempto parser), FrameNet, and BabelNet, that is necessary in order to understand the proposed approach and make the paper self-contained. Section 3 describes the framework of KALM, its frame-based parser and the role-filler disambiguation algorithms. Section 4 describes the parallelization and the other optimizations that make role-filler disambiguation feasible. Section 5 describes the explainability aspect of KALM. Section 6 presents an evaluation of our approach, which indicates very high accuracy. Section 7 concludes the paper with a discussion of related work and future extensions.

2   Background

This section provides background on the systems used by KALM; specifically, the *Attempto parsing engine* (APE), the *FrameNet* methodology for representing the meaning of sentences, and the *BabelNet* knowledge graph.

Attempto. KALM accepts sentences that follow the grammar and interpretation rules of Attempto Controlled English, *ACE*.[3] ACE represents the semantics of text in a logical form, called *discourse representation structure* (DRS) [7], relying on seven predicates: `object/6`, `predicate/4`, `property/3`, `relation/3`, `modifier_adv/3`, `modifier_pp/3`, and `has_part/2` (in p/N, N is the number of arguments in predicate p). An `object`-fact represents an entity—a noun-word with some properties (e.g., countable or uncountable, quantity). A `predicate`-fact represents an event—a verb-word and its participating entities. A `property`-fact represents the syntactic relation between a noun and its adjective modifier. A `modifier_adv`-fact represents the syntactic relation between a verb and its adverbial modifier. A `modifier_pp`-fact represents the syntactic relation of a verb, its prepositional modifier and its prepositional complement. A `relation`-fact represents the genitive relation between two noun-words. For conjunctions of noun phrases, the Attempto Parsing Engine, APE, uses an additional predicate, `has_part/2`, to represent the grouping of these entities. Each `object`-,

---

[1] https://github.com/Attempto/APE.

[2] https://github.com/tiantiangao7/kalm.

[3] http://attempto.ifi.uzh.ch/site/docs/syntax_report.html.

`predicate`-, or `has_part`-fact has a unique identifier. Lastly, each fact has an *index* (e.g., `-1/2` in the first fact) showing the position of the word in the original sentence that generates this fact. For example, the sentence *A customer buys a watch for a friend* is represented using Prolog terms of the form:

```
object(A,customer,countable,na,eq,1)-1/2.
object(B,watch,countable,na,eq,1)-1/5.
object(C,friend,countable,na,eq,1)-1/8.
predicate(D,buy,A,B)-1/3.
modifier_pp(D,for,C)-1/6.
```

where A, B, and C are identifiers that represent the *customer*-, *watch*- and *friend*-entities, respectively, and D the *buy*-event. In each `object`-fact, the second argument represents the stem form of the word the fact represents; the rest of the arguments are the properties of this entity. In each `predicate`-fact, the third argument represents the subject of the event and the fourth argument represents the object of the event. In this case, the identifier A (resp. B) indicates that *customer* (resp. *watch*) is the subject (resp. object) of the event. A `modifier_pp`-fact connects the *buy*-event and its prepositional complement, the *friend*-entity.

As explained in the introduction, a very serious issue with Attempto Controlled English, ACE, is that sentences that have the same meaning may be represented by very different logical terms, preventing logic engines from making useful inferences from ACE parses. The often proposed workaround to manually build bridge rules is impractical. This paper solves this and related problems.

FrameNet. FrameNet is a knowledge base of semantic relations based on a theory of meaning called *frame semantics* [1]. The meaning of a sentence is understood as a semantic *frame* along with the semantic *roles* that the various words in the sentence play in the frame. FrameNet calls these roles *frame elements*. For example, in a sentence about purchasing goods, the frame `Commerce_Buy`[4] typically involves an individual purchasing a good (i.e., `Buyer`), the items that are purchased (i.e., `Goods`), the thing given in exchange for goods in the transaction (i.e., `Money`), the individual that has the possession of the goods and exchanges them with the buyer (i.e., `Seller`), the individual intended by the buyer to receive the goods (i.e., `Recipient`), the place and time of purchase (i.e., `Place` and `Time`), and so on. A frame is associated with a list of *lexical units* (words plus their part-of-speech). A lexical unit represents the basic language unit in a sentence that can *trigger* an application of the frame. For example, the lexical units `buy.v`, `purchase.v`, `buyer.n`, and `purchaser.n` can trigger the `Commerce_Buy` frame. But not only: the lexical unit `buy.v` can also trigger the frame, `Fall_for`.

Given the flexibility of natural languages, the same lexical unit can be used in multiple ways in sentences that match the same frame. To capture this, each pair (*lexical unit, frame*) in FrameNet is associated with a set of *valence patterns*, which represent the syntactic contexts in which a particular lexical unit and some of the frame elements can appear in sentences. For instance, one valence pattern

---

[4] https://framenet2.icsi.berkeley.edu/fnReports/data/frame/Commerce_buy.xml.

for (buy.v, Commerce_Buy) says that the Buyer-role is the subject of the *buy*-event and the Goods-role is the object of that event. Therefore, the sentence *Mary buys a watch* matches the frame Commerce_Buy via the lexical unit buy.v and the valence pattern that extracts *Mary* as the filler for the Buyer-role and *watch* as the filler for the Goods-role.

BabelNet. BabelNet is a multilingual knowledge base that contains a rich semantic network for words with their linguistic and semantic information. It is constructed by integrating multiple well-known structured knowledge bases, such as WordNet [17], DBpedia [3], and Wikidata [26]. Similarly to WordNet, each word has a part-of-speech tag and a gloss representing its meaning. Words with similar meanings are grouped into *synsets* that have unique identifiers (of the form bn:*dddddddp*, where *d* is a digit and *p* is a part of speech symbol v, n, etc.). BabelNet is structured as a knowledge graph where synset nodes are connected by directed edges representing semantic relations (i.e., *hypernym*, *hyponym*, etc.) Compared to WordNet, BabelNet has a much larger vocabulary and richer semantic relations. For instance, there are many *named entities* like famous people, locations, songs, books, etc. Besides, each edge in the knowledge graph has a weight that intends to capture the degree of relevance between two connected synset nodes with respect to the type of the edge. This abundance of information is the main reason we ended up using BabelNet as the underlying semantic network of words after trying many knowledge bases, such as WordNet, DBpedia, and Wikidata. Along with the richness, however, comes certain amount of noise and incompleteness—in part because integration of the data sources in BabelNet is done algorithmically and without much further curation by domain experts. While BabelNet is very large and rich in synsets and semantic relations, it also contains rarely used meanings of words, wrong semantic links, and words incorrectly associated with various synsets. Such errors can (and do) lead semantic parsers astray and therefore analysis and countermeasures are required to mitigate the impact of such noise in the knowledge base.

3   The KALM Framework

The KALM's frame-based parser is designed to parse CNL sentences and extract frame relations. Before embarking on building our own, we tried a number of semantic relation extraction tools, including Ollie [15], Stanford CoreNLP [14], the LCC system [13], SEMAFOR [4], and SLING [21]. These tools are designed for general text understanding and are strong contenders in that difficult domain, but their accuracy is far below the quality required for the knowledge that would be acceptable for logical knowledge bases. By *accuracy* we mean both precision and recall because, as mentioned earlier, our aim is to provide high-quality data and rules for logic-based reasoners, and these systems are very sensitive both to errors in the data as well as to missing data. In the KALM framework, high accuracy is achieved both through reliance on CNL, which makes our job much simpler compared to the aforesaid Open IE extractors, due to the extensive use of rich off-the-shelf knowledge bases, and due to the algorithms unique to KALM.

Our frame-based parser uses a model that contains a set of *logical frames* and *logical valence patterns*. The logical frames are mostly modeled after FrameNet's frames, but we represent them in logical form and disambiguate the semantic meaning of each role via BabelNet synsets. The logical valence patterns are modeled after FrameNet's valence patterns, but we represent them in a form compatible with APE parses. These logical valence patterns are constructed in an automatic way by learning linguistic structures from annotated training sentences. For the rest of the paper, we use the acronyms *frame* and *lvp* to denote the concept of a logical frame and logical valence pattern, respectively.

3.1 *FrameOnt*– The Logical Model of Frames

FrameNet is not formal enough—it contains only textual descriptions of frames and valence patterns, so FrameNet cannot be directly used for frame-based parsing. We formalize FrameNet as *FrameOnt*, an ontology that models frames and valence patterns using logical facts and rules. A frame consists of a set of *roles* (or "frame elements" in the terminology of FrameNet), each representing the semantic role an entity plays in the frame relation. Unlike FrameNet, *FrameOnt* disambiguates each role via a set of BabelNet synsets that capture the relevant meanings of the role. In addition, *constraints* may be imposed on roles. For instance, a data type constraint may state that the *Money* role must be a number representing an amount in some currency.

The below `fp-fact` represents the `Commerce_Buy` frame that describes purchases involving buyers, sellers, goods, etc.

```
fp('Commerce_Buy',[
  role('Buyer',['bn:00014332n'],[]),
  role('Seller',['bn:00053479n'],[]),
  role('Goods',['bn:00006126n','bn:00021045n'],[]),
  role('Recipient',['bn:00066495n'],[]),
  role('Money',['bn:00017803n'],['Currency'])]).
```

The first argument here is the name of a frame; the second is a list of role descriptors in the frame. In each *role* descriptor, the first part is the name of the role, the second is a list of BabelNet synset IDs representing the meaning of the role (there can be several: `Goods` above can mean *article of commerce* or *article of a sale*), and the third lists data type constraints for that role. To extract an instance of the frame from a sentence, we use lexical units (from the previous section) and *logical valence patterns*, or *lvps*. We call the word extracted from a sentence to correspond to a role a *role-filler*. For instance, the `Commerce_Buy` frame has this logical valence pattern:

$$
\begin{aligned}
&\texttt{lvp(buy,v,'Commerce\_Buy', [} \\
&\qquad \texttt{pattern('Buyer','verb}\rightarrow\texttt{subject',required),} \\
&\qquad \texttt{pattern('Goods','verb}\rightarrow\texttt{object',required),} \\
&\qquad \texttt{pattern('Recipient','verb}\rightarrow\texttt{dep[for]',optnl),} \\
&\qquad \texttt{pattern('Money','verb}\rightarrow\texttt{dep[for]',optnl),} \\
&\qquad \texttt{pattern('Seller','verb}\rightarrow\texttt{dep[from]',optnl)]).}
\end{aligned}
\tag{1}
$$

The first three arguments of an lvp-fact identify the lexical unit and the frame. The fourth argument is a set of **pattern**-terms, each having three parts: the first is the name of a role in the frame; the second is the *grammatical pattern* that specifies the grammatical context that relates the lexical unit, the role, and suitable role-filler words; and the third says whether the pattern is required in order to trigger the lvp or is optional. Each grammatical pattern is bound to a separate *parsing rule* that may be applied to extract the role-filler based on the APE parses. For example, in the first **pattern**-term, verb→subject says that the role-filler for the Buyer-role must be the subject of the *buy*-event. Based on the format of APE output described in Sect. 2, the corresponding parsing rule will find a suitable **object**-fact whose identifier equals the third argument (the subject) of a **predicate**-fact representing the *buy*-event. If so, the word representing the **object**-fact will be extracted as the role-filler of the Buyer-role. For example, given the sentence *Mary buys a watch for John from Bob*, the above lvp applies the Commerce_Buy frame and extracts *Mary* as the Buyer, *Bob* as the Seller, *watch* as the Goods, and *John* as the Recipient. The lvp is used even though a filler for the optional Money role was not present.

Both the lexical units and the associated lvps are generated by KALM when a knowledge engineer designs and marks up sentences to train the parser to recognize frames and roles in various linguistic structures. This aspect is discussed next.

3.2   Frame Construction

Figure 1 shows the pipeline for frame and lvp construction. The frames and roles are designed by a knowledge engineer in advance, based on FrameNet and Babel-Net. For each frame, the knowledge engineer must provide the semantics for the roles. In KALM, this requires searching BabelNet to find the most appropriate synsets for the roles in question. This has to be done because role-words tend to have multiple senses, and disambiguation of the role senses is key to ensuring accuracy of the extracted information. New frames may also have to be created, if the target domain requires that. (For instance, some important relations, such as human gender are not provided by FrameNet.) Some other frames in FrameNet must also be made more precise or expanded.

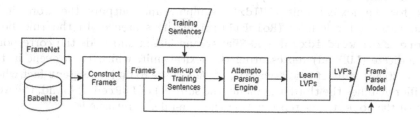

Fig. 1. Pipeline for frame and lvp construction

Once a frame and its roles are identified, the lvps are *learned* automatically from a set of marked-up *training sentences* designed by a knowledge engineer. In FrameNet, each valence pattern is associated with a set of exemplar sentences. Since KALM uses CNL, the knowledge engineer needs to rephrase sentences so that they will follow the ACE grammar. For each sentence, the engineer needs to mark the frame type, the lexical unit, the relevant roles, and the synonyms of the lexical unit. For instance, for a sentence like *Mary buys a watch for John from Bob for 200 dollars*, the knowledge engineer would create the following mark-up sentence and ask this query:

```
?- train('Mary buys a watch for John from Bob for 200 dollars',
   'Commerce_Buy', 'LUIdx'=2,
   ['Buyer'=1+required, 'Goods'=4+required,
   'Recipient'=6+optnl, 'Seller'=8+optnl, 'Money'=11+optnl],
   [purchase, acquire] ).
```

This says that the training sentence triggers the frame Commerce_Buy with the word *buy* as the lexical unit (*buy* is identified by the word index 2), that *Mary* (identified by the word index 1) is a filler for the *required* role Buyer, *Bob* (word index 8) fills in the *optional* role Seller, *watch* (word index 4) is a filler for the role Goods (also required), *200 dollars* (word index 11) fills in the optional role Money, and *John* is the Recipient. The words purchase and acquire are defined as the synonyms of *buy* which can trigger an instance of the Commerce_Buy frame the same way as *buy* does.

Our *lvp generator* is a Prolog program that takes marked-up sentences described above and *learns* the appropriate grammatical patterns and parsing rules. These parsing rules can check if the syntactical context of the lexical unit with respect to the role-fillers in the marked-up sentence can be applied to new sentences and extract role-fillers from that sentence. For instance, the aforementioned marked-up sentence will lead to the lvp (1) shown earlier. An example of such a learned parsing rule is given below. It takes an APE parse and extracts the role-filler for Buyer according to the grammatical pattern verb→subject.

```
apply_pattern_to_target('verb→subject',APEParse,LUIdx,RoleFilIdx) :-
    get_pred_from_word_idx(APEParse,LUIdx,LUPred),                    (2)
    get_subj_from_verb(APEParse,LUPred,RoleFilIdx).
```

The rule takes an Attempto parse (APEParse) of a sentence and the word index for the lexical unit (LUIdx) as input, and outputs the word index of the extracted role-filler (RoleFilIdx) in the sentence. In the rule body, get_pred_from_word_idx takes APEParse and LUIdx and finds the corresponding predicate (LUPred) representing the lexical unit, which is an event in this case. Next, get_subj_from_verb searches APEParse to find an object-fact whose identifier matches the third argument (the subject) of LUPred. If found, the word index of the object-fact representing the role-filler is returned.

3.3   Frame Parsing

Having parsed a CNL sentence, the next step is to identify the frames and lvps (described in Sect. 3.2) that match the sentence. To this end, the sentence is scanned for lexical units of the existing lvps and then one checks if these lvps can be applied. If an lvp is applicable, all the extracted role-fillers from the sentence are collected and candidate frame-based parses are constructed. A *candidate frame-based parse* (abbr., *candidate parse*) has the form <FN, {(RN$_i$,RF$_i$)$_{i=1,...k}$}>, where FN is the name of a frame the sentence possibly belongs to, and the second component in the tuple is a set of extracted role-name/role-filler pairs. This is a purely syntactic check and some parses may be rejected later on semantic grounds. For example, consider the following lvps:

lvp(buy,v,'Commerce_Buy',[pattern('Buyer','verb→subject',required),
  pattern('Goods','verb→object',required),
  pattern('Recipient','verb→dep[for]',optnl),   (3)
  pattern('Money','verb→dep[at]→rel→dep',optnl),
  pattern('Seller','verb→dep[from]',optnl)]).

lvp(buy,v,'Commerce_Buy',[pattern('Buyer','verb→subject',required),
  pattern('Goods','verb→object',required),
  pattern('Recipient','verb→dep[for]',optnl),   (4)
  pattern('Money','verb→dep[for]',optnl),
  pattern('Seller','verb→dep[from]',optnl)]).

lvp(buy,v,'Commerce_Buy', [pattern('Buyer,'verb→subject',required),
  pattern('Goods,'verb→object',required),
  pattern('Recipient,'verb→dep[for]',optnl),   (5)
  pattern('Money,'verb→dep[for]→rel→dep',optnl),
  pattern('Seller','verb→dep[from]',optnl)]).

In our running example, the sentence *Mary buys a watch from John for Bob for 200 dollars*, the word *buys* triggers the above lvps. In all three cases, the pattern verb→subject lets rule (2) extract *Mary* as the Buyer. The pattern verb→object triggers another rule in the parser, which will extract *watch* as the Goods, and so on.

Based on these lvps, the system will construct several candidate parses, but some will be wrong, useless, or redundant. First, some candidate parses may be subsumed by others. For example, lvp (3) above yields a candidate parse where *Mary* is a Buyer, *watch* is the Goods, *Bob* is the Recipient, and *John* is the Seller. However, this parse is subsumed by the parse obtained from lvp (4) because our sentence contains all the components mentioned in lvp (4).

Second, the parser may misidentify the roles for the words extracted from the CNL sentence, so wrong role-fillers may get associated with some of the frame's roles in the candidate parses. For example, in lvp (4) the grammatical patterns for Recipient and Money are the same. Therefore, it will generate two candidate parses: in one case *Bob* is a role-filler for the `Recipient` role and *200 dollars* is a role-filler for `Money`; in another case, *Bob* is the role-filler for the `Money` and *200 dollars* is the role-filler for `Recipient`.

The third problem arises when a candidate parse extracts wrong role-fillers. For example, given the sentence *Mary buys a watch from John for Bob for a price of 200 dollars*, lvp (5) will give the right result. However, lvp (4) also applies, so we will get *price* as a role-filler for either the `Recipient` or the `Money`.

All of these problems are solved in the following subsection, via an algorithm for semantic *role-filler disambiguation*—a process related to word-sense disambiguation [18] but more narrow and so it has higher-accuracy solutions than the general problem of word-sense disambiguation.

3.4   Role-Filler Disambiguation

Role-filler disambiguation is akin to word-sense disambiguation but it does not try to disambiguate entire sentences. Instead, the goal is to disambiguate different senses of the extracted role-fillers and find the best sense for each role-filler with respect to the roles in particular logical frames. Consider the sentence *Mary grows a macintosh*, which belongs to the `Growing_Food` frame where *Mary* is the `Grower` and *macintosh* is the `Food`. In BabelNet, *macintosh* has several meanings like *an early-ripening apple* (`bn:00053981n`), *a computer sold by Apple Inc.* (`bn:21706136n`) and *a kind of waterproof fabric* (`bn:00052580n`). Since `Food` is much more semantically related to an apple than to a computer or a fabric, *macintosh* should be disambiguated with the synset `bn:00053981n` denoting *an apple*.

Role-filler disambiguation works on candidate parses produced by frame parsing, as explained in the previous subsection. Each role-filler is often associated with several synsets. The disambiguation process first scores BabelNet synsets in relation to the frame roles filled by the role-filler words and then combines the individual scores into scores for entire candidate parses, ranks the parses, and removes the ones that score below a threshold.

The disambiguation algorithm for candidate parses queries BabelNet for each role-filler and gets a list of *candidate role-filler synsets*, which are BabelNet synsets for the role-filler words. Then it performs a heuristic breadth-first search to find all semantic paths that start at each candidate role-filler synset and end at a role synset, or vice versa. A heuristic scoring function assigns a score to each path, prunes the unpromising paths, and selects the path with the highest score. The starting (or ending) point of that path is the role-filler synset chosen as the semantically most likely BabelNet synset for the role-filler in question. At this stage, each role-filler in a candidate parse is disambiguated, yielding a *disambiguated candidate parse* of the form <FN, {(RN$_i$,RF$_i$, BNSyn$_i$, Score$_i$)}>, where FN is a frame name, RN$_i$ a synset for a role in FN, RF$_i$ a role filler synset for the role RN$_i$, and Score$_i$ is a score that signifies the semantic relatedness of the role filler RF$_i$ to the particular meaning of the frame role represented by the synset RN$_i$. This disambiguated candidate parse thus extends the notion of a candidate parse described previously by adding the disambiguating information (in the form of the synsets RN$_i$ and RF$_i$ along with the relatedness score). For the score of the entire disambiguated parse, we take the geometric mean of all the individual role-filler scores. Candidate parses with lower scores are then discarded. The key to this process is choosing an appropriate scoring function, which is described next.

Computing Semantic Scores. Ideally, each role should be a direct or indirect *hypernym* of its role-filler, or vice versa. Consider the sentence *A person buys a car that* belongs to Commerce_Buy frame, where *person* is the Buyer and *car* is the Goods. Here, *person* is a hypernym of Buyer and Goods is a hypernym of *car*. At the first glance, one might try to focus on hypernym paths between the role-filler synsets and the role synsets, but this would have been too easy to actually work. First, BabelNet does not contain the entire knowledge of the world and many hypernym links are missing. Second, despite the overall high quality of this knowledge base, it still contains many wrong hypernym relations. Therefore, one must consider a broader class of semantic relations (like *derivationally related, gloss related,* and more) in building semantic paths between pairs of synsets. Note that some of the errors can be detected and corrected— see Sect. 5. Since it is impractical to fix all the wrong semantic relations or add all the missing ones, one must consider all kinds of semantic paths, not only the shortest ones. Also, not all links are created equal. As mentioned, hypernym links are probably a good bet, but following hyponym or gloss-related links (which connect words with related glossaries) is riskier. To compute the semantic score, we consider three factors: the semantic connection number (total number of semantic links connected to each synset node), the edge type and weight, and the path length. The first two can be obtained by querying BabelNet, but the edge weight information there is rather sparse and cannot be relied upon too much. For instance, many good hypernym links have the weight of zero in BabelNet. We therefore bump up the weight of hypernym and other links by various constants (e.g., larger for hypernyms, lower for hyponyms).

The scoring function in KALM was chosen to encourage the paths with higher semantic connection numbers and edge weights, and to penalize the longer paths. Additionally, different *relevance factors* are given to different types of edges in a path. For instance, the hypernym edges have the highest relevance factor. Derivationally-related and gloss-related edges are given the next highest relevance factor, etc. Formally, let n_1 be a role-filler synset node, n_l be a role synset node and $L = \{n_1, e_{12}, n_2, \cdots, n_l\}$ be a semantic path from n_1 to n_l, where n_i represents a BabelNet synset node and $e_{i,i+1}$ represents an edge between n_i and n_{i+1}. The semantic score of the path is computed by the following formula based on the above principles:[5]

$$score = \frac{\sum_{i=1}^{n-1} \sqrt{f_n(n_i)} \times f_w(e_{i,i+1})}{5^{\sum_{i=1}^{n-1} f_p(e_{i,i+1})}} \tag{6}$$

where $f_n(n_i)$ is n_i's semantic connection number, $f_w(e_{i,i+1})$ is the sum of $e_{i,i+1}$'s BabelNet edge weight and its relevance factor, and $f_p(e_{i,i+1})$ is the penalty value for $e_{i,i+1}$, defined based on the edge type. The *base* of the exponent in the denominator is 5, which imposes a serious penalty for longer paths.

The above algorithm is fairly naive and takes hours to compute the score of a disambiguated candidate parse. This is because BabelNet is very large, the number of BabelNet queries required by this algorithm is in millions, and even a *local* such query takes about 10 ms. On average, each word is associated with 15 synsets and each synset is semantically related to a few hundred other synsets, so the number of semantic paths can be huge. Section 4 deals with this complexity, reducing the time to seconds.

3.5   Constructing Unique Logical Representation from Parses

We now show how frame parsing and role-filler disambiguation work in tandem to yield *unique logical representation (ULR)* for sentences. The process is shown in Fig. 2.

---

[5] The parameters were chosen experimentally. As part of future work, we will explore using a neural net to fine-tune this formula.

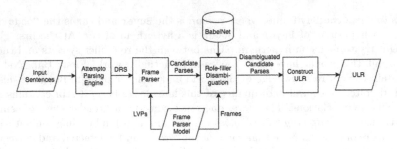

Fig. 2. Pipeline for translating a sentence into ULR

ULR uses the predicates `frame/2` and `role/2` for representing instances of the frames and the roles. The predicates `synset/2` and `text/2` are used to provide synset and textual information. Consider these sentences: *Mary buys a watch for Bob at a cost of 200 dollars, Mary buys a watch for Bob for 200 dollars*, and *Mary buys a watch for Bob for a price of 200 dollars*. Although these sentences are different in structure, they trigger the same frame (`Commerce_Buy`) because they match the lvps (3), (4), and (5) in Sect. 3.3, respectively, and this leads to *exactly the same* candidate parses. Therefore, when these sentences are stated as facts, they would be translated into exactly the same logical representation, shown below.

```
frame(id_1,'Commerce_Buy').
    role(id_1,'Buyer',id_2).    role(id_1,'Recipient',id_3).
    role(id_1,'Goods',id_4).    role(id_1,'Money',id_5).
    synset(id_2,'bn:00046516n').    // person synset
    text(id_2,'Mary').
    synset(id_3,'bn:00046516n').    // person synset
    text(id_3,'Bob').
    synset(id_4,'bn:00077172n').    // watch synset
    text(id_4,'watch').
    synset(id_5,'bn:00024507n').    // currency synset
    text(id_5,'200 dollars').
```

The symbol `id_1` here is a unique ID given to the event of Mary buying a watch. The other IDs are assigned to the various role-filler entities extracted from the sentence. For instance, `id_2` represents the entity corresponding to *Mary* and `id_3` to *Bob*. These entities are further described by the predicates `synset/2` and `text/2`.

4   Taming the Complexity of Role-Filler Disambiguation

BabelNet is a very large knowledge graph and the role-filler disambiguation relies on massive amount of querying of that graph, while each query is relatively expensive (even when BabelNet instance runs locally and is called directly, via Java). To solve the performance problems with the naive disambiguation algorithm of Sect. 3.4, we developed a number of optimizations whose collective effect is reducing the computation time from hours to seconds. These techniques are described below.

Parallel Computation. The first obvious observation is that the base algorithm is easily parallelizable, since finding semantic paths connecting different synsets pairs can be done independently. To this end, we create a thread pool where each separate thread finds paths from a specific candidate role-filler synset to a role synset. Moreover, if one such path is found, the highest current score among such a paths is shared with all the parallel threads and is used as a cut-off for pruning the computation of any low-score path that is in progress. Our test machine had 12 CPU cores; with more cores, more threads could be created by elaborating on the above idea. Parallelization reduces the running time by an order of magnitude in some cases. Role-filler disambiguation could also be done in parallel across the different candidate parses, and one could further parallelize the process across sentences.

Caching BabelNet Queries. BabelNet queries are relatively expensive and collectively take most of the computing time. Our experiments showed that in role-filler disambiguation about 70% of such queries are repeated more than once. Although BabelNet does some caching on its own, it is insufficient. To hasten the search for paths between pairs of synsets, KALM caches the results of BabelNet queries internally, which results in a big speedup (3–5 times, depending on specifics of the case).

No Duplicate Computation in Role-Filler Disambiguation. For a sentence, different candidate parses (generated from different lvps) that represent the same frame often share some of the role/role-filler pairs. We avoid such duplicate computations by creating one thread for each unique role/role-filler pair.

Priority-Based BabelNet Path Search. Given the complexity of BabelNet, any pair of synsets can have many connecting paths and even more paths wonder astray without connecting the requisite nodes. Although we prune away paths that score low, naive breadth-first search for connecting paths can get stuck exploring wrong parts of the graph for a long time. To avoid this problem, we use adaptive priority-based search with a priority queue in which unpromising paths get downgraded and eventually pruned.

Inverse Path Search. The aforementioned algorithm is designed to find a semantic path from the role-filler synset to the role synset. However, in the car-buying example of Sect. 3.4, the role could be either a hypernym of the role-filler, as in (*car*, Goods), or a hyponym, as in (*person*, Buyer). In principle, we could use the same priority-queue based approach to find a hyponym path from the *person* synset to the Buyer synset. Once the path is found, we could compute one semantic score based on the hyponym path and another based on the inverse semantic path that goes from Buyer to *person* and uses hypernym links. We could then pick the best-scoring path.

However, not all BabelNet edges have semantically inverse edges (e.g., *entailment* edges do not). Besides, the fan-out in the BabelNet graph at a role-filler synset and that at the frame role synset can be very different. For example, the *person*-synset (bn:00046516n) has more than a thousand hyponyms, and starting the search from that synset is almost always costlier than going from, say, the role Buyer to the role-filler *person*. To take advantage of this asymmetry, separate threads are created to search from role synsets to their candidate role-filler synsets. This inverse path search is also based on the priority queue and is computed similarly.

5   Explaining Semantic Parses

This section discusses the explainability aspect of the KALM approach. This includes both explaining the correct semantic parses and also why errors are made.

5.1   Explaining Correct Parses

Section 3.4 explained the process of role-filler disambiguation, which assigns a BabelNet synset to each role-filler word. This is done by finding highest-scoring semantic paths that connect the candidate synsets for role-filler words and the synsets for the roles in selected *FrameOnt* frames. The KALM explanation mechanism is based on analysis of these paths. Consider the sentence *Robin Li is a founder of Baidu*, which has three candidate parses with the following lvps:

$$
\begin{aligned}
&\texttt{lvp(founder,n,Create\_Organization, [}\\
&\quad \texttt{pattern(Creator,}object|\rightarrow\texttt{verb}\rightarrow\texttt{subject,required),}\\
&\quad \texttt{pattern(Organization,object}\rightarrow\texttt{rel}\rightarrow\texttt{object,required)]).}
\end{aligned} \tag{7}
$$

$$
\begin{aligned}
&\texttt{lvp(be,v,People\_by\_Origin, [}\\
&\quad \texttt{pattern(Person,verb}\rightarrow\texttt{subject,required),}\\
&\quad \texttt{pattern(Origin,verb}\rightarrow\texttt{object,required)]).}
\end{aligned} \tag{8}
$$

$$
\begin{aligned}
&\texttt{lvp(be,v,Being\_Employed, [}\\
&\quad \texttt{pattern(Employee,verb}\rightarrow\texttt{subject,required),}\\
&\quad \texttt{pattern(Position,verb}\rightarrow\texttt{object,required)]).}
\end{aligned} \tag{9}
$$

Here, the lvp (7) belongs to the **Create_Organiazation** frame, where *Robin Li* fills the **Creator**-role and *Baidu* fills the **Organization**-role. The lvp (8) belongs to the **People_by_Origin** frame, where *Robin Li* fills the **Person**-role and *founder* fills the **Origin**-role. The last lvp, (9), belongs to the **Being_Employed** frame, where *Robin Li* fills the **Employee**-role and *founder* fills the **Position**-role. The parse corresponding to the first lvp (7) gets the highest score with the following semantic paths that can be shown to the user (who is the domain expert in this case) as explanations:

Creator: *Robin Li* (**bn:03307893n**) $-hypernym\rightarrow$ *a person who founds or establishes some institution* (**bn:00009631n**)

Organization: *Baidu* (**bn:00914124n**) $-hypernym\rightarrow$ *an institution created to conduct business* (**bn:00021286n**) $-hypernym\rightarrow$ *an organization* (**bn:00059480n**)

These paths justify the chosen parse by demonstrating the semantic connections in BabelNet between each role (**Creator** and **Organization** in this case) and their role-fillers. The alternative disambiguations, like **Origin:** *founder* (that stems from the lvp (8)) and **Position:** *founder* (that stems from the lvp (9)) receive very low scores because the concepts represented by these roles and their role-fillers (*founder* for both) are semantically incompatible, which results in low-scoring connecting BabelNet paths.

5.2   Explaining Erroneous Parses

Along with plethora of useful data, BabelNet contains fair amount of uncurated noise due to the fact that much of this knowledge graph was created automatically, by merging information from various sources with the help of sophisticated heuristics. Like any algorithm of that kind, this process admits certain amount of errors, including wrong synset assignments to words, incorrect semantic links, and missing links. For instance, BabelNet makes the concept of *job position* a hypernym of the concept of *womanhood* and the concept of *engineering science* a hypernym of the concept of *building structure*. It also wrongly assigns the concept of engineering science as one of the meanings of the word *engineer*. These errors can throw role-filler disambiguation off-course and hurt the accuracy of knowledge authoring.

To deal with such errors, it is necessary to be able to both explain (to a domain expert) why KALM has selected a wrong semantic parse and then to provide the means to correct or mitigate the noise in BabelNet that was responsible for that particular error. We illustrate these issues using three examples where errors in BabelNet cause wrong parsing results and show how a domain expert can deal with such problems.

First, consider the case of a wrong synset assignment to words in BabelNet. This problem arises in the sentence *Mary buys a watch for Susan's daughter*, among others. Here the frame parser selects the **Commerce_Buy** frame where *Mary* fills the role of **Buyer**, *watch* fills the role of **Goods**, and *daughter* fills the role of **Recipient**. The word *daughter* is disambiguated with the BabelNet synset **bn:00018346n** (*a human offspring—son or daughter—of any age*). Although this synset has a connection with the **Recipient** role, it is not equivalent to the *daughter* concept which only refers to *a female human offspring*. The domain expert can record this synset assignment error and add it to an *exception* list, so KALM will not associate *daughter* with synset **bn:00018346n** in the next run.

Now consider a case of incorrect semantic links using the sentence *Mary works in Rockefeller Center* as an example. Our semantic parser will generate three parses based on three different lvps—all belonging to the same frame **Being_Employed**:

```
{(Employee,Mary),(Place,Rockefeller Center)}
{(Employee,Mary),(Field,Rockefeller Center)}
{(Employee,Mary),(Employer,Rockefeller Center)}
```

Obviously, only the first parse is intended, but the second one gets the highest score. The reason is that *Rockefeller Center* is connected to **Field** (as a branch of knowledge) via the following path which has a very high score:

Field: *Rockefeller Center* (**bn:00897288n**) −*hypernym*→ *a building structure* (**bn:00013722n**) −*hypernym*→ *a discipline dealing with art or science* (**bn:00005105n**) −*hypernym*→ *a branch of knowledge*(**bn:00007985n**).

Clearly, the second link is wrong because *a building structure* is not a special case of *a discipline dealing with art or science*. A domain expert can record this incorrect semantic link and KALM will not consider it as a valid link next time.

Finally, consider the case when BabelNet has a missing semantic link using the sentence *John travels to Los Angeles*. The frame parser would select the **Travel** frame where *John* is the **Traveler** and *Los Angeles* is the **Goal**. Surprisingly, the synset **bn:00019336n**, which refers to the city of *Los Angeles* in California, does not get the highest score because BabelNet is missing an important *hypernym* link connecting **bn:00019336n** (*Los Angeles, CA*) and the concept of municipality with the synset **bn:00056337n**. The highest score gets a relatively small city in Argentina (**bn:02084491n**) under the same name. This fact is immediately clear when one compares the semantic path from Los Angeles in Argentina to the role **Goal** (the highest-scoring path) to the path from the intended synset of Los Angeles, CA to that same role. This simple analysis immediately suggests to the user that the missing link should be added.

Another source of errors is when BabelNet associates different synsets to the same meaning. For instance, BabelNet synsets **bn:00071215n** (which comes from WordNet) and **bn:15385545n** (which comes from Wikidata) denote the same concept as *a place where items or services are sold*. This can be corrected by establishing an equivalence between these two synsets.

6   Evaluation

Dataset. Acting as knowledge engineers, we used the methodology described in Sect. 3.2 and created a total of 50 logical frames,[6] mostly derived from FrameNet but also some that FrameNet is missing (like *Restaurant*, *Human_Gender*). We then used KALM to learn 213 logical valence patterns from 213 *training* sentences.(see footnote 6) We used 28 additional *tuning* sentences to adjust the parameters of the scoring function (6) used for role-filler disambiguation and to deal with noise in BabelNet.

We evaluated the KALM system using 250 test sentences(see footnote 6) (distinct from the training sentences) and verified whether the system returns the expected frames and disambiguates each role-filler correctly. Note that our approach is based on CNL and so public and standardized data sets are not available for comparison. The test sentences were instead constructed by rephrasing the sentences from FrameNet into CNL. While Attempto CNL and KALM can handle quite complex sentences, the test sentences were on purpose selected to be very simple and common, to rule out the possibility of a bias towards KALM. We claim that to be of any use for knowledge acquisition or authoring, any system should grok such sentences out of the box. Here is a sample of the typical test sentences:

> *Mary buys a laptop.*
> *Kate obtains a master degree in biology from Harvard University.*
> *Kate makes a trip from Beijing to Shanghai.*
> *John works at IBM.*
> *Kate Winslet co-stars with Leonardo DiCaprio in Titanic.*
> *Warren Buffett stays in Omaha.*
> *A student borrows a textbook from a library.*

Comparison Systems. The aim of this work is to create a technology to enable domain experts to author high-quality knowledge using CNL. This goal is quite unique in the literature and there do not seem to be systems that are directly comparable to our work. It is interesting, however, to compare KALM with systems designed for general text understanding, like SEMAFOR, SLING, and Stanford CoreNLP. Since these systems are much more general than KALM and tackle a much more difficult problem, it cannot be expected that they would produce the same quality of knowledge as KALM. However, given the simplicity of our test sentences, it is still reasonable to anticipate that these systems would do well. Nevertheless, KALM bested all of them by a margin much wider than expected.

A few more observations about the differences between KALM and other systems are in order. First, none of the other systems do disambiguation or attempt to find

---

[6] https://datahub.csail.mit.edu/browse/pfodor/kalm/files.

synsets for role-fillers, so in this aspect KALM does more and is better attuned to the task of knowledge authoring. Second, none of these systems can explain their results, nor do they provide ways to analyze and correct errors. Third, two of the comparison systems use ontological frameworks that differ from *FrameOnt*. Whereas SEMAFOR is based on FrameNet and is similar in this respect to KALM, SLING is based on PropBank [20], and Stanford CoreNLP is based on Knowledge Base Population (KBP) relations [16]. In our view, PropBank is not well-suited to support disambiguation because it does not maintain equivalence among frames well enough. For instance, given the sentences *Mary buys a car* and *Mary purchases a car*, the word *buy* and *purchase* would trigger *buy.01* and *purchase.01* frames, respectively. Although these sentences mean the same, they are not mapped to the same frame in PropBank. As to KBP, it has too few types of semantic relations usable for knowledge acquisition compared to FrameNet and PropBank. In any case, although the three ontological frameworks are different, *FrameOnt*, FrameNet, and PropBank all cover the concepts used in the test sentences, and KBP covers many of them as well. Therefore, the comparison systems were expected to parse our test sentences and extract correct semantic relations.

Results. The evaluation is based on the following metrics.

FrSynC all frames and roles (semantic relations) are identified correctly
        and all role-fillers are disambiguated
  FrC all frames and roles are identified correctly
PFrC some frames/roles are identified, but some are not
Wrong some frames or roles are misidentified

KALM: 239 sentences are *FrSynC* (**95.6%**), 248 sentences are *FrC* (>99%), and 2 sentences are *Wrong* (<1%). Note that *FrSynC* applies only to KALM, since none of the comparison systems can disambiguate the senses of the extracted entities.
SEMAFOR: parses 236 sentences out of the 250 test sentences, where 59 sentences are *FrC* (**25%**), 44 sentences are *PFrC* (18.6%), and 133 sentences are *Wrong* (56.4%).
SLING: parses 233 sentences, where 98 sentences are *FrC* (**42.1%**), 63 are *PFrC* (27%), and 72 sentences are *Wrong* (30.9%).
Stanford CoreNLP: parses 26 sentences, out of which 14 sentences are *FrC* (**53.8%**), 10 sentences are *PrC* (38.5%), and 2 sentences are *Wrong* (7.7%).

Compared to the other three systems, KALM is by far more accurate: in only two cases it misidentifies the semantic frames. In one of these cases SEMAFOR succeeds partially (*PFrC*) and in the second case all other systems fail also. An example of such a difficult sentence is *Kate makes a purchase of a company*, which belongs to the frame Commerce_Buy, where *Kate* is supposed to fill the role of Buyer and *company* the role of Goods. However, KALM selects the Building frame instead and marks *Kate* as the Agent and *purchase* as the Created_Entity.

In the other 9 cases where KALM is less than perfect, all frames and roles are identified correctly, but some of the synsets are misidentified. For instance, in the sentence *Kate purchases a house*, KALM assigns the synset of a "public building for gambling and entertainment" to the role-filler *house*, but *house* was correctly extracted to fill the role Goods. Recall that the comparison systems do not have the means for assigning any synsets at all.

7   Conclusion

Controlled natural languages were proposed as a technology designed to enable domain experts who have no skills in knowledge representation to become effective as knowledge engineers. Unfortunately CNLs fell short of this promise due to insufficient attention to the semantics, which led to serious gaps in accuracy between what CNLs provide as knowledge authoring tools and what logic knowledge bases actually require. In this paper, we introduced a logic-based knowledge authoring approach, KALM, and demonstrated that bridging this gap is possible if CNLs are combined with linguistic frameworks, like FrameNet and knowledge bases like BabelNet, and with role-filler disambiguation. We have shown that this approach can be made efficient and that it achieves the unprecedented accuracy of 95.6% for CNL sentences. We also believe that this result can be further improved with machine learning techniques for tuning the relatedness scoring functions in KALM.

Before converging on FrameNet and BabelNet, we considered a number of other linguistic and general knowledge bases, such as ConceptNet [25], VerbNet [23], PropBank, DBpedia, Wikidata, and of course, the original WordNet. However, none of these systems could match the breadth of BabelNet, and we found the FrameNet-based methodology to be a good match for a logic-based approach such as ours. We also considered SEMAFOR, SLING, and Stanford CoreNLP as alternative frame extractors, but found that they target unrestricted natural language and have accuracy that is too low for our purposes.

For future work, we plan to extend the KALM framework to enable high-accuracy authoring of complex rules and to deal with rules that have exceptions, which are common in human knowledge.

Acknowledgements. We thank Niranjan Balasubramanian and H. Andrew Schwartz for the helpful discussions. This work was partially supported by NSF grant 1814457.

References

1. Allan, K.: Natural Language Semantics. Wiley, Hoboken (2001)
2. Angeli, G., Premkumar, M.J.J., Manning, C.D.: Leveraging linguistic structure for open domain information extraction. In: 53rd Annual Meeting of the Association for Computational Linguistics, Beijing, China, pp. 344–354 (2015)
3. Auer, S., Bizer, C., Kobilarov, G., Lehmann, J., Cyganiak, R., Ives, Z.G.: DBpedia: a nucleus for a web of open data. In: 6th International Semantic Web Conference, pp. 722–735 (2007)
4. Das, D., Chen, D., Martins, A.F.T., Schneider, N., Smith, N.A.: Frame-semantic parsing. Comput. Linguist. **40**(1), 9–56 (2014)
5. Erdem, E., Erdogan, H., Öztok, U.: BIOQUERY-ASP: querying biomedical ontologies using answer set programming. In: 5th International RuleML2011@BRF Challenge, pp. 1–8 (2011)
6. Fuchs, N.E., Kaljurand, K., Kuhn, T.: Attempto controlled english for knowledge representation. In: Baroglio, C., Bonatti, P.A., Małuszyński, J., Marchiori, M., Polleres, A., Schaffert, S. (eds.) Reasoning Web. LNCS, vol. 5224, pp. 104–124. Springer, Heidelberg (2008). https://doi.org/10.1007/978-3-540-85658-0_3
7. Fuchs, N.E., Kaljurand, K., Kuhn, T.: Discourse representation structures for ACE 6.6. Technical report 2010.0010, Department of Informatics, University of Zurich, Switzerland (2010)

8. Gebser, M., Kaufmann, B., Kaminski, R., Ostrowski, M., Schaub, T., Schneider, M.T.: Potassco: the potsdam answer set solving collection. AI Commun. **24**(2), 107–124 (2011)
9. Gomez, F.: The acquisition of common sense knowledge by being told: an application of NLP to itself. In: Kapetanios, E., Sugumaran, V., Spiliopoulou, M. (eds.) NLDB 2008. LNCS, vol. 5039, pp. 40–51. Springer, Heidelberg (2008). https://doi.org/10.1007/978-3-540-69858-6_6
10. Johnson, C.R., et al.: FrameNet: Theory and Practice (2002)
11. Kifer, M.: Knowledge representation & reasoning with Flora-2 (2018). http://flora.sourceforge.net
12. Kuhn, T.: A survey and classification of controlled natural languages. Comp. Linguist. **40**(1), 121–170 (2014)
13. Lehmann, J., Monahan, S., Nezda, L., Jung, A., Shi, Y.: LCC approaches to knowledge base population. In: 3D Text Analysis Conference, TAC, pp. 1–11. NIST, Gaithersburg (2010)
14. Manning, C.D., Surdeanu, M., Bauer, J., Finkel, J.R., Bethard, S., McClosky, D.: The stanford CoreNLP natural language processing toolkit. In: 52nd Annual Meeting of the Association for Computational Linguistics, ACL, System Demonstrations, Baltimore, MD, USA, pp. 55–60 (2014)
15. Schmitz, M., Soderland, S., Bart, R., Etzioni, O.: Open language learning for information extraction. In: The Joint Conference on Empirical Methods in Natural Language Processing and Computational Natural Language Learning, EMNLP-CoNLL, Jeju Island, Korea, pp. 523–534 (2012)
16. McNamee, P., Dang, H.T., Simpson, H., Schone, P., Strassel, S.M.: An evaluation of technologies for knowledge base population. In: 7th International Conference on Language Resources and Evaluation (LREC 2010), Valletta, Malta, p. 4, May 2010
17. Miller, G.A.: WordNet: a lexical database for english. Commun. ACM **38**(11), 39–41 (1995)
18. Navigli, R.: Word sense disambiguation: a survey. ACM Comput. Surv. **41**(2), 10 (2009)
19. Navigli, R., Ponzetto, S.P.: BabelNet: the automatic construction, evaluation and application of a wide-coverage multilingual semantic network. Artif. Intell. **193**, 217–250 (2012)
20. Palmer, M., Kingsbury, P., Gildea, D.: The PropBank: an annotated corpus of semantic roles. Comput. Linguist. **31**(1), 71–106 (2005)
21. Ringgaard, M., Gupta, R., Pereira, F.C.N.: SLING: a framework for frame semantic parsing. CoRR 1710.07032, pp. 1–9 (2017). http://arxiv.org/abs/1710.07032
22. Sagonas, K., Swift, T., Warren, D.S.: XSB as an efficient deductive database engine. In: ACM Conference on the Management of Data, New York, USA, pp. 442–453 (1994)
23. Schuler, K.K.: VerbNet: a Broad-coverage, comprehensive Verb Lexicon. Ph.D. thesis, University of Pennsylvania (2005). aAI3179808
24. Schwitter, R.: English as a formal specification language. In: 13th International Workshop on Database and Expert Systems Applicationa (DEXA 2002), Aix-en-Provence, France, pp. 228–232 (2002)
25. Speer, R., Chin, J., Havasi, C.: Conceptnet 5.5: an open multilingual graph of general knowledge. In: 31st AAAI Conference on AI, CA, USA, San Francisco, pp. 4444–4451 (2017)

26. Vrandečić, D., Krötzsch, M.: Wikidata: a free collaborative knowledgebase. Commun. ACM **57**(10), 78–85 (2014)
27. Yang, G., Kifer, M., Zhao, C.: $\mathcal{F}$LORA-2: a rule-based knowledge representation and inference infrastructure for the semantic web. In: Meersman, R., Tari, Z., Schmidt, D.C. (eds.) OTM 2003. LNCS, vol. 2888, pp. 671–688. Springer, Heidelberg (2003). https://doi.org/10.1007/978-3-540-39964-3_43

On Generating Stories from Semantically Annotated Tourism-Related Content

Zaenal Akbar[1]([✉]), Anna Fensel[2], and Dieter Fensel[2]

[1] Research Center for Informatics, Indonesian Institute of Sciences,
Jl. Raya Bogor Km. 47, Cibinong 16916, Indonesia
`zaenal.akbar@lipi.go.id`
[2] Semantic Technology Institute (STI) Innsbruck, University of Innsbruck,
Technikerstraße 21a, 6020 Innsbruck, Austria
`{anna.fensel,dieter.fensel}@sti2.at`

Abstract. In online marketing communication, publication consistency and content diversity are two important factors for marketing success. Especially in the tourism industry, having a strong online presence through the dissemination of high-quality content is highly desired. A method to maintain these two factors is by collecting and remixing various user-generated contents available on the Web and presenting them more interestingly. This method, known as content curation, has been widely used in social media. Multiple social media content can be aggregated for further consumption, for instance by listing them in historical order or grouping them according to particular topics. While the amount of user-generated content available on the Web is continuously increased, finding and selecting content to be mixed into a meaningful story are mainly performed manually by humans. These are challenging tasks due to the vast amount of accessible content on the Web, presented in various formats, and available in distributed sources. In this paper, we propose a method to automatically generate stories in the tourism industry by leveraging rule-based system over a collection of semantically annotated content. The method utilizes data dynamics of annotations, detected through a rule-based system, to identify the relevant content to be selected and mixed. We evaluated our method with a collection of semantically annotated tourism-related content from the region of Tyrol, Austria with promising results.

Keywords: Semantic annotation · Automatic story generation
Rule-based system · Online marketing · Tourism marketing

1 Introduction

The Internet enables organizations to connect, communicate, and engage with a wide range of audiences in multiple online communication channels. Social media, in particular, has been used as a significant communication means for maintaining relationships with customers [16]. Frequent use of multiple social

© Springer Nature Switzerland AG 2018
H. Panetto et al. (Eds.): OTM 2018 Conferences, LNCS 11230, pp. 481–497, 2018.
https://doi.org/10.1007/978-3-030-02671-4_29

media platforms, such as YouTube and Facebook, could positively affect consumers' attitudes toward marketing information [1]. Exposure to organizations' social media activities is another factor that could affect audiences perception towards organization's reputation [9]. More than that, online communication channels have been developed into platforms for influencing audiences [11], where providing the information needed by customers is a key to influence them. In the tourism industry, the Internet has become the top source for travel planning, where 83% of travelers were using social networking, video and photo sharing sites as their top online sources for travel inspiration, followed by search engines (61%), and travel's review sites/apps (42%)[1].

Besides creating content in every channel directly, organizations also could collect and share relevant content created by other organizations or individuals. The latter solution has been widely used in social networking environments, where social media content will be re-shared or re-mixed. Social curation for example, as a process to collect and organize a collection of social media content and re-publish them [10], the process could help organizations to maintain a persistent existence on social media. More than that, the source of content could be any online communication channel, including website or blog. Organizations could cooperate with bloggers to share posts, where a link to the original posts is vital to introduce content diversity as well as increase platform diversity [8].

With the vast amount and continuously growing available content on the Web, the task of identifying and collecting relevant content for publication is becoming more challenging. Content is organized in various data format, stored in different data stores, maintained by different organizations with different policies. Apart from those obstacles, a capability to identify and collect relevant content from distributed sources is highly valuable, especially for marketing purpose. With consistent activity and diversity of interests in publishing curated content, individuals or organizations could attract more followers [18]. In the field of tourism, a few efforts have been made to annotate tourism-related content with the primary purpose is to increase the online visibility of service providers [3].

In this paper, we propose a method to generate stories automatically in the field of tourism marketing. A story can be seen as a collection of relevant content, ordered and grouped according to specific criteria. Storify[2], Wakelet[3], and Paper.li[4] are a few examples of online services that enable users to create this kind of stories by importing and mixing multiple content from the Web especially social media. Our method would generate a similar kind of stories. While those existing solutions rely mainly on humans to identify and select relevant content, our method performs the story generation automatically. Our method utilizes a collection of semantically annotated content, where a rule-based system is used to detect data dynamics in the collection. The detected dynamics

---

[1] Think with Google, "The 2014 traveler's road to decision", https://www.thinkwithgoogle.com/consumer-insights/2014-travelers-road-to-decision/.

[2] https://en.wikipedia.org/wiki/Storify.

[3] https://wakelet.com/.

[4] https://paper.li/.

then used to identify and select multiple relevant content to be imported and mixed into meaningful stories. Further, the generated stories can be published to multiple online marketing communication channels, where publication should be consistent and at the same time keep published stories to be diversified. Our main contributions are: (i) three different formats of rules to detect dynamics in a collection of semantically annotated content, (ii) two metrics to measure performance of content publication to multiple channels, namely publication consistency and content diversity, (iii) a prototype and evaluations of the method with annotated content from the tourism industry. The rest of the paper is structured as follows: Sect. 2 lists related works. After that, we explain in detail our method to generate stories in Sect. 3, followed by our implementation prototype in Sect. 4. Section 5 demonstrates results from two evaluations based on data from the tourism industry. Finally, Sect. 6 summarizes our findings and provides a discussion on the future work.

2 Related Work

We align our work to a few research topics. First, Web content curation and stories generation which includes a few necessary activities including collecting (e.g. selecting, categorizing) and organizing content from the Web for further use. The second topic is rule-based automation, where rules will be defined to react to certain conditions and perform specific actions based on detected conditions. After describing related works on each topic, we summarize our contribution in the end.

Web Content Curation and Stories Generation. Identifying and selecting the relevant content from the Web is challenging. The amount of content available on the Web is growing very fast. A solution to deals with the challenge is using a topic recommendation system to assists a content curation [14]. The recommender system could assign webpages to the right collection, automatically or semi-automatically, based on the intrinsic features (such as page title, snippet text) and extrinsic features (based on how other users curated similar pages in the past). On Twitter, users have different motivations for creating lists of tweets, including interest in topics, recording conversation, splitting a long article, summarizing an event, etc [10]. On Pinterest, it is possible to re-pin images into users' boards automatically by predicting the category of the image [17]. The prediction was performed based on user-related features (e.g. users preference, profile), image-related features (e.g. quality, objects in the image), as well as crowd features (e.g. majority categories). The recommendation also can be constructed by considering re-pin path, explicit social relations, content-based social relation features [12]. On Flickr, curation is highly affected by tags specified manually by users or automatically extracted by the platform including location, time, camera model, etc [5]. On Twitter, relationships between tweets, hashtags, text units, URLs can be used to discover tweets which are related to events [13]. In Web archive systems, relevant content can be identified through metadata of file headers, links and URL strings [15].

For stories generation, integration between social and Web archives is also possible, where relevant content will be selected from the archives, ordered chronologically, and then visualized in storytelling tools to show how a story has evolved over time [4]. In this case, stories will be generated from a set of seed URIs, where each seed has many copies through time. Therefore, four types of stories can be generated according to: (i) different representation of content (fixed page, fixed time), (ii) different URI at different time (sliding page, sliding time), (iii) same URI at different time (fixed page, sliding time), (iv) different perspectives at a point of time (sliding page, fixed time).

Rule-Based Automation. A method to achieve an automatic system is through a rule-based system where a set of users' defined rules will be consumed by a rule-engine to make automatic inferences. This kind of system has been widely used in a variety of web applications, mainly to incorporate reactive capabilities to overcome the dynamics of the Web [6]. New information can be added, modified or deleted from the Web at any time. It is impossible to monitor those changes manually, an automatic solution is required. Reactive (active) rules provide reactive behavior that activated according to changes in the states of a monitored system. Including in this kind of rules are [7]: (i) Event-Condition-Action (ECA) rules, where the 'Action' will be executed if the 'Event' occurs where the 'Condition' holds, (ii) Condition-Action (CA) rules, also known as production rules, where the 'Action' part will be executed whenever a change to the system makes 'Condition' true. In online communication, reactive rules can be used to align semantically defined concepts to potential output channels in a way a semi-automatic publication can be performed [2].

Contribution. In alignment with those works, our work proposes a method to detect dynamics in a content source such that relevant content can be identified and used further, namely to be mixed as a meaningful story ready to be published to multiple marketing channels. The content source is a collection of semantically annotated content available on the Web, and the dynamics are detected through rules.

3   Automated Story Generation

In this section, we describe our solution to leverage semantically annotated content to drive automatic content selection to be weaved into a meaningful story. First, we show our conceptual solution where a rule engine as the core. After that, we describe a few formats of rules to detect annotation dynamics. Then, based on the detected dynamics, we develop our metrics to measure publication to multiple channels of the generated stories. Finally, we summarize our solution in the end.

3.1   The Conceptual Solution

As mentioned in Sect. 1, a story will be generated by identifying and selecting multiple relevant contents from the Web and order them according to specific criteria.

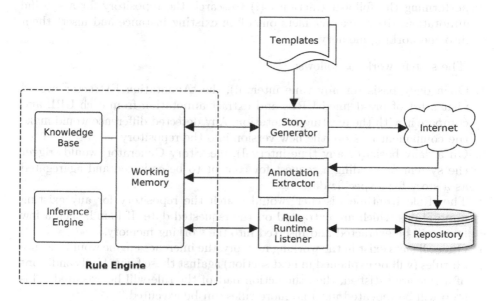

Fig. 1. Our conceptual solution for an automated story generation

Figure 1 shows our conceptual solution to leverage semantically annotated content available on the Internet for generating stories automatically. Multiple semantically annotated content from the Internet are extracted and stored in a repository. Then, a rule-engine would make use those collected annotations to detect a few data dynamics such that relevant content can be identified to be mixed into a story. The main components of the solution are:

1. Story generator, i.e. a collection of relevant content, collected through defined rules and mixed according to defined templates. A template defines which type of content would be aggregated, including how each content will be presented, grouped and ordered.
2. Annotation extractor and repository, i.e. a component to extract annotations from given URLs and stored them into the repository as well as into the rule engine. The repository would store all extracted annotations, use versioning where annotations from the same URL could be stored multiple times differentiated based on the date of extractions.
3. Rule engine, which is typically composed of three main components[5]: (i) a knowledge base, holds a list of rules, (ii) a working memory, holds temporary

---

[5] https://en.wikipedia.org/wiki/Rule-based_system.

facts, (iii) an inference engine, which performs inference by executing the defined rules over known facts in the working memory, including performing actions specified in the rules.

4. A component so-called 'Rule Runtime Listener' would bridges the repository and the rule engine, especially to monitor the working memory as well performing the following actions: (i) to search the repository for a specific annotation, (ii) to extract facts out of an existing instance and insert them into the working memory.

The system works as follows:

1. On a daily basis (or any time interval), the 'Annotation Extractor' would visit a list of pre-defined URLs and extract annotation from each URL and compare it with the existing annotation. Any detected difference would make the component to store the new version into the repository.
2. On a daily basis (or any time interval), the 'Story Generator' would trigger the system by sending a request for content to be collected and aggregated as a story for a specific date.
3. The 'Rule Runtime Listener' would search the repository for any existing annotations which are extracted on the requested date. If found, then a few facts will be extracted and inserted into the working memory.
4. Once all facts exist in the working memory, the inference engine would execute all rules (will be explained in next section) against those facts. If all conditions of a rule are satisfied, then the action part of the rule will be executed. This step will be repeated until no more rules can be executed.

3.2   Detection of Annotation Dynamics

Our solution utilizes the dynamics of annotations to identify relevant content to be aggregated as a story. Therefore, the most important thing that needs to be done is to detect those dynamics. Three generic dynamic indicators that would be possible to be detected, as follow:

1. **Detection of annotation existence,** to detect if a new annotation is detected in the repository. In this case, the annotation has no previous version yet. This first type of rules will be useful to detect if a web page, identified through a URL, has been annotated or not, or to check whenever new content is available on the Web.
2. **Detection of annotation alteration,** consisting of two types:
   (a) **Alteration of data property value,** to detect if the value of a data property of annotation has been altered. The detection will be based on the datatype of the value, such as string, integer, boolean, etc. Two data values can be compared based on their types by using operators such as equality, inequality, greater (or equal) than, less (or equal) than comparison. As an example, a 'LocalBusiness'[6] has a data property 'priceRange' which range as 'Text' that can be compared with a string matching.

---

[6] http://schema.org/LocalBusiness.

(b) **Alteration of object property value,** to detect if the value of an object property of annotation has been altered. A few operators can be used to compare two values such as sub- or super-class relationships, set memberships comparison, etc. As an example, a 'LocalBusiness' has an object property 'images' which might contain a list 'ImageObject' where a set membership comparison can be used to determine if a new image has been added.

In this alteration detection, a detection will be performed not only to determine if a value has been altered but also to identify the impact of the alteration. For example, whenever the value of the maximum price of property 'priceRange' of a 'LocalBusiness' has been altered, then the impact of this alteration could affect the price to be increased or decreased. This type of rules is essential to add contexts, such as time, price, location during detection of annotation dynamics.

Rules will be constructed in the format of `IF Condition THEN Action`, where the `Action` part is a collection of activities that will be executed whenever the part `Condition` is true. The `Condition` part contains one of the above-described detection, while the `Action` part would modify the working memory or collect the relevant content to be aggregated. In our case, this kind of rule is used to define the logic of content selection and story generation.

3.3   Multi-channel Publication Metrics

After defining our approach for detecting annotation dynamics and selecting relevant content through a rule-based system, then we use the detected dynamics and selected content to define metrics for content publication to multiple channels. As mentioned in the Sect. 1, two important publication strategies required to maintain online visibility on multiple channels:

1. Publication consistency, i.e there should be enough distinctive content items available to be published to every channel. Publishing a similar item repeatedly is not desired because it means that there is no new information available in the publication.
2. Publication diversity, i.e. there should be enough items from unique content type to be published to every channel. To make the publication more interesting, a different type of content should be published to every channel. For example, it will be more interesting to have an item about an event published to a channel and at the same time an item about prices of an accommodation published to another channel.

Let T as the collection of targeted channels, D as the collection of detected annotation dynamics, and C as the collection of selected content where a content $c \in C$ can be selected by one or more $d \in D$.

1. For publication consistency, for every publication date, content must be published to one channel only. Therefore, we define the publication consistency

metric as $P_c = |C| \geq |T|$, meaning that the number of selected content for the particular date is equal or bigger than the number of targeted channels.

2. For publication diversity, for every publication date, each dynamic detection must select one content to be published to one channel only. In this case, a diversify publication will also be a consistent publication. We define publication diversity metric as $P_d = |D| \geq |T|$, meaning that the number of distinctive dynamics must be equal or bigger than the number of targeted channels.

As mentioned in Sect. 1, two essential factors for marketing success on multiple online communication channels are publication consistency and content diversity. Above defined metrics would measure those two factors.

3.4   Discussion

As explained above, our solution utilizes the dynamics of a collection of semantically annotated content to identify and select relevant content to generate stories. To detect those dynamics, a rule-based system will be used. Rules will be constructed where various dynamics detection will be used as conditions of the rules. We specified three different types of rules that can be used to detect those dynamics, as well as defined two metrics to measure publication to multiple channels.

During the selection process, multiple items of content can be selected. The selected contents can be combined into a story or more than one stories depends on the purpose of each story. For example, to provide tourists with the latest situation of a region, then we collect only the most recent changes of information in the collection. But, if we would like to provide an overview of the region, then we gather all relevant information on various topics from all over the region.

4   Implementation

In this section, we describe our rule-based system implementation for generating stories from semantically annotated content. First, we describe how to represent facts, before discussing how to construct different types of rules. We use Schema.org vocabulary[7], a set of types and properties that can be used to mark-up Web content where a rule is represented using the Drools Rule Language[8].

4.1   Facts Representation

Facts need to be constructed based on the used vocabulary, where a type will be represented as a class and a property as a field. Figure 2 shows an example of a fact's representation. In this example, a type of "LodgingBusiness"[9] is represented as a class "LodgingBusiness" that consists of several fields such as name,

---

[7] http://schema.org.
[8] http://drools.org.
[9] https://schema.org/LodgingBusiness.

aggregate rating, image, and so on. Based on its specification, "LodgingBusiness" has a few more specific types, such as "BedAndBreakfast", "Hostel", "Hotel", and so on. Therefore a class "Hotel" would be recognized as a class "LodgingBusiness" as well. This semantic relationship will be applied to facts and rules as well.

```
package at.sti2.schema;

public enum Status {NEW, PREVIOUS}
public class LodgingBusiness {
    private String id;
    private Status status;
    private String name;
    private PostalAddress address;
    private AggregateRating aggregateRating;
    private List<ImageObject> image;
    private List<Offer> makesOffer;
    ...
}
```

Fig. 2. Facts representation used in the system

To track the changes of every annotation, a field "id" is introduced that specify the source of the annotation and the date when it was created, and therefore we might have several annotations for a web page, depending on how many times the annotation for the web page changed. For rule processing, we introduce a field "status" with possible value as one of "NEW" or "PREVIOUS" to represent the currently available annotation on the web page and the previous version of the annotation.

4.2   Rules Construction

Based on the generated facts, rules can be constructed by comparing the type of the class or the value of a field.

Detection Rules for Annotation Existence. Figure 3 shows a rule to detect if an annotation with the main type of *LodgingBusiness* is new or not. In this rule, if an annotation for the same URL has not been stored before (status is equal to "PREVIOUS"), then we would have an identical identification number because the dates for both versions of annotations will be same, namely today.

Detection Rules for Data Property Value Alteration. Figure 4 shows an example of rules for detecting qualitative data changed. In this example, the rules will detect if the maximum price of a lodging business has decreased or increased. Since the value range of "priceRange" property of Schema.org[10] is textual, then

---

[10] http://schema.org/priceRange.

```
import at.sti2.schema.*;
import at.sti2.model.Status;

global Set<LodgingBusiness> selection;

rule "New LodgingBusiness detection"
when
    item : LodgingBusiness(status == Status.NEW, cid : id)
    LodgingBusiness(status == Status.PREVIOUS, id == cid)
then
    selection.add(item);
end
```

Fig. 3. Example of rule for detecting the existence of a new annotation

```
import at.sti2.model.PriceRange;

rule "Decreased price detection"
when
    PriceRange(status == Status.PREVIOUS, max : maxPrice)
    PriceRange(status == Status.NEW, maxPrice < max, cid : id)
    item : LodgingBusiness(status == Status.NEW, id == cid)
then
    selection.add(item);
end

rule "Increased price detection"
when
    PriceRange(status == Status.PREVIOUS, max : maxPrice)
    PriceRange(status == Status.NEW, maxPrice > max, cid : id)
    item : LodgingBusiness(status == Status.NEW, id == cid)
then
    selection.add(item);
end
```

Fig. 4. Example of rules for detecting data property value alteration

a data pre-processing is required which is modeled by "PriceRange" class. The first rule detects if there is a lodging business with the maximum price of the new annotation is lower than the price in the previous annotation. Same case with the second rule which detects if the maximum price is higher than the previous one.

Detection Rules for Object Property Value Alteration. Figure 5 shows an example of rules to detect if new images have been added to an annotation by comparing the collection of images (through theirs URLs) from both versions of annotations. The first rule will remove (retract) all facts about images whose have similar URLs, and the second rule collects the remaining facts as the newly inserted images.

```
rule "Similar images detection"
when
    ImageObject(status == Status.PREVIOUS, u : url)
    item : ImageObject(status == Status.NEW, url == u)
then
    retract (item);
end

rule "Changed images collecting"
salience -100
when
    ImageObject(status == Status.NEW, cid : id)
    item : LodgingBusiness(status == Status.NEW, id == cid)
then
    selection.add(item);
end
```

Fig. 5. Example of rules for detecting object property value alteration

5   Result and Evaluation

In this section, we show results of our experiment and evaluation of the proposed solution with data from the tourism industry. In the following sections, we explain our experiments including the datasets and experimental procedures. After that, we show and discuss the obtained results, before summarizing our findings in the end.

5.1   Experiment

For experiment, we collected semantically annotated data from the tourism industry. Below, we explain our datasets, followed by the experimental procedures.

Datasets. We constructed our datasets from semantically annotated content in a various topic of tourism-related information, such as accommodation, events, infrastructure from the region of Tyrol, Austria [3]. In this work, we would like to demonstrate how to utilize a rule-based system to identify relevant content for story generation. Therefore, we selected annotations from one topic only, namely accommodation as follows: (i) limited to annotation in English only, (ii) limited to the main type *LodgingBusiness* (See footnote 9) and contains other sub-types including *BedAndBreakfast, Hotel, Motel,* (iii) limited to annotations that were generated from October 1, 2017 until January 31, 2018. We collected annotations from three tourist organizations in the region, namely the Destination Management Organization (DMO) Mayrhofen, Seefeld, and Fügen. A DMO is an organization that offers services and information to visitors about a destination as well as coordinating the tourism development of the destination. We obtained more than three thousand (3,556) of instances, correspond to more than nine hundred thousand (911,245) of statements.

Experimental Procedure. We performed our experiments as follows:

1. We constructed rules (as explained in the previous section) to detect seven conditions, where each condition will be associated with a different indication of knowledge dynamic:
   (a) *New.Annotation* as the rule to detect if a new instance of a lodging business is available,
   (b) *New.Images* and *New.Offer* as rules to detect changes in the collection of images and offers of a lodging business respectively,
   (c) *Price.Down* and *Price.Down* as rules to detect changes in the price range of a lodging business, decreased or increased,
   (d) *Rating.Down* and *Rating.Up* as rules to detect changes in the aggregate rating of a lodging business, decreased or increased.
2. For every instance generated in the selected date:
   (a) Extract the following facts: *LodgingBusiness* (main type or its sub-types), *ImageObject*, *Offer*, *PriceRange*, and *AverageRating* using the facts representation as explained in the previous section,
   (b) Insert those facts into the working memory,
   (c) Search the repository for the previous version of this instance. If found, then repeat the extraction process (step (a)) where their status values will be "PREVIOUS".
3. Fire all rules and collect all selected annotations
4. To measure rules daily performance, for every selected annotation:
   (a) identify the day of the week (Monday to Friday) when it was generated,
   (b) identify the rule that was selecting it.
5. To measure multi-channel publication performance we simulate the number of channels between 2 and 5, where we categorize every selected annotation into three categories as follows:
   (a) Compute publication diversity P_d, and if it is equal or bigger than the number of channels, then categorize the content as "2".
   (b) If P_d is less than the number of channels then compute publication consistency P_c, and if P_c is equal or bigger than the number of channels, then categorize the content as "1".
   (c) Other than that, categorize the content as "0".

This procedure was applied to the three available datasets, where each rule performances will be discussed in the following sub-section. A rule performance refers to its capability to identify a data dynamic in a collection of semantically annotated content, such that relevant content can be identified and selected for publication. After that, publication performance will also be discussed.

5.2 Evaluation: Rules Daily Performance

Figure 6 shows the daily performances of defined rules in DMO Mayrhofen dataset. For Monday and Tuesday, rule *New.Image* was dominant followed by rule *Price.Up*. And for the other days, rule *Price.Up* was dominant followed by *Price.Down*. An interesting result also was obtained for Wednesday; rules were contributed relatively equal except for the rule *New.Annotation*. This situation indicates that for Wednesday we could use any rules. The rule *New.Offer* contributed a high number of annotations equally to the rule *Price.Up* on Tuesday. The organization seems to modify its offers during this day.

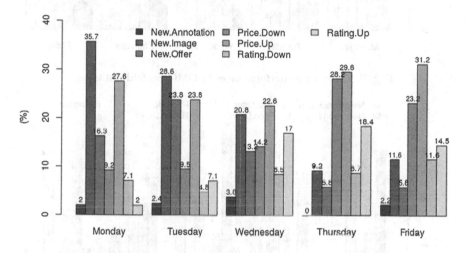

Fig. 6. Daily rules performances in DMO Mayrhofen dataset

For DMO Seefeld dataset, the daily performances of defined rules are shown in Fig. 7. The rule *New.Image* was dominant almost on all days except on Monday. For Monday, rule *Price.Up* was contributed the most of selected annotations. An interesting result was obtained for Thursday, where the rule *New.Offer* was contributed equally to *Price.Up*. Most likely, the organization changes most of their offers within this day.

Figure 8 shows the rules daily performance for DMO Fügen dataset. The rule *New.Image* was dominant on Monday, Wednesday, and Friday. This rule generated more than 35% of selected annotations from Wednesday. For the other days, Tuesday and Thursday, the selection was dominated by the rule *Price.Up*. The rule *New.Offer* contributed a high number of annotations on Monday and Thursday.

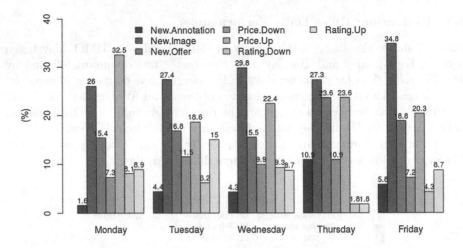

Fig. 7. Daily rules performances in DMO Seefeld dataset

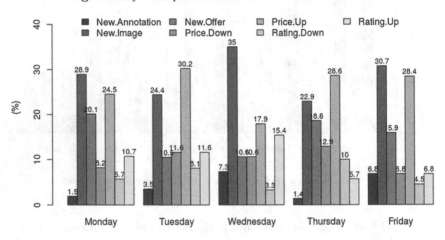

Fig. 8. Daily rules performances in DMO Fügen dataset

5.3   Evaluation: Multi-channel Publication Performance

For the second evaluation, we compute two multi-channel publication metrics as described in Sect. 3, namely publication consistency and diversity. Figure 9 shows the comparison of these two metrics in our three datasets, namely for DMO Mayrhofen (left), DMO Seefeld (center), and DMO Fügen (right). The values of publication consistency (dashed lines) will be increased until a certain point whenever the number of channels is increased, four channels in the case of DMO Mayrhofen, and three channels in the case of DMO Seefeld. In all datasets, the values of publication diversity (dotted lines) will be decreasing significantly whenever the number of channels is increased.

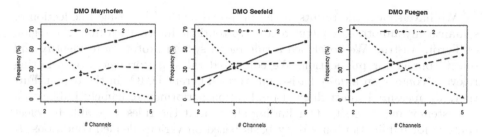

Fig. 9. Comparison of multi-channel publication performance based on publication consistency and diversity

5.4 Summary

We performed two types of evaluation, namely rules' daily performance and multi-channel publication performance. In the first evaluation, we measured how rules performed on selecting content during days of a week. From the results, we identified several distinctions between each rule in every organization. Most of the selected content was produced based on the change in information related to the organizations as business entities, for example, an addition of new images. A few content selections were triggered by changes in the business activities of the organizations as well, for example, the increasing/decreasing price which contributed a high number of annotations. In the second evaluation, we measured two publication metrics to measure publication consistency and diversity. From the results, seven annotation dynamics could provide relatively similar values for publication consistency and diversity between three and four channels.

6   Conclusion

In this paper, we introduce a method to identify and select user generated content to be aggregated into stories ready for publication to multiple online marketing channels. The method leverages semantically annotated content as data sources, where a variety of annotation dynamics is detected by rules to identify and select the most relevant content to be mixed as a meaningful story. Three different formats of rules are proposed, namely: (i) detection of annotation existence, i.e. detecting if a new annotation is available in a specific web page, (ii) detection of object property value alteration, i.e. comparing the value of an object property from an entity in an annotation, (iii) detection of data property value alteration, i.e. comparing the value of a data property from an entity in an annotation. The generated stories were used in the context of content publication to multiple channels, where two publication metrics were defined: (i) publication consistency, i.e. there is enough distinctive content items to be published to every channel, (ii) publication diversity, i.e. there is enough items from distinctive type of content to be published to every channel.

We have shown the results of the proposed method by using a collection of semantically annotated content related to touristic information from the region of Tyrol, Austria. We developed a rule-based system prototype to identify and select content for publication. We compared rules' performances on selecting relevant content on a daily basis from three different DMOs in the region. Further, we measured multi-channel publication performance, namely publication consistency and diversity. Our finding shows that the rules were able to select content for publication on a daily basis based on various defined conditions. It indicates that the proposed method could help organizations to have consistent and diverse publications to multiple communication channels.

In this work, we use English annotations for accommodations only. In the future, we would like to extend our work to another topic, such as event, infrastructure, points of interest, etc. Multilingual support will also be our next step, as well as using data from a different domain such as geographical data. More importantly, we would like to collect complete data for a whole year, such that we will able to analyze rules performances during weekends or specific session. This work could benefit multi-channel online marketing strategy of organizations by automating the creation of their marketing content.

Acknowledgements. We would like to thank all the members of the Online Communication working group (http://oc.sti2.at) of the Semantic Technology Institute (STI) Innsbruck for their valuable feedback and suggestions. The work is partially supported by the Indonesian Institute of Sciences (http://www.lipi.go.id).

References

1. Akar, E., Topçu, B.: An examination of the factors influencing consumers' attitudes toward social media marketing. J. Internet Commer. **10**(1), 35–67 (2011). https://doi.org/10.1080/15332861.2011.558456
2. Akbar, Z., García, J.M., Toma, I., Fensel, D.: On using semantically-aware rules for efficient online communication. In: Bikakis, A., Fodor, P., Roman, D. (eds.) RuleML 2014. LNCS, vol. 8620, pp. 37–51. Springer, Cham (2014). https://doi.org/10.1007/978-3-319-09870-8_3
3. Akbar, Z., Kärle, E., Panasiuk, O., Şimşek, U., Toma, I., Fensel, D.: Complete semantics to empower touristic service providers. In: Panetto, H., et al. (eds.) OTM 2017. LNCS. Springer, Cham (2017). https://doi.org/10.1007/978-3-319-69459-7_24
4. AlNoamany, Y., Weigle, M.C., Nelson, M.L.: Generating stories from archived collections. In: Proceedings of the 2017 ACM on Web Science Conference (WebSci 2017), pp. 309–318. ACM (2017). https://doi.org/10.1145/3091478.3091508
5. Barton, D.: The roles of tagging in the online curation of photographs. Discourse, Context Media **22** (2018). https://doi.org/10.1016/j.dcm.2017.06.001
6. Berstel, B., Bonnard, P., Bry, F., Eckert, M., Pătrânjan, P.-L.: Reactive rules on the web. In: Antoniou, G., et al. (eds.) Reasoning Web 2007. LNCS, vol. 4636, pp. 183–239. Springer, Heidelberg (2007). https://doi.org/10.1007/978-3-540-74615-7_3

7. Boley, H., Kifer, M., Pătrânjan, P.-L., Polleres, A.: Rule interchange on the web. In: Antoniou, G., et al. (eds.) Reasoning Web 2007. LNCS, vol. 4636, pp. 269–309. Springer, Heidelberg (2007). https://doi.org/10.1007/978-3-540-74615-7_5
8. Chang, Y.T., Yu, H., Lu, H.P.: Persuasive messages, popularity cohesion, and message diffusion in social media marketing. J. Bus. Res. **68**(4), 777–782 (2015). https://doi.org/10.1016/j.jbusres.2014.11.027. Special issue on global entrepreneurship and innovation in management
9. Dijkmans, C., Kerkhof, P., Buyukcan-Tetik, A., Beukeboom, C.J.: Online conversation and corporate reputation: a two-wave longitudinal study on the effects of exposure to the social media activities of a highly interactive company. J. Comput.-Mediat. Commun. **20**(6), 632–648 (2015). https://doi.org/10.1111/jcc4.12132
10. Duh, K., Hirao, T., Kimura, A., Ishiguro, K., Iwata, T., Yeung, C.M.A.: Creating stories: social curation of twitter messages. In: Proceedings of the 6th International AAAI Conference on Weblogs and Social Media (ICWSM 2012), pp. 447–450. AAAI Press (2012)
11. Hanna, R., Rohm, A., Crittenden, V.L.: We're all connected: the power of the social media ecosystem. Bus. Horiz. **54**(3), 265–273 (2011). https://doi.org/10.1016/j.bushor.2011.01.007
12. Liu, H., Wu, L., Zhang, D., Jian, M., Zhang, X.: Multi-perspective User2Vec: exploiting re-pin activity for user representation learning in content curation social network. Sig. Process. **142**(Suppl. C), 450–456 (2018). https://doi.org/10.1016/j.sigpro.2017.07.002
13. Mahata, D., Talburt, J.R., Singh, V.K.: From chirps to whistles: discovering event-specific informative content from twitter. In: Proceedings of the ACM Web Science Conference (WebSci 2015), pp. 1–17. ACM (2015). https://doi.org/10.1145/2786451.2786476
14. Saaya, Z., Schaal, M., Rafter, R., Smyth, B.: Recommending topics for web curation. In: Carberry, S., Weibelzahl, S., Micarelli, A., Semeraro, G. (eds.) UMAP 2013. LNCS, vol. 7899, pp. 242–253. Springer, Heidelberg (2013). https://doi.org/10.1007/978-3-642-38844-6_20
15. Vo, K.D., Tran, T., Nguyen, T.N., Zhu, X., Nejdl, W.: Can we find documents in web archives without knowing their contents? In: Proceedings of the 8th ACM Conference on Web Science (WebSci 2016), pp. 173–182. ACM (2016). https://doi.org/10.1145/2908131.2908165
16. de Vries, L., Gensler, S., Leeflang, P.S.: Popularity of brand posts on brand fan pages: an investigation of the effects of social media marketing. J. Interact. Mark. **26**(2), 83–91 (2012). https://doi.org/10.1016/j.intmar.2012.01.003
17. Zhong, C., Karamshuk, D., Sastry, N.: Predicting pinterest: automating a distributed human computation. In: Proceedings of the 24th International Conference on World Wide Web (WWW 2015), pp. 1417–1426 (2015). https://doi.org/10.1145/2736277.2741671
18. Zhong, C., Shah, S., Sundaravadivelan, K., Sastry, N.: Sharing the loves: understanding the how and why of online content curation. In: Proceedings of the 7th International AAAI Conference on Weblogs and Social Media (ICWSM 2013), pp. 659–667. AAAI Press (2013)

A Big Linked Data Toolkit for Social Media Analysis and Visualization Based on W3C Web Components

J. Fernando Sánchez-Rada[✉], Alberto Pascual, Enrique Conde,
and Carlos A. Iglesias

Grupo de Sistemas Inteligentes, Universidad Politécnica de Madrid, Madrid, Spain
{jf.sanchez,carlosangel.iglesias}@upm.es, a.pascuals@alumnos.upm.es
http://www.gsi.dit.upm.es

Abstract. Social media generates a massive amount of data at a very fast pace. Objective information such as news, and subjective content such as opinions and emotions are intertwined and readily available. This data is very appealing from both a research and a commercial point of view, for applications such as public polling or marketing purposes. A complete understanding requires a combined view of information from different sources which are usually enriched (e.g. sentiment analysis) and visualized in a dashboard.

In this work, we present a toolkit that tackles these issues on different levels: (1) to extract heterogeneous information, it provides independent data extractors and web scrapers; (2) data processing is done with independent semantic analysis services that are easily deployed; (3) a configurable Big Data orchestrator controls the execution of extraction and processing tasks; (4) the end result is presented in a sensible and interactive format with a modular visualization framework based on Web Components that connects to different sources such as SPARQL and ElasticSearch endpoints. Data workflows can be defined by connecting different extractors and analysis services. The different elements of this toolkit interoperate through a linked data principled approach and a set of common ontologies. To illustrate the usefulness of this toolkit, this work describes several use cases in which the toolkit has been successfully applied.

Keywords: Linked Data · Web Components · Visualization
Social media · Big Data

1 Introduction

We are used to the never-ending stream of data coming at us from social media. Social media has become a way to get informed about the latest facts, faster than traditional media. It is also an outlet for our complaints, celebrations and feelings, in general. This mix of factual and subjective information has drawn the

© Springer Nature Switzerland AG 2018
H. Panetto et al. (Eds.): OTM 2018 Conferences, LNCS 11230, pp. 498–515, 2018.
https://doi.org/10.1007/978-3-030-02671-4_30

interest of research and business alike. The former, because social media could be used as a proxy to public opinion, a probe for the sentiment of the people. The latter, because knowing the interests and experience of potential users is the holy grail of marketing and advertisement.

However, making sense of such a big stream of data is costly in several ways. The main areas that need to be covered are: extraction, analysis, storage, visualization and orchestration. All these aspects are further influenced by the typical attributes of Big Data such as large volume, large throughput and heterogeneity. We will cover each of them in more detail.

First of all, in order to analyze this data, it needs to be extracted. The volume of data and metadata available in today's media can be overwhelming. For instance, a simple tweet, which in principle consists of roughly 140 characters, contains dozens of metadata fields such as creation date, number of retweets, links to users mentioned in the text, geolocation, plus tens of fields about the original poster. Some of this data is very useful, whereas some information (e.g. the background color of the author's profile) are seldom used. Furthermore, Twitter is one of the best case scenarios, because it provides a well documented API. Other media require collecting unstructured information, or using more cumbersome techniques.

The extracted data needs to be stored and made available for analysis and visualization. Since the volume of data is potentially very large, the data store needs to keep up with this pace, and provide means to quickly query parts of the data. Modern databases such as ElasticSearch or Cassandra have been designed for such types of loads. However, analysis requires using data from different sources. For the sake of interoperability and simplicity, data from different sources should be structured and queried using the same formats. Hence, using vocabularies and semantic technologies such as RDF and SPARQL would be highly beneficial.

The next area is data analysis. The analysis serves different purposes, such as enriching the data (e.g. sentiment analysis), transforming it (e.g. normalization and filtering) or calculating higher order metrics (e.g. aggregation of results). Unfortunately, different analysis processes usually require different tooling, formatting and APIs, which further complicates matters.

Finally, there is visualization, where the results of the analysis are finally presented to users, in a way that allows them to explore the data. This visualization needs to be adaptable to different applications, integrated with other analysis tools, and performance. In practice, visualization is either done with highly specialized tools such as Kibana [13], with little integration with other products, or custom-tailored to each specific application, which hinders reusability.

And, lastly, all these steps need to be repeated for every application. This is, once again, typically done on an ad-hoc basis, and every step in the process is manually programmed or configured via specialized tools.

This work presents a toolkit that that deals with these issues on different levels: (1) to extract heterogeneous information, it provides independent data extractors and web scrapers; (2) data processing is done with independent semantic analysis services that are easily deployed; (3) a configurable Big Data orchestrator controls the execution of extraction and processing tasks; (4) the end result is presented in a sensible and interactive format with a modular visualization framework based on Web Components that connects to different sources such as SPARQL and ElasticSearch endpoints. Data workflows can be defined by connecting different extractors and analysis services. The different elements of this toolkit interoperate through a Linked Data principled approach and a set of common ontologies. The combination of Linked Data principles and Big Data is often referred to as Big Linked Data. The toolkit has been successfully used in several use cases, in different domains, which indicates that it is useful in real scenarios.

The remaining sections are structured as follows: Sect. 2 presents technologies and concepts that this work is based on. Section 3 explains the architecture of the toolkit, and its different modules. Section 4 illustrates the use of this toolkit in different use cases. Lastly, Sect. 5 presents our conclusions and future lines of work.

2   Enabling Technologies

2.1   W3C Web Components

W3C Web components are a set of web platform APIs that allow the creation of new custom, reusable, encapsulated HTML tags to use in web pages and web apps. This Web Components idea comes from the union of four main standards: custom HTML elements, HTML imports, templates and shadow DOMs.

- *Custom Elements:* Custom Elements [47] let the user define his own element types with custom tag names. JavaScript code is associated with the custom tags and uses them as an standard tag. Custom elements specification is being incorporated into the W3C HTML specification and will be supported natively in HTML5.3.
- *HTML imports:* HTML Imports [26] let users include and reuse HTML documents in other HTML documents, as 'script' tags let include external JavaScript in pages.
- *Templates:* Templates [9] define a new 'template' element which describes a standard DOM-based approach for client-side template. Templates allow developers to declare fragments of markup which are parsed as HTML.
- *Shadow DOM:* Shadow DOM [17] is a new DOM feature that helps users build components. Shadow DOMs can be seen as a scoped sub-tree inside your element.

In order to make compatible these W3C Web components with modern browsers, a number frameworks have emerged to foster their use.

Polymer is one of these emerging frameworks for constructing Web Components that was developed by Google[1]. Polymer simplifies building customized

---

[1]   https://www.polymer-project.org/.

and reusable HTML components. In addition, Polymer has been designed to be flexible, fast and close. It uses the best specifications of the web platform in a direct way to simply custom elements creation.

2.2 Emotion and Sentiment Models and Vocabularies

Linked Data and open vocabularies play a key role in this work. The semantic model used enables both the use of interchangeable services and the integration of results from different services. It focuses on Natural Language Processing (NLP) service definition, the result of such services, sentiments and emotions. Following a Linked Data approach, the model used is based on the following existing vocabularies:

- NLP Interchange Format (NIF) 2.0 [15] defines a semantic format for improving interoperability among natural language processing services. To this end, texts are converted to RDF literals and an URI is generated so that annotations can be defined for that text in a linked data way. NIF offers different URI Schemes to identify text fragments inside a string, e.g. a scheme based on RFC5147 [49], and a custom scheme based on context.
- Marl [46], a vocabulary designed to annotate and describe subjective opinions expressed on the web or in information systems.
- Onyx [31], which is built on the same principles as Marl to annotate and describe emotions, and provides interoperability with Emotion Markup Language (EmotionML) [37].
- Schema.org [12] provides entities and relationships for the elements that are outside the realm of the social media itself. For instance, it can be used to annotate product reviews.
- FOAF [11] provides the description of relationships and interactions between people.
- SIOC [4] is used to annotate blog posts, online forums and similar media.
- PROV-O [24] provides provenance information, linking the final results that can be visualized with the original data extracted, the processes that transformed the data, and the agents that took part in the transformation.

Additionally, NIF [15] provides an API for NLP services. This API has been extended for multimodal emotion analysis in previous works [33,34]. This extension also enables the automatic conversion between different emotion models.

2.3 Senpy

Senpy [32] is a framework for sentiment and emotion analysis services. Services built with Senpy are interchangeable and easy to use because they share a common API and Examples. It also simplifies service development.

All services built using Senpy share a common interface, based on the NIF API [14] and public ontologies. This allows users to use them (almost) interchangeably. Senpy takes care of:

- Interfacing with the user: parameter validation, error handling.
- Formatting: JSON-LD [39], Turtle/n-triples input and output, or simple text input.
- Linked Data: Senpy results are semantically annotated, using a series of well established vocabularies.
- User interface: a web UI where users can explore your service and test different settings.
- A client to interact with the service. Currently only available in Python.

Senpy services are made up of individual modules (plugins) that perform a specific type of analysis (e.g. sentiment analysis). Plugins are developed independently. Senpy ships with a plugin auto-discovery mechanism to detect plugins locally. There are a number of plugins for different types of analysis (sentiment, emotion, etc.), as well as plugins that wrap external services such as Sentiment140, MeaningCloud and IBM Watson[2].

3   Architecture

This work presents a modular toolkit for processing Big Linked Data encouraging scalability and reusability. The high level architecture of this toolkit, which we call Soneti, is depicted in Fig. 1. It integrates existing open source tools with other built specifically for the toolkit. The main modules are orchestration, data ingestion, processing and analysis, storage and visualization and management, which are described below.

Orchestration. The *orchestration module* (Sect. 3.1) is responsible of managing the interaction of the rest modules by automating complex data pipelines and handling failures. This module enables *reusability* at the data pipeline level, In addition, it enables *scalability*, since every task of the workflow can be executed in a Big Data platform, such as a Hadoop job [48], a Spark job [50] or a Hive query [43], to name a few. Finally, this module helps to recover from failures gracefully and rerun only the uncompleted task dependencies in the case of a failure.

The *Data Ingestion module* (Sect. 3.2) involves obtaining data from the structured and unstructured data sources and transforming these data into linked data formats, using scraping techniques and APIs, respectively. The use of linked data enables *reusability* of ingestion modules as well as *interoperability* and provides a uniform schema for processing data.

The *Processing and Analysis module* (Sect. 3.3) collects the different analysis tasks that enrich the incoming data, such as entity detection and linking, sentiment analysis or personality classification. Analysis is based on the NIF recommendation, which has been extended for multimodal data sources. Each

---

[2] Sentiment140, MeaningCloud and IBM Watson are online sentiment analysis services available at http://www.sentiment140.com/, https://www.meaningcloud.com/ and https://www.ibm.com/watson/services/natural-language-understanding/, respectively.

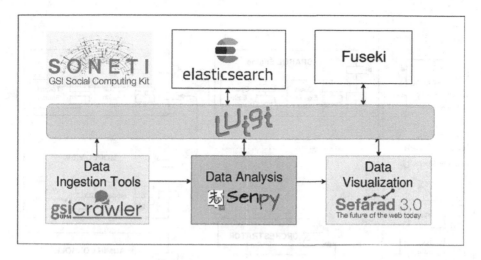

Fig. 1. High-level architecture.

analysis task has been modelled as a plugin of Senpy, presented in Sect. 2.3. In this way, analysis modules can be easily *reused*.

The *Storage module* (Sect. 3.4) is responsible for storing data in a nonSQL database. We have selected ElasticSearch [10], since it provides scalability, text search as well as a RESTful server based on a Query DSL language. For our purposes, JSON-LD [39] is used, with the aim of preserving linked data expressivity in a format compatible with the Elasticsearch ecosystem.

The *Visualization and Querying module* (Sect. 3.5) enables building dashboards as well as executing semantic queries. Visualisation is based on W3C Web Components. A library of interconnected Web Component based widgets have been developed to enable faceted search. In addition, one widget has been developed for providing semantic SPARQL queries to a SPARQL endpoint Apache Fuseki [19]. Fuseki is provisioned by the data pipeline.

Figure 2 provides a more detailed view of the architecture, focused on the Visualization and Querying module, to explain its connection to the rest of the modules. The following subsections describe each module in more detail.

3.1 Orchestration

Workflow management systems are usually required for managing the complex and demanding pipelines in Big Data environments. There are a number of open source tools for workflow management, such as Knime [45], Luigi [40], SciLuigi [23], Styx [41], Pinterest's pinball [29] or Airbnb's Airflow [20]. The interested reader can find a detailed comparison in [23,30].

We have selected as workflow orchestrator the open source software Luigi [40], developed by Spotify. It allows the definition and execution of complex dependency graphs of tasks and handles possible errors during execution. In addition,

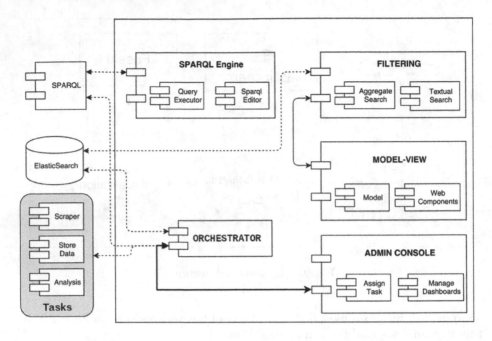

Fig. 2. Detailed architecture of the visualization components.

Luigi provides a web interface to check pipeline dependencies as well as a visual overview of tasks execution.

Luigi is released as a Python module, which provides an homogeneous language since machine learning and natural language processing tasks are also developed in this language.

A pipeline is a series of interdependent tasks that are executed in order. Each task is defined by its input (its dependencies), its computation, and its output.

Some examples of the most common pipelines we have reused in a number of projects are shown in Fig. 3:

- *Extract and Store:* this workflow extracts data from a number of sources and store them in a JSON-LD format, as shown in Fig. 3a.
- *Extract and Store in noSQL database and a LD-Server:* this worflow extends the previous worflow by storing in parallel in a noSQL database and a SPARQL endpoint the extracted triples, as depicted in Fig. 3b.
- *Extract, Analyze and Store workflow:* this workflow analyze the data before storing it, as shown in Fig. 3c. The analysis consists in a data pipeline where each analyzer adds semantic metadata, being the analyzers Senpy plugins. Some examples of these analyzers are sentiment and emotion detection as well as entity recognition and linking.

The processed data in most workflows is stored in one or multiple datastores and formats. Figure 4 illustrates the type of semantic annotations that would

(a) Extract and Store

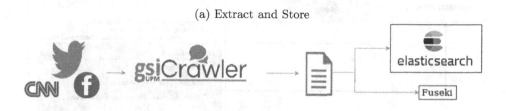

(b) Extract and Store in a NoSQL database and an LD-Serve

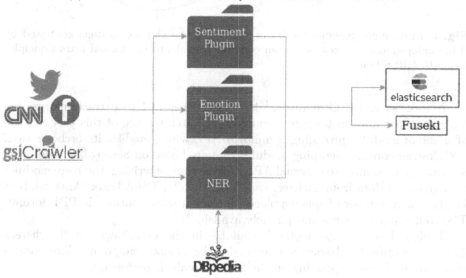

(c) Extract, Analyze and Store

Fig. 3. Examples of different Luigi workflows.

be generated by a combination of three different services (Sentiment Analysis, Emotion Analysis and Named Entity Recognition Analysis).

3.2 Data Ingestion

The objective of this module is extracting the information from external sources, map it to linked data formats for process and storage.

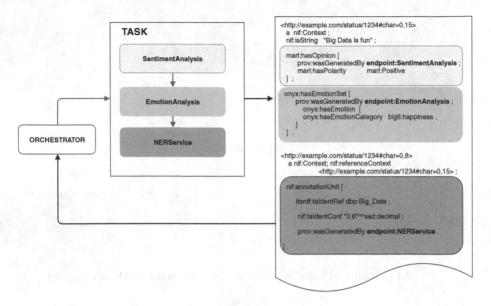

Fig. 4. Enrichment pipeline results in turtle format. The annotations generated by three independent services have been combined thanks to the Linked Data principles and NIF URI schemes.

A tool, so called GSICrawler[3] has been developed to extract information for structured and unstructured sources. The architecture of this tool consists of a set of modules providing a uniform API, which enables its orchestration. GSICrawler contains scraping modules that are based on Scrapy [21], and other modules that connect to external APIs. At the time of writing, there are modules for extracting data from Twitter, Facebook, Reddit, TripAdvisor, Amazon, RSS Feeds, and a number of specific places, including some journals in PDF format. The tool is Open Source and publicly available[4].

Table 1 describes the method available in the GSICrawler API, whereas Table 2 contains the basic parameters for the /tasks endpoint. More parameters are available, depending on the type of analysis performed.

Table 1. API endpoints to access tasks and jobs in GSICrawler

Endpoint	Description
GET/tasks/	Get a list of available tasks in JSON-LD format
GET/jobs/	Get a list of jobs. It can be limited to pending/running jobs by specifying ?pending=True
POST/jobs/	Start a new job, from an available task and a set of parameters

---

[3] GSICrawler's documentation: https://gsicrawler.readthedocs.io.

[4] https://github.com/gsi-upm/gsicrawler.

Table 2. Basic parameters for a new job. Other parameters may be needed or available, depending on the task.

Parameter	Description
task_id	Identifier of the task. Example: pdf-crawl
output	Where to store the results. Available options: `none`, `file`, `elasticsearch`
retries	If the task fails, retry at most this many times. Optional
delay	If specified, the job will be run in `delay` seconds instead of immediately. Optional
timeout	Time in seconds to wait for the results. If the timeout is reached, consider the task failed. Optional

3.3 Data Processing and Analysis

There is an array of processing tasks that are relevant for social media analysis. The most common are text-based processes such as sentiment and emotion analysis, named entity recognition, or spam detection. These types of processes are covered both from an API point of view (Sect. 2.3) and from a modelling point of view (Sect. 2.2), with NIF and its extensions.

Having a common API for analysis services, as covered in Sect. 2.3, avoids coupling other parts of the system to the idiosyncrasies of the specific services used. As a result, services that provide equivalent types of annotation (e.g. two sentiment services) are interchangeable as far as the rest of the system is concerned. The obvious downside is that, in order to reach this level of decoupling, external services need to be adapted either natively or through the use of additional layers such as proxies and wrappers. Fortunately, the number of services is much lower than the number of applications using them, which makes adapting services much more efficient than having to adapt systems to include other services.

Using a common semantic model for results and annotations means that other modules in the system, especially the visualization module, do not need to rely on specific schemata or formats for every service or type of service. They can focus only on representing the information itself. Semantic standards such as RDF also ensure that applications can be agnostic of the specific serialization format used (e.g. JSON or XML). This independence is exploited in other modules of the toolkit. For example, more than one type of datastore can be used as storage modules, each of them with their own formats. An ElasticSearch database (JSON-based) may co-exist with a Fuseki (RDF-based) datastore, provided the annotations are correct and the appropriate conversion mechanisms (e.g. framing in the case of JSON-LD) are in place.

All services that are compatible with Senpy's API and format can be used with the toolkit proposed in this paper. An updated list is available at Senpy's documentation and, it includes services for sentiment analysis, emotion analysis, NER, age and gender detection, radicalization detection, spam detection, etc.

3.4   Storage

Our toolkit takes two types of storage into consideration: SPARQL endpoints and traditional datastores with a REST API. In practice, we have employed Fuseki's SPARQL endpoint [19], and ElasticSearch's REST API [10].

One of the main reasons to support other datastores is the need for Big Data analysis. In particular, we focused on ElasticSearch. Elasticsearch is a search server based on Lucene. It provides a distributed, full-text search engine with an HTTP web interface and schema-free JSON documents. ElasticSearch has been widely used in Big Data applications due to its performance and scalability. ElasticSearch nodes can be distributed, it divides indices into shards, each of which can have zero or more replicas. Each node hosts one or more shards, and acts as a coordinator to delegate operations to the correct shard(s).

To retain semantics, we use a subset (or dialect) of JSON, JSON-LD [39], which adds semantic annotation to plain JSON objects.

3.5   Visualization and Querying

One of the main goals of the toolkit is to provide a component-based UI framework that can be used to quickly develop custom data visualizations that lead to insights.

Re-usability and composability were two of our main requirements for the framework. For this reason, we chose to base the visualization module on W3C Web Components. Web Components is an increasingly popular set of standards that enable the development of reusable components. Using Web Components adds a layer of complexity, especially when it is combined with the usual visualization libraries (e.g. D3.js[5]). Fortunately, the additional effort is outweighed by the growing community behind Web Components and the increasing number of compatible libraries.

Nevertheless, several aspects were not fully covered by the current standard. In particular, we wanted to provide faceted search combined with text search and web component communication. To do so, components need to communicate with each other, which requires a set of conventions on top of Web Components.

There are several alternatives for web component communication [42], such as custom events between components and publish-subscribe pattern [22]. After considering these alternatives, we chose to follow a Model-View-Controller (MVC) architecture (Fig. 2). In MVC, a single element is in charge of connecting to the data sources, filtering the results, and exposing it to other components, which can them present it.

Since this visualization should also be interactive, visualization components also contain their own set of filters. When interacting with these components, a

---

[5]   https://d3js.org/.

user may modify the filters, and the component will communicate the change of filters back to the filtering component. This allows storing which elements have been selected and thus making more complex queries to data sources (e.g. Elastic-Search). The communication between components is achieved through observers and computed properties, which allow changes to be seamlessly propagated to all components.

The result of combining Web Components with these conventions to organize data is Sefarad[6], an Open Source code[7] framework which is the core of the visualization module in the toolkit. Visualizations in Sefarad are composed of individual dashboards, which are web pages oriented to display all groups of related information (e.g. visualization of the activity of a brand in social media). In turn, these dashboards are further divided into widgets (e.g. charts and lists), which are connected to present a coherent and interactive view.

Dashboards serve the purpose of integrating a collection of widgets and connecting them to the data sources (e.g. Fuseki). Hence, dashboards are custom-tailored to specific applications, and are not as reusable as widgets. There are two main types of dashboards. On one hand, there are dashboards that provide a simple interface with interactive widgets, filters and textual search. This type of dashboards is aimed towards inexperienced users. Hence, their actions are guided with pre-defined queries and suggestions. On the other hand, we find dashboards that cater to more advanced users, who can explore the dataset through more complex queries using a SPARQL editor. These results can be viewed in raw format, using pivot tables, and through compatible widgets.

As shown in Fig. 5, Serafad is also capable of retrieving semantic data from external sources, such as Elasticsearch, Fuseki or DBPedia. Data retrieving is done by an client (e.g. Elasticsearch) located at the dashboard. This client stores data and it is shared with all the widgets within that dashboard.

At the time of writing, this is a categorized list of popular widgets in the toolkit:

– **Data statistics widgets:** These widgets are used to visualize data statistics from an Elasticsearch index at a glance. We include inside this category Google-chart-elasticsearch, number-chart, spider-chart, Liquid-fluid-d3, wordcloud...
– **Sentiment widgets:** These widgets are used to visualize sentiment information. We include inside this category chernoff-faces, field-chart, tweet-chart, wheel-chart, youtube-sentiment...
– **NER widgets:** These widgets are used to visualize recognized entities from an Elasticsearch index. We include inside this category entities-chart, people-chart, aspect-chart, wheel-chart...
– **Location widgets:** This group of widgets visualize data geolocated in different maps. Spain-chart, happymap and leaflet-maps are some examples of this kind of widgets.

---

[6] Sefarad's documentation: http://sefarad.readthedocs.io/.
[7] https://github.com/gsi-upm/sefarad.

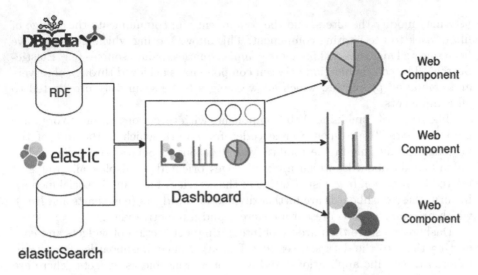

Fig. 5. Architecture of the visualization module

- **Document widgets:** Inside this group we can find tweet-chart and news-chart. These widgets are used to visualize all documents within an Elastic-search index.
- **Query widgets:** This widgets add more functionalities to Sefarad framework, they are used to modify or ask queries to different endpoints. We include inside this category material-search, YASGUI-polymer, date-slider...

4 Case Studies

The platform has been used in a number of national and European R&D projects, such as Financial Twitter Tracker [3,35], FP7 SmartOpenData [7,36], H2020 Trivalent [2], and ITEA Somedi. In addition, the platform has been applied in several master thesis in sentiment and emotion detection in Twitter, Facebook and web sites in different domains, such as football [25,27,28], song lyrics [18], geolocated media [8], political parties [1], financial news [6,44] and e-commerce [5]. It has also been applied for detection of insomnia [38] and radicalism [16] in Twitter [38]. For illustration purposes, we will describe three scases were the platform has been used.

Figure 6a shows the Trivalent dashboard. In this case, the purpose of the dashboard is to analyze radicalization sources, including Twitter, news papers (CNN, New York Times and Aljazeera) and radicalist magazines (Dabiq and Rumiyah). The crawler collects all the information and processes in different ways. In particular, the current version includes entity recognition and linking, topic identification and sentiment and emotion analysis. Future versions will also include narrative detection.

The second case is brand monitoring and analysis of competitors, within the SoMeDi project. The goal was to compare the social media activity related

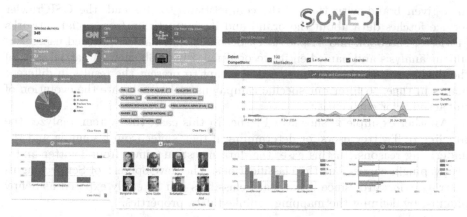

(a) Screenshot from the Trivalent (b) Brand monitoring for the SoMeDi
Dashboard   project.

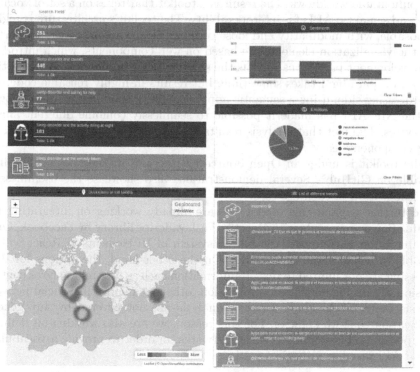

(c) Example of analysis of insommia in Twitter.

Fig. 6. Case studies

to a given brand with that of the competition. To this end, the GSICrawler service fetches data about the brand and its competition from social networks (Twitter, Facebook and Tripadvisor). Secondly, this data is enriched using sentiment analysis and named entity recognition. Figure 6b shows a partial view of the dashboard. In this case, it was important to present the results in different points in time, to filter out specific campaigns and to compare the evolution of the activity for each entity.

Another example is shown in Fig. 6c. In this case, the system analyzes the timeline of Twitter users for determining if they suffer from insommia and the underlying reasons. In this case, the data ingestion comes from Twitter and a Senpy plugin carries out the classifications. The development of Senpy plugins is straight forward, since Scikit-learn classifiers can be easily exposed as Senpy plugins, by defining the mapping to linked data properties.

5   Conclusions

The motivation of this work was to leverage Linked Data to enable the analysis of social media, and later visualization of the results, with reusable components and configurable workflows. The result is a toolkit that relies on a set of vocabularies and semantic APIs for interoperability. The toolkit's architecture is highly composable, with modularity and loose coupling as driving principles. In particular, the visualization elements are based on web components, which introduce new development paradigms such as the shadow DOM and templates. Adapting to this new paradigm takes some time, but results in highly reusable code. On the processing side, using a semantic approach with a combination of ontologies and the NIF API has made it possible to seamlessly combine different analysis services. The fact that analysis results are semantically annotated has made using components easy.

The toolkit is under an Open Source license, and its modules are publicly available on GitHub[8]. Several demonstrations also showcase the usefulness of the visualization in each use case.

To further expand this toolkit, we are already working on integrating the visualization components with React[9], the JavaScript library by Facebook. Once the integration is complete, the full ecosystem of UI elements in React will be available in widgets and dashboards. On the other hand, the options for data processing are not limited to text. If information such as user relevance or content diffusion are important for an application, other techniques like social network analysis are needed. These types of analysis are not covered by any generic specification that we know of. For this reason, we are also working on defining the types of analysis of online social networks, in order to provide a vocabulary and an API just like NIF did for NLP.

---

[8] Soneti's documentation: https://soneti.readthedocs.io/.
[9] https://reactjs.org/.

Acknowledgements. The authors want to thank Roberto Bermejo, Alejandro Saura, Rubén Díaz and José Carmona for working on previous versions of the toolkit. In addition, we want to thank Marcos Torres, Jorge García-Castaño, Pablo Aramburu, Rodrigo Barbado, Jose Mª Izquierdo, Mario Hernando, Carlos Moreno, Javier Ochoa and Daniel Souto, who have applied the toolkit in different domains. Lastly, we also thank our partners at Taiger and HI-Iberia for using the toolkit and collaborating in the integration of their analysis services with the toolkit as part of project SoMeDi (ITEA3 16011).

This work is supported by ITEA 3 EUREKA Cluster programme together with the National Spanish Funding Agencies CDTI (INNO-20161089) and MINETAD (TSI-102600-2016-1), the Spanish Ministry of Economy and Competitiveness under the R&D project SEMOLA (TEC2015-68284-R) and by the European Union through the project Trivalent (Grant Agreement no: 740934).

References

1. Aramburu García, P.: Design and development of a sentiment analysis system on Facebook from political domain. Master's thesis, ETSI Telecomunicación, June 2017
2. Barbado, R.: Design of a prototype of a big data analysis system of online radicalism based on semantic and deep learning technologies. TFM, ETSI Telecomunicación, June 2018
3. Bermejo, R.: Desarrollo de un framework HTML5 de Visualización y Consulta Semántica de Repositorios RDF. Master's thesis, Universidad Politécnica de Madrid, June 2014
4. Breslin, J.G., Decker, S., Harth, A., Bojars, U.: SIOC: an approach to connect web-based communities. Int. J. Web Based Commun. **2**(2), 133–142 (2006)
5. Carmona, J.E.: Development of a social media crawler for sentiment analysis. Master's thesis, ETSI Telecomunicación, February 2016
6. Conde-Sánchez, E.: Development of a social media monitoring system based on elasticsearch and web components technologies. Master's thesis, ETSI Telecomunicación, June 2016
7. Díaz-Vega, R.: Design and implementation of an HTML5 framework for biodiversity and environmental information visualization based on geo linked data. Master's thesis, ETSI Telecomunicación, December 2014
8. García-Castaño, J.: Development of a monitoring dashboard for sentiment and emotion in geolocated social media. Master's thesis, ETSI Telecomunicación, July 2017
9. Glazkov, D., Weinstein, R., Ross, T.: HTML templates W3C working group note 18. Technical report, W3C, March 2014
10. Gormley, C., Tong, Z.: Elasticsearch: The Definitive Guide: A Distributed Real-Time Search and Analytics Engine. O'Reilly Media, Inc., Newton (2015)
11. Graves, M., Constabaris, A., Brickley, D.: FOAF: connecting people on the semantic web. Cat. Classif. Q. **43**(3–4), 191–202 (2007)
12. Guha, R.V., Brickley, D., Macbeth, S.: Schema.org: evolution of structured data on the web. Commun. ACM **59**(2), 44–51 (2016)
13. Gupta, Y.: Kibana Essentials. Packt Publishing Ltd., Birmingham (2015)
14. Hellmann, S.: Integrating natural language processing (NLP) and language resources using linked data. Ph.D. thesis, Universität Leipzig (2013)

15. Hellmann, S., Lehmann, J., Auer, S., Brümmer, M.: Integrating NLP using linked data. In: Alani, H., et al. (eds.) ISWC 2013. LNCS, vol. 8219, pp. 98–113. Springer, Heidelberg (2013). https://doi.org/10.1007/978-3-642-41338-4_7

16. Hernando, M.: Development of a classifier of radical tweets using machine learning algorithms. Master's thesis, ETSI Telecomunicación, January 2018

17. Ito, H.: Shadow DOM. Technical report, W3C, March 2018

18. Izquierdo-Mora, J.M.: Design and development of a lyrics emotion analysis system for creative industries. Master's thesis, ETSI Telecomunicación, January 2018

19. Jena, A.: Apache Jena Fuseki. The Apache Software Foundation (2014)

20. Kotliar, M., Kartashov, A., Barski, A.: CWL-Airflow: a lightweight pipeline manager supporting common workflow language. bioRxiv p. 249243 (2018)

21. Kouzis-Loukas, D.: Learning Scrapy. Packt Publishing Ltd., Birmingham (2016)

22. Krug, M.: Distributed event-based communication for web components. In: Proceedings of Studierendensymposium Informatik 2016 der TU Chemnitz, pp. 133–136 (2016)

23. Lampa, S., Alvarsson, J., Spjuth, O.: Towards agile large-scale predictive modelling in drug discovery with flow-based programming design principles. J. Cheminform. **8**(1), 67 (2016)

24. Missier, P., Belhajjame, K., Cheney, J.: The W3C PROV family of specifications for modelling provenance metadata. In: Proceedings of the 16th International Conference on Extending Database Technology, pp. 773–776. ACM (2013)

25. Moreno Sánchez, C.: Design and development of an affect analysis system for football matches in Twitter based on a corpus annotated with a crowdsourcing platform. Master's thesis, ETSI Telecomunicación (2018)

26. Morita, H., Glazkov, D.: HTML imports. W3C working draft, W3C, February 2016

27. Ochoa, J.: Design and Implementation of a scraping system for sport news. Master's thesis, ETSI Telecomunicación, February 2017

28. Pascual-Saavedra, A.: Development of a dashboard for sentiment analysis of football in Twitter based on web components and D3.js. Master's thesis, ETSI Telecomunicación, June 2016

29. Pinterest: Pinball. https://github.com/pinterest/pinball

30. Ranic, T., Gusev, M.: Overview of workflow management systems. In: Proceedings of the 14th International Conference for Informatics and Information Technology, CIIT 2017. Faculty of Computer Science and Engineering, Ss. Cyril and Methodius University in Skopje, Macedonia (2017)

31. Sánchez-Rada, J.F., Iglesias, C.A.: Onyx: a linked data approach to emotion representation. Inf. Process. Manag. **52**(1), 99–114 (2016)

32. Sánchez-Rada, J.F., Iglesias, C.A., Corcuera, I., Araque, O.: Senpy: a pragmatic linked sentiment analysis framework. In: 2016 IEEE International Conference on Data Science and Advanced Analytics (DSAA), pp. 735–742. IEEE (2016)

33. Sánchez-Rada, J.F., Iglesias, C.A., Gil, R.: A linked data model for multimodal sentiment and emotion analysis. In: Proceedings of the 4th Workshop on Linked Data in Linguistics: Resources and Applications, pp. 11–19. Association for Computational Linguistics, Beijing, July 2015

34. Sánchez-Rada, J.F., Iglesias, C.A., Sagha, H., Schuller, B., Wood, I., Buitelaar, P.: Multimodal multimodel emotion analysis as linked data. In: 2017 Seventh International Conference on Affective Computing and Intelligent Interaction Workshops and Demos (ACIIW), pp. 111–116. IEEE (2017)

35. Sánchez-Rada, J.F., Torres, M., Iglesias, C.A., Maestre, R., Peinado, R.: A linked data approach to sentiment and emotion analysis of Twitter in the financial domain. In: Second International Workshop on Finance and Economics on the Semantic Web, FEOSW 2014, vol. 1240, pp. 51–62, May 2014. http://ceur-ws.org/Vol-1240/

36. Saura Villanueva, A.: Development of a framework for geolinked data query and visualization based on web components. PFC, ETSI Telecomunicación, June 2015

37. Schröder, M., Baggia, P., Burkhardt, F., Pelachaud, C., Peter, C., Zovato, E.: EmotionML – an upcoming standard for representing emotions and related states. In: D'Mello, S., Graesser, A., Schuller, B., Martin, J.-C. (eds.) ACII 2011. LNCS, vol. 6974, pp. 316–325. Springer, Heidelberg (2011). https://doi.org/10.1007/978-3-642-24600-5_35

38. Souto, D.S.: Design and development of a system for sleep disorder characterization using social media mining. Master's thesis, ETSI Telecomunicación, ETSIT, Madrid, June 2018

39. Sporny, M., Kellogg, G., Lanthaler, M.: JSON-LD 1.0, January 2014. http://json-ld.org/spec/latest/json-ld/

40. Spotify: Luigi. https://github.com/spotify/luigi

41. Stephen, J.J., Savvides, S., Sundaram, V., Ardekani, M.S., Eugster, P.: STYX: stream processing with trustworthy cloud-based execution. In: Proceedings of the Seventh ACM Symposium on Cloud Computing, pp. 348–360. ACM (2016)

42. Stokolosa, V.: Communication between components (2018). https://hackernoon.com/communication-between-components-7898467ce15b

43. Thusoo, A., et al.: Hive-a petabyte scale data warehouse using Hadoop. In: 2010 IEEE 26th International Conference on Data Engineering (ICDE), pp. 996–1005. IEEE (2010)

44. Torres, M.: Prototype of stock prediction system based on Twitter emotion and sentiment analysis. Master's thesis, ETSI Telecomunicación, July 2014

45. Warr, W.A.: Scientific workflow systems: pipeline pilot and Knime. J. Comput.-Aided Mol. Des. 26(7), 801–804 (2012)

46. Westerski, A., Iglesias, C.A., Tapia, F.: Linked opinions: describing sentiments on the structured web of data. In: Proceedings of the Fourth International Workshop on Social Data on the Web, SDoW2011, pp. 21–32. CEUR, October 2011

47. WHATWG (Apple, Google, Mozilla, Microsoft): HTML living standard. Technical report, W3C, July 2018

48. White, T.: Hadoop: The Definitive Guide. O'Reilly Media Inc., Newton (2012)

49. Wilde, E., Duerst, M.: URI fragment identifiers for the text/plain media type, April 2008

50. Zaharia, M., et al.: Apache spark: a unified engine for big data processing. Commun. ACM 59(11), 56–65 (2016)

Modeling Industrial Business Processes for Querying and Retrieving Using OWL+SWRL

Suman Roy[1]([⊠]), Gabriel Silvatici Dayan[2], and V. Devaraja Holla[3]

[1] Optum Global Solutions India Pvt. Ltd. (UnitedHealth Group),
Bangalore 560 103, India
Suman.Roy@optum.com
[2] Software Engineering, Instituto Tecnologico de Buenos Aires (ITBA),
Buenos Aires, Argentina
gsilvati@itba.edu.ar
[3] Infosys Ltd., # 44 Electronics City, Hosur Road, Bangalore 560 100, India
devaraja_vaderahobli@infosys.com

Abstract. Process modeling forms a core activity in many organizations in which different entities and stakeholders interact for smooth operation and management of enterprises. There have been few work on semantically labeling business processes using OWL-DL that formalize business process structure and query them. However, all these methods suffer from few limitations such as lack of a modular approach of ontology design, no guarantee of a consistent ontology development with TBox and ABox axioms and no provision of combining control flow relations of the main process and its sub-processes. In this work, we propose an approach for labeling and specifying business processes by using hybrid programs which offers modular ontology design, consistent ontology design of each module and unified control flow for process and its sub-processes. This formalism of hybrid programs integrates ontology specified in OWL-DL with SWRL (Semantic Web Rules Language) rules. Further we report on our experimental effort on modeling industrial business processes with this hybrid formalism. We also present a case study of an industrial business process to illustrate our modeling approach which can aid in business knowledge management.

Keywords: Business process management
Business processes modeling · Patterns · Ontology · OWL-DL
SWRL · Querying · Case study

1 Introduction

Hundreds of business process models are developed by enterprises to manage the flow of work through an organization. For a process model one needs to con-

G. S. Dayan—This work was done when the author was an intern with Infoys Ltd, Bangalore during Mar–May'17.

H. Panetto et al. (Eds.): OTM 2018 Conferences, LNCS 11230, pp. 516–536, 2018.
https://doi.org/10.1007/978-3-030-02671-4_31

sider the semantics of the meta-model elements when different representations
are used, and as well as the terms that describe the model elements. The realization of such a semantic modeling of processes can be achieved by extracting
ontology from process models using appropriate semantic web formalisms which
can facilitate querying and retrieving process models [12].

Several approaches have been proposed for semantic modeling of processes
and subsequent retrieval of them using keywords, or data, or process properties.
In one such approach Groener and Staab have proposed an ontology modeling
of a process capturing explicitly various hierarchical and ordering relationships
between activities in [8]. Moreover, they can query for retrieving process structures with specified control flow characteristics and modalities as well as process
traces. However, such a modeling suffers from a few drawbacks which we shall
discuss using an example of a process model below.

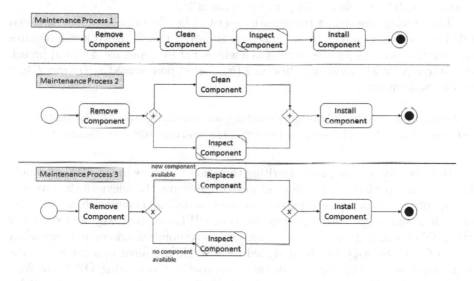

Fig. 1. Different variants of a maintenance process

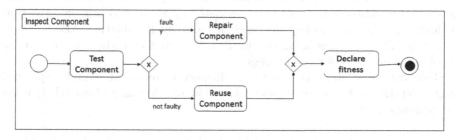

Fig. 2. Inspect component subprocess

A Motivation for New Modeling Framework. In Fig. 1 we describe three maintenance processes, Maintenance Process 1 (*MProcess1*), Maintenance Process 2 (*MProcess2*) and Maintenance Process 3 (*MProcess3*), with three different characteristics. In these process diagrams there are four main activities, 'Remove Component (RC)', 'Clean Component (CC)', 'Replace Component (RpC)' and 'Install Component (IC)'. There is also a sub-process invocation activity, Inspect Component (SPIC) - this sub-process activity can be further decomposed into constituent activities (in Fig. 2), 'Test Component (TC)', 'Repair Component (RepC)', 'Reuse Component (ReuC)' and 'Declare Fitness (DF)'. We assume that the class (node) Activity can be instantiated with individuals in different cases as follows, *actRC* ('Remove Component'), *actCC* ('Clean Component'), *actRpC* ('Replace Component') and *actIC* ('Install Component'), *actTC* ('Test Component'), *actRepC* ('Repair Component'), *actRC* ('Reuse Component'), *actDF* ('Declare Fitness') etc. The sub-process invocation activity is instantiated as *spIC* (stands for 'Inspect Component')[1].

The ontology modeling framework described in [8] would be able to model a OWL-DL ontology out of these processes. However, this framework still requires writing the ontology for the process as a whole. For example, using this approach the ontology for Maintenance Process 2 (its control flow named as *followedBy2*) can be written as:

$$MProcess2 \equiv Start\sqcap = 1 followedBy2.(RC \sqcap \exists followedBy2.(CC\sqcap = 1 followedBy2.(IC \sqcap$$
$$\exists followedBy2.End)) \sqcap \exists followedBy2.(SPIC\sqcap = 1 followedBy2.(IC\sqcap = 1 followedBy2.End))).$$

However, for a large process writing the whole ontology in one attempt would be tedious, especially in presence of nested gateways. To alleviate this, we aim to capture ontology for each pattern as one module and combine them to obtain the whole ontology. Although any piece of OWL can be easily added to any other OWL ontology just by merging the corresponding triples it is not clear how a OWL ontology can be designed for a single fragment of a process in the framework of [8]. Our pattern-oriented approach of capturing OWL ontology facilitates this. We specify each such pattern in a process as a complex OWL concept using TBox axioms, see Table 1. Also in [8] it is not mentioned how one can write ABox axioms so that the ontology remains consistent. For that we design consistent ontology for each pattern by formulating ABox axioms along with TBox axioms as shown in Table 1[2] and merge them to obtain the consolidated ontology for the process.

Moreover, the sub-process activity 'Inspect Component' can be specified using OWL-DL as below (with its control flow relation as *followedBy4*) using the approach of [8]:

$$SPIC \equiv Start \sqcap \exists followedBy4.(TC \sqcap \exists followedBy4.(((RepC \sqcap fault) \sqcup (ReuC \sqcap$$
$$nofault)) \sqcap \exists followedBy4.(DF \sqcap \exists followedBy4.End)))$$

---

[1] Wlog we assume same individuals for all the three processes.

[2] For brevity of space we specify only a couple of patterns here.

Table 1. A pattern-oriented modeling of maintenance process 2

Patterns	TBox axioms	ABox axioms
	$MProcess2 \equiv Start \sqcap$ $= 1followedBy2.C_{RC}$	$Start(start1), Task(actRC),$ $followedBy2(start1, actRC)$
	$C_{RC} \equiv Task \sqcap (\exists followedBy2.$ $C_{CC}) \sqcap (\exists followedBy2.\sqcap$ $C_{SPIC}) \sqcap = 2\, followedBy2$	$Task(actCC), SubProcess(spIC),$ $followedBy2(actRC, CC)$ $followedBy2(actRC, spIC)$

It is evident that the $MProcess2$ and $InstallComponent$ share different workflow relations $followedBy2$ and $followedBy4$ respectively. In [8] the authors do not mention any way of combining workflows for a main process and its constituent sub-processes. Our modeling framework is able to combine the control flow for the process and its sub-processes by using SWRL rules. For example, we can define a control flow relation $followedBy$ at the main process level and specify that the a task in Maintenance Process 2 is followed by the next task in sub-process 'Install Component' by use of the following rule:

$$followedBy(?x, ?z) \leftarrow Process(?p), Node(?x), SubProcess1(?sp), followedBy2(?x, ?sp),$$
$$beginsWith1(?sp, ?s), Start(?s), Node(?z), followedBy4(?s, ?z)$$

Contributions. In this work, we adopt the framework of hybrid programs which integrates OWL-DL ontology with SWRL rules, to model and specify business processes. We adhere to a decidable fragment of SWRL rules *a la* DL-safe rules [15] to make querying and other reasoning tasks decidable in this framework. Not only we are able to model the control flow of the process capturing hierarchical and ordering relationships between nodes for querying, we also advocate an explicit modular design of process ontology that helps building the ontology in stages. We also adequately model ABox axioms to maintain the consistency at each stage of the creation of ontology. This kind of consistent and modular ontology design can facilitate efficient process modeling in different industrial applications and business knowledge management.

The paper is organized as follows. In Sect. 2 we briefly describe the main notions of a business process. Process models are formalized using OWL-DL with SWRL rules in Sect. 3. We study patterns for querying and retrieving processes in Sect. 4. In Sect. 5 we describe an implementation of our framework and narrate our experimental effort. A case study of an industrial business process modeling in this formalism is described in Sect. 6. The discussion on related work is in Sect. 7. Finally we conclude in Sect. 8.

2   A Primer on Business Process

In this paper we work with Business Process Diagrams (BPD) captured using standard Business Process Modeling Notation (BPMN), which consist of nodes and control flow relation linking two nodes. A *node* can be a task (also called an activity here), an event, a fork (AND-split), a choice (XOR-split), a synchronizer (AND-join), and a merge (XOR-join) gateway. In a BPD, there are *start events* (also called *start nodes*) denoting the beginning of a process, and *end events* (also called *end nodes*) denoting the end of a process. A *start activity* is an activity which follows a start node. An activity is called a *sink activity* (or *end activity*) if it is immediately followed by an end event. We do not take into consideration message passing, timer events etc. in our model. A process can reside within another process. In this case, the former is called a *sub-process invocation activity* or simply *sub-process*. A business process is *well-formed* if it has exactly one start node with no incoming edges and one outgoing edge from it, there is only one incoming edge to a task and exactly one outgoing edge from a task, each fork and choice has exactly one incoming edge and at least two outgoing edges, each synchronizer and merge has at least two incoming edges and exactly one outgoing edge, every node is on a path from the start node to some end node, and there exists at least one task in between two gateways (this is to avoid triviality). Also we can safely assume that an end event is immediately preceded by a task, in absence of which we can introduce a dummy/silent task (which does not do anything). From now on without loss of generality, we shall consider only well-formed business processes.

The semantics of control elements of a business process are similar to that of work-flows discussed in [14]. There are two typical control flow related errors that can take place in processes: deadlock and lack of synchronization. A deadlock implies that the process will never terminate. A lack of synchronization allows multiple instances of the same task to occur in a process. A business process is *sound* if it does not produce deadlock and lack of synchronization. There are standard techniques to check the soundness of processes, for example see [4]. For this work, we consider only sound processes.

3   Formalizing Business Processes in OWL

We shall extract OWL-DL ontologies out of business processes in a constructive manner using OWL-DL [1,18] in conjunction with SWRL rules [16]. The satisfiability of OWL-DL in conjunction with SWRL is undecidable [15] as the latter is not DL-safe. It can be made decidable by adding a non-DL atom of the form $O(?x)$ in the body of a rule for every variable $?x$ appearing in it and adding a fact $O(a)$ for every individual a to the list of ABox axioms. In our case it would be possible to turn all the rules that we use into DL-safe rules.

3.1 Process Vocabulary

For extracting ontology out of arbitrary business processes we decompose the diagram into atomic patterns (originally introduced by Van der Aalst *et al.* for workflow diagrams in [20]) and generate an independent OWL concept for each of the patterns. Then using equivalence (and substitution) the concepts are merged to get the complex concept for the whole diagram in a modular fashion. The complex concept is generated in a top-down fashion from the model starting from the start activity of the diagram to an end activity. Our method is motivated by a construction of CSP[3] process from a business process [17] and conversion UML models to CSP expressions [2].

Below is the description of vocabulary for processes. There is a base class *Process* representing the Business Process Diagram in question. *ConceptTask* stands for a complex concept representing a pattern of a task, it will have subconcepts *ConceptTaskA, ConceptTaskB* corresponding to tasks A, B respectively and so on. Nodes are represented by the class *Node*. It has subclasses, *Task* for a task, *Start* for a start node, *End* for a final node and $\mathcal{J}$ for a synchronizer. The control flow relation is modeled by the role *followedBy* which is defined on nodes. For composing different sub-process diagrams the role *followedBy* for each diagrams may be denoted with a subscript (*e.g.*, *followedByi*), (where *followedByi* $\sqsubseteq$ *followedBy*). Thus we may use *followedBy1* for denoting the control flow for the sub-process at its first level embedding in the process, *followedBy0* for the control flow relation for the main process etc. Finally the role *followedBy* is defined to denote the control flow relation of whole process. The transitive role *followedByTran* is a super role of *followedBy*. We use the role *contains* with *Process* as domain and *Node* as range to denote that a process contains certain nodes. Further, there is a role *containedIn* with *Node* as domain and *Process* as range to denote that a node is contained in a certain process. There is also a role *beginsWith* which indicates that a process begins with a certain start node, similarly the role *endsWith* says that a process ends with an end node. Table 2 describes the roles used for building the process ontology. Similar conventions using suffix like the role *followedBy* for these roles, can be introduced when we deal with sub-processes. Lastly, we also consider a datatype role *pairWith* on *Task* and is string valued. This is used to capture the conditions on the outgoing edges of a XOR-split which can assume mutually exclusive values.

3.2 Modeling Basic Control Flow Patterns in OWL-DL

We consider basic control flow patterns [20] of a business process (see Fig. 3(a)), and translate them to OWL-DL complex concepts preserving the graphical structure of the process diagrams. This is done using a modular approach in which

---

[3] CSP here stands for Communicating Sequential Process.

Table 2. The roles used for building the process ontology (using ABox axioms)

Role	Type of properties	Description
$followedBy(node1, task2)$	Object	Node $node1$ is followed by task $task2$
$beginsWith(process1, start2)$	Object	The Business Process $process1$ starts with start node $start2$
$endsWith(process1, end3)$	Object	The Business Process $process1$ ends with end node $end3$
$contains(process1, task2)$	Object	The Business Process $process1$ contains a task node $task2$
$containedIn(task3, process2)$	Object	A task node $task3$ occurs in the Business Process $process2$
$pairsWith(task4, \text{“}yes\text{)”}$	Datatype	Instantiated Task $task4$ is associated with the condition denoted by the string "yes" on an XOR-split outgoing edge

each pattern is modeled as an OWL concept (which can be thought of a module). These concepts are then suitably merged to obtain the final ontology. The atomic patterns used for process ontology are shown in Fig. 3(b). Below we supply the TBox axioms for each pattern. Later we shall provide corresponding ABox axioms.

Start Event: As mentioned earlier, a *Start* activity is defined for the corresponding start event in the process. The expression $\mathcal{C}_0$ denotes the complex concept for the whole process (this is also called concept *Process*). The concept expression for the pattern in Fig. 3(a) is modeled as a conjunction of Start class and the existential restriction of concept class for activity A with $followedBy$ role. This convention will be followed throughout for generating concept expressions for other patterns of a business process.

$$\mathcal{C}_0 \equiv (Start \sqcap\; = 1 followedBy.\mathcal{C}_A).$$

Sequential Activities: In Fig. 3(a)(b) task A is followed by task B. Let $\mathcal{C}_A$ denote the concept associated with the task node A[4]. We assume that concept $\mathcal{C}_A$ is equivalent to the task class $Task$ and a following existentially quantified concept $\mathcal{C}_B$.

$$\mathcal{C}_A \equiv (Task \sqcap\; = 1 followedBy.\mathcal{C}_B).$$

---

[4] Denoted with a small rectangle.

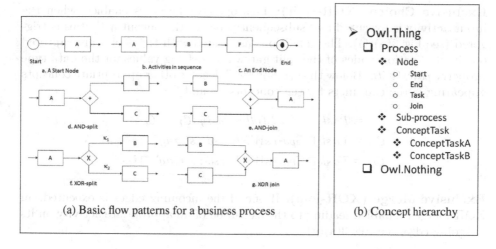

(a) Basic flow patterns for a business process   (b) Concept hierarchy

Fig. 3. Pattern-based OWL ontology modeling for business processes

End Activity: In particular, for the pattern shown in Fig. 3(a)(c) the process terminates with an end node[5] which is preceded by a task F. We capture this as,

$$\mathcal{C}_F \equiv (Task \sqcap\ = 1\ followedBy.End).$$

Parallel Split (AND-split): To ensure that the parallel concepts originating at an AND-split are synchronized (see Fig. 3(a)(d)) we use an axiom that states there exist multiple follower sequences, which are captured in terms of an intersection of sequences. In the conjunct we also use a cardinality constraint role to denote the number of outgoing edges out of the AND-split.

$$\mathcal{C}_A \equiv Task\ \sqcap\ (\exists followedBy.\mathcal{C}_B) \sqcap\ (\exists followedBy.\mathcal{C}_C)\ \sqcap\ (= 2.followedBy).$$

Synchronizer (AND-join): The behavioral property of the synchronizer states that it can be executed only after the end of the execution of all the input activities. For example, in Fig. 3(a)(e) A can be executed only after both B and C are executed. We define another class for AND-join (subclass of node $Node$), denoted as $\mathcal{J}$ (stands for $Join$ class).

$$\mathcal{C}_B \equiv\ Task \sqcap\ = 1.followedBy.(\mathcal{J} \sqcap\ = 1.followedBy.\mathcal{C}_A).$$
$$\mathcal{C}_C \equiv\ Task \sqcap\ = 1.followedBy.(\mathcal{J} \sqcap\ = 1.followedBy.\mathcal{C}_A).$$

---

[5] Denoted with a shaded circle inscribed within another circle.

Exclusive Choice (XOR-split): This operator becomes enabled when the input activity is executed and subsequently, one of the output activities is triggered (see Fig. 3(a)(f)). The conditions associated with the choice are captured on the destination nodes of the split gateways as string values for the data type property *pairsWith*. Below the symbol "$\cdots$" denotes other appropriate concepts appearing in the conjuncts for the concepts $\mathcal{C}_B$ and $\mathcal{C}_C$.

$$\mathcal{C}_A \equiv Task \; \sqcap \; (= 1 followedBy.(\mathcal{C}_B \sqcup \mathcal{C}_C))$$
$$\mathcal{C}_B \equiv Task \sqcap \exists pairsWith\, \text{``}xsd : string\text{''} \sqcap \cdots$$
$$\mathcal{C}_C \equiv Task \sqcap \exists pairsWith\, \text{``}xsd : string\text{''} \sqcap \cdots$$

Exclusive Merge (XOR-join): If one of the incoming edges is executed, an XOR-merge is enabled leading to the execution of an appropriate activity on its outgoing edge, see Fig. 3(a)(g).

$$\mathcal{C}_B \equiv \; Task \sqcap \; = 1.followedBy.\mathcal{C}_A$$
$$\mathcal{C}_C \equiv \; Task \sqcap \; = 1.followedBy.\mathcal{C}_A$$

Iteration of Activities. Each loop is assumed to contain a choice and a join, this is to avoid interminable looping. Thus a loop may be executed a certain number of times depending on the exit condition. Such a process can be specified by breaking it into patterns and writing the concepts accordingly. Consider an example of a loop in Fig. 4(a). Here the process begins with task A. Then tasks B and C can occur in a loop if the condition at the split gateway is false. If the condition evaluates to true then activity D occurs which marks the end of the process. Notice there is a choice gateway after B which splits into C and D, and there is a merge gateway which joins A and C to produce B. Then we write concepts corresponding to these gateways as formulated before. This may lead to cyclic terminology which need not be definitorial [1]. However, we can argue that this terminology will have an interpretation which is a fixpoint and hence will have a model. The cycle (due to the loop) in the dependency graph of this terminology contains zero negative arc and so, it will have a fix point interpretation [1].

$$\mathcal{C}_0 \equiv (Start \; \sqcap \; = 1 followedBy.\mathcal{C}_A)$$
$$\mathcal{C}_A \equiv (Task \; \sqcap \; = 1 followedBy.\mathcal{C}_B)$$
$$\mathcal{C}_B \equiv Task \; \sqcap \; (= 1 followedBy.(\mathcal{C}_C \sqcup \mathcal{C}_D))$$
$$\mathcal{C}_C \equiv Task \sqcap \exists pairsWith\, \text{``}xsd : string\text{''} \sqcap \; = 1 followedBy.\mathcal{C}_B$$
$$\mathcal{C}_D \equiv Task \sqcap \exists pairsWith\, \text{``}xsd : string\text{''} \sqcap \; = 1 followedBy.End$$

Sub-process Invocation Activities. A process may have a sub-process invocation activity which denotes another process. In Fig. 4(b), the original process P begins with the activity A which is followed by a sub-process invocation activity SP, which in turn, is followed by another activity B. Further in SP activity C is preceded by a start node and is followed by an end node. We write some of the axioms and rules which model this process. The last two rules link the control flow relation of the original process with that of the sub-process. These start and end activities of the main process and its sub-process will be disjoint from each other.

$$Process \equiv (Start \sqcap = 1 followedBy0.\mathcal{C}_A); SubProcess1 \equiv (Start \sqcap = 1 followedBy1.\mathcal{C}_C)$$

$$\mathcal{C}_A \equiv (Task \sqcap = 1 followedBy0.\mathcal{C}_{SP}); \mathcal{C}_{SP} \equiv (SubProcess1 \sqcap = 1 followedBy0.\mathcal{C}_B)$$

$$\mathcal{C}_B \equiv (Task \sqcap = 1 \, followedBy0.End); \mathcal{C}_C \equiv (Task \sqcap = 1 \, followedBy1.End)$$

$$SubProcess1 \sqsubseteq Process; followedBy0 \sqsubseteq followedBy; followedBy1 \sqsubseteq followedBy$$

$$Process \sqsubseteq \exists followedBy0.Node. SubProcess1 \sqsubseteq \exists followedBy1.Node$$

$$Process \sqsubseteq \exists contains0.Node. SubProcess1 \sqsubseteq \exists contains1.Node$$

$$Process \sqsubseteq \exists beginsWith0.Start. SubProcess1 \sqsubseteq \exists beginsWith1.Start$$

$$Process \sqsubseteq \exists endsWith0.End; SubProcess1 \sqsubseteq \exists endsWith1.End$$

$$followedBy(?x, ?z) \leftarrow Process(?p), Node(?x), contains0(?p, ?x), SubProcess1(?sp),$$
$$followedBy0(?x, ?sp), beginsWith1(?sp, ?s), Start(?s), Node(?z), contains1(?sp, ?z),$$
$$followedBy1(?s, ?z)$$

$$followedBy(?x, ?z) \leftarrow Process(?p), SubProcess1(?sp), Node(?x), contains1(?sp, ?x),$$
$$endsWith1(?sp, ?e), End(?e), followedBy1(?x, ?e), Node(?z), contains0(?p, ?z),$$
$$followedBy0(?sp, ?z).$$

We add few more axioms in the process ontology some of which are borrowed from [8]; they are listed in Table 3. Here $\perp$ denotes contradiction, akin to owl:Nothing.

The above set of axioms constitute the TBox axioms for the ontology created corresponding to any business process. The process diagram itself serves as the meta-model for the process from which those (TBox) axioms are to be extracted, whereas the specific process model would lead to the generation of ABox axioms. We consider the process patterns in Fig. 3(a) and list sample ABox axioms corresponding to those basic patterns in Table 4. In this way we can construct the ontology for a business process which can be shown to be consistent by taking induction on the structure of the process and showing that ontology (TBox and ABox axioms) corresponding to each pattern is consistent, a formal argument of which is left out for a future work.

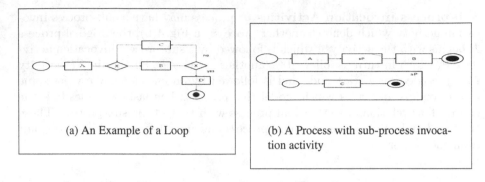

Fig. 4. Other patterns for business processes

Table 3. Axiomatization for business process diagrams

Statement	OWL-DL axioms
Start and End activities and Task are subclasses of class node	$Start, End, Task \sqsubseteq Node$
An AND-join is a subclass of class node	$Join \sqsubseteq Node$
$followedByTran$ is the super role of $followedBy$	$followedByi \sqsubseteq followedBy$, and $followedBy \sqsubseteq followedByTran$ $(i = 0, 1, \ldots)$
Start Activity has no predecessor	$(Node \sqcap \forall containedIn.Process \sqcap\ =1followedBy.Start) \sqsubseteq \bot$
End Activity has no follower	$(End \sqcap\ =1followedBy.Node) \sqsubseteq \bot$
A Process contains some nodes	$Process \sqsubseteq \exists contains.Node$
A Process begins with a start node	$Process \sqsubseteq= 1beginsWith.Start$
A Process ends on an end node	$Process \sqsubseteq \exists endsWith.End$
$contains$ and $containedIn$ shares a reciprocal relation	$containedIn(?y, ?x) \leftarrow contains(?x, ?y)$ $contains(?x, ?y) \leftarrow containedIn(?y, ?x)$

Table 4. ABox axioms for basic patterns

Basic patterns	ABox axioms
Start event	$Process(process1), Start(startS), Task(taskA), followedBy(startS, taskA),$ $contains(process1, startS), containedIn(startS, process1)$ etc
Sequential activities	$Task(taskA), Task(taskB), followedBy(taskA, taskB)$ etc.
End event	$End(endS), Task(taskF), followedBy(taskF, endS)$ etc.
Parallel split	$Task(taskA), Task(taskB), Task(taskC),$ $followedBy(taskA, taskB), followedBy(taskA, taskC)$
Synchronizer	$Task(taskA), Task(taskB), Task(taskC), Join(join1), followedBy(taskB, taskA),$ $followedBy(taskC, taskA), followedBy(taskB, join1), followedBy(taskC, join1)$
Exclusive choice	$Task(taskA), Task(taskB), Task(taskC), followedBy(taskA, taskB),$ $followedBy(taskA, taskB), pairsWith(taskB, "yes"), pairsWith(taskC, "no")$
Exclusive merge	$Task(taskA), Task(taskB), Task(taskC),$ $followedBy(taskB, taskA), followedBy(taskC, taskA)$

4 Semantic Query Patterns for Querying and Retrieving Processes

We now specify a few requirements on the process models shown in Fig. 1 to query them and retrieve process information. These queries will be posed using DL query on three processes, $MProcess1$ (Maintenance Process 1), $MProcess2$ (Maintenance Process 2) and $MProcess3$ (Maintenance Process 3).

4.1 Querying Processes

We show how we capture requirements for an individual process using the proposed ontology modeling. In particular, we consider Maintenance Process 1. Below **Req** will stand for requirement and **Spec** will denote the corresponding specification of the requirement.

– **Req1** Cleaning component is preceded by removing component.
  Spec1: $Start \sqcap (\exists followedByTran(value\,"actRC" \sqcap \exists followedByTran\ value\,"actCC"))$.
– **Req2** Repairing component is always followed by installing the component.
  Spec2: $Start \sqcap \exists followedByTran(value\,"actRep" \sqcap \exists followedByTran\ value\ "actIC")$
  $\sqcap \neg \exists followedByTran(value\,"actRep" \sqcap \exists followedByTran\ value\,"actX" \sqcap differentFrom(actX, actIC))$.
– **Req3** Installing component can mark the end to the maintenance process.
  Spec3: $Start \sqcap \exists followedByTran(value\,"actIC" \sqcap \exists followedBy.End)$.

4.2 Querying for Process Retrieval

We use three different query patterns with respect to the control flow of the process [8] to retrieve processes. The first pattern is about the execution order. The second pattern is used to query a process for modality. The third pattern is related to terminology which facilitates merging flow relations from the original process and its sub-process. The **Query** input depicts a process description. **Result** prints out the relevant processes (as individuals). We use DL queries for querying using concept subsumption as inference.

Pattern for Execution Order. A query related to execution pattern is described below.

  Query: Which processes do execute Inspect Component after Remove Component?
  $\{P \equiv Start \sqcap \exists followedByTran.(value\,"actRC" \sqcap \exists followedByTran.value\ "actIC")\}$
  Result: {MProcess1, MProcess2, MProcess3}
  The result contains all processes that execute Inspect Component after Remove Component with an arbitrary number of activities between them.

Pattern for Process Modality. This pattern deals with queries which refers to the modality of the processes as described below.

> **Query:** Which process does offer Replace Component?
> $\{P \equiv \exists contains.\,value\,"actRC"\}$

> **Result:** {MProcess3}
> The query will search for the processes that are related to Replace Component via the *contains* role. Only the MProcess3 has the Replace Component Task.

Pattern for Process Terminology. By using this pattern one can query details about the original process and its constituent sub-process using terminological knowledge.

> **Query:** Which processes execute Declare fitness before Install Component?
> $\{P \equiv Start \sqcap \exists followedByTran.(value\,"actDF"\sqcap\exists followedByTran.value$
> $"actIC")\}$
> **Result:** {MProcess1, MProcess2, MProcess3}
> As Declare Fitness is related to Install Component using the merged control flow relation of the original process and the sub-process (captured using SWRL rules), we can query processes with different levels of process hierarchy.
> **Query:** Which process does allow the execution of Clean Component and Test Component in an interleaving manner?
> $\{P \equiv Start \sqcap ((\exists followedByTran.(value\,"actCC"\sqcap\exists followedByTran.value$
> $"actTC")$
> $\sqcup(\exists followedByTran.(value\,"actTC"\sqcap\exists followedByTran.value\,"actCC")\}$
> **Result:** {MProcess2}
> The process obtained thus allows an interleaving of the execution of Clean Component and Test Component.

5   Experimental Results

In this section we describe our implementation efforts. Also we report on the experiments that we perform on industrial process models.

5.1   Implementation

We implement our framework using Java and OWL API. At the front end we use a BPM modeler for capturing business process models. For this purpose we use Camunda[6] which is an open source platform for workflow and business process management. Camunda Modeler provides a desktop application for editing BPMN process diagrams (using BPMN 2.0) which comes with a graphical user interface. Moreover, a business process drawn in Camunda can be exported as an xml file. We have written a translator in Java that can parse the xml

---

[6] Available at https://camunda.org/.

file, generate basic patterns out of the process and create OWL ontology with SWRL rules for each of them using OWL API which are subsequently merged. The OWL ontology can be uploaded on Protégé framework for viewing. A Java implementation with some example processes can be found in "https://github.com/gsilvatici/DiagramOntologyParser".

5.2   Experiments and Evaluation

Dataset. For experimental purposes we consider a total of 29 different industrial process models. These processes are modeled on Infosys in-house requirements modeling tool called InFlux Requirements Studio (RS).[7]. Influx RS has a process modeling editor interface which uses BPMN for capturing processes and produces xmi (a kind of xml) output files for these processes. We consider these xmi files produced from processes modeled on InFlux and translate them into OWL using our algorithm. These process models contain tasks, exclusive gateway, parallel gateways, loops and sub-processes. We create a KB for evaluating the process retrieval by using process multipliers on original processes.

Methodology. For the evaluation we use the HemriT 1.3.8.413 reasoner in Java 1.8 running on a computer with 3.2, 4-core GHz CPU and 16 GB RAM. We create four knowledge bases with different sizes (with processes chosen with replacement) on which process retrieval is evaluated. The first KB contains 9, the second 15, and the third 20 and fourth contains 29 process models. The Protègè 5.2 framework (with HemriT 1.3.8.413) is used for querying and reasoning. For each of the KBs, the evaluation consists of 10 to 20 queries similar to the queries illustrated in Sect. 4.

Result. We present our evaluation result concerning process retrieval in Table 5. KB size refers to the number of processes and their constituent sub-processes. By KB node size we mean the number of nodes (activities, gateways and events) of the processes comprising the KB. The quantity sub-process per process denotes the (average and maximum) number of sub-processes in each process in the KB. We also capture the number of axioms and rules present in each KB. We show the (average and maximum) retrieval time (in milliseconds (ms)) for both simple and complex queries. Simple queries include only one activity or a negated activity. Complex queries consist of multiple (at least three) activities. The average retrieval time for concept satisfiability is also shown. By concept satisfiability[8] we mean checking the consistency of the conjunction of the complex concepts for a process with all other relevant axioms like class hierarchy, object property hierarchy, datatype property hierarchy, class assertions, object property assertions and the like.

---

[7] InFlux process models have created high impact on Infosys business by bringing in formalism and repeatability into the process of translation of business objectives into IT solutions.

[8] This is like consistency checking of the whole ontology created on Protégé.

Table 5. Result on process retrieval

No.	KB size	KB node size	Sub-process per process size		KB axioms	KB rules	Simple query time [msec]		Complex query time [msec]		Concept sat time [msec]
			Avg	Max			*Avg*	*Max*	*Avg*	*Max*	*Avg*
1	20	151	2	3	1746	179	4390	4482	4201	4270	6806
2	20	143	3	5	1632	183	5820	6020	5750	5826	18909
3	29	214	2	3	2498	258	6721	6851	6515	6684	20310
4	29	217	3	5	5442	261	12213	12773	12228	12307	42322

The performance evaluation has the following outcomes. The number of sub-processes in a process makes considerable difference in query retrieval and concept satisfiability time, as evidenced by the 3rd and 4th KB. Both these KBs have the same process size of 29, but the average number of sub-processes per process in 3rd KB is higher than that in 4th KB, so much so, the retrieval time of queries differs by almost 100% for them. The 1st and the 2nd KB show comparable performances. However, the 1st KB though having larger KB node size, shows lower retrieval time for simple and as well as complex queries. It seems the retrieval time is also greatly influenced by the number of sub-processes per process in the KB as mentioned before. This is because the number of rules in the KB increases with the increase in the number of sub-processes (every sub-process generates two lengthy SWRL rules). It is interesting to note that except for the 2nd KB, the retrieval time for both kinds of queries goes up with an increase in KB node size.

The retrieval time for queries is directly proportional to KB size. As indicated for all the KBs, the retrieval time for queries is more than 50% high for a KB with 29 processes than the KB with 20 processes, while the number of sub-process per process remains almost constant. Also the number of sub-processes per process seems to affect the concept satisfiability time a lot. For the same KB size of 1st and 2nd KBs, concept satisfiability time increases by three times for the latter. Similar trend is shown in 3rd and 4th KBs, the concept satisfiability time for 4th KB is two times more than 3rd KB.

The evaluation realizes the following qualitative results. (1) Processes from the KB are subsumed by the more general query processes using the roles *followedBy* and *followedByTran*. (2) The presence of unique activities inside a process lends an advantage on the use of the *contains* role, as using it with along the *followedBy* role leads to a more expressive query. (3) The retrieval of processes with queries that use activities occurring inside sub-processes are made possible by the use of SWRL rules that links the control flow relation of the original process with that of its sub-processes at different levels of hierarchy.

Limitations. Our experimentation is restricted in scope due to KB size. This is because, for KB with more than 40 process models, concept satisfiability for most of the cases does not terminate. This is mainly due to the number of rules that are present in the KB (and of course, consistency checking and querying in OWL-DL is NEXPTime complete [15]). This is confirmed by the fact that consistency checking without SWRL rules in the KB leads to appreciable decrease in time. It is obvious that use of SWRL degrades the performance of querying and consistency checking. However, from Fig. 5 we can see that consistency (concept satisfiability) checking time is only about 45000 ms more for KB with no rules compared to KB with rules in limit. Also the former rises appreciably in comparison to the latter when the KB size is close to 20.

6 Business Process Modeling as Part of Knowledge Management: A Case Study

As the business centers are becoming more process-oriented they have started to adopt process modeling methods and tools to effectively manage the complexity of these systems. This has led to the development of integrated business process modeling tools which are capable of delivering valuable business objectives. Each BPM software application is made of a combination of several compo-

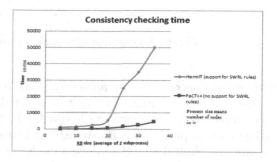

Fig. 5. Consistency checking time for KBs with and without rules

nents: process modeling and design, process monitoring, process operation (automation and integration) and technology platforms and interfaces. Although each of these components is important for selecting a BPM tool the ability to model process and maintain process repository would be the most important yardstick for choosing such tools. Even if modeling tools adequately support the modeling and enactment of business processes, they still do not provide much support for knowledge-related activities. By proper ontology modeling of processes it will be possible to extract existing knowledge that can be made explicit to the user. This is the reason we consider a case study of a business process and follow a step-by-step approach of extracting OWL+SWRL ontology that explicitly integrates knowledge management activities into the business process environment.

Figure 6 represents an example of business process in a banking domain (related to opening of a savings account) arising in an IT application scenario. This is an abridged version of a process model in Infosys business process repository. In this process the bank receives request (A) for opening an account from a client. The bank then obtains client information (B) and selects service (C). Getting client information reduces to getting driver's license (D) and analyzing customer relationship (E) whereas select service forks into record information (F) and submit deposit (G). After analyzing customer relation and recording information, document is prepared (H) followed by preparing for account opening (I). For final phase of account opening, a review process is scheduled (J)

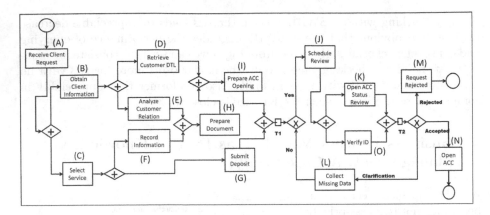

Fig. 6. An example of a bank account opening process

which follows account status review (K) and ID verification (O). Finally there is a decision where either a request is rejected (M), or an account is opened successfully (N), or missing data is sought (L) for. Note that the activities are marked using capital letters in parentheses corresponding to the activities in the diagram. We shall divide this process modeling effort into the following steps, - sub-process identification, vocabulary fixing, concept hierarchy design, pattern identification, pattern to ontology creation, axiom listing and ontology merging.

Sub-process identification. One needs to identify all the sub-processes as each sub-process will be characterized by a separate control flow relation. So, if there are n processes then we should have assigned n control flow relations, $followedBy1, \ldots, followedByn$. If a sub-process is embedded in another sub-process then we use another subscript, for example, if a sub-process with control flow relation $followedBy2$ contains another sub-process then the control flow of the latter will be denoted by $followedBy21$, and so forth. However, this particular process does not contain any sub-process, and hence can be modeled by a single control flow relation $followedBy$ and its transitive closure.

Vocabulary fixing. Once the control flow relation associated with each sub-process and the main control flow relation with the original process are decided one needs to identify a naming convention for all the nodes in the process. Activities are provided with named individuals, for example, task A will be represented as an individual $actA$, task B as $actB$ etc. Similarly, start and end nodes are instantiated as $start1, end1, \ldots$ etc. Each join node is also associated with an individual like $join1, \ldots$ etc. The naming convention is that join nodes are marked from left to right in the figure with the word 'join' appended with appropriate natural numbers. The naming convention for roles will be as described in Sect. 3.1. For ease of notation we may adopt the unique name assumption which states that different names always refer to different entities in the world, although it is not a requirement in OWL modeling.

Concept hierarchy design. In most of the cases the concept hierarchy in Fig. 3(b) is adopted.

Pattern identification. It is known that a well-formed process can be decomposed into atomic patterns as proposed by Van der Aalst *et. al* in [20]. Hence we can identify those patterns (as depicted in Fig. 3(a)) in the process considered.

Pattern to ontology creation. Once a business process is associated with well-designated patterns one can start writing ontology for each of these patterns. For some of these patterns we specify TBox axioms as below. Also for these patterns we list the ABox axioms in Table 6.

Axiom listing. Some extra axioms like the ones in Table 3 are also added. For sub-processes similar axioms need to be listed specific to each of them.

Ontology merging. Finally, the ontology specified in the last two steps are merged. By construction the created ontology as argued in Sect. 3.2, will be consistent.

Table 6. A partial specification of ontology for the business process in Fig. 6

Patterns	TBox axioms	ABox axioms
Start node followed by task A	$C_0 \equiv (Start \sqcap = 1 followedBy.C_A)$	$Start(start1), Task(actA),$ $followedBy(start1, actA)$
Task A is split into two parallel branches containing tasks B and C respectively	$C_A \equiv Task \sqcap$ $(\exists followedBy.C_B) \sqcap$ $(\exists followedBy.C_C) \sqcap$ $(= 2.followedBy)$	$Task(actB), Task(actC),$ $followedBy(actA, actB),$ $followedBy(actA, actC)$
Task B is split into two parallel branches containing tasks D and E respectively	$C_B \equiv Task \sqcap$ $(\exists followedBy.C_D) \sqcap$ $(\exists followedBy.C_E) \sqcap$ $(= 2.followedBy)$	$Task(actD), Task(actE),$ $followedBy(actB, actD),$ $followedBy(actB, actE)$
. . .	. . .	. . .
Tasks E and F get synchronized into task H	$C_E \equiv Task \sqcap =$ $1.followedBy.(\mathcal{J} \sqcap =$ $1.followedBy.C_H),$ $C_F \equiv$ $Task \sqcap =$ $1.followedBy.(\mathcal{J} \sqcap =$ $1.followedBy.C_H)$	$Task(actH), Join(join1),$ $followedBy(actE, actH),$ $followedBy(actF, actH),$ $followedBy(actE, join1),$ $followedBy(actF, join1)$
. . .	. . .	. . .
Task N is followed by end node	$C_N \equiv (Task \sqcap = 1 followedBy.End)$	$Task(actN), End(end1),$ $followedBy(actN, end1)$

In this way, one can create ontology for each process in a repository and merge those ontologies to create useful organizational knowledge repository. As nowadays, most of the organizations are involved in the projects related to business process management this work could facilitate adopting an integrated business process and knowledge management centric approach. Such a modeling framework should encourage the development of integrated BPM and Knowledge management software tools that should enable the transformation of business process models into knowledge repository.

7   Related Work

There are some existing research work on annotating business processes using semantic web formalisms. Business processes have been tagged with semantic labels as a part of knowledge base with a view to formalize business process structure, business domains, and a set of criteria describing correct semantic marking in [5]. In another work [6], the authors propose semantic web language OWL to formalize business process diagrams, and automatically verify sets of constraints on them, that deal with knowledge about the domain and process structure. There have been earlier attempts to model processes and retrieve process structures. Sequences arising in a business process have been modeled in [10]. Processes are retrieved using process information and annotation in [23]. Process reuse has been advocated in [7] by using DL-based process models, but complex control flow is not captured. In [9], the authors build on these approaches of process modeling, and attempt to analyze requirements for modeling and querying process models. They also present a pattern-oriented approach for process modeling and information retrieval. For this purpose they specify the execution order of a process in OWL and also express the modality and process activities and structures in the same formalism. In a recent work [11] Käfer and Harth design an ontology for representing workflows over components with Read-Write Linked Data interfaces and give an operational semantics to the ontology via a rule language, however they do not deal with explicit business process models. As mentioned before, our work offers some advantage over this work as it allows a modular design of process models and combines control flows of an original process and constituent sub-processes using SWRL rules.

These semantic annotation techniques of business processes lead to the possibility of semantic validation, *i.e.,* whether the tasks in business processes are consistent with respect to each other in the underlying framework of semantic annotation. Such issues are investigated in [22], where the authors introduce a formalism for business processes, which combines concepts from work flow with that from AI. A rule-based method for modeling processes and workflows has been proposed in [13], where the authors introduce an extended Event-Condition-Action (ECA) notation for refining business rules, and perform a consistent decomposition of business processes. Cicekli and Cickeli have used event calculus, a kind of logic programming formalism for specification and execution of workflows in [3]. They express control flow graph of a work flow specification as a set of logical formulas. Using a similar framework of Constraint Logic Programming the authors propose a method for representing and reasoning about business processes from both the workflow and data perspective [19]. However most of these techniques lead to undecidable reasoning problem.

Let us also contrast our OWL modeling of business processes with possible modeling of the same with OWL-S [21]. OWL-S is one of the first attempts to present an OWL ontology for semantic modeling of processes. OWL-S differentiates between atomic and composite processes. Our modeling technique does not require such a differentiation. OWL-S Sequence allows arbitrary processes as components. As a result, the semantics of a sequence of two splits is unclear and unintuitive. Suppose a split A has components $A_1, \ldots, A_m$ and split B has components $B_1, \ldots, B_n$. When A and B are composed in a sequence such that A is followed by B, it may still happen that a B_i is finished before an A_j. Our modeling technique requires the first component to be a start event. OWL-S process model proposes a complicated way for modeling input and output parameters with OWL. We do not model input and output parameters of activities in our approach.

8   Conclusion

In this work we provide a formalization of business processes in OWL-DL with SWRL rules for modeling and retrieving purposes. Our modeling technique offers some advantages over the existing repertoire by the way of offering a modular approach of modeling, linking control flow relations of a process and its subprocess using rules and providing a consistent way of modeling ontologies. The framework can be successfully integrated with different applications involving requirement engineering, business process information systems etc. In future we would like to design a natural language query interface for querying business processes in this framework. Sentences expressed in a controlled subset of natural language will be used as query languages on the user interface which will be converted to SQWRL queries at the back end for information retrieval.

References

1. Baader, F., Nutt, W.: Basic description logics. In: Description Logic Handbook, pp. 43–95 (2003)
2. Bisztray, D., Heckel, R.: Rule-level verification of business process transformations using CSP. ECEASST **6** (2007)
3. Cicekli, N.K., Cicekli, I.: Formalizing the specification and execution of workflows using the event calculus. Inf. Sci. **176**(15), 2227–2267 (2006)
4. Fahland, D., et al.: Analysis on demand: instantaneous soundness checking of industrial business process models. Data Knowl. Eng. **70**(5), 448–466 (2011)
5. Di Francescomarino, C., Ghidini, C., Rospocher, M., Serafini, L., Tonella, P.: Reasoning on semantically annotated processes. In: Bouguettaya, A., Krueger, I., Margaria, T. (eds.) ICSOC 2008. LNCS, vol. 5364, pp. 132–146. Springer, Heidelberg (2008). https://doi.org/10.1007/978-3-540-89652-4_13
6. Di Francescomarino, C., Ghidini, C., Rospocher, M., Serafini, L., Tonella, P.: Semantically-aided business process modeling. In: Bernstein, A., et al. (eds.) ISWC 2009. LNCS, vol. 5823, pp. 114–129. Springer, Heidelberg (2009). https://doi.org/10.1007/978-3-642-04930-9_8
7. Goderis, A., Sattler, U., Goble, C.A.: Applying description logics for workflow reuse and repurposing. In: Proceedings of the International Workshop on Description Logics (DL 2005) (2005)
8. Gröner, G., Staab, S.: Modeling and query pattern for process retrieval in OWL. In: Proceedings of the 5th International Conference on Knowledge Capture (K-CAP 2009), 1–4 September 2009, Redondo Beach, California, USA, pp. 189–190. ACM (2009)

9. Groener, G., Staab, S.: Modeling and query patterns for process retrieval in OWL. In: Bernstein, A., Karger, D.R., Heath, T., Feigenbaum, L., Maynard, D., Motta, E., Thirunarayan, K. (eds.) ISWC 2009. LNCS, vol. 5823, pp. 243–259. Springer, Heidelberg (2009). https://doi.org/10.1007/978-3-642-04930-9_16

10. Hirsh, H., Kudenko, D.: Representing sequences in description logics. In: Proceedings of the Fourteenth National Conference on Artificial Intelligence and Ninth Innovative Applications of Artificial Intelligence Conference, AAAI 1997, pp. 384–389 (1997)

11. Käfer, T., Harth, A.: Specifying, monitoring, and executing workflows in linked data environments. CoRR abs/1804.05044 (2018). http://arxiv.org/abs/1804.05044

12. Kiefer, C., Bernstein, A., Lee, H.J., Klein, M., Stocker, M.: Semantic process retrieval with iSPARQL. In: Franconi, E., Kifer, M., May, W. (eds.) ESWC 2007. LNCS, vol. 4519, pp. 609–623. Springer, Heidelberg (2007). https://doi.org/10.1007/978-3-540-72667-8_43

13. Knolmayer, G., Endl, R., Pfahrer, M.: Modeling processes and workflows by business rules. In: van der Aalst, W., Desel, J., Oberweis, A. (eds.) Business Process Management. LNCS, vol. 1806, pp. 16–29. Springer, Heidelberg (2000). https://doi.org/10.1007/3-540-45594-9_2

14. Liu, R., Kumar, A.: An analysis and taxonomy of unstructured workflows. In: van der Aalst, W.M.P., Benatallah, B., Casati, F., Curbera, F. (eds.) BPM 2005. LNCS, vol. 3649, pp. 268–284. Springer, Heidelberg (2005). https://doi.org/10.1007/11538394_18

15. Motik, B., Sattler, U., Studer, R.: Query answering for OWL-DL with rules. J. Web Semant. 3, 41–60 (2005)

16. O'Connor, M., Tu, S., Nyulas, C., Das, A., Musen, M.: Querying the semantic web with SWRL. In: Paschke, A., Biletskiy, Y. (eds.) RuleML 2007. LNCS, vol. 4824, pp. 155–159. Springer, Heidelberg (2007). https://doi.org/10.1007/978-3-540-75975-1_13

17. Roy, S., Bihary, S., Laos, J.A.C.: A CSP-theoretic framework of checking conformance of business processes. In: 19th Asia-Pacific Software Engineering Conference, APSEC 2012, pp. 30–39 (2012)

18. Schmidt-Schauß, M., Smolka, G.: Attributive concept descriptions with complements. Artif. Intell. 48(1), 1–26 (1991)

19. Smith, F., Proietti, M.: Reasoning on data-aware business processes with constraint logic. In: Proceedings of the 4th International Symposium on Data-Driven Process Discovery and Analysis (SIMPDA 2014), pp. 60–75 (2014)

20. Van Der Aalst, W.M.P., Ter Hofstede, A.H.M., Kiepuszewski, B., Barros, A.P.: Workflow patterns. Distrib. Parallel Databases 14(1), 5–51 (2003)

21. W3C Recommendation: OWL-S Semantic Markup for Web Services (2004). http://www.w3.org/Submissions/OWL-S

22. Weber, I., Hoffman, J., Mendling, J.: Beyond soundness: on the verification of semantic business process models. Distrib. Parallel Databases 27, 271–343 (2010)

23. Wolverton, M., Martin, D.L., Harrison, I.W., Thoméré, J.: A process catalog for workflow generation. In: Proceedings of 7th International Semantic Web Conference, ISWC 2008, pp. 833–846 (2008)

Understanding Information Professionals: A Survey on the Quality of Linked Data Sources for Digital Libraries

Jeremy Debattista$^{(\boxtimes)}$, Lucy McKenna, and Rob Brennan

ADAPT Centre, School of Computer Science and Statistics,
Trinity College Dublin, Dublin, Ireland
debattij@scss.tcd.ie, lucy.mckenna@adaptcentre.ie,
rob.brennan@cs.tcd.ie

Abstract. In this paper we provide an in-depth analysis of a survey related to Information Professionals (IPs) experiences with Linked Data quality. We discuss and highlight shortcomings in linked data sources following a survey related to the quality issues IPs find when using such sources for their daily tasks such as metadata creation.

Keywords: Metadata quality · Digital libraries · Linked Data

1 Introduction

The success of a digital library (DL) is said to be dependent on the quality of the available metadata [7]. In such a broad sense, one could easily answer the question *"what is a good digital library?"*, however, in reality one cannot generalise which digital library is the absolute best for all cases and for everyone. This is due to the fact that defining what constitutes good metadata quality is subjective. Many researchers and librarians themselves tried to define metadata quality, however, their definition is mainly geared towards their institutional needs. These needs are coupled with the Information Professionals' (IP) experience and the role within the library setting, as this would also play an important part of formulating a definition of quality. Furthermore, metadata quality is not just the human's perception that defines quality, but similar to *data quality*, the task-at-hand is a decisive factor for defining quality. The use of Linked Data is gaining momentum within IPs and digital libraries[1]. IPs realised that Linked Data offers many benefits, such as better resource discovery and interoperability [5]. However, Linked Data implementation

This research has received funding from the Irish Research Council Government of Ireland Postdoctoral Fellowship award (GOIPD/2017/1204) and the ADAPT Centre for Digital Content Technology, funded under the SFI Research Centres Programme (Grant 13/RC/2106) and co-funded by the European Regional Development Fund.

[1] https://www.oclc.org/research/themes/data-science/linkeddata/linked-data-survey.html Date Accessed: 11th July 2018.

© Springer Nature Switzerland AG 2018
H. Panetto et al. (Eds.): OTM 2018 Conferences, LNCS 11230, pp. 537–545, 2018.
https://doi.org/10.1007/978-3-030-02671-4_32

by IPs has been relatively slow, with issues in relation to the quality of currently available Linked Data resources being a notable challenge [5,8].

We have recently conducted a survey, amongst 185 IPs worldwide, whose purpose is twofold: (a) to have a better understanding of the quality criteria IPs with different experiences and expertise; and (b) to understand better the kind of quality problems these IPs are facing when searching for, or using external data sources. In this short paper we discuss our findings for the latter, that is, discussing the different quality problems these IPs are facing in their day-to-day tasks. The rest of the paper is structured as follows; In Sect. 2 we discuss the related work. The survey's methodology is described in Sect. 3. Discussion on the survey findings are discussed in Sect. 4, whilst in Sect. 5 we conclude this article with our final remarks and next steps building upon this survey.

2   Related Work

Quality in digital libraries has been discussed in various works throughout the years. However, to the best of our knowledge, there is no large-scale survey that gathers knowledge about metadata quality from IPs. These IPs provide the unique insight based on their varied experience and the institutions they belong to. Identifying and defining *what makes a good digital library* is dependent on a lot of factors, which makes it a statement that cannot be generalised for all. These factors include the stakeholder using the digital library and the task at hand. In order to try and address this statement, Gonçalves et al. [2] defined a formal model for understanding the quality of digital libraries based on the 5S (stream, structural, spatial, scenarios, and societies) theory. Supporting this model, the authors defined 16 dimensions each having a set of measurable metrics. The dimensions *accuracy, completeness, conformance to standards*, and *consistency* were proposed as candidate quality dimensions affecting the metadata concept. The majority of research work investigating digital library or metadata quality suggested a number of different quality measures, most of them based on their particular use case at hand, but as Park suggested in his work [6], most of the literatures' metric suggestions overlapped.

The broad survey literature on metadata quality in digital libraries led the foundations to our work. The introduction of digital libraries together with the Web of Data brought an upheaval in the way data catalogers generate metadata. More metadata and web resources are being re-used, nonetheless, it does not mean that quality has improved (or otherwise). In this short paper, we discuss the current data quality pitfalls IPs face in their daily tasks.

3   Survey Methodology

The survey analysed for our research formed part of a more extensive survey conducted to explore the attitudes and experiences of Information Professionals (IPs), such as librarians, archivists and metadata cataloguers, with regards to Linked Data. In this paper we refer to these as *digital library consumers*.

Participants in our questionnaire were primarily IPs with experience working in the LAM domain (N = 172). IPs were encouraged to participate regardless of whether they had any prior experience working with the Linked Data. This was done in an attempt to recruit a broad range of participants, rather than just IPs who are highly experienced in Linked Data. Also recruited were researchers and academics with experience in the LAM and/or LD domain (N = 13). This was done in order to gain the perspective of those engaging in current LD and LAM research. The 185 questionnaires that were analysed were classified into two groups: participants who have experience working with Linked Data (N = 54) (group 1), and participants who do not have experience working with Linked Data (N = 131) (group 2). For more information on the survey methodology and participants, we refer the reader to [5].

4   Creating (Linked) Metadata in Digital Libraries - Quality Problems in External Data Sources

Linked Data quality varies from one dataset to another, as Debattista et al. [1] discuss in their recent study of the quality of the 2015 version of the LOD Cloud[2]. In this section we discuss our findings in relation to the various quality issues IPs encounter when consuming these external sources for metadata creation tasks. In order to better understand the kind of quality problems the participants face when consuming external data sources for creating metadata, we asked the following question:

> *Can you give an example of a data quality issue or concern you experience frequently?*

Out of 185 participants, 92 addressed this question. From these 92, answers from 77 could be classified into 14 different quality dimensions. The remaining 15 answers could not be classified as quality problems and are out of scope for this article. Furthermore, some of the respondents mentioned more than one problem in their response and thus in total the number of problems identified is 90. Table 1 aggregates the 14 problems identified by the participants. Overall *semantic accuracy* problems are the most commonly mentioned amongst the 77 participants, whilst lack of *verbosity* was listed as the most commonly cited problem within Group 2 participants.

Semantic Accuracy Problems. The major concern mentioned in both groups was the fact that they have to work with a lot of incorrect data, more specifically dataset not representing the real world library object. The most common pitfall was the presence of incorrect values in data in various fields of catalogue resources. Whilst such issues cannot be pinpointed down to a particular one, there are various metrics that can be deployed in a publishing lifecycle that

---

[2] http://lod-cloud.net.

Table 1. Quality pitfalls within external sources.

Problem - quality dimension	Group 1	Group 2	Total
Semantic accuracy	6	9	15
Completeness	7	6	13
Interoperability	6	6	12
Conciseness	2	10	12
Data formatting/syntactic validity	6	4	10
Language versatility	4	2	6
Availability	3	2	5
Trustworthiness	2	2	4
Interpretability	3	0	3
Licensing	1	2	3
Timeliness	1	2	3
Provenance	0	2	2
Interlinking	0	1	1
Documentation	0	1	1

assess the datasets being produced. For example, one participant mentioned that they often find wrong ISBNs in e-books, as data providers mint their own identifiers rather than using the actual correct one. Another participant highlighted that data extracted using OCR techniques are usually prone to incorrect values. Semantic accuracy can also be a consequence of problems in syntactic validity, but not vice-versa.

Completeness (Data Coverage) Problems. In data quality, a dataset is said to be complete if it is comprehensive enough for the task at hand. This means that even if a dataset is not 100% complete when compared to the real world object, it can still be considered as complete if it meets the consumers' expectations. Participants mentioned that they do not trust that information is correct and complete in crowdsourcing efforts. One of these participants also noted that some content vendors dump their data into shared databases without following any best practices, thus creating noise for data consumers. Another participant noted that completeness of old records is lacking due to them not being updated for compliance with newer standards.

Interoperability Problems. Interoperability is one of the main strengths of the RDF data model, however, in order to ensure maximum interoperability, publishers should try and re-use existing terminology and semantic vocabularies for a particular domain as much as possible. Apart from metadata schemas, in digital libraries we also find a number of controlled vocabularies[3] that can be used when describing a resource. Nonetheless, the responses suggest that there is no consensus on which vocabularies should be used for which purpose. Furthermore, these controlled vocabularies and digital libraries might use different formats, which makes metadata consumption for re-use more challenging. One participant noted that metadata formats (e.g. BIBFRAME[4]) are changing significantly and rapidly from one version to another which might cause interoperability issues between different catalogues that were not updated to the new version. Therefore, ontology maintainers should ensure that appropriate versioning techniques are used, in order to ensure seamless interoperability between the various agents using different versions of a particular dataset.

Conciseness Problems. Ambiguity within resources and duplicate copies of the same resource will lead to poor overall quality since it would make it difficult for data consumers to decide which resources one should use for various tasks. The survey shows that in this dimension, ambiguity is a major problem, which could be resolved if a disambiguation process (or authority control in library science) is enforced and unique persistent IDs are used throughout. This could also be linked to an argument one participant raised that local authorities are creating their own resources and that databases such as the Library of Congress should harmonise with the said authorities in order to prevent problems with data duplication within a dataset distribution.

Data Formatting (Syntactic Validity) Problems. When dealing with machine-readable formats, syntactic validity is an important aspect in datasets, otherwise such problems might hinder their use as machines would not be able to parse them correctly. These problems are mostly related to the violation of syntactical rules. Common problems mentioned by the participants were incorrect formatting of dates, inconsistencies in names (eg. first name, last name vs last name, first name), and problems caused by OCRd data. Problems in this dimension can directly affect the quality in the semantic accuracy dimension.

Language Versatility Problems. Datasets, especially those on the Web, are meant to be used by anyone. A multi-lingual data catalogue is more likely to be re-used by different users/institutes who require the data to be in a specific language. Nonetheless, this does not mean that a dataset should have some resources in one language and some others in another language. One issue raised is regarding the inconsistency of using American English and UK English in terminologies in the authority and subject control data. Another problem is related to the localisation of the machine and the application, where for example one has to use cyrillic alphabet, which is not supported in some international

---

[3] For example http://www.w3.org/2005/Incubator/lld/XGR-lld-vocabdataset/.
[4] https://www.loc.gov/bibframe/.

standard authority data (for example Getty Vocabularies http://www.getty.edu/research/tools/vocabularies/). In Linked Data, the use of language tags (eg. @en) in string literals is strongly suggested so that data consumers (users, machines) can determine to what extent they can use the data [4]. Nonetheless, processes has to be in place to help encode different transliteration schemes as language tags on their own would not be sufficient.

Availability Problems. One of the main Linked Data principles is that resources are decentralised and interlinked together through the Unique Resource Identifiers (URI). Therefore, it is of utmost importance that resources on the web are maintained and are ready to be consumed by machines and humans alike at any time. The most common problems mentioned were, the presence of dead or broken links and the reliability of online services.

Trustworthiness Problems. If the data is deemed to be credible, and correct, then the data consumer might consider a data source to be trustworthy. In this survey, some participants voiced different opinion on how they consider a dataset to be trustworthy. For example, one participant noted that *"collaborative effort across multiple industries is required to have trustworthy, unbiased sets of data to work from"*. Another participant mentioned that one of the quality criteria he looks at when choosing a fit dataset is whether the work was carried out in his/her institution, implying that the participant trusts (or distrusts) the work done in his/her institution more than others.

Interpretability Problems. In Linked Data, interpretability is mostly related to whether a machine is able to process and interpret the data. The concerns mentioned by the participants here are mostly related to the quality of schemas used. An ontology provides formal semantics of a class or a property, therefore, a machine can make sense out of the values that are defined in a dataset. Therefore, having a defunct vocabulary or inconsistencies within the schema itself means that a machine cannot process the data correctly as this data would be without formal meaning. The most pressing issues highlighted by the participants in this regard include (a) Links to published vocabularies go dead; (b) abandoned vocabularies are heading to their death due to the lack of maintainer information; and (c) datasets are using vocabularies with inconsistencies. In Linked Data, these problems have further consequences, for example one would not be able to reason upon data, or it could lead to wrong interlinking in automatic interlinking processes.

Licensing Problems. Data, being open or not, should have a license defined in its metadata in order for a data consumer to understand to what extent they can (re-)use the data [1]. If the license is not clearly defined, one might run into intellectual property rights and copyright complications. The three participants highlighting this issue are on a common ground with regard to this topic. On the other hand, when talking about Linked Data datasets **published on the web,** Heath and Bizer [3] state that "it is a common assumption that content and data made publicly available on the Web can be re-used at will. However, the absence of a licensing statement does not grant consumers the automatic right to use that content/data".

Timeliness Problems. Freshness and relevance of data sources is also important in metadata creation. Whilst certain values such as book name and author in data catalogues might not be changing frequently, there are some that require changing from time to time, as explained by two participants in the case of out-dated authority files[5]. Furthermore, using outdated or broken links as reference pointers is not just an availability problem, but it also a dataset freshness problem, as highlighted by one of the participants. Another common issue mentioned in the survey is that catalogued archives are not being updated in authority files, and thus causing a freshness issue.

Provenance Problems. Provenance metadata provides data consumers with the necessary information to understand where the data comes from, who produced it and how. The W3C Data on the Web Best Practices WG [4] highlights the importance of the provision of provenance stating that "published data outlives the lifespan of the data provider projects or organisations". Therefore, it is important that data publishers provide both basic contact information about themselves, but also provenance at a resource or statement level such that these are traceable to the original source. These problems are highly related to trustworthiness, as data consumers might look at provenance information to make decisions on whether to trust a particular dataset or data publisher [1].

Interlinking Problems. One of Linked Data principles, having interlinks between resources enable data consumers to discover more (in a follow-your-nose fashion) about a particular entity. For example, data catalogues might not tell us who the spouse of a particular author was, but by linking the author to a data source such as DBpedia, a data consumer might be able to know this information and more. Having interlinks is also a requirement for 5-star Linked Open Data according to Tim Berners-Lee's scheme https://5stardata.info/en/.

Documentation Problems. Whilst most data resources on the Web should allow for both machine and human consumption, data consumers should be able to understand how to access and use this data. For example, a data source might have a mailing list or even provide information in a human readable format. Nonetheless, when it comes to Linked Data, data publishers can publish such documentation in the dataset metadata using vocabularies such as voID

---

[5] In library science, authority control is the establishment and maintenance of consistent terminology for the identification of concepts across library collections.

to define regular expressions of typical resource URIs, or even an indication of the vocabularies used in the published dataset. Such documentation makes the dataset more understandable, which in turn could result in more re-use.

5   Final Remarks and Future Direction

When it comes to quality problems within external Linked Data source, IPs point out that most problems are intrinsic in nature, with *semantic accuracy*, *completeness*, *interoperability* and *conciseness* in the top three places. These survey results are worrying especially for the *semantic accuracy* and *interoperability* dimensions, where Linked Data should excel in. When comparing back to the work in [1], we find that even in the LOD cloud, the average for the usage of undefined classes and properties (related to the *interoperability* dimension) stands around 55%, with a very high standard deviation value. On the other hand, the LOD cloud average for the extensional conciseness metric (related to the *conciseness* dimension) is higher and is around 92%. Therefore, whilst this user study is an indication of the quality gaps within Linked Data sources, it is also an opportunity for the Linked Data publishers to update their publishing mechanisms in order to serve the digital library community better.

This user study is the first step of our quest to support digital libraries and their communities to adopt and improve their services using Linked Data. The next step is to assess the quality of Linked Data sources used in Digital Libraries, making quality metadata publicly available in a quality-based data portal. Furthermore, these quality metadata will be used in an interlinking framework for IPs, where a mechanism suggests different external data sources based on different quality criteria for the task at hand.

References

1. Debattista, J., Lange, C., Auer, S., Cortis, D.: Evaluating the quality of the LOD cloud: an empirical investigation. Semantic Web, November 2017 (to appear)
2. Gonçalves, M.A., Moreira, B.L., Fox, E.A., Watson, L.T.: "What is a good digital library?" - a quality model for digital libraries. Inf. Process. Manag. **43**(5), 1416–1437 (2007)
3. Heath, T., Bizer, C.: Linked Data: Evolving the Web into a Global Data Space, 1st edn. Morgan & Claypool, San Rafael (2011)
4. Lóscio, B.F., Burle, C., Calegari, N.: Data on the web best practices. W3C recommendation, World Wide Web Consortium, January 2017. https://www.w3.org/TR/2017/REC-dwbp-20170131/
5. McKenna, L., Debruyne, C., O'Sullivan, D.: Understanding the position of information professionals with regards to linked data: a survey of libraries, archives and museums. In: Proceedings of the 18th ACM/IEEE on Joint Conference on Digital Libraries (JCDL 2018), Fort Worth, Texas, USA, pp. 7–16 (2018)
6. Park, J.R.: Metadata quality in digital repositories: a survey of the current state of the art. Cat. Classif. Q. **47**(3–4), 213–228 (2009)

7. Tani, A., Candela, L., Castelli, D.: Dealing with metadata quality: the legacy of digital library efforts. Inf. Process. Manag. **49**(6), 1194–1205 (2013). https://doi.org/10.1016/j.ipm.2013.05.003. http://www.sciencedirect.com/science/article/pii/S0306457313000526
8. Yoshimura, K.S.: Analysis of an international linked data survey for implementers. D-Lib Mag. **22**(7), 6 (2016)

Challenges in Value-Driven
Data Governance

Judie Attard[(✉)] and Rob Brennan

KDEG, ADAPT Centre, School of Computer Science and Statistics,
O'Reilly Institute, Trinity College Dublin, Dublin 2, Ireland
{attardj,rob.brennan}@cs.tcd.ie

Abstract. Data is quite popularly considered to be the new oil since
it has become a valuable commodity. This has resulted in many entities
and businesses that hoard data with the aim of exploiting it. Yet, the
'simple' exploitation of data results in entities who are not obtaining
the highest benefits from the data, which as yet is not considered to
be a fully-fledged enterprise asset. Such data can exist in a duplicated,
fragmented, and isolated form, and the sheer volume of available data
further complicates the situation. Issues such as the latter highlight the
need for value-based data governance, where the management of data
assets is based on the quantification of the data value. This paper has the
purpose of creating awareness and further understanding of challenges
that result in untapped data value. We identify niches in related work,
and through our experience with businesses who use data assets, we here
analyse four main context-independent challenges that hinder entities
from achieving the full benefits of using their data. This will aid in the
advancement of the field of value-driven data governance and therefore
directly affect data asset exploitation.

Keywords: Data governance · Data value · Data asset
Data exploitation

1 Introduction

The exponential growth in the availability of data has led to an evident increase
of companies that use data as an enterprise asset. While money and people
have been considered to be enterprise assets for a long time, data is as yet
hardly considered to be so [12]. Yet, organisations and companies are increasingly
relying on their data to become more competitive, for example, by having greater
knowledge of their customers, by taking more informed decisions, by finding new
innovative uses for the data, by controlling risks and cutting costs, and also by
innovating upon this data. Such use of data assets enables companies to not only
better achieve their goals, but also to improve their financial performance.

As the volumes of data continue to rise, and enterprises and organisations are
increasingly relying on data, data is being duplicated, fragmented, and isolated

© Springer Nature Switzerland AG 2018
H. Panetto et al. (Eds.): OTM 2018 Conferences, LNCS 11230, pp. 546–554, 2018.
https://doi.org/10.1007/978-3-030-02671-4_33

into various silos [1]. The sheer volume of data also affects data quality, since data standards cannot be enforced so easily. Such data may lead to additional risks, increased costs, non efficient processes, and therefore potential business losses [1,6]. Moreover, although there is the general understanding that data of a high quality leads to more benefits when the data is exploited, there might be a lack of understanding on the process of managing this data, as well as the resulting business impact of using it.

These issues already show a clear need to manage data assets. Since data governance and management efforts and investments are on the rise, it is becoming increasingly relevant to identify the economic value of data and the return on investment. Data value has been used as a basis for organisational decision making on quality [10], but also as a part of automated control systems for data lifecycles [7] and file retention [20]. Failing to value data will result in a number of consequences such as retaining information that has little to no value, reduction in data usage, and leaving data investments vulnerable to budget cuts [13]. Hence, data value is an aspect that plays a very important role in data governance. The issue is that although gaining recognition as a valuable asset, data has as yet resisted quantitative measurement.

The aim of this paper is to identify and analyse the challenges that hinder entities from enjoying the full benefits of exploiting data as assets, in context of value-driven data governance. Existing literature cover various aspects of data value, however there is as yet no consensus on how to measure or quantify the value of data. There are also additional challenges that hinder the valuation of data, and this in turn makes data governance efforts more demanding. The contribution of this paper is therefore aimed towards any entity that exploits data as an asset, in an effort to optimise data governance efforts.

The rest of the paper is structured as follows: in Sect. 2 we provide an overview of identified challenges within a real use case, where a business exploits data assets with the aim of gaining competitive advantage, in Sect. 3 we analyse and discuss value-driven data governance challenges (as identified in niches in related work, and through our experience with businesses who use data assets), and finally in Sect. 4 we deliver our concluding remarks.

2   Use Case

In this section we present MyVolts; a company that uses data assets in order to obtain a competitive edge, as a use case with the aim of providing a first overview of challenges in value-driven data governance.

MyVolts is a successful SME with a 15 year track record that develops and operates a highly automated internet retail and business intelligence system. They currently operate in 4 countries in Europe, namely Ireland, the UK, France, and Germany, and also in the USA. In these countries MyVolts is a leading source for consumer device power supplies. They perform the following data value processes (amongst others) on their data assets:

- **Data Acquisition:** This company gathers data which includes data on their customers, the evolving market of power supply device specifications, and the power supply needs of all consumer electronics. They collect this data by monitoring social media, web sales data such as Amazon top seller lists, and device manufacturer homepages. New consumer electronic devices must be discovered, categorised, profiled for potential sales value and have their power supply technical specifications mined from open web data.
- **Data Curation:** The lack of standardised machine-readable repositories means that PDF is the dominant data publication format. Integrating this data while maintaining strict quality control is a major challenge for MyVolts.
- **Data Exploitation:** In this process MyVolts use their data assets to create adverts for their products. This process is a decision-rich process that requires to identify which products need advertising and which consumers to target. Data exploitation is therefore a process that also requires tapping into various data assets and potentially also integrating them.
- **Data Generation:** This process is an ongoing process resulting from product sales through the MyVolts website. This information, as specified above, will be used to create targeted adverts to optimise sales, and therefore also increase profits.

2.1   Challenges in MyVolts Use Case

The sample data value chain detailed above already provides us with a number of challenges that stem from using data assets as a basis for competitive advantage.

The first challenge is the quantification of the value of data as it is being acquired. MyVolts need to be able to **measure the value** of this data in order to identify whether this data is worth their effort and/or money. This quantification will not only enable MyVolts to reduce the risk of investing poorly in the data acquisition process, but also help target company efforts and aid decision making in the data exploitation and data curation processes.

The first challenge is directly related to the second challenge; **what makes data valuable?** In this use case, in order to be valuable, data needs to be reliable, timely, relevant, accurate, with good potential for impact once its used, and preferably even unique (not available to other competitors).

In general, all four data value processes described above highlight the requirement for data governance. A successful effort to exploit data assets and achieve competitive advantage requires various data governance tasks, including the definition of roles; data policies, standards, and procedures; the definition of an interoperable data architecture; and data storage and organisation. Therefore, we here identify the need of a **value-driven data governance model**.

Finally, we also identify the challenge of **optimising data governance** for the specific use case. An ideal data governance approach does not only encompass data governance tasks, but is also tailored to the use case in question. In this use case, decision making is a recurring process that exists throughout the data value chain. For instance, MyVolts employees need to decide which data to acquire, how much is it worth paying for, what data to maintain and what data to discard, what products to advertise, etc. Building upon the previously-mentioned challenges, the optimisation of data governance will result in efficient and effective use of data assets whilst minimising costs and achieving company goals (such as increasing profits, innovative use of data, etc.).

3 Challenges in Value-Driven Data Governance

In the following section we discuss challenges that hinder entities from effectively exploiting data assets. We base our analysis on existing related work and on our experience with businesses exploiting data assets.

3.1 Defining Data Value

Data value is recognised as a *"key issue in information systems management"* [6]. Yet, while most research on information or data value seeks to identify dimensions that characterise it, there is still **no consensus on the definition of data value**. In fact, the multi-dimensional nature of value, as well as the role context plays in data value quantifying efforts, make the definition of data value quite challenging. The interdisciplinary nature of this field also adds to the complexity of this task.

Different data has varied value in different contexts (e.g. different points in time [7], different consumers [12]) depending on a number of dimensions [18]. Ahituv [2], for example, suggests timeliness, content, and cost as data value dimensions. Even and Shankaranarayanan follow a similar reasoning where they focus on the intrinsic value of data and consider data quality dimensions that are both context independent and context dependent [10]. Chen, on the other hand, presents an information valuation approach that quantifies the value of a given piece of information based on its usage over time [7]. Along with usage, Sajko et al. also define data value dimensions to consist of meaning to business (through profits evaluation and utility), cost, and timeliness of data [15].

The above dimensions, are but a few of the existing dimensions that are used in literature to characterise data value. Whilst initial efforts have already been made with regards to providing a semantic data value vocabulary that can be used to comprehensively define data value [4], this heterogeneity of dimensions in literature indicates the need for terminological unification, which would also aid in developing a common understanding of the domain.

3.2 Measuring Data Value

To build adaptive, value-driven systems, it is necessary to have concrete value assessment techniques that report over time. Without assessment, the effective management of value, and hence efficient exploitation of data is highly unlikely [5]. Despite the growing literature on data as a valuable asset and on data exploitation, there is little to no work on how to **directly assess or quantify the value** of specific datasets held or used by an organisation within an information system. Moreover, existing methods for measuring the value of data often require intensive human effort and are also case-specific [7].

The lack of consensus on the definition of data value as described in Sect. 3.1 is hindering progress on data value assessment since entities and organisations are still fundamentally challenged to understand what characterises data value. Viscusi et al. [18] recently reconfirmed Moody and Walsh's [14] earlier assertion that there is no consensus on how to measure information value.

Usage, cost, and quality are three recurring data value dimensions that are measured in existing literature. Chen, for example, devises an approach to measure data value based on two measurable and observable metrics; usage and time [7]. Wijnhoven et al. extended Chens usage-based data valuation approach with a utility-based estimation based on file metadata [20]. Turczyk et al. also calculate the value of files from usage information [17], and Jin et al. similarly also measure data usage through information sharing and number of users accessing the information [11].

Various cost metrics are used in literature to measure data value. Stander breaks 'cost' into two categories; (i) the purchase price of the data asset, and (ii) the direct costs attributed to preparing the data for use [16]. DAMA International also focus on cost as a data value characterising dimension [8]. They use the cost of losing a data asset and the resulting impacts of not having the current amount and quality level of data as metrics of the value of a data asset.

Data quality metrics are the focus of Even and Shankaranarayanan's paper, where the authors describe a quantitative approach for assessing the business value attributed to data assets [10]. The data value aspects assessed include completeness, validity, accuracy, and currency. On the other hand, Stander considers the frequency and accuracy aspects of data assets [16]. Other literature such as [9,18] also mention quality aspects as data value dimensions, yet they do not specifically mention metrics that can be used to quantify this value.

Whilst usage, cost, and quality are three of the most popular data value dimensions that are quantified in literature, other data value dimensions are also discussed. For example, Laney focuses on utility functions [12], however this provides for abstract measures that are very challenging to realise as concrete metrics. Al-Saffar and Heileman provide an information valuation model with the aim of measuring the impact that a data asset can have [3]. The authors however acknowledge that this metric is subjective.

The existing literature therefore not only highlights the lack of existing metrics to quantify value, but also points out the need for more efforts in defining data value. Moreover, the literature also makes evident the complexity of quantifying data value, also due to its dependence on the context of use and its subjectivity. Yet, the subjective nature of some dimensions that characterise data value certainly does not rule out their quantification. Similar to some data quality aspects such as timeliness, such dimensions can still be accurately quantified in an objective manner, if only relevant for a specific context of use.

3.3   Modelling Value-Driven Data Governance

Whether using the 'data governance' term explicitly or not, many organisations and entities are exploring new strategies and approaches towards governing and managing their data assets. Such strategies may include both direct data manipulation (e.g. data quality, security, access) and also business plans on how the data asset is exploited. The issue here is that to date most data governance models are either proprietary, or otherwise human-process oriented and thus **do not support interoperable systems specification**.

Weill and Ross define an organisational approach to data governance where they establish a set of processes and delegation of authorities for making decisions and providing input [19]. This approach however focuses on roles and responsibilities rather than information system architectures, interfaces, processes or algorithms. The view of DAMA International [8] is more concrete and defines processes, roles and formal goals; for better decision-making, assuring compliance, increasing efficiency and business integration. Abed defines a framework based on four value pillars; agility, trust, intelligence, and transparency, focusing on enabling business sustainability and supporting economical growth [1]. Brous et al. document a systematic review of data governance principles [6]. The authors identify four main principles based on the review; the organisation of data management, ensuring alignment with business needs, ensuring compliance, and ensuring a common understanding of data.

Realistically, it is quite doubtful to have a one size fits all data governance solution. That being said, current approaches lack the link between data assets and organisational value. Such a strategy is essential in exploiting data assets to achieve competitive advantage that provides both short and long term value, therefore ensuring business success and sustainability [1]. We therefore identify the requirement for an interoperable, standardised, machine readable data governance model that caters for data assets, roles, and processes.

3.4   Optimising Data Governance

Effective data value chain governance, and hence optimised exploitation of data assets, depends on an understanding and representation of the context of use, the exploitation processes, data value measures, and hence also the nature of data value. In fact, one of the goals of data governance is *"to understand and promote the value of data assets"* [8]. Many data processing systems include "black-box" processes that do not provide any insight or reasoning behind their outputs, results or motivations. This lack of data understanding undermines the specification and enforcement of data governance policies, and provision of robust auditing. Moreover, although there is some literature where data value monitoring/measurement has been used with the aim of enhancing control of processes within a data value chain [7,16,17] such literature focuses on the management of individual processes within the system, such as file storage, and not on overarching data governance optimisation.

This challenge is also directly related to the challenge of measuring data value, as discussed in Sect. 3.2. The quantification of data value (even if just estimates) would enable the optimised governance of data assets in an enterprise. Examples of data governance processes that can be optimised can include data storage, where more valuable data can be stored in more reliable, more secure storage, whilst less valuable data can be stored using cheaper options; and data acquisition, where data can be acquired depending on whether its value for the enterprise is worth its cost.

4   Conclusion

The aim of this paper is to raise awareness about the potential impact of value-driven data governance, and guide further research. Therefore, based on existing literature and experience of existing businesses that exploit data assets, we explored four main challenges that hinder value-driven data governance. As data has been established as a requirement for most businesses to remain competitive, it has become vital to implement data governance to enable successful data asset exploitation. Figure 1 provides an overview of the challenges covered in this paper, as well as the resulting impacts that can be achieved with relevant solutions. As the figure indicates, the challenges build on top of each other. Therefore, in an ideal world, the solution of the first challenge would contribute towards the solution of the next challenge. Any relevant solutions for the challenges explored in this paper will contribute towards an overall more efficient and effective data governance and therefore data asset exploitation. In turn, this will enable the more successful achievement of data-driven business or company goals.

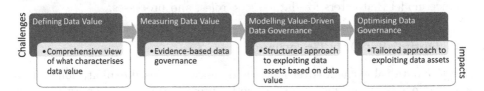

Fig. 1. Overview of challenges and impacts that can be achieved with relevant solutions

Acknowledgements. This research has received funding from the ADAPT Centre for Digital Content Technology, funded under the SFI Research Centres Programme (Grant 13/RC/2106), co-funded by the European Regional Development Fund and the European Unions Horizon 2020 research and innovation programme under the Marie Sklodowska-Curie grant agreement No. 713567.

References

1. el Abed, W.: Data governance: a business value-driven approach, pp. 1–16. Global Data Excellence (2011)
2. Ahituv, N.: A systematic approach toward assessing the value of an information system. MIS Q. 4(4), 61 (1980)
3. Al-Saffar, S., Heileman, G.L.: Semantic impact graphs for information valuation. In: Proceedings of the Eighth ACM Symposium on Document Engineering, DocEng 2008, pp. 209–212. ACM, New York (2008)
4. Attard, J., Brennan, R.: A semantic data value vocabulary supporting data value assessment and measurement integration. In: Proceedings of the 20th International Conference on Enterprise Information Systems. SciTePress (2018)
5. Brennan, R., Attard, J., Helfert, M.: Management of data value chains, a value monitoring capability maturity model. In: ICEIS (2018)
6. Brous, P., Janssen, M., Vilminko-Heikkinen, R.: Coordinating decision-making in data management activities: a systematic review of data governance principles. In: Scholl, H., et al. (eds.) EGOVIS 2016. LNCS, vol. 9820, pp. 115–125. Springer, Cham (2016). https://doi.org/10.1007/978-3-319-44421-5_9
7. Chen, Y.: Information valuation for information lifecycle management. In: Second International Conference on Autonomic Computing, ICAC 2005, pp. 135–146. IEEE, June 2005. https://doi.org/10.1109/ICAC.2005.35
8. DAMA International: The DAMA Guide to the Data Management Body of Knowledge, p. 430. DAMA (2009)
9. Engelsman, W.: Information assets and their value (2007)
10. Even, A., Shankaranarayanan, G.: Value-driven data quality assessment. In: Proceedings of the 2005 International Conference on Information Quality (2005)
11. Jin, H., Xiong, M., Wu, S.: Information value evaluation model for ILM. In: 2008 Ninth ACIS International Conference on Software Engineering, Artificial Intelligence, Networking, and Parallel/Distributed Computing. IEEE (2008)
12. Laney, D.: Infonomics: the economics of information and principles of information asset management. In: The Fifth MIT Information Quality Industry Symposium, 13–15 July 2011, pp. 590–603 (2011)
13. Maina, C.K.: Valuing information in an information age: the price model and the emerging information divide among individuals, societies, and nations (2003). http://www.cais-acsi.ca/search.asp?year=3002
14. Moody, D., Walsh, P.: Measuring the value of information: an asset valuation approach. In: Seventh European Conference on Information Systems, ECIS 1999, pp. 1–17 (1999). http://www.org/citeulike:9316228
15. Sajko, M., Rabuzin, K., Bača, M.: How to calculate information value for effective security risk assessment. J. Inf. Organ. Sci. 30(2), 263–278 (2006)
16. Stander, J.B.: The modern asset: big data and information valuation. Ph.D. thesis, Stellenbosch University (2015)
17. Turczyk, L.A., Heckmann, O., Steinmetz, R.: File valuation in information lifecycle management. In: Proceedings of the Thirteenth Americas Conference on Information Systems, Keystone, Colorado (2007)
18. Viscusi, G., Batini, C.: Digital information asset evaluation: characteristics and dimensions. In: Caporarello, L., Di Martino, B., Martinez, M. (eds.) Smart Organizations and Smart Artifacts. LNISO, vol. 7, pp. 77–86. Springer, Cham (2014). https://doi.org/10.1007/978-3-319-07040-7_9

19. Weill, P., Ross, J.W.: IT Governance How Top Performers Manage IT Decision Rights for Superior Results. Harvard Business School Press, Boston (2004)
20. Wijnhoven, F., Amrit, C., Dietz, P.: Value-based file retention. J. Data Inf. Qual. 4(4), 1–17 (2014). https://doi.org/10.1145/2567656

Automatic Extraction of Data Governance Knowledge from Slack Chat Channels

Rob Brennan[1(✉)], Simon Quigley[1], Pieter De Leenheer[2],
and Alfredo Maldonado[1]

[1] ADAPT Centre, Computer Science and Statistics, Trinity College Dublin,
Dublin 2, Ireland
{rob.brennan,siquigle,maldona}@scss.tcd.ie
[2] Collibra Research Lab, New York, USA
pieter@collibra.com

Abstract. This paper describes a data governance knowledge extraction prototype for Slack channels based on an OWL ontology abstracted from the Collibra data governance operating model and the application of statistical techniques for named entity recognition. This addresses the need to convert unstructured information flows about data assets in an organisation into structured knowledge that can easily be queried for data governance. The abstract nature of the data governance entities to be detected and the informal language of the Slack channel increased the knowledge extraction challenge. In evaluation, the system identified entities in a Slack channel with precision but low recall. This has shown that it is possible to identify data assets and data management tasks in a Slack channel so this is a fruitful topic for further research.

Keywords: Ontologies · Data management · Systems of engagement

1 Introduction

Data governance is increasingly important, and formal systems of data governance that audit and channel communication about data have become widespread. However large amounts of intra-organisational communication, including data governance information, is carried over unstructured channels such as Slack, and thus is not easily captured by a traditional data governance system.

Natural language processing (NLP) techniques have matured greatly over the last decade and can convert this unstructured human communication into machine-processable structured data for analysis and audit. Transformation into

This research has received funding from the ADAPT Centre for Digital Content Technology, funded under the SFI Research Centres Programme (Grant 13/RC/2106) and co-funded by the European Regional Development Fund.

© Springer Nature Switzerland AG 2018
H. Panetto et al. (Eds.): OTM 2018 Conferences, LNCS 11230, pp. 555–564, 2018.
https://doi.org/10.1007/978-3-030-02671-4_34

open knowledge models, such as RDF and OWL, provides the greatest flexibility to support inference, interlinking and global knowledge sharing. However data governance knowledge extraction from Slack chat has many challenges: short interactions, informal use of language, lack of standard test corpora, small datasets compared with global Twitter feeds, expert domain knowledge required to annotate training data and the abstract nature of data governance concepts compared with traditional NLP concepts used for named entity recognition (NER) tasks.

Given the lack of published training data for this task and the vast data requirements for neural NLP approaches, it was decided to investigate the performance of a state-of-the-art NER system based on conditional random fields (CRF). Thus the following research question is proposed: *To what extent can CRF-based Named Entity Recognition be used to extract data governance knowledge from an enterprise chat channel?* Data governance information is defined here as a set of data governance assets, processes, rules, roles and users.

This paper provides the following contributions: a new, open, data governance ontology and a trained data governance NER system and evaluation of the system performance using real-world enterprise Slack data.

The rest of this paper is structured as follows: Sect. 2 use case and requirements, Sect. 3 related work, Sect. 4 our approach to data governance knowledge extraction, Sect. 5 evaluation of the prototype system and finally Sect. 6 provides conclusions.

2   Use Case: Slack Channels as Data Governance Systems of Engagement

This paper is a first step in linking semantics-driven AI and user-centred data governance Systems of Engagement (SoE) [10]. The following diagram shows the systemic interaction between the Collibra DGC (Data Governance Centre) platform, being the System of Record (SoR), and a set of systems of engagement e.g. based on a Slack channel. The diagram was adapted from our work on community-based business semantics management [4] which was foundational for Collibra (Fig. 1).

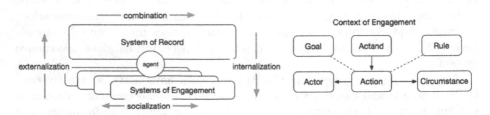

Fig. 1. LHS: SECI knowledge conversions between one SoR and many SoEs, through intelligent agents (on e.g., Slack). RHS: engagement contexts.

Both components consist of multiple instances of data governance operating concepts. In the Collibra platform SoR these concepts are shared, explicit and understood, i.e. based on a shared ontology. We refer to this ontology as the Collibra data governance operating model. Yet the ontology of these data governance concepts may differ widely in the various SoE applications we wish to integrate. On the SoE side, instances of these concepts are typically less explicit and usually scattered. They can be more of a socio-technical of nature, i.e. tacitly shared among humans, resulting in a poor unified record for supporting data governance as opposed to a SoR. E.g., your actor identity in Slack may be different from Confluence and Collibra. Also references to actands and actions may suffer wide differences in vocabulary and grammar, requiring (named) entity resolution. Slack has become a key corporate system of engagement and a hence a source of vital data governance context as data assets are discussed, evaluated, located and exchanged through Slack. Now it becomes imperative to enable the data governance SoR to engage with that unstructured context.

Enterprise data management traditionally focuses on centralizing formal management of operational and analytical data. This conservative view inhibits us from seeing the underlying fabric that glues all the data together. This data is scattered across engagement platforms and largely unstructured, usually expressed by humans in context-heavy natural language. Data governance systems must tap into this unstructured data and interactions to bring greater insights into how people, workplaces, and perhaps societies interact.

Derived Requirements: (1) A common ontology of data governance concepts and context that can span data governance in both systems of record and systems of engagement. For widespread adoption it is important that this uses an open, standards-based model such as W3C's OWL/RDF; and (2) Ability to convert unstructured communications into machine-readable data. This requires a knowledge extraction framework that is specialised both for the data governance domain and for the style and content of the communications channel (Slack).

3   Related Work

Here we discuss relevant work in: knowledge models for data governance, and NER for data governance in Chat channels.

Knowledge Models for Data Governance: Data governance is defined here as the organisational function aimed at the definition and enforcement of data policies to enable data collaboration, understanding and trust. To our knowledge there is no over-arching semantic model for data governance, e.g. ISO 38505-1 addresses foundations for data governance, but it does not provide a knowledge model of the domain.

However there are many existing standards-based metadata vocabularies that are important for data governance, e.g. the W3C provenance (PROV) standard

[7], DBpedia's DataID to describe data assets, the H2020 ALIGNED project knowledge models of data lifecycles and tools. W3C PROV can be used as a basis for specifying activities, agents and entities in a data governance model. This would enable interoperability with standard PROV services such as meta-data repositories and wider enterprise workflow and information integration applications. The W3C data quality vocabulary (DQV) standard can be used to describe a dataset's quality, whilst the data value vocabulary (DaVE) [1] could act as basis for describing data value metrics and dimensions. Thus there is a need for an upper governance ontology to glue together these individual vocabularies to describe the data governance domain as a knowledge model.

NER for Data Governance in Chat Communications Channels: To the best of our knowledge, this is the first usage of an NER approach to extract data governance concepts. NER aims to identify individual words or phrases in running text that refer to information units such as person names. We employ a state-of-the-art machine learning NER method called conditional random fields (CRF). In addition to being able to extract traditional entities, CRF has been shown to be able to successfully extract other types of information, e.g. headers, citations and key phrases from research papers [2]. Given the success of CRF-based methods in such a diverse array of problems and languages [8], we consider them to be a good candidate for extracting data governance information.

CRF systems in the NLP literature are typically trained and used on formal and well-formatted texts like news articles. There has been less attention on informal text, e.g. Slack chat logs. Informal text characteristics such as incomplete sentences, non-standard capitalisation and misspellings generally lead to a loss of accuracy for NER systems. There are some papers on the application of NER systems to informal texts, typically on social media. For example, [5] investigates the main sources of error in extracting entities in tweets, and how these errors could be addressed. It found that non-standard capitalisation had a particularly negative impact on NER performance, with greater impact than slang or abbreviations. It investigated the use of part-of-speech tagging and normalisation to reduce the impact of noise in tweets, but ultimately found that precision and recall scores remained low using NER standard algorithms. Similarly, [3] explores the use of word representations to improve the effectiveness of a NER in labelling Twitter messages. This work found that general NER systems performed very poorly in labelling tweets.

4   Data Governance Knowledge Extraction Approach

Before integrating the knowledge extraction tool into the Slack channel as a bot it was necessary to train and evaluate a NER system capable of detecting the data governance entities defined by the new open data governance ontology based upon the Collibra data governance operating model and the state of the art semantic web data governance ontologies.

4.1   Knowledge Architecture

The knowledge model used to classify the data governance entities and relationships detected in the Slack channel was based upon the Collibra data governance operating model but generalised as an OWL ontology.

Collibra Data Governance Operating Model. This Model[1] has been implemented by hundreds of companies. It establishes the foundation for and drives all data stewardship and data management activities. It has three sub-categories each addressing a key design question.

1. What is to be governed in terms of Structural Concepts, including asset types, (complex) relation types, attribute types.
2. Who governs it, in terms of Organisational Concepts. These include Communities, domains, users, user groups.
3. How is it to be governed in terms of Execution and Monitoring Concepts, including role types, status types and workflow definitions.

Data stewardship activities align and coordinate data management operations. Data Management concerns the integration of stewardship activities with third-party applications (such as data profilers, scanners, metadata repositories, etc.). In this work we only extracted (data) Asset Types. An Asset is the capital building block in data governance. An Asset Type formally defines the semantics of an asset. There core asset types, or asset classes as illustrated below. An asset captures the authoritative lifecycle metadata, in terms of attributes and relations with other assets, for one of the following five classes of assets:

- a governance asset (such as a policy or data quality rule): e.g., 'Customer Data Protection Policy' is the name of an asset of type 'Policy';
- a business asset (such as a business term or metric): e.g., 'Client' is the name of an asset of type 'Business Term';
- a data asset (such as e.g., reports or predictive models): e.g., 'first_name' is the name of an asset of type 'Column';
- a technology asset (such as a database or system): e.g., 'CRM' is the name of an asset of type 'System';
- an issue (such as a data quality issue): e.g., 'Customer Lifetime Value Report data is of too low quality' is the name for an asset of type 'Data Issue'.

The Open Data Governance Ontology (odgov). Conversion of the entire Collibra Data Governance Operating Model into an OWL ontology is a large task beyond the scope of this paper. However here we have created the first upper data governance ontology that serves the knowledge extraction and annotation needs of the data governance NER system.

This required the creation of eight main OWL classes (GovernanceAsset, BusinessAsset, DataAsset, TechnologyAsset, Role, Issue, and User) and parent

---

[1] https://university.collibra.com/courses/introduction-to-the-operating-model-5-x/.

classes for Assets and data governance execution and monitoring concepts. In addition a data management task class was created to hold the frequent references to data management activities (e.g. importing, copying, and backing up data) that appear in the Slack channel. This last class was an extension to Collibra data governance operating model as these activities are not separately modelled from business processes within that model. In addition three relation types from the Collibra model are included: the generic relation between assets, the uses asset relation and the is governed by relation.

Then these upper data governance terms were linked to the W3C provenance ontology by defining all odgov:Asset as subclasses of prov:entity, odgov:DataAssets as subclasses of dataid:dataset, dgov:DataManagementTask as a subclass of prov:Activity and odgov:User as a subclass of prov:Activity. Then a set of machine-readable metadata fields were defined so that the ontology is publishable via the live OWL documentation (LODE) environment. The final ontology and html documentation is available on the web[2].

4.2   NLP/NER Toolchain

Stanford NER [6] was used for the experiments reported in this paper. It is a widely used open source implementation of a CRF system that performs well with minimal fine-tuning requirements as it includes many built in feature extractors to enhance performance. The Collibra slack chat dump was tokenised using the Stanford Tokeniser (part of the Stanford CoreNLP toolkit [9]). In addition, the authors developed Python scripts for additional data pre-processing, conversion, experiment automation and evaluation. We have made these scripts available online[3]. The annotation of the chat dump was done through the Brat annotation tool by the authors. Section 5.1 details the annotation scheme.

5   Evaluation

We evaluated the effectiveness of the NER system at extracting data governance information from a real Slack chat channel. Section 5.1 describes the slack chat dataset and the scheme used to annotate it. Next we present the experimental protocol. The results (Sect. 5.3) show the accuracy of the NER system varies according to the actual Data Governance Information Category it seeks to predict. We present a correlation analysis to explain these variations.

5.1   Data Annotation

The test dataset is a raw dump of messages from Collibra's Data Governance team Slack. The resulting data consisted of 7,022 messages totalling about 300,000 tokens. These messages were first filtered to detect those most directly

---

[2] http://theme-e.adaptcentre.ie/odgov.
[3] https://github.com/simonq80/datagovernancenter.

related to data governance using Shah et al.'s binary classifier [11], this produced a final dataset of 800 messages, totalling 4,749 tokens. The entities annotated in the dataset were based on our data governance ontology detailed earlier. This approach used the initial entity types: Governance Assets(Gov), Business Assets(Bus), Data Assets(Data), Technology Assets(Tech), Governance Roles(Role), Users(User) and Issues(Issue). However, upon annotating a sample of the dataset with this scheme, the Business Asset class was found to be overloaded and an additional entity types was used: Dmtask to label text representing a data management task, such as upgrading or backing up a database. The actual annotation work was conducted by the authors using the BRAT annotation tool. The number of annotated tokens for each data governance entity was as follows: Governance Assets 182, Business Assets 196, Data Assets 503, Technology Assets 236, Users 153, Governance Roles 14 and Issues 310 for a total of 1738 word tokens. Of the total 4,749 tokens, 3,011 were not related.

5.2 Experimental Protocol

We evaluate the accuracy of our system using standard precision, recall and F-1 scores, which are commonly used for evaluating NER systems. We compute these scores on each entity type as well as overall scores for all categories.

The computation of these scores require the dataset to be partitioned into training and test sets. In order to produce robust evaluation scores, we followed the k-fold cross validation evaluation scheme. Under this scheme, the dataset is divided into k equally sized sections. Each of the k sections is used as the test set once, with the remaining $k-1$ sections used as the training set. This results in k test results which are averaged to get a performance estimate of the model. Larger values of k result in a smaller test set and larger training set for each fold. Cross validation tends to have low variance and generally low bias.

10-fold cross validation (i.e. $k = 10$) is typically used as it is generally considered to be optimal for reducing bias and variance for accuracy estimation. However, due to the small size of our dataset, test portions tended to be too small in 10-fold cross validation to represent all Data Governance Information Categories reliably. So we experimented as well with 5- and 4-fold cross validation variants and 4-fold validation was found to have the best F1 score. Evaluation results for these experiments are presented in the following section.

5.3 Results

Results for each Data Governance Information category from 4-fold cross-validation can be seen Table 1. Across all metrics, the NER performed by far the best on the User category. It also performed well on both Data and Tech, achieving relatively high precision, but with worse performance in recall. Aside from Role, which was never predicted due to its rarity in the dataset (hence the N/A values in the table), the NER performed the worst on the Gov, Issue and Bus categories, all of which had very low recall and relatively low precision. With the exception of User, all entity types had notably higher precision than recall.

Table 1. 4-fold cross-validation results per category

Category	Precision	Recall	F-1 Score
Bus	0.3611	0.0663	0.1121
Data	0.6139	0.493	0.5469
Dmtask	0.4918	0.2083	0.2927
Gov	0.3684	0.0385	0.0697
Issue	0.3889	0.0675	0.1151
Role	N/A	0.0000	N/A
Tech	0.6423	0.3347	0.4401
User	0.8831	0.8889	0.886

Different Data Governance Information Categories perform differently. We find that this variation in performance correlates with the number of annotated instances for each category (the more instances a category has, the better its performance) as well as with its type-token ratio (the lower the category's type-token ration, the better its performance). We now look into these two correlations.

Number of Annotated Instances Per Category. As expected, Data Governance Information Categories that have more annotated instances in the dataset will tend perform better. This is simply because the CRF algorithm is exposed to more examples and is thus able to learn relevant features more reliably. Figure 2a plots this correlation for the F-1 measure (precision and recall show a similar correlation). The Pearson correlation coefficient is 0.32. A least-squares polynomial line is shown in the figure to make this correlation more visible.

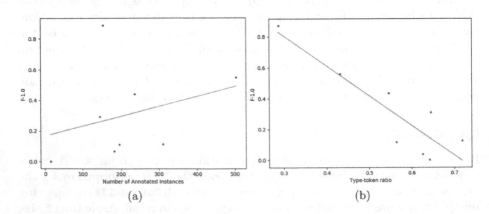

(a)   (b)

Fig. 2. Correlation between F-1 score and (a) the number of annotated instances of a category and (b) the type-token ratio of a category

Type-token ratio is the number of unique words (types) of a category divided by the total number of words (tokens) of that category. It is a measure of word diversity in each category: the higher the type-token ration, the more word diversity there is in the category. Categories with low type-token ratios tend to use more or less the same words (little word diversity). So it is not surprising that Fig. 2b shows a very strong negative correlation between the type-token ratio of categories and their F-1 score. The Pearson correlation coefficient is -0.89. Again, a least-squares polynomial line is shown to visualise the correlation. Precision and recall plots show similar correlations.

6   Conclusions and Future Work

This paper has demonstrated that CRF-based NER is a promising approach for extraction of data governance knowledge based on a new open upper ontology for data governance. Given the limitations of the current training data set (c. 5,000 annotated tokens) it is a positive result to see two categories of governance entity detected with over 0.6 precision and one at 0.88. The recall scores are poor, but we hope that precision is more important for the planned application as an interactive bot on the Slack channel system of engagement who must minimise their number of incorrect interventions to avoid frustrating the user.

References

1. Attard, J., Brennan, R.: A semantic data value vocabulary supporting data value assessment and measurement integration. In: Proceedings of 20th International Conference on Enterprise Information Systems, pp. 133–144. INSTICC, SciTePress (2018)
2. Augenstein, I., Das, M., Riedel, S., Vikraman, L., McCallum, A.: Semeval 2017 task 10: scienceIE-extracting keyphrases and relations from scientific publications. arXiv preprint arXiv:1704.02853 (2017)
3. Cherry, C., Guo, H.: The unreasonable effectiveness of word representations for Twitter named entity recognition. In: Proceedings of 2015 Conference of the North American Chapter of the Association for Computational Linguistics: Human Language Technologies, pp. 735–745 (2015)
4. De Leenheer, P., Debruyne, C., Peeters, J.: Towards social performance indicators for community-based ontology evolution. In: Workshop on Collaborative Construction, Management and Linking of Structured Knowledge at ISWC (2009)
5. Derczynski, L., et al.: Analysis of named entity recognition and linking for tweets. Inf. Process. Manag. **51**(2), 32–49 (2015)
6. Finkel, J.R., Grenager, T., Manning, C.: Incorporating non-local information into information extraction systems by Gibbs sampling. In: Proceedings of 43rd Annual Meeting of the Association for Computational Linguistics, pp. 363–370 (2005)
7. Lebo, T., et al.: PROV-O: the PROV ontology. Technical report (2012). http://www.w3.org/TR/prov-o/
8. Maldonado, A., et al.: Detection of verbal multi-word expressions via conditional random fields with syntactic dependency features and semantic re-ranking. In: Proceedings of 13th Workshop on Multiword Expressions, Valencia, pp. 114–120 (2017)

9. Manning, C.D., Surdeanu, M., Bauer, J., Finkel, J., Bethard, S.J., McClosky, D.: The Stanford CoreNLP natural language processing toolkit. In: Association for Computational Linguistics (ACL) System Demonstrations, pp. 55–60 (2014)
10. Moore, G.: Systems of engagement and the future of enterprise IT - a sea change in enterprise IT. Technical report, AIIM, Silver Spring, Maryland (2011)
11. Shah, J.: Utilizing natural language processing and artificial intelligence to identify plausible data requests on slack and linking it to Collibras system of record tool DGC. Technical report, Collibra (2017)

Factors of Efficient Semantic Web Application Development

Martin Ledvinka(✉), Miroslav Blaško, and Petr Křemen

Department of Cybernetics, Faculty of Electrical Engineering,
Czech Technical University in Prague, Prague 6 - Dejvice, Prague, Czech Republic
{martin.ledvinka,miroslav.blasko,petr.kremen}@fel.cvut.cz

Abstract. Creating domain-specific Linked Data applications is a complex endeavor as they need to work with ontological knowledge, consume/produce Linked Data and perform nontrivial business logic. In this work, we analyze several domain-specific Linked Data applications and introduce a set of features which influence the efficiency of development and maintenance of these applications. For each feature, we also list examples of software libraries supporting it.

Keywords: Object-oriented · Domain-specific · Linked Data Application

1 Introduction

Most of the Semantic Web applications to date fall into the category of generic tools like ontology editors or Linked Data publishing platforms [1]. Such applications are domain-independent and require their users to understand the underlying principles of the Semantic Web. The nature of these applications reflects also in the software tools upon which they are built. Thus, the most popular Semantic Web software libraries are triple stores like RDF4J [2], SPARQL query engines like Jena ARQ[1], ontology editors like Protége [3] and statement-based data access APIs like RDF4J API [2], Jena [4] or OWL API [5].

We claim that the Semantic Web can offer significant benefits also to users of domain-specific applications like enterprise and business software, content management systems or business intelligence solutions. Such benefits may reside in the support for *inference* based on an accurate *domain model*, implicit production and consumption of machine readable *Linked Data* (LD) or advanced data integration. However, hand in hand with applications must also come the tools which enable their development.

In this paper, we consider several domain-specific Linked Data-based applications. We analyze their architecture and, most importantly, the ways in which their semantic nature influences the design. Based on this analysis, we define a set of features or typical tasks a developer of such an application needs to

---

[1] https://jena.apache.org/documentation/query/, accessed 2018-06-11.

© Springer Nature Switzerland AG 2018
H. Panetto et al. (Eds.): OTM 2018 Conferences, LNCS 11230, pp. 565–572, 2018.
https://doi.org/10.1007/978-3-030-02671-4_35

accomplish. For each of these features, we list a few example software libraries which support them.

The remainder of this work is structured as follows: Sect. 2 presents an analysis of the selected applications. Section 3 presents the discovered features. Section 4 briefly reviews related work and Sect. 5 concludes the paper.

2   Analysis of Domain-Specific Linked Data Applications

LD-based applications are often used in a read-only scenario where the application can be queried but it is not possible to directly create new data. For instance, in a study conducted by Barbosa et al. [6], 78% of the examined articles discuss systems providing access to semantic data. Nevertheless, our interest is in both read only and data modifying applications.

We examined eight LD-based applications – four of them were developed by creators around the world, their source code is not available but their description can be used to get an understanding of functions they provide and support they need. The other four were developed by ourselves or with our participation and we have full access to their source code and know the details of their design and functions.

The following paragraphs provide a brief description of each of the examined applications.

Financial Data Integrating Application developed by O'Riain et al. [7] integrates financial and company data from multiple heterogeneous (mostly non-RDF) sources. Its users are not able to modify the data, it is used to query and visualize knowledge about companies, publicly available financial statements, news regarding the companies etc.

The system provides keyword search, mash ups of data about a company from different sources, visualization using various plots or faceted display.

BBC Content Publishing and Linking. A well-known example of using Linked Data to improve data structure and usability is BBC's content linking and integration [8], and data publishing[2]. The content integration and linking platform allows to transform data to RDF and interlink entities and documents with the help of external vocabularies such as the DBPedia ontology. In addition, it is able to semi-automatically annotate and link terms in documents. This way, entities mentioned in content from different domains can be connected. Then, the platform is able to generate topic pages, integrating content regarding one topic from various domains.

GetThere [9] is a system gathering and providing information about public transportation. It integrates data from semantic and non-semantic sources like timetables, geographical data, public transportation access point databases etc.

---

[2] https://bbc.in/1SLBRLO, accessed 2018-06-27.

In addition, a mobile application is used to gather real-time data about public transportation vehicle location.

The mobile application essentially serves two purposes – it provides users with information about public transportation services and in turn, once the user enters a public transportation vehicle, it is able to upload sensory data to the server, where it is used to ascertain the vehicle's current location and compare it to its expected schedule.

Accident Investigation Support Tool was created by Carvalho et al. [10] originally for NASA. This ontology-based system is used to manage findings during an accident investigation and provide investigators with easy access to this knowledge. Data entered into the system vary from textual documents to photos and videos. The system was, for example, used to support the investigation of the *Columbia* space shuttle accident.

Reporting Tool[3] is a system supporting safety management in high risk industries. Its current domain is aviation safety, but the concept is general enough to support, for example, marine transportation, power plants etc. The tool allows users to create *occurrence reports* where they record events potentially affecting safety in the domain and are able to further investigate them. The tool is then able to provide statistical data about most common causes of occurrences, their severity and so on.

SISel [11] grew from the roots of the Reporting Tool. Its target user group are civil aviation authorities. It is able to integrate safety occurrence reports with audit data and safety issues (commonly occurring safety patterns), providing a more comprehensive view of the safety situation. Besides data entered into the system by its users, it also has to import data from international occurrence report repositories like ECCAIRS[4].

Dataset Dashboard. The problem of many Linked Data datasets is that very little is known about their content. Dataset Dashboard [12] is an online application for exploration of SPARQL endpoints. It is based on the notion of *dataset descriptors* which characterize the dataset content and structure. The application is able to generate these descriptors, providing users with information about datasets of their choosing.

Study Manager [13] is an ontology-based manager for clinical trials. Its model consists of a static part concerning user and organization management and a dynamic part which deals with actual studies. Each type of study requires the users to enter different data, so declaratively described forms are used for the individual studies. UI and code handling these forms are then generated by the application at runtime.

---

[3] https://github.com/kbss-cvut/reporting-tool, accessed 2018-08-29.
[4] http://eccairsportal.jrc.ec.europa.eu/, access 2018-08-29.

3   Features for Linked Data Application Development

We generalize the examined systems into a class of information systems called *Domain-specific Linked Data Applications* (DSLDAs). Such applications are primarily based on Linked Data, they produce Linked Data and use them internally. They provide web services for integration with other systems, whether these are LD-based or not. They can integrate data from multiple heterogeneous data sources but the primary storage is a triple store. They are based on a domain-specific ontology which may reuse external ontologies/vocabularies to facilitate system interoperability. Their business logic is nontrivial and may encompass both reading and editing data. This type of architecture is visualized in Fig. 1.

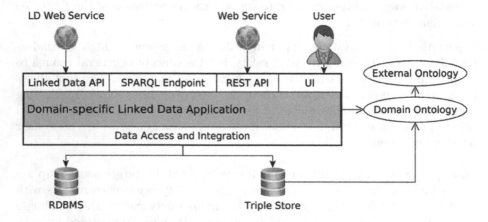

Fig. 1. DSLDA architecture. Arrows with a full head represent interaction direction, arrows with an open head represent ontology dependence.

According to project EUCLID [14], a DSLDA may be classified as using Semantic Web technologies *intrinsically*, it *produces* and *consumes* Linked Data, it may use both *shallow* (RDF(S)) and *strong* (OWL) models and can be both *isolated* and *integrated* in terms of vocabulary interconnection.

Based on an analysis of the applications presented above, we have identified a set of features which influence the efficiency of developing DSLDAs and, in some cases, could be relevant to the actual functionality of the system as well. The features are introduced below together with examples of software libraries fulfilling them. Our experience with developing ontology-based applications has led us to create several software libraries which support most of the listed features. These libraries are *highlighted*.

F1 – Domain-Specific Data Access Paradigm. As discussed in [15], Linked Data may be accessed using either domain-independent or domain-specific libraries. While domain-independent access (using, for instance, Jena [4] or RDF4J [2]) is generic and able to accommodate any kind of domain model, it also requires a significantly larger amount of code and is more difficult to maintain [16]. For domain-specific applications, the developer would either end up transforming the statements to domain objects manually, or they would have to write the application business logic against the statement-based API, which is extremely cumbersome and error prone. Thus, for the purpose of DSLDA development, we consider domain-specific data access libraries more efficient.

Supported by AliBaba [17], Empire [18], *JOPA* [16].

F2 – Static and Dynamic Domain Model. When building an information system in a complex domain, the domain model tends to change with time [19]. However, changing the object model requires modifications to the application code as well. Thus, it is handy to split the model into a *static* part, which is already settled and is not likely to change, and a *dynamic* part, where changes are frequent and is represented on the code level using some generic structure. As the DSLDA design evolves, portions of the dynamic model become static, providing more domain-specific business and user interface logic to the end users. Another case could be an application where a part of the model is highly dynamic and dependent on contextual information and creating a static mapping for it would be infeasible.

Supported by ActiveRDF [20], *JOPA*.

F3 – Data Provenance. Domain applications (and thus also DSLDAs) gather provenance metadata, e.g., author, last editor, date of creation, about their data in order to aid auditing and data provenance resolution. Semantic Web offers standards like the *reification* vocabulary [21] or PROV [22] to facilitate this task. Using a standardized approach allows the provenance data to be processed automatically by independent tools, e.g., when data origin is validated. Compare this approach to the approaches using relational databases, where vendor-specific mechanisms have to be used to create provenance data and query them.

Supported by *SPipes*[5].

F4 – Linked Data-Compatible API. The primary goal of Linked Data applications is usually to produce LD for others to consume. In order to do that, an API must be provided by the application. Although not strictly a Linked Data API (it does not satisfy the LD principles [1]), many applications provide a SPARQL endpoint to the consumers. A true Linked Data API can be, for instance, a Pubby server [23]. An important extension of plain Linked Data APIs, which are read-only, is the ability to modify the data as well. Using such APIs, DSLDA users can not only read but also author new data.

Supported by Carbon LDP[6], *JB4JSON-LD*[7], Pubby [23].

F5 – Quality Data Gathering. One of the key issues of user-entered data is their quality. The reason may be misinterpretation of the form field semantics, lack of contextual information or ambiguous input formats. Most of these reasons relate to the interaction between the user and the application form UI – an extensively

---

[5] https://kbss.felk.cvut.cz/web/kbss/s-pipes, accessed 2018-08-29.
[6] https://carbonldp.com/, accessed 2018-08-29.
[7] https://github.com/kbss-cvut/jb4jsonld, accessed 2018-08-29.

researched topic [24–26]. Introducing ontologies to the user during data gathering can provide form fields with clear semantics (e.g., type information, explanatory comments, historical data) and thus improve quality of the gathered data.

Supported by *SForms*[8].

F6 – Access to Inferred Data. The ability to *infer* implicit knowledge from explicit data is one of the biggest assets of expressive ontological languages. A properly built domain model expressed in a formal language like OWL 2 [27] may uncover hidden dependencies in the data. For example, causality chains in the Reporting Tool or related topics in BBC's content publishing platform. However, the software library providing access to the data needs to distinguish between asserted and inferred statements as inferred statements cannot be directly modified.

Supported by *JOPA*, OWL API [5], Jena [4].

4   Related Work

Literature concerning Linked Data-based application is relatively scarce. As a survey in [28] shows, most of documented Linked Data applications are in fact triple stores or data access libraries. Even rarer is literature on the design and development of LD-based applications. Hausenblas in [29] describes principles of building LD applications, mainly on top of existing non-RDF data. A comprehensive review of LD application architectures is also provided in [14].

On the other hand, besides specific features of the Semantic Web, one may, in developing DSLDAs, apply general design principles known from software engineering, e.g., Domain-driven Design [19] or design patterns [30].

5   Conclusions

We have examined several Linked Data-based applications. Based on this analysis, we have introduced a class of domain-specific Linked Data applications and discussed a set of features which influence the development of such applications.

In the future, a deeper analysis of different Semantic Web application architectural styles should be performed, so that the set of features influencing their development can be expanded and software libraries can be developed/extended to support these features. In addition, attention should be paid to the documentation and integration of Semantic Web software libraries with established tools and frameworks.

Acknowledgment. This work was supported by grant No. GA 16-09713S Efficient Exploration of Linked Data Cloud of the Grant Agency of the Czech Republic and by grant No. SGS16/229/OHK3/3T/13 Supporting ontological data quality in information systems of the Czech Technical University in Prague.

---

[8]   https://kbss.felk.cvut.cz/web/kbss/s-forms, accessed 2018-08-29.

References

1. Wood, D., Zaidman, M., Ruth, L., Hausenblas, M.: Linked Data: Structured Data on the Web. Manning Publications Co., Shelter Island (2014)
2. Broekstra, J., Kampman, A., van Harmelen, F.: Sesame: a generic architecture for storing and querying RDF and RDF schema. In: Proceedings of the First International Semantic Web Conference on the Semantic Web, pp. 54–68 (2002)
3. Protégé. http://protege.stanford.edu. Accessed 12 Feb 2017
4. Carroll, J.J., Dickinson, I., Dollin, C., Reynolds, D., Seaborne, A., Wilkinson, K.: Jena: implementing the semantic web recommendations. In: Proceedings of the 13th International World Wide Web Conference (Alternate Track Papers & Posters), pp. 74–83 (2004)
5. Horridge, M., Bechhofer, S.: The OWL API: a Java API for OWL ontologies. Semantic Web – Interoperability, Usability, Applicability (2011)
6. Barbosa, A., Bittencourt, I.I., Siqueira, S.W.M., de Amorim Silva, R., Calado, I.: The use of software tools in linked data publication and consumption: a systematic literature review. Int. J. Semant. Web Inf. Syst. **13**(4), 68–88 (2017). https://doi.org/10.4018/IJSWIS.2017100104
7. O'Riain, S., Harth, A., Curry, E.: Linked data driven information systems as an enabler for integrating financial data. In: Information Systems for Global Financial Markets: Emerging Developments and Effects, pp. 239–270. IGI Global (2012). https://doi.org/10.4018/978-1-61350-162-7.ch010
8. Kobilarov, G., et al.: Media meets semantic web – how the BBC uses DBpedia and linked data to make connections. In: Aroyo, L., et al. (eds.) ESWC 2009. LNCS, vol. 5554, pp. 723–737. Springer, Heidelberg (2009). https://doi.org/10.1007/978-3-642-02121-3_53
9. Corsar, D., Edwards, P., Nelson, J., Baillie, C., Papangelis, K., Velaga, N.: Linking open data and the crowd for real-time passenger information. Web Semant. **43**(C), 18–24 (2017). https://doi.org/10.1016/j.websem.2017.02.002
10. Carvalho, R.E., Williams, J., Sturken, I., Keller, R., Panontin, T.: Investigation organizer: the development and testing of a web-based tool to support mishap investigations. In: 2005 IEEE Aerospace Conference, pp. 89–98, March 2005. https://doi.org/10.1109/AERO.2005.1559302
11. Ledvinka, M., Křemen, P., Kostov, B., Blaško, M.: SISel: aviation safety powered by semantic technologies. In: Data a znalosti 2017, pp. 77–82 (2017). https://daz2017.kiv.zcu.cz/data/DaZ2017-Sbornik-final.pdf
12. Křemen, P., Saeeda, L., Blaško, M., Med, M.: Dataset dashboard – a SPARQL endpoint explorer. In: CEUR Workshop Proceedings of Fourth International Workshop on Visualization and Interaction for Ontologies and Linked Data, VOILA 2018, October 2018 (to appear)
13. Klíma, T.: Sémantický manažer prospektivní klinické studie. B.S. thesis, České vysoké učení technické v Praze. Vypočetní a informační centrum (2018)
14. EUCLID: Building Linked Data Applications (2014). http://euclid-project.eu/modules/chapter5.html. Accessed 25 June 2018
15. Křemen, P., Kouba, Z.: Ontology-driven information system design. IEEE Trans. Syst. Man Cybern.: Part C **42**(3), 334–344 (2012)
16. Ledvinka, M., Křemen, P.: JOPA: accessing ontologies in an object-oriented way. In: Proceedings of the 17th International Conference on Enterprise Information Systems (2015)

17. Leigh, J.: AliBaba (2007). https://bitbucket.org/openrdf/alibaba/. Accessed 2 Jan 2018
18. Grove, M.: Empire: RDF & SPARQL Meet JPA. semanticweb.com, April 2010. http://semanticweb.com/empire-rdf-sparql-meet-jpa_b15617
19. Evans, E.: Domain-Driven Design: Tacking Complexity in the Heart of Software. Addison-Wesley Longman Publishing Co., Inc., Boston (2003)
20. Oren, E., Heitmann, B., Decker, S.: ActiveRDF: embedding SemanticWeb data into object-oriented languages. Web Semant.: Sci. Serv. Agents World Wide Web 6(3) (2008). https://doi.org/10.1016/j.websem.2008.04.003
21. Brickley, D., Guha, R.V.: RDF schema 1.1. W3C Recommendation (2014)
22. Belhajjame, K., et al.: PROV-O: the PROV ontology. Technical report (2012). http://www.w3.org/TR/prov-o/
23. Cyganiak, R., Bizer, C.: Pubby – a linked data frontend for SPARQL endpoints (2007). http://wifo5-03.informatik.uni-mannheim.de/pubby/. Accessed 30 June 2018
24. Graesser, A.C., Black, J.B.: The Psychology of Questions. Routledge, Abingdon (2017)
25. Wright, P.: Strategy and tactics in the design of forms. Visible Lang. 14(2), 151–193 (1980)
26. Jansen, C., Steehouder, M.: Forms as a source of communication problems. J. Tech. Writ. Commun. 22(2), 179–194 (1992)
27. Motik, B., Parsia, B., Patel-Schneider, P.F.: OWL 2 web ontology language structural specification and functional-style syntax. W3C Recommendation (2009)
28. Heitmann, B., Cyganiak, R., Hayes, C., Decker, S.: Architecture of linked data applications. In: Linked Data Management, pp. 69–91 (2014). https://doi.org/10.1201/b16859-5
29. Hausenblas, M.: Exploiting linked data to build web applications. IEEE Internet Comput. 13(4), 68–73 (2009). https://doi.org/10.1109/MIC.2009.79
30. Gamma, E., Helm, R., Johnson, R., Vlissides, J.: Design Patterns: Elements of Reusable Object-Oriented Software. Addison-Wesley Longman Publishing Co., Inc., Boston (1995)

Evaluating a Faceted Search Index
for Graph Data

Vidar Klungre[(✉)] and Martin Giese

University of Oslo, Oslo, Norway
vidarkl@ifi.uio.no

Abstract. We discuss the problem of implementing real-time faceted search interfaces over graph data, specifically the "value suggestion problem" of presenting the user with options that makes sense in the context of a partially constructed query. For queries that include many object properties, this task is computationally expensive. We show that good approximations to the value suggestion problem can be achieved by only looking at parts of queries, and we present an index structure that supports this approximation and is designed to scale gracefully to both very large datasets and complex queries. In a series of experiments, we show that the loss of accuracy is often minor, and additional accuracy can in many cases be achieved with a modest increase of index size.

1 Introduction

Faceted search [7] is a popular search and exploration paradigm (used by e.g. Ebay), which enables users to extract information from structured data sources without needing to know the relevant formal query language. Systems providing faceted search present multiple orthogonal dimensions (facets) of the data to the user, and allows him to apply or remove filters via an intuitive UI. As this is done, the system immediately updates the lists of results and new filter suggestions. To support this functionality, the system needs fast access to the underlying data. This is often provided by specialised software like e.g Lucene, Sphinx or Elasticsearch, which provides better performance for the queries required by faceted search than standard triple stores and RDB-based implementations.

In this paper we focus on ontology-based *Visual query systems* (VQSs) like Rhizomer [2], SemFacet [1], and OptiqueVQS [5]. The purpose of these systems is to allow non-experts to construct SPARQL queries and execute them over RDF-graphs. A good overview of VQSs and their target audience is described in [6]. Most VQSs provide an intuitive UI, and allow the user to apply or remove filters on different facets, similar to standard faceted search systems. For each variable in the SPARQL query, every datatype property is considered to be a facet. Furthermore, object properties are used to connect the variables, and they allow the user to construct complex *graph queries*. This is a difference from standard faceted search, where only one variable of exactly one type is considered.

In particular we look at one specific feature of faceted search: The ability to suggest reasonable filter values for each facet. One way of doing this, is to

© Springer Nature Switzerland AG 2018
H. Panetto et al. (Eds.): OTM 2018 Conferences, LNCS 11230, pp. 573–583, 2018.
https://doi.org/10.1007/978-3-030-02671-4_36

pre-compute and present all the values from the RDF-graph that are related to the given datatype property. This method is very straightforward, and since it does not depend on the current state of the query, all computations can be done outside the query session starts. However, some of these values may feel superfluous to the user, because they are incompatible with existing filters. So instead we aim for what we call *adaptive value suggestions*:

> **Adaptive Value Suggestion:** Calculate and suggest the complete set of filter values for a facet that are compatible with both the existing filters and underlying data, in order to avoid a query that returns no results.

Unfortunately, the indices used to acheive adaptive value suggestions for faceted search, like Lucene, do not support querying graph data. The obvious way of achieving this over the original graph data (i.e. without an index) requires running the whole partial query once for every facet (see $\mathcal{S}_o$ in Sect. 2). For very large datasets and queries with many joins, this will be too slow. Some of the queries constructed with OptiqueVQS include up to 9 object properties, and are intended to be run over data stores of several PB. Even with very fast hardware, these queries cannot be executed within tenths of seconds as required for interactive systems. It becomes clear that some kind of custom-built solution is needed to achieve our goal sufficiently fast.

Based on the visual query system OptiqueVQS [5], we have devised a system that combines faceted search with graph queries, and that uses an indexing structure for suggesting facet values that can easily be scaled out arbitrarily. In return, it compromises some accuracy in the presented values, but in a highly configurable manner.

Formal Framework. For the purpose of this paper, we work with a number of simplified notions of ontology, dataset, and query. These are less general than OWL, RDF, and SPARQL, respectively, but they cover the essential notions for VQSs that we require. See [3] and [4] for a more complete description and examples.

We assume that the VQS supports tree-shaped conjunctive queries Q that conforms to the given ontology $\mathcal{O}$. In addition each variable must be associated with either a concept in $\mathcal{O}$ (concept variables), or a data type (datatype variables). Filters are specified by a filter function $\mathcal{F}$ that returns a set of values for each datatype variable in Q. We do not include an "optional" operator, i.e. all variables of Q have to be bound. Furthermore, we assume that the system is given a dataset (RDF graph) $\mathcal{D}$, and when the query is finished, he will be running it over $\mathcal{D}$ in order to retrieve results. We use $Ans(Q, \mathcal{D})$ to denote the set of tuples we get by running Q over $\mathcal{D}$. We also assume that the user can select and focus on one specific variable v of Q, called the *focus variable*. It is convenient to define Q as a tree rooted in v (possibly reversing the direction of some triples), and for the reminder of this paper we assume this is the case. And for convenience we also let $\mathcal{C}$ denote the type of v.

During query construction, the user is presented with a list of suggestions for every relevant property t of v. These suggestions are based on the current state of the session, i.e Q, in addition to the underlying dataset $\mathcal{D}$. Before we continue, we need to formalize the idea of a *suggestion function*:

Definition 1. *Suggestion function:* *A suggestion function S takes as input a dataset $\mathcal{D}$, a query Q, and some datatype property t linked to the focus variable v of Q, and returns a set of literal values $Sugg = S(\mathcal{D}, Q, t)$.*

By selecting values $X \subseteq Sugg$, the user modifies the filter related to w, where w is the datatype variable linked to v via t. I.e. Q is updated to $Q \wedge t(v, w)$, and $\mathcal{F}(w) = X$. Notice that the Definition 1 does not restrict S on neither its computation time nor the quality of suggested values. However, it should be clear by now that we are looking for functions that return adaptive value suggestions without spending so much time that it ruins the user experience of the VQS. In this work we target the following problem:

Value Suggestion Problem. Find a suggestion function S that
1. is efficiently enough for interactive use, even for large $\mathcal{D}$ and complex Q
2. includes all values, that can be filtered on without making the answer set empty, i.e. $Ans(Q \wedge t(v, x), \mathcal{D}) \neq \emptyset \implies x \in S(\mathcal{D}, Q, t)$ for all values s in $\mathcal{D}$
3. includes as few values as possible that will make the answer set empty, i.e. $S(\mathcal{D}, Q, t)$ is as small as possible while satisfying condition 2.

Condition 1 is necessary because suggestions have to be calculated after every user interaction with the UI, and the user should not have to wait for suggestions. So they have to be calculated efficiently, and scale with respect to both $\mathcal{D}$ and Q. The second condition formalizes the idea that all values that are compatible with the partial query should also be suggested to the user. Otherwise, some sensible queries could not be constructed. I.e. we want perfect *recall*. Finally, condition 3 reflects that we want to suggest as few options as possible to the user that are incompatible with the partial query. I.e. the suggestion function should be as *precise* as possible. These three conditions are in conflict, and as indicated in the problem description, we consider conditions 1 and 2 to be non-negotiable.

2   Suggestion Functions and Indexing

Optimal Suggestion Function S_o. Based on standard faceted search systems, we will now define what we consider to be the gold standard for the value suggestion problem (with respect to accuracy), namely the *optimal suggestion function S_o*:

$$S_o(\mathcal{D}, Q, t) = Ans(Q_o(x), \mathcal{D}) \text{ where } Q_o(x) = Q \wedge t(v, x).$$

It considers both the underlying dataset $\mathcal{D}$ and the partial query Q, and calculates suggestions that never lead the user into a combination of filters that are too restrictive, i.e. it returns adaptive value suggestions. Unfortunately, $\mathcal{S}_o$ does not scale for large Q and $\mathcal{D}$, because it has to calculate the answers to the query $Q_o(x) = Q \wedge t(v,x)$, which is more complex than Q itself.

Range-Based Suggestion Function $\mathcal{S}_r$. Another important suggestion function is the function that computes suggestions based only on the value range of t for instances of type $\mathcal{C}$ found in $\mathcal{D}$. We call this function the *range-based suggestion function $\mathcal{S}_r$*:

$$\mathcal{S}_r(\mathcal{D}, Q, t) = Ans(Q_r(x), \mathcal{D}) \text{ where } Q_r(x) = \mathcal{C}(v) \wedge t(v,x).$$

Notice that $\mathcal{C}$ and t are the only two parameters used by $\mathcal{S}_r$ that change during the query session: $\mathcal{D}$ is fixed during the session, and except for the focus concept $\mathcal{C}$, Q is just ignored. This means that we can calculate the suggestion set for each possible combination of $\mathcal{C}$ and t offline, and providing suggestions is then just a matter of fetching the correct pre-calculated set. The number of such combinations is limited, and Q_r is a very simple query, so any system based on $\mathcal{S}_r$ is efficient w.r.t. both time and space.

Approximate Suggestion Function $\mathcal{S}_a$. The optimal suggestion function $\mathcal{S}_o$ is too costly to compute in practice, while the range-based function, on the other hand, is quite inaccurate but can be pre-computed with reasonable effort. There is a gap between these two suggestion functions, and we now present a family of approximate suggestion functions $\mathcal{S}_a$ to fill this gap.

Each member $\mathcal{S}_a^{\mathcal{Z}}$ of $\mathcal{S}_a$ is configured by what we call a *facet configuration* $\mathcal{Z}$, which is a function returning one tree-shaped query (with root of type $\mathcal{C}$) $\mathcal{Z}_{\mathcal{C}}$ for every concept $\mathcal{C}$. We call $\mathcal{Z}_{\mathcal{C}}$ the *concept configuration* of $\mathcal{C}$. Now, given Q and the corresponding focus concept $\mathcal{C}$, $\mathcal{S}_a^{\mathcal{Z}}$ computes a pruned version of Q: $Q_{pr} = Q \cap \mathcal{Z}_{\mathcal{C}}$. Q_{pr} is then used together with the underlying dataset $\mathcal{D}$ to calculate value suggestions:

$$\mathcal{S}_a^{\mathcal{Z}}(\mathcal{D}, Q, t) = Ans(Q_a(x), \mathcal{D}) \text{ where } Q_a(x) = Q_{pr} \wedge t(v,x) = Q \cap \mathcal{Z}_{\mathcal{C}} \wedge t(v,x).$$

Intuitively the concept configuration $\mathcal{Z}_{\mathcal{C}}$ just defines what to consider when calculating suggestions. Every part of Q which is not covered by $\mathcal{Z}_{\mathcal{C}}$ is simply ignored, and removed as the intersection $Q \cap \mathcal{Z}_{\mathcal{C}}$ is calculated.

The most aggressive member of $\mathcal{S}_a$ is the suggestion function defined by concept configurations that only contains the root, i.e. $\mathcal{Z}_{\mathcal{C}} = \mathcal{C}(v)$ for all concepts $\mathcal{C}$. This member will actually return $Q_{pr} = \mathcal{C}(v)$ for any partial query given to it, regardless of its shape, size and focus concept. But this means that $Q_a(x) = \mathcal{C}(v) \wedge t(v,x) = Q_r(x)$, so this particular member of $\mathcal{S}_a$ returns exactly the same suggestions as $\mathcal{S}_r$. And in fact, the range-based suggestion function is just the special case of $\mathcal{S}_a$ where only the root of the partial query is considered, and everything else is ignored.

Now let us consider the opposite case: instances of $\mathcal{S}_a$ with very large concept configurations. If the partial query is completely covered by the tree defined by the concept configuration i.e. $\mathcal{Z}_\mathcal{C} \subseteq Q$, we get $Q_{pr} = Q$. Hence $Q_a(x) = Q \wedge t(v, x) = Q_o(x)$, which shows that $\mathcal{S}_o$ is the limit case of $\mathcal{S}_a$ for configurations that cover all possible queries. In general, for every partial query Q and facet configuration $\mathcal{Z}$, the following holds:

$$Q \subseteq Q_{pr} \subseteq \mathcal{C}(v) \Rightarrow Q_o \subseteq Q_a \subseteq Q_r \Rightarrow \mathcal{S}_o \subseteq \mathcal{S}_a^{\mathcal{Z}} \subseteq \mathcal{S}_r. \tag{1}$$

As we focus on a certain query, we can ignore large parts of the facet configuration $\mathcal{Z}$, since only one concept configuration $\mathcal{Z}_\mathcal{C}$ is needed to calculate value suggestions. In some cases, we will therefore use $\mathcal{S}_a^{\mathcal{Z}_\mathcal{C}}$ instead of $\mathcal{S}_a^{\mathcal{Z}}$, as short hand notation. Similarly, we may only use the word "configuration" if it is clear whether we mean "facet configuration" or "concept configuration".

Index Structure for $\mathcal{S}_a$. As seen above, $\mathcal{S}_a$ reduces the complexity of calculating suggestions by only considering Q_{pr} instead of Q. This will often reduce the query execution time, but it is not guaranteed to be good enough for our purpose: If Q_{pr} combines several concepts, it will result in bad user experience due to the time consuming join operations it requires.

The solution to this problem is to pre-compute all joins covered by the facet configuration $\mathcal{Z}$, and store the results in an index structure. The system can then execute Q_a over this index structure instead of the original dataset $\mathcal{D}$, in order to retrieve answers fast enough. It is important though, that the final constructed query is executed over the original dataset. $\mathcal{S}_a$ and its index should only be used to support adaptive value suggestion, not to answer the user's final information need.

The index is guaranteed to contain all the data needed to answer Q_a since they both are limited by the variables defined by $\mathcal{Z}_\mathcal{C}$. Notice that constructing such an index would not be possible if we wanted a perfect system described by $\mathcal{S}_o$ – it is impossible to construct an index that fits all the data needed to cover any possible query, because there are infinitely many of them. By using $\mathcal{S}_a$, we only need to consider Q_{pr}, which is limited by $\mathcal{Z}_\mathcal{C}$, hence pre-computing and indexing is possible.

We now describe how to construct and use the index. It will consist of multiple tables – one for each concept $\mathcal{C}$. Each table is based on the corresponding concept configuration $\mathcal{Z}_\mathcal{C}$, and is constructed as follows:

1. One column is added for each variable in the query defined by $\mathcal{Z}_\mathcal{C}$.
2. One row is added for each *distinct* tuple of $\mathrm{Ans}(\mathcal{Z}_\mathcal{C}', \mathcal{D})$, where $\mathcal{Z}_\mathcal{C}'$ is a modified version of $\mathcal{Z}_\mathcal{C}$, where everything except for the root node is made optional.

The result is a large denormalized table containing all the data that is covered by $\mathcal{Z}_\mathcal{C}$. By using the optional version $\mathcal{Z}_\mathcal{C}'$ instead of $\mathcal{Z}_\mathcal{C}$ directly, we ensure that we also get the data that is just partly covered by $\mathcal{Z}_\mathcal{C}$.

Answering Q_a over this table is then just a simple table scan, and the query response time can be reduced to a satisfactory level by indexing the columns and/or parallellizing the storage and processing, similar to what state of the art search engines do. Such scaling out is much easier for a single pre-joined table than for relational or graph storage. But it requires the pruning defined by a fixed configuration, which is precisely the point of our approximate suggestion functions.

With data stored denormalized, we essentially have the same situation as for standard faceted search with only one concept: We just act like every column (i.e. variable of the configuration) is a facet. This means that we can achieve adaptive value suggestions (over the variables in the configuration) with the same performance as standard faceted search systems by simply using the same underlying search engine technology.

Earlier we stated that $\mathcal{Z}_\mathcal{C} = \mathcal{C}(v)$ is the smallest possible concept configuration one can use for $\mathcal{S}_a$. This is true if we use the original dataset, but not if we use the index, because we need to answer $\mathcal{C}(v) \wedge t(v, x)$ for each datatype property t we want suggestions for, which cannot be done if a data column for t does not exist. We want to provide suggestions for each local datatype property $t \in T$, hence $\mathcal{Z}_\mathcal{C} = \mathcal{C}(v) \wedge \bigwedge_{t_i \in T} t_i(v, x_i)$ is the smallest configuration we allow.

With the index construction method described above, we get one column containing only URIs for each concept variable included in the concept configuration. But this is just a waste of space, since only filtering on datatype variables are allowed. So instead of storing the full URI, we use a boolean value to indicate whether an instance assignment exists or not. This reduces the index size considerably, compared to the case where all URIs are stored, because multiple rows where only one URI differs can now be collapsed into only one row. In our first experiment, we explored how much the accuracy increases by adding another layer of these existential concepts nodes to the index, which is a comparatively cheap investment.

3   Evaluation

We have implemented a faceted search module for OptiqueVQS based on $\mathcal{S}_a$ and the index structure described in Sect. 2. Furthermore, we implemented both $\mathcal{S}_r$ and $\mathcal{S}_o$ in order to compare them to $\mathcal{S}_a$ in our experiments.

In Sect. 2 we argued that our system is at least as efficient (w.r.t. index access) as state of the art faceted search engines using only one concept, so we have not spent any effort on measuring the time our system uses. We have also not measured the performance of the index construction process, since it is not as time crucial as index access. In other words, we do not claim that our implementation is suited for systems that require real-time update. Instead, we explored how facet configurations of different size and shape affect the constructed index, and how accurately they can suggest values for different kinds of queries. In total we conducted two experiments with the goal of answering the following three questions about $\mathcal{S}_a$:

1. How does the accuracy increase as the size of $\mathcal{Z}_\mathcal{C}$ increases?
2. How much does the accuracy rise by adding existential concept variables to $\mathcal{Z}_\mathcal{C}$?
3. How much does the index size have to be increased in order to obtain a given increase in accuracy?

Dataset, Ontology and Queries. In the experiments we used the RDF version of the NPD Factpages[1] – a dataset covering details about oil and gas drilling activities in Norway. This dataset contains 2.342.597 triples, and it has a corresponding OWL ontology containing 209 concepts and 375 properties. The NPD Factpages is actually a RDB, containing information that all oil companies in Norway are legally required to report to the authorities. This means that the RDF version, which is generated from this RDB, is fairly complete and homogeneous. This is optimal for persons who want answers to complex queries. Among the different concepts we considered in our queries, each have on average 14.1 different outgoing datatype properties, and 6.4 outgoing object properties in NPD Factpages. The number of distinct individuals/literals each such property leads to is 572 on average (with a median of 12).

The query catalogue[2] we used for the experiments consists of complex queries covering a wide set of possible cases. It consists of 29 queries ranging from 5 to 8 concept variables and 0 to 12 datatype variables, and the corresponding result sets over the NPD dataset range from just 12 tuples, to over 5 million tuples.

Accuracy Measure. Providing the value suggestions is an information retrieval problem, where S_o defines the set of relevant values. We therefore use the well established measures of precision and recall to measure the accuracy of S_a (and S_r). From Eq. 1 we know that $S_o \cap S_a = S_o$ and $S_o \cap S_r = S_o$ which gives: $pre(S_a) = \frac{|S_o|}{|S_a|}$, $pre(S_r) = \frac{|S_o|}{|S_r|}$ and $rec(S_a) = rec(S_r) = 1$.

Both S_a and S_r have perfect recall. Hence, when evaluating these systems, only the precision matters, so in the reminder of this paper, we will use and mention precision instead of accuracy. Furthermore, since the user is exposed to several local datatype properties at the same time, and we want to do more high-level experiments on the system, we average the precision over all the local datatype properties.

So given Q, D, Z_C, we will use this average as the overall measure of precision. From Eq. 1, we can derive the following relationship between the precision of our three suggestion functions: $pre(S_r) \leq pre(S_a^Z) \leq pre(S_o) = 1$.

Test Cases and General Setup. In both of our experiments we ran multiple test cases, where each test case was based on one of the 29 queries from the query catalogue, and a generated concept configuration Z_C covered by the tree defined by this query. Since each test case only considers one query and one concept configuration, the index based on the configuration will only contain one table, so we use the number of cells in the table as a measure for index size. Value suggestions are then calculated by running Q_a over the table, and precision is calculated by comparing to S_o as explained above.

Notice that a real world scenario would be more complex than this. The success of a concept configuration and its corresponding table index would not

---

[1] https://gitlab.com/logid/npd-factpages.

[2] https://github.com/Alopex8064/npd-factpages-experiments.

only depend on the success of one single query, but rather a large set of possibly very different queries. One of our future goals is to develop methods for finding configurations that works well for a large set of queries.

Exp. 1 - Configuration Type/Size vs Precision. In Experiment 1 we wanted to show how the accuracy of $\mathcal{S}_a$ changes as configurations of different size and shape are used. To do this, we first generated a set of random "configurations cores" c for each query Q in the query catalogue. Each core consisted of one or more connected concept variables from Q, and was just used as a basis for generating two other concept configurations:

– $Dat(c)$: Every possible datatype property is added to the concept variables in c.
– $ObjDat(c)$: Every possible datatype property *and* object property is added to the concept variables in c.

The only difference between these two configurations, is that $ObjDat(c)$ contains one extra layer of concept variables. As explained earlier, it is relatively cheap (w.r.t. storage usage) to add these concept variables, but the precision will (potentially) increase by doing it. So the split between $Dat(c)$ and $ObjDat(c)$ was created in order to measure how much the precision increases, and thereby answering question 2.

Both $Dat(c)$ and $ObjDat(c)$ were used in one test each, and in general the following holds: $pre(\mathcal{S}_r) \leq pre(\mathcal{S}_a^{Dat(c)}) \leq pre(\mathcal{S}_a^{ObjDat(c)}) \leq pre(\mathcal{S}_o) = 1$. After running through every test case, the results were grouped by both the configuration type (Dat or $ObjDat$) and the size of the configuration, where the size of a configuration is defined by the number of concept variables in the configuration core c. Finally the average precision of each group was calculated and the results visualized.

Figure 1 displays the average precision for all the queries of size 6 (15 of the 29 queries). Similar charts for queries of size 5, 7 and 8 are omitted from the paper, but can be found on Github[3] together with charts for each individual query.

The yellow line shows the precision of the range-based function $\mathcal{S}_r$, which is always constant. Since this is the suggestion function with the lowest precision we consider, it acts as a baseline – marking the worst case scenario for $\mathcal{S}_a$. The blue and red curves show the average precision of $\mathcal{S}_a^{Dat}$ and $\mathcal{S}_a^{ObjDat}$ respectively. As expected, these two curves are non-decreasing and $pre(\mathcal{S}_a^{Dat}) \leq pre(\mathcal{S}_a^{ObjDat})$ for all configuration sizes.

It is worth noting the relatively high precision of the range-based function. In our experiment, its precision ranged from 0.22 to 0.96 (depending on the query), with an average of 0.56. This does not sound too bad, but user studies on OptiqueVQS show that the users are not always satisfied with $\mathcal{S}_r$.

---

[3] https://github.com/Alopex8064/npd-factpages-experiments.

In the cases where key restrictions are associated with object properties, S_a^{ObjDat} performs much better than S_a^{Dat}. In fact, it quite often returns suggestions with perfect precision, which was the case for many of our individual queries. The average difference between S_a^{ObjDat} and S_a^{Dat}, shown in Fig. 1, indicates that it is worth adding this extra layer of object properties to the configuration, especially since the resulting increase in the index size is relatively small (one extra boolean column).

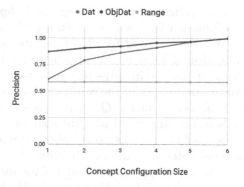

Fig. 1. Average precision of size 6 queries. (Color figure online)

Exp. 2 - Index Size vs Precision. In Experiment 2 we made a direct comparison between the index size and the precision. We did this by first making one test case for every query Q, and each possible configuration Z_C covered by it. Then, for each such test case, we calculated both the size of the table generated by Z_C, and the precision of $S_a^{Z_C}$. Finally we analysed and visualized the results.

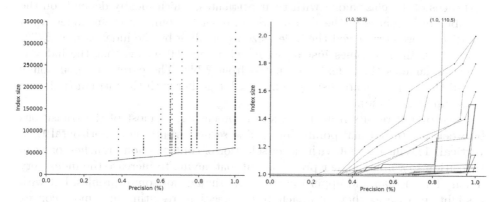

Fig. 2. Scatter plot for Query 6.2. Pareto optimal configurations are connected. Index size is not normalized.

Fig. 3. Pareto optimal configurations for all queries with median (red) and upper quartile (blue). Index size is normalized. (Color figure online)

Figure 2 shows the results for Query 6.2 visualized as a scatter plot, where each point represents a test case/concept configuration/index table. Some of the points are *pareto optimal*, which means that neither of the two dimensions (precision and index size) can be improved without weakening the other. These points are located in the bottom right part of the plot (smaller index and higher precision are better), and are connected by line segments. The frontier of pareto optimal points shows how large the index must be in order to achieve a given precision in a *best-case scenario*, i.e. when the configuration is chosen optimally.

We cannot *expect* to achieve results like this consistently, but it does give an indication of what might be achieved with an optimal choice of configuration. The fact that we investigate the best-case scenario also explains why it is sufficient to only consider the configurations covered by Q: For any configuration $\mathcal{Z}_C{}'$ with branches outside Q, there exists another concept configuration $\mathcal{Z}_C$ which leads to the same precision, but a smaller index. Visually, the set of all such test cases would appear as points above the already existing points, and hence not be candidates for pareto-optimality.

The set of pareto-optimal points for each query defines a monotonically increasing curve. Let $\mathcal{Z}_C^{min}$ and $\mathcal{Z}_C^{max}$ denote the configurations used for the first and last of these points. $\mathcal{Z}_C^{max}$ is the configurations that is isomorphic to Q. I.e. it fully covers Q, but it has no branches outside of it. The precision given by this configuration is perfect, but it also uses the largest index of the pareto-optimal configurations. $\mathcal{Z}_C^{min}$ on the other hand contains only the root and all local datatype properties. This is the smallest configuration that can provide value suggestions for each of the local datatype properties.

When we look at the pareto-optimal configurations for all the different queries, we see that the index size of $\mathcal{Z}_C^{min}$ differs depending on the focus concept of the query: we can't expect the index to become smaller than a table of the instances of the class along with their attributes, which mostly depends on the number of instances in the dataset. So in order to compare them under equal conditions, we normalized the index size by dividing by the index size of $\mathcal{Z}_C^{min}$. The y-axis then becomes just a factor, where e.g 2.0 means that the index is twice as large as the index constructed from $\mathcal{Z}_C^{min}$. The pareto-optimal points for all the 29 queries are displayed in Fig. 3, together with the median (red) and upper quartile (blue).

The overall results from Fig. 3 seems promising, as most of the transitions between pareto optimal points (black line segments) are more horizontal than vertical. This means that with clever selection of configuration branches, one can transition to a much higher precision without having to increase the index very much. The median and upper quartile have similar horizontal profiles, but with a slight increase as they approach 100% precision, resulting in a more convex curve.

From Experiment 1 and Fig. 1 we know that the average precision of $\mathcal{S}_a$ when using the smallest possible configuration for each query ($\mathcal{Z}_C^{min}$) is 0.61. Figure 3 shows that this precision can be increased to 100% with an index that is less than 2.1 times larger, with the exception of three queries that are orders of magnitude higher. This is caused by their highly restrictive filters on branches far away from the root.

4   Conclusion and Future Work

We discussed the combination of visual query systems for graph queries with the adaptive value suggestions of faceted search. After defining the "value suggestion problem", we introduced three suggestion functions: an optimal one that is slow for large datasets and complex queries; a range based one that is rather inaccurate, but allows fast implementation; and a configurable family of intermediate (precise enough and fast enough) solutions to the problem, based on only looking at a part of the constructed query. We conducted a series of experiments to conclude that

1. good approximations to the value suggestion problem can often be reached by taking into account only relatively small parts of the constructed query.
2. the precision of the approximations can often be improved dramatically by including the presence of required object properties in the configuration, rather than only connected datatype properties.
3. modest increases in index size often leads to a significant increase in accuracy.

In future work we intend to study alternative storage formats for the prejoined index. In particular a document database like MongoDB could be suitable. A related question is how to share storage space between indices for sub- and super-classes in the type hierarchy. The viability of our approach depends on a good choice of the facet configuration: it should be possible to determine an optimal configuration given a log of previous user queries. Another approach to reducing the index size is to work with "buckets" that combine ranges of facet values. Also suitable bucketing strategies can be determined from the query log and data.

Acknowledgement. This project is partially funded by NFR through the SIRIUS center.

References

1. Arenas, M., Grau, B.C., Kharlamov, E., Marciuška, Š., Zheleznyakov, D.: Faceted search over RDF-based knowledge graphs. J. Web Semant. **37**, 55–74 (2016)
2. Brunetti, J.M., García, R., Auer, S.: From overview to facets and pivoting for interactive exploration of semantic web data. IJSWIS **9**(1), 1–20 (2013)
3. Klungre, V.N.: A faceted search index for graph queries. Technical report 469, University of Oslo, Department of Informatics (2017). https://www.duo.uio.no/handle/10852/56755
4. Klungre, V.N., Giese, M.: Approximating faceted search for graph queries. In: 12th Scalable Semantic Web Systems (SWSS) (2018)
5. Soylu, G., Giese, M., et al.: Experiencing OptiqueVQS: a multi-paradigm and ontology-based visual query system for end users. UAIS **15**(1), 129–152 (2016). https://doi.org/10.1007/s10209-015-0404-5
6. Soylu, A., Giese, M., et al.: Ontology-based end-user visual query formulation: why, what, who, how, and which? UAIS **16**(2), 435–467 (2017). https://doi.org/10.1007/s10209-016-0465-0
7. Tunkelang, D.: Faceted search. Synthesis lectures on information concepts, retrieval, and services, **1**(1), 1–80 (2009)

Object-Relational Rules for Medical Devices: Classification and Conformity

Sofia Almpani[1(✉)], Petros Stefaneas[2], Harold Boley[3], Theodoros Mitsikas[1], and Panayiotis Frangos[1]

[1] School of Electrical and Computer Engineering,
National Technical University of Athens, Athens, Greece
salmpani@mail.ntua.gr, {mitsikas,pfrangos}@central.ntua.gr
[2] School of Applied Mathematics, National Technical University of Athens,
Athens, Greece
petrosstefaneas@gmail.com
[3] Faculty of Computer Science, University of New Brunswick, Fredericton, Canada
harold.boley@unb.ca

Abstract. This work focuses on formalizing the rules enacted by Regulation (EU) 2017/745, for risk-based classification and for class-based conformity assessment options regarding medical devices marketability, in Positional-Slotted Object-Applicative (PSOA) RuleML. The knowledge base represents knowledge by integrating F-logic-like frames with Prolog-like relationships for atoms used as facts and in the conditions and conclusions of rules. We tested this open-source knowledge base by querying it in the open-source PSOATransRun system which provided a feedback loop for refinement and extension. This can support the licensing process for stakeholders and the registration of medical devices with a CE conformity mark.

1 Introduction

Regulations are usually represented as moderately controlled natural-language text. While logical reasoning on knowledge representations is rather well-understood, there are no established methods to convert a given medical legal text to an appropriate knowledge representation [1]. The increased use of computational medical records requires ontologies to support taxonomic organization of information, as well as legal-based rules for medical tests, procedures, and registrations, so that the quality of healthcare is secured and improved.

Medical applications that combine ontologies with rule languages can be used, e.g., as clinical guidelines [2] and for medical decision support [3]. In the literature, there are various languages for modeling rules such as SWRL, KIF, RuleML, etc. In this work, Positional-Slotted Object-Applicative (PSOA) RuleML is used for its simplicity and its suitability to express deductions by rules over enriched atoms. EU Regulations of medical devices concerning the classification rules and

H. Panetto et al. (Eds.): OTM 2018 Conferences, LNCS 11230, pp. 584–591, 2018.
https://doi.org/10.1007/978-3-030-02671-4_37

the declaration of conformity procedures were formalized in PSOA RuleML presentation syntax [4,5][1]. This use case—Medical Devices Rules—illustrates how PSOA RuleML integrates the data and knowledge representation paradigms of *relationship atoms* with those of *frame atoms*. PSOA RuleML has also been used for legal rules formalization in other use cases, such as Port Clearance Rules [5] and Air Traffic Control Regulations [6] providing evidence that PSOA RuleML is well-suited to express real-world legal texts. This paper, in conjunction with our previous work [7], is an initial attempt to formalize, in a computational manner, a regulation of medical devices. However, other medically relevant EU regulations have been subject of formalization, e.g. Huth, in [8], focuses on developing concepts and awareness in the implementation of a company's specific GDPR requirements.

The main objectives of our work concerning Regulation (EU) 2017/745 are: (a) to develop a computational rule format of the core parts of Regulation (EU) 2017/745, realized with object-relational facts and rules about medical devices, and an explicit taxonomy of medical devices to form a Knowledge Base (KB), (b) to test the accuracy, interpretability, and reliability of the developed computational model with PSOATransRun queries (permitting validation by humans), and (c) to create a basis for computational guidelines to assist stakeholders of medical devices in the classification and registration of medical devices.

The resulting prototype, Medical Devices Rules, can only complement the classification and registration of medical devices by medical experts – it is an informative computational model of the regulation for stakeholders (i.e. regulators, manufacturers, importers, distributors, wholesalers etc.), rather than constituting expert knowledge.

The paper is organized as follows: Sect. 2 describes the formalization in PSOA RuleML and its challenges. Section 3 demonstrates queries and evaluates the results. Section 4 concludes the paper and outlines future directions.

2 Formalization of Medical Devices Rules

The **Regulation (EU) 2017/745** [9] of the European Parliament and of the Council of 5 April 2017 on medical devices presents a framework of risk-based classification, leading to risk-appropriate conformity requirements. The classification criteria for the four classes (Class I, IIa, IIb, III) are described with 22 rules in the form of moderately controlled natural language and are grouped based on kinds of devices, i.e. non-invasive, invasive, active, and medical devices with special rules (Annex VII of the Regulation). Manufacturers of medical devices will need to state the classification of their products (Annex VIII of the Regulation). The **CE marking** ("CE" is an abbreviation of "Conformité Européenne") on a medical device is a declaration from the manufacturer that the device complies with the necessary class-based conformity requirements.

---

[1] Details of PSOA RuleML syntax, terms, and PSOATransRun can be found in [5] and in PSOA RuleML wiki page http://wiki.ruleml.org/index.php/PSOA_RuleML.

Our formalization of Regulation (EU) 2017/745 consists of four parts, exemplified below by the classification and declaration of conformity of medical device code MDN1204a.

The 22 Classification Rules of Medical Devices: The original rules are expressed with a three-level-deep description of medical devices characteristics, connected for abbreviation with (informal) three-symbol categories as in the following clause for Rule 4[2].

```
% Rule 4: Devices in contact with injured skin.
Forall ?m (:CategoryOfMedicalDevice(?m :N4a) :-
  ?m#:MedicalDevice(:kind->:NonInvasive
                    :use->:ContactInjuredSkin
                    :specificCase->:MechanicalBarrier))
```

Subsequently, the aforementioned categories are connected with the class they reside in, forming an 'Or' branch (disjunction). The categories e.g. in Class I are expressed as follows:

```
% Classification Grouping: Class I
  Forall ?m (:IsClassifiedIn(?m :I) :-
           Or(:CategoryOfMedicalDevice(?m :N1)
             :CategoryOfMedicalDevice(?m :N4a)
             :CategoryOfMedicalDevice(?m :I5a)
             :CategoryOfMedicalDevice(?m :I6b)
             :CategoryOfMedicalDevice(?m :A10a)
             :CategoryOfMedicalDevice(?m :A11c)
             :CategoryOfMedicalDevice(?m :A13)))
```

Class-Based Conformity Requirements for Marketability: All the different conformity assessment routes of each class (e.g., Class I) for the CE marking and the implied marketability of medical devices are described[3].

```
% Requirements for Class I
Forall ?m (:DeclarationOfConformity (?m) :-
        And(:IsClassifiedIn(?m :I)
            :RegisterWithTheECA(?m)
            :AppointingAnEAR(?m)
            :ConformityAssessment(:device->?m :technicalFile->:Yes
                :vigilanceSystem->:Yes :harmonizedStandards->:No)))
```

---

[2] It formalizes the sentence *"All non-invasive devices which come into contact with injured skin or mucous membrane are classified as: class I if they are intended to be used as a mechanical barrier, for compression or for absorption of exudates"* [9]. The present work is restricted to the English version of the Regulation.

[3] ECA: European Competent Authorities, EAR: European Authorized Representative.

An Explicit Taxonomy of Medical Devices: The 'subclass' relation (denoted in PSOA as '##') (e.g., :AbsorbentPads##mdcode:MDN1204a) and the 'instance' relation (e.g., :AbsorbentPadsUDI#:AbsorbentPads) are used for building a variable-depth multi-layer **taxonomy**, containing more than 150 different medical device products.

Sample Data (Facts) of Medical Devices: Data are added to the Medical Devices Rules KB as needed, e.g. for facts about medical device code MDN1204a:

```
% Requirements of MDN1204a: Class I, 2Yes, No ECA
mdcode:MDN1204a#:MedicalDevice(
    :kind->:NonInvasive :use->:ContactInjuredSkin
    :specificCase->:MechanicalBarrier)
:AppointingAnEAR(mdcode:MDN1204a)
:ConformityAssessment(:device->mdcode:MDN1204a :technicalFile->:Yes
    :vigilanceSystem->:Yes :harmonizedStandards->:No)
```

Notice that because of the randomly chosen facts concerning marketability requirements for each medical device, this medical device example does not satisfy all conditions to be marketable.

A more detailed description of the formalization of Medical Devices Rules KB[4] can be found in [7]. The current paper focuses on the challenges of the formalization and the deductive quering answering of the Medical Devices Rules KB.

Some of the principles and challenges of the rule formalization are described below.

- The explicit numbering of classification rules is helpful for their formalization. Every natural language rule of the regulation is shown before its formal representation in the Medical Devices Rules KB.
- In the text of the regulation, there is no aggregation of devices belonging to the same class (e.g., Class I), neither a clear separation of the different cases in each rule. A knowledge schema and data mapping is required for the needs of the computational formalization. In particular, the original 22 rules are represented with additional three-symbol categories based on their differentiated characteristics as abbreviations. Subsequently, these categories form classification groups, as shown in [7].
- Medical devices facts are based on the list of codes (2017/2185) [10] and the corresponding types of devices under Regulation (EU) 2017/745. Since there is no explicit connection of these codes with the categories of medical devices, an association[5] is made based on the commonly-described characteristics. However, this connection is used for enhancement of the KB with

---

[4] The code source and PSOATransRun queries of the KB and detailed explanatory diagrams can be found in: http://psoa.ruleml.org/usecases/MedicalDevices/. See also the wiki page: http://wiki.ruleml.org/index.php/Medical_Devices_Rules.

[5] In cases where the codes do not describe specifically a category a random coding is applied (e.g.,:DeviceR3a), while in cases where more than one category belongs in the same code, letters a,b,c,ST are used (e.g., mdcode:MDN1202c).

representative medical devices facts and for general documentation of the regulation and not for providing actual legal knowledge. Moreover, representative
marketability requirements for each medical device fact are chosen randomly.
- Hence, while the current KB does not use an actual dataset of medical devices
  facts, in the future a standard dataset could be obtained from Eudamed,
  which is currently under development. Eudamed, the European data bank of
  medical devices, is being overhauled in order to increase capabilities and allow
  wider access in accordance with the new regulation. Thus, Unique Device Identification (UDI) of medical devices—which could be used for that purpose—
  will be phased in and be added to Eudamed over several years.
- For obtaining a more detailed, complete and usable KB, an hierarchical taxonomy of medical devices was created, where the aforementioned codes are also
  connected with specific examples of medical devices. This taxonomy was created based on pertinent guidelines but does not reflect medical-devices expert
  knowledge (there are numerous different types of medical devices, with this
  number growing constantly).

3   Query Answering by PSOATransRun

In this section, we pose representative copy&paste-ready queries to the KB and
demonstrate the answers obtained by PSOATransRun. The Prolog instantiation
of PSOATransRun [4], currently in version 1.3.1, is the reference implementation
of PSOA RuleML.

Queries and Answers for Medical Devices Classification: To obtain the
medical devices with one or more specific characteristics, e.g. for the devices
using derivatives, the following query can be used.

```
> ?m#:MedicalDevice(:use->:Derivatives)
?m=<http://eur-lex.europa.eu/legal-content/EN/TXT/CODES/...#MDS1003>
?m=<http://eur-lex.europa.eu/legal-content/EN/TXT/CODES/...#MDS1002>
```

The multiple ?m-answer bindings are shown as full IRIs expanded from the
':'-prefixed abbreviations in the KB.

Similarly, to obtain the category of a specific medical device, the following
deductive query is employed, binding the answer to the output variable ?g.

```
> :CategoryOfMedicalDevice(mdcode:MDN1204a ?g)
?g=<http://psoa.ruleml.org/usecases/MedicalDevices#N4a>
```

Using the top-level predicate :IsClassifiedIn we can ask whether a certain
medical device code, e.g. :IsClassifiedIn(mdcode:MDA0204 :IIb), belongs to
a specific class, i.e. IIb (Answer: Yes). Moreover, we can ask for the classification
of a medical device, even if we do not know its specific code, by asking for an
OID with certain characteristics, getting all the possible answers, e.g.:

```
> :IsClassifiedIn(?m#:MedicalDevice(:use->:ModifyingComposition) :III)
?m=<http://eur-lex.europa.eu/legal-content/EN/TXT/CODES/...5#MDN1212>
```

Abstracting this query (e.g., the constant :III becomes the variable ?c), we could also pose the generalized, symbolic-execution-style non-ground query :IsClassifiedIn(?m ?c), to deduce all medical devices and their corresponding classes, using two output variables (?m and ?c).

Queries and Answers for Medical Devices Marketability: More queries can be asked on the marketability and conformity requirements of medical devices. In the example of medical devices represented by the code :MDN1214, PSOATransRun returns a 'Yes'-answer in the following queries.

```
:IsClassifiedIn(mdcode:MDN1214 :I)
:RegisterWithTheECA(mdcode:MDN1214)
:AppointingAnEAR(mdcode:MDN1214)
:ConformityAssessment(:device->mdcode:MDN1214 :technicalFile->:Yes
                      :vigilanceSystem->:Yes :harmonizedStandards->:No)
:DeclarationOfConformity(mdcode:MDN1214)
:HasCEwithNBN(mdcode:MDN1214)
:MarketableMedicalDevice(mdcode:MDN1214)    % Answer for all: Yes %
```

We can also ask for all the marketable devices, using e.g. the input variable ?m, by posing the query :MarketableMedicalDevice(?m). Moreover, we can obtain all medical devices that satisfy one or more specific marketability requirements.

Queries and Answers for Medical Devices Taxonomy: For the description of the explicit relations between the hierarchical levels of medical devices, a separate taxonomy was created, which facilitates the complement of more medical devices products and UDIs in the future. When using PSOA's '##' infix, one instance-level relation is required for PSOATransRun to deduce answers. We can ask about the upper classes of a medical device product UDI-instance, e.g. using the output variable ?c, to deduce all the upper layers of the taxonomy (Bottom-to-Top Taxonomy Queries). We can also ask queries about the instances belonging in the lower levels, e.g. using the variable ?m (Top-to-Bottom Taxonomy Queries). In this query, all the UDIs of the relevant medical devices will be exported, but not the sub-classes between (i.e., the intermediate sub-class with the code 'MDN1202b').

```
> :DevicesToStoreOrgansUDI#?c %Bottom-to-Top%
?c=<http://psoa.ruleml.org/usecases/MedicalDevices#DevicesToStoreOrgans>
?c=<http://eur-lex.europa.eu/legal-content/EN/TXT/CODES/...#MDN1202b>
?c=<http://psoa.ruleml.org/usecases/MedicalDevices#N2b>
?c=<http://psoa.ruleml.org/usecases/MedicalDevices#NonActiveNonInvasive>
?c=<http://psoa.ruleml.org/usecases/MedicalDevices#MedicalDevices>

> ?m#:N2b   %Top-to-Bottom%
?m=<http://psoa.ruleml.org/.../MedicalDevices#TubesForBloodTransfusionUDI>
?m=<http://psoa.ruleml.org/.../MedicalDevices#DevicesToStoreOrgansUDI>
```

Discussion and Evaluation: The above queries are posed at a logical KB which integrates object and relational modeling.

These query examples also indicate that in both typical and complex queries the answers provided by PSOATransRun were accurate and the results can be validated by a human with audit trails, which is a critical parameter in medical domain.

There are limitations on the kinds of answers that can be obtained. One limitation of the queries is that even though we can obtain all the medical devices that are in compliance with a specific marketability requirement, we cannot retrieve at once all non-compliant devices. Similarly, we cannot retrieve all requirements to be fulfilled in order to establish the compliance of a device. Another query limitation in the taxonomy is that we can ask about all upper classes only from a lower instance level (medical device product UDI), and in the top-to-bottom direction we can obtain only the instances of the lowest level, without the middle levels. The run-time performance of PSOATransRun has also been evaluated. For our testing laptop (Intel Core 2 Duo P7550 2.26 GHz CPU, 4 GB RAM, running on Linux) query answering was instantaneous for the provided data set, which includes 55 categories in the KB and more than 150 examples of products in the taxonomy, even with queries with three different variables, as in the example below:

```
And(:DeclarationOfConformity(?m) :QualityType(?m ?q)
    :IsClassifiedIn(?m ?c))
```

4   Conclusions and Future Work

We have demonstrated a formalization of medical devices regulation as part of a logical KB leading to a computational decision model in PSOA RuleML. The resulting KB is capable of answering queries regarding the classification and marketability of medical devices aiming at compliance with the Regulation (EU) 2017/745. This has created an initial opportunity for decision support using this rule formalization via formal query, analysis, and proof, as well as permitting translation to other formalisms.

Future work includes extensions and improvements of the Medical Devices Rules KB, e.g. enrichment of products with UDIs for medical devices as well as post-marketability and clinical evaluation requirements. Aiming to correlate medical devices regulation with robotics regulation (e.g., wearables), future work can also include the formalization of further relevant regulations concerning robot technology and safety (e.g., ISO for robotics, General Data Protection Regulation). This can contribute to the effort of unifying both legal frameworks, such as in [11] for Non-social Personal Care Robots, evolved to a computational format, as part of legal-informatics efforts (e.g., OASIS LegalRuleML).

Acknowledgments. We want to thank Dr. Gen Zou (UNB) for realizing PSOATransRun and for his early comments on this work. Moreover, we thank Dr. Vasileios Aravantinos (Council of State of Greece) for his hints on the expressiveness, interpretability and accuracy of Medical Devices Rules.

References

1. Holzinger, A., Biemann, C., Pattichis, C.S., Kell, D.B.: What do we need to build explainable AI systems for the medical domain? CoRR abs/1712.09923 (2017)
2. Casteleiro, M.A., Diz, J.J.D.: Clinical practice guidelines: a case study of combining OWL-S, OWL, and SWRL. Knowl.-Based Syst. **21**(3), 247–255 (2008)
3. Djedidi R, A.M.: Medical domain ontology construction approach: a basis for medical decision support. In: Computer-Based Medical Systems, vol. 44, pp. 509–511 (2007)
4. Zou, G., Boley, H.: PSOA2Prolog: object-relational rule interoperation and implementation by translation from PSOA RuleML to ISO prolog. In: Bassiliades, N., Gottlob, G., Sadri, F., Paschke, A., Roman, D. (eds.) RuleML 2015. LNCS, vol. 9202, pp. 176–192. Springer, Cham (2015). https://doi.org/10.1007/978-3-319-21542-6_12
5. Zou, G., Boley, H., Wood, D., Lea, K.: Port clearance rules in PSOA RuleML: from controlled-English regulation to object-relational logic. In: Proceedings of the RuleML+RR 2017 Challenge, vol. 1875. CEUR, July 2017. http://ceur-ws.org/Vol-1875/paper6.pdf
6. Mitsikas, T., Almpani, S., Stefaneas, P., Frangos, P., Ouranos, I.: Formalizing air traffic control regulations in PSOA RuleML. In: Proceedings of the Doctoral Consortium and Challenge @ RuleML+RR 2018 hosted by 2nd International Joint Conference on Rules and Reasoning, vol. 2204. CEUR, September 2018. http://ceur-ws.org/Vol-2204/paper9.pdf
7. Almpani, S., Stefaneas, P., Boley, H., Mitsikas, T., Frangos, P.: Computational regulation of medical devices in PSOA RuleML. In: Benzmüller, C., Ricca, F., Parent, X., Roman, D. (eds.) RuleML+RR 2018. LNCS, vol. 11092, pp. 203–210. Springer, Cham (2018). https://doi.org/10.1007/978-3-319-99906-7_13
8. Huth, D.: A pattern catalog for GDPR compliant data protection. In: PoEM Doctoral Consortium (2017)
9. European Parliament: Regulation (EU) 2017/745 of the European Parliament and of the Council of 5 April 2017 on medical devices. Off. J. Eur. Union **L 117** (2017)
10. European Parliament: Regulation (EU) 2017/2185 of 23 November 2017 on the list of codes and corresponding types of devices. Off. J. Eur. Union **L 309/7** (2017)
11. Fosch Villaronga, E.: Legal frame of non-social personal care robots. In: Husty, M., Hofbaur, M. (eds.) MESROB 2016. MMS, vol. 48, pp. 229–242. Springer, Cham (2018). https://doi.org/10.1007/978-3-319-59972-4_17

Reducing the Cost of the Linear Growth Effect Using Adaptive Rules with Unlinking and Lazy Rule Evaluation

Mark Proctor[1,2](✉)(iD), Mario Fusco[2], Davide Sottara[3](iD), and Tibor Zimányi[2]

[1] Department of Electrical and Electronic Engineering, Imperial College London, London, UK
mdproctor@gmail.com
[2] Red Hat Inc., Raleigh, USA
[3] Biomedical Informatics Department., Arizona State University, Scottsdale, AZ, USA
http://www.imperial.ac.uk, http://www.redhat.com, http://www.bmi.asu.edu

Abstract. The match cost of Rete [8] increases significantly and approximately linearly with the number of rules [2]. A major part of that cost is the eager creation of cross products within the join nodes in an attempt to materialize rule instantiations. This paper builds on the idea of adaptive rules [1] using the unlinking of nodes, segments of nodes and rules to delay join attempts, which helps mitigate some aspects of the linear growth effect. By delaying the evaluation of a rule until after it's linked and restricting the propagation to a single path, a lazy goal-driven evaluation behaviour is introduced. The algorithm also preserves node sharing by organising the network into segments and paths of segments; with memory now at node, segment and path levels. This paper presents the design and implementation of this work within the popular Open Source Drools rule engine. Drools also provides a baseline Rete implementation, without these enhancements, against which this work can be benchmarked. The evaluation of the results shows positive improvements over Rete, with no downsides.

Keywords: RETE · Production rules · Pattern matching
Rule engines · Refraction

1 Introduction

Rete [8], developed by Charles Forgy in 1979, is a popular rule engine algorithm for production rule systems, that is characterised by its eager and data driven nature. The Rete algorithm presents a number of challenges when trying to scale up both the number of rules and amount of data. There are many texts on the subject of providing techniques to help avoid these performance issues, like "Programming Expert Systems with OPS5" [3]. However this pushes the complexity of the problem onto the programmer and the program itself, undermining the goal of declarative rule bases. Nevertheless, there is a limit to how

© Springer Nature Switzerland AG 2018
H. Panetto et al. (Eds.): OTM 2018 Conferences, LNCS 11230, pp. 592–601, 2018.
https://doi.org/10.1007/978-3-030-02671-4_38

much these techniques can help with the existing technology - making it necessary to improve the engine itself to achieve better performance. When looking to improve the engine it helps to understand that there are two cycles, recognise and act. The act cycle performs the execution of rule actions. The recognise cycle, which is the most costly of the two [9], matches data to rule conditions to produce rule instantiations that may execute. When analysing the matching process and resulting rule instantiations [11] notes that not all produced rule instantiations are fired, and refers to this effort as "wasted" work. [1] further notes that not all efforts to produce partial matches, result in rule instantiations, which he also classifies as wasted work. This wasted work means the engine exhibits a linear growth effect in slow down, for each rule that is added. This was covered by [1] where he defines and discusses three categories of research for consideration when scaling up a rule engine. Those three categories are titled "Taming the combinatorial explosion", "Improved memory subsystem performance" and "Eliminating linear average growth effect". This paper builds on the idea of adaptive rules from "Eliminating linear average growth effect" category. The algorithm presented by this paper achieves this by unlinking the nodes, segments of nodes and rules to delay the beta matching attempts from rule evaluation. To support node sharing two levels of memory were introduced, segment and path memory in addition to existing node memory. This allows the current rule to continue its evaluation, while making materialized partial matches available to peered segments that have the same parent segments. By delaying the evaluation of a rule until after it's linked and restricting the propagation to a single path, a lazy goal-driven evaluation behaviour is introduced. The open source Drools engine was used for this implementation as it already has a number of well known Rete enhancements, and provides a baseline Rete implementation, without these enhancements, against which this work can be benchmarked. The evaluation of the results shows <results exist, still need to add results>.

2   Related Research

TREAT [10] was one of the earlier attempts at adaptive rules, with its 'rule-active' flag. Unlike Rete, Treat has no sharing of the network between rules and each rule has its own flag. Without the ability to exploit network sharing, there is a linear time cost to maintain this flag [1], with regards to the number of productions in the system. This paper presents an efficient way to maintain this 'rule-active' flag, while also supporting sharing of the network. It achieves this by using node, segment and path linking, via setting and unsetting bits on a bitmask, ensuring that a rule is only active when it has data at all of its inputs. It should be possible for this algorithm to be applied to TREAT, as an enhancement to TREAT to avoid that linear slow down - although TREAT would still not benefit from the network sharing during it's matching phase. The linking of this algorithm was inspired by the Rete/UL [7] node linking, although for this version they solve two different problems. Rete/UL addresses the issue of propagation through a wide fanout, in a large systems, which would result in "null left activations" and "null right activations". While this saves wasted propagations in a wide fanout, it does not address the wasted beta matching that this paper focuses on. With Rete/UL, it will not stop or delay eager partial matching within the beta network. It will still undertake this matching, even if there is no data in a descendant child node and thus no resulting rule instantiations could occur. The version of the algorithm in this paper does not address the alpha network fan out propagation that Rete/UL does, but this should be possible and could be future work. Further, while Rete/UL unlinking physically disconnects parts of the network to block propagation, the linking and unlinking of this paper refers to the setting and unsetting of the bits in the mask, which are used to control propagation flow and rule network evaluation. Lastly, Rete/UL remains an eager data driven algorithm whereas this paper introduces a lazy goal driven algorithm. LEAPS [11] is another well known lazy algorithm, both will delay when a rule is eventually evaluated, but there are two main differences. LEAPS will lazily materialise the partial and full matches of the rule, whereas the algorithm in this paper will fully materialise all matches using set oriented propagation. For this reason under certain use cases LEAPS will maintain lower latency levels and use less memory. Those use cases are typically when a context object is used to select a small subset of the data which on change results in other rules firing. When the flow of rules loops to repeat the current rule the selected data has changed, and thus it wouldn't benefit that much from remembering partial matching - this is the model of execution followed by the manners and waltz benchmarks. LEAPS does not have any network sharing and does not maintain beta memory, which can result in exponential slow down for some rules. An example of this would be stream style rules, where you continuously receive updates to partial matches, especially towards the tip, as each insert would have to recalculate all it's previous partial matches. As with TREAT, the linking technique could probably be applied to the LEAPS algorithm too. The reason to choose a set oriented propagation was to ensure this algorithm remained general purposes, especially with regards to working on aggregations of data, and that future work intends to adopt collection oriented match [2] - which helps collapse the cross product costs.

3   Implementation

Network sharing and segmentation, is key to reducing the linear growth cost of maintaining the 'rule-active' flag, as incurred in algorithms like TREAT, [1]. To understand segmentation the reader must first understand node sharing. As with Rete [8], node sharing means that each node may be associated with 1..n rules. If a beta node has a single child then it will have the same rule association as the child node. A segment consists of 1..n beta nodes that have the same rule association. A network split occurs if the beta node has two or more child nodes, where each child will have a different rule association to the parent. The parent is the end of the current segment and each child is the start of a new segment (Figs. 1 and 2).

A subnetwork, a form of network split, is formed when a conditional element, such as not, exists or accumulate, contains two or more patterns. The parent node creates a split, with one side going to the subnetwork, that contains the two or more child nodes, and the other to a child join node. The subnetwork feeds back into the right input of that join. A path consists of 1..n segments. A Path always starts at the root left input adapter node, sometimes referred to as a Dummy node, and ends either at the rule terminal node or at the end of a subnetwork before it feeds back into the outer join. All nodes in a segment must belong to the same set of paths. If there is no sharing and no subnetworks the path for the rule will have a single segment. In additional to Rete's beta node memory two new types of memory, for those segments and paths, have been added. This allows for much more contextual understanding during evaluation of a Rule. The path memory is subclassed depending on whether it is for a rule (the outermost path) or a subnetwork path. Each path mem-

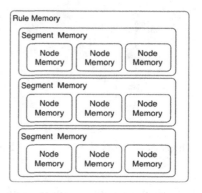

Fig. 1. Rule, segment and node memories

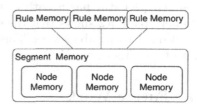

Fig. 2. Segment to path memory

ory has 1..n segment memories. Each segment can be associated with 1..n path memories, for each rule it is shared by. Rete will churn away producing partial match attempts for all nodes, even if the last join is empty. The unlinking technique ensures that no evaluation will be done for partial matches, unless a potential rule instantiation can materialise and data exists at all the inputs. When data inserted, updated or deleted it is propagated through the alpha network until it arrives at one or more beta nodes. For each node the data is stored in a linked list, and the node is "linked" - which means its bit is set in a bitmask for the segment containing the node. When all the nodes for a segment are linked, the segment is linked. Not nodes with constraints and accumulate nodes have special behaviour and can never unlink a segment, and are always considered to have their bits on. When all the segments in a path are linked, the path is linked and the rule is scheduled for evaluation on the agenda. The schedule order is determined by a conflict resolution strategy, which is implemented as salience followed by rule order. This further delays rule evaluation. Once a scheduled rule starts evaluation it will incrementally materialize all new rule instantiations, for this rule, while updating existing ones and removing old ones that are no longer true. Memory example 1 shows a single rule, with three patterns; A, B and C. It forms a single segment, with bits 1, 2 and 4 for the nodes. Memory example 2 adds two more rules. This results in 3 paths, with A and B shared by all and D shared by R2 and R3. Subnetworks are formed when a Not, Exists or Accu-

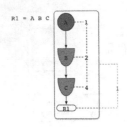

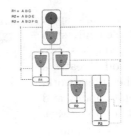

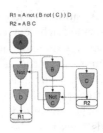

Fig. 3. Memory 1   **Fig. 4.** Memory 2   **Fig. 5.** Memory 3

mulate node contain more than one element. In example 3 *"B not(C)"* forms the subnetwork, note that *"not(C)"* is a single element and does not require a subnetwork and is merged inside of the Not node. The subnetwork gets its own segment. R1 still has a path of two segments. The subnetwork forms another "inner" path. R2 shows that the subnetwork nodes can be shared by a rule that does not have a subnetwork. This results in the subnetwork segment being split into two (Figs. 3, 4 and 5).

4   Future Work

The original work by Doorenbos [6] unlinked at the alpha network level, pulling data on demand from the object type node. The work in this paper only unlinks the beta network. When adding alpha network level unlinking, it is important the overhead costs of tracking this, do not become too high. The engine uses a fairly basic heuristic, that all inputs must have data, to determining when a rule is linked and a goal created and scheduled for evaluation. Future work would attempt to delay the linking even further; using techniques such as arc consistency [13] to determine whether or not matching will result in rule instance firings. Dirty segment tracking could be used to skip whole segments during rule evaluation. While this algorithm does implement set propagation, significant performance gains and memory reduction can be achieved by the introduction of set oriented matching [2]. Lastly segmentation paging would be a positive way to reduce memory consumption in large systems. If a rule is not evaluated for a given period of time the engine should remove the tuple structures for that segment, so they can be garbage collected. Although it does need to keep track on which of those rule instantiations it has already fired. When the rule is eventually asked to be evaluated again, it can rematerialise the tuple structures using the previously fired data to discard rule instances that have already fired. Efficiency, and thus performance, can be measured by the number of partial matches (tokens) processed by each algorithm [12]. As standard Rete and unlinking Rete both produce the same number of partial matches, for a given rule evaluation, the time to evaluate one rule between the two systems should be fairly similar. The benchmarks are classified into two focus areas, the cost of unlinking and the efficiencies gained. The cost of unlinking category looks to find the worst case scenarios and their cost and also the cut over point to where the cost is less than the efficiency gained. The other category looks at efficiency gains by avoiding wasted work that does not result in rule firings.

5 Benchmarks and Results

The benchmarks were executed on Drools 6.5, which supports both Rete and unlinking lazy executions. Both execute with as much shared code as is possible. How the network is built, the tuple data structures, the expression evaluations are all the same code. The lazy algorithm adds some set wrappers around the tuples, and their existing data structures. The other lazy implementation details, linking etc., are all layered onto the same Rete code base. A rule generation tool was developed that could generate 1..n rules, using two main parameters. The first parameter controls the segment fanout, per level, i.e. how many children will a segment have. This value is the same for all segments at that level. The second parameters controls the number of nodes per segment. Given these two parameters it will generate the rules, such that the patterns and constraints support the sharing necessary to fit the segmentation requirements. This is then used as the supporting base, using different consequences and rules priorities, for four different benchmarks. For the benchmarks, the generated data would have a single root fact with two options for the leaf fact. The first is a leaf fact per rule, the second was single leaf fact. Each leaf fact is always constrained to a single rule at a time, using the rule id. For the nodes inbetween the root and leaf a parameterised value was used to generate the facts. The given value would determine the number of generated facts for the second pattern. To avoid combinatorial problems the value is halved for the next pattern, and halved again for the pattern after that and so on until the last pattern. The benchmark used 32 for the fact parameter, as this was the largest size that would work on both algorithms. It then used five different network configurations. (1) 1 level, 1 segment (in total) with 8 nodes. (2) 3 levels, 2 child segments a level, with 2 nodes a segment. (3) 4 levels, 2 child segments a level, with 2 nodes a segment. (4) 2 levels, 3 child segments a level, with 2 nodes a segment. (5) 4 levels, 3 child segments a level, with 2 nodes a segment. There is only ever a single root object, which always matches true against the first pattern. The last pattern is generated to constrain the leaf fact id to the rule id. The generated data and tests ensure there is only ever a single root fact and an optional single matching leaf fact, per rule. All other patterns are generated with constraints that always return true. This ensures a full cross product is produced for each join, to really stress the system. All data was shuffled before inserting, using a given seed number to ensure the shuffled order was repeatable. The Java Microbenchmark Harness (JMH) tool was used to execute the benchmarks, using *SingleShotTime* mode, with suitable warm up iterations before executing the timed benchmark iterations. **Match And Fire All Rules.** While the other benchmarks attempt to show the cost of wasted work for Rete this one produces full cross products and full rule instantiations and then attempts to fire each in turn, from highest to lowest salience, with no wasted work. Each rule's consequence updates a counter, which is not in the working memory, and does not result in any forward chaining. When the last rule is fired it updates the root fact, which reproduces full cross products and full instantiations for all rules and repeats the process. After 100 loops the program exits. This is a pure throughput benchmark, with no wasted work, comparing the join and propagation performance of each algorithm. **Repeat First Rule Fire.** With Rete semantics, when the data is inserted, it will result in full cross products and rule instantiations for all rules. The first rule, having the highest salience, fires first and updates the root object. This causes all cross products for all rules to be re-evaluated and their rule instantiations to be reproduced. All rule instantiations that did not fire that iteration, were wasted work. The first rule will then fire again and this repeats for 100 iterations, where it then exits. The lazy algorithm will only attempt to match and fire the first rule, avoiding the wasted work of Rete. **Repeat Last Rule Fire.** This is implemented as per the benchmark "Repeat First Rule Fire". Except this time, the last rule has the highest salience. Which means after all the data is inserted the loop will be around the last rule. This test is primarily to demonstrate that the algorithm in this paper is not optimised for certain rule positions, and will exhibit similar performance gains regardless of which rule has the highest salience. **Iterate And Fire All Rules.** This benchmark has a single leaf fact, that starts of constrained to first rule. With Rete semantics, when the data is inserted, it will produce partial matches up until the leaf for all but the first rule. Those rules will not produce rule instantiations, as there is no final leaf fact to match. The first rule will have full matches and rule instantiation. When the first rule fires it updates the root and leaf fact so that they match the next rule. This results in the first, and all other rules, producing partial matches only. This rule fires and the process repeats to iterate all rules until the last rule. The last rule resets values for the root and leaf fact back to 0, causing the program to loop again. The benchmark iterates for 100 loops. This demonstrates the Rete cost of the wasted partial matches and that the algorithm works well with forward chaining across all rules in a given program (Fig. 7).

6   Discussion

The benchmark came with some unexpected results. For "Match And Fire All Rules" (Fig. 6) it was expected the two algorithms to have similar levels of performance, as there is no wasted work here, all cross products result in rule instantiations and all of which are fired. However the lazy algorithm was twice as fast and improving with larger cross products. Configuration 5 is showing 25.9% to 74.1%. This behaviour would be an ideal investigation for the future; an initial speculation believes this may be due to two reasons. The first reason may be due to the lazy algorithm not sorting each individual rule instantiation on the agenda, which it does with a binary heap queue. Every time a rule instantiates it is added to the queue and every time it is fired, the binary heap undergoes some sorting operations. Instead it just sorts the rule itself, the instantiations

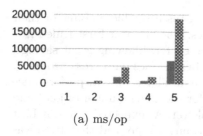
(a) ms/op

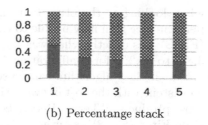
(b) Percentange stack

Fig. 6. Match And Fire All Rules (rete is hatched, lazy is solid)

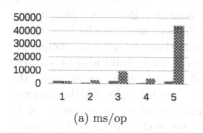
(a) ms/op

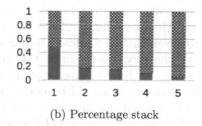
(b) Percentage stack

Fig. 7. Repeat First Rule Fire (rete is hatched, lazy is solid)

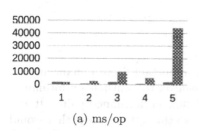
(a) ms/op

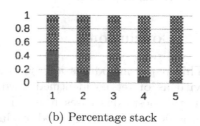
(b) Percentage stack

Fig. 8. Repeat Last Rule Fire (rete is hatched, lazy is solid)

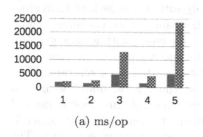
(a) ms/op

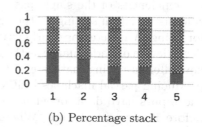
(b) Percentage stack

Fig. 9. Iterate And Fire All Rules (rete is hatched, lazy is solid)

are held on a linked list. The second may be due to method recursion used for the depth first tuple oriented propagation. It will use a lot of cpu cycles to repeatedly walk the tree, and constant 'create and destroy' for the method stack frames will make cpu cache less efficient. This needs to be taken into account when looking at the other benchmarks, as it means a sizable amount of their performance gain may be due to these efficiencies. The "Repeat First Rule Fire" (Fig. 8) was exactly what was hoped and expected for. Showing great savings, 3.8% to 96.2%, for configuration 5. As the number of rules, and cross products, grows the lazy algorithm can be seen to keep good, almost linear, performance consistent with the cost of evaluating one rule, for the given number of joins and cross products. Whereas Rete gets slower and slower. As expected "Repeat Last Rule Fire" (Fig. 8) has exactly the same behaviour. We noticed that Rete was further disadvantaged due to much larger GC cycles, this would also create a larger error for the score variation. "Iterate And Fire All Rules" (Fig. 9) at first glance also has great improvements at 16.7% to 83.3%. However "Match And Fire All Rules" had a 25.9% to 74.1% difference. Meaning that the bulk of the improvements were most likely due to the propagation and agenda efficiencies, with the lazy aspects impacting to a lesser degree. This would also be an area needing for further investigation, to understand what is going on between the two systems. It should be noted that by only sorting the rules (goals) and not the individual rule instantiations it is not possible to implement advanced OPS5 conflict strategies, such as LEX and MEA [8]. However the author believes there are better alternatives to rule orchestration, such as using defeasible rules [4] or rule modularity [5].

7   Conclusion

This paper introduces and successfully proves important Rete enhancements, with as of yet no identified downsides with regards to runtime performance. In the best edge cases it is achieving around 30x performance gains. It did provide for some unexpected results with regards to throughput tests, that would not benefit from any lazy behaviour. With the lazy algorithm still achieving almost 4x performance gains in comparison. It is speculated this is down to the efficiencies of the single pass propagation algorithm and lack of individual rule instantiation sorting on the agenda. The algorithm can be considered more forgiving than Rete, for poorly written and large rule bases, with a more graceful degradation of performance as the number of rules and complexity increases. The key difference being that Rete will undertake a lot of wasted work, churning away producing partial machines - either for rules that could never match as not all the inputs have data, or where it does have data the rule instance is deleted before it ever gets to fire. Whereas the algorithm presented in this paper is available to avoid this wasted work and gain better performance as a result. The algorithm does come with some considerable implementation complexity, over standard Rete, hardening this took some time, involved writing a lot of unit tests and continuous end user testing and feedback. The three levels of memory, node, segment and rule, is not something (to the best knowledge of the author) that has been seen in any other research on production rules before and brings a high level of innovation to this work and research area. The future work highlights some interesting next steps. Alpha network unlinking should be introduced, so that the algorithm can also provide the benefits of Rete/UL. Also increasing the heuristic to further delay evaluation through arc consistency would be very welcome.

References

1. Acharya, A.: scaling up production systems: issues, approaches and targets **9**(01), 67 (1994). https://doi.org/10.1017/s0269888900006603
2. Acharya, A., Tambe, M.: Collection oriented match (1993)
3. Brownston, L., et al.: Programming Expert Systems in OPS5. Addison-Wesley Publishing Co. Inc., Reading (1985)
4. Bassiliades, N., Antoniou, G., Vlahavas, I.: DR-DEVICE: a defeasible logic system for the semantic web. In: Ohlbach, H.J., Schaffert, S. (eds.) PPSWR 2004. LNCS, vol. 3208, pp. 134–148. Springer, Heidelberg (2004). https://doi.org/10.1007/978-3-540-30122-6_10
5. Browne, J.C., et al.: A new approach to modularity in rule-based programming. In: 1994 Proceedings of the Sixth International Conference on Tools with Artificial Intelligence, pp. 18–25. IEEE (1994)
6. Doorenbos, R.B.: Combining left and right unlinking for matching a large number of learned rules (1994)
7. Doorenbos, R.B.: Production matching for large learning systems (1995)
8. Forgy, C.L.: Rete: a fast algorithm for the many pattern/many object pattern match problem. Artif. Intell. **19**(1), 17–37 (1982). https://doi.org/10.1016/0004-3702(82)90020-0
9. McDermott, J., Newell, A., Moore, J.: The efficiency of certain production system implementations (63), 38 (1977). https://doi.org/10.1145/1045343.1045366
10. Miranker, D.P.: TREAT: a better match algorithm for AI production systems; long version. Technical report, Austin, TX, USA (1987)
11. Miranker, D.P., Brant, D.A., Lofaso, B.J., Gadbois, D.: On the performance of lazy matching in production systems, pp. 685–692 (1990)
12. Nayak, P.P., Gupta, A., Rosenbloom, P.S.: Comparison of the rete and treat production matchers for soar, pp. 693–698 (1988)
13. Perlin, M.: Arc consistency for factorable relations. Artif. Intell. **53**(2–3), 340–345 (1991)

Author Index

Printed in the United States
By Bookmasters